General Studies

Paper II

for

Civil Services Main Examination

Second Edition

CONSTITUTION | POLITY | SOCIAL JUSTICE
GOVERNANCE | INTERNATIONAL RELATIONS

D V K RAO

Member (Retd), Ordnance Factory Board (Ministry of Defence)

G. K. PUBLICATIONS (P) LTD.

Title : General Studies Paper II: For UPSC Civil Services Main Examination Second Edition

Language : English

Author's Name : D V K Rao

Typeset & Published by :

Career Launcher Infrastructure (P) Ltd.
A-45, Mohan Cooperative Industrial Area, Near Mohan Estate Metro Station, New Delhi - 110044

Marketed by :

G.K. Publications (P) Ltd.
Plot No. 9A, Sector-27A, Mathura Road, Faridabad, Haryana-121003

ISBN : **978-93-91061-98-2**

Printer's Details : Print in India, New Delhi.

For product information :
Visit ***www.gkpublications.com*** or email to ***gkp@gkpublications.com***

ABOUT THE AUTHOR

Shri D V K Rao graduated from Delhi's prestigious St. Stephen's College and joined the Indian Ordnance Factories Services (IOFS) through the civil services examination in 1974. He is a Post Graduate in Public Administration from the Indian Institute of Public Administration (IIPA), Delhi. After 36 years of Service, he retired from the post of Member of the apex Ordnance Factory Board under the Ministry of Defence.

He has authored a book for the General Studies Paper III (main examination) published by GK Publications (part of the Career Launcher group). He can be reached at dvkrau@gmail.com.

ACKNOWLEDGEMENTS

This book, covering the syllabus of Paper II of Civil Services (Mains) is the result of a single minded pursuit to provide quality content to aspirants and to make the learning process simple and exciting. A single volume, having simplified text as per syllabus, model questions, practice questions, and previous years' questions with answers will no doubt be a great support for all aspirants.

At the outset, I would like to acknowledge the support and guidance of Mr. Kannath Prakash of GK Publications (Career Launcher group), whose perseverance and patience encouraged and motivated me. His contribution is gratefully acknowledged.

Ms Meenakshi Subramaniam, my sister who is an ex-IRS officer, contributed immensely and extensively in finalising the text and also with the last five years questions and answers. Her remarkable ability to present answers in a cogent, comprehensive and conclusive manner gives this book a ready advantage. My heartfelt thanks go to her.

PREFACE

General Studies Paper II of the Civil Services Main Examination is all about constitution, governance and international relations with a focus on Indian polity and social justice. While the Constitution at one end provides the context, the topic International Relations gives a nice complementarity to the whole chain. It should therefore be understood and realised that the paper is all about India and its political and policy aspects.

Crafted with care, this book tries to disseminate the required knowledge about the above mentioned topics in a calibrated and systematic manner.

While the conceptual part of each topic has been dealt with extensively, it is supported by

(a) Model questions with answers

(b) Solved questions of previous 8 years (providing the candidates with a unique opportunity to understand how answers are attempted).

(c) 'General Guidelines and Strategies for Success in Prelims and Mains' is another valuable addition that gives a keen insight on how to approach the Civil Services examination.

Practice questions offer both a challenge as well as an opportunity to sharpen the skills and shape to simulate actual attempt. Material given in Boxes is to alert the candidates on possible topics; it is expected candidates would search for more data.

The book attempts a wide coverage with sufficient depth and is written in simple language.

I am sure aspirants would find this a valuable asset in their preparation for the civil services examination.

I wish the best of luck to the aspirants in all their endeavours.

D V K RAO

INTRODUCTION

General Studies Paper II of the Civil Services Main examination is a challenging paper as it covers dynamic subjects like Constitution, Governance, Polity, Social Justice and International relations. These topics require in- depth study and a grasp of the finer, intricate points and interpretations. At the same time there is a need to understand the application of various laws, plans, schemes etc.

In this book, the topics dealing with constitution are arranged in a meaningful, methodical way, whereby the role, structure and functions of all the agencies involved are covered. The remarkable document that the Indian constitution is, it relates to governance with a structured and systematic approach that accommodates and assimilates the interplay of all the agencies to strike a balance. If one decided to read the whole constitution, it would be difficult to understand the topics. Effort has therefore been made to strictly cover the topics as given in the syllabus. Coverage of the relevant topics of the constitution has been made interesting, lively and enjoyable to read. The essence and spirit of the constitution has been captured to present it in a manner that is at once simple, satisfying yet serious. What emerges is the momentous task of capturing the key features of a monumental document to equip the aspirant to attempt any type of question.

Governance is dynamic, evolving, exciting and structured. It draws sustenance from the will of the people, sanctity from the constitution and satisfaction from the performance it delivers. Governance has to strike a balance between change and continuity, executive exuberance and administrative processes, systems and structures on the one side and response and results on the other. Governance is a concern for results and results for the concerned. Governance is also working today, with a vision for tomorrow. It is working to achieve goals through institutions, through interaction, through intervention, through incentives, through inclusion, through inputs and finally through inspiration. The syllabus covers governance in a matter-of-fact manner: constitutional bodies, statutory bodies, regulatory bodies, quasi-judicial bodies, governance policies and interventions. Yet, all the policies, best of institutions, best of will, wish and intent cannot deliver unless the involvement of the people exists. Hence, the role of all stakeholders. All these topics have been covered with eye for details and care for facts.

'Social Justice' has a ring of seriousness; a moral undertone and a sense of urgency also surround it. Welfare schemes, issues relating to poverty and hunger are the topics forming the bedrock of social justice. These topics have been covered with passion and purpose. The very laudable and commendable schemes of both the union and state governments, how they are being implemented in our federal structure, what is the gap between promise and reality are all dealt with. Compassion should rule our hearts, that's evidently the undertone even if not intended. India's poverty is historical, so are the causes. British rule accentuated it, is a theme now popular.

What of governance and role of civil service in a democracy? How does civil service deliver in an environment of probity, openness, accountability and empowerment? How does a civil servant get used to the idea of being called, questioned, advised, observed and penalised? Today's civil servant has to monitor, master and deliver. The tools are automation and technology. The role of civil servants in democracy has been covered showing the historical underpinnings and current manifestations. Today's civil servant has manifold challenges, multitude of issues and magnificent opportunities. He is however blessed with tools of technology, temperament of science and a tradition of self-actualisation.

The subject 'International Relations' stands alone. India and its neighbourhood with its historical problems, challenges and opportunities is indeed a task for any government. However with a fast forward and proactive outlook, the country's policies present a fresh look. Although in the past too, the country had some notable successes and there was a remarkable continuity in policies, yet it was always the case of being reactive. Today the challenges are different. Terrorism, nuclear policy, energy security, communications, trade deals, environmental concerns, sea line safety and security are major concerns. Economics has dwarfed politics.

It is here that agreements, bilateral, regional, multilateral are becoming important. No permanent friends, no permanent foes, only permanent interests. International institutions are part of the game. The world is engaged, like never before, in an integrated manner. WTO, UN and its agencies, BRICS, SAARC, ASEAN, EU, BIMSTEC are all engaged to further the cause of prosperity, progress and peace. Measure for measure, the world is integrated through communication networks, trade networks, social networks, travel network and ironically terror networks too.

India always believed in 'Vasudeva Kutumbakham,' a truly global outlook with the thought that 'Peace is indivisible'. The chapters on 'International Relations' are written to initiate the layman and ignite the learned. With adequate coverage of the past, understanding of the present and insight into emerging trends for the future, the chapters present a roadmap to understanding International Relations.

Civil service aspirants will find this single volume book, covering Paper II of Civil Service Exams (Mains), rewarding and will be happily surprised to see how much their task has been made simpler. The book also has model questions and past years' solved papers which makes the book complete. Do we need to say more?

GENERAL GUIDELINES AND STRATEGIES FOR SUCCESS IN PRELIMS AND MAINS

The civil services examination is both a challenge in terms of the amount of factual knowledge to be imbibed as well as honing the interpretative and analytical skills. Preparation must however essentially be result-oriented and based on clear objectives.

Let us look at some key issues and strategies for success in this highly competitive and taxing examination.

THE PRELIMINARY EXAMINATION

In the **preliminaries**, the expectation is 'spread' of knowledge and it involves grasp of the same over a wide range of subjects and topics. *As a strategy, one has to look at the key result areas (KRAs) where the common pitfalls while preparing for prelims are:*

(a) Too much effort to grasp everything leaves one gasping.

(b) Trying to read and assimilate matter from too many books, magazines, journals, and newspapers. It's best to focus on some good standard books.

(c) There's a tendency to answer all the questions in the prelims forgetting the negative marking. It would be wise not to stretch one's luck too much.

(e) Considering the sheer number of students in the prelims and the fact that nearly 90% candidates get filtered out in this stage, this stage is too competitive and this must ingrained in the minds of the aspirant.

What then are the 'Key Result Areas' for a balanced preparation? Key Result Areas:

1. Constitution.
2. Environment.
3. Economy.
4. History, Freedom struggle.
5. Geography.
6. Science (Biology).

Constitution: It calls for in depth study and the important aspect is to look at current developments that have a direct bearing on the Constitution. For example, the debate on Article 35 (A), or Article 44 or Article 370 etc are in news and must be thoroughly prepared. **Environment:**

Topics on environment involve 5 broad areas.

1. Environment issues.
2. Indian environmental issues and legislation.
3. Ecology and related matters.
4. Inter disciplinary matters involving environment and other topics like Geography, Economy, Biology, Law etc.
5. Global challenges and issues.

The spread here is huge and some detailed attention is called for. Current initiatives and issues are important. Development versus environment is an ongoing debate. Constitutional provisions related to the environment must not be ignored. Judicial verdicts and activism on environment should not be overlooked either. As environment is a global issue, developments in the global arena have also to be noted.

Economy: It is interesting; the coverage is huge but the focus should be on Indian economy. Current developments in plans, policies and performance must rank high. Money and banking are important as also areas like infrastructure development.

Knowledge of basic concepts like budgets, inflation, fiscal consolidation, taxation and subsidies is needed. Note that it is the application of concepts in economy that usually forms the basis for framing of questions. Social sector, poverty and employment too need attention. However, don't engage too much on figures and fanciful data.

Indian economy has agriculture at its root and cannot be ignored. WTO and subsidy issues are core.

The best way to go about is to evolve a sequence.

For example, the Indian economy at the time of Independence, the five year plans, development versus social issues, budgets, infrastructure, money and banking, agriculture, poverty, foreign trade etc.

Once a pattern is followed, continuity and cohesion are achieved.

History: Here it is vast and varied; the general tendency is to get into political history, battles and bugles, successions and accessions. However, it is seen that the questions are usually about art, architecture, archaeology etc.

Ancient India and its history are vast, here also questions mostly relate to arts, music, and architecture. Even so, there are maximum of only one or two questions for all that investment in time and energy.

On the contrary, there are many questions on freedom movement, and modern history of India etc.

Social, cultural, economic and art issues are more important than battles, wars and intrigues.

Geography: It is a key issue, whether it is economic geography or physical or social or environmental. The subject is not that vast as is mistakenly believed to be so. Indian Geography holds the key here. A good standard book covering these aspects is needed; many questions come from traditional geography. Current issues are important too.

An imaginative preparation is called for, and this involves general understanding of various geographical phenomena, distribution of resources and materials, flora and fauna etc. Economic geography cannot be neglected altogether.

Science: This is a huge subject what with Physics, Chemistry, Biology, Space, Earth, etc. It is an advantage to have a science background but only just. UPSC expects awareness about day to day science matters and understanding of common scientific facts. Achievements of India in space and technology too are useful. Issues linking science with environment too are very important.

Now we come to Current Affairs; the topics are vast and varied. Here the emphasis should be 'need to know'; an association is good, no need for detailed investigation.

One good magazine is a good investment and good idea.

Now we come to topics that you ***need not*** *focus.*

Some useful suggestions would be: Sports, films, awards, personalities, day to day politics, local news, speeches etc. These can divert and distract you.

THE MAIN EXAMINATION

Now on the Main Examination:

In so far as mains are concerned, there are two points of view:

(i) Prepare for the prelims; take up preparation for mains later. One step at a time: Focus on the task at hand.

(ii) Prepare for the mains; simultaneously look out for prelim based issues. Go for an integrated approach.

It is the considered opinion that the best course is to be using option (ii) and prepare for the mains, but two months before the prelims, entire effort should focus on prelims.

Two issues emerge in the context of the 'mains':

(a) The main examination is oriented towards depth. What is being tested here is your depth of understanding of the topic and how well you can express yourself on the topic. Therefore, a sort of précis writing skill is important.

(b) Also, in the mains, the weightage is to be understood as far the strategy of preparation go.

- 40% weightage to be given to 'Basic knowledge'.
- 30% weightage to be given to 'Application of this knowledge'.
- 30% weightage to be given to 'Inter-disciplinary' matters.

To elaborate, if a question is like this 'Constitution is biased towards the Centre which has overriding powers over the States. With recent clamour from States on this, examine the issues involved.'

Here, you should know about the constitutional provisions regarding federalism and as per its application, you should focus on issues that are hurting the state.

Only such an approach would make your answer concise and correct.

What of 'inter-disciplinary 'approach? It is of utmost importance and least understood. The approach involves 'scanning'. It means looking at the issue in a holistic and wholesome manner. If a question is asked, 'Examine the impact of liberalisation on Indian Economy,' your answer should not confine itself to data from pure economics but must look at growth scenario, rise of private sector, easing of imports, exports, ease of doing business, tax reforms, licensing changes and global integration.

You should be able to see the full picture and *show* it in your answer. Your answer should expand and throw light on the issue. A question on social justice may involve Directive Principles from the Constitution, may cover important institutions involved in governance, may have a connect with some important judicial pronouncements, could have the role of the Centre as well state governments. In short, take out your telescope and not the microscope.

What then are the strategies while writing the answer?

First and foremost, sharpen two skills (i) of making 'précis' and (ii) of 'expansion'. This needs practice, more practice.

Secondly, understand that a precise and proper answer is worth its weight in gold; there are no totally correct or totally wrong answers. The important thing is the ability to sum up; that is to get to the heart of the matter. Separate the grain from the chaff.

How does one build an answer? Here are some ways and methods.

(i) Make a mental note of the key issues involved. Don't straight away launch into writing.

(ii) Avoid using literary and bombastic language which will certainly put off the examiner. Be original in your views even if you are not fully equipped with facts.

(iii) Don't go off the word limit by a huge margin by going too much into the background of the issue.

(iv) Remember the 'C' formula; your answer must be cohesive and should have continuity. Continuity and cohesiveness ranks high in priority while writing for the main examination.

(v) Avoid digressions into other topics, they are like 'speed breakers'.

Some do's and don'ts

Do's

(a) Stay in context throughout and follow the theme

(b) Maintain continuity and sequence.

(c) Maintain word limit discipline.

(d) Sum up your answer in one or two lines at the end.

Don'ts'

(a) Avoid repeating the question.

(b) Avoid quotes unless very essential.

(c) Don't support your answer with too many figures and statistics

(d) No personal opinions, don't be judgemental.

(e) No unsubstantiated passages

(f) Avoid BRICS Language–No Bombastic, Repetitive, Idiomatic, Cynical and Sarcastic language.

(g) Avoid humour and also 'I agree' or 'I don't agree', statements.

Now let's analyse how questions are worded differently and how they should be approached. The most common ways in which questions are framed are as follows:

(1) Discuss the issues.

(2) Discuss critically.

(3) Justify your answer.

(4) Critically examine.

(5) Assess.

(6) Comment.

(7) Briefly outline.

(8) Elucidate.

(9) Analyse.

(10) Give reasons.

For (1) above, candidates are expected to discuss the issues objectively as emerging from the question. Most important arguments in favour or against must be brought out. It is basically evaluation.

For (2) above, it should not be taken that you to criticise. 'Critically' means dispassionately and objectively. One may have three reasons in favour and only one against. No effort should be made to balance 'for' and 'against'

Justify your answer at (3) means you have to choose between two options and may have to justify that choice. Such a choice has to be unequivocal and final; no 'ifs' and 'buts', no 'perhaps', no 'under the circumstance', no 'conditions permitting'.

Critically examine as at (4) may happen at places where the question is suggestive of an answer and you are expected to expand on its merits or demerits. You can draw your conclusions to be in agreement or otherwise.

Assess as at (5) above is simple, you may have to bring out the strong points in the question and assess them either in favour or against. You have scope to bring logic to substantiate your views.

Comment as at (6) is also simple; generally, the questions leave open- ended issues and you are expected to comment. Here the field is open for you to bring forth your views in the form of comments.

'Briefly outline' as at (7) above may have various points scattered in the questions, you have to outline them. In other cases, where they do not appear so, you may have to fall back on your experience and outline them.

Elucidate as at (8) above means expansion; the question is put with the idea that you will see the same and elucidate on them. Here generally one or two points are given and you are expected to expand them. You can give examples, similar instances.

Analyse at (9) above could be tricky. Arguments in favour and against are required to be brought out. Wrong or illogical arguments are to be contested and stamped out. Personal views however are to be avoided.

Lastly, 'give reasons' as at (10) above calls for reasons to be adduced either for or against in answer. If the question says 'give reasons in favour', it must be the goal. Prioritise important reasons in front and less important later. Do not fall in the trap of banking on only one reason to exhaust your word limit.

In conclusion two more issues remain; one is the 'close' and other is 'summing up'. Both are essential in presenting a good answer. In some instances, it is best to close by emphatic statement either in favour or against. Where the issues are open or are futuristic 'time will decide or tell' is the right way.

At times a 'proverb' or a 'punch line' can also come in handy. Conclusion should never be contrived or abrupt or loose. It is always a good idea to let the end come up by summing up the issues.

Summing up, is a challenge, owing to many a reason. One, the word limit may not permit such a luxury; two, summing up may not be really necessary; three, summing up may be difficult; four, summing up may be possible with a one liner or a proverb.

If the opportunity is there and it fits into the scheme of things, go ahead and sum it up but never impose a summation. It should be smooth and seamless.

It should always be borne in mind that it also is an examination but with some notable differences too. It is a merit based exam where ranking matters. There's a fight out there for each mark.

Secondly, it may well be expected that unlike the prelims, in the mains, the candidates are more or less equally well prepared; it is the presentation and ability to grasp, analyse and address the core issues that makes all the difference. Civil Service officers often face voluminous notes that have to be deciphered, unimportant matters to be segregated from the important ones; priorities to be kept in sight, implications understood, complications addressed, future envisioned and road map unfolded. Sounds interesting, but in practice it is a daunting task.

As already explained earlier, the three stages for success in this exam are knowledge, application and interdisciplinary approach.

Linkages are most important while looking at the interdisciplinary aspects. As for example, a question on governance may have a linkage with Constitutional amendment, a question on social justice may have link with Directive Principles of State Policy and so on.

SUMMING UP

What then is the workmanlike, workable solution?

Quintessentially, the answer would be to look at the issues in a holistic manner and answer the same keeping some broad guidelines. *Here are some of the guidelines.*

1. Read the question carefully and find out what are the 'core issues'.
2. Think of the answer purely in terms of points.
3. Assign importance to the points and prioritise.
4. Does the answer have issues related to current affairs?
5. Any linkage with the Constitution, law, court judgements?
6. Is there any connection with environment, ecology, etc.?
7. Any plans, policies or programmes of the government that have a bearing on your answer?
8. Any apt quotes?
9. Can a 'punch line' be found?

In nutshell, once you prepare and organise the answer through a scientific process, it will all look simple.

Best wishes in your preparation!

SYLLABUS: GS PAPER II

- Indian Constitution- historical underpinnings, evolution, features, amendments, significant provisions and basic structure.
- Functions and responsibilities of the Union and the States, issues and challenges pertaining to the federal structure, devolution of powers and finances up to local levels and challenges therein.
- Separation of powers between various organs dispute redressal mechanisms and institutions.
- Comparison of the Indian constitutional scheme with that of other countries
- Parliament and State Legislatures – structure, functioning, conduct of business, powers & privileges and issues arising out of these.
- Structure, organization and functioning of the Executive and the Judiciary Ministries and Departments of the Government; pressure groups and formal/informal associations and their role in the Polity.
- Salient features of the Representation of People's Act.
- Appointment to various Constitutional posts, powers, functions and responsibilities of various Constitutional Bodies.
- Statutory, regulatory and various quasi-judicial bodies
- Government policies and interventions for development in various sectors and issues arising out of their design and implementation.
- Development processes and the development industry- the role of NGOs, SHGs, various groups and associations, donors, charities, institutional and other stakeholders
- Welfare schemes for vulnerable sections of the population by the Centre and States and the performance of these schemes; mechanisms, laws, institutions and Bodies constituted for the protection and betterment of these vulnerable sections.
- Issues relating to development and management of Social Sector/Services relating to Health, Education, Human Resources.
- Issues relating to poverty and hunger.
- Important aspects of governance, transparency and accountability, e-governance- applications, models, successes, limitations, and potential; citizens charters, transparency & accountability and institutional and other measures.
- Role of civil services in a democracy.
- India and its neighborhood- relations.
- Bilateral, regional and global groupings and agreements involving India and/or affecting India's interests
- Effect of policies and politics of developed and developing countries on India's interests, Indian Diaspora.
- Important International institutions, agencies and fora- their structure, mandate.

CONTENTS

PART I : CONSTITUTION

PART II : POLITY

11. Development Processes and Development Industry–Role of NGOs, SHGs and Other Stakeholders 11.1 - 11.13

PART III: SOCIAL JUSTICE

12. Welfare Schemes for the Vulnerable 12.1 - 12.21

PART IV: GOVERNANCE

PART V : INTERNATIONAL RELATIONS

PART VI: PREVIOUS YEARS' SOLVED PAPERS

PART I

Constitution

CHAPTER 1

Evolution of Our Constitution

OVERVIEW

The Indian Constitution is both a journey as well as a destination; in a unique manner it lists out the objectives as also the processes to be followed to meet the desired objectives. How our Constitution evolved, what are its features, what are its significant provisions; these are the questions answered here. The Indian Constitution is a vibrant, dynamic, detailed document. It permits amendments while retaining its basic structure. The longest written Constitution has evolved putting in place the institutions of legislature, judiciary, and executive with due and definite separation of powers, but with a commonality of interests.

"No other constitution has provided so much impetus towards changing and rebuilding society for common good." **Granville Austin (on Indian Constitution)**

THE DOCUMENT SIZE

The Indian Constitution is the largest Constitution in the world–395 Articles, 12 Schedules, divided into 22 parts, and amended more than 100 times. The Indian Constitution is for both the Union as also the States; it has provisions for Union Territories too.

There's a Preamble declaring the objective behind the Constitution. Logically, the Constitution follows this path: The Preamble, Who is making this Constitution? → Who will be its citizens? → What will be their Fundamental Rights ? → How will the state look after their welfare? → What are the citizen's Fundamental Duties? → How will the executive under the Union function? → How will the Parliament be organised? → How will the Judiciary be organised and function? → CAG its role, functions → How will States function, its executive, legislature, High Courts → Subordinate courts → How will the Union Territories be placed → Panchayats and municipalities → Cooperatives → Scheduled and tribal areas → Relations between the Union and the States → How will Union transact business? Property and suits → Trade and commerce → Services under the Union → UPSC, EC → Official language → Emergencies → Amendments → Temporary Provisions → Schedules.

CHAPTERS

	Preamble	Articles
Part I	The Union and its territory	1, 2, 3, 4
Part II	Citizenship	5-11
Part III	Fundamental Rights	12-35
Part IV	Directive Principles of State Policy	36-51
Part IV A	Fundamental Duties	51A
Part V	The Executive (President & Vice President)	52-73
	Council of Ministers	74-75
	The Attorney-General for India	76
	Duties of Prime Minister & conduct of business of govt. of India	77-78
	Parliament, Functions, Duties, officers, Procedures, conduct of business	79-122
	Legislative powers of the President	123
	The Union judiciary	124-147
	Comptroller and Auditor General of India	148-151
Part VI	The States : General	152
	Governor, Council of Ministers & Conduct of business, state legislative composition, Procedure	153-212
Part VI (Contd.)	Legislative power of the governor	213
	High Courts	214-231 Article: 232 Omitted
	Subordinate courts	233-237
Part VII	The States in Part B of the First Schedule	238 (Repealed)
Part VIII	Union Territories	239-241 242 (Repealed)
Part IX	The Panchayats	243, 243A-243O
Part IX A	The Municipalities	243P-243ZG

Part X	The Scheduled & Tribal Areas	244 & 244A
Part XI	Relations between union & states	245-263
Part XII	Finance, property, contracts & Suits	264-300A
Part XIII	Trade & Commerce with territory & India	301-307
Part XIV	Services under the union & the states	308-323
Part XIVA	Tribunals	323A, 323B
Part XV	Elections	324-329
Part XVI	Special provisions relating to certain classes	330-342
Part XVII	Official Language & Regional Languages	343-351
Part XVIII	Emergency Provisions	352-360
Part XIX	Miscellaneous	361-367
Part XX	Amendment of the Constitution	368
Part XXI	Temporary, Transitional and special provisions	369-392
Part XXII	Short title, Commencement, Authoritative Text in Hindi and Repeals	393-395

SCHEDULES

I	The States, Union Territories.
II	Provisions as to the President and the Governors of States. Judges of Supreme Court and of High Courts, Comptroller and Auditor general.
III	Forms of Oaths or Affirmations.
IV	Allocation of seats in the Council of States.
V	Provisions as to the administration and control of Scheduled Areas and Scheduled Tribes.
VI	Provisions as to the Administration of Tribal Areas in the States of Assam, Meghalaya, Tripura and Mizoram.
VII	Union, State, Concurrent Lists.
VIII	Languages.
IX	Validation of certain Acts and Regulations.
X	Provisions as to disqualification on grounds of defections.
XI	Powers, authority and responsibilities of Panchayats.
XII	Powers, authority and responsibilities of Municipalities.

The Preamble

WE, THE PEOPLE OF INDIA, having solemnly resolved to constitute India into a SOVEREIGN SOCIALIST SECULAR DEMOCRTIC REPUBLIC and to secure to all its citizens;

JUSTICE, Social, economic and political

LIBERTY of thought, expression, belief, faith and worship

EQUALITY of status and of opportunity.

FRATERNITY assuring the dignity of the individual and the unity and integrity of the nation.

IN OUR CONSTITUENT ASSEMBLY, this twenty sixth day of November, 1949 do HEREBY ADOPT, ENACT AND GIVE TO OURSELVES THIS CONSTITUTION.

The preamble provides a key to the understanding and interpretation of the Constitution. It was not treated as a part of the Constitution by the Supreme Court in *Berubari case* (1960) but later in the *Kesavananda Bharati Case* (1973), the apex court held the Preamble to be part of the Constitution.

The word, 'SOCIALIST, SECULAR' and "Unity and integrity" (of nation) were inserted by the 42nd constitution amendment of 1976; called the 'mini-constitution'.

Fundamental Duties

(Part IV-A, Inserted by the Constitution 42th amendment act, 1976)

(a) to abide by the Constitution and respect its ideals and institutions, the National Flag and the National Anthem.

(b) to cherish and follow the noble ideals which inspired our national struggle for freedom.

(c) to uphold and protect the sovereignty, unity and integrity of India.

(d) to defend the country and render national service when called upon to do so.

(e) to promote harmony and the spirit of common brotherhood amongst all the people of India transcending religious, linguistic and regional or sectional diversities; to renounce practices derogatory to the dignity of women.

(f) to value and preserve the rich heritage of our composite culture.

(g) to protect and improve the natural environment including forests, lakes, rivers and wildlife and to have compassion for living creatures.

(h) to develop the scientific temper, humanism and the spirit of inquiry and reform.

(i) to safeguard public property and abjure violence.

(j) to strive towards excellence in all spheres of individual and collective activity so that the nation constantly rises to higher levels of endeavour and achievement.

(k) who is a parent or guardian to provide opportunities for education to his child or, as the case may be, ward between the age of six and fourteen years (inserted by the constitution 86th amendment act, 2002).

All these duties are not legally enforceable.

EVOLUTION

Constitutions are of two types; one that evolve over a period of time with gathered experience of change and of continuity. This type of Constitution is built on values, rationale, balance, and inclusiveness. Examples are Britain, India, Canada, etc.

The other types of Constitutions are the result of war, revolution, or cataclysmic changes. Such Constitutions are often caused by shift in power equations too. Constitutions of Soviet Russia (1917-war), France (1789- revolution), USA (1789-changes) are examples of this type.

The Indian Constitution is an example of collection of good practices and prescriptions. It draws from the example of Britain, USA, Ireland, Canada, Australia, Soviet Union, Weimar Germany, Republican France, and a whole host of others but the thought is Indian, the essence is Indian, and the flavour is Indian; both in spirit as well as practice. The East India Company (EIC) came to trade but gradually found it more profitable and engaging to administer. Profit was its goal, loot was its method. It was hardly to be expected that EIC would advance the cause of Constitution making in the country, for most part the emphasis was on changing and chopping the Governor General's Council and extended interest by the British Parliament to rein in the Company. Responsible government, Representative government, Rational government were not the agenda and a people groaning under enslavement were not the lot to stand and question.

Stand and question they did in 1857, putting an end to the Company rule and bring in Crown rule. 1858 Act transferred the power to the Crown which now began in earnest to rule this country. Act, Act, Act.....one Act followed by another.....another by another. Rule by Act, but never act by rule: this was the 'Crowning' glory of its rule (1858–1947).

YEAR/ACT

1858: Act for the good Governance of India. Rule by East India Company is over. British Crown takes control. Administrative machinery in India is improved, not so the governance.

1861: Indian Councils Act. It enabled the Governor General to associate representatives of the Indian people by nominating them to the council to help in legislation; second, it decentralised the legislative powers of the Governor General and vested them with the governments of Bombay and Madras.

1892: Council expanded (min 10, max 16). Discussions now allowed on annual financial statement (Budget) but within limits. Questions could be asked on matters of public interest. The Act brought in representative element.

1909: Enlarged the council to 60 members. Injected the concept of communal representation, separate representation for Muslim, S. P. Sinha became the first Indian to join the viceroy or Governor Generals' council. Powers of legislative councils, central and provincial, were increased.

1919: Government of India Act 1919. It was a step towards gradual development of self-governing institutions, with a view to progressive realisation of responsible government. It was British determination, not self-determination; a reasoning government, not responsible government. The Act introduced two Houses at the Centre, Lower and Upper, and separated powers between Centre and the provinces. 'Dyarchy' was in. Separate electorate for Sikhs, Anglo-Indians, Christians. Public service commission established.

Congress was not impressed, agitation was intensified. Rowlatt Act and Jallianwala Bagh massacre Bagh added fuel to the fire. Simon Commission, appointed ahead of time to study the working of 1919 Act was boycotted by the Congress. At the Lahore Session of the Congress in 1929"30, Nehru called for 'Purna Swaraj'. The Government of India stirred to action, action to discussion. Three Round Table Conferences were held in London, amidst growing turmoil in British politics, rising spectre of fascism in Europe, and creeping Hindu- Muslim dissensions in India.

1935: Cynically called the last throw of the dice by the British Government of India: Government of India Act, 1935. It envisaged 'Federation of All India', consisting of British Provinces, Indian States willing to join, Princely States, Chief Commissioner's Provinces (subsequent Union Territories).

It wanted to break up the unitary system under which India had been administered hitherto. The 1919 Act gave delegated powers to the provinces, 1935 Act took them on board in a federation. Devolution, not delegation, was a significant shift. Powers of Centre and provinces were demarcated; provinces were recognised as separate entities exercising executive and legislative powers in their own right.

Elections were held and Congress swept the polls and formed governments in the provinces to gain significant insight and experience in governance.

1935 Act suggested, very significantly, that the country ought to have a Constitution; a far sighted move that would occupy the minds and means of the country in years to come. Meanwhile, war broke out in Europe and the British India Government joined the war without as much consulting the country and the Congress. Miffed with this, the Congress ministries in the provinces resigned. In the war, the British took the bashing to retreat heroically (Dunkirk 1940) sometimes, hysterically at others (South-East Asia, Malaysia, and Singapore). Japan was singeing the English Lion and mauling the British Empire in Asia. Britain needed India's support; enter Cripps mission. Sir Stafford Cripps was sent by the National Government in Britain but was a failure, as his promises didn't impress the Congress: result was 'Quit India' movement of 1942. British repression cast Congress to confinement, all the leaders were jailed, barring Subhas Chandra Bose who preferred to enlist support of Japan and Germany and led the fight from abroad.

By 1944 the tide was turning, Nazi Germany was in full retreat, mortal blows from the east by Soviets and invasion in the west (June, 1944) by the resurgent British and pugnacious Americans. In India, the Congress leaders were released and soon parleys were resumed between a fatigued British Government and a fervent Congress leadership. Jinnah with his Muslim League joined the meet to chip in with his demands. The Princes, a historical anachronism, too joined with proposals. They were out of sync with the times. The chessboard was getting messy, pawns seemed to set their own rules for moves. The British hand was getting uncertain, slow, and at times hindered by its previous moves. Their policy of divide and rule was coming home to roost.

Congress leadership was excited, surprised at the welcome and reception the masses gave, and it infused a new vigour and spirit in them. India was tired of the British.

Viceroy Wavell was a spent force, exhausted by the endless wrangling among the parties, exacerbated by the lack of support from the British government, and excluded from the quintessence of political snap deals. Wavell exploded at Gandhi and Nehru, 'I don't understand you both, don't talk to me like lawyers. Talk straight.' 'Is it our fault that we are lawyers?' retorted Gandhi. Wavell, was a trained soldier, not a tuned politician. 'Wavell Plan', failed and none lamented. For Wavell, it was not a game of chess or chequers but of snakes and ladders, with the snakes coming alive at times and ladders collapsing at all times. Meanwhile, elections to the Central Assembly and Provincial Assemblies were completed and Britain announced the sending of a Cabinet Mission to India, comprising Lord Pethick Lawrence, First Lord of Admirality, A.V. Alexander and Sir Stafford Cripps. Cabinet Mission set in motion the machinery for Constitution–making, drawing sustenance from the Government of India Act 1935 which had suggested the same.

India now embarked upon a phase of Constitution making, a phase of astute bargaining, a phase of intense debate and discussion and above all a phase of aspirations, hopes, pledges, promises and mutual understanding.

CONSTITUENT ASSEMBLY

'Freedom without Constitution is like a bird to fly without wings, Constitution without freedom is like a cage to a bird with wings'. Dr. Ambedkar, the chairman of the drafting committee held freedoms, personal and institutional, dear to his heart. For him, both the bird and the cage were important; freedom with just and due restriction.

Fact File

The president of the Constituent Assembly was Dr. Rajendra Prasad. Members of the Constituent Assembly were elected by the Provincial Legislative Assemblies, which in turn, were represented by people elected by a limited electorate base. There were 17 committees, as listed in the Annexure. It took the constituent assembly two years, eleven months and eight days to finalise the Constitution. It first met on December 9, 1946 and the Constitution was signed on November 26, 1949 and came into force with effect from Jan 26, 1950 (the occasion being the anniversary dating to January 26, 1930 when Congress declared 'Purna Swaraj' to be its cherished goal).

Total number of members was 385, of whom 93 were representatives from the Indian States, 292 from the provinces. After partition the number come down to 299.

Members of the Drafting Committee

1. N. Gopalaswamy Ayyangar.
2. Alladi Krishnaswamy Iyer.
3. K. M. Munshi.
4. Mohammad Saadullah.
5. B. L. Mitter, replaced later by N. Madhava Rau.
6. Dr. D. P. Khaitan, replaced by T. T. Krishnamachari after Dr. Khaitan expired.

CONSTITUENT ASSEMBLY: A WORK IN PROGRESS

The Constituent Assembly appointed several committees for framing the Constitution and these committees submitted their reports between April and August, 1947. Based on these reports, Sir B. N. Rau, the indefatigable Constitution Advisor submitted a draft of the Constitution by October 1947. It had 240 Articles and 13 Schedules. This draft was submitted to the Drafting Committee headed by Dr. B. R. Ambedkar, then Union Law Minister.

The Drafting Committee with remarkable openness and transparency circulated the first draft to jurists, lawyers, judges, and other men in public life for comments, validations, criticism, and considered opinions.

(a) Based on comments, views, and criticisms, the drafting committee placed before the Constituent Assembly a second draft with 315 Articles, 9 Schedules.

(b) Based on third reading clause by clause, the Constituent Assembly adopted the draft on November 26, 1949.

(c) 'Consensus' was the watchword and all decisions, were taken in a spirit of unanimity or near unanimity; the route of 'majority vote was avoided to foster a spirit of accommodation. The towering presence of Nehru, Patel, Azad, and Rajendra Prasad brought calmness, conviction, consent, and control to the proceedings. Dr. Ambedkar steered the proceedings with tact, understanding, vision, and insight to tide over many a hurdle.

(d) There were hurdles aplenty: what should be the relations between the Union and the States, what should be the role of judiciary, should property rights be protected, why should India have a decentralised system of government, why should there be a Preamble, should not the States have their own Constitutions? All vital questions, impinging on the vitality of the nation. Wit, wisdom, and will were used to sort out all issues smoothly.

(e) One issue brought rare unanimity and remarkable consensus: Universal suffrage, the bedrock of our democracy. The poor, the illiterate, the scholar, all stood enfranchised. Women too were fully enfranchised, even ahead of many a democracy in the world.

(f) The issue of minorities took centrestage, but the majority batted for the minorities in the true spirit of secularism. Constitution makers had the remarkable turn of foresight and forbearance to bring it as fundamental to the Constitution in the form of fundamental rights.

All in all, despite the lingering criticism that the Constituent Assembly took a long while to draft the Constitution, (they had 161 sittings) the moot point is that the task was daunting, issues daring, and outcomes decidedly uncertain. In those years of the whiff of fresh air of freedom, it was possible to make people to agree, agree to disagree.

A critical point has not been given the due it deserves. With the transfer of power on Aug14/15, 1947, the Constituent Assembly became not only the Constitution framing body but also the law-making body. These two tasks were to be performed on separate days. Dr. Rajendra Prasad continued as the President of the Constituent Assembly for framing the Constitution and G. V. Mavalankar was elected as the Speaker of the Constituent Assembly for legislative functions of law-making. This was a remarkable solution with remarkable foresight, a seamless separation with a smooth application.

Constitutent Assembly: Committees

Sl. No.	Committee	Chairman
1.	Committee on the Rules of Procedure	Dr. Rajendra Prasad
2.	Steering Committee	"
3.	Finance and Staff Committee	Jawaharlal Nehru
4.	Ad hoc Committee on National Flag	"
5.	Union Constitution Committee	"
6.	Union Power Committee	"
7.	State Committee	"
8.	Advisory Committee on Fundamental Rights, Minorities and Tribals and Excluded Areas.	"
9.	Drafting Committee	Dr. B.R. Ambedkar
10.	Credential Committee	Alladi Krishnaswami Ayyar
11.	House Committee	Pattabhi Sitaramayya
12.	Order of Business Committee	K.M. Munshi
13.	Committee on Functions of the Constituent Assembly	G.V. Mavalankar
14.	Minorities Subcommittee	H.C. Mookerjee
15.	Fundamentals Rights Subcommittee	J.B. Kripalani
16.	North-East Frontier Tribal Areas and Assam Excluded and Partially Excluded Areas Subcommittee	Gopinath Bordoloi
17.	Excluded and Partially Excluded Areas (Other than those in Assam) Subcommittee	A.V. Thakkar

HISTORICAL UNDERPINNINGS

What does the word 'underpinning' means? It means 'to support or corroborate' or technically 'to support (a structure) from beneath, usually temporarily, with brickwork or a prop'. Underpinning, thus means support for a structure.

Historically, India was yearning for a Constitution. All the free countries were already governing themselves with a Constitution whether, democratic or communist or even a monarchy or a dictatorship; all had a Constitution to swear by. India, a colony, was longing for a Constitution. Its traditions, its temperament, and all pointedly demanded a Constitution to move forward. Thus, the foremost underpinning was the Indian peoples desire to have a Constitution. They knew it was not only right that they have one, but also it was theirs to be had by right.

The second underpinning was the growing clamour and demand by the Congress party. Galvanised and energised by Mohandas Gandhi, who now took it to the masses, Congress was raising the pitch for a Constitution. 'Congress, Constitution and the country' was no longer a cry in wilderness; it was the full throated anguished cry of a nation. At its sessions, the Congress leadership always rent the air with slogans for Constitution. Gandhi, Nehru, Patel, and a whole host of leaders busied themselves with issues concerning Constitution making, it was an investment for the future, and Nehru was the guiding spirit.

In 1934, the demand of a Constitution for the country being 'framed by its own people without outside interference', was made by the Indian National Congress. Congress had been agitating for Constitution; matters came to a head in 1928 when Lord Birkenhead, secretary of State challenged Indian politicians to produce an 'agreed Constitution' and submit it to Parliament. Motilal Nehru chaired a committee to produce a report, which called for responsible elected government, fundamental rights, secular state, and protection to minorities: a commendable effort with vision and versatility. It was an example of how countrymen could, when challenged, produce a report with remarkable consensus, unity of thought, purpose, and manageable perfection. The Report embodied not only the perspective of the contemporary nationalist opinion but an outline of a draft Constitution for India.

Earlier, the country had energetically participated in the First World War to respond to the call of the British, on the fobbed promise of Dominion status after the war. It was the first of 'post-dated cheques on a crashing bank', even with a 'forged' signature. The War ended His Majesty's Government, gave India Rowlatt Act (1919) and Jallianwala Bagh Massacre (1919). Congress felt betrayed, country felt besieged. By 1927, 'Simple Simon' arrived with no Indian representation to review 1919 Act, and Congress was aflame yet again. In 1936, the Lucknow session of the Congress proclaimed: 'no Constitution imposed by an outside authority and no Constitution which curtails the sovereignty of the people would be acceptable to the Congress',

Meanwhile, many socialists would be so impressed by Stalinist Soviet Russia and its Constitution that they would clamour for communism. M.N. Roy in 1920s, back from Russia, was the first to raise the pitch. Meanwhile, the Liberal party in Britain was split, giving way to left learning Labour. Many of the Labourites favoured governance of India by Indians. This underpinning ultimately proved to be the soft underbelly for the British in 1947 when Labour swept the polls to emerge winners. Many British thinkers, writers, politicians, activists, and academicians stood by India and its rights. They shaped the opinion in Britain although they could not size it.

The United States, that cradle of democracy, kept urging Britain for freedom and rule of law, as envisaged by Indians. It was a factor which was not exerting pressure, yet always gently nudged Britain: 'might is always not right.' US stood for values: freedom and democracy. It was a moral persuasion at one level. The Congress grew aggressive and more aggressive until 1942, when patience gave way to petulance to call for 'Quit India'. Even Gandhi condoned violence as 'just against the unjust violence of the State'.

FEATURES OF THE CONSTITUTION

Features

The Indian Constitution has some unique features that at once stand out to make it one of the most comprehensive and cohesive, documents in the world. These features are the binding spirit that forms the essence of the Constitution. By features, it is to be understood to mean the facts and not provisions.

(a) **Longest written Constitution in the world:** Distinctly, yes. One of the reasons is that India does not have a separate Constitution for the States, like in the United States. Secondly, our Constitution covers both powers and procedures, always an elaborate exercise.

(b) **Different Sources:** Indian Constitution is called a 'bag of borrowings', which is true to an extent, as we picked up the best principles, practices and precedents from other constitutions.

(c) **Secularism:** The Preamble has, through the 42nd amendment, made a clear insertion that the country is secular. It does not mean tnat the state will be indifferent to religious beliefs and practices, but that the state will be aggressively neutral.

(d) **Single Citizenship:** The Constitution prescribes single citizenship for all, unlike many other countries. Constitution uploads only one Citizenship: Indian.

(e) **Parliamentary form of Government:** India has opted for Parliamentary form of democracy and elected Government. Parliamentary form of government is based on universal adult franchise and devoid of discriminations. Largely, patterned after the British form, sans monarchy. President is the head of the State and Vice-President, the chairman of Rajya Sabha. Full powers are given to the Parliament and devolution and accountability are the paramount features.

(f) **Union and State Governments:** A shared power arrangement where, as per Schedule seven, powers of Union, state and common grounds are defined. Finance Commission (Art. 280), constituted every 5 years, prescribes form of division of revenue. It is a federal arrangement with mutual concurrence.

(g) **Balance between Parliament and Judiciary:** Constitution has worked to a nicety to strike a balance between Parliament and the Judiciary. Notwithstanding an occasional bout of contest, and a distinct one in 1967 (Golaknath) and 1973 (Kesavanda Bharati) respectively, the issue is laid to rest with a mutually congruous 'Basic Structure.' Framers of the Constitution were farsighted and ultimately Constitution only guided to work out a solution.

(h) **Independent Judiciary:** An abiding feature of our Constitution is that we have an 'Independent Judiciary' much respected and much accepted. The judges draw their salaries from the central and state consolidated found, to be independent of the executive.

(i) **Unitary, but federal bias is towards unitary:** Indian Constitution has a remarkable feature–flexibility. Indian is a 'Union of States' but given the compulsion of an emergency, the country becomes unitary. Moreover, Union has the power to take over state governance in the event of crisis (Art. 356), financial emergency (360), and external emergency (352). Largely, the balance of bias is towards the Union. Articles 249, 250, and 251 distinctly give the power to the Parliament to legislate over the state.

(j) Another unique feature of our Constitution is that it not only prescribes the powers, be it for the Parliament, executive, or judiciary, but also the process through which to use the powers. For instance, Article 368 lays down the power to amend the Constitution and the process too. A very sagacious move on part of the framers of the Constitution to remove ambiguity and restrain exuberance, thereby avoid litigation, delays, dilemmas, and discursiveness.

Working of Committees: A remarkable feature of Parliamentary democracy is the working of committees. Transcending party lines, personal views, and public opinions, parliamentary work takes place in an atmosphere of rare unanimity and understanding. Often aided and assisted by a civil servant who works in complete anonymity and neutrality, these committees work to fill in a large volume of parliamentary work. Subordinate legislation is another area where parliamentarians and civil servants work together to frame rules to support enacted legislation.

FAUX PAS..... MR. PRIME MINISTER

If you thought parliamentarians were all work-charged, grim, humourless, sardonic personalities, you could be in for a happy surprise. Humour in parliament is well known over the years. The funny repartees in British Parliament by Churchill are part of the lore. Back home, a few to recount: First time Prime Minister, Vajpayee rose to address the Parliament and looking at the leader of the opposition he addressed, 'Respectable, Mr. Prime Minister......er...' The house broke into peals and peals of laughter, guffaws filled the air. Unfazed, Vajpayee also joined the laughter, 'what can I do.....sitting in the opposition for years... year after year, I am now a prisoner of habit..... so, you can appreciate how it is'. The laughter continued, easing the monotony and the tension of the moment. Or of another instance when a visibly disturbed finance minister began his speech by asserting glibly that economy was indeed looking up, when an opposition MP quipped, 'yes true. That's because economy is flat on the ground'. Laughter all round, may be the solitary occasion when topic of economy brought cheers, laughter, and mirth.

CONSTITUTIONAL PROVISIONS

Areas covered

Briefly, the following areas are covered through significant provisions.

(a) Union and its territory, citizenship.
(b) Fundamental Rights, Directive Principles of State Policy, Fundamental Duties.
(c) The Executive–The President and Vice President, Council of Ministers, Attorney General,
(d) Parliament and its Procedures, Legislative Powers of the President.
(e) Union Judiciary, CAG.
(f) The States: Executive, Legislative and its Procedures. Legislative powers of the Governor.
(g) High Courts in the States, Subordinate Courts,
(h) Union Territories.
(i) Panchayats, Municipalities, Cooperative Societies.
(j) Scheduled and Tribal Areas.
(k) Relations between the Union and the States.
(l) Finances, Property, Contracts, Suits.
(m) Distribution of Revenue between the Union and the States. Trade, Commerce and Intercourse within the territory of India.

(n) Services under the Union and the State, Public Service Commissions.
(o) Elections.
(p) Special provisions relating to certain classes.
(q) Official Language, Special directives.
(r) Emergency Provisions.
(s) Amendment to the Constitution.
(t) Temporary, Transitional, and special provisions.
(u) Schedules.

While some of the provisions, covered by relevant articles, are purely procedural or functional, some other provisions are critical. Here, the significant provisions become vital, as they are the heart and soul of the Constitution.

Significant provisions of the constitution

(i) **Preamble:** The Preamble is significant as it only outlines the essence of the Constitution. The word 'secular' was inserted by the 42nd amendment.

(ii) **Articles 14 to 35:** Fundamental Rights–They are the heart of the Constitution. Individual freedoms; right to equality, right to freedom, right to freedom of religion, right against exploitation, cultural and educational rights.

While on the one hand (1) Right to Equality, (2) Right to freedom, (3) Right against Exploitation are rights available in a positive way to individuals, on the other hand (1) Right to freedom or religion (2) Cultural and Educational Rights are rights available to minorities to stand by their conviction and conscience. All these rights are taken from the US Constitution. Dr. Ambedkar, called the Fundamental Rights the heart of the Constitution.

All these rights are justiciable.

(iii) **Articles 36 to 51:** Directive Principles of State Policy–Borrowed from the Irish Constitution, these are principles of governance in a welfare state. They are not justiciable, but justifiable always. Governments often have ideas but no money, governments often know the best way forward, but no capability to carry all, governments often have plans to implement but don't know when. Accumulated are such plans and schemes in the Directive Principles of State Policy.

(iv) **Universal Adult Franchise:** Art. 326 prescribes adult franchise in elections. India is among the first countries, even ahead of US, to go for it and reposing faith and trust in our adults. The illiterates, rural or urban can vote. The women can vote. A historic, bold, and dynamic assertion. Democracy to the grassroots, empowerment to roots, inclusive to all.

(v) **Autonomous Bodies:** It is said pithily, 'Give bureaucracy an inch, it grabs a yard.' Constitution has provisions for autonomous bodies which are independent, self-sustaining, and standing to serve a mandate. The bodies have a stature and status: they are Constitutional bodies. Salaries of its officials are drawn from the central or state consolidated funds, as applicable.

They submit their annual reports to the President, and he in turn causes them to be laid on the table of the Parliament (for Union autonomous bodies) and Governor similarly, for the state legislature (for state autonomous bodies).

1. Comptroller and Auditor General (Art. 148 to 151)
2. Union Public Service Commission (Art. 315 to 323)
3. Election Commission (Art. 324 to 329 A)
4. State Public Service Commission (Art. 315 to 323)

The autonomous bodies are independent, performing, and neutral. They are more in the nature of 'watch over bodies'.

(vi) **Minorities, SCs, and STs:** Significant provisions also cover the issues of Minorities, SCs, and STs to ensure that they get their rights, dues, and authorisations. Constitutional mandates have to be honoured and safeguards maintained.

National Commission for SCs: Art. 338

National Commission for STs: Art. 338

Part XVI (Art. 330 to 342) is about special provisions for certain classes. These are significant in our Constitution for adding to our commitment toward minorities, SCs, and STs.

(vii) **Emergency Provisions:** Borrowing from the concept of Article 48 of the inter war years, namely Weimer Constitution of Germany, the framers of our Constitution brought the provisions of Emergency into our Constitution.

Art. 352: External Emergency: used in 1962

Art. 356: Applicable internally in States due to breakdown of machinery

Art. 360: Financial Emergency: Never applied so far.

These articles are significant for they are meant for emergencies; internal or external. The Union of India takes charge and States take a back seat. There are cries in anguish that Art. 356 is often misused for political ends; there's some truth to it and courts have intervened often.

(viii) **Amendments:** If Articles 352, 356, and 360 are for bloodletting in an emergency, Art. 368 is like a purgative. Article 368 deals with the power of Parliament to amend the Constitution. The Articles cover both the powers and process for amendment. It is this article which was the bone of contention between the Parliament and the Supreme Court in *Golaknath* (1967) and *Kesavanda Bharati* (1973) and *Minerva Mills* (1980) cases. On balance, the power has to be there but with power comes responsibility and with responsibility comes maturity and with maturity comes wisdom and with wisdom comes sagacity. So far Art. 368 have been used mostly for routine needs like joining of new States, reservations, new names to States etc. However, the 42nd (1976) and 44th (1978) amendments were historic. 42nd went for revisiting the whole Constitution and 44th made that visit less memorable by drawing a line.

(ix) **Temporary, transitional, and special provisions:** Part XXI of the Constitution deals with a tricky and tumultuous issue relating to temporary, transitional, and special provisions, the creation of historical compulsions. They are real, persuasive, and pestering issues. Art. 370 relating to Jammu and Kashmir is a milestone, not a millstone.

(x) **Articles relating to revenue, sharing etc.:** Article 268 to 281 covers very significant issues: the distribution of revenues between the Union and the States. Article 280 deals with the Finance Commission. The entire gamut of Articles from 268 to 281 can be said to be so very essential to our federal structure! It has left no ambiguity, no doubts but a little bickering, but these provisions are historically significant and eternally lasting. No wonder the Union-State relationship often revolves round this.

(xi) **Tenth Schedule:** A lid on defections has strengthened our democracy, improved our image. It's an honourable end to Aaya Rams, Gaya Rams of our democracy, a very significant issue for all times to come.

There indeed was one MLA, Aaya Ram who changed his party affiliations thrice in a single day in 1967, prompting Home Minister Y.B. Chavan to lament in the parliament, 'How do we bring stability to our work when we have Aaya Rams and Gaya Rams defecting at will?' For record, Chavan also defected subsequently!

RIGHT TO CONSTITUTIONAL REMEDIES

An interesting inclusion is the right to Constitutional remedies, as a fundamental right. It is an astute and convincing recognition that the state and others may trample upon citizens' rights and that courts may have to step in to prevent violations. Ordinary remedy through recourse to courts may be delaying, thereby, denying justice. Through Article 32 of the Constitution and Article 226 of the same, the Supreme Court and High Court respectively across the country can be approached for redressal of wrongs; both actual and intended. Writs are the mode through which the Supreme Court and High Court across the country can be approached for instant and independent consideration of violations of the law of the land. Courts can intervene, adjudicate, instruct, and even stay the proceedings.

Essential difference between the role of the Supreme Court and the High Court

'Supreme Court has the power to issue writs *only* for the purpose of enforcement of Fundamental Rights whereas Under Art. 226, a High Court can issue writs for the purpose of enforcement of Fundamental Rights and/or for the redress of any other *injury or illegality*.'

WRIT

What is a Writ? 'A legal document issued by a court in the name of the sovereign, by which someone is summoned, or required to do or refrain from doing something.'

Types of Writs

Writs are of ***five*** types.

I. **Habeas Corpus:** 'meaning produce the body'.

Around 1640, King Charles I of England peeved with the growing vocal dissent and belligerence of members of parliament against royal edicts, chose to enter the house with armed retainers to arrest Cromwell and Hampden and others. The two having fled, the king carried away three others. The Parliament passed the 'Habeas Corpus' motion. Thus, began the chapter in civil liberties and the civil war, which cost the king his head and the Parliament its unity.

A writ of Habeas Corpus calls upon the person who has detained another, to produce the latter before the court, in order to let the court known on what grounds the person has been confined and to set the person free if there is no legal justification for detention.

II. **Mandamus:** It means a 'Command'. It commands the person to whom it is addressed to perform some public or quasi-public legal duty which the person has refused to perform and the performance of which cannot be enforced by any other adequate legal remedy.

III. **Prohibition:** It is a writ issued by the Supreme Court or High Court to lower court forbidding the latter to continue proceedings there in excess of its jurisdiction or to usurp a jurisdiction with which it is not legally vested.

Prohibition is issued only against judicial or quasi-judicial authorities, not administrative authorities. Prohibition is available during the pendency of the proceedings and before the order is made.

IV. **Certiorari:** Certiorari is available against courts or tribunals exercising judicial or quasi-judicial powers.

Certiorari is issued to quash order or decision of the court or tribunal. It is issued only after the order is made.

Certiorari is against erring lower courts.

V. **Quo Warrants:** This writ is a proceeding whereby the court enquires into the legality of the claim which a party asserts to a public office and to oust the person from its enjoyment if the claim is not founded.

Certain conditions need to be fulfilled for Quo warrants

(a) The office must be public.

(b) It must be created by a statute or Constitution.

(c) Office must be substantive.

(d) There must be some contravention of the Constitution or a statute or statutory instrument in appointing such a person to that post.

Writs are serving an important function in a public cause. They go a long way in instilling confidence among the public and re-assuring that rule of law prevails, and further that none is above the law.

BASIC FEATURES CONTENTION: 'PARADIGM SHIFT'

The phrase 'Basic structure' does not appear anywhere in the Constitution; it was uttered for the first time in the *Golaknath vs State of Punjab* (1967) case (in the Supreme Court) by the petitioner's lawyer, more out of vehemence than validation, more out of persuasion than pressure.

The moot point was whether Parliament has the power to amend any or all the provisions of the Constitution. Until the case of Golaknath, Supreme Court held that no part of Constitution is unamendable.

(I) **1951:** In the *Shankari Prasad Singh Deo vs Union of Indian* case, the Supreme Court unanimously held that the terms of Article 368 were perfectly general and empowered that Parliament to amend the Constitution without any exception whatever.

(II) **1955:** In *Sajjan Singh vs State of Rajasthan* the Supreme Court held that when Article 368 confers on Parliament the right to amend the Constitution, the power in question can be exercised over all the provisions of the Constitution.

In the *Golaknath vs State of Punjab* (1967) this position of equilibrium was given a hard shove; in a 6:5 judgement, the Supreme Court held the position that Article 368 did not confer upon Parliament the power to amend the Constitution. The Chief Justice himself took an extreme view that Article 368 merely outlines the procedure for amendment and that it does not give the power.

This opened up a piquant position, as to who is supreme. Parliament held on to its right to amend the Constitution and passed two more amendments. In 1973, in *Kesavananda Bharati vs State of Kerala* case the Supreme Court reversed its position of *Golaknath vs State of Punjab* case to hold that Article 368 indeed gives Parliament the power to amend any part of the Constitution, but without altering the 'Basic Structure'. The court however did not define what indeed constitutes the 'Basic Structure'. It gave the judiciary the power of judicial review.

Even so, the deliberations did outline what could perhaps be called 'Basic Structure'.

(a) Supremacy of the Constitution.

(b) Republican and Democratic form of Government.

(c) Secular character of the Constitution.

(d) Separation of powers between the legislature, executive, and the judiciary.

(e) Federal character of the Constitution.

(f) Unity of the country.

(g) Mandate to build a welfare state.

(h) Fundamental Rights.

(i) Judicial Review.

(j) Article 368 in its construction.

This averted a showdown between Parliament and the judiciary. Parliament felt it had the power to amend the Constitution to usher in a welfare state, and verily honour the mandate of the people. Judiciary felt that fundamental rights cannot be a plaything of the Parliament of the day. The political party in power whipped up a campaign against what they called 'vested interests,' blocking welfare. Anger filled the air, mobs the street. By 1976, during national emergency, under the 42nd amendment, the Parliament put amendments beyond judicial review. 44th Amendment in 1978 redressed the issue. The paradigm had not shifted, but it was sifted.

BASIC STRUCTURE

Basic structure concept may be comparable in essence to the human body structure. The bones, muscles, heart, kidneys, lungs, liver, eyes, ears, nose, teeth, hands, and legs may be said to be forming the basic structure and need not be altered. Nails, hair, appendix may not be part of the basic structure and could be trimmed, chopped off.

It was best left to examine issues on case to case basis. Putting basic structure into a cast iron or a straitjacket would have led to more controversies, more disputes, and more litigation. Judiciary held to its own by asserting that judicial review itself is part of the basic structure, and that says it all; so eloquently.

SOME ASPECTS OF THE INDIAN CONSTITUTION

Articles 1, 2, & 3

India is s unitary state, not a federation. It is plainly a Union of States, both historically and culturally. The few federal features such as separation of powers are only intended to strengthen the Union. The Constitution supports the view that the Union is the most supreme authority, but it is obliged also to protect and strengthen the States. There is only one citizenship and one domicile. Trade and commerce are free throughout the land. Any disputes which may arise between and among the States are subject to arbitration by the Union only. Defence and Foreign affairs are sole prerogative of the Union only. Also, in administration of justice, the Supreme Court exercises jurisdiction over the entire territory of India. The mere fact that just because the Constitution provided for separation of powers between Union and States, it can't be said that India is federal, or is unitary with several federal characteristics. No State has a right to alienate itself from the Union. On the other hand, all the States are duty bound to implement the directions of the Union.

The Union laws extend to the whole of India, States, and Union Territories. India's territory includes the whole country. If the applicability of some laws do not extend over State of Jammu and Kashmir, it only means that the expression 'territory of India' includes Jammu and Kashmir. Disputed areas like Pak occupied Kashmir (Pok) and the area forcibly occupied by China are part of India.

The Union Government holds the power to form new States, alter the boundaries of the States but, of course, subject to the condition that the States concerned are given an opportunity to express themselves through their own legislatures. However, the opinion expressed by the States is not binding on the Union. In case of new state formation, the laws applicable to the areas transferred shall continue to be the same laws until the new authority alters the same.

The Union alone has the important power to cede any territory to any other country. It alone can accept merger of any foreign territory into the Union either as a State or a Union territory. But, where such additions or deletions are made, there is a necessity to amend the Constitution in a manner which includes or excludes the territories, specified in the Schedule. Where certain areas are ceded to Bangladesh or certain areas are brought in such as Goa and Pondicherry and when Sikkim was merged with India, the Constitution was accordingly amended. If a surrogate child is born to Indian woman but whose biological father is a foreign national, the child is an Indian citizen entitled to Indian passport.

Articles 5 to 11

Who are entitled to citizenship? It s a natural right of all persons born in India and have been ordinarily resident for not less than five years immediately preceding the commencement of the Constitution, in 1950. Special provisions have been created because of the partition of the country into India and Pakistan because many immigrated to Pakistan and many migrated to India. The provisions, hence, have been made under Articles 6 and 7 which provide for a prior registration at the respective consulates within a particular period and proof of actual residence at the time of application for citizenship. Article 8 talks about acquisition of citizenship by persons of Indian origin residing in former British colonies, whose parents originally belong to India. Regarding the important question of conferring citizenship as well as the perplexing question of disputed citizenship, the Central Government is the only authority as per the provisions of Citizenship Act of 1955. If question of citizenship is disputed, the person concerned shall not be deported till the question of citizenship is settled.

The Chakmas who are foreigners are entitled to right to life under Article 21. If they are prepared to apply for Indian citizenship and their applications are pending, they cannot be forcibly evicted from India.

Articles 12 to 35

A Narrative

The fundamental rights guaranteed by Constitution are equality before law [Art. 14]; Prohibition of discrimination on grounds of religion, race, caste, sex or place of birth [Art. 15]; equality of opportunity in matters of public employment [Art. 16]; abolition of untouchability [Art.17]; abolition of titles [Art. 18]; freedom of speech etc.; freedom to assemble; freedom to form associations; freedom to move freely throughout India [Art. 19]; protection against double jeopardy [Art. 20]; protection to life and personal liberty [Art. 21]; right to education [Art. 21-A]; protection against detention [Art. 22]; prohibition of traffic in human beings and forced labour [Art. 23]; prohibition of employment of children [Art. 24]; right to conscience and right to profess religion [Art. 25]; freedom to carry on religious affairs [Art. 26]; freedom from paying taxes for promotion of any particular religion [Art. 27]; freedom as to attendance at religious instructions or religious worship in educational institutions [Art. 28]; protection of interest of minorities [Art. 29]; right of minorities to establish and administer educational institutions [Art. 30]; compulsory acquisition of property [Art. 31]; (since repealed under 44th Amendment Act of 1978); Arts. 31-A, 31-B and 31-C are additional clauses relating to the acquisition of properties; remedies for enforcement of fundamental rights [Art. 32]; exemption of armed forces from the application of fundamental rights [Art. 33]; restriction on fundamental rights during martial law [Art. 34].

Who has legislative competence to give effect to fundamental rights? It is Parliament and not state legislatures.

On the significant issues of enforcement, protection, or implementation of the fundamental rights, the Union Government may issue executive orders or legislate enactments. Judiciary holds the power to interdict any order or legislation which affects the fundamental rights. Mala fide orders, unreasonable orders, and orders which do not contain any reasons are directly hit by Art. 14. Classification of persons for conferring benefits into distinct groups is allowed only if such classifications achieve the purposes for which classification is made. The reservation of posts for socially and economically backward classes in public employment and in seats in educational institutions is valid, provided the backward classes are identified properly by the commissions specially constituted for the purpose. It should be noted that the classification of reserved categories into creamy layer and others and the classification of Scheduled Tribes, Scheduled Castes, and Backward Classes into A, B, C, and D does not offend Art. 14. Freedom of Press is part of the freedom of speech. It is noteworthy that no man can be punished twice for the same offence. The principle will not apply to different punishments under different enactments which follow different procedures. For example, a person prosecuted for excise offence can be punished under disciplinary proceedings relating to his employment. Freedom of conscience is protected if the person at a prayer meeting stands up showing respect for National Anthem without singing or participating in chorus at religious congregations. Right to religious and linguistic minorities to establish their own institutions is placed under the general rules of supervision and control when such institution receives grants or recognition. Labour laws apply to all institutions irrespective whether they belong to religious or linguistic minorities or otherwise.

Repeal of Art. 31 and its reincorporation in Art. 300-A does not, in fact, effect the basic right to compensation for property acquired by State except for the fact that the amount of compensation now payable after amendment depends more on the discretion of the Government by "fixing" the amount of compensation in some particular cases involving land reforms. However, as discretion can't be arbitrary and fanciful, determination of compensation can still be questioned a person, as arbitrary. The old law says, a citizen can be deprived of his property if there a law and if such law describes the method of calculating compensation. After the new change, the Estate Abolition Acts which prescribed the procedure for arriving at the amount of compensation and the Land Ceiling Acts and the Bank Nationalisation Act which "fixed" the compensation have become valid.

The big effect of Arts. 31-A and 31-B is that no law providing for acquisition of eStates shall be declared invalid on the ground that it offends a fundamental right and that all such laws when they are included in the 9th Schedule should not be treated as having become invalid for the reason that any of the provisions offend the Constitution. It is also worth observing that the effect of Art. 31-C is that no law which purports to have been made in pursuance of the directive principles of State policy shall be declared as invalid on the ground that the said Act does not achieve the purpose intended. It is left to the Court to decide whether the impugned enactment encroaches upon any of the basic features of the Constitution and whether the impugned enactment does not achieve the objects of State policy. Because, the latter part of Art. 31-C that "and no law containing declaration that it is giving effect to such policy shall be called in question in any court on the ground that it does not give effect to such policy" was struck down by the Supreme Court in *Kesavananda Bharati vs State of Kerala case.*

By inclusion of Art. 32 within the part dealing with fundamental rights, the right to approach the Supreme Court for enforcement of fundamental rights itself has been made a fundamental right and the right to approach the Supreme Court being the basic feature this right cannot be restricted by any law including by an Amendment to the Constitution. Under this power the Supreme Court, it must be noted, cannot legislate any enactment giving effect to any of the fundamental rights. However, it can direct their enforcement or interdict any act which infringes on any of the fundamental rights. To give an example, where preventive detention is ordered, the court can prevent the arrest in very exceptional circumstances. Therefore, it is advised that a writ of mandamus be filed. In recent times, however, the Supreme Court has been issuing what are called guidelines judgements with a direction that the said guidelines may be enforced by all authorities. The guidelines issued by the Supreme Court on foreign adoptions, on opening of blood banks, and for protection of women in public places are being enforced by all the authorities concerned.

Supreme Court's power to enforce fundamental rights along with a right conferred on the citizen means in substance that the court can not only interdict the orders which may infringe upon the citizen's fundamental rights but also issue orders to the executive to make appropriate rules in this regard which enable the citizens to enjoy fundamental rights. The series of judgements rendered by the Supreme Court on environment can be referred. The court has also clarified that the applicability of fundamental rights which are also human rights do apply to foreigners also. For example, the court has ordered that Chakmas cannot be deported by force without following lawful procedure and that foreign women are entitled to the rights under Protection of Women from Domestic Violence Act.

Fundamental Rights are conferred on citizens by the Constitution and fundamental duties are the obligations the Constitution has cast upon the States in relation to directive principles of state policy. The orders which may be given by the Courts in relation to the objectives of State policy can be only recommendations, because no effective writ can be issued in this regard. That is why guidelines jurisprudence has come into being. For example, in the case of foreign adoptions, blood banks, and protection of women at work places, it is the guidelines themselves that are being followed and acted upon. Proceeding further, in the case of irretrievable breakdown of marriage as a ground for divorce, the Supreme Court itself has directed that the High Courts may adopt this ground while granting divorce. Shortly, the lower judiciary also may adopt it as a rule saying that they are bound by the law laid down by the Supreme Court.

That all the fundamental rights or human rights are granted only to the citizens does not deprive the foreigners to claim protection of such fundamental rights like right to life. The foreigners are entitled to the protection of those which come under human rights.

Articles 36 to 51

A Narrative

While penning a chapter on directive principles of State policy, the Constitution has made it clear that the State in India is a welfare State, its economy is inclusive of all sections of the people, particularly the lowest of the low and also expressly non-exploitative in character. It is true, the Supreme Court cannot issue any directives in the nature of mandamus to the State to legislate a law in conformity with the principles stated in this chapter, but the Courts can take into consideration the objectives of the principles while making any orders, where said principles are involved. The court cannot direct any State to make any law on full employment, yet, the Court will certainly sustain any law in the direction of creating employment such as Rural Employment Guarantee Act, notwithstanding the fact that it will not cover all the rural unemployed. A law made by the State to control the industry by means of regulation will be upheld by the Court on the ground that it discourages monopoly. When any legislation is made to take over excess properties above the ceiling fixed, such law will surely get the go-ahead from the judiciary applying the principles contained in the directive principles of State policy and such law cannot be treated as a law authorising total expropriation of property. If a legislation satisfies the declaration contained therein that it is designed to achieve the directives of State policy, it does not preclude the Supreme Court to examine whether such law satisfies the declaration contained therein.

CONSTITUTIONAL AMENDMENTS

Constituent Assembly has not only refrained from putting a seal of finality and infallibility upon this Constitution by denying the people the right to amend the Constitution...or by making the amendment of the Constitution subject to the fulfilment of extraordinary terms and conditions but has provided for a facile procedure for amending the Constitution. –Dr. B.R. Ambedkar

The need for a flexible, operational, rational, reasonable and up-to-date Constitution is paramount and proven. A Constitution not in tune with people's hopes and aspirations, will and wants, thinking and believing is more likely to be cause of irritation, upsurge, and upheaval. Constitutions are a necessary concomitant for rule of law.

Amendments are like surgeries to keep the system alive, they are necessary incisions to remove the infected part. In some countries, amendments are an anathema, they are abhorred; in others they are a way of life. In the Indian Constitution, amendments are not very difficult, nor too easy for comfort.

Article 368 in part XX of the Constitution deals with both power and procedure for amendments. Amendments of three types have been covered by the said article, while power has been questioned by courts, and Parliament held on, but, of course, procedure has never been in doubt or question.

Art. 368

Power of Parliament to amend the Constitution and procedure thereof

[(1) Notwithstanding anything in this Constitution, Parliament may in exercise of its constituent power amend by way of addition, variation or repeal any provision of this Constitution in accordance with the procedure laid down in this article.]

[(2)] An amendment of this Constitution may be initiated only by the introduction of a Bill for the purpose in either House of Parliament, and when the Bill is passed in each House by a majority of the total membership of that House and by a majority of not less than two-thirds of the members of that House present and voting, [it shall be presented to the President who shall give his assent to the Bill and thereupon] the Constitution shall stand amended in accordance with the terms of the Bill:

Provided that if such amendment seeks to make any change in-

(a) Article 54, Article 55, Article 73, Article 162 or Article 241, or

(b) Chapter IV of part V, Chapter V of Part VI, or Chapter I of Part XI, or

(c) any of the Lists in the Seventh Schedule, or

(d) the representation of States in Parliament, or

(e) the provisions of this Article,

the amendment shall also require to be ratified by the Legislature of not less than one-half of the States by resolution to that effect passed by those Legislatures before the Bill making provision for such amendment is presented to the President for assent.

[(3) Nothing in Article 13 shall apply to any amendment made under this article.]

[(4) No amendment of this Constitution (including the provisions of Part III) made or purporting to have been made under this article [whether before or after the commencement of Section 55 of the Constitution (Forty-second Amendment) Act, 1976] shall be called in question in any court on any ground.

[(5) For the removal of doubts, it is hereby declared that there shall be no limitation whatever on the constituent power of Parliament to amend by way of addition, variation or repeal the provisions of this Constitution under this article.]

Types of Amendments:

Procedural

(1) Amendment by a simple majority: It means majority, a simple majority, of those present and voting.

(2) Amendment by special majority: It means a majority of the total membership of that house and by a majority of not less than two-thirds of the members of the house present and voting.

(3) Amendment by Special Majority and Ratification by States.

To elaborate:

(a) While amendment by simple majority to bring about amendment is fine as a process, there exist many items which do not come within the purview of Art. 368. They stand there by their own logic: As for example, several Articles of the Constitution make provisions of a tentative nature and Parliament has been given power to make laws regarding these provisions by ordinary legislative process and it is not to be regarded as an amendment of the Constitution and is also not subject to the special procedure prescribed in Article 368.

Some Examples:

(i) Abolition of a legislative council in a state.

(ii) Administration and control of Scheduled Areas and Scheduled Tribes.

(iii) Parliament may make any provision for citizenship.

(iv) Part XXI of the Constitution–Temporary, transitional, and special provisions, where Parliament is empowered to make laws with respect to certain matters included in the state list.

(v) Second Schedule: emoluments and privileges of the President.

(b) Regarding amendment by special majority: Amendment Bill must be passed by each House of Parliament by a majority of the total membership of the House, and by a majority of not less than two-thirds of the members of the House present. Then the Bill is presented to the President.

(c) Regarding amendment by special majority with ratification, it must be remembered that India is a Union of States and interests of the States must be protected. Under the third category, an amendment bill has to be passed by Parliament by special majority and in addition to that, a ratification by the legislatures of not less than one half of the States by resolution to that effect is also required before the bill is sent to the President for his assent. There's however no time frame within which the States must ratify a Constitution amendment bill.

Cases covered are:

(1) Election of the President.

(2) Representation of States in Parliament.

(3) Procedure for Constitution amendment bill.
(4) Distribution of legislative powers between the Union and the States.
(5) The Supreme Court and High Courts.
(6) Extent of the executive power of the Union.

Now regarding the amendment process itself, following points are significant.

(a) An amendment can be initiated only by the introduction of a bill in either house of Parliament, state legislatures cannot initiate amendments.
(b) There is no provision for a joint sitting in case of disagreement between the two houses in the case of amendment bills; each house has to pass the bill separately as specified.
(c) No specific time limit for ratification of an amending bill by state legislatures is laid down.
(d) An amendment bill may be introduced by a minister, or a private member.
(e) When the bill is passed as per conditions prescribed, it must be presented to the President who shall give his assent; he can't return it or withhold assent.

Thus, we have covered the amendment process and types of amendments, it leaves us with the crucial issue of Parliament's power to amend the Constitution under Art. 368. Parliament and the judiciary have engagingly asserted themselves. Briefly, outlined below is the genesis of the posturing and positioning that verily led both the Parliament and the Supreme Court to the very edge.

S No	Case	Year	Judgement
1.	*Shankari Prasad Singh Deo vs Union of India*	1951	Art. 368 is general and Parliament can amend the Constitution
2.	*Sajjan Singh vs State of Rajasthan*	1965	Parliament can amend any part of the Constitution, including fundamental rights.
3.	*Golaknath vs State of Punjab*	1967	In a 6:5 majority judgement the Supreme Court held the fundamental freedoms to be beyond Parliament's power to modify, restrict, or impair.
4.	*Kesavananda Bharati vs State of Kerala*	1973	By a 7:6 majority the Supreme Court over turned the Golaknath judgement, giving nod to Parliament the right to amend any part of the Constitution, but basic structure of the Constitution is not to be changed.
5.	*Minerva Mills vs Union of India*	1980	4:1 majority judgement upheld the power of judicial review of Constitutional amendments, but also upheld the power of parliament to amend within the confines of basic structure.Court held that power of judicial review was also the basic feature of the Constitution.

In *Waman Rao vs Union of India*, the Supreme Court upheld the *Minerva Mills* judgement. Curtain was coming down, albeit slowly; Parliament and the Supreme Court made their positions clear and clarity was accepted.

NOTABLE AMENDMENTS

The Constitution (Fourth Amendment) Act, 1955

Article 31 (2) of the Constitution was amended to re-state more precisely the state's power of compulsory acquisition and requisitioning of private property and distinguish it from cases where the operation of regulatory or prohibitory laws of the States results in "deprivation of property". Article 31A of the Constitution was also amended to extend its scope to cover categories of essential welfare legislation like abolition of zamindars, proper planning of urban and rural areas, and for effecting a full control over the mineral and oil resources of the country, etc. Six Acts were also included in the Ninth Schedule. Article 305 was also amended to save certain laws providing for State Monopolies.

The Constitution (Twenty-fourth Amendment) Act, 1971

This amendment was passed in the context of a situation that emerged with the verdict in Golaknath's case by the Supreme Court. Accordingly, this Act amended Article 13 and Article 368 to remove all doubts regarding the power of Parliament to amend the Constitution including the Fundamental Rights.

The Constitution (Twenty-fifth Amendment) Act, 1971

This amendment further amended Article 31 in the wake of the Bank Nationalisation case. The word 'amount' was substituted in place of 'compensation' in the light of the judicial interpretation of the word 'compensation' meaning 'adequate compensation'.

The Constitution (Forty-second Amendment) Act, 1976

This act made a number of important amendments in the Constitution. These amendments were mainly for the purpose of giving effect to the recommendation of Swaran Singh Committee.

Some of the important amendments made are for the purpose of spelling out expressly the high ideals of socialism, secularism, and the integrity of the nation, to make the Directive Principles more comprehensive, and giving them precedence over those Fundamental Rights which have been allowed to be relied upon to frustrate socio-economic reforms. The amendment Act also inserted a new chapter on the Fundamental Duties of citizens and made special provisions for dealing with anti-national activities, whether by individuals or by associations. The judiciary provisions were also amended by providing for a requirement as to the minimum number of judges for determining question as to the Constitutional validity of law, and for a special majority of not less than two-third for declaring any law to be Constitutionally invalid.

To reduce the mounting arrears in High Courts and to secure the speedy disposal of service matters, revenue matters, and certain other matters of special importance in the context of socio-economic development and progress, this amendment Act provided for the creation of administrative and other tribunals for dealing with such matters while preserving the jurisdiction of the Supreme Court in regard to such matters under Article 136 of the Constitution. Certain modifications in the writ jurisdiction of High Courts under Article 226 were also made.

The Constitution (Forty-fourth Amendment) Act, 1978

The right to property which had been the occasion for more than one amendment of Constitution was omitted as a Fundamental Right and it was made only as a legal right. It was, however, ensured that the removal of the right to property from the list of Fundamental Rights would not affect the right of minorities to establish and administer educational institutions of their choice. Article 352 of the Constitution was amended to provide "armed rebellion" as one of the circumstances for declaration of emergency. Internal disturbance not amounting to armed rebellion would not be a ground for the issuance of a Proclamation. The right to personal liberty as contained in Articles 21 and 22 is further strengthened by the provision that a law for preventive detention cannot authorise, in any case, detention for a longer period than two months unless an Advisory Board has reported that there is sufficient cause for such detention. The additional safeguard has also been provided by the requirements that the Chairman of an Advisory Board shall be a serving Judge of the appropriate High Court and that the Board shall be constituted in accordance with the recommendations of the Chief Justice of that High Court.

With a view to avoid delays, Articles 132 and 134 were amended and a new Article 134A was inserted to provide that a High Court should consider the question of granting a certificate for appeal to Supreme Court immediately after the delivery of the judgement, final order, or sentence concerned on the basis of an oral application by a party or, if the High Court deems it so to do, on its own. The other amendments made by the Act are mainly for removing or correcting the distortions which came into the Constitution by reason of the amendment initiated during the period of internal emergency.

The Constitution (Fifty-second Amendment) Act, 1985

It amends the Constitution to provide that a Member of Parliament or a State Legislature who defects, or is expelled from the party which set him up as a candidate in the election, or if an independent member of the House, joins a political party after expiry of six months from the date on which he takes seat in the House, shall be disqualified to remain a member of the House. The Act also makes suitable provisions with respect to splits and merger of political parties.

The Constitution (Sixty-fifth Amendment) Act, 1990—Article 338 of the Constitution provides for a special Officer for the Scheduled Castes and Scheduled Tribes to investigate all matters relating to the safeguards provided for the Scheduled Castes and Scheduled Tribes under the Constitution and to report to the President on their working. The Article has been amended for the constitution of a National Commission for Scheduled Castes and Scheduled Tribes consisting of a Chairperson, Vice Chairperson and five other Members who shall be appointed by the President by warrant under his hand and seal. The amended Article elaborates the duties of the said Commission and covers measures that should be taken by the Union or any state for the effective implementation of the reports presented by the Commission. It also provides that the Commission shall, while investigating any matter or inquiring into any complaint have all the powers of a Civil Court trying a suit and the reports of the said Commission shall be laid before Parliament and the Legislature of the States.

The Constitution (Seventy-third Amendment) Act, 1993

Article 40 of the Constitution which enshrines one of the Directive Principles of State Policy, lays down that the State shall take steps to organise village Panchayats and endow them with such powers and authority as may be necessary to enable them to function as units of self-government.

In the light of the above, a new part IX relating to the Panchayats has been inserted in the Constitution to provide for among other things, Gram Sabha in a village or group of villages; Constitution of Panchayats at village and other level or levels; direct elections to all seats in Panchayats at the village and intermediate level if any, and to the offices of Chairpersons of Panchayats at such levels; reservation of seats for the Scheduled Castes and Scheduled Tribes in proportion to their population for membership of Panchayats and office of Chairpersons in Panchayats at each level; reservation of not less than one-third of the seats for women; fixing tenure of five years for Panchayats and holding elections within a period of six months in the event of supersession of any Panchayat.

The Constitution (Seventy-fourth Amendment) Act, 1993

In many States, local bodies have become weak and ineffective on account of a variety of reasons, including the failure to hold regular elections, prolonged supersession, and inadequate devolutions of powers and functions. As a result, Urban Local Bodies are not able to perform effectively as vibrant democratic units of self-government.

Having regard to these inadequacies, a new part IX-A relating to the municipalities has been incorporated in the Constitution to provide for among other things, constitution of three types of Municipalities, i.e., Nagar Panchayats for areas in transition from a rural area to urban areas.

The Constitution (Eighty-first Amendment) Act, 2000

By this amendment the unfilled vacancies of a year which were reserved for the Scheduled Castes and the Scheduled Tribes for being filled up in that year in accordance with any provision for reservations made under Article 16 of the Constitution, shall be considered as a separate class of vacancies to be filled up in any succeeding years or years, and such class of vacancies shall not be considered together with the vacancies of the year in which they were filled up for determining the ceiling of fifty per cent reservation against total number of vacancies of that year.

The Constitution (Eighty-second Amendment) Act, 2000

The amendment provides that nothing in Article 335 shall prevent the state from making any provision in favour of the members of the Scheduled Castes and the Scheduled Tribes for relaxation in qualifying marks in any examination or lowering the standards of evaluation for reservation in matters of promotion to any class or classes of services or posts in connection with affairs of the Union or of a State.

The Constitution (Ninety-first Amendment), Act, 2003–In Article 75 of the Constitution, after clause (1), the following clauses shall be inserted, namely:

"(1A) –The total number of Ministers, including the Prime Minister, in the Council of Ministers shall not exceed fifteen per cent of the total number of members of the House of the people.

(1B) – A member of either House of Parliament belonging to any political party who is disqualified for being a member of that House under paragraph 2 of the Tenth Schedule shall also be disqualified to be appointed as a Minister under clause (1) for duration of the period commencing from the date of his disqualification till the date on which the term of his office as such member would expire or where he contests any election to either House of Parliament before the expiry of such period, till the date on which he is declared elected, whichever is earlier"

In Article 164 of the Constitution, after clause (i), the following clauses shall be inserted namely:

"(1A) – the total number of Ministers, including the Chief Minister, in the Council of Ministers in a state shall not exceed fifteen per cent of the total number of members of the Legislative Assembly of the state:

[Provided that the number of Ministers, including the Chief Minister, in a state shall not be less than twelve:

Provided further that where the total number of Ministers, including the Chief Minister, in the Council of Ministers in any state of the commencement of the Constitution (Ninety-first Amendment) Act,2003 exceeds the said fifteen per cent or the number specified in the first proviso, as the case may be, then, the total number of Ministers in that state shall be brought in conformity with the provisions of this clause within six months from such date as the President may by public notification appoint.]

(1B) – A member of the Legislative Assembly of a state or either House of the legislature of a state having Legislative Council belonging to any political party who is disqualified for being a member of that House under paragraph 2 of the Tenth Schedule shall also be disqualified to be appointed as a Minister under clause (1) for duration of the period commencing from the date of his disqualification till the date on which the term of his office as such member would expire or where he contests any election to the Legislative Assembly of a state or either House of the Legislature of a state having Legislative Council, as the case may be, before the expiry of such period, till the date on which he is declared elected, whichever is earlier"

After Article 361A of the Constitution, the following article shall be inserted, namely:

361B– A member of a House belonging to any political party who is disqualified for being a member of the House under Paragraph 2 of the Tenth Schedule shall also be disqualified to hold any remunerative political post for duration of the period commencing from the date of his disqualification till the date on which the term of his office as such member would expire or till the date on which he contests an election to a House and is declared elected, whichever is earlier.

The Constitution (One Hundredth Amendment) Act, 2015

amended the First Schedule of the Constitution, for the purpose of giving effect to the acquiring of territories by India and transfer of territories to Bangladesh through retaining of adverse possession and exchange of enclaves, in pursuance of the Agreement between India and Bangladesh concerning the demarcation of the land boundary, signed on 16th May 1974 and its protocol, signed on 6th September, 2011.

The Constitution (One Hundred and First Amendment)

Act, 2016–The Constitution was amended to introduce "The Goods and services Tax (GST)". It amended the Articles 248, 249, 250, 268, 269, 270,286, 366, &368. It amended the Sixth & Seventh Schedules, omitted Article 268A, and inserted new Articles 246A (special provision with respect to goods and services tax), 269A (levy and collection of goods and services tax in course of inter-state trade or commerce), and 279A (Goods and services Tax council). The act also provided for compensation to States for loss of revenue on account of introduction of goods and services tax.

ART. 368

Power of Parliament to Amend the Constitution and Procedure

Parliament has power to amend the Constitution in any of its provisions. There is no requirement to convene any new Constituent Assembly to amend or re-enact any provision in the Constitution. To deal with the amendments to the Constitution, the Parliament itself sits as Constituent Assembly. Barring certain matters, Parliament may approve the amendments with simple majority of the members attending. In any other matter, the Parliament shall vote by a majority of the strength of the Parliament or by a majority of 2/3rd members present and voting. The expression 'persons present in voting' means, in simple terms, 'those who are actually present in the Parliament at the time of voting'. It can be clarified that those who walk out, or those who abstain from voting are not taken into account. Regarding certain matters in which the States are interested, a ratification of the amendment by majority of the States is necessary. Here too, if any State or States do not send their resolutions, their opinion or abstention is not taken into consideration. Sometimes, the opinion of States is called for. In such cases, only the opinion is considered by the Union. What is essential is that a mere consideration of the opinion of the State takes place. But the Union is not obliged to follow the opinion of the State Legislatures. As per Article 368, the Parliament is competent to amend any part of the Constitution or any Article. In *Golaknath's* case, the Supreme Court gave verdict that Parliament is not competent to amend the fundamental rights. This view was totally reversed in *Kesavananda Bharati's* case but the Supreme Court, however, put a condition that the Parliament, even though it can amend the fundamental rights, cannot amend the Constitution in a manner which negates the basic features of the Constitution. The Supreme Court has spelt the following as basic features: (1) Parliamentary system; (2) Principle of equality; (3) Rule of law; and (4) Judicial review.

[(1) Notwithstanding anything in this Constitution, Parliament may in exercise of its constituent power amend by way of addition, variation or repeal any provision of this Constitution in accordance with the procedure laid down in this article.]

[(2)] An amendment of this Constitution may be initiated only by the introduction of a Bill for the purpose in either House of Parliament, and when the Bill is passed in each House by a majority of the total membership of that House and by a majority of not less than two-thirds of the members of that House present and voting, [it shall be presented to the President who shall give his assent to the Bill and thereupon] the Constitution shall stand amended in accordance with the terms of the Bill:

[Provided that if such amendment seeks to make any change in

(a) Article 54, Article 55, Article 73, Article 162 or Article 241, or

(b) Chapter IV of part V, Chapter V of Part VI, or Chapter I of Part XI, or

(c) any of the Lists in the Seventh Schedule, or

(d) the representation of States in Parliament, or

(e) the provisions of this article,

the amendment shall also require to be ratified by the Legislature of not less than one-half of the States by resolution to that effect passed by those Legislatures before the Bill making provision for such amendment is presented to the President for assent.]

[(3) Nothing in Article 13 shall apply to any amendment made under this article.]

[(4) No amendment of this Constitution (including the provisions of Part III) made or purporting to have been made under this article [whether before or after the commencement of Section 55 of the Constitution (Forty-second Amendment) Act, 1976] shall be called in question in any court on any ground.

[(5) For the removal of doubts, it is hereby declared that there shall be no limitation whatever on the constituent power of Parliament to amend by way of addition, variation or repeal the provisions of this Constitution under this article.]

HAS OUR CONSTITUTION DELIVERED?

An oft repeated question is, 'Has our Constitution delivered? 'Have we succeeded? Is our Constitution the best that we could give to ourselves? Many agree that it is so; some agree to disagree. There are doubting Thomases, yet the remarkable feature is that the Constitution has survived to strengthen our faith. It has shown us the way to usher in a system of rights, checks and balances, social justice, rule of law, and above all governance based on order, integrity and values.

Our constitution was framed at a time when the British had just left, leaving the country divided. Expectations were many, so were the compulsions. Loyalties were in conflict, people were in distress. Food situation was pathetic, the economy was attuned to the war needs, refugee problem was looking insurmountable, Pakistan was set on fomenting trouble with India, princes were stirring the pot of trouble, prejudice against institutions nurtured by the British was running high, and above all Gandhiji's life had been ended by a madman's bullet. Under such circumstances of anger, anxiety, acrimony, and animosity, the framers of our Constitution still kept their wit and wisdom together to give us this Constitution. Equality prevailed over exclusion, equanimity over exuberance, excellence over emptiness, experience over expediency and expectation over excuses. The truth however is that our Constitution has stood the test of time, test of challenges, test of emergent situations, and test of credibility. Countries in our neighbourhood have experimented with peel and repeal type constitution and then moved over to fresh engagement.

Pakistan has had constitutional crisis, leading even to the division of that country. Afghanistan moved from monarchy to anarchy to Taliban to tailspin to treaty-based settlement. Nepal is battling to find a right Constitution with rights for all. Myanmar is emerging out of the shadows of army rule with a debate on 'army's vice and people's voice. Sri Lanka has settled for a Constitution after some uncertainty over Tamil issues. Bangladesh has alternated between army and civil rule; both having their vision and version of what Constitutions should be like. China too has had revisions. Single party rule too considered need for change!

The truth however is that our Constitution has stood the test of time, test of challenges, test of emergent situations, and test of credibility. Countries in our neighbourhood have experimented with peel and repeal type constitution and then moved over to fresh engagement.

Indian Constitution has seen many an amendment: quite a few being procedural and perfunctory. Even so, our Constitution though it took close to three years to enact, has remained firmly rooted. We have had spectacular successes as also singular failures, although it must be said that some of the failures are failures of the institutions created by the Constitution, not of the Constitution itself.

The success story continues. The Constitution has created many institutions; sanctified some existing ones and these have taken firm roots even in our psyche. Parliament, courts, government-led institutions are some of them. Constitution has created posts like the President, Prime Minister, Comptroller and Auditor General, Speaker, etc. and these too have been accepted by the country, although one would rather have a better view of Governors.

Elections have been held when due and the succession has been smooth and satisfactory. It is a tribute to the vast majority that they have participated in the process happily and with maturity.

We were bold enough to go in from British era limited franchise to Universal Adult Suffrage and gave women the right to vote, even ahead of the United States.

Democracy has reached the grassroot level with the ushering in of the Panchayati Raj consequent to Constitutional amendments (73rd/74th). Our Constitution has the flexibility for accommodation through means that are well established.

Unforeseen situations like Chinese aggression of 1962 have been met with proclamation of external emergency. The Punjab militant crisis of 80s was met through a series of amendments to extended President's rule. Constitution has provisions to meet such unforeseen events. Country is ruled by unitary mechanisms putting the federal ones to secondary positions. When the need was felt the country reverted back to normalcy.

Constitution has provisions for welfare of the scheduled castes, tribes, and other backward classes who have suffered over centuries socially and economically. It is a case for all to be partners in prosperity; not doles, but dignity. Yet it is not roses, roses all the way, thorns too have been there. There have been instances of failure or feeling of failure. As already hinted, success of governance or failure of the same is a different issue altogether and it cannot be directly linked to the Constitution. Success of Green Revolution or expansion of telecommunication or education or infrastructure or healthcare or industry services can be a matter of pride and satisfaction doubtless, and one can even say that institutions created by the Constitution have a large role in that, but per se it is the governance which is responsible. In the same vein, failure to curb population, poverty, corruption, casteism, criminalisation, social prejudices, etc. cannot be blamed on the Constitution: it's the governance.

> Frequent amendments have dented the credibility of the Constitution though the causes for the same are justifiable. Amendments are like lifelines to support the system to avoid rigidities, but overdose of amendments leaves the system weak, worried, and withered.

We are concerned with failures that can be traced to the provisions set out in the Constitution. There are many who still do not believe in the idea of a Constitution; they are dogged dissenters, such as left-wing extremists, fundamentalists, groups seeking secession in the north-east, etc. Many have come on board since 1950 but some have not. It is an area of uncertainty.

Article 356 regarding proclamation of President's role has invited bickerings alleging misuse; a charge not altogether misplaced. Many commissions have sought its modification but the party in power always resists. Even courts have intervened to set matters right. Sooner or later the issue will have to be resolved, one hopes it is sooner.

There however exist many areas of concern, causes for conflict, and cases for consideration, which if not attended to will undermine the concept of Constitution. These are festering wounds needing urgent attention. Foremost, economic disparities are widening; Constitutional framework is just not able to address itself to it. India's global rank in various indices such as corruption, poverty, women and child health, ease of doing business is still not worth mentioning. Bureaucracy is still creaky. Reform process is slow.

Electoral reforms, police reforms, judicial reforms, social reforms, economic reforms, etc. are all moving, but not at a satisfactory pace. Technology is the key but it still seems to go through the mire and maze of bureaucracy. What of the Parliament? Adjournments, disruptions, walkouts, slogan shouting, tearing papers, sitting in the well of the house; the list is endless, not so the Parliament time.

What of the honourable members? A few of them have lowered the dignity of the exalted body; cash for questions, bribes, sleaze, gratifications, etc. Parliament today is not given that respect it once commanded. The conflict between the legislature and the judiciary which rocked the 70s and early 80s is still too fresh in our minds to be forgotten. *Golaknath, Kesavananda Bharti*, and *Minerva Mills* cases saw the conflict and the consensus. Judicial review is held to be supreme now but parliament can amend the Constitution, sans 'Basic structure' which remains ill-defined but well-debated.

Conflicts also exist between the executive and the judiciary: many a scam cases are ample testimony to that. Judiciary has moved in quite often to order court monitored progress.

Fundamental Rights need to be expanded and fundamental duties need to be enforced. Union's role need to be redefined as it has a commanding role in the Constitution. Many commissions constituted to examine Centre-State relations have been clear about many issues but their implementation remains tardy. Sarkaria Commission and Punchhi Commission reports have gathered dust, not momentum (for implementation). Justice Venkatachaliah Commission appointed in 2002 (National commission to review the working of the Constitution) laboured hard to hand down a voluminous report but its labours remain confined to debates, discussions, and deliberations.

The commission suggested enlargement of provisions of Art.15 (prohibition of discrimination on grounds of religion, race, caste, sex, or place of birth) to include ethnic or social origin, colour, age, language, and political or other opinion, property, etc.

The commission suggested amendments to the contentious Art. 356 and recommended that all trials of strength should be on the floor of the house. It recommended setting up of a panel with the Prime Minister, Lok Sabha Speaker, and the Chief Minister concerned for the appointment of the Governor who should have fixed tenure. State legislature should have provisions to impeach the Governor. The commission also suggested expansion of fundamental rights, like rights to privacy, clean environment, etc.

JUSTICE VENKATACHALIAH'S VIEW

According to the National Commission to Review the Working of the Constitution (NCRWC) chairman Mr. Justice M. Venkatachaliah, the vast majority of the suggestions eventually be made by the body will not require amendments to the Constitution.

He has said that the bulk of the Commission's recommendations would relate to reforming existing legislation or be in the nature of suggestions for administrative reform. ``That on the Constitutional side will be very minimal," he stated. ``And even here there is no question of tampering with the basic features."

The former Chief Justice of India also pointed out that in many areas parliamentary democracy could be strengthened if the Government were to adopt certain conventions. As an example of this, he referred to the appointment of the Comptroller and Auditor General (CAG) and said that nothing in Article 148 prevented a Government from seeking a broader political consensus on this. The same held for the Chief Vigilance Commissioner but it had taken the Supreme Court to chalk up an impartial procedure for making the appointment.

Mr. Venkatachaliah has said that he was personally not in favour of the idea of indirect elections (one of the suggestions in a consultation paper that had sparked off a controversy). To a question about whether he favoured run-off elections, another major proposal relating to election reform, he said he was open- minded about this. (Under the run-off system, a second election is proposed whenever no candidate gets 50 per cent of the votes polled. The second election will be held between the candidate who polled the maximum number of votes and the one who polled the second most number of votes.)

CONSTITUTIONAL PRESCRIPTIONS AS REGARDS TIME PERIOD		
(1)	Those who left for Pakistan earlier to 19th July 1948 and those who left for Pakistan between 19rth July, 1948 upto the commencement of the Constitution and migrated to India are entitled to the Indian citizenship on certain terms and conditions	Art. 5-11
(2)	Detention beyond 24 hours in police custody is illegal	Art. 22
(3)	Preventive detention beyond three months without obtaining the opinion of the Advisory Board is illegal	Art. 22
(4)	The term of office of the President is five years	Art. 56
(5)	Election of President shall be held within six months of the date of vacancy	Art. 62
(6)	Notice of impeachment of President shall be 14 days	Art. 61
(7)	Notice for the removal of the office of the Vice-President is 14 days	Art. 67
(8)	If the Minister is not a member of the Parliament/State Assembly for six months, he ceases to be a Minister	Art. 75
(9)	Life of Parliament is five years. It can be extended during emergency by one year each time and shall end by sixth month after emergency ceases	Art. 83
(10)	Not more than six months' time shall elapse between one session and the other of the Parliament / State Assembly	Art. 85
(11)	The period of notice to be given for the removal of Speaker and Deputy Speaker is 14 days	Art. 94
(12)	If a member of the Parliament / Assembly is absent for sixty days without the permission of the House, he shall cease to be a member	Art. 101 & Art. 168
(13)	Penalty is imposable on every day of sitting on the member who is not entitled to participate in the Parliament / Assembly	Art. 104 & Art.193

(14)	If more than six months' elapse after the dispute between the Lok Sabha and Rajya Sabha the President shall convene a joint session of both Houses	Art. 108
(15)	Rajya Sabha must complete the discussion on the money bill within 14 days from the day it is received at the Rajya Sabha from the Parliament. Other than money bill the discussion must be completed within 6 weeks	Art. 109
(16)	Qualification for appointment of Supreme Court Judge is 5 Years' experience as High Court Judge and 10 Years' experience as Advocate	Art. 124
(17)	Term of office of the Governor is 5 Years	Art. 156
(18)	Reduction in the number of Ministers which should be 15% of the total members of the House shall be effected within six months from the date of the Presidential notification made in this regard	Art. 164
(19)	Ordinance shall expire after six weeks from the first meeting of the Parliament or Rajya Sabha whichever is later	Art. 123
(20)	Duration of State Legislature is five years. There is no such restriction on the Rajya Sabha or on the Legislative Council of the States	Art. 172
(21)	If more than three months elapsed after the bill is submitted to the Council, it may again be considered as passed by Legislature	Art. 197
(22)	If the President refuses his assent and Governor sends back the bill to the legislature for reconsideration, the legislature shall take up the bill within six months	Art. 201
(23)	Retirement of High Court Judge is 62 Years	Art. 207
(24)	Qualification of appointment of High Court judge is 10 years' experience as judicial officer or 10 years' experience as advocate	Art. 207
(25)	When exparte order is made by High Court under Art. 226, it will expire by end of two weeks unless the matter is taken up and disposed of within that period or extended during the continuance of the interim application	Art. 226
(26)	Duration of panchayat/municipality is five years	Art. 243E & Art 243U
(27)	On dissolution of the panchayat and municipality, fresh elections shall be held within six months	Art. 243E, 243U
(28)	Term of office of the Public Service Commission is six years	Art. 316
(29)	During emergency if 1/10th members of the Parliament request for a meeting of Parliament for condemning emergency, the President shall convene the Parliament forthwith	Art. 352
(30)	Maximum duration of President's rule over State subject to extensions is 3 years	Art. 356
(31)	President's power to adopt laws to bring them in conformity with the Constitution is 3 years from the commencement of the Constitution	Art. 372A

Did you know?

The Indian Constitution with 448 articles, 12 Schedules is the largest written constitution in the world.

It is lengthy because both the Union and the States are covered in it. It not only lays down the basis of governance but also creates institutions to see the enforcement through administrative procedure.

It took three years, eleven months and twenty-six days to frame the constitution.

Did you know?

In the *Sankari Prasad Singh Deo Vs Union of India* case of 1952 and the1955 *Sajjan Singh Vs Rajasthan* case, the Supreme Court upheld the power of Parliament to amend any part of the constitution. But in 1967, an eleven bench of the Supreme Court reversed the position in the *Golaknath Vs State of Punjab* case. In a 6:5 majority judgement, the Supreme Court held that Article 368 merely outlined the procedure for amendment and did not grant parliament the power.

The term 'Basic Structure' was used by one of the counsels in the case. The stage now was set for confrontation between the Parliament and the Judiciary as the former insisted on its primacy.

In 1973, in the *Kesavananda Bharti case* The Supreme Court now held that Parliament had the right to amend any part of the Constitution so long as the 'Basic Structure' was not altered.

'Basic Structure' is not defined the constitution and in the 1973 *Kesavananda Bharti case* each judge held forth as to what he felt constituted the 'Basic Structure'.

Broadly, it was construed to mean:

1. Unity and integrity of the nation.
2. Parliamentary form of democracy.
3. Supremacy of the constitution.
4. Fundamental Rights and Directive Principles.
5. Secular character of the Constitution.

The parliament got its supremacy endorsed but in the ultimate analysis, the judiciary emerged with the power to rule what constituted the 'Basic Structure'. It was a way forward.

Constitution ...Other Provisions

Here are some more provisions contained in the Constitution and the same are shown here briefly;

1) **Part XVI:** Special provisions pertaining to certain cases:
   Articles 330 to 342 covers the special provisions relating to Scheduled Castes and Scheduled Tribes as also Anglo-Indians
2) **Part XVII:** Relates to official language through Articles 343, 344 ;Regional languages from 345 to 347; language of Supreme Court , 348 and 349; Special directives 350, 350A, B and 351
3) **Part XXI:** Temporary, transitional and special provisions. Articles 369 to 392 deal with temporary, transitional and special provisions that relate to specified articles in respect of some states. *Briefly* :

Articles 370, 371A to J: All about states

Article 369: Power of Parliament about items in State List as though they were in Concurrent List

Article 373: Power of President to make orders in respect of preventive detention in certain cases

Article 374, 375, 376: About court matters

Article 377: About CAG (Comptroller and Auditor General)

Article 376: About PSC (Public Service Commission)

Article 370: Gives autonomous status to the state of Jammu and Kashmir. It is always in the news

Did you know?

The Constituent Assembly was created by the British Government to draw a constitution under the framework of the Cabinet Mission plan. The British Parliament retained the right to veto any constitution framed by the Constituent Assembly; to this extent the Assembly was not sovereign.

The Constituent Assembly, however, declared itself sovereign and passed a resolution that it could not be dissolved except through its own resolution with two thirds majority.

Dawn of independence on August 15, 1947 removed this anomaly, as now the Constituent Assembly became sovereign by right and by reason. The next issue was now that this body had to perform two functions: both complementary:

1. Constituent Assembly..as a constitution framing body.
2. Constituent Assembly..as a law making body.

A committee was appointed by the Assembly with Shri G.V Mavalankar to study and submit a report on how to address these twin functions. Based on the recommendations of the committee, rules were amended and a new body called Constituent Assembly (Legislative) was at once constituted with Mavalankar elected as the Speaker (November 17, 1947).

Dr. Rajendra Prasad continued as the Chairman of the original Constituent Assembly to progress further the work of completing the constitution framing. On November 26, 1949 the work was completed. We had our Constitution.

2

CHAPTER

Functions of The Union and The States

OVERVIEW

The Constitution has the Union and the States amalgamated in a unique bond of a federation, with set and defined functions and responsibilities; it is not a bond of dependence, but of interdependence. The powers, both political and economic, are defined and detailed to the lowest level. Constitution has drawn the boundaries, set the lines, and defined the divisions; all to ensure that the Union and the States work together in a spirit of 'Cooperative Federalism'. This chapter therefore covers functions and responsibilities of the Union and the States; issues and challenges pertaining to the federal structure; devolution of powers and finances up to local levels and challenges therein.

The Union functions have two parts; one the powers of the President, second powers of the Union.

The Union and the States are bound in a federal set up with mutuality of interest and commonality of purpose. The federal system has a strong bias towards the Union, but it is neither coercive nor compulsive. The States have a reasonable degree of freedom and autonomy with defined set of administrative, legislative and financial articles. What makes the constitution further unique is that it is dynamic with a fair degree of flexibility too.

The federal set up is not without its critics, which is reasonable to expect, given the diversity of interests and degree of intricacies. Of particular significance are the emergency articles; notably Article 356 which has been the cause of some concern and consternation. Even so, the arrangement has withstood the test of times and found acceptance; its a tribute not only to the wisdom of the framers of our Constitution but also their maturity.

The devolution of powers with the constitutional amendments (73rd and 74th,1992) have taken democracy to the grassroots and brought huge excitement and enthusiasm to the masses. Similarly, regular holding of elections have ensured that our democracy stays vibrant and visible. This is due in a large measure to the institutions that the Constitution has created. The Union and the States, both have their roles to play in a spirit of acceptance and accomodation; this has been guided by the Constitution.

THE PRESIDENT

Article 52.

There shall be a President of India.

Article 53.

(1) The executive power of the Union shall be vested in the President and shall be exercised by him either directly or through officers subordinate to him in accordance with this Constitution.

(2) Without prejudice to the generality of the foregoing provision, the supreme command of the Defence Forces of the Union shall be vested in the President and the exercise thereof shall be regulated by law.

(3) Nothing in this article shall–

(a) be deemed to transfer to the President any functions conferred by any existing law on the Government of any State or other authority; or

(b) prevent Parliament from conferring by law functions on authorities other than the President.

Article 54.

The President shall be elected by the members of an electoral college consisting of–

(a) the elected members of both Houses of Parliament; and

(b) the elected members of the Legislative Assemblies of the States.

Article 55.

(1) As far as practicable, there shall be uniformity in the scale of representation of the different States at the election of the President.

(2) For the purpose of securing such uniformity among the States interse as well as parity between the States as a whole and the Union, the number of votes which each elected member of Parliament and of the Legislative Assembly of each State is entitled to cast at such election shall be determined in the following manner:–

(a) every elected member of the Legislative Assembly of a State shall have as many votes as there are multiples of one thousand in the quotient obtained by dividing the population of the State by the total number of the elected members of the Assembly;

(b) if, after taking the said multiples of one thousand, the remainder is not less than five hundred, then the vote of each member referred to in sub-clause (a) shall be further increased by one;

(c) each elected member of either House of Parliament shall have such number of votes as maybe obtained by dividing the total number of votes assigned to the members of the Legislative Assemblies of the States under sub-clauses (a) and (b) by the total number of the elected members of both Houses of Parliament, fractions exceeding one-half being counted as one and other fractions being disregarded.

(3) The election of the President shall be held in accordance with the system of proportional representation by means of the single transferable vote and the voting at such election shall be by secret ballot.

Article 56.

(1) The President shall hold office for a term of five years from the date on which he enters upon his office : *Provided that–*

(a) the President may, by writing under his hand addressed to the Vice-President, resign his office;

(b) the President may, for violation of the Constitution, be removed from office by impeachment in the manner provided in article 61;

(c) the President shall, notwithstanding the expiration of his term, continue to hold office until his successor enters upon his office.

(2) Any resignation addressed to the Vice-President under clause (a) of the proviso to clause (1) shall forth with be communicated by him to the Speaker of the House of the People.

Article 57.

A person who holds, or who has held, office as President shall, subject to the other provisions of this Constitution, be eligible for re-election to that office.

Article 58.

(1) No person shall be eligible for election as President unless he–

(a) is a citizen of India,

(b) has completed the age of thirty-five years, and

(c) is qualified for election as a member of the House of the People.

(2) A person shall not be eligible for election as President if he holds any office of profit under the Government of India or the Government of any State or under any local or other authority subject to the control of any of the said Governments.

Article 59.

(1) The President shall not be a member of either House of Parliament or of a House of the Legislature of any State, and if a member of either House of Parliamentor of a House of the Legislature of any State be elected President, he shall be deemed to have vacated his seat in that House on the date on which he enters upon his office as President.

(2) The President shall not hold any other office of profit.

(3) The President shall be entitled without payment of rent to the use of his official residences and shall be also entitled to such emoluments, allowances and privileges as may be determined by Parliament by law and, until provision in that behalf is so made, such emoluments, allowances and privileges as are specified in the Second Schedule.

(4) The emoluments and allowances of the President shall not be diminished during his term of office.

Article 60.

Every President and every person acting as President or discharging the functions of the President shall, before entering upon his office, make and subscribe in the presence of the Chief Justice of India or, in his absence, the senior-most Judge of the Supreme Court available, an oath or affirmation in the following form, that is to say—

"I, A.B., do swear in the name of God / solemnly affirm that I will faith- fully execute the office of President (or discharge the functions of the President) of India and will to the best of my ability preserve, protect and defend the Constitution and the law and that I will devote myself to the service and well-being of the people of India".

Article 61.

(1) When a President is to be impeached for violation of the Constitution, the charge shall be preferred by either House of Parliament.

(2) No such charge shall be preferred unless—

(a) the proposal to prefer such charge is contained in a resolution which has been moved after at least fourteen days' notice in writing signed by not less than one-fourth of the total number of members of the House has been given of their intention to move the resolution, and

(b) such resolution has been passed by a majority of not less than two-thirds of the total membership of the House.

(3) When a charge has been so preferred by either House of Parliament, the other House shall investigate the charge or cause the charge to be investigated and the President shall have the right to appear and to be represented at such investigation.

(4) If as a result of the investigation a resolution is passed by a majority of not less than two-thirds of the total membership of the House by which the charge was investigated or caused to be investigated, declaring that the charge preferred against the President has been sustained, such resolution shall have the effect of removing the President from his office as from the date on which the resolution is so passed.

Article 62.

(1) An election to fill a vacancy caused by the expiration of the term of office of President shall be completed before the expiration of the term.

(2) An election to fill a vacancy in the office of President occurring by reason of his death, resignation or removal, or otherwise shall be held as soon as possible after, and in no case later than six months from, the date of occurrence of the vacancy; and the person elected to fill the vacancy shall, subject to the provisions of article 56, be entitled to hold office for the full term of five years from the date on which he enters upon his office.

Article 70.

Parliament may make such provisions as it thinks fit for the discharge of the functions of the President in any contingency not provided for in this Chapter.

Article 71.

(1) All doubts and disputes arising out of or in connection with the election of a President or Vice-President shall be inquired into and decided by the Supreme Court whose decision shall be final.

(2) If the election of a person as President or Vice-President is declared void by the Supreme Court, acts done by him in the exercise and performance of the powers and duties of the office of President or Vice-President, as the case may be, on or before the date of the decision of the Supreme Court shall not be invalidated by reason of that declaration.

(3) Subject to the provisions of this Constitution, Parliament may by law regulate any matter relating to or connected with the election of a President or Vice-President.

(4) The election of a person as President or Vice-President shall not be called in question on the ground of the existence of any vacancy for whatever reason among the members of the electoral college electing him.

Article 72.

(1) The President shall have the power to grant pardons, reprieves, respites or remissions of punishment or to suspend, remit or commute the sentence of any person convicted of any offence–

(a) in all cases where the punishment or sentence is by a Court Martial;

(b) in all cases where the punishment or sentence is for an offence against any law relating to a matter to which the executive power of the Union extends;

(c) in all cases where the sentence is a sentence of death.

(2) Nothing in sub-clause (a) of clause (1) shall affect the power conferred by law on any officer of the Armed Forces of the Union to suspend, remit or commute a sentence passed by a Court Martial.

(3) Nothing in sub-clause (c) of clause (1) shall affect the power to suspend, remit or commute a sentence of death exercisable by the Governor of a State under any law for the time being in force.

Article 73: Extent of Executive Power of the Union

(I) Subject to the provisions of this Constitution, the executive power of the Union shall extend

(a) to the matters with respect to which Parliament has power to make laws; and

(b) to the exercise of such rights, authority and jurisdiction as are exercisable by the Government of India by virtue of any treaty or agreement.

[Provided that the executive power referred to in the sub-clause (a) shall not, save as expressly provided in this Constitution or in any law made by Parliament extend in any state to matters with respect to which legislature of the state has also power to make laws.]

(II) Until otherwise provided by Parliament, a state and any officer or authority of the state may, notwithstanding anything in this Article, continue to exercise in matters with respect to which Parliament has power to make laws for that state such executive power or functions as the state or authority thereof could exercise immediately before the commencement of this Constitution.

Article 74: Council of Ministers to Aid and Advise President

(I) There shall be a Council of Ministers with the Prime Minister as the head to aid and advise the President who shall, in the exercise of his functions, act in accordance with such advice.

[Provided that the President may require the Council of Ministers to reconsider such advice either generally or otherwise, and the President shall act in accordance, the advice tendered after such reconsideration.

(Inserted by 44th amendment)

(II) The question whether any, and if so what advice was tendered by Ministers to President shall not be inquired into in any court.

Article 76: Attorney-General for India.

(1) The president shall appoint a person who qualified to be appointed a Judge of the Supreme Court to be Attorney-General for India.

(2) It shall be the duty of the Attorney-General to give advice to the Government of India upon such legal matters, and to perform such other duties of a legal character, as may from time to time be referred or assigned to him by the President, and to discharge the functions conferred on him by or under this Constitution or any other law for the time being in force.

(3) In the performance of his duties the Attorney-General shall have right of audience in all courts in the territory of India.

The Attorney-General shall hold office during the pleasure of the President, and shall receive such remuneration as the President may determine.

Article 77: Conduct of Business of the Government of India

(1) All executive action of the Government of India shall be expressed to be taken in the name of the President.

(2) Orders and other instruments made and executed in the name of the President shall be authenticated in such a manner as may be specified in rules to be made by the President, and the validity of an order or instrument which is so authenticated shall not be called in question on the ground that it is not an order or instrument made or executed by the President.

(3) The President shall make rules for the more convenient transactions of the business of the Government of India and for the allocation among ministers of the said business.

Article 78: Duties Of the Prime Minister with Respect to the Furnishing Of Information to the President

It shall be the duty of the Prime Minister

(a) To communicate to President all decisions of the Council of Ministers relating to administration of the Union and proposals for legislation.

(b) To furnish such information relating to the administration of the affairs of the Union and proposals for legislation as the President may call for;

(c) If the President so requires to submit for the consideration of the Council of Ministers any matter on which a decision has been taken by a minister but which has not been considered by the Council.

Article 123: Power of the President to Promulgate Ordinances During Recess of Parliament

(1) If at any time, except when both Houses of Parliament are in session, the President is satisfied that circumstances exist which render it necessary for him to take immediate action, he may promulgate such ordinances as the circumstances appear to him to require.

(2) An ordinance promulgated under this Article shall have the same force and effect as an Act of Parliament, but every such ordinance,

  (a) shall be laid before both Houses of Parliament and shall cease to operate at the expiration of six weeks from the reassembly of Parliament, or, if before expiration of the period resolutions disapproving it are passed by both Houses, upon the passing of the second of those resolutions; and

  (b) may be withdrawn at any time by the President.

(3) If and so far as an ordinance under this Article makes any provisions which the Parliament would not under this Constitution be competent to enact, it shall be void.

ARTICLE 77: CONDUCT OF BUSINESS OF THE GOVERNMENT OF INDIA

A Narrative

The business of Government of India is in the name of the President. Nobody can question that order has not been made by the President under his direct authorisation. The party named shall be the Union of India represented by the Secretary to the Government. If it is not so styled, the suit is liable to be dismissed as against the Union Minister. A decision involving financial implications without consulting Finance Department would be acting contrary to the business rules.

ARTICLE 123: ORDINANCES

A Narrative

What is the legislative power of the President? When the Parliament is not in session, the President may promulgate an Ordinance which is equal to the legislation passed by Parliament. The

Ordinance remains in force till the expiry of six weeks from the date of a next meeting of the next session of the Parliament or earlier before that date the Ordinance is substituted by a bill and Parliament. If Parliament does not ratify the Ordinance within six weeks, the Ordinance lapses. When the Parliament disapproves the Ordinance, it shall cease to be in force. Actions taken under the Ordinance continue to be valid during the period when it is in force; there may be cases that Ordinance fulfils itself before it is disapproved. In such situations, the Parliament has to make a law invalidating the actions taken under the Ordinance. Sometimes, Ordinance is promulgated with a view to achieve a particular purpose, in such cases even when the Ordinance lapses the action taken will continue to be valid. On the provisions of the Ordinance being incorporated in the Act subsequently passed, such Act will be retrospective as and from when the Ordinance is passed. Any Arbitration and Conciliation Ordinance has to be issued twice. When subsequently enacted into the Act it is brought into force as and from the date of the Ordinance, first issued. It should be remembered that existence of circumstances necessitating urgency is necessary before the President promulgates Ordinance.

ARTICLES OF THE CONSTITUTION RELATED TO THE PRESIDENT OF INDIA

A Narrative

The President of India is the Head of the Union and its executive head too. The executive power of the Union President embraces all subjects other than those covered by legislature and judiciary. The election is by system of proportional representation by single transferable vote. The electoral college of Presidential election comprises of all the elected members of Lok Sabha and all the elected Members of Legislative Assemblies of the States and Union Territories (except those nominated).

The Presidential election can be questioned in the Supreme Court only which sits as election tribunal and no other court.

The President always acts on the advice of the Prime Minister and never differs. If for any reason he dissents, he holds option to send back the file to the Cabinet for reconsideration. But, where the Cabinet resubmits its recommendations as originally framed or modified in accordance with the suggestions of the President either fully or partly, the President has to accept the new recommendations of the Cabinet.

In a few cases, the Presidential interference changed the course of action proposed by the Cabinet. President Dr. Babu Rajendra Prasad was not agreeable to the Hindu Code Bill unless it was divided into different parts such as Hindu Marriage Act of 1955, Hindu Succession Act, 1956, Hindu Minority and Guardianship Act of 1956, Hindu Adoption and Maintenance Act, 1956, and the subject of coparcenary was deleted. Hence, it is seen that the Hindu Law reforms took the form of four enactments instead of a single code. President Zail Singh did not agree with Mr. Rajiv Gandhi on a suggested postal Bill. The Bill died quietly because it failed to secure the Presidential assent. There was also the time where President A.P.J. Abdul Kalam recommended that a comprehensive enactment on the subject of "office of profit" should be passed, instead of making exemption enactments every time such tricky problem arose. The Prime Minister did not accept and got passed the enactment granting exemption to a particular office of profit.

Thus, in order that Cabinet reigns supreme, the Constitution has made it obligatory for the President to grant the assent when the Cabinet resubmits its opinion on a Presidential objection.

The President possesses some discretionary powers connected with Cabinet recommendations. He is not at all bound by the advice of the outgoing Prime Minister who has lost the confidence of the House. But, he has to okay the recommendations of outgoing Prime Minister if for any reason he desires to go for early polls and for that purpose seeks dissolution of the House. Yet, the President has to seek bona fide alternatives for the formation of a new Ministry, in cases of crisis. Where the President is required to follow the recommendation of any particular Minister holding a special charge of a specified portfolio, he has option to avoid the Cabinet but where the President dissents with the opinion of the Minister, he can refer the subject to the Cabinet for its approval. The President has the important power to grant pardon and can convert the sentence of death to life imprisonment. The President also has power to grant reprieves, and can whittle sentence for life to any lower punishment. But, it should be remembered that the President has no powers to convert the conviction to acquittal. The President has power to grant pardon in respect of cases of court martial and also power to give pardon in cases of death sentence when the Governor of the State has chosen not to grant the pardon.

The President has the important power to grant pardon and can convert the sentence of death to life imprisonment. The President also has power to grant reprieves, and can whittle sentence for life to any lower punishment. But, it should be remembered that the President has no powers to convert the conviction to acquittal. The President has power to grant pardon in respect of cases of court martial and also power to give pardon in cases of death sentence when the Governor of the State has chosen not to grant the pardon.

The President has the power to refer a question of law of Constitutional importance to the Supreme Court for opinion. But, the opinion rendered by the Supreme Court is not binding on the Government. The Supreme Court has to take up reference and is compulsorily bound to consider the questions submitted to it for its opinion. The Court has powers to reject the questions, if the facts of the dispute so warrant. The Supreme Court can refuse to record opinion. In one case the Supreme Court after hearing on the Presidential reference omitted to render its opinion.

It was the case arising out of Babri Masjid. The Supreme Court queried from the Attorney General whether the Government would follow the opinion of the Supreme Court, and the Attorney General failed to give any such assurance. During a hearing of the Presidential reference, the Supreme Court must hear all the persons interested and also all those who apply for an opportunity of hearing. The Presidential reference is styled as "In re: Presidential reference".

The Vice President, who is elected by the Members of Rajya Sabha and the Members of the Lok Sabha is the ex-officio Chairman of Rajya Sabha and conducts its proceedings in the same manner as the Speaker conducts the proceedings of the Lok Sabha.

The term of the office of the President and Vice President is five years, but they may continue in the post till next elected President and Vice President takes charge. Thus, the election of the President and Vice President shall take place before the period of the expiry of their term. Where any vacancy occurs on account of the death of incumbent or otherwise the election must be held as early as possible. Just like the election of the President can be questioned only in the Supreme Court, the election of the Vice President also can be questioned in the Supreme Court only.

The business of the Union shall be carried on in President's name and all orders issued shall be duly authenticated. Once a document is duly authenticated, it is not open for any Court to enquire whether such order is in fact made by the President personally. The business rules also say that the President should allot the subjects to several Ministries. If Minister concerned is the final authority and the President dissents with his view, the President may direct the matter to be considered by the Cabinet. Then, the Cabinet decision may be treated as reconsidered recommendation and the same shall be accepted by the President.

The question as to what advice the Cabinet has tendered to the President being confidential is protected under the Official Secrets Act. The Cabinet cannot be compelled to disclose such advice. However, the Commission of Information under the Right to Information Act held that the recommendation of the Cabinet can be disclosed after the decision is made on the subject matter under consideration.

The President using his discretion appoints the Prime Minister whom he considers to be the Leader of the House. The Leader of the majority party or group of parties becomes the Leader of the House. The President appoints Ministers, as recommended by the Prime Minister. The number of Ministers to be appointed shall not exceed 15% of the members of the Lok Sabha.

The expression "pleasure of President" means that the persons can be removed by the President if they lose the President's confidence. Yet, the removal of Constitutional functionaries is governed by some special procedures. For example, judges and the Chief Election Commissioner can be removed only through the procedure of impeachment.

There is nothing as noteworthy as a Minister losing the confidence of the House. A no-confidence motion is moved against the Prime Minister and his entire Cabinet since, the whole Cabinet functions as a unit and is jointly responsible to the Parliament. If a Minister loses the confidence of the Prime Minister, such a Member can be removed by the President, if the Prime Minister recommends his removal. A Minister may be facing a barrage of criticism in the Parliament yet, he cannot be removed unless the Prime Minister recommends his removal. Of course, the Prime Minister may in some embarrassing circumstances tell the Minister to resign voluntarily.

The President appoints all the big Constitutional functionaries such as the Judges of the Supreme Court and the Judges of the High Court, the Attorney General, the Comptroller and Auditor General, and Commissions like the Election Commission, Finance Commission, and all such other Commissions as the Constitution and the law order to be appointed by the President. Unless the law otherwise provides, all of them hold office at the pleasure of President. The expression "pleasure of President" means that the persons can be removed by the President if they lose the President's confidence. Yet, the removal of Constitutional functionaries is governed by some special procedures. For example, judges and the Chief Election Commissioner can be removed only through the procedure of impeachment.

The Attorney General, the Comptroller and Auditor General are removed if the Government loses its confidence and recommends their removal to President. The Election Commissioners other than Chief Election Commissioner can be removed solely on the recommendation by the Chief Election Commissioner who is required to make his recommendation of the President. Other Constitutional functionaries can be removed only on the recommendation of the Cabinet. Sometimes, a person is also removed from his position by abolishing o the post he occupies. Commissions appointed for some special purposes are dismantled by not renewing their term or by abolishing the commissions itself.

The President holds the power to convene all the sessions of the Parliament. He always addresses the first session of the Parliament after General Elections and also the first session of the Parliament at the beginning of each year. His address notwithstanding all the interruptions, is treated as read and the same is followed by the motion of thanks which is also treated as passed in spite of no voting by reason of disturbances. The President has also power to send messages to the Parliament ordering discussion of any question of importance under Art. 87. He can also send messages if any bill is pending. If the Parliamentarians are following dilatory tactics or otherwise delaying the discussion, Parliament is bound to take up the matter and conclude business, forthwith.

VICE-PRESIDENT

Article 63.

There shall be a Vice-President of India.

Article 64.

The Vice-President shall be ex officio Chairman of the Council of States and shall not hold any other office of profit:

Provided that during any period when the Vice-President acts as President or discharges the functions of the President under article 65, he shall not perform the duties of the office of Chairman of the Council of State sand shall not be entitled to any salary or allowance payable to the Chairman of the Council of States under article 97.

A Narrative

Vice-President holds two posts, one as Vice-President and another as ex-officio Chairman of Rajya Sabha. If removed from office as Vice-President by a simple majority of both Houses separately voting, he shall cease to be the Chairman of Rajya Sabha as well. When acting as President, he shall not function as Chairman of Rajya Sabha during which period, the Dy. Chairman takes the place of Chairman. However, it does not mean that Dy. Chairman can function as Vice-President.

Article 65.

(1) In the event of the occurrence of any vacancy in the office of the President by reason of his death, resignation or removal, or otherwise, the Vice-President shall act as President until the date on which a new President elected in accordance with the provisions of this Chapter to fill such vacancy enters upon his office.

(2) When the President is unable to discharge his functions owing to absence, illness or any other cause, the Vice-President shall discharge his functions until the date on which the President resumes his duties.

(3) The Vice-President shall, during, and in respect of, the period while he is so acting as, or discharging the functions of, President, have all the powers and immunities of the President and be entitled to such emoluments, allowances and privileges as may be determined by Parliament by law and, until provision in that behalf is so made, such emoluments, allowances and privileges as are specified in the Second Schedule.

Article 66.

(1) The Vice-President shall be elected by the members of an electoral college consisting of the members of both Houses of Parliament in accordance with the system of proportional representation by means of the single transferable vote and the voting at such election shall be by secret ballot.

(2) The Vice-President shall not be a member of either House of Parliament or of a House of the Legislature of any State, and if a member of either House of Parliamentor of a House of the Legislature of any State be elected Vice-President, he shall be deemed to have vacated his seat in that House on the date on which he enters upon his office as Vice-President.

(3) No person shall be eligible for election as Vice-President unless he–

(a) is a citizen of India;

(b) has completed the age of thirty-five years; and

(c) is qualified for election as a member of the Council of States.

(4) A person shall not be eligible for election as Vice-President if he holds any office of profit under the Government of India or the Government of any State or under any local or other authority subject to the control of any of the said Governments.

Article 67.

The Vice-President shall hold office for a term of five years from the date on which he enters upon his office:

Provided that–

(a) a Vice-President may, by writing under his hand addressed to the President, resign his office;

(b) a Vice-President may be removed from his office by a resolution of the Council of States passed by a majority of all the then members of the Council and agreed to by the House of the People; but no resolution for the purpose of this clause shall be moved unless at least fourteen days' notice has been given of the intention to move the resolution;

(c) a Vice-President shall, notwithstanding the expiration of his term, continue to hold office until his successor enters upon his office.

Article 68.

(1) An election to fill a vacancy caused by the expiration of the term of office of Vice-President shall be completed before the expiration of the term.

(2) An election to fill a vacancy in the office of Vice-President occurring by reason of his death, resignation or removal, or otherwise shall be held as soon as possible after the occurrence of the vacancy, and the person elected to fill the vacancy shall, subject to the provisions of article 67, be entitled to hold office for the full term of five years from the date on which he enters upon his office.

Article 69.

Every Vice-President shall, before entering upon his office, make and subscribe before the President, or some person appointed in that behalf by him, an oath or affirmation in the following form, that is to say–

"I, A.B., do swear in the name of God/ solemnly affirm that I will bear true faith and allegiance to the Constitution of India as by law established and that I will faithfully discharge the duty upon which I am about to enter."

ARTICLE 365: ADMINISTRATION OF STATE

A Narrative

The failure of the State Government to comply with the directions issued by the Union amounts to a situation in which Government of the State cannot be carried on in accordance with the Constitution. It implies that the States are bound to comply with each and every direction the Union may issue. This Article lends weight to the view that India is a unitary State and that the Union is supreme and it governs the country through Governors. The argument that the post of the Governor shall be abolished is not tenable. Without the Governor looking over the State, administration and the laws the Union Government cannot effectively function and discharge its duties and obligations to the people. Without the power to issue directions to the State and the compelling need for the State to observe them, Union Government itself cannot function with success.

ART. 260: JURISDICTION OF THE UNION IN RELATION TO TERRITORIES OUTSIDE INDIA

The Government of India may by agreement with the Government of any territory not being part of the territory of India undertake any executive, legislative, or judicial functions vested in the Government of such territory, but every such agreement shall be subject to and governed by, any law relating to the exercise of foreign jurisdiction for the time being in force.

DISPUTES RELATING TO WATERS

Art. 262: Adjudication of disputes relating to waters and inter-State rivers or river valleys

(1) Parliament may by law provide for the adjudication of any dispute or complaint with respect to the use, distribution or control of the waters of, or in, any inter-State river or river valley.

(2) Notwithstanding anything in this Constitution, Parliament may by law provide that neither the Supreme Court nor any other court shall exercise jurisdiction in respect of any such dispute or complaint as is referred to in clause (1).

CO-ORDINATION BETWEEN STATES

Art. 263: Provisions with Respect to an Inter-State Council

If at any time it appears to the President that the public interests would be served by the establishment of a Council charged with the duty of

(a) enquring into and advising upon disputes which may have arisen between States;

(b) investigating and discussing subjects in which some or all of the States, or the Union and one or more of the States, have a common interest; or

(c) making recommendations upon any such subject and, in particular, recommendations for the better co-ordination of policy and action with respect to that subject, in shall be lawful for the President by order to establish such a Council, and to define the nature of the duties to be performed by it and its organisation and procedure.

ADMINISTRATIVE RELATIONS : UNION AND STATES

Articles 256 To 263: Executive Powers

Article 256: Obligation of States and Union

The executive power of every state shall be so exercised as to ensure compliance with the laws made by Parliament and any existing laws which apply in that State, and the executive power of theUnion shall extend to the giving of such directions to a State as may appear to the Government of India to be necessary for that purpose.

Article 257: Control of the Union over states in certain cases

(1) The executive power of every State shall be so exercised as not to impede or prejudice the exercise of the executive power of the Union, and the executive power of the Union shall extend to the giving of such directions to a State as may appear to the Government of India to be necessary for that purpose.

(2) The executive power of the Union shall also extend to the giving of directions to a State as to the construction and maintenance of means of communication declared in the direction to be of national or military importance.

[Provided that nothing in this clause shall be taken as restricting the power of Parliament to declare highways or waterways to be national highways or national waterways, or the power of the Union with respect to the highways or waterways so declared or the power of the Union to construct and maintain means of communication as part of its functions with respect to naval, military and air force works.]

(3) The executive power of the Union shall also extend to the giving of directions to a State as to the measures to be taken for the protection of the railways within the State.

(4) Where in carrying out any direction given to a State under clause (2) as to the construction or maintenance of any means of communication or under clause (3) as to the measures to be taken for the protection of any railway, costs have been incurred in excess of those which would have been incurred in the discharge of the normal duties of the State if such direction had not been given, there shall be paid by the Government of India to the

State such sum as may be agreed, or, in default of agreement, as may be determined by an arbitrator appointed by the Chief Justice of India, in respect of the extra costs so incurred by the State.

Article 258: Power of Union to confer power etc; on states in certain cases

(1) Notwithstanding anything in this Constitution, the President may, with the consent of the Governor of a State, entrust either conditionally or unconditionally to that Government or to its officers functions in relation to any matter to which the executive power of the Union extends.

(2) A law made by Parliament which applies in any State may, notwithstanding that it relates to a matter with respect to which the Legislature of the State has no power to make laws, confer powers, and impose duties, or authorise the conferring of powers and the imposition of duties, upon the State or officers and authorities thereof.

(3) Where by virtue of this Article powers and duties have been conferred or imposed upon a State or officers or authorities thereof, there shall be paid by the Government of India to the State such sum as may be agreed, or, in default of agreement, as may be determined by an arbitrator appointed by the Chief Justice of India, in respect of any extra costs of administration incurred by the State in connection with the exercise of those powers and duties.

Article 258-A: Power of states to entrust functions to Union

Notwithstanding anything in this Constitution, the Governor of a State may, with the consent of the Government of India, entrust either conditionally or unconditionally to that Government or to its officers functions in relation to any matter to which the executive power of the State extends.

Article 260: Jurisdiction of Union in relation to territories outside India

Article 261: Public acts, records and judicial proceedings to be given full faith and credit

Article 262: Adjudication of disputes relating to waters and inter-state rivers or river valleys

Article 263: Provisions with respect to an inter-state council

A Narrative

The expression 'executive power' is obviously wider than 'administrative power'. All the powers which laws confer on the State and are implied in the sovereign rights and obligations are executive powers and entering into international agreements too comes within the scope of executive power. The power to implement laws as well as power to execute them is also executive power. The power to enforce the law and order and the obligations to promote peace and good government are part of executive power. The obligation to promote good environment and the obligation to protect people from hazards of nature also comes under the field of executive power. It should be noted that it is within the scope of executive power to protect persons and groups against discrimination and prevent their degradation. Ensuring an inclusive society, thus, comes within the scope of executive power whether there exists any legislation on the subject or not. On other hand, wherever there is law, it is the obligations of the Government to administer it and the power so vested for this purpose is called the administrative power. Land laws need administration to survey the lands, determine the ownership of every plot surveyed, and also assess the tax payable. Yet, it is under the executive power, the Government creates facilities to carry out administrative functions by the administrative authorities. Again, under executive power all the orders made by the administrative authorities are duly executed. While the process of levy and assessment of tax is done by tax administrators, the recovery of tax is done by the executive created thereof. Union Government as under the Constitution may order the State Governments under its executive power to take and fulfil all such administrative and executive actions as it could have done through its officers. Similarly, when the State Government needs assistance of the Union Government it can require the Union to undertake such tasks which it could have not done otherwise by itself. The Constitution of India has created a machinery for the settlement of inter-State disputes. Such wrangles may arise out of sharing water of inter-State rivers and in other connected disputes. For such disputes, Parliament enacted the law called Inter-State Water Disputes Act, 1956. In the case of other disputes the Union Government may appoint Councils as and when necessary to investigate such disputes and make recommendations. But, while Inter-State Commission on River Waters can make an award, the inter-State Councils make only recommendations. The jurisdiction of the Courts including Supreme Court to entertain any complaints in both the cases is, however barred. The apex Court may however entertain any applications to enforce any claim arising out of the award or recommendations.

ARTICLES 239, 239-A, 239-B, 240, 241 AND 242: UNION TERRITORIES

Article 239. Administration of Union territories.

(1) Save as otherwise provided by Parliament by law, every Union territory shall be administered by the President acting, to such extent as he thinks fit, through an administrator to be appointed by him with such designation as he may specify.

(2) Notwithstanding anything contained in Part VI, the president may appoint the Governor of a State as the administrator of an adjoining Union territory, and where a Governor is so appointed, he shall exercise his function as such administrator independently of his Council of Ministers

Article 239AA. Special provisions with respect to Delhi.

(1) As from the date of commencement of the Constitution (Sixty-ninth Amendment) Act, 1991, the Union territory of Delhi shall be called the National Capital Territory of Delhi (hereafter in this Part referred to as the National Capital Territory) and the administrator thereof appointed under Article 239 shall be designated as the Lieutenant Governor.

(2) (a) There shall be a Legislative Assembly for the National Capital Territory and the seats in such Assembly shall be filled by members chosen by direct election from territorial constituencies in the National Capital Territory.

(b) The total number of seats in the Legislative Assembly, the number of seats reserved for Scheduled Castes, the division of the National Capital Territory into territorial constituencies (including the basis for such division) and all other matters relating to the functioning of the Legislative Assembly shall be regulated by law made by Parliament.

(c) The provisions of Articles 324 to 327 and 329 shall apply in relation to the National Capital Territory, the Legislative Assembly of the National Capital Territory and the members thereof as they apply, in relation to a State, the Legislative Assembly of a State and the members thereof respectively; and any reference in Articles 326 and 329 to 'appropriate Legislature' shall be deemed to be a reference to Parliament.

(3) (a) Subject to the provisions of this Constitution, the Legislative Assembly shall have power to make laws for the whole or any part of the National Capital Territory with respect to any matters enumerated in the State List or in the Concurrent List in so far as any such matter is applicable to Union territories except matters with respect to Entries 1, 2 and 18 of the State List and Entries 64, 65 and 66 of that List in so far as they relate to the said Entries 1, 2 and 18.

(b) Nothing in sub clause (a) shall derogate from the powers of Parliament under this Constitution to make laws with respect to any matter for a Union territory or any part thereof.

A Narrative

Union Territories are: (1) Delhi; (2) Andaman and Nicobar Islands; (3) Lakshadweep; (4) Dadra and Nagar Haveli; (5) Daman and Diu; (6) Pondicherry; and (7) Chandigarh. The Administration of a Union Territory is different from that of the States. It is directly administered by the President who may appoint Ministers. If the Parliament provides for creating a Legislative Assembly, then the Union Territory will have an Assembly and Cabinet. The President administers a Union Territory through administrator instead of Governor. In the case of Pondicherry and Delhi (Delhi-since renamed as National Capital Territory) they are legislatures and administrator called Lt. Governor. The powers of legislatures cover all subjects in the State List and Concurrent List, excluding those which cover the subjects of law and order. If difference of opinion arises between the Cabinet and the Lt. Governor, the matter is referred to the President and the decision of the President is final. A reference may be pending, yet the Lt. Governor is competent to take all steps as may be necessary, pending decision of the President except in the case of Pondicherry and Delhi. The administration in all other Union Territories is carried on with regulations made by the President for peace, progress and good Government. The expression 'peace, progress and good government' means all Governmental functions including positive steps for economic and social welfare, and also their protection and safety. Parliament may create a High Court for each Union Territory or extend the jurisdiction of the neighbouring High Court to the Union Territory. For example, the Union Territory of Delhi boasts of an independent High Court for itself. The High Court of Calcutta's jurisdiction sway holds over Andamans. However, the status of the High Court of the Union Territory is the same as that of any other High Court. Any Judge of the High Court of Union Territory can be elevated to the Supreme Court. *T. Deen Dayal vs Union of India.*

FEDERALISM

Article 153: Governor

There shall be a Governor for each State.

[Provided that nothing in this Article shall prevent the appointment of the same person as Governor for two or more States.]

Article 154: Executive power of State

(1) The executive power of the State shall be vested in the Governor and shall be exercised by him either by him either directly or through officers subordinate to him in accordance with this Constitution.

(2) Nothing in this Article shall

(a) be deemed to transfer to the Governor any functions conferred by any existing law on any other authority; or

(b) prevent Parliament or the Legislature of the State from conferring by law functions on any authority subordinate to the Governor.

Article 213: Power of Governor to Promulgate Ordinances During Recess of Legislature

(1) If at any time, except when the Legislative Assembly of a State is in session, or where there is a Legislative Council in a State, except when both Houses of the Legislature are in session, the Governor is satisfied that circumstances exist which render it necessary for him to take immediate action, he may promulgate such Ordinances as the circumstances appear to him to require:

[Provided that the Governor shall not, without instructions from the President, promulgate any such Ordinance if

(a) a Bill containing the same provisions would under this Constitution have required the previous sanction of the President for the introduction thereof into the Legislature; or

(b) he would have deemed it necessary to reserve a Bill containing the same provisions for the consideration of the President; or

(c) an Act of the Legislature of the State containing the same provisions would under this Constitution have been invalid unless, having been reserved for the consideration of the President, it had received the assent of the President.]

(2) An Ordinance promulgated under this Article shall have the same force and effect as an Act of the Legislature of the State assented to by the Governor, but every such Ordinance

(a) shall be laid before the Legislative Assembly of the State, or where there is a Legislative Council in the State, before both the Houses, and shall cease to operate at the expiration of six weeks from the reassembly of the Legislature, or if before the expiration of that period a resolution disapproving it is passed by the Legislative Assembly and agreed to by the Legislative Council, if any, upon the passing of the resolution or, as the case may be, on the resolution being agreed to by the Council; and may be withdrawn at any time by the Governor.

(b) may be withdrawn at any time by the Governor.

Explanation: Where the Houses of the Legislature of a State having a Legislative Council are summoned to reassemble on different dates, the period of six weeks shall be reckoned from the later of those dates for the purposes of this clause.

(3) If and so far as an Ordinance under this Article makes any provision which would not be valid if enacted in an Act of the Legislature of the State assented to by the Governor, it shall be void:

[Provided that, for the purposes of the provisions of this Constitution relating to the effect of an Act of the Legislature of a State which is repugnant to an Act of Parliament or an existing law with respect to a matter enumerated in the Concurrent List, an Ordinance promulgated under this Article in pursuance of instructions from the President shall be deemed to be an Act of the Legislature of the State which has been reserved for the consideration of the President and assented to by him.]

The Governor's legislative powers encompass issuing Ordinance on subjects in which the State Legislative Assembly has jurisdiction. The power is restricted to the period when the Legislative Assembly and the Legislative Council are not in session and prorogued. This Ordinance issued will not be in force after six weeks counted from the date of the first meeting of the Assembly or the Council during which it must either be approved or disapproved by both Houses. The Governor cannot promulgate the Ordinance without the assent of the President when the subject matter requires the prior assent of the President. Though the Constitution specifically gives power to the Governor for issue of Ordinance, he can do so only if he is satisfied about the urgency and the necessity in promulgating the Ordinance. There are instances where with a view to issue Ordinances the Governor is prorogating the Legislatures. This practice is severely deprecated.

Article 162: Extent of Executive Power of State

Subject to the provisions of this Constitution, the executive power of a State shall extend to the matters with respect to which Legislature of the State has power to make laws:

[Provided that in any matter with respect to which Legislature of a State and Parliament have power to make laws, the executive power of the State shall be subject to, and limited by, the executive power expressly conferred by this Constitution or by any law made by Parliament upon the Union or authorities thereof.]

Article 165: Advocate-General for the State.

(1) The Governor of each state shall appoint a person who is qualified to be appointed a Judge of a High Court to be Advocate -General for the State.

(2) It shall be the duty of the Advocate-General to give advice to the Government of the State upon such legal matters and to perform such other duties of a legal character, as may from time to time be referred or assigned to him by the Governor, and to discharge the functions conferred on him by or under this Constitution or any other law for the time being in force.

The Advocate-General shall hold office during the pleasure of the Governor, and shall receive such remuneration as the Governor may determine

Article 167: Duties of Chief Minister as Respects the Furnishing of Information of Governor

It shall be the duty of the Chief Minister of each State

(a) to communicate to the Governor of the State all decisions of the Council of Ministers relating to the administration of the affairs of the State and proposals for legislation;

(b) to furnish such information relating to the administration of the affairs of the State and proposals for legislation as the Governor may call for; and

(c) if the Governor so requires, to submit for the consideration of the Council of Ministers any matter on which a decision has been taken by a Minister but which has not been considered by the Council.

GOVERNOR VS STATE LEGISLATURE

Articles 153 to 164

A Narrative

The executive powers of the State extend to all subjects reserved for the State in the State List under Schedule VII and over subjects covered by concurrent list with the concurrence of theUnion. The Governor is the repository of all executive powers. He can act only on the advice of the Chief Minister on all matters except those for which he is conferred with discretion to act. The subjects on which he acts on his own discretion is the appointment of Chief Minister. The Governor of Assam and the Governor who is appointed as administrator of Union territories have certain social responsibilities. As Governor of Assam he enjoys independent discretionary powers in the matters arising out of tribal areas. As administrator of Union territories, he has to function under the Union Government. In the matter of special responsibilities entrusted to him under some of the provisions of Articles 371, 371-A(1)(vi), 37A(c)(i), and 37A(f) and (g), Governor is conferred with several discretionary powers which he should discharge as directed by the President.

The Governor is appointed by the President and he holds the post during the pleasure of the President only. It implies the Governor may be removed at any time at the pleasure of the President without any notice. As the President can act on the advice of the Prime Minister, it is possible to assume that the Governor holds the post at the pleasure of the Prime Minister.

The Governor is appointed by the President and he holds the post during the pleasure of the President only. It implies the Governor may be removed at any time at the pleasure of the President without any notice. As the President can act on the advice of the Prime Minister, it is possible to assume that the Governor holds the post at the pleasure of the Prime Minister.

The important case of removal of the Governors occurred during emergency and after emergency and after the re-emergence of the Congress rule on the fall of Janata coalition Governments. There is no other case of removal of Governors in other normal times. The term of office of the Governor is five years and he continues to hold office after the expiry of the term till his successor takes charge. A Governor can be appointed for two or more States in which case the salary, etc. of the Governors are apportioned between and among the States concerned by the Union Government. The minimum age of the Governor is 35 years at the time he is appointed. He has power to grant pardons, reprieves and remission, and to suspend, remit, or commute sentences. However, his power is exercisable only under bona fide reasons and not to serve any personal or political interest. As the Governor is repository of all executive power, all actions of the Governor shall be expressed to have been taken in his name and under his seal. If any document is duly authenticated, it is not open to any Court to enquire into any allegation that the order has not been made by the Governor.

Executive power of the State is co-extensive with the legislative power of the legislature. Such instructions shall not contradict law made by the legislature. The executive cannot issue any instructions in the field in which the State Government has to necessarily make a law, i.e., no tax can be imposed by executive instruction, for there cannot be any imposition of tax without a law made by a legislature. No executive instruction can be issued by the State Government in the field which by law is reserved for the Union. The State Government can't issue any executive instructions in any matter relating to tax on inter-State transactions or relating to any matter covered by inter-State dealings. When once any law is made by the State legislature, the executive instructions issued in relation cease to operate. The orders of the Board of Revenue of the former Madras Government were subsequently found to be mere executive instructions. When found that the land revenue was levied on the basis of such executive instructions, the Andhra Pradesh High Court struck down the levy of land revenue and its enhancement which necessitated the Government of Andhra Pradesh to make a law on the levy and collection of land revenue in Andhra area.

ARTICLES 165 TO 167: ADVOCATE GENERAL

A Narrative

It is the Governor who makes the appointment of the Advocate General. Such appointment is, however, made on the advice of the Chief Minister. The Advocate General holds office at the pleasure of the Governor. It is discernible that he holds office at the pleasure of the political authority. The functions of the Advocate General are independent. He being an advisor is not expected to subordinate himself regarding his opinions to the Government. That is why the Advocate General generally resigns from his post every time the political authority changes. The Advocate General has a duty not only to tender his advice but also argues for the Government in all matters before the Court. Thus, he shall not only be competent to advice the Government on any point of law and facts, but he shall also be competent to substantiate the case of the Government before the Court. The Advocate General is bound to carry out other functions of legal nature such as the advice on the proposed legislation, appearance before any commission which may be set up by the Government. The Advocate General, if so requested may also appear before the legislature or before any Committee set up by the legislature. He can speak and participate in discussion and shall not be entitled to vote. The Advocate General is the authority for permitting the filing of any contempt applications by private parties. If he himself chooses to file such applications, he can always prevent the private parties to file the applications by refusing to grant them the permission. The Advocate General can withdraw a prosecution against any party in public interest. The Advocate General can make concessions in the Court on behalf of the Government without there being any special authorisation to do so from the Government as, he is an independent advisor and no servant of the Government. The Advocate General shall not appear against the State on behalf of any private party but he can appear as Advocate in private litigation between parties in which the Government has no interest. The Advocate General is entitled to primacy of audience in Court. That is, the case in which he appears shall have precedence over the others in the day's cause list.

RESPONSIBILITY OF THE UNION AND STATES

A Narrative

Welfare of the citizens is the prime responsibility of the state. As per the constitution, 'state' means Union, parliament, state, and state legislature. Although the constitution spells out 'Directive principles of state policy' as a prescribed measure of state policy for welfare of citizens, these are not justiciable. Even so, these principles form the road map for ushering in a welfare state.

Union and State Governments are charged with the responsibility of implementing the Directive Principles. Borrowed from the constitution of Ireland, the said principles are the backbone of the welfare measures. The government, at the Union and state levels, may have constraints of money, lack of unanimity, absence of institutions, lack of awareness, divergence of interests, and clash with fundamental rights, but progress in the right direction is the primary aim.

Over the years, a steady effort has ensured that substantial progress has been made. State has built consensus very assiduously, brought in legislation, and created awareness to ensure smooth implementation. There have been problems with Union and state governments having divergent views; more about method than (matter), more about money than manner, more about measure than management. At times, courts also had their moments of doubts, delays, and differences but ultimately predominance of Directive Principles has been recognised. State has a duty to discharge. Citizens can't demand it as a right, but expect it as the right way that the state would be obliged to act.

DIRECTIVE PRINCIPLES OF STATE POLICY

Art. 36

'Definition': State means Union Government, Parliament, State Government, and State legislature.

Art. 37

'Application of the principles contained in this part': The provisions contained in this part shall not be enforceable by any court, but the principles therein laid down are fundamental in the governance of the country and it shall be the duty of the state to apply these principles in making laws.

Art. 38

'State to secure a social order for the promotion of welfare of the people.' State to secure and protect a social order in which justice, social, economic, and political is ensured. Inequalities, both social and economic, are reduced.

Art. 39

'Certain principles of policy to be followed by the state.' Men and women should have equal status and rights. Concentration of wealth is to be checked and health of workers, men, and women should be protected.

Art. 39A

'Equal justice and free legal aid'.

Art. 40

'Organisation of village panchayats'.

Art. 41

'Right to work to education and to public assistance in certain cases.' Right to education for children has become a fundamental right (86th amendment, 2002)

Art. 42

'Provision for just and humane conditions of work and maternity relief'.

Art. 43

'Living Wage etc. for workers.'

Art. 43A

'Participation of workers in management of Industries.' 42nd amendment introduced this in 1976.

Art. 43B

'Promotion of Cooperative Societies'. Constitution amendment (97th), 2011 has made right to form cooperative societies a fundamental right.

Art. 44

'Uniform civil code for the citizens'. Contentious issue defying progress. Only Goa has a uniform civil code for citizens.

Art. 45

'Provision for early childhood care and education to children below the age of six years'. 86th (Constitution) amendment brought in Art. 21A, 51A (K) bringing the issues as fundamental rights (21A) and fundamental duties (51(A)K).

Art. 46

'Promotion of educational and economic interests of Scheduled Castes, Scheduled Tribes and other weaker sections'.

Art. 47

'Duty of the state to raise the level of nutrition and the standard of living and to improve public health'.

Art. 48

'Organisation of agriculture and animal husbandry'.

Art. 48A

'Protection and improvement of environment and safeguarding of forests and wild life'.

Art. 49

'Protection of monuments and places and objects of national importance.' 7th Amendment (1956) amplified by stating the monuments, places, objects to be those "declared by Parliament by Law".

Art. 50

'Separation of judiciary from the executive'. This has been accomplished; judiciary and executive can look at each other more intently, more intensely.

Art. 51

'Promotion of International peace and security'

It becomes clear that while some of the Directive Principles are action-oriented, pointed, and directed, others are idealistic and somewhat utopian. However, the general aim of these principles is altruistic and well-intentioned. These principles go a long way in establishing a classless, harmonious, self-sustaining society; a society where care, concern, and compassion are a way of life; not only rule of law. A society where wealth is not worship, where wants are not waived and work is not woeful. Directive principles seek to bring a seamless transition, bringing everyone on board. A country like India, driven by dissensions, divide, and dilemmas has a particular need for such principles. After centuries of class, caste barriers, centuries of inequalities, ignorance can't be just wished away by a constitution or a course of instruction. What is needed is a path, a way of life, and a life of belief; this can come about only through dedication to these Directive Principles. They may be inconvenient, they may be invasive, they may be incompatible, but they have a role to play. It's the role that we have assigned them, it was our choice and it was historical.

THE FEDERAL STRUCTURE

Introduction

The phrase 'federal structure' does not appear in the Indian Constitution, yet quintessentially the spirit of federalism permeates everywhere. Article I of the Constitution opens with a fierce assertion, 'India, that is Bharat, shall be a Union of States.' It is intent of faith, declaration of belief, and a proclamation of action. These are not empty words, not statements of casual content but reflect essence of pragmatism and intensity. India at the time of Independence was more a 'Geographical Expression,' than an integrated country. There were the territories held by the British, there were States under princes, there were territories under the British but governed by political parties under the provisions of 1935 Act. India presented variety, vexation, and vacuity. Post-Independence, the foremost challenge was integration of States, five hundred odd princely States; some very small, some big, some very big, but all steeped in tradition, outmoded thoughts, and rituals.

These States had seen centuries of princely rule, royal traditions, unbelievable wealth, and appalling poverty.

Not all princely States were ruled badly; a few had good social order and well advanced education systems. Rights might be missing but concern for values and social justice ranked high. Some of the Princes looked after their subjects, some looked after the British, and quite a few others looked after themselves first.

By and large the Princes were afflicted with pompousness which meant pomp and pageantry, pleasures and pastimes, patronage and pleasantries, and postures and platitudes. They were living in a world of make-believe, a world which rested on loyalty, leverage, lease, and legacy.

India was on the move. A surge of nationalism, a belief that we could rule, and an urgency that it was to be now or never, filled the hearts with hopes. Slowly but steadily, a picture was emerging; one of integration, even as another was beginning to take shape: communalism, but more of that later.

At the time of adoption of the Constitution in 1950 there were four categories of States and territories:

Categories of States and Territories in 1950

Part A: Erstwhile Provinces of British India

1. Assam.
2. Bihar.
3. Bombay.
4. Madhya Pradesh.
5. Madras.
6. Orissa.
7. Punjab.
8. United Provinces.
9. West Bengal.

Part B: Six Princely States with Legislatures

1. Hyderabad.
2. Jammu and Kashmir.
3. Madhya Pradesh.
4. Mysore.
5. Patiala.
6. Eastern Punjab.

Part C: Centrally administered States

1. Ajmer.
2. Bhopal.

3. Cooch Bihar.
4. Coorg.

Part D

1. Andaman and Nicobar Islands.

The seventh amendment (1956) removed the distinction between Part 'A' and 'B'. Now there exist three categories of territories-States, Union territories, and other territories as may be acquired by the Government of India. Three features stand out.

(a) The state of Jammu and Kashmir has its own Constitution and an umbilical relationship through special status under Art. 370.

(b) Fifth and sixth Schedules outline Scheduled Areas and Tribal areas within the States of Northeast; Assam, Meghalaya, Tripura, and Mizoram as per 6th Schedule, and other States excluding the States covered in 6th Schedule.

(c) In the States of Andhra Pradesh, Gujarat, Nagaland, Maharashtra, Assam, Manipur, Sikkim, Arunachal Pradesh, and Mizoram, certain special provisions override the general provisions as a class.

Presently there are 29 States and 7 Union Territories.

With this federal structure, what are the issues and challenges?

ISSUES AND CHALLENGES IN A FEDERAL STRUCTURE

A federal structure, involving the Union and the States, could always be having issues; issues of power, perception, pressure, privilege, principles, and people's will. Foremost, however, the loyalty to the Constitution remains as an unshakeable article of faith. On this point there are no issues except that left wing extremists who swear by violence do not give their allegiance to the Constitution. The Constitution of India is acceptable to all others and the institutions created by it are also sacrosanct and respected.

First issue is Centre-State relations. The Constitution has given the Centre, referred to as 'Union', a dominant, not dormant role. In the three areas, Legislation, Executive Power and the Finances, the Centre holds a commanding position. States have to conform not confront.

In Union-State relations, ruptures often come from the role, function, and acts of the Governor. The Governor is appointed by the President on the recommendations of the Prime Minister. It has been suggested that the Union government follow some norms while appointing a person to be the Governor.

(a) The concerned State must be consulted before the appointment of a person to the office of Governor.

(b) The person should be an eminent figure from any walk of life.

(c) The person should have detached himself from local politics of the state.

(d) The person should not be a politician of the ruling party at the Centre if the State to which he is being appointed is ruled by the opposition party.

(e) The Governor should not be appointed to his own State.

(f) Persons of minority groups have to be given a chance.

Notwithstanding the lofty recommendations of Sarkaria Commission and Punchhi Commission (2007), it is still the practice that appointees to the post of Governor often are politicians, inconvenient leaders in the state, retired bureaucrats, retired service officers, friendly party leaders, and even retired judges.

Centre-State relations often go sour on how the Governor conducts himself. The raging controversy in Arunachal Pradesh, Jharkhand some years back, as also Gujarat are all illustrations. Sometimes, the post of Governor is so preferred by incumbents that it becomes a puzzling matter; why, there's even a case of a chief minister of a state under division who preferred the post of Governor to Governance in times of crisis!

The three functional areas where there's friction between the Centre and the States are:

(a) Executive

(b) Legislative

(c) Financial

Although the framers of the Constitution had anticipated, in a manner of sorts, the issues of friction and created an ambience for their resolution, yet the fact remains that over the years issues have multiplied. This can't be put to the institutions entirely, but to the persons handling the issues too. Politics has also changed over the years when these days attitudes harden easily, yielding is rare and animosity is always there.

EXECUTIVE

Centre, through its executive power, can intervene in States; notably through use of Article 356 of the Constitution. Article 356 is an emergency provision and has its uses but it is often the view of the States that it is misused more than perhaps needed.

Article 356

Provisions in Case of Failure of Constitutional Machinery in States

If the President, on receipt of report from the Governor of a state or otherwise, is satisfied that a situation has arisen in which the Government of the state cannot be carried out in accordance with the provisions of this Constitution, the President may by proclamation

(a) Assume to himself all or any of the functions of the Government of the state and all or any of the powers vested in or exercisable by the Governor or anybody or authority in the state other than the Legislature of the state.

(b) Declare that the powers of the Legislature of the state shall be exercisable by or under the authority of the Parliament.

(c) Make such incidental and consequential provisions as appear to the President to be necessary or desirable for giving effect to the objects of the Proclamation, including provisions for suspending in whole of this Constitution relating to anybody or authority of the state.

Each proclamation shall be laid before each house of Parliament for approval.

The powers Art. 356 confer on the President are indeed for reaching and sweeping. Governor has a role to play too: for reaching and sweeping, in a way. Art 356 has created countless controversies, often due to political vendetta.

Reasons for resorting to Art. 356 are varied and very many:

(a) Loss of mandate during mid-way. In 1977 after Janata Government come to power sweeping Congress party and the polls, Congress governments in the States were rolled over; Congress repaid the compliment in 1980 when voted back.

(b) Previously, before anti-defection law, (10th Schedule) usage of Art. 356 was a necessity due to political uncertainties and horse trading.

(c) Other factors like breakdown of law and order; 1992 UP Government after Babari Masjid communal flare up, etc.

(d) Conducive conditions didn't exist for elections; Punjab in mid-eighties due to fear psychosis.

(e) Defeat of ruling party on the floor of the house and no viable options available for alternate Government.

Sarkaria Commission has observed that Art 356 has been misused for political purposes. It suggested:

(i) As far as possible, the Çentre should issue a warning to the state government before resorting to the use of Art. 356.

(ii) Art 356 be amended so that it can be used only after parliament approval to dissolve state legislature.

(iii) President proclamation should include 'reasons' as to why the state cannot be run as per normal provisions of the Constitution.

In the recent case of Uttaranchal, the High Court at Nainital has intervened, not to challenge the power itself to use but the basis of such usage.

Court here also ruled that show of results based on test of strength among elected representatives be done on the floor of the house, not elsewhere like the Governor's house, hotels etc.; or lately resorts, combining business with pleasure.

In a landmark judgement in the S. R. Bommai vs Union of India case (1994), the Supreme Court held that the power of the President in issuing a proclamation of emergency in state is subject to judicial review to the extent of:

(a) Examining whether it was issued on the basis of any material at all.

(b) Whether the material was relevant; or

(c) Whether the proclamation was mala fide exercise of power.

The court also declared that the power of dissolving a State Legislative Assembly can be exercised by the President, only after the proclamation is approved by both houses of Parliament (Sarkaria Commission's similar stand).

Another issue of contention between Centre and the States is the deployment of Central Armed Forces and para military forces to States. The States see this as encroachment. Constitution provides that such forces can be deployed only with the consent of the States.

42nd amendment introduced Article 257-A which catered for deployment of Armed Forces and other forces as assistance, notwithstanding States' opposition. This was repealed by the 44th Amendment by 1978. Even so, the States have a fear and the Centre a feel; both have their points of view, one having a district impression that once in, the central forces won't move out in a hurry and the other that they are charged with the duty of securing and protecting the country as the country witnessed the Mumbai terror attack in November, 2008. The Centre has tried to sort out this issue but quite a few States had their own apprehensions.

Yet another issue is the control by Centre of state legislation. Constitution provides for Centre's assent before state legislature can pass a bill to make it a law. This provision has been introduced to ensure that the country has uniformity and also conformity with central laws.

Art.	Legislation
31A	Any legislation passed by the state legislature for acquisition of private property for public purpose will not become law unless it has the assent of the President.
200	Directs the Governor of a state to reserve a Bill passed by a state legislature for consideration of the President, if in his opinion, the bill if passed into law would derogate the functions, dignity, and endanger the position which High Court is designed to fill.
288 (2)	State is authorised to impose taxes on water, electricity; stored, generated, consumed or distributed by central authority (NTPC, NHPC), etc. but any such law is effective only after assent by the President.
304 (b)	State legislature can pass bills regarding imposition of reasonable restrictions on freedom of trade, commerce, and intercourse within the state in public interest, but such a bill needs prior approval of the President.
274	Prior recommendation of President required to Bills affecting taxation in which States are interested. The expression 'tax or duty in which States are interested means: (a) A tax or duty the whole or part of the net proceeds whereof are assigned to any state; or (b) A tax or duty by reference to the net proceeds whereof sums are for the time being payable out of the consolidated Fund of India to any state.
365	Effect of failure to comply with, or to give effect to, directions by the Union: Where any state has failed to comply with or to give effect to, any directions given in the exercise of the executive power of the Union under any of the provisions of the Constitution, it shall be lawful for the President to hold that a situation has arisen in which Government of the state cannot be carried on in accordance with the provisions of the Constitution.

LEGISLATION

Indian Constitution has a significant, pronounced bias towards the Union. Being a deliberate choice, a decided outcome, and a decision made unanimously the States cannot complain. 'Theirs not to reason why, theirs but to do and die', seems significantly an adage close to their condition. Yet, it is not the Constitutional provisions per se but their usage, the vehemence behind their application and sadly sometimes, the timing that hurts the States.

States feel done in, States feel cornered, States feel pushed around but they cannot complain. True, sometimes courts can intervene but in legislative matters the scope is exceedingly small. Till 1967, one party strode like a colossal over the Indian scene and generally there were no dissensions, save a Madras (now Tamil Nadu) or Kerala or some organisations. Post 1967; scenario changed, the mighty fell. Era of desperate, disparate coalitions set in. Regionalism, casteism, extremism, communalism, all as seen through a 'prism' took hold. Union and States were no longer on the same page, not even the same book. Article 356 began to be used with frightening regularity, for example, in Kerala (1959), ousting a popularly elected left front government.

Administrative Reforms Commission (Ist, headed by Morarji Desai)

Recommended an inter-state council to strengthen the functioning of Centre?state model. It noted with consternation that Centre had moved into areas earmarked for the States. The commission's report was largely relevant but found few takers, as a result.

Setalvad Study Team

Held out for Constitution of an inter-state council with the Prime Minister, Central Ministers, Chief Ministers, and others constituting the council. It also gave a stern look at the post, position and posting of Governors, seeking ability, objectivity, and independence in their term. A far cry as subsequent years would prove.

Rajamannar Committee

An initiative of the DMK (Dravida Munnetra Kazhagam) government in Tamil Nadu. The committee recommended:

(a) Transfer of several subjects from the Union and concurrent lists to the state list. 'Residuary Power' of legislation and taxation to be with the state.

(b) Abolition of Planning Commission, to be replaced by a statutory body comprising experts from various fields.

(c) Sitting up of an inter-state council with the Prime Minister as chairman and Chief Ministers as members.

(d) Deletion from the Constitution of those articles that empower the Centre to issue directives to States and take over the administration of the States.

(e) Article 312 to be amended to omit the provisions of creation of any new All India Cadre in future.

We have already seen how legislation in the Constitution as a subject has strong tilt towards the Centre. It must however be said to the eternal credit of the leadership in the country, that many of these provisions have not been used, or used only sparingly.

Art.	Legislation
245	Extent of laws made by Parliament and by the legislatures of States.
246	Subject matter of law made by Parliament and by the legislatures of States.
248	Residuary Power of Legislation.
249	Power of Parliament to legislate with respect to a matter in the state list in national interest.
250	Power of Parliament to legislate to any matter in the state list, if a proclamation of emergency is in operation.
251	Inconsistency between laws made by Parliament under Article 249 and 250 and laws made by the legislatures of States.
252	Power of Parliament to legislate for two or more States by consent and adoption of such legislation by any other state.
254	Inconsistency between laws made by the Parliament and the laws made by legislatures of States.

All these articles ultimately reveal that the will of the Parliament prevails over that of the legislatures of the States. However, under Article 368 of the Constitution, States have some protection in amendments to articles involving their interests. In such cases, besides two-thirds majority in Parliament of those present and voting and a simple majority from the total of the house, at least half the States have to ratify.

FINANCE

The framers of the Constitution had an onerous task to attend to. It was how to ensure that there was fair and equitable distribution of revenues and how to ensure a dynamic, acceptable system was in place for redistribution of Centre and States' share of revenue in the context of a changing environment. Foremost, a distinction needed to be made outlining exclusive preserves of Centre and the States and also where the interests might overlap.

Seventh Schedule, covering provisions of Article 246, of the Constitution lists:

		Originally	Currently
List I	Union list	97 items	100
List II	State list	66 items	61
List III	Concurrent list	47 items	52

42nd Amendment (1976) took 5 items out of the state list to move them over to the concurrent list.

Union List

It reveals the nature and extent of the Union's control with vital areas like Foreign affairs, Defence, Industries, Communications, Post and Telegraph, Foreign trade, Atomic Energy, Railways, Ports, Parliament, Reserve Bank, etc. under its control. Quite a few items have a bearing on Union?State relations and can be used to increase influence.

State List

It includes Law and Order, Police, Administration of Justice, Agriculture, Local Government, Money Lending, Gambling, Treasure Trove, etc.

Art 249 empowers Rajya Sabha to transfer any matter in the state list to the legislative jurisdiction of the Parliament by two-thirds majority. Under Article 356, the Centre could take over a state legislative authority if there is a breakdown of constitutional machinery.

Art 252

According to Art 252, if the legislatures of two or more States pass resolution to the effect that it is desirable to have a law passed by Parliament on any matter in the state list, Parliament can make laws regulating the matter. Any other state may also adopt such a law by adopting a resolution to that effect.

Art 253

Parliament under Art 253 can make laws for the whole country or any part of the territory of India implementing international agreements and conventions of which India is a part, even if subjects covered by such treaties and agreements fall within the state list.

Concurrent List

Both Parliament and the state legislature can make laws on the subjects listed in the concurrent but the Parliament has a superior claim. List includes criminal law, civil procedure, Divorce & Marriages, Factories, social security, Electricity and Economic and Social Planning. [Inserted by 42nd Amendment (1976)]

1. Administration of Justice, Constitution, and organisation of all courts except Supreme Court and High Courts.
2. Forests.
3. Population control and Family Planning.
4. Education, including Technical Education, medical Education and Universities subject to entries 63, 64, 65 of List I, vocational and technical training of labour.
5. Weights and Measures except establishment of standards.

With this broad view of division of subjects in the three considered domains, we now move over to Art 280 of the Constitution which relates to the Finance Commission. The very purpose of having a Finance Commission every five years is to acknowledge that in a dynamic environment of economy and social milieu, there are bound to be changes, changes both in terms of generation of revenue as well as its distribution. In the context what should be the share of Centre and States? What principle should be applied for a workable division?

Art 280

(1) 'The President shall, within two years from the commencement of this Constitution and thereafter at the expiration of every fifth year or at such earlier time as the President considers necessary, by order constitute a Finance Commission which shall consist of a Chairman and four other members to be appointed by the President.

(2) Parliament may now determine the qualifications which shall be requisite for appointment as members of the commission and the manner in which they shall be selected.

(3) It shall be duty of the commission to make recommendations to the President as to

(a) The distribution between the Union and the States to the net proceeds of taxes which are to be divided between them under this chapter and the allocation between the States of the respective shares of such proceeds;

(b). The principle which should govern the grants-in-aid of the revenues of the States out of the consolidated Fund of India. The measures needed to augment the consolidated Fund of a state to supplement the resource of the Panchayats in the state on the basis of recommendations made by the Finance Commission of the state.

[Inserted by 73rd amendment 1992]

(c) The measures needed to augment the consolidated Fund of a state to supplement the resources of the Municipalities in the state on the basis made by the Finance Commission of the State. (Inserted by the 74th amendment 1992)

(d) The commission shall determine their procedure and shall have such powers in the performance of their functions as the Parliament may by law confer on them.

Art 281

The President shall cause every recommendation made by the Finance Commission under the provision of this Constitution together with an explanatory memorandum as to the action taken to be laid before each house of Parliament.

Finance Commission is a major conduit between the Centre and the States for distribution of taxes. The 14 th Finance Commission has increased the share of States by 10% and the Centre has promptly shifted some of their programmes to the States.

Finance Commissions have, over the years, rationalised the process and principles of sharing between the Centre and the States, scope of raising additional revenues, etc.

Grievances of the States

(1) The States find the resources inadequate and request the Centre for more finance. The States have to cater to unforeseen expenditure, calamities, etc.

(2) States and Centre are never in agreement about the States overdraft issues, debt re-payment emergencies, etc.

(3) Centre decides on new projects and their location. Delays eat into time and resources, States suffer. There's conflict too between the Centre and the States over location of new projects.

(4) Centre okays Pay Commission for its staff and States feel the rebound. Staff in the state agitate throwing work out of Schedule, States budget take a hit.

(5) Centre moves into state list with resultant distress, pressed for funds, States tap environmentally hazardous and socially degrading areas like mining, liquor business, etc. In the long run it is self-defeating.

Some States have resorted to heavy taxation on aviation fuel with evangelical fury under the mistaken belief that they are loosening rich man's purse strings. Actually, it's the middle class which suffers, and the airlines industry takes a hit.

(6) Some historical issues like 'cess' on coal, iron ore, etc. that the central government gives to States from where mining is done are not yet settled to satisfaction, Centre cites helplessness, state hopelessness; year after years game goes on in this "cess pool".

DISTRIBUTION OF REVENUES BETWEEN THE UNION AND THE STATES

Art 268

Article 268 outlines the scheme for the distribution, between the Union and the States, of revenue. Union is entitled to the proceeds of the taxes in the union list, and states have exclusive right to taxes from the state list while.

Concurrent list includes no taxes. Union list taxes are allotted, wholly or partially, to the states as per following categories.

(a) Duties levied by the union but collected and appropriated by the states.

Stamp duties, duties of excise on medicinal and toiletry preparations, share transfer, debentures.

(b) Taxes levied and collected by the Union but assigned to states.

Inter-state sales tax on goods other than newspapers consignment tax. Taxes on railway fares and freights.

(c) Taxes levied and collected by the Union and distributed between the Union and states.

Income tax after deducting for emoluments and that amount attributable to union territories rest to union and states as per prescription by law. All items in taxes in union list (except those covered by Art 268, 268 A, 269) and any cess for specific purpose also are distributable between union and states as per Finance Commission prescription.

(d) Proceeds of surcharges go to the union exclusively.

(e) Taxes levied and retained by the state

Sales Tax, Land Revenue, tax on agricultural income, tax on land and buildings, mineral rights, road vehicles, boats, entertainment, animals, electricity, alcohol, profession tax, tolls, stamp duty other than in union list.

Every five years' finance commission gives its recommendations on sharing of taxes which after action taken is laid before the Parliament.

Two amendments, 80th and the 88th have brought in sea change in the whole matter of tax revenues.

88th Amendment (2003) introduced a new entry (92C) in the Union List: tax on services. A new article 268A on appropriation and sharing of service tax.

86th Amendment (2000) introduced with retrospective effect from April 1996; this amendment deleted Art. 272. As per the provisions of this amendment, all taxes and duties referred to in the Union List, except surcharges on taxes and duties and cess levied for special purpose are divisible between the union and the states. Thus duties of customs, corporation tax have become available for division and distribution. This was done as per the recommendations of the Xth Finance Commission.

Thus, the grievances of the states do get handled by the Finance Commissions. Some states have gone to the extreme as well: West Bengal, under Left front rule, 1977 preferred that the centre be left with Foreign Affairs, Defence, Communications, Currency and economic coordination.

Goods And Services Tax: GST

Everyone agrees that GST is good for the country and will rationalise things. Everyone agrees that GST will speed up business transactions by subsuming multiple taxes, and will bring about transparency, traceability and accountability GST will boost the GDP, and bring about financial awareness, but some States will gain and some will lose. GST is now more a political issue than an economic one. Success of GST ultimately depends on automation and computerizsation. Yet no one knows how GST will affect them in the long run and how it will affect the country.

Art 269

Taxes levied and collected by the Union but assigned to States

Inter-States sales tax on goods other than newspapers, consignment tax.

Taxes on railway fares and freights.

Art 270

Taxes levied and collected by the Union and distributed between the Union and States

Income tax after deducting for emoluments and that amount attributable to Union territories rest to Union and States as per prescription by law.

All items in taxes in Union list (except those covered by Art 268, 268A, 269) and any cess for specific purpose also are distributable between Union and States as per Finance Commission prescription.

Proceeds of surcharges go to the Union exclusively.

Taxes levied and retained by the States

A Narrative

Sales tax, land revenue, Tax on agricultural income, Tax on land and buildings, Mineral rights, Road vehicles, Boats, Entertainment, Animals, Electricity, Alcohol, Profession tax, Tolls, Stamp Duty other than in Union list.

Every five years, the Finance Commission gives its recommendations on sharing of taxes after which action taken is laid before the Parliament.

Two amendments, 80th and the 88th have brought in a sea change in the whole matter.

80th Amendment (2000) introduced a new entry (992c) in the Union list: tax on services. A new Article 268A on appropriation and sharing of service tax has been introduced.

88th Amendment (2000) introduced with retrospective effect from April 1996, this amendment deleted Art 272. As per the provisions of this amendment, all taxes and duties referred to in the Union list, except surcharges on taxes and duties and cess levied for special purpose are divisible between the Union and the States. Thus, duties of customs and corporation tax have become available for division and distribution. This was done as per the recommendations of the 10th Finance Commission.

Thus, the grievances of the States do get handled by the Finance Commission. Some States have gone to the other extreme as well: West Bengal, under left front rule, 1977 preferred that the Centre be left with Foreign Affairs, Defence, Communications, Currency, and economic co-ordination while all others, including residuary be left with the States, repeal of Articles 356, 357, 360, and abolition of All India Services.

A veritable surgery of the Constitution, without anesthesia! The Akali government in Punjab adopted the Anandpur Sahib Resolution in 1973: Centre be restricted to Defence, Foreign Affairs, Communications and Currency and all residuary powers to the States, equal representation for States.

Such demands become a rallying point for all the elements inimical to India, both as a country and concept.

TWO COMMISSIONS

Sarkaria Commission (Report Submitted in 1988)

The commission favoured a strong Centre but held that centralising heavily did not mean a strong Centre. It called for extensive use of Art 258 to confer more authority on the States and also stronger say for the States in the concurrent list.

Regarding Articles 246 and 254, the commission recommended Constitutional amendment giving more power to the States, such as ability to amend Parliament on the subjects on the States list under 252 with the assent of the President.

The Commission also states that the net proceeds of the corporation tax may be made sharable with the States. Centre should not impose surcharge or income tax, except for a specific purpose and that too for a limited purpose.

The recommendations of the commission have found favour with the States who have been demanding their implementation. The Centre has proceeded cautiously to implement them piece-meal.

Punchhi Commission

Headed by M.M. Punchhi, former chief justice of India, the Commission's report, vast, voluminous, and vociferous makes the following recommendations as far financial matters are concerned:

(a) Articles 256, 257 relating to obligation of Union and States (256) and control of Union over States in some cases (257) should be sparingly used. It is less a safety valve than a lightning conductor.

(b) Commission recommended a continuing audit role for inter-States council for concurrent or overlapping jurisdiction.

(c) Commission was concerned about the increase in the revenue collected through cesses and surcharges.

(d) Commission feels the vastness or absoluteness of powers under Art 253 needs to be regulated. Art 253 concerns legislation for giving effect to international agreements. Commission States that where States interest is involved, they should be negotiated with involvement of States. Treaty with Bangladesh on sharing, of Teesta waters with involvement of West Bengal States the point.

(e) Finance commission to be permanent body, with members changing every five years.

(f) Higher central transfers to backward States to enable them to improve their physical, human infrastructure.

(g) Royalty rates on major minerals to be revised every three years.

(h) Introduction of Goods and Services Tax.

(i) Additional expenditure on central schemes to be borne by the Centre.

(j) Scope for more revenue to States through Art 268 be examined afresh, either by next Finance Commission or an expert committee may be appointed to look into the matter.

(k) States-specific targets for fiscal deficit in the Fiscal Responsibility Budget Management legislation by the States.

EMERGENCY PROVISIONS

Art. 352: Proclamation of Emergency

(1) If the President is satisfied that a grave emergency exists whereby the security of India or of any part of the territory thereof is threatened, whether by war or external aggression or [armed rebellion], he may, by Proclamation, make a declaration to that effect [in respect of the whole of India or of such part of the territory thereof as may be specified in the Proclamation].

[Explanation- A Proclamation of Emergency declaring that the security of India or any part of the territory thereof is threatened by war or by external aggression or by armed rebellion may be made before the actual occurrence of war or of any such aggression or rebellion, if the President is satisfied that there is imminent danger thereof.]

(2) A Proclamation issued under clause (1) may be varied or revoked by a subsequent Proclamation.

(3) The President shall not issue a Proclamation under clause(1) or a Proclamation varying such Proclamation unless the decision of the Union Cabinet (that is to say, the Council consisting of the Prime Minister and other Ministers of Cabinet rank under Article 75) that such a Proclamation may be issued has been communicated to him in writing.

(4) Every Proclamation issued under this Article shall be laid before each House of Parliament and shall, except where it is a Proclamation revoking a previous Proclamation, cease to operate at the expiration of one month unless before the expiration of that period it has been approved by resolutions of both Houses of Parliament:

[Provided that if any such Proclamation (not being a Proclamation revoking a previous Proclamation) is issued at a time when the House of the People has been dissolved, or the dissolution of the House of the People takes place during the period of one month referred to in this clause, and if a resolution approving the Proclamation has been passed by the Council of States, but no resolution with respect to such Proclamation has been passed by the House of the People before the expiration of that period, the Proclamation shall cease to operate at the expiration of thirty days from the date on which the House of the People first sits after its reConstitution, unless before the expiration of the said period of thirty days a resolution approving the Proclamation has been also passed by the House of the People.]

(5) A Proclamation so approved shall, unless revoked, cease to operate on the expiration of a period of six months from the date of the passing of the second of the resolutions approving the Proclamation under clause (4):

[Provided that if and so often as a resolution approving the continuance in force of such a Proclamation is passed by both Houses of Parliament the Proclamation shall, unless revoked, continue in force for a further period of six months from the date on which it would otherwise have ceased to operate under this clause:

Provided further that if the dissolution of the House of the People takes place during any such period of six months and a resolution approving the continuance in force of such Proclamation has been passed by the Council of States but no resolution with respect to the continuance in force of such Proclamation has been passed by the House of the People during the said period, the Proclamation shall cease to operate at the expiration of thirty days from the date on which the House of the People first sits after its reConstitution unless before the expiration of the said period of thirty days, a resolution approving the continuance in force of the Proclamation has been also passed by the House of the People.]

(6) For the purposes of clauses (4) and (5), a resolution may be passed by either House of Parliament only by a majority of the total membership of that House and by a majority of not less than two-thirds of the members of that House present and voting.

(7) Notwithstanding anything contained in the foregoing clauses, the President shall revoke a Proclamation issued under clause (1) or a Proclamation varying such Proclamation if the House of the People passes a resolution disapproving, or, as the case may be, disapproving the continuance in force of, such Proclamation.

(8) Where a notice in writing signed by not less than one-tenth of the total number of members of the House of the People has been given, of their intention to move a resolution for disapproving or, as the case may be, for disapproving the continuance in force of, a Proclamation issued under clause (1) or a Proclamation varying such Proclamation,

(a) to the Speaker, if the House is in session; or

(b) to the President, if the House is not in session, a special sitting of the House shall be held within fourteen days from the date on which such notice is received by the Speaker, or, as the case may be, by the President, for the purpose of considering such resolution.

(9) The power conferred on the President by this Article shall include the power to issue different Proclamations on different grounds, being war or external aggression or [armed rebellion] or imminent danger of war or external aggression or [armed rebellion], whether or not there is a Proclamation already issued by the President under clause (I) and such Proclamation is in operation.

Art. 353: Effect of Proclamation of Emergency

While a Proclamation of Emergency is in operation, then

(a) notwithstanding anything in this Constitution, the executive power of the Union shall extend to the giving of directions to any State as to the manner in which the executive power thereof is to be exercised;

(b) the power of Parliament to make laws with respect to any matter shall include power to make laws conferring powers and imposing duties, upon the Union or officers and authorities of the Union as respects that matter, notwithstanding that it is one which is not enumerated in the Union List:

[Provided that where a Proclamation of Emergency is in operation only in any part of the territory of India,

(i) the executive power of the Union to give directions under clause (a), and

(ii) the power of Parliament to make laws under clause

(b) shall also extend to any State other than a State in which or in any part of which the Proclamation of Emergency is in operation if and in so far as the security of India or any part of the territory thereof is threatened by activities in or in relation to the part of the territory of India in which the Proclamation of Emergency is in operation.]

Art. 354: Application of provisions relating to distribution of revenues while a Proclamation of Emergency is in operation

(1) The President may, while a Proclamation of Emergency is in operation, by order direct that all or any of the provisions of Articles 268 to 279 shall for such period, not extending in any case beyond the expiration of the financial year in which such Proclamation ceases to operate, as may be specified in the order, have effect subject to such exceptions or modifications as he thinks fit.

(2) Every order made under clause (1) shall, as soon as may be after it is made, be laid before each House of Parliament.

Art. 355: Duty of Union to Protect States Against External Aggression and Internal Disturbance

It shall be the duty of the Union to protect every State against external aggression and internal disturbance and to ensure that the Government of every State is carried on in accordance with the provisions of this Constitution.

Art. 356: Provisions in Case of Failure of Constitutional Machinery in States

(1) If the President, on receipt of report from the Governor of a state or otherwise, is satisfied that a situation has arisen in which the Government of the state cannot be carried on in accordance with the provisions of this Constitution, the President may by Proclamation

(a) assume to himself all or any of the functions of the Government of the State and all or any of the powers vested in or exercisable by the Governor or anybody or authority in the States other than the Legislature of the States;

(b) declare that the powers of the Legislature of the State shall be exercisable by or under the authority of Parliament;

(c) make such incidental and consequential provisions as appear to the President to be necessary or desirable for giving effect to the objects of the proclamation, including provisions for suspending in whole or in part the operation of any provisions of this Constitution relating to anybody or authority in the State:

[Provided that nothing in this clause shall authorise the President to assume to himself any of the powers vested in or exercisable by a High Court, or to suspend in whole or in part the operation of any provision of this Constitution relating to High Courts.]

(2) Any such Proclamation may be revoked or varied by a subsequent Proclamation.

(3) Every Proclamation issued under this Article shall be laid before each House of Parliament and shall, except where it is a Proclamation revoking a previous Proclamation, cease to operate at the expiration of two months unless before the expiration of that period it has been approved by resolutions of both Houses of Parliament:

[Provided that if any such Proclamation (not being a Proclamation revoking a previous Proclamation) is issued at a time when the House of the People is dissolved or the dissolution of the House of the People takes place during the period of two months referred to in this clause, and if a resolution approving the Proclamation has been passed by the House of the People before the expiration of that period, the Proclamation shall cease to operate at the expiration of thirty days from the date on which the House of the People first sits after its reConstitution unless before the expiration of the said period of thirty days a resolution approving the Proclamation has been also passed by the House of the People.]

(4) A Proclamation so approved shall, unless revoked, cease to operate on the expiration of a period of [six months] from the date of issue of the Proclamation.

[Provided that if and so often as a resolution approving the continuance in force of such a Proclamation is passed by both Houses of Parliament, the Proclamation shall, unless revoked, continue in force for a further period of [six months] from the date on which under this clause it would otherwise have ceased to operate, but no such Proclamation shall in any case remain in force for more than three years:

Provided further that if the dissolution of the Houses of the People takes place during any such period of [six months] and a resolution approving the continuance in force of such Proclamation has been passed by the Council of States, but no resolution with respect to the continuance in force of such Proclamation has been passed by the House of the People during the said period, the Proclamation shall cease to operate at the expiration of thirty days from the date on which the House of the People first sits after its reconstitution unless before the expiration of the said period of thirty days a resolution approving the continuance in force of the Proclamation has been also passed by the House of the People.]

[Provided also that in the case of the Proclamation issued under clause (1) on the 11th day of May, 1987, with respect to the state of Punjab, the reference in the first provision to this clause to "three years" shall be construed as a reference to [" five years"].]

(5) Notwithstanding anything contained in clause (4), a resolution with respect to the continuance in force of a Proclamation approved under clause (3) for any period beyond the expiration of one year from the date of issue of such Proclamation shall not be passed by either House of Parliament unless- (a) a Proclamation of Emergency is in operation, in the whole of India or, as the case may be, in the whole or any part of the State, at the time of the passing of such resolution, and

(b) The Election Commission certifies that the continuance in force of the Proclamation approved under clause (3) during the period specified in such resolution is necessary on account of difficulties in holding general elections to the Legislative Assembly of the State concerned.

Art. 357: Exercise of Legislative Powers Under Proclamation Issued Under Article 356

(1) Where by a Proclamation issued under clause (1) of Article 356, it has been declared that the powers of the Legislature of the State shall be exercisable by or under the authority of Parliament, it shall be competent

(a) for Parliament to confer on the President the power of the Legislature of the State to make laws, and to authorise the President to delegate, subject to such conditions as he may think fit to impose, the power so conferred to any other authority to be specified by him in that behalf;

(b) for Parliament, or for the President or other authority in whom such power to make laws is vested under sub-clause (a), to make laws conferring powers and imposing duties, or authorising the conferring of powers and the imposition of duties, upon the Union or officers and authorities thereof;

(c) for the President to authorise when the House of the People is not in session expenditure from the Consolidated Fund of the State pending the sanction of such expenditure by Parliament.

(2) Any law made in exercise of the power of the Legislature of the State by Parliament of the President or other authority referred to in sub-clause (a) of clause (1) which Parliament or the President or such other authority would not, but for the issue of a Proclamation under Article 356, have been competent to make shall, after the Proclamation has ceased to operate, continue in force until altered or repealed or amended by a competent legislature or other authority.

Art. 358: Suspension of Provisions of Article 19 During Emergencies

[While a Proclamation of Emergency declaring that the security of India or any part of the territory thereof is threatened by war or by external aggression is in operation], nothing in Article 19 shall restrict the power of the State as defined in Part III to make any law or to take any executive action which the State would but for the provisions contained in that Part be competent to make or to take, but any law so made shall, to the extent of the incompetency, cease to have effect as soon as the Proclamation ceases to operate, except as respects things done or omitted to be done before the law so ceases to have effect:

[Provided that where such Proclamation of Emergency is in operation only in any part of the territory of India, any such law may be made, or any such executive action may be taken, under this Article in relation to or in any State or Union territory in which or in any part of which the Proclamation of Emergency is not in operation, if and in so far as the security of India or any part of the territory thereof is threatened by activities in or in relation to the part of the territory of India in which the Proclamation of Emergency is in operation.]

(2) Nothing in clause (1) shall apply

(a) to any law which does not contain a recital to the effect that such law is in relation to the Proclamation of Emergency in operation when it is made; or

(b) to any executive action taken otherwise than under a law containing such a recital.]

Art. 359: Suspension of the Enforcement of the Rights Conferred by Part III During Emergencies

(1) Where a Proclamation of Emergency is in operation, the President may by order declare that the right to move any court for the enforcement of such of [the rights conferred by Part III (except Articles 20 and 21)] as may be mentioned in the order and all proceedings pending in any court for the enforcement of the rights so mentioned shall remain suspended for the period during which the Proclamation is in force or for such order shorter period as may be specified in the order.

[(1-A) while an order made under clause (1) mentioning any of [the rights conferred by Part III (except Articles 20 and 21)] is in operation, nothing in that part conferring those rights shall restrict the power of the state as defined in the said part to make any law or to take any executive action which the state would but for the provisions contained in that part be competent to make or to take, but any law so made shall, to the extent of the incompetency, cease to have effect as soon as the order aforesaid ceases to operate, except as respects things done or omitted to be done before the law so ceases to have effect]

[Provided that where a Proclamation of Emergency is in operation only in any part of the territory of India, any such law may be made, or any such executive action may be taken, under this Article in relation to or in any State or Union territory in which or in any part of which the Proclamation of Emergency is not in operation, if and in so far as the security of India or any part of the territory thereof is threatened by activities in or in relation to the part of the territory of India in which the Proclamation of Emergency is in operation.]

[(1-B) Nothing in clause (1A) shall apply

(a) to any law which does not contain a recital to the effect that such law is in relation to the Proclamation of Emergency in operation when it is made; or

(b) to any executive action taken otherwise than under a law containing such a recital.]

(2) An order made as aforesaid may extend to the whole or any part of the territory of India:

[Provided that where a Proclamation of Emergency is in operation only in a part of the territory of India, any such order shall not extend to any other part of the territory of India unless the President, being satisfied that the security of India or any part of the territory thereof is threatened by activities in or in relation to the part of the territory of India in which the Proclamation of Emergency is in operation, considers such extension to be necessary.]

(3) Every order made under clause (1) shall, as soon as may be after it is made, be laid before each House of Parliament.

Art. 360: Provisions as to Financial Emergency

(1) If the President is satisfied that a situation has arisen whereby the financial stability or credit of India or of any part of the territory thereof is threatened, he may by a Proclamation make a declaration to that effect.

(2) A Proclamation issued under clause (1)

(a) may be revoked or varied by a subsequent Proclamation;

(b) shall be laid before each House of Parliament;

(c) shall cease to operate at the expiration of two months, unless before the expiration of that period it has been approved by resolutions of both Houses of Parliament:

[Provided that if any such Proclamation is issued at a time when the House of the People has been dissolved or the dissolution of the House of the People takes place during the period of two months referred to in sub-clause (c), and if a resolution approving the Proclamation has been passed by the Council of States, but no resolution with respect to such Proclamation has been passed by the House of the People before the expiration of that period, the Proclamation shall cease to operate at the expiration of thirty days from the date on which the House of the People first sits after its reConstitution, unless before the expiration of the said period of thirty days a resolution approving the Proclamation has been also passed by the House of the People.]

(3) During the period any such Proclamation as is mentioned in clause (1) is in operation, the executive authority of the Union shall extend to the giving of directions to any State to observe such canons of financial propriety as may be specified in the directions, and to the giving of such other directions as the President may deem necessary and adequate for the purpose.

(4) Notwithstanding anything in this Constitution-

(a) (i) provision requiring the reduction of salaries and allowances of all or any class of persons serving in connection with the affairs of a State;

(ii) a provision requiring all Money Bills or other Bills to which the provisions of Article 207 apply to be reserved for the consideration of the President after they are passed by the Legislative of the State;

(b) it shall be competent for the President during the period any Proclamation issued under this Article is in operation to issue directions for the reduction of salaries and allowances of all or any class of persons serving in connection with the affairs of the Union including the Judges of the Supreme Court and the High Courts.

Art. 365: Effect of Failure to Comply with, or to Give Effect to, Directions Given by the Union

Where any State has failed to comply with, or to give effect to, any directions given in the exercise of the executive power of the Union under any of the provisions of this Constitution, it shall be lawful for the President to hold that a situation has arisen in which the Government of the State cannot be carried on in accordance with the provisions of this Constitution.

ARTICLES 352 TO 360: EMERGENCIES

A Narrative

There are three types of emergencies:

(1) National emergency;

(2) Emergency in the State; and

(3) Financial emergency.

President has powers to impose any of these three emergencies. A national emergency can be imposed after the full Cabinet requests the President to do so, in writing.

> Financial emergency means a situation where creditworthiness of the Union Government and of the States is in jeopardy. Yet, mere financial difficulty in meeting any expenditure is not a ground for imposing financial emergency. During the financial emergency the President is empowered to issue directives to the Union and States to practice economy in expenditure. He may even direct salaries payable to the staff, including the Judges, be reduced.

It becomes clear and essential that there should be full consideration about the necessity of emergency by the full Cabinet and secondly the request made to the President to impose emergency must be in writing. The Cabinet means all the members of the Cabinet rank excluding such members who are not Cabinet members. The national emergency can be invoked only in cases where there exists a state of war or impending war with foreign countries. It can also be imposed in cases where there exists internal rebellion. Popular agitations against the Government do not warrant emergency as they are mere law and order problems and cannot be treated as internal rebellion. Rebellion signifies an armed insurrection. It should be noted that a mere extortion to the Government servants, to the army personnel, or to police personnel to refuse to accept the orders from the executive does not amount to rebellion. In State emergency, the conditions required for issuance of Presidential proclamation are that there exists a situation when the administration of State cannot be carried on in accordance with the Constitution and that there exist widespread internal disturbances.

It is important to note that the expression 'administration cannot be carried on in accordance with the Constitution' includes defiance by the States to comply with the directions of the Union Government. If no Ministry whether by the majority or by a minority or by coalition can be formed, it is also a ground for imposition of President's rule. During emergency days, the President has power to suspend the operation of any of the fundamental rights. That is, the Courts, during the emergency, cannot interfere in any manner if breaches of fundamental rights occur. Claims arising out of the breaches can, however, be raised after the emergency ends. That is the reason why after the national emergency ceases the Parliament enacts a law called the statute of indemnity so that no such claim can be raised even after the emergency. If no such act of indemnity is passed, all acts which infringe the fundamental rights during emergency may be easily questioned in a Court of law and compensation claimed. A very important point is that it is not open to the President to suspend the operation of any fundamental right guaranteed under Article 20 and 21 of the Constitution of India. Financial emergency means a situation where creditworthiness of the Union Government and of the States is in jeopardy. Yet, mere financial difficulty in meeting any expenditure is not a ground for imposing financial emergency. During the financial emergency the President is empowered to issue directives to the Union and States to practice economy in expenditure. He may even direct salaries payable to the staff, including the Judges, be reduced.

The cuts in salary so effected may be returned immediately after the declaration of emergency ceases to operate. Though the Constitution does not speak of payment of the withheld part of the salary it is reasonably assumed that payment of the arrears can be made when the Union and the State regain solvency. The President may during the financial emergency also suspend fulfilment of contractual obligations. If any payments are withheld, they may be paid after the financial emergency ends. Yet, if withheld obligations and payments are not satisfied after the financial emergency it shall not be counted as a Constitutional infringement. These provisions have given rise to several confrontations. It was even once held that imposition of emergency can deprive the people of right to life itself and that the President has power to suspend Articles 20 and 21. This situation has since been changed because of the Constitutional amendment whereby the President has no power to suspend the operation of Articles 20 and 21 during the emergency. Another dispute is about President's power to promulgate emergency in the State. Regarding the question whether the Governor while recommending the President's rule has or has not acted bona fide the Courts have since held that the Governor shall act bona fide, without any other motivation. The Supreme Court has in fact held in a Bihar case that since the Governor acted mala fide a declaration of emergency was unconstitutional and set aside.

DEVOLUTION OF POWERS AND FINANCES UPTO LOCAL LEVELS AND CHALLENGES THEREIN

Introduction

India has a history and heritage of governance at local levels without outside influence or intervention. Ancient India has numerous instances of local governance with active, willing participation of local people, including women. The word 'Panchayat' has its origin dating back to those times, with five member councils forming the apex body. Decisions of the panchayats were widely welcomed and respected.

In ancient India, the villages were self-regulating, self-sufficient, and self-sustaining; crafts, arts, technologies and service segments were widespread and met all the needs of local people. Fairs and meets were common and popular with all kinds of merchandise and offerings. Villages had enough food and livestock, satisfactory transportation, abundant skills, and fair share of entertainment. The word 'Panchayat' had a positive vibe about it; it had an aura of authority, fairness, and efficiency. Respect and fear also came to be associated with it. Mughal India, and before that the Sultanate period, left the local governance and related institutions largely unaltered.

Then came the British, and then came the trouble, and the transition. As early as 1727, the East India Company established the municipalities in Calcutta, Bombay, and Madras. Gradually, after 1727, the Company started centralising the administration trodding heavily on local governance and institutions. Post 1857, with the exit of the company, the British Crown administration established Cantonment Boards, municipalities to strengthen the administration. Lord Ripon earned a name for himself in 1880s as the "father of local government in India", through some pioneering effort in decentralisation. Powers and Finances, both were given a liberal look; equally liberal look was given at involvement of local people. The outlook was 'Drain, Train, Gain'. Memory of Ripon lived on, Lord Curzon by the turn of the century, however came round to intervene heavily, notably in Calcutta municipality, to bring in Central authority.

By 1909, the Indian National Congress was adopting a resolution for the revival of Panchayats in India. Gandhi who arrived in India in 1915, soon started talking about the glory of Panchayats and the Indian psyche being attuned to it. Congress Party would neither condone, nor confirm, or concur as it did not want its influence to wane or wear off; decentralisation so soon after Independence was more of a scare. In the Constitution, as a measure of abundant grace and attendant concession to Gandhiji's memory, Article 40 was included in 'Directive Principles of States Policy'.

Organisation of Village Panchayats (Art 40)

The States shall take steps to organise village panchayats and endow them with such powers and authority as may be necessary to enable them to function as units of self-government.'

No initiatives were taken to progress the prophecy. Even so, Community Development Programme in association with Ford Foundation of USA was launched on October 2, 1952 only to soon realise that the ground situation of the aims were laudable, objectives lively, and spirit leavening. People, in the early years of freedom, were excited too, but the bureaucracy was caught in its own web: it was neither ready nor receptive. Years later National Extension Services (NES), a bureaucratic prescription, was created.

Balwant Rai Mehta was appointed to review the working of the two schemes, in January 1956.

Balwant Rai Mehta Committee Report

The Committee proposed adoption of 'Democratic Decentralisation', meaning thereby that decentralisation was to be on democratic principles. A 3-tier arrangement was suggested.

Three Tier Decentralisation			
I	Panchayat	Village Level	Direct Election
II	Panchayat Samitis	Block Level	Indirect Election
III	Zilla Parishads	District Level	Indirect Election

Panchayati Samiti was to be formed with all the sarpanchs elected at the Ist level. Panchayat, Zilla Parishad was to comprise of all the Presidents of Panchayat Samitis: IInd level. Zilla Parishad would have co-opted and ex-officio members too. All these, the Zilla Parishad members, coopted, ex-officio members were to elect their president or chairman. National Development Council (1958) endorsed the recommendations of the Balwant Rai Mehta committee and country was ready to step into Panchayati Raj–the dawn of a new era of hopes, aspirations, and expectations; self-government by countrymen.

Rajasthan was the first State to experiment with Panchayati Raj, Andhra Pradesh followed soon. Results were: dismal failure. Country was too far steeped into old habits and systems. Panchayati Raj was seen as an intrusion, inconvenience, inept, and inefficient, it was also seen as inconsequential.

Reasons were not far to seek:

(a) Members were illiterate, ignorant, and in most cases lacked political awareness.

(b) Panchayati Raj Institutions had no powers to raise funds, could not find ways and means to go forward.

(c) They were dependent on States Governments which had other priorities.

(d) Higher organs in the Panchayati Raj dominated lower ones leading to immobility.

(e) Higher castes, landlords, rich persons thoroughly misused the institutions for their own benefits, others became indifferent, if not hostile too.

(f) There was total confusion about role, responsibility, and functions. Often it led to the States Government getting involved to create more confusion.

(g) Some States Governments saw the whole arrangement as a ploy by the Centre to create power equations, to their detriment.

(h) Choice of Rajasthan, Andhra both caste ridden States had been selected to launch the panchayat system.

Numerous study groups, working analysis groups, and committees to improve procedures and processes were formed until December 1977 when Ashok Mehta committee was set up to study the whole system. This was initiated by the Janata Government under Morarji Desai.

Ashok Mehta Committee: 1978

The committee recommended replacement of the existing three-tier arrangement with a two-tier one.

Two-tier Decentralisation		
I Mandal Panchayat	15 members directly elected by voters	President to be elected by the members
II Zilla Parishad	Members to be elected from suitably demarcated wards, Presidents of panchayat samitis nominees of municipalities, 2 women, 2 co-opted members. All MLAs/ MPs to be ex-officio members of the Zilla Parishad	

Committee brought in the concept of electoral system at the Zilla Parishad besides the following:

(a) Reduced dependence on States governments; amend the Constitution to give power of taxation.

(b) Open participation of political parties.

(c) A monitoring system to look after the interests of vulnerable social and economic groups.

(d) Political grounds not to be used for suppressing Panchayats.

Turning of the Tide: Coming of 73rd/ 74th Amendments

A feeling was now well entrenched that local self-government, as envisaged through Panchayati Raj Institutions, was always going to be a far cry, a distinct dream, a hope against hope. By now the country was politically awakened, the dominance of one party was over; India was now open to coalitions, regional parties moving up the ladder, parties' with common minimum programmes, parties' minimum common programmes, programmed parties, parties galore, parties coming to party... it was party time. It was the case of party with a difference, differences in the party, and 'Vox Populi'.

Constitution amendment (64th) proved inadequate and now the mood turned to giving Panchayati Raj Constitutional status, safeguards. Idea was to bring in uniformity as also standardisation. It was achieved in 1993 through 73rd amendment to the Constitution. Part IX was inserted in Article 243 to make it 243?343(O). Exemptions were given to Jammu and Kashmir, Nagaland, Meghalaya, Mizoram, and hill areas of Manipur through Art 243 (M). Darjeeling, under Darjeeling Gurkha Hill council, was exempt too.

Panchayati Raj: Composition

Three-Tier System

(a) Village Level

(b) Intermediate Level: Between village and district with States having population of 20 lakh and above.

(c) District Level

States having population below 20 lakh need not have the intermediate level.

POWERS AND RESPONSIBILITIES (ART. 243G, 243H)

The eleventh (11th) Schedule to the Constitution lists out subjects (29) that the Panchayats may be empowered by the States to deal with to usher in local self-government. To appreciate it better, one has to understand the significance of Art. 243 (G) and Art. 243(H).

Art. 243 G: Power Authority and Responsibility of Panchayat

Subject to the provisions of this Constitution, the legislature of a States may, by law, endow the Panchayats with such powers and authority as may be necessary to enable them to function as institutions of self-government and such law may contain provisions for the devolution of powers and responsibilities upon Panchayats at the appropriate levels, subjects to such conditions as may be specified therein, with respect to:

(a) The preparation of plans for economic development and social justice.

(b) The implementation of schemes for economic development and social justice as may be entrusted to them including those in relation to matters listed in the Eleventh Schedule.

Art 243 H: Powers to Impose Taxes by, and Funds of the Panchayats

The legislature of a States may, by law:

(a) Authorise a Panchayat to levy, collect, and appropriate such taxes, duties, tolls, and fees in accordance with such procedure and subject to such limits;

(b) Assign to a Panchayat such taxes, duties, tolls, and fees levied and collected by the States Government for such purpose and subject to such conditions and limits.

(c) Provide for making such grants-in-aid to the Panchayats from the Consolidated Fund of the States; and

(d) Provide for Constitution of such Funds for crediting all moneys received, respectively by or on behalf of the Panchayats and also for the withdrawal of such moneys therefrom as may be specified in the law.

Thus, with the Constitutional base aided by Articles 243 (G) and 243(H), panchayats have a sound footing to levy and collect taxes. Much depends on the States government regarding sharing of the power base. If both at the panchayat and States government levels there's a confluence of views and congruity of approach, matters will work to a nicety. Synergy will be in operation; should it be not, there will be divergence, dissent, dichotomy, and disturbance. As one wag put it, 'Hoping States government to delegate powers to panchayats with an expectation of mutual growth is like a turkey welcoming the prospects of a good Christmas'.

Finance: Devolution and Delegation

States Finance Commissions, which has a five year term, under Art. 243 (I) has to review the financial position of panchayats and to make recommendations on the following issues:-

(a) Distribution between the States and the Panchayats of the net proceeds of taxes, duties, tolls, and fees leviable by the States which may be divided between them and how the allocation is to be made among the various tiers.

(b) What taxes, tolls, and fees may be assigned to the panchayats

Grants-in-aid to the panchayats from the Consolidated Fund of States

(c) the States, controlled by the legislature.

(d) Measures needed to improve the financial position of the panchayats.

(e) Any other matter referred to the finance commission by the Governor in the interest of sound finance of the panchayats.

It is clear that the arrangement is dynamic and evolving. States government holds a major responsibility for the performance of the panchayats. Finance plays a critical role in the scheme of things.

MISCELLANEOUS

Trade, Commerce, and Intercourse Within The Territory of India

Art. 303: Restrictions on the Legislative Powers of the Union and of the States with Regard to Trade and Commerce

(1) Notwithstanding anything in Article 302, neither Parliament nor the Legislature of a State shall have power to make any law giving, or authorising the giving of, any preference to one State over another, or making, or authorising the making of, any discrimination between one State and another, by virtue of any entry relating to trade and commerce in any of the Lists in the Seventh Schedule.

(2) Nothing in clause (1) shall prevent Parliament from making any law giving, or authorising the giving of, any preference or making, or authorising the making of, any discrimination if it is declared by such law that it is necessary to do so for the purpose of dealing with a situation arising from scarcity of goods in any part of the territory of India.

Art. 304: Restrictions On Trade, Commerce, And Intercourse Among States

Notwithstanding anything in Article 301 or Article 303, the Legislative of a State may by law

(a) Impose on goods imported from other States [or the Union territories] any tax to which similar goods manufactured or produced in that State are subject, so, however, as not to discriminate between goods so imported and goods so manufactured or produced; and

(b) Impose such reasonable restrictions on the freedom of trade, commerce, or intercourse with or within that State as may be required in the public interest:

[Provided that no Bill or amendment for the purposes of clause (b) shall be introduced or moved in the Legislature of a State without the previous sanction of the President.]

Articles 243, 243-A To 243Z E: Gram Panchayats and Municipalities

A Narrative

Panchayat Raj signifies a political system applicable to village panchayats and municipalities to govern themselves. As it has to be essentially democratic, the entire village is declared as the Parliament of the village in which all voters are members. It is akin to a general body of the village. The villagers vote for an executive committee which is called Gram Panchayat. The minimum age to be a member of the Panchayat is fixed at 21 years. In the elections to be held for gram panchayat, seats are reserved for Scheduled Tribes and Scheduled Castes and women too. There is a further sub-classification for women to be reserved for SC and ST women. There is similar reservation in Mandal Panchayats and Zilla Panchayats for SCs and STs and also for women. When a seat for Mandal Panchayat is reserved for SC, it is only the SC woman who was elected to the reserved seat in the Gram Panchayat can compete. It means when Zilla Panchayat president seat is reserved for SC woman, it is only that SC woman who was elected to the Gram Panchayat and Mandal Panchayat in the reserved quota who can compete and not any SC woman. The powers and functions of the Gram Panchayat are allotted by all the State Legislatures.

Gram Panchayat has power to levy taxes. It can prepare and approve plans for the development of the village and incur the expenditure required thereof. The State Government appoints a Finance Commission every five years to study the financial condition of the Panchayats and moots measures in regard to their finances and for improving their condition.

The powers and functions of the Gram Panchayat are allotted by all the State Legislatures. Gram Panchayat has power to levy taxes. It can prepare and approve plans for the development of the village and incur the expenditure required thereof. The State Government appoints a Finance Commission every five years to study the financial condition of the Panchayats and moots measures in regard to their finances and for improving their condition.

Gram Panchayat must meet at least once in a year and can meet as often as possible. In the context of the Rural Employment Guarantee Scheme the Gram Panchayats are now holding meetings very frequently.The members of the Gram Panchayat who are directly elected, elect the members of the Mandal Panchayat and the members of the Mandal Panchayat in turn, elect the members of Zilla Panchayat. Schemes framed by the Village Panchayats, if they cover more than one village, are taken up by the village panchayats and mandal panchayats. Schemes prepared by the Mandal Panchayats, if they cover more than one Mandal Panchayat, are left to be implemented by the Village Panchayats concerned, Mandal Panchayats, and Zilla Panchayats. The schemes made by the Zilla Panchayats are implemented by the Zilla Panchayats with the cooperation of the Mandal and Village Panchayats. The Constitution specifies the subjects which shall be allotted by the State Government to Village Panchayats and the States are slowly making the subjects devolve on the Panchayats. There is now a new controversy in all the States that the State Governments are very slow in devolving powers on the Gram Panchayats. Electoral rolls of the Gram Panchayats get updated as on 1st January of the year of election. The reservation of seats for SCs and STs is constituency-wise where SC and ST population have the maximum number of voters. Seat reservation is on the basis of population only and it cannot be made by lottery. The superintendence, direction and control of the election, vests with the State Election Commission. However, the delimitation of constituency within the Panchayats or the election of any candidate cannot be questioned in any Court except by Election Petition. The life of the Gram Panchayat is full five years. If due to any reason the Panchayat is dissolved, the re-election shall take place within six months and if such six months period falls within the period when the general elections fall due, there is no need to conduct any election. Panchayats at village level, panchayats at intermediate level and panchayats at district level are totally different from the municipalities, town area committees, and cantonments in urban areas. The law applicable to municipalities is specified out in Part IX-A, Articles 243-P to 243-Z(F).

All over India and in almost all the States there are laws governing the Constitution of Panchayats and Municipalities detailing their duties and responsibilities. The provisions contained in Articles 243 and 243-A to 243-Z(F) require that those laws must be updated to accord with the principles laid down in the Constitution with direction to the State Government to transfer the subjects specified in XI th and XII th Schedule.

ARTICLE 243ZF: CONTINUANCE OF EXISTING LAWS AND MUNICIPALITIES

Notwithstanding anything in this Part, any existing provision of any law relating to Municipalities in force in a State immediately before the commencement of the Constitution (Seventy-fourth Amendment) Act, 1992, which is inconsistent with the provisions of this Part, shall continue to be in force until amended or repealed by a competent Legislature or other competent authority or until the expiration of one year from such commencement, whichever is earlier:

[Provided that all the municipalities existing immediately before such commencement shall continue till the expiration of their duration, unless sooner dissolved by a resolution passed to that effect by the Legislative Assembly of that State, or in the case of a State having a Legislative Council, by each House of the Legislature of that State.]

243ZG: BAR TO INTERFERENCE BY COURTS IN ELECTORAL MATTERS

Nothwithstanding anything in this Constitution,

(a) the validity of any law relating to the delimitation of constituencies or the allotment of seats to such constituencies, made or purporting to be made under Article 243ZA shall not be called in question in any court;

(b) no election to any Municipality shall be called in question except by an election petition presented to such authority and in such manner as is provided for by or under any law made by the Legislature of a State.

ARTICLES 294 TO 300: OWNERSHIP

A Narrative

After the transfer of power on August 15, 1947 all the properties vested in the British Crown had been vested with the Union Government and the State Governments. There had been a controversy, for years whether the sovereign was the owner of the land or the people who cultivate the land are owners. According to the Roman Law and Mohammedan jurisprudence, all the lands within the domain of the sovereign belong to sovereign and the holders of the land were only granted such rights as the sovereign desired. But under the Hindu jurisprudence the finders and occupiers and the cultivators are the owners of the land. During the British regime the ryot was said to own a permanent rights of occupancy only and the Government had a superior domain over the land whereby it can acquire the lands, if the Government so chooses or without compensation at the discretion of the Government. This controversy has come to an end by the Government making appropriate revenue laws conferring on the ryots the ownership and issuing passbooks which are equivalent to title deeds. Wherever there is no owner of any property, movable or immovable, it vests with the Government. The law made in this regard provides elaborate enquiry to trace the owners and it is only after the expiry of thirty years, that vesting of the property with the Government becomes absolute.

All the properties situated within the territorial waters, continental shelf, and exclusive economic zone are declared by the Constitution to be the property of the Union. These areas being located beyond the sea belt, the State Governments do not have a proprietary right in those properties.

It is within the executive power of the Government to carry on trade and also it is within the scope of the executive power of the Union and State Governments to enter into contracts. They have also a right to sue and be sued in their name. It is absolutely wrong to sue the State or the Union without describing the Union as represented by its Secretary and the State as represented by the Secretary. Any suit described otherwise is always liable to be dismissed. Where by reason of change in the law, any other person or authority is substituted in the place of the government; there is no need to add such other party as the plaintiff or the defendant in addition to the Government. The cause title only must be amended by an application made in this behalf.

The contract with the Government shall always be expressly executed by the President in his name and it must be so stated and signed by the person duly authorised. That being a mandatory term any contract otherwise made won't bind the Government. When the contract is expressed as signed on behalf of the Government it is not open to anybody to question whether it was or was not done with the consent of the President. Though the Government is not bound to carry out the terms of the contract which was made contrary to the above position, it is yet bound to return the advantage the Government has received under the contract. The Government is also bound to all torts actions of its employees if such acts are done in the course of their employment and when such acts are in excess of their authority.

ARTICLE 271: SURCHARGE AND TAXES

Article 271: Surcharge on certain duties and taxes for the purpose of the Union:-

Notwithstanding anything in Article 269 and 270, Parliament may at any time increase any of the duties or taxes referred to in those articles by a surcharge for purposes of the Union and the whole proceeds of any such surcharge shall form part of the Consolidated Fund of India.

A Narrative

If the Central Government imposes any surcharge over an already levied tax, the total amount realised by the surcharge belongs to the Union Government. No part of it shall be shared with the State. For example, Bangladesh surcharge is totally utilised by the Union. The amount realised by the surcharge, whatever be the amount or purpose, it can be used by the Union Government for its general purposes including the purpose which is indicated. The State Government has also powers to impose surcharge on the tax already levied. It is not even necessary that any special purpose need to be pleaded. But if the State Government levies any surcharge mentioning the purpose, the amount realised must be utilised for the said purpose only. Surcharge upon Court fee is to be spent for purpose of enforcement of law and justice. Surcharge for education, on the tax levied over the buildings must be used by the local authority for the purposes of education only and for no other purpose.

Article 274: Prior recommendation of President required to Bills affecting taxation in which States are interested.

(1) No Bill or amendment which imposes or varies any tax or duty in which States are interested, or which varies the meaning of the expression "agricultural income" as defined for the purposes of the enactments relating to Indian income-tax, or which affects the principles on which under any of the foregoing provisions of this Chapter moneys are or may be distributable to States, or which imposes any such surcharge for the purposes of the Union as is mentioned in the foregoing provisions of this Chapter, shall be introduced or moved in either House of Parliament except on the recommendation of the President.

In this article, the expression "tax or duty in which States are interested" means-

(a) a tax or duty the whole or part of the net proceeds whereof are assigned to any State; or

(b) a tax or duty by reference to the net proceeds whereof sums are for the time being payable out of the Consolidated Fund of India to any State.

Articles 264 to 291

A Narrative

The Union and State Governments maintain three accounts: (1) Consolidated Fund of the Union/State; (2) the public accounts of theUnion/State; (3) the Contingency Accounts of theUnion/State. All the amounts received as revenue taxes collected are deposited into the Consolidated Fund of India and all other moneys received by theUnion or the State as the case may be shall be deposited in the public account of the Union/State. The contingency fund is the account into which the funds from the Consolidated Funds are transferred. Though amounts in the Consolidated Fund of India and the public account are spent in accordance with the sanctions provided in the budget, the amounts of the contingency fund are spent by the orders of the Governor to meet the expenses arising out of unprovided contingencies, unexpected expenditure, or the excess expenditure pending sanction of the Parliament. Supplementary and additional grants may be sanctioned by the Parliament.

There are four methods by which the revenues received are apportioned. First, stamp duties and duties on the toilet and medical preparations are levied in the name of the Union and collected by the State. The amounts received are apportioned by the respective States. The second method is levy and collection of service tax. This tax is collected by theUnion as well as by the State and is apportioned to the Union and the States in accordance with the principle laid down by the Parliament. The third method is levy and collection of tax on the inter-State sale and purchase of goods and on consignment sales. The tax collected by theUnion is assigned to the State in which the tax is collected. The fourth method is related to all taxes levied and collected by theUnion in exercise of its power to levy tax and they shall be appropriated among the States in accordance with orders of the President issued following the recommendations of the Finance Commission.

It is seen that surcharges and cesses over and above the tax are levied for the purposes of theUnion and such amounts are not divisible between the State and theUnion. Also, the Union

Government is competent to make special grants to such of those States which might lose their revenue by reason of levy of import and export duties on goods which have special importance to States. The States of Assam, Bihar, Orissa, and West Bengal receive grants in lieu of the export duty on jute. Further, the Union Government hands over specific grants to certain States which may incur additional expenditure while executing projects of national importance. There are also special grants called grants-in-aid. The Parliament may sanction these to such of the States which need assistance depending on their need. All these grants are made out of the Consolidated Fund of India.

There are a few general provisions in the chapter on finance. The first one is that there is no tax without there being a law. In other words, there shall be a law defining the tax and its incidence. Such law should lay down the procedure to make assessment. Unless the tax is duly levied against a person liable to pay the tax, the liability to pay tax does not arise. The law should lay down the rules to be observed for recovery of the tax. Tax collected without authority of law and without observing the provisions of assessment and collection is liable to be refunded. The amount of tax paid whether it is in full settlement of the demand or for part satisfaction or in protest shall be received and acknowledged. All the monies received otherwise shall be accounted as received under public account. The second rule is all deposits made with the Government including Court deposits shall be kept in the public account. The third rule is that all the properties of the Union are exempt from State taxation. The electricity generated and water bodies created by the Union in relation to inter-State rivers and development of inter-State river basins shall not be taxed by the State. The fourth rule is that the State Government is not competent to impose any tax on inter-State sale and purchase of goods. In a secular State, no Government has powers to make financial provision for maintenance of any religious institutions. But an interesting situation arose when the Cochin Princely State was merged into the Indian Union. Here, some properties, the income from which was being used for purpose of Guruvayur temple came to Travancore State and some properties have come to Tamil Nadu State. Then, the Constitution by Article 290-A provided that an amount of Rs. 46,50,0000/- shall be paid out of the Consolidated Fund of Kerala and a sum of Rs.13,50,000/- shall be paid out of the Consolidated Fund of Tamil Nadu every year to Devaswom Fund established by the State of Kerala towards maintenance of the Hindu temple.

Articles 292 and 293

A Narrative

The Government of India and the Government of State have power to borrow funds from the public on the security of their assets of guarantees furnished. While the Government of India can borrow from foreign agencies, the State Government cannot borrow except through the Government of India. For the borrowing of the State, it is open to the Government of India to furnish guarantee but the Government of India does not furnish additional guarantees for additional State loans unless the State Governments clear the earlier loans for which the Government of India furnished guarantee.

DUTIES AND FUNCTIONS OF THE PRESIDENT OF INDIA		
(1)	Appointment of Prime Minister	Art. 74
(2)	Appointment of Attorney General	Art. 76
(3)	Can call for information on any subject from the Prime Minister	Art. 78
(4)	To decide on disqualification of M.Ps. (Other than for defection)	Art. 103
(5)	Summoning of joint session of the Parliament and making rules for the joint session	Art. 108 & Art. 118
(6)	Assent to the bills	Art. 111
(7)	Recommendation to the Parliament on demands for grants	Art. 117
(8)	Power to promulgate ordinances	Art. 123
(9)	Appointment of Judges	Art. 124
(10)	Consent for appointment of ad hoc judges	Art. 127
(11)	Approval of the rules made by Supreme Court for itself	Art. 145
(12)	Presidential reference to Supreme Court	Art. 143
(13)	Approval to the salaries of the staff of Supreme Court	Art. 146
(14)	Appointment of Comptroller and Auditor General	Art. 148
(15)	Appointment of Governors	Art. 155
(16)	Apportionment of expenditure of States which have a common Governor	Art. 158
(17)	President's power to entrust duties to any person otherwise not provided for	Art. 160
(18)	President's power to make rules as regards the persons who are elected to two or more States	Art. 190
(19)	Money bill cannot be introduced in Parliament without recommendation of the President	Art. 117
(20)	President's power to transfer judges of the High Courts	Art. 222
(21)	President's power to appoint administrators for Union Territories	Art. 239
(22)	President's power to decide disputes between the administrator of Union territories and his Ministry	Art. 239
(23)	President's power to make regulations for peace and good government for Andamans, Lakshadweep, Dadra, Nagar Haveli, Daman & Diu & Pondicherry	Art. 240
(24)	Assent to the laws made by the States on subjects in concurrent list	Art. 254
(25)	Appointment of Finance Commission	Art. 280
(26)	President's assent to the proposals of the States to impose tax on water and electricity	Art. 288
(27)	All contracts shall be expressed to have been signed by the President	Art. 299
(28)	Service rules shall be framed by the President till the Parliament makes a law	Art. 309
(29)	Persons appointed by the President shall hold their posts at his pleasure	Art. 310

(30)	Power to dispense with the enquiry in the interests of security in the case of disciplinary proceedings against employees	Art. 311
(31)	Effective constitution of appeal (memorial) of the President	Art. 311
(32)	Appointment of Union Public Service Commission	Art. 316
(33)	Appointment of Election Commission	Art. 324
(34)	Appointment of National Commissions for S Cs, STs, & BCs.	Art. 338
(35)	Appointment of Commission for scheduled areas	Art. 339
(36)	Issue notification containing the list of SCs, STs, & BCs. for purpose of reservation	Art. 341 & Art. 342
(37)	Appointment of Language Commission	Art. 344
(38)	Proclamation of emergency in the country	Art. 352
(39)	Proclamation of emergency in the states	Art. 356
(40)	Proclamation of financial emergency	Art. 360
(41)	Administration over major ports and aerodromes	Art. 364
(42)	President shall get translated the Constitution of India into Hindi	Art. 394-A

IMMUNITY OF PRESIDENT AND GOVERNOR

Article 361: Article 361 speaks of immunity of the President and the Governor from the proceeding in court of law, civil and criminal.

The position in this regard may be summarized as follows:

	ISSUE	STATUS/POSITION
(1)	Acts done by the President or the Governor in official capacity during the period of their office.	Action can be questioned through proceedings initiated against the Government. The President or the Governor shall not be made parties. If they are made parties, their names would be struck off.
(2)	Acts done by the President or the Governor in personal capacity during the period of office.	No civil proceedings can be filed except after serving them a two months' notice.
(3)	Acts done by the President in personal capacity prior to taking office.	No civil proceedings can be filed except after serving on them a two months' notice.
(4)	Acts done by the President and the Governor in official capacity when bona fides are questioned.	Proceeding can be taken against government only. Officers may represent the President or the Governor.
(5)	Criminal acts done by the President or Governor prior to taking office.	No action can be taken against the President or the Governor during the time they hold office. After they remit office, the proceedings if already initiated, will get revived and if not already initiated they can be initiated afresh after they remit office.

(6)	Criminal acts done by the President and Governor during the period of office.	No action can be taken during the period when they hold office. They can be initiated and proceeded with, after they remit office.
(7)	Can contempt proceedings be taken against the President and the Governor?	No contempt proceedings can be taken.
(8)	Can any court insist on the presence of the President or the Governor in the Court?	No. If the President or the Governor so chooses, he can appear before the Court. There is one instance in which President V.V. Giri appeared in person before the Supreme Court in his election case.
(9)	Acts for which the President can be impeached.	Enquiry into the charges against the President can be enquired into by a Committee set up by the Parliament, even as the President is functioning in his office. There is no case of impeachment of the President of India so far. The only case of impeachment is that of Justice Ramaswamy of the Supreme Court.

State Legislature Constitution has provisions for the State legislature regarding position, power and procedures along the similar lines as the House of People.

Chapter III Articles 168-177: About constitution of Assembly, composition, duration, qualifications of membership and rights of Ministers

Officers of the State Legislature: Article 178-187 : About Speaker, Dy. Speaker of the legislative Assembly and Chairman, Dy.Chairman of the Legislative Council. Seven states: Jammu and Kashmir, Bihar, Telangana, Andhra Pradesh, Uttar Pradesh, Maharashtra and Karnataka have legislative councils in addition to Legislative Assemblies.

Disqualification of members: Articles 190 -193

Articles 194 and 195 deal with powers, privileges and immunities of State legislatures and their members

Articles 196-201 cover legislative procedure and Articles 202-207, the procedure in financial matters

Articles 2018-212 are all about procedure, generally.

Article 155: Appointment of Governor: The Governor shall be appointed by the President by warrant under his hand and seal.

Article 156: Term of office of Governor:

1) Governor shall hold office during the pleasure of the President.
2) The Governor may, by writing under his hand addressed to the President, resign his office.

3) Subject to the foregoing provisions of this article, a Governor shall hold office for a term of five years from the date on which he enters upon his office.

Article 157: No person shall be eligible for appointment as Governor unless he is a citizen of India and has completed the age of thirty-five years.

Article 158: Conditions of Governor's office:

1) The Governor shall not be a member of either House of Parliament or of a House of the Legislature of any State.
2) The Governor shall not hold any other office of profit.
3) The Governor shall be entitled without payment of rent to the use of his official residence and shall also be entitled to such emoluments, allowances and privileges as may be determined by the Parliament by law.

Article 159: Oath and affirmation by the Governor.

Every Governor and every person discharging the functions of the Governor shall, before entering upon his office, make and subscribe in the presence of the Chief Justice of the High Court exercising jurisdiction in relation to the state, or, in his absence, the senior most judge of that court available, an oath or affirmation (as per prescribed form)

Article 160: Discharge of the functions of the Governor in certain contingencies:

The President may make such provision as he thinks fit for the discharge of the functions of the Governor of a state in any emergency not provided for in this chapter.

Article 161: Power of the Governor to grant pardons etc and to suspend, remit or commute sentences in certain cases:

The Governor of a state shall have the power to grand pardons, reprieves, respites or remissions of punishment or to suspend, remit or commute the sentence of any person convicted of any offence against any law relating to a matter to which the executive power of the state extends.

(*Note*: The Governor has no power in case of death sentence matters which are with the President alone)

The 69th amendment to the Constitution (1991) inserted a new article Art. 239 AA bringing new special provisions with respect to Delhi. *With this the following changes took place:*

239(AA) (1)

Union Territory of Delhi will be called National Capital Territory of Delhi and the administrator will be called Lieutenant Governor.

239(AA)(2)(a)

There shall be a legislative assembly whose member shall be elected directly.

239(AA)(2)(b)

Total number of sets will be regulated by the Parliament.

239(AA)(2)(c)

Provisions of articles 324 to 327 and 329 shall apply (Elections).

239(AA) (3)

Subject to this constitution, the Legislative Assembly shall have power to make laws for the whole or any part of the National Capital Territory (The subjects will be from state list or concurrent list bound by some restrictions)

239(AA) (4)

There shall be a council of Ministers consisting of not more than ten percent of the total number of members in the Legislative Assembly with the chief Minister at the head.

In case of difference of opinion between lieutenant governor and his ministers on any matter, the lieutenant governor will refer it to the President.

239(AA) (5)

The Chief Minister will be appointed by the President.

239(AA) (6)

The council of ministers shall be responsible collectively to the Legislative Assembly. Thus it may be seen that though Delhi has an Assembly and a Chief Minister, it still not at par with other states.

3

CHAPTER

Separation of Powers & Dispute Redressal

OVERVIEW

The Constitution has created institutions like the Parliament, Judiciary, and the Executive with defined powers, functions and responsibilities to work with freedom and focus. In this their powers have been separated to obviate any intrusion or incursion. Even so, there would always be a case for concern and cause for consternation. The Constitution has dispute redressal mechanisms and institutions to sort such matters out. The tussle between the Legislature and the Judiciary in recent times has left lasting footprints; it is too fresh in our memory.

""There are checks and balances and broad separation of powers under the constitution. Each organ of the state i.e. the Legislature, the Executive and the Judiciary must have respect for the others and not encroach into each other's domain."" ***(P. Sathasivam, former Chief Justice of India and presently Governor of Kerala)***

INTRODUCTION

'The Constitution brings into existence three different Constitutional entities, namely the Union, the States and the Union Territories. It creates three major instruments for power, namely the legislature, the executive and the judiciary. It demarcates the jurisdiction minutely and expects them to exercise their respective powers without overstepping their limits. They should function within the spheres allotted to them,' declared Chief Justice Koka Subba Rao in the *Golaknath case* of 1967.

This may appear so upon reading the Constitution but the underlying spirit does not indicate rigidity of exclusive zones and compartments; rather it permits cohesiveness and integration.

Let us first analyse the various provisions of the Constitution in so far as they relate to the three organs.

Parliament (Legislature) and the States (Legislature)

India has opted for a bicameral form of legislation; the Lok Sabha representing the will of the people and the Rajya Sabha, the interest of the states. This is the basic separation of powers.

Lok Sabha has a life of 5 years and Rajya Sabha, a permanent body with 1/3rd (one-third) members being replaced after every two years.

Powers of Rajya Sabha (Council of States) which Lok Sabha doesn't have

Art. 249

Parliament can assume temporary power to legislate on state list subjects, if the Rajya Sabha passes a resolution, supported by not less than 2/3rds of its members present and voting that it is in national interest to do so.

Art. 312

Creation of an All India Service depends on Council of States (Rajya Sabha) passing a resolution supported by two-thirds of its members present and voting that it is in national interest to do so.

Art. 80

12 persons of eminence can be nominated to the Rajya Sabha.

Art. 67 (b)

Rajya Sabha alone can initiate the proposals for removal of Vice-President of India.

Powers of the Lok Sabha that Rajya Sabha (Council of States) doesn't have

Art 109

- A Money Bill shall not be introduced in the Council of States. 'Money Bill' is defined in Art. 110; decision of the Speaker of Lok Sabha is final as to whether the Bill is a Money Bill or not. Rajya Sabha has no power to amend or reject a money bill, not even vote.
- In case of joint parliamentary committees, the proportion of Lok Sabha members is more than that of Rajya Sabha.
- Only the Lok Sabha can discontinue a national emergency by a resolution to the effect.
- The Estimates Committee, the largest committee of Parliament (30 members) is constituted only with Lok Sabha members.
- No confidence motion by the opposition can be moved only in the Lok Sabha.
- Censure motion by the opposition can be moved only in the Lok Sabha.

Art. 116

Exceptional grants or vote on account; only Lok Sabha has the power to make grants.

Art. 118(4)

In Joint sitting of both houses, Speaker of Lok Sabha will preside.

The above are the exclusive powers of both the Rajya Sabha and the Lok Sabha. Lok Sabha has a higher status given its functions and domain. All Money Bills must originate in the Lok Sabha. Rajya Sabha has its exclusive powers as well; it is a permanent body.

NO WATERTIGHT COMPARTMENT

The three pillars of democracy are the Legislature, Judiciary, and the Executive. All three are sovereign, independent, and have their core areas of competence and authority. There exists a system of checks and balances to ensure that any one organ does not dictate or dominate or decide to the detriment of others. The Constitution also envisages a system where dependence or independence are suggestively unwelcome, whereas interdependence is permissible to the point it does not create friction.

In the event, however, it is also not possible to have three watertight compartments of legislature, judiciary, and executive as such a situation can only lead to battle for primacy, privacy, and policies. It can also lead to friction and exclusiveness; both being detrimental for democracy. By separation of powers, it does not mean separation of interests or goals or objectives. Powers are so separated that there's no overlapping, nor more importantly, there is no gap. Commonality of interests and mutuality of goals remains same, separation only strengthens that. Broadly, the legislature makes the laws, executive executes them, and judiciary examines the laws for their legality and the execution for its rightness. Legislature has to, in the first instance; ensure that laws are valid, right, and legally enforceable. Executive must execute orders to meet the objective of laws fully and in the right manner with the right means. Judiciary must balance its vision to judge the right from the wrong. It cannot question the basis of using that power. Similarly, executive cannot question the legislature but it can, if called to do so, offer its views. In the same measure, executive can answer the judiciary with all details to support its point of view and expect judiciary not to be judgemental.

SEPARATION OF POWERS

Evolution of Thought

Separation of power has evolved over the years; both as a thought as well as process. Ancient India, Greece, Roman empire all practised it. Separation of power as a thought emerged more intensely with the decline of influence of religion, notably the church in the west. With the onset of reformation and renaissance, men began to question, question use of power and arbitrariness too. England had its civil war in 1640s with the King (executive) and the Parliament (Legislature) at loggerheads with each other. The King was beheaded and Parliament became supreme. England woke up to the dangers of tilt in balance and restored the monarchy. A little later, when the monarchy went beyond reason, the country let Parliament call the shots and usher in the 'Glorious Revolution' in 1688-89. A King of Parliament's choice, and a Parliament without choice, settled down to a truce in a new equation of balance of power through separation of powers.

Hundred years later, in 1789, two things of world importance happened; France representing the old order slipped into chaos disturbing the frail and fragile separation of powers, and the United States representing the brave new world of order and opportunity, gave itself a new Constitution heralding the dawn of a new era of democracy founded on separation of powers. France beheaded its king, curtailed its church, and fell into anarchy till Napoleon arrived to give the country a new order where he ruled supreme. Legislature folded up and the church signed a deal.

Two prominent thinkers, one French and the other English, ignited the minds of their countrymen. **Montesquieu (1689-1755)** from France developed a theory of separation of powers to espouse the cause of liberty of the people. He viewed that concentration of legislative, executive, and judicial functions either in a single person or a body of persons, results in abuse of authority, and such a system becomes tyrannical. 'There is no liberty if the judicial power is not separate from the legislative and executive powers. Where it is joined with the legislative power, the life and liberty of the subject would be exposed to arbitrary control; for the judge would then be a legislator. Where it is joined with the executive power, the judge might behave with violence and oppression', Montesquieu cautioned. Words of wisdom, succinctly coupled. Subsequent events in France proved how right he was, but the croning irony remains that he was quoted as the inspiration for the revolution!

(Oh! Liberty what crimes are being committed in thy name!)

John Locke (English philosopher), much before Montesquieu, argued that the executive and legislative powers should be separated as, 'the same persons who have the powers of making laws have also in their hands the power to execute them'. Locke outlined the government power into the three parts.

(a) Continuous Executive Power : Executive
(b) Continuous Executive Power : Judiciary
(c) Discontinuous Legislative Power : Rule making power along with the power regulating foreign affairs.

Both Locke and Montesquieu argued for separation of powers as the best guarantee for the liberty of the people as also to promote efficiency in the administration, democratic discourse, and ensuring of checks and balance. Unfortunately, both were readily espoused by the very forces they wanted to rein in through a system of checks and balances. Locke's ideas gave fillip to the legislature in England; Montesquieu's to the mobs seeking to curb the monarchy in France. Both succeeded, for a while.

Practices in Perspective

To separate the powers is easier said than done. Rigid separation is neither feasible nor recommended to be tried. All three organs, the legislature, the judiciary, and the executive have their roles to play. Each nation has its own tradition and trust. It is unreasonable to expect that all three organs will have equal powers, even more unreasonable to hope that there should be no checks and balances, and most unreasonable to even assume that separation of powers can be achieved without the accompanying spirit of give and take. Let us see how the United Kingdom fared in this pursuit.

Power Sharing in the United Kingdom

England in 1215, witnessed the signing of 'Magna Carta' by King John I; a historic document and a concession by the King acknowledging the rights of people. Even in 1295, the King had to seek Parliamentary approval to tax the people. Tudor kings ruled with grace and balance and tried not to antagonise the Parliament, but subsequent rulers, the Stuarts claimed a 'divine right' which was challenged by the Parliament in the civil war. 1688 saw the triumph of Parliament and in 1689, the bill of rights made way for Parliamentary dominance:

(a) Limit on the powers of the Crown

(b) Rights of Parliament outlined

(c) Rules for freedom of speech

(d) Right to petition the monarch

England has a parliamentary form of government with the monarch as the head. Monarch is the executive head as also part of the legislature. It is more a case of fusion of powers than separation of powers. Courts in England cannot call to question the legislature or parliament.

For most part of the later half of nineteenth century and a good part of the twentieth century, England has battled to reform the House of Lords. This issue revolved round separation of judiciary from the legislature too. Even so, the United Kingdom comprising England, Scotland, Northern Ireland, Wales, and Isle of Man presents a curious picture of tradition-driven parliamentary democracy with a relic-ridden Monarchy, defence oriented judiciary, and European Union-commanded executive. United Kingdom has a point to prove yet: separation of powers is organic and the spirit behind it matters; mere statutes and declarations of intent and faith are not enough. Separation of powers is actually a happy fusion of forces where the last word is of the Monarch, on the ground it is tradition not transgression, trust not threat, that matters.

DISPUTE REDRESSAL MECHANISM AND INSTITUTIONS

Dispute redressal mechanism relates to systems in vogue through institutions for settlement of disputes, grievances, and claims. These could be individual against the State, States vs States, institutions vs the State, etc. Constitution provides both the provisions as well as mechanisms to redress the same.

At the level of an individual there could be disputes regarding his rights against others. Constitution protects individual's fundamental rights alongside minorities' specific rights. Aggrieved persons or minorities can seek relief through usage of writs, Article 32 in Supreme Court, and Article 226 in High Courts. There is however one issue, that Supreme Court can be approached only for relief in violation of fundamental rights whereas High courts can be approached for violation of fundamental rights as also other legal rights. Judicial review under Articles 32 and 226 is a basic feature of the Constitution beyond the scope of amendability.

FUNDAMENTAL AND OTHER RIGHTS

Fundamental Rights

Art.	Right to Equality
14.	Equality before law.
15.	Prohibition of discrimination on grounds of religion, race, caste, sex, place of birth, etc.
16.	Equality of opportunity in matters of public employment.
17.	Abolition of untouchability.
18.	Abolition of titles.
Art.	**Right to Freedom**
19.	Protection of certain rights regarding freedom of speech, etc.
20.	Protection in respect of conviction for offences.
21.	Protection of life and personal liberty.
21-A.	Right to education (86th amendment, 2002).
22.	Protection against arrest and detention in certain cases.
Art.	**Right against exploitation**
23.	Prohibition of traffic in human beings and forced labour.
24.	Prohibition of employment of children in factories, etc.
Art.	**Right to freedom of religion**
25.	Freedom of conscience and free profession, practice, and propagation.
26.	Freedom to manage religious affairs.
27.	Freedom as to payment of taxes for promotion of any particular religion.
28.	Freedom as to attendance at religious instruction or religious worship in certain educational institutions.
Art.	**Cultural and educational rights**
29.	Protection of interest of minorities.
30.	Right of minorities to establish and administer educational institutions.
31.	Compulsory acquisition of property; repealed and replaced by Art. 300-A which makes it an ordinary legal right, not a fundamental right (44th amendment, 1978).
Art.	**Saving of certain laws**
31A.	Savings of laws providing for acquisition of estates, etc.
31B.	Validation of certain acts and regulations.
31C.	Savings of laws to give effect to Directive Principles.
31D.	Repeal.

Art.	Right to Constitutional Remedies
32.	Remedies for enforcement of rights conferred by this part.
32A.	Repealed
33.	Power of the parliament to modify rights conferred by this part in their application to forces, etc.
34.	Restrictions on rights conferred by this part while martial law is in force in any area.
35.	Legislation to give effect to the provisions in this part.

It may however be of relevance to note that rights to equality and rights to freedom are not absolute; the state may impose reasonable restrictions. These may be in pursuance of policies to give extra support to the less privileged like reservations in jobs. Right to freedom ends where other rights get in force; one may have full freedom to wield a stick but it ends where the tip of someone's nose begins.

Court Cases, Parliamentary Legislation, and Fundamental Rights

Such legislation may restrict the fundamental rights:

(a) **Equality :** *F.R. Jesuratnam vs Chief of Air Staff* (1976)

(b) **Freedom of expression :** *Lt. Col Prithi Pal Singh Bedi vs Union of India*, 1982 and also personal liberty, same case.

(c) **Freedom of association :** *Achudan Nair vs Union of India* (1976)

Other Rights

(i) Constitutional rights (given by the Constitution) not having the status of fundamental rights

(ii) Statutory rights

(iii) Rights flowing from subordinate legislation

(iv) Rights based on case law

(v) Customary rights

(vi) Contractual rights

Thus, it may be seen that in dispute resolution involving individuals and their rights, be it fundamental or others, courts are part of the mechanism at the level of High Courts and Supreme Court. Writs of Habeas Corpus, Mandamus, Certiorari, Prohibition, and Quo Warranto can be used singly or in combination to agitate for redressal. Constitution provides for establishment of tribunals as mechanism for redressal of grievances and disputes.

TYPES OF TRIBUNALS

There exist various types of tribunals, some created under Constitutional provisions, others under the provisions of the specific organisational act flowing from the parliament, and those created by amending the Constitution. All these have quasi-judicial functions, but the power of judicial review, a basic feature of the Constitution, cannot be taken away.

Constitutional

I. Election Commission : Election Commission as a tribunal adjudicates in all matters of disputes, be it election symbols or unfair practices or influence. Even so, ultimate appeal lies in the Supreme Court.

II. Administrative Tribunals : The Parliament, in 1976 through 42nd amendment (3.1.77) inserted the following two articles:

323-A

Parliament may by law provide for administrative tribunals to adjudicate disputes.

323-B

Parliament, as the case may be, or a state legislature competent to make laws, by law provide for administrative tribunals and other tribunals to adjudicate disputes.

To elaborate further:

323-A

"Administrative Tribunals" (I) : Parliament may, by law provide for the adjudication or trial by administrative tribunals of disputes and complaints with respect to recruitment and conditions of service of persons appointed to public services and posts in connection with the affairs of the Union or of any state or of any local or other authority within the territory of India or under the control of the Government of India or of any corporation owned or controlled by the Government.

323-B : (1)

The appropriate legislature may, by law, provide for the adjudication or trial by tribunals of any disputes, complaints, or offences with respect to all or any of the matters specified in clause (2) with respect to which such legislature has power to make laws:

(2) (a) Levy, assessment, collection, enforcement of any tax.

(b) Foreign exchange, import, and export across custom frontiers.

(c) Industrial and labour disputes.

(d) Land reforms

(e) Ceiling on urban property.

(f) Election to either house of Parliament

(g) Food stuffs: Production, procurement, supply, and distribution.

(h) Rent and tenancy.

In both these, 323-A and B, the jurisdiction of High Court was exempted in the awards given by the Tribunals. In 1977, Supreme Court in *Chandra Kumar vs Union of India* struck down the exemption and declared that judicial review, a basic feature cannot be done away with by the amendment. Administrative and other Tribunals follow the principles of Natural Justice but are not bound down by the technicalities of civil procedure.

Other Tribunals

Various acts passed by the parliament have provisions to set up departmental tribunals to resolve disputes. *The necessity for setting up such tribunals was two-fold:*

(a) To reduce the burden on courts; especially as when socio-economic legislation was bound to expand the activities of the state.

(b) Many of the cases would involve technical matters which in best of times too, the courts would find in, may be in a manner of thought somewhat complex in the first instance, perhaps; to put it mildly but methodically.

(c) Issues would be less legal, more departmental, more technical; more departmental violations than legal infringements.

(d) Courts operate within the provisions of civil procedure code where the burden of proof is strictly legal, whereas tribunals being quasi-judicial bodies go by principles of natural justice. Strictly speaking, these two bodies; courts and tribunals, are in two different domains. If the tribunal domain cases went to the courts, delays would be endemic and endless. 'Burden of proof will be buried under proof of burden'. Even so, Supreme Court has ruled that consistent with the need for judicial review, all decisions appealed against the tribunals have a final way up–to the Supreme Court, the apex court.

Tribunal	Set up by	Domain
1. Industrial tribunal	Industrial Disputes Act, 1947	Centre and States can set up tribunals. These relate to disputes between employer and the workers. Conditions of work, wages, allowances, closure, retrenchment, and gratuity are the domain issues. Appeal lies with the Supreme Court.
2. Railway Rates Tribunal	Indian Railways Act, 1989	Unreasonable rates, unfair practices, preferential treatment, discrimination : all by the Railway administration. Appeal lies with the Supreme Court.
3. Customs and Excise Revenue Appellate Tribunal (CERAT)	CERAT Act, 1986	Disputes, Complaints, levying of duties in excess, offences relating to customs and excise. Appeal lies with the Supreme Court.

ADMINISTRATIVE TRIBUNALS: ADVANTAGES VS DISADVANTAGES

Advantages	Disadvantages
1. Big relief to courts, already burdened with cases.	1. Administrators have problems appreciating issues of law. Sometimes judgements go wrong. Judges may take time but justice handed down is well and truly remarkable.
2. System operates quite fast and in a manner understood by both the parties.	2. Administrative Tribunals go too much by interpretation of rules and regulations. This often brings in a tilt. Cases get skewed.
3. It is less expensive as too many issues of law, and liberty to add to litigation is not there. No expenses like court fee, stamp fee, incidentals, lawyers' recurring expenses, and dates.	3. There's always a tendency not to question closely, issues of discretion, as it is felt that the same are the prerogative of the executive.
4. Its more flexible, not bound by tradition, rules, and precedents. Rules and regulations and their implementation, interpretation matters; not legal cannons, bullet points, and other points to fire.	4. Since decisions or judgements of tribunals are subject to review and appeal, if so desired, cases do add up in High Courts and Supreme Court defeating the very purpose of having tribunals. In fact, cases get more tangled and twisted at times.
5. Justice handed down is adequate, appropriate, and acceptable. Parties know their bonds and bindings; evidence is mostly documented. What is questionable is discretion.	5. A uniform code of procedure is not there for tribunals unlike with courts. This leads to case- by-case consideration, case- by-case construction.
6. Heavy technical matters, complex departmental rules, and relaxations are known better to those who have worked through them. This experience is invaluable and cannot be assimilated overnight.	6. On occasions, members of tribunals carry their own predilections, preferences, and choices; they are conditioned. It affects judgements.

The CAT

The decision of the Government in 1985 to set up Central Administrative Tribunal (CAT) to exclusively handle cases of Central Government Employees and similarly placed persons barring them from going to High Courts was received with some trepidation and lot of apprehension. The composition of the Tribunal with a Judicial Member and another Administrative, with former as chairman also did not enthuse. Soon cases started piling up and adjournments also set in; this was some relief to the employees. Engagement of lawyers by both sides was further comfort. Departments of the Government of India and its litigant employees now settled to a game of 'date and fate'. In all intent and content, it was like other courts.

Soon voices began to be heard, cases are piling, there are delays. Delays, more delays. Lawyers started blaming the Government departments for inadequacy, ignorance, and incompetence. Government departments started blaming the systems of the tribunal and also the lawyers. The cantankerous litigants started blaming both, the lawyers and the Tribunal.

Finally, debate was afoot, who is responsible for all this. Some government departments started voicing a plea that they should have their own tribunals. The final word went to a wag who said in all mock seriousness, "I say cat (Central Administrative Tribunal) is alone responsible for all this we see? No, the dog is also responsible!" Dog who? Dog what, Dog how? Dog is Department of Government. Dog with its orders, clarifications, corrigendums, corrections, concurrences........ The tail wags the dog!!

Arbitration: A tool for redressal mechanism

Arbitration is emerging as the preferred mode of grievance redressal mechanism; there are many reasons for this. It is less protracted compared to litigation, not so messy and never so intense as to leave scars behind. Arbitration involves submission of substantive points for decision by both parties with an understanding that the decision delivered would be binding. The decision would be based on canons of law and consideration of principles of natural justice.

The Arbitration and Conciliation Act 2015 is in fact an amendment to the 1996 Act which had to be so amended as to meet the challenges of changing times and environment.

With a huge load of court cases, the judiciary is already burdened; the present Act will help reduce further pressure on the judiciary. Changes will make arbitration user friendly, cost effective and speedy. The Act as amended now, will facilitate ease of doing business and build levels of confidence.

The other significant changes now are:

(i) Arbitration Tribunal will be empowered to grant all kinds of interim measures which a regular court is empowered to grant.

(ii) Awards have to be made in 12 months' time, extendable by six months. Fast track awards, on choice, within 6 months.

(iii) To ensure fairness and neutrality, Arbitrator will have to give a certificate that he has no interest or relationship of any kind.

(iv) In case of International Arbitration, the relevant court would have to be High Court with original ordinary jurisdiction.

(v) Appointment of Arbitrators shall be made by Supreme Court or High Court. Electronic Communication will be equivalent to written communication.

CHAPTER 4

Our Constitution Vis-a-Vis Other Countries

OVERVIEW

The Indian Constitution has been drawn partly based on the experience of other countries, not as an expediency or exigency, but more out of an express need to emulate what is good in them. In doing so, the framers of our Constitution have acknowledged the universality of values, utility of norms, and uniqueness of evolution. These have been adopted or adapted, tailoring to our needs. We did not want to reinvent the wheel, perhaps add some spokes or set it rolling on our soil; either way we never allowed a situation of 'wheels within wheels'.

"India would do as she had done for centuries, take what she desired from other cultures and bend it to her needs."

Granville Austin

It is a trite but well-worn cliché that the Indian constitution is a 'bag of borrowings'; there's a measure of truth in this, if one considers adapting good, compatible, universal features from others as 'borrowing'. The idea was noble, intent fair, and purpose eternally pure. In their pursuit of establishing democracy, the framers of our constitution leaned on the experience of democracies, their struggles, and evolution. It was a graceful tribute and a generous acknowledgement of a soul-stirring saga involving sacrifice and suffering that democracies underwent. To call it a borrowing is to demean their own effort in securing democracies in their countries.

Secondly, human values, dignity, rights, compassion, and consideration are all universal in nature. No one country can claim exclusive right to them. The essence of democracy is protection and preservation of these values, these beliefs, and these faiths. After all, aren't all men created equal? To call integration of all these values, rights as a 'borrowing' is an insult to universal fraternity ad brotherhood.

Thirdly, India as a country has a long history and heritage. Traditions of tolerance, trust, and temperance are rooted in our psyche; they form the basis of their own institutions. If perchance other countries featured themes similar in their constitutions, it can't be called 'borrowing' but coincidence, a matter of happening.

Fourthly, India suffered at least two centuries of British colonial rule. Many institutions by the British took roots here and got accepted. India, post-independence continued persisting with them. Again, this cannot be termed as 'borrowing'. These institutions were nurtured, grown, and developed here. By this analogy, all constitutions, American, Australian, Canadian, etc. owe their existence to the British who ruled them and the features of their constitutions are not called 'borrowing'.

Finally, even under the colonial rule we participated very energetically and effectively in nation-building and gained significant experience in running institutions. Be it the imperial legislature, be it the courts, be it the local self-government, be it finance, property, contracts, or even trade, commerce etc., the country had developed its own mechanisms. These institutions were running our day to day lives and a very special place in our minds was dedicated to them. Although started by colonial masters, yet they came to be regarded as our very own since the best minds of our countrymen were directed to run them. To call these a bag of borrowings is to insult their memory.

Even so, the moot point is comparison of India's constitutional scheme with that of other countries. As already recounted, there are two types of constitutions; one made for the country due to exigencies of war, revolution, or internal upheavals, the other laboriously over the years balancing expectations with expedience, progress with pursuits, reason with rationale, and tradition with trust. The Constitution of the United States (1789), Soviet Union (1919), France (1790), and Ireland (1921) are all examples of war, revolution and upheaval driven constitutions. The British Constitution is an example of the latter kind: an unwritten constitution built on traditions, trust, and thoroughness. Overall, an enduring document and endearing dispensation.

Let us rate the features of our constitution and their relationship with the constitution of other countries.

From U.K.	• Nominal Head President (like Queen) • Cabinet System of Ministers • Post of PM • Parliamentary Type of Govt. • Bicameral Parliament • Lower House more powerful • Council of Ministers responsible to Lowe House • Speaker in Lok Sabha

From U.S.	• Written Constitution • Executive head of state known as President and his being the Supreme Commander of the Armed Forces • Vice-President as the ex-officio Chairman of Rajya Sabha • Fundamental Rights • Supreme Court • Provision of States • Independence of judiciary and judicial review • Preamble • Removal of Supreme court and High court Judges
From USSR	• Fundamental Duties • Five year Plan
From Australia	• Concurrent list • Language of the Preamble • Provision regarding trade, commerce and intercourse
From Japan	• Law on which the Supreme Court functions
From Weimar Constituion of Germany	• Suspension of Fundamental Rights during the emergency
From Canada	• Scheme of federation with a strong Centre • Distribution of powers between Centre and the States and placing, Residuary Powers with the Centre
From Ireland	• Concept of Directive Principles of States Policy(Ireland borrowed it from Spain) • Method of election of President • Nomination of members in the Rajya Sabha by the President

India was bound to follow the traditions established by the United Kingdom and the United States as a parliamentary democracy following the twin principles of equality and rule of law.

The Constitution of the United States has given us the idea of pre-dominance of the constitution, rule of law and separation of powers, checks, and balances. India, however, has not followed the principle of the states having their own constitution as in United States, nor the Indian judiciary has the same footing or foundation as with the United States judiciary which has sweeping powers, commanding status. We took the idea of a written constitution from the United States.

The United Kingdom, which has largely an unwritten constitution, has given the idea of Parliamentary from of democracy, post of Prime Minister, Bicameral legislature, and a nominal head of state. The cornerstone of the constitution is flexibility and foundation of accountability.

What we have not taken from the United Kingdom are the following.

(a) In the United Kingdom there's no system of judicial review; parliament rules and reigns, courts can't overturn laws.

(b) Local governments are under the control of central Government which can throw them over and out. We have given some constitutional safeguards.

(c) United Kingdom is a unitary state, federalism is not known to it.

(d) There's a world of difference between our Rajya Sabha and the House of Lords of the United Kingdom, although in one respect they are similar; they cannot touch the money bills except to advice. Rajya Sabha is constituted through elections from State legislatures whereas the House of Lords comprises of hereditary peers and nominated members.

Once we take a look at the Head of the State as in the United States, United Kingdom, and India we come across substantial difference in nature, scope, and functions.

United Kingdom

The United Kingdom is a parliamentary democracy under a constitutional monarch. The constitutional monarch is a symbolic, titular head with lot of ceremonial functions, emotional appeal, and a historical legacy. From the time James II the King abandoned rule and fled in 1688, England got its parliament to rule, regulate, and relegate. Why, even when King Edward VIII wanted to marry an American divorcee, Mrs. Wallis Simpson, Parliament said, 'No'. The king abdicated the throne, not his love; parliament set terms for the new king.

India

Contrast with the Indian President, he is the Head of the State. He is elected through a process involving members of the Lok Sabha, Rajya Sabha, legislators of the State, etc. He has a claim to legitimacy through choice, not chance of a hereditary breeding. Indian President has a whole host of functions, lots of duties, and obligations. He has legislative powers, financial powers, military powers, and executive powers. He is the face of the country abroad, he has ceremonial functions. He is forever busy with ordinances, promulgation of rule under Article 356, making speeches about the achievements of the government of the day, busy with reports of the CAG, Finance Commission, UPSC, and other constitutional bodies, giving away awards, consulting Supreme court, and going through petitions appointing civil servants carefully with concern. He is functional and purposeful and has a fixed tenure of 5 years.

The Indian constitutional schemes have placed the President at the apex, much like with the tradition of a viceroy in India. He has a duty to the constitution, a devotion to the Parliament, and a dedication to the will of the people.

The United States

The President of the United States is both head of state as also head of Government. The US constitution vests the President with executive power to charge him with execution of federal law along with responsibility of appointing federal executive, diplomatic, regulatory, and judicial officers, and concluding treaties with foreign powers with the advice and consent of the senate.

He is elected by an electoral college constituted for the purpose. The members of this college are elected directly by the people of all states. He holds the office for a term of 4 years and cannot serve more than two terms.

Thus, when we consider the Indian constitutional scheme with that of other democratic countries we at once find that we have taken a golden mean, the best of both worlds and attuned to our needs and conditions. We have captured the essence and the spirit while retaining our flavour and fragrance. Our society with its divisions and spoils, its historical evolution and specially, its twists and turns are all unique as they are singularly difficult to comprehend too. All these had to be integrated in a constitution with a marked bias for unitary form in a flexible mould. India's challenge to make its constitution functional, evolving, inclusive, and flexible was indeed huge. It was like manufacturing a telescope which could be turned into microscope and yet give readings for both.

In communists or centrally controlled countries like the erstwhile Soviet Union or China, the emphasis rests with the party and the government has to follow the party diktat. Focus is on equality and meeting of objectives. Direction is known and deviations are suspect. Communist country constitution has role for dissent but within the party apparent criticism and self-criticism are permitted only to the extent the party permits. Governance is strictly not within the scope of constitutional construction.

Countries like Japan and Germany, both ravaged by the Second World War, had historical issues, the issue with war mongering being ingrained in the psyche. Japan through an Article of its constitution abandoned recourse to war. Germany forced its citizens to partake benefits of freedom and rights. Both these countries have evolved their constitutions on the principles of separation of powers between legislature, executive and the judiciary with nominal heads of state. Constitutions of both these countries have stressed on economic reconstruction and individual liberty. Hiroshima and Hamburg are painful reminders of a horror visiting them not so long ago. Constitutions emphasise on federalism and rights and functional division of powers among the organs of the state. India achieved all this through debate, discussion, and devolution. True, we did not reinvent the wheel; there was no need for us, the wheel had come to us turning a full circle. No, our constitution is not a bag of borrowings, nor a blog of borrowings, but a living, vibrant, inclusive, action-oriented document of hope and expectation. It is a unique document that covers both the powers and process in a harmonious construction.

Comparing Indian Constitution with other Countries.

India	America	Britain	Soviet Union	France	Japan
1950	1789	-	1977	1946	1946
Written	Written	Unwritten largely	Written	Written	Written
Flexible	Rigid	Flexible	Rigid	Rigid	Rigid
Parliamentary Democracy	Presidential	Parliamentary	Single Party	President Parliamentary	Parliamentary
Federal	Federal	Unitary	Federal	Unitary	Unitary
Bicameralism	Bicameralism	Bicameralism	Bicameralism	Bicameralism	Bicameralism
Fundamental Rights	Bill of Rights	Rule of law	Fundamental Rights	Bill of Rights	Fundamental Rights

When we compare the Indian constitution with that of the other countries, a couple of things emerge. Indian constitution is the first edition dating back to 1950 whereas country like France has had many a constitution before the present one. Japanese constitution of 1946 is largely shaped by American occupying forces led by Gen. Douglas Mcarthur; constitution gave sizeable personal freedom in a highly monarchial state valuing obedience and subservience to order, authority and hierarchy. Japanese emperor was the 'monarch of all that he surveyed': Japan valued order, obedience and oligarchy: constitution vaunted freedom; fair play and franchise. America has two sets of constitutions, one federal and other for each state. "Bill of Rights" enumerating individual liberties and freedoms is the cornerstone of American constitution. American President is both the Head of the state as also the Head of the Government. The constitution spells out checks and balances the Legislature, Executives and the Judiciary. American president is much more powerful than the Indian president. Judiciary too has sweeping powers under the American constitution. Upper House, the senate in the US, elected for a term of six years is much more powerful than the House of Representatives, elected for two years period. In India, the Lower House is more powerful and has a term of 5 years; Upper House is a permanent body with 1/3rd of members retiring after every 2 years.

US President is elected on the principle 'Winner takes it all' ie. if California has 55 votes, the candidate winning the state of California takes all 55 votes in the electoral college. In India, the President is elected by an electoral college comprising of members of Lok Sabha, Rajya Sabha, State legislatures and Union Territories on the principle of 'representation by proportion';value of vote of an MP representing the size of population.

In the British constitution, all the powers of the government are vested in a single, supreme central government. Local governments are created only for administrative convenience and work under the control of Central Government; they can be established by Central Government.

Britain has an institution called 'Privy Council' presided over by Lord President and is an advisory body to the cabinet. India has no such system. Similarly, Britain has system of 'shadow cabinet' where the party in opposition runs a parallel government tracking the ruling party. 'Shadow cabinet' a unique system of Britain is officially recognised. India has no such system.

France has part quasi-presidential, part quasi-parliamentary government. It has a President directly elected by the people and is powerful. France has a Parliament and a nominated council of ministers who are not members of the Parliament, but responsible to the Government. India has a President who is not a member of the Parliament but draws powers from it. In India, the ministers are members of the Parliament and are responsible to it. Collective responsibility is the operating principle.

France has a constitutional council with nine members appointed for nine years serving as a judicial watchdog to ensure that executives decrees and parliamentary laws conform to the constitution. It is an advisory body, its opinions are not binding. India doesn't have such a body but Supreme Court can, in its jurisdiction, can step in if executive powers and parliamentary laws are at variance.

Japan's constitution has 31 Articles (out of 103 Articles) devoted to the rights and duties of the people. Indian constitution too has rights and duties, although not in the aggressive manner the Japanese have; In Japan, right to property is a prominent right.

Article 9 of the Japanese constitution declares renunciation of war to settle international disputes. Now, this article is being amended. India doesn't have such issues, we have a fundamental belief as brought out in Art. 5' to work for peace.

Japanese constitution has not seen a single amendment, barring the move to amend Article '9'; it is a rigid, frozen and stiff constitution although political instability in Japan is endemic. Indian constitution has been subject to amendments but good number of such amendments are procedural, for administrative reasons and for convenience. They are not to set a deep rooted flaw right, nor for any fundamental issue. By and large, the sanctity of the constitution is being maintained. It is a document that has shown a way, shown a destination and shown faith can move mountains. Aberration, if any, was the 42nd Amendment Act of 1976 during emergency, when the party in power applied the scalpel to prune, pare and pave the constitution for specific ends. 44th amendment Act of 1978 by a government of coalition did away with some of 42nd Amendments. Pendulum swings both ways ultimately to settle to rest at a golden mean.

United Kingdom : England in 1215, witnessed the signing of 'Magna Carta' by King John I; a historic document and a concession by the king acknowledging the rights of people. Even in 1295, the king had to seek parliamentary approval to tax the people. Tudor kings ruled with grace and balance not to antagonise the Parliament, but subsequent rulers, the Stuarts claimed a 'divine right' which was challenged by the Parliament in the civil war. 1688 saw the triumph of Parliament and 1689, the bill of rights making way for parliamentary dominance :-

a. Limit on the powers of the crown
b. Rights of Parliament outlined
c. Rules for freedom of speech
d. Right to petition the monarch.

England has a parliamentary form of government with the monarch as the head. Monarch is the executive head as also part of the legislature. It is more a case of fusion of powers than separation of powers. Courts in England cannot call to question the legislature or parliament.

For most part of later half of nineteenth century and good part of twentieth century, England has battled to reform the House of Lords. This issue revolved around separation of judiciary from the legislature too. Even so, the United Kingdom comprising England, Scotland, Northern Ireland, Wales and Isle of Man presents a curious picture of traditionally driven parliamentary democracy with a relic ridden monarchy, defence oriented judiciary and European Union commanded executive. United Kingdom has a point to prove yet: Separation of powers is organic and the spirit behind it matters; mere statutes and declarations of intent and faith are not enough. Separation of powers is actually a happy fusion of forces where the last word is of the Monarch. On the ground, it is tradition not transgression, trust not threat, that matters. United Kingdom has its uniqueness and that has its uses, conveniences, conformity and compulsion: all in the name of the constitution.

5

CHAPTER

Parliament and State Legislatures

OVERVIEW

Our Constitution has given the legislature the prime position of pristine glory, pivotal power, and predominant status. This brings power and privileges; often a heady mixture which inevitably leads to issues that need handling with care and caution. The legislatures at theUnion and the States are structured with defined powers, detailed rules for conduct of business, and a demarcation that seamlessly draws the jurisdiction between the Houses; as between the Lok Sabha and the Rajya Sabha and legislative council and legislative Assembly. The legislature is the bedrock of our Parliamentary system.

INTRODUCTION

India has opted for a parliamentary form of democracy; option is for a government of the people, by the people, and for the people, and the mechanism is through a government responsible to the Parliament. The process is by the Parliament getting elected in the first place, by the people, through open and fair elections and conducted through participation on basis of universal adult franchise. People are the stakeholders, people are sovereign, people are the ultimate masters.

The Preamble itself begins with the declaration, 'We the people of India having solemnly resolved to constitute India into a Sovereign, Socialist, Secular, Democratic Republic...' It is a clear affirmation that the Constitution is the result of people's resolve. Parliament is the means and mechanism to implement the provisions of the Constitution through elected representatives. Legislation to enact the law of the land is done by the Parliament and only Parliament ensures the enactment of rules and regulations through subordinate legislation, etc. Parliament also ensures accountability through audit and accounting. Parliament has the judiciary and the executive to work alongside in a manner such that harmony with harness is achieved with seamless integration. Supremacy of Parliament is acknowledged, superiority of judicial review is conceded, speciality of executive is affirmed, and sanctity of the Constitution is universally accepted. It is a fine balance of powers, a balance based on convictions, not convenience, a balance based on reason, not rhetoric, a balance based on necessity, not narrative. The parliamentary form of government first evolved in England, laboriously over centuries, with checks and balances, with claims and counter claims, with power and perils.

England went to civil war to engage for parliamentary supremacy, restored monarchy after seeing despotism in the name of parliamentary pursuit, in the name of republicanism, in the name of people's power. Parliament too suffered under Cromwell as he purged it to replace with his 'protectorate'. England evolved its largely unwritten constitution based on conventions, practices, and beliefs. Two significant developments took place, almost without any stir. First, when King Charles I went to the Parliament with armed soldiers, Cromwell, Hampden John, and Pym and others fled. Enraged, the King addressed the Speaker, 'I see that the birds have flown away...'

'Aye, Sir. I do not have the eyes to see nor the ears to hear except what the Parliament commands me to see or hear. I am but a servant of the house.'

This set the precedent for the Speaker for the House. The position of 'Speaker' got entrenched.

Second, Robert Walpole leading the Whigs became a minister in the government. The king took fancy to his unflappable demeanour and easy ways. Walpole started calling on the king in settings of mutual admiration, discussing issues and affairs of the state. Soon, he began to be known as the 'Prime' Minister. The institution of Prime Minister came to be recognised with awe and admiration. 'First among equals, not equal among firsts.' England found it expedient to have a Prime Minister; it was good to have a leader, good to have a spokesperson, good to have a perspective. Both Tories and the Whigs found the practice purposeful. Soon conventions started building around the position of the 'Prime Minister'. The 'accidental' Prime Minister Walpole, as was his wont to say, would have amused himself with his celebrated saying, 'Let sleeping dogs lie.' England now had a Prime Minister, the political world an institution. Years later, under Queen Victoria, Disraeli, and Gladstone, both vied with each other to occupy Prime Minister's position; it had gained respectability, status, and an exalted position.

The parliamentary form of government first evolved in England, laboriously over centuries, with checks and balances, with claims and counter claims, with power and perils.

Bicameral legislation involving two Houses also traces its origin to England; the House of Commons and the House of Lords, the Commons representing people with ever enlarged franchise over the years, and Lords representing people with privilege across the years with hereditary lineage. Tussle between Commons and Lords was not uncommon. Through the years, Lords yielded to the Commons, money bills being among them. India has taken the cue to have Lok Sabha representing the popular interest and Rajya Sabha the interests of States; mercifully not of privileged class, nor on hereditary basis. Rajya Sabha is a permanent body with infusion of fresh entrants every two years at the rate of one-third of the House. Lok Sabha goes for elections every five years to respond to the voice of the people. People express themselves, political system moves on. Both the Lok Sabha as well as the Rajya Sabha have their own rules for conduct of business. Parliamentary democracy depends a great deal on working collectively. It's best achieved through a system of committees having diverse talent but common goals. Critical issues, crucial matters, and conflicting interests all get resolved in a spirit of togetherness and commonality of purpose. Dignity of the House and devotion to integrity matters above all else. Rule of law and common good are the prime movers; country first, government next. Yet all is not honky dory.

It is not roses, roses all the way. Tussles, scandals, waste of time, lack of respect, criminalisation of politics, lack of quality discussions, caste driven loyalties, and concern for regionalism are a blot on the parliamentary system. Corruption and sexual escapades are in evidence too. There's a belief gaining ground that we need to cleanse the system, beginning with electoral reforms, parties next.

It's easy to find faults always but there's a growing tendency now to fault the find; shoot the messenger.

Yet, when we see the countries around us, we see how elusive democracy is. We see army takeovers, single party rules, same set of leadership over decades, experimentation with democracy, communist party rule, guided democracies, religious rule by religious dogmas, limited democracies and sheikhdoms. We present an example of an oasis in a vast desert of doom, despair, and devastation. We are an example unto ourselves, unto others: we are an example of what might have been.

I. STRUCTURE OF PARLIAMENT

Bicameral Legislature

Under the Constitution, the legislature of the Union, called the Parliament is constituted on the basis of the principle 'bicameralism': i.e legislature having two Houses. A federal system of government envisaged a balance between the two Houses, one representing the people as a whole and the other the States. House of the people, Lok Sabha, is composed of representatives elected directly by electorate on the basis of adult franchise and territorial constitutions. It reflects the will of the people and has a term of five years. Council of States, Rajya Sabha, comprises of representatives elected by state assemblies. This House is permanent with one-third of the members retiring after every two years. This House reveals the wisdom of the States; called the elders, it has its role to showcase the feel of States. Both Houses supplement each other; spirit is of cooperation, not confrontation, clash and cynicism.

Article 79

'There shall be a Parliament for theUnion which shall consist of the President and two Houses to be known as Council of States and House of the People. (President is not a member of either of the Houses).

A Narrative

The legislature of a State can be unicameral or bicameral. It is left to the State's wishes to have two Chambers or one Chamber. The State Legislature must pass a resolution on the creation or abolition of the second Chamber. It can do so by a resolution adopted by a majority of members of Legislative Assembly or by 2/3rd majority of the members present. When such resolution is forwarded to theUnion, Parliament enacts a law creating the second Chamber. However, there is no time limit within which the Parliament should act on the resolution of the Assembly. The Legislative Assembly gets elected by the people of the State at the general elections from constituencies, the demarcation of which is determined by the Delimitation Commission in such a way that the population of each constituency is as nearly as possible the same. Population figures taken into consideration for delimiting constituencies are the population figures of the year 2001 and it continues to be so till the population figured are published in 2026. The Legislative Council is elected by special constituencies created like teachers' constituency, graduates' constituency, local bodies' constituency, and the Assembly constituency. In teachers' constituency, persons who are teachers by profession for over three years and residing in the State are enrolled as voters and they elect 1/12th of the total number of the council. Similarly, graduates of any university residing in the State for over three years and enrolled as voters may elect 1/12th of the members of the council. Elected members of local bodies form local bodies' constituency and they elect 1/3rd of the total number of members of the council. Another 1/3rd members of the council get elected by the elected members of the Legislative Assembly. The total number of members of the Legislative Council stands at 1/3rd of the total members of the Legislative Assembly. For example, if the elected number of members of the Legislative Assembly is 324, the members of the Legislative Council shall be 108 and 1/3rd of that, i.e., 36 are elected by the members of the Legislative Assembly, 36 are elected by the local bodies, 9 are elected by the graduates, and 9 others are elected by teachers. The balance 18 is nominated. Members who are elected at the first time after the Constitution of the Council will hold their membership for six years, four years, and two years, as may be determined by the lottery and thereafter every member then elected will hold membership for six years. The next elections to the council are held every two years for 1/3rd of the members for each class.

Article 80

The Council of States shall consist of:

(a) Twelve members to be nominated by the President. The members to be nominated by the President shall consist of persons having special knowledge or practical experience in respect of such matters as the following, namely, literature, science, art and social service. ('Sports' was added later).

(b) Not more than two hundred and thirty eight representatives of States and Union Territories. The allocation of seats in the Council of States to be filled by representatives of the States and Union territories shall be in accordance with the provisions in that behalf contained in the Fourth Schedule. The representative of each state shall be elected by the elected members of the legislative assembly of the state in accordance with the system of proportional representation by means of the single transferable vote.

Article 81: Composition of the House of the People

The House of the People shall consist of:

(a) Not more than five hundred thirty members chosen by direct election from territorial constituencies of the States and

(b) Not more than twenty members to represent the Union Territories, chosen in such a manner as the Parliament may by law provide. (only Union Territories of Delhi and Pondicherry have representation in the Rajya Sabha).

Two points are relevant:

(i) 84th (Eighty Fourth) Amendment Act, 2002 has frozen the allocation of seats in Lok Sabha and State Assemblies up to 2026. Presently, 2001 Census is the base.

(ii) Article 331 States that 'The President may, if he is of the opinion that the Anglo-Indian community is not adequately represented in the House of the People, nominate not more than two members of that community to the House of the People; notwithstanding provisions of Article 81 (Eighty One).

A Narrative

The number of Lok Sabha members is fixed at 550. The number of Members of Rajya Sabha stands at 238 elected plus 12 nominated Members. The members of Lok Sabha are directly elected under Universal Adult Franchise in which all citizens both men and women above the age of 18 years are voters. The whole country is divided into 543 territorial constituencies and each constituency elects one Member. Of these, 79 are reserved for Scheduled Castes and 49 are reserved for Scheduled Tribes. It may be noted that six constituencies are located in Pakistan occupied Kashmir (Pok) and one seat reserved for Anglo Indians lapsed. Reservation means only persons belonging to SCs and STs only can stand for election and the whole electorate votes for such a candidate. Reserved constituency does not mean that those who belong to reserved classes only vote their own representative. The delimitation commission physically defines the constituencies and their reservation. There is no judicial review. The proposal for reserving seats for Muslims as a Community and for women is under consideration. The Backward Castes among Muslims already enjoy reservation.

Article 82: Re-adjustment after each Census

Readjustment after each census, now frozen up to 2026 census, shall not affect representation in the House of the People until dissolution of the existing House.

Readjustment of the number of seats for Parliament and State Assemblies on the basis of changes in population can take place only after publication of the final census figures in 2026. Till then, the number of constituencies for the Parliament and State Assemblies shall remain fixed. The boundaries of the constituencies can be so altered as to make the population covered by the constituencies as far as possible equal and shall be as nearly as possible equal to the total population of the State divided by the number of constituencies. It is quite possible under this scheme that a parliamentary constituency in Bihar may have more number of voters because of the higher density of population than a parliamentary constituency of Assam where density of population is lower. Presently, the population for each assembly constituency and accordingly the parliamentary constituency is calculated on the basis of census figures published in 2001. The situation will continue up to the year 2026.

A Narrative

Parliament shall meet in such a way that the time between the last date of one session and the first day of the next session shall not exceed six months. So it is compulsory that there shall be three sessions in a year. These sessions are called Budget Session, Monsoon Session, and Winter Session. The meetings in the session can be adjourned but the session continues till it ends. The session ends when prorogued. The recess between the session which is prorogued and the next session can be called the time when the Parliament is said to be not in session. The President's right to issue Ordinances is to be exercised only when the Parliament is not in session. Repeated prorogations to enable the President to promulgate or re-promulgate Ordinance have been criticised by the Supreme Court.

The time lag between the last meeting of one session of Lok Sabha and the first meeting of the next session must not exceed six months. The implication is Lok Sabha can have any number of sessions in a year and the minimum shall be three as per the present practice. The President may prorogue the Lok Sabha at any time, even while it is in session. The meaning of Prorogation is that the Lok Sabha is not in session. Otherwise, when Lok Sabha adjourns from time to time, it is deemed to be in session. The practice of proroguing the session to enable the President to issue an Ordinance and repeated prorogations to reissue the same ordinance without legislating an enactment is worthy of criticism both in the case of Lok Sabha and particularly in the case of State Assemblies. Lok Sabha, presided by Speaker and Rajya Sabha by Chairman conduct the meetings of the Houses which shall be in accordance with the rules. The quorum for meeting is fixed at 1/10th of the strength of the House. If discovered that the attendance at the House is less than 1/10th, the meeting shall be adjourned to meet again, after the quorum is achieved. All matters put to vote may be treated as approved by the House when they are voted by the majority of the members present. In case of equality of votes, the Speaker or Chairman shall have the right to exercise his casting vote. Speaker elected to the post remains independent of the party to which he belongs. Where the House wants that the voting must be physically counted, the House divides and cast their votes in boxes kept on the corridors of the Parliament. The names of the Members along with how they voted are published in the official records of the Parliament.

Article 83: Duration of House of Parliament

(1) Council of States shall not be subject to dissolution, one-third of the members shall retire at the end of two years.

(2) The House of the People, unless sooner dissolved, shall continue for five years from the date appointed. However, while a Proclamation of Emergency is in operation, it can be extended by a period not extending one year at a time and not extending in any case beyond six months after the Proclamation has ceased to operate. (This has come about due to the 44th Amendment).

Article 84: Qualification for Membership of Parliament

A person shall not be qualified to be chosen to fill a seat in Parliament unless he

(a) Is a citizen of India, and makes and subscribes before some person authorised in that behalf by the Election Commission an Oath or affirmation according to the form set out for the purpose in the Third Schedule.

(b) Is, in the case of a seat in the Council of States, not less than thirty (30) years of age and in the case of a seat in the House of People not less than twenty five years of age (25), and

(c) Possesses such other qualifications as may be prescribed in that behalf by or under any law made by Parliament.

A Narrative

There may be cases where a person gets disqualified after the election by reason of insolvency, insanity, or some other reason as the Parliament may provide, or, by reason of defection or by reason of holding an office of profit. The question of disqualification has to be decided by the Speaker alone and not by any other authority, and till such disqualification is decided, the member continues to function as member. Similarly where a person resigns, then also the Speaker has to compulsorily hold an enquiry and decide upon the genuineness of the resignation. A member of Parliament ceases to be a Member if he gets himself elected to the State Legislature, if within a period prescribed he does not resign his seat in the Assembly. The meaning is, if he does not resign his seat in the Assembly, he continues to be a Member of the State Assembly and ceases to be a Member of the Parliament, and if he resigns his membership in the Parliament, thereafter his seat in the Assembly shall be treated as confirmed. If after resignation from Parliament he subsequently resigns from the State Assembly within the time prescribed, he shall not regain his parliamentary seat.

Article 85: Session of Parliament, Prorogue, and Dissolution

(1) The President shall from time to time summon each House of Parliament to meet at such time and place as he thinks fit, but six (6) months shall not intervene between its last sitting in one session and the date appointed for its sitting in the next session.

(2) The President may from time to time

(a) Prorogue the Houses or either House.

(b) Dissolve the House of the People.

Article 86: Right of President to Address and Send Messages to Houses

(1) The President may address either House or both Houses assembled together and for that purpose require the attendance of members.

(2) The President may send messages to either House of Parliament, whether with respect to a bill pending with them in Parliament or otherwise, and a House to which any message is so sent shall with all convenient despatch consider any matter required by the message to be taken into consideration.

Article 87: Special Address by the President

(1) At the commencement of the first session after each general election to the House of People and at the commencement of the first session of each year, the President shall address both Houses of Parliament assembled together and inform Parliament of the causes of its summons.

(2) Provisions shall be made by the rules regulating the procedure of either House for the allotment of time for discussion of matters referred to in such rules.

Article 88: Rights of Ministers and Attorney—General as Respects Houses

Every Minister and the Attorney-General shall have the right to speak in, and otherwise to take part in the proceedings of, either House, any joint sitting of the Houses, but shall not by virtue of this Article be entitled to vote.

RAJYA SABHA: PURPOSE AND POSITION

1. Rajya Sabha is the face of our federalism where States are represented. With the dynamic nature of our politics, where changes do take place in States, Rajya Sabha having 1/3rd members retiring every two years, the realities of situation of people's aspirations are reflected.
2. Senior politicians, elders, statesmen get access to Rajya Sabha without having to go through the rough and tumble of politics, caste equations, and above all party dispensations. Their experience is an asset and their talent an added value.
3. Rajya Sabha is a House of revision and restraint; it often looks for a course for caution to Lok Sabha's bills of enthusiasm and haste.

II. OFFICERS OF PARLIAMENT IN THE COUNCIL OF STATES

Article 89: The Chairman and Deputy Chairman of the Council of States

(1) The Vice-President of India shall be the ex-officio chairman of Council of States. (Note: Only Council of States can remove him.)

(2) The Council of States, as soon as may be, chooses a member of the council to be Deputy Chairman thereof and as soon as the office of the Deputy Chairman becomes vacant, the council shall choose another member to be Deputy Chairman thereof.

Article 90: Vacation and Resignation of, and Removal from, the Office of Deputy Chairman

A member holding office as Deputy Chairman of the Council of States

(a) Shall vacate his office if he ceases to be a member of the council

(b) May at any time, by writing under his hand addressed to the Chairman resign his office; and

(c) May be removed from his office by a resolution of the council passed by a majority of all the then members of the council (with 14 days' notice)

Article 91: Power of the Deputy Chairman or any Other Person to Perform the Duties of the Office of, or to Act as Chairman

(1) While the office of chairman is vacant, or during any period when the Vice-President is acting as, or discharging the functions of President, the duties of the office shall be performed by the Deputy Chairman, or if the office of Deputy Chairman is also vacant, by such member of the Council of States as the President may appoint for the purpose.

(2) During the absence of the chairman from any sitting of the Council of States the Deputy Chairman, or, if he is also absent, such person as may be determined by the rules of procedure of the council, or, if no such person is present, such other person as may be determined by the council, shall act as chairman.

Article 92: The Chairman or the Deputy Chairman not to Preside while a Resolution for Removal from His Office is Under Consideration

The chairman shall have the right to speak in, and otherwise to take part in proceedings of, the Council of States while any resolution for the removal of Vice-President from his office is under consideration in the council, but notwithstanding anything in Article 100 shall not be entitled to vote at all on such resolution or any other matter during such proceedings.

(**Note:** Article 100: The chairman or Speaker or person acting as such, shall not vote in the first instance, but shall have and exercise a casting vote in the case of equalities of votes.)

HOUSE OF PEOPLE

Article 93: The Speaker and Deputy Speaker of the House of the People

The House of the people shall, as soon as may be, choose two members of the House to be respectively Speaker and Deputy Speaker thereof and so often as the office of the Speaker or Deputy Speaker becomes vacant the House shall choose another member to be Speaker or Deputy Speaker, as the case may be.

Article 94: Vacation and Resignation of, and Removal from, the Offices of Speaker and Deputy Speaker

A member holding office as Speaker or Deputy Speaker of the House of the People

(a) Shall vacate his office if he ceases to be a member of the House of the People;

(b) May at any time, by writing under his hand addressed, if such member is Speaker, to the Deputy Speaker, and if such member is the Deputy Speaker, to the Speaker, resign his office; and

Article 95: Power of the Deputy Speaker or Other Person to Perform the Duties of the Office of, or to act as Speaker

(1) While the office of Speaker is vacant, the duties of the office shall be performed by the Deputy Speaker, or if the office of the Deputy Speaker is also vacant, by such member of the House of the People as the President may appoint for the purpose.

(2) During the absence of the Speaker from any sitting of the House of the People the Deputy Speaker or, if he is also absent, such person as may be determined by the rules of procedure of the House, or, if no such person is present, such other person as may be determined by the House, shall act as Speaker.

Article 96: The Speaker or the Deputy Speaker not to Preside While a Resolution for his Removal from Office is Under Consideration

(1) At any sitting of the House of the People, while any resolution for the removal of the Speakers from his office is under consideration, the Speaker, or while any resolution for

the removal of the Deputy Speaker from his office under consideration, the Deputy Speaker, shall not, though he is present preside, and the provisions of clause 2 of Article 95 shall apply in relation to every such sitting as they apply in relation to a sitting from which the Speaker, or, as the case may be, the Deputy Speaker is absent.

(2) The Speaker shall have the right to speak in, and otherwise to take part in the proceedings of the House of the People while any resolution for his removal from office is under consideration in the House and shall, notwithstanding anything in Article 100, be entitled to vote in the first instance on such resolution or any other matter during such proceedings but not in the case of equality of votes.

Article 97: Salaries and Allowances of the Chairman and Deputy Chairman, Speaker and Deputy Speaker

These shall be fixed by the Parliament by law and until provision in that behalf is so made, such salaries and allowances as are specified in the second Schedule.

Article 98: Secretariat of Parliament

Each House of Parliament shall have a separate secretarial staff.

(1) Provided that nothing in this clause shall be construed as preventing the creation of posts common to both Houses of Parliament.

(2) Parliament may by law regulate the recruitment, and the conditions of service of persons appointed, to the secretarial staff of either House of Parliament.

(3) Until provision is made by Parliament under clause (2), the President may, after consultation with the Speaker of the House of the People or chairman of the Council of States, as the case may be, make rules regulating the recruitment, and the conditions of service of persons appointed, to the secretarial staff of the House of the People, or the Council of States, and any rules so made shall have effect subject to the provisions of any law made under the said clause.

SPEAKER AND DEPUTY SPEAKER

A Narrative

The Speaker of the Assembly and the Deputy Speaker of the Assembly, the Chairman and Deputy Chairman of the Council are all elected by respective Houses by a simple majority of the members present and voting but in the case of their removal, the Assembly and the Council as the case may be, has to vote by a majority of the members of the respective Houses. The Speaker and the Deputy Speaker when he acts as a Speaker presiding over the Assembly, the Chairman and the Deputy Chairman when he acts as Chairman presiding over the Council are not competent to vote on any matter under discussion but he can exercise his casting vote only when the House is equally divided. It must be noted that in case of a motion for their removal, the Speaker and Deputy Speaker and the Chairman and the Deputy Chairman are competent to participate in the discussion. They are allowed to vote on any matter which is ancillary to the main motion as well as on the motion itself but not entitled to the casting vote when the House is equally divided. It is seen that though Article 181(2) and Article 185(2) do not specifically refer to the Deputy Speaker in the case of the Assembly and the Deputy Chairman in the case of Council, the omission can be supplied by the theory of inclusive interpretation. To make things clear, the person presiding over any meeting shall not vote on any motion in the first instance. It implies he shall not exercise his personal vote. Such person who has what is called casting vote, can exercise his right to vote when the House is divided equally. Hence, he cannot by casting his personal vote create equality and then cast his vote to secure the verdict in his favour. From whatever angle we see, a person has only one vote. Where the law permits him to exercise his personal vote, he cannot exercise his casting vote for a second time. And where the person is entitled to exercise casting the vote, he shall not exercise his personal vote. The Speaker's position is questioned often. His decisions and proceedings under Schedule X have become subject matters of the High Courts. His decisions on contempt matters can be questioned, too. If summoned by the High Court or the Supreme Court, he should appear in person.

The position of the Speaker has become very delicate. If Speaker is made answerable for every action taken by the Legislature on the recommendations of the Lokpal and Lokayuktas, he will spend his whole time in Courts only instead of attending to the work of Legislature. It is necessary that suitable amendments are made in the relevant Articles so that the Speaker is given dignity of post.

The Speaker's position is questioned often. His decisions and proceedings under Schedule X have become subject matters of the High Courts. His decisions on contempt matters can be questioned, too. If summoned by the High Court or the Supreme Court, he should appear in person.

The Supreme Court is often found exercising jurisdiction over the Speaker and Speakers are found to be resisting the Court's interference. Where the Speaker issued a warrant of arrest, the court's interference was upheld under Presidential reference. Supreme Court's interference with the orders of the Speaker in the case of corruption of MPs occurring within the premises, notwithstanding the protest of the Speaker against making him a party, the order of the Speaker was upheld. On the contrary, Speaker's orders were dismissed in the case of bribery of MPs who voted on the confidence resolution receiving heavy bribes, on the ground that the alleged bribery took place outside the Parliament. There are instances where the Supreme Court insisted on the presence of the Speaker in the Court but conduct of the business of the House shall not invalidate the proceedings. The participation of a person who is unqualified is made punishable with penalty of Rs. 500/- for each day of his presence and the same may be recovered from him as a debt due to the Government.

III. CONDUCT OF BUSINESS

Article 99: Oath or Affirmation by Members

Each member of either House of Parliament shall, before taking his seat, make and subscribe before the President, or some person appointed in that behalf by him, an oath or affirmation according to the form set out for that purpose in the Third Schedule.

(**Note:** Oath is in the name of God. Solemn affirmation is a grave declaration of conduct)

Article 100: Voting in Houses, Power of Houses to Act Notwithstanding Vacancies, And Quorum

(1) Save as otherwise provided in this constitution, all questions at any sitting of either House or joint sitting of the Houses shall be determined by the majority of votes by the members present and voting, other than the Speaker or person acting as chairman or Speaker.

The chairman or Speaker, or the person acting as such, shall not vote in the first instance, but shall have and exercise a casting vote in the case of equality of votes.

(2) Either House of Parliament shall have power to act notwithstanding any vacancy in the membership thereof, and any proceedings in Parliament shall be valid notwithstanding that it is discovered subsequently that some person who was not entitled so to do sat or voted or otherwise took part in the proceedings.

(3) Until Parliament by law otherwise provides, the quorum to constitute a meeting of either House of Parliament shall be one-tenth of the total number of members of the House.

(4) If at any time during a meeting of a House there is no quorum, it shall be the duty of the chairman or Speaker or person acting as such, either to adjourn the House or to suspend the meeting until there is quorum.

PASSING OF BILLS (OTHER THAN MONEY BILLS)

A Narrative

Regarding the passing of bills other than money bills there is a difference in the procedures adopted by the Lok Sabha vis-a-vis Rajya Sabha. For instance, if the bill is passed in Lok Sabha and is sent to Rajya Sabha for its approval, and the Rajya Sabha dissents and returns the bill with the comments and if the Lok Sabha does not agree with the amendment proposed by the Rajya Sabha, the President will convene a meeting of the joint session of both the Houses and the bill as adopted by the joint session is deemed to have been passed by both the Houses. But in the case of State Legislative Assembly vis-a-vis the Council, the bill returned by the Council is adopted by the Assembly with or without amendments suggested by the Council and will be treated as passed by both the Houses. In the States, there is no question of joint session. The second adoption of the Assembly is held to be final. Even regarding the passing of money bills also there is variation in the procedure between Lok Sabha vis-a-vis Rajya Sabha and the State Assembly vis-a-vis Legislative Council. If money bills passed by the Assembly are sent to the Council, and the Council proposes any amendments, the Assembly considers the same for the second time and pass the bill with or without amendments suggested by the Council. A money bill passed by the Assembly in the first instance as passed by the second time becomes final. It will be then be treated as approved by both the Houses.

Except the money bills, all the bills are to be moved either in the Lok Sabha or in the Rajya Sabha. A money bill can be defined as the bill, the purpose of which is the imposition and collection of tax for the purpose of the general revenue and relating to such subjects as public debt, Consolidated Fund, and audit of accounts. It should be noted that bills dealing with levy of any fees or those relating to tax or fees of local bodies are not money bills.

It is the important duty of the Speaker to certify the bill as money bill or general bill. The Speaker's decision in this regard is full and final. His certificate to the effect that the bill is passed accompanying all the bills presented to the President is absolutely necessary.

The procedure followed by the Parliament is laid down in the business rules. The Constitution itself says that a bill is declared as passed only after it is adopted by both the Houses. If Lok Sabha is dissolved, the bill introduced and pending before it automatically lapses. In case the bill which is introduced in Rajya Sabha after it is passed, is sent to Lok Sabha and while the said bill is pending the Lok Sabha is dissolved, such bill will not lapse and can be taken up by the succeeding Lok Sabha. Where the bill introduced in Lok Sabha after it is passed, is sent to Rajya Sabha and the Lok Sabha is dissolved, the bill pending in Rajya Sabha will lapse subject to the condition that if Rajya Sabha dissents with the bill as passed by Lok Sabha, the President may call for joint session (of course the Lok Sabha naturally will then be a body constituted after the election).

It is the important duty of the Speaker to certify the bill as money bill or general bill. The Speaker's decision in this regard is full and final. His certificate to the effect that the bill is passed accompanying all the bills presented to the President is absolutely necessary.

Annual financial statements which are called the Budget are presented in the Parliament every year. The date of budget presentation was the last day of February. It used to be presented at 5 p.m. which happens to coincide with the time at which the British Parliament meets in London. That was only a tradition started during the British Rule. It has been given up. The budget is now presented in the morning hour of the opening of Lok Sabha on February the budget has two parts–one deals with income and expenditure already incurred up to the end of the previous financial year and the estimates of the income and expenditure for the coming financial year. The budget is divided into two sections–one dealing with capital revenue and capital expenditure and the other dealing with current revenue and expenditure.

Capital revenue includes all such revenue with does not recur and the capital expenditure is all that which is spent once and for all. Capital income is that which is derived from grant, loans, and debt instruments and the capital expenditure is that spent for creating permanent and durable assets. Revenue receipts are recurring receipts such as from taxes and revenue expenditure means all that expenditure which is incurred for administration and for welfare of the people. Unless the budget is passed by 31st March of a financial year, there can't be any authorisation to draw from the Consolidated Fund of India. Hence, it is the procedure by which Parliament approves what is called vote-on-account. Vote-on-account may mean sanction of all additional expenditure incurred on items of the previous year and to sanction expenditure of items proposed for the coming year till the passing of the full budget. Presentation of budget, discussion thereon and its passing by approving all the demands are, in fact, the three stages in the budget discussions. Where the Parliament has no time enough to discuss all items by the last day of the budget session, the Parliament adopts the budget in full without discussion. The procedure taken up by the Speaker declares all the undiscussed items are guillotine and accordingly are deemed to have been discussed and voted upon. If a member moves what is called cut motion, there is discussion on that item of expenditure either fully or partly. All such motions are rejected by the House and the full budget is treated as passed. Guillotine part of the budget or adoption of a budget cannot be questioned in any Court including the Supreme Court. Apart from passing the budget, the Parliament may also approve what are called supplementary, additional, and excess grants at any time during the course of the year whenever such supplementary expenditure is called for or ratification of such additional expenditure is required. If the Speaker adjourns the House, Court has no powers to question the adjournment nor can it call upon the Speaker to convene the House.

JOINT SITTING OF BOTH HOUSES

Article 108

Article 108 of the Constitution provides for Joint sitting of both Houses of Parliament in certain cases. Of course it is a fact that the Lok Sabha having more members will have a pronounced say in the matter, but given the nature of politics and seat sharing, possibilities always remain of an outcome significantly otherwise.The President can summon the Houses to a joint sitting for deliberations and voting, through public notification. The central theme is to discuss, debate, and deliberate using all the experience and expertise to break the deadlock. Idea is to bring all points of view across in a mature and meaningful manner so that due consideration is given to all issues. It could even be an accommodation of opinions, views, and sinews. The framers of our constitution kept this window of opportunity open so that, in the ultimate analysis, the Parliamentarians will sit and resolve matters in the interest of the nation all matters of concern, even if all are not in agreement, nor the agreed resolution will leave all in agreement; agree to disagree but overall interests prevail. So far on three occasions, Joint Sittings have taken place.1961: Dowry Prohibition Act. Lok Sabha and Rajya Sabha disagreed but joint sitting resolved it 1978: Banking Service Commission Repealed. (Act) 2002: Prevention of Terrorism Act. 2017 : Launch of GST

IV. FUNCTIONS OF PARLIAMENT

Both the Council of States and the House of the People have certain functions to perform; some independently and many in togetherness and all within the framework of the Constitution. Constitution has laid down the demarcated functions of the Lok Sabha, the House of the People and Rajya Sabha, the StatesCouncil of States.

Under the cabinet system of Government, functions of the Parliament are as given below:

(i) Select the party or group which will form the Government and let it have its confidence as long as it endures and sustains it. If the confidence is gone, the power is lost.

(ii) Make necessary legislation to enact necessary laws. Parliament frames the laws for various fields; finance, executive, judicial and others.

(iii) Control the finances: ways and means to raise the requisite revenues, authorise expenditure, and specify purpose for which expenditure will be appropriated, ensure that money is spent for the authorised purpose. Budget, called the Annual Financial Statement (Article 112), Appropriation Bills (ArticleArticle 114), and Audit (Article 149) are some of the relevant provisions for Union Parliament as also similar ones for States.

(iv) Scrutiny and control of the executive through debates, motions, and committees in the Parliament.

(v) To amend the Constitution as per procedure laid down to meet the emergent needs consistent with hopes and aspirations of a growing, dynamic, complex, and versatile society.

(vi) To serve as an electoral college to elect the President, Vice-President; impeach them, Judges and others as a court of Justice. Initiate action for contempt if one crosses the limits.

(vii) Conduct its own business as per procedure laid down and in a manner that upholds its dignity and presents a picture of solemnity of purpose and perfection.

(viii) Resort to enforcement of emergency; internal, external, and financial, should the need be compelling and considerable. More an exception than a rule, more a compulsion than convention, more a caution than a casual option.

(ix) Hold Centre the State relations on an even keel, respecting the spirit of federalism in a true, the transparent, and tolerant way making Centre and States feel the bond of aUnion.

Parliament, Judiciary, and the Executive are three organs on which our parliamentary democracy rests. Parliament is the one which is linked to the people through elections, unlike the Judiciary and the Executive in many ways. Parliament reflects the will of the people, Judiciary the hope, and the Executive the aspirations. All three are independent yet interdependent. Both the Lok Sabha as well as Rajya Sabha broadly has the following functions:

(a) Legislative Functions
(b) Financial Functions
(c) Administrative Functions
(d) Constituent Functions and
(e) Miscellaneous Functions

COUNCIL OF STATES (RAJYA SABHA)

Article 249

Article 249 provides that Rajya Sabha is empowered to declare by a resolution, supported by not less than two-thirds (2/3[rds]) of the members present and voting, a special majority that Parliament should make laws with respect to any matter enumerated in the state list. Such a resolution can originate only in Rajya Sabha and cannot remain in force beyond one year.

Article 312

Article 312 empowers the Rajya Sabha to declare by a resolution supported by not less than two-thirds of the members present and voting that it is expedient in the national interest, that Parliament should create one or more All India Services, including All India Judicial Service (42nd amendment) common to the Union and States, and also to regulate the recruitment and conditions of service of persons appointed to such services. Only Rajya Sabha can initiate this.

Note: *When it is stated two-thirds of the members present and voting, it also means that it should have majority of the total strength. Nominated members, for most part do not have voting rights. Example, if Rajya Sabha strength is 238, majority would mean 119 and 2/3rds of those present and voting, as the case may be.*

Article 352 & 356

In cases of declaration of emergency under Article 352 and Article 356 by the President, these must be approved by Rajya Sabha within a period of one month (Article 352) and two months (Article 356) respectively.

Article 368

In case of constitution amendment bills, they must be passed by Rajya Sabha separately. There is no provision for joint sitting. Those affecting interests of the States by 2/3rds (Two-thirds) majority of members present and voting, with a simple majority plus ratification by at least half the States.

LEGISLATIVE FUNCTIONS OF RAJYA SABHA

Rajya Sabha cannot do anything without the involvement of Lok Sabha.

(a) **Article 55:** The members of Rajya Sabha (except nominated ones) can participate in the election of the President.

(b) **Article 61:** For the impeachment of the President, a resolution to the effect must have 2/3rd (Two-thirds) of the members of Rajya Sabha separately.

(c) **Article 66:** The Vice-President shall be elected by the members of an electoral college consisting of members of both Houses of Parliament.

(d) **Article 67:** Under Article 67, a resolution seeking the removal of the Vice-President can originate only in the Rajya Sabha. After the Rajya Sabha passes such a resolution by a majority of the members of the House, it goes for approval to the Lok Sabha.

(e) **Article 75:** Members of the council of ministers could also be from Rajya Sabha, allowing for the States a say in governance and policy-making.

(f) **Article 107:** All bills, except money bills, can originate in the Rajya Sabha but cannot become law without the acceptance by Lok Sabha. Both Houses are on equal footing for ordinary bills.

(g) Rajya Sabha can delay a bill but not deny. It cannot reject a bill passed by Lok Sabha but delay up to six months.

(h) **Article 108:** Ordinary and financial bills should have the approval of the Rajya Sabha; there are provisions for joint sittings in case Rajya Sabha disagrees A question arises: what are the similarities and differences between a money bill and a finance bill. a money bill cannot be introduced in the Rajya Sabha, a finance bill also cannot be introduced in the Rajya Sabha.

(i) **Article 123:** Power of the President to promulgate Ordinance during recess of Parliament:

(1) If at any time, except when both Houses of Parliament are in session, the President is satisfied that circumstances exist which render it necessary for him to take immediate action, he may promulgate such ordinances as the circumstances appear to him to require.

(2) An ordinance promulgated under this Article shall have the same force and effect as an Act of Parliament, but every such ordinance shall be laid before both Houses of Parliament.

OTHER FUNCTIONS OF THE RAJYA SABHA

Financial Functions

Rajya Sabha has very little control over financial matters. Speaker of Lok Sabha decides whether a bill is a money bill or not and his decision is final. A money bill passed by Lok Sabha is sent to Rajya Sabha which has to send it back with or without recommendation within 14 days. If 14 days are over, the bills is deemed to have been passed. Lok Sabha may or may not accept Rajya Sabha's recommendations.

Administrative Functions

Ministers are appointed from both Houses and are allowed to attend both Houses. Rajya Sabha can question the ministers and also help in framing laws.

Constituent Functions

Article 368, dealing with amendments to the Constitution has a specific role for the Rajya Sabha. Constitution amendment bill can be introduced in either of the Houses. All three types of amendments must have Rajya Sabha voting as at (i), (ii), and (iii) listed below.

(i) Simple majority

(ii) Two-thirds majority among those present and voting, and a majority in the House, and

(iii) Two-thirds majority among those present and voting, and a majority in the House as also at least half the States ratifying.

Rajya Sabha adds to the safeguards.

Miscellaneous Functions

Rajya Sabha considers, along with Lok Sabha, reports of CAG, UPSC, Finance commission, SC, and ST Commissions.

Rajya Sabha is at par with Lok Sabha in power in the process of impeachment of the President, removal of judges, chief election commissioner, and CAG.

HOUSE OF PEOPLE (LOK SABHA)

The House of the People, Lok Sabha, has lots of functions to discharge. It has a term of 5 years and is an elected body. It has legislative functions, financial functions, control over executive, constituent functions, and miscellaneous functions. In essence, it controls the purse strings keeping money in its fold as well as control over ministers for their removal, etc.

Legislative Functions

(i) A confidence or non-confidence motion can be initiated and passed only in the Lok Sabha.

(ii) The Lok Sabha, under Article 352, in a special sitting can disapprove the continuation of emergency proclaimed by the President. The President in such a case shall revoke the national emergency.

Financial Functions

All Money Bills, including Finance Bills can originate in the Lok Sabha. Rajya Sabha can keep money bills for fourteen days maximum after which it is deemed to have been passed. Rajya Sabha can delay but not deny.

Executive Functions

(1) Lok Sabha controls the executive through checks and balances. Parliamentary committees regularly work and report on functioning. Public Accounts Committee (PAC), committee on Public Sector undertakings, and Estimates Committee are some of the committees reporting or controlling the executive.

(2) Comptroller and Auditor General (CAG) audits all government departments to see if expenditure has been made as authorised or not. It also audits sanctions and systems showing loopholes or leakages. CAG's report is placed on the table of Lok Sabha for discussion. Some examples are 2G Report, Commonwealth Games, coal auction, etc.

(3) **Article 75 (3):** Vote of No Confidence: In the Parliamentary system of Government provided under the Indian Constitution, the Council of Ministers, which is the real executive, stays in office as long as it enjoys the confidence of Parliament. Thus, there is accountability to Lok Sabha.

No confidence motion can be moved only in the Lok Sabha.

(4) **Article 265:** Revenue: No taxation except as by law authorised: As regards revenue, it is expressly laid down by the Constitution (Article 265) that no tax shall be levied or collected except by authority of law. Executive cannot levy and tax without legislative sanction; if it is done, courts are there to hand down relief at once.

Minister not being a member of either House

If a person appointed as a Minister in the State by the Governor, happens to be a member of Rajya Sabha, he can resign his Rajya Sabha membership and get elected to the State Assembly or the Council within six months. If the Central Minister is a member of State Legislature, he can within a period of six months resign his membership of the State Legislature and get elected to Lok Sabha or Rajya Sabha.

LEGISLATIVE RELATIONS

Article 245: Extent of laws made by Parliament and by the Legislatures of States

(1) Subject to the provisions of this Constitution, Parliament may make laws for the whole or any part of the territory of India, and the Legislature of a State may make laws for the whole or any part of the State

(2) No law made by Parliament shall be deemed to be invalid on the ground that it would have extra territorial operation

Article 246: Subject matter of laws made by Parliament and by the Legislatures of States

(1) Notwithstanding anything in clauses (2) and (3), Parliament has exclusive power to make laws with respect to any of the matters enumerated in List I in the Seventh Schedule (in this Constitution referred to as the Union List)

(2) Notwithstanding anything in clause (3), Parliament, and, subject to clause (1), the Legislature of any State also, have power to make laws with respect to any of the matters enumerated in List III in the Seventh Schedule (in this Constitution referred to as the Concurrent List)

(3) Subject to clauses 1 & 2, the legislature of any state has exclusive power to make laws for such state or any part thereof with respect to any of the matter enumerated in List II in the Seventh Schedule (in the Constitution referred to as the `State List')

(4) Parliament has power to make laws with respect to any matter for any part of the territory of India not included (in a State) notwithstanding that such matter is a matter enumerated in the State List

Article 249: Power of Parliament to Legislate with Respect to a Matter in the State List in the National Interest

(1) Notwithstanding anything in the foregoing provisions of this Chapter, if the Council of States has declared by resolution supported by not less than two-thirds of the members present and voting that it is necessary or expedient in national interest that Parliament should make laws with respect to any matter enumerated in the State List specified in the resolution, it shall be lawful for Parliament to make laws for the whole or any part of the territory of India with respect to that matter while the resolution remains in force.

(2) A resolution passed under clause (1) shall remain in force for such period not exceeding one year as may be specified therein (can be extended by another one year with a same similar resolution).

Article 250 : Power of Parliament to legislate with Respect to any Matter in the State List if a Proclamation of Emergency is in Operation

(1) Notwithstanding anything in this Chapter, Parliament shall, while a Proclamation of Emergency is in operation, have power to make laws for the whole or any part of the territory of India with respect to any of the matters enumerated in the State List.

(2) A law made by Parliament which Parliament would not but for the issue of a Proclamation of Emergency have been competent to make shall, to the extent of the incompetency, cease to have effect on the expiration of a period of six months after the Proclamation has ceased to operate, except as respects things done or omitted to be done before the expiration of the said period.

Article 251: Inconsistency between Laws made by Parliament under Articles 249 and 250 and Laws made by the Legislatures of States

Nothing in Articles 249 and 250 shall restrict the power of the Legislature of a State to make any law which under this Constitution it has power to make, but if any provision of a law made by the Legislature of a State is repugnant to any provision of law made by Parliament which Parliament has under either of the said Articles power to make, the law made by Parliament, whether passed before or after the law made by the Legislature of the State, shall prevail, and the law made by the Legislature of the State shall to the extent of the repugnancy, but so long only as the law made by Parliament continues to have effect, be inoperative.

Article 252: Power of Parliament to legislate for two or more States by Consent and Adoption of such legislation by any other State

(1) If it appears to the Legislatures of two or more States to be desirable that any of the matters with respect to which Parliament has no power to make laws for the States except as provided in Articles 249 and 250 should be regulated in such States by Parliament by law, and if resolutions to that effect are passed by all the Houses of the Legislatures of those States, it shall be lawful for Parliament to pass an Act for regulating that matter accordingly, and any Act so passed shall apply to such States and to any other State by which it is adopted afterwards by resolution passed in that behalf by the House or, where there are two Houses, by each of the Houses of the Legislature of that State.

(2) Any Act so passed by Parliament may be amended or repealed by an Act of Parliament passed or adopted in like manner but shall not, as respects any State to which it applies, be amended or repealed by an Act of the Legislature of that State.

Article 254: Inconsistency Between Laws made by Parliament and Laws made by the Legislatures of States

(1) If any provision of a law made by the Legislature of a State is repugnant to any provision of a law made by Parliament which Parliament is competent to enact, or to any provision of an existing law with respect to one of the matters enumerated in the Concurrent List, then, subject to the provisions of clause (2), the law made by Parliament, whether passed before or after the law made by the Legislature of such State, or, as the case may be, the existing law, shall prevail and the law made by the Legislature of the State shall, to the extent of the repugnancy, be void.

(2) Where a law made by the Legislature of a State with respect to one of the matters enumerated in the Concurrent List contains any provision repugnant to the provisions of an earlier law made by Parliament or an existing law with respect to that matter, then,

the law so made by the Legislature of such State shall, if it has been reserved for the consideration of the President and has received his assent, prevail in that State.

[Provided that nothing in this clause shall prevent Parliament from enacting at any time any law with respect to the same matter including a law adding to, amending, varying, or repealing the law so made by the Legislature of the State.]

ADMINISTRATIVE RELATIONS

Article 256: Obligation of States and the Union

The executive power of every state shall be so exercised as to ensure compliance with the laws made by Parliament and any existing laws which apply in that State, and the executive power of theUnion shall extend to the giving of such directions to a State as may appear to the Government of India to be necessary for that purpose.

Article 257: Control of the Union over States in Certain Cases

(1) The executive power of every State shall be so exercised as not to impede or prejudice the exercise of the executive power of the Union, and the executive power of the Union shall extend to the giving of such directions to a State as may appear to the Government of India to be necessary for that purpose.

(2) The executive power of the Union shall also extend to the giving of directions to a State as to the construction and maintenance of means of communication declared in the direction to be of national or military importance.

[Provided that nothing in this clause shall be taken as restricting the power of Parliament to declare highways or waterways to be national highways or national waterways, or the power of the Union with respect to the highways or waterways so declared or the power of the Union to construct and maintain means of communication as part of its functions with respect to naval, military and air force works.]

(3) The executive power of the Union shall also extend to the giving of directions to a State as to the measures to be taken for the protection of the railways within the State.

(4) Where in carrying out any direction given to a State under clause (2) as to the construction or maintenance of any means of communication or under clause (3) as to the measures to be taken for the protection of any railway, costs have been incurred in excess of those which would have been incurred in the discharge of the normal duties of the State if such direction had not been given, there shall be paid by the Government of India to the State such sum as may be agreed, or, in default of agreement, as may be determined by an arbitrator appointed by the Chief Justice of India, in respect of the extra costs so incurred by the State.

Article 258: Power of the Union to Confer Powers, etc., on States in Certain Cases

(1) Notwithstanding anything in this Constitution, the President may, with the consent of the Governor of a State, entrust either conditionally or unconditionally to that Government

or to its officers functions in relation to any matter to which the executive power of the Union extends.

(2) A law made by Parliament which applies in any State may, notwithstanding that it relates to a matter with respect to which the Legislature of the State has no power to make laws, confer powers, and impose duties, or authorise the conferring of powers and the imposition of duties, upon the State or officers and authorities thereof.

(3) Where by virtue of this Article powers and duties have been conferred or imposed upon a State or officers or authorities thereof, there shall be paid by the Government of India to the State such sum as may be agreed, or, in default of agreement, as may be determined by an arbitrator appointed by the Chief Justice of India, in respect of any extra costs of administration incurred by the State in connection with the exercise of those powers and duties.

Article 258-A: Power of the States to Entrust Functions to the Union

Notwithstanding anything in this Constitution, the Governor of a State may, with the consent of the Government of India, entrust either conditionally or unconditionally to that Government or to its officers functions in relation to any matter to which the executive power of the State extends.

Articles 245 to 255

A Narrative

This is a crucial part of the Constitution. It points out that the legislative competence of the Parliament to make laws applicable, becomes operative only after each of the States individually repeal the Central enactment. Take the case of Urban Land Ceiling Act which having been enacted at the instance of few States and subsequently adopted by several other States has come to be repealed by the Centre; all the States implementing the Urban Land Ceiling Act had to repeal the Central Act one after the other. Tamil Nadu was one of the States which did not adopt the Central Act and made an Urban Land Ceiling Act separately for itself. That State did not have to repeal the Central law. Andhra Pradesh which adopted the Central Law repealed the Central enactment in the same terms as the Centre. The third scenario is when a national emergency is enforced–the Parliament can make any law covering the subjects under the State legislature. This law will continue to be in force for a period of six months after emergency ceases.

Parliament has power to make laws by which it may require any State to implement international obligations. On such law being passed by the Parliament, the State shall implement the same without any protest. Enumeration of subjects under theUnion List, State List, and Concurrent List gives rise to a knotty problem. The issue is whether a particular legislation falls within the scope of the entry under which it is purported to have been made and whether the subject matter of the legislation falls within the scope of the entry or whether it falls under a different entry in another list. In deciding the issue under the first situation, the pith and substance doctrine shall be applied to know what in substance the Act is purported to cover. Where the enactment is held to cover one item of the list and also covers another claim of a different list, the legislation is declared ultra vires. In such cases the law to the extent of its repugnancy will be declared invalid. The confrontation between the State law and the Central law is not limited to the terms of legislation. It also includes the conflict in rules and procedures made under the respective Acts. Regarding matters arising under Concurrent List, the reference to the prior Presidential assent should be treated as mandatory. Presidential assent obtained after the enactment is enforced, cannot validate actions taken under the Act. There is no term like post Presidential assent.

There are two examples of Andhra Pradesh. The first one is non-implementation of provisions in spite of Presidential assent. This arose in the case of Land Reforms and Ceilings on Agricultural Holdings. The amendment proposed was that when land holder transfers his excess holding in favour of another under oral or written agreement, the same transfer cannot be recognised. The proviso to the amendment added that the amendment shall not apply in case the transferee's holding does not exceed the ceiling. As it is felt that there will not be any landholder with any sense of reason to transfer his excess holding to another who is also an excess landholder, the exemption became meaningless. Accordingly, the Government has decided not to implement the provision which is infructuous. The second instance was the case of Land Revenue Code enacted by the Andhra Pradesh Legislature in which as many as 196 Central Acts, Ordinances, and Government Orders were repealed. In this case the President did not grant assent.

When is a Special Session of Lok Sabha Convened

If not less than $1/10^{th}$ members of Lok Sabha give in writing to the Speaker, and if Lok Sabha is already in session or if it is not in session and express their intention to disapproving the continuance of national emergency, then a special session of Lok Sabha shall be convened within 14 days. By convention this resolution is given to the President only. The Lok Sabha then takes a decision on continuance or not of the emergency.

Whip

Each party appoints a Whip to control and discipline its members elected to the legislature (either House of the Parliament or of the State Legislature). He is called party whip and he must be a member of the legislature.

On crucial occasions like voting on no-confidence motion and important Bills, he exercises the'whip' to the members of the legislate wing of his party to attend the meeting and vote as directed by the party leadership.

HOW A BILL BECOMES AN ACT

A Bill is the draft of a legislative proposal which has to pass through various stages before it becomes an Act of Parliament.

Step 1 First Reading

The legislative process starts with the introduction of a Bill in either House of Parliament–Lok Sabha or Rajya Sabha. A Bill can be introduced either by a Minister or by a Private Member. In the former case, it is known as a Government Bill and in the latter case it is called as a Private Member's Bill. It is necessary for a member-in-charge of the Bill to ask for leave to introduce the Bill. If leave is granted by the House, the Bill is introduced. This stage is known as the First Reading of the Bill. If the motion for Leave to introduce a Bill is opposed, the Speaker may, in his discretion, allow brief explanatory statement to be made by the member who opposes the motion and the member-in-charge who moved the motion. Where a motion for leave to introduce a Bill is opposed on the ground that the Bill initiates legislation outside the legislative competence of the House, the Speaker may permit a full discussion thereon. Thereafter, the question is put to the vote of the House. However, the motion for leave to introduce a Finance Bill or an Appropriation Bill is forthwith put to the vote of the House.

Step 2 Publication in the *Gazette of India*

After a Bill has been introduced, it is published in the Official Gazette called *The Gazette of India*. Even before introduction, a Bill might, with the permission of the Speaker, be published in the *Gazette*. In such cases, leave to introduce the Bill in the House is not asked for and the Bill is straightaway introduced.

PRIVATE MEMBER'S BILL

- Every MP, who is not a Minister, is called a Private Member. Private Members' Bills are introduced by these MPs.
- In Lok Sabha, the last two and a half hours of a sitting on every Friday are generally allotted for transaction of Private Members' Business, i.e., Private Members' Bills and Private Members' Resolutions.
- Till date, Parliament has passed 14 Private Members' Bills. Six of these were passed in 1956 alone.
- In the current term of Parliament, 264 Private Members' Bills have been introduced in Lok Sabha and 160 in Rajya Sabha. Of these, only 14 have been discussed in Lok Sabha and 11 in Rajya Sabha.

Step 3 Reference of Bill to Standing Committee

After a Bill has been introduced, the Presiding Officer of the concerned House can refer the Bill to the Standing Committee concerned for examination and make report thereon. If a Bill is referred to the Standing Committee, the Committee shall consider the general principles and clauses of the Bill referred to them and make report thereon. The Committee can also take expert opinion or the opinion of the general public who are interested in the measure. After the Bill has thus been considered, the Committee submits its report to the House. The report of the Committee, being of persuasive value, shall be treated as considered advice given by the Committee.

Step 4 Second Reading

The Second Reading consists of consideration of the Bill which is in **two** stages.

The **first stage** consists of general discussion on the Bill as a whole when the principle underlying the Bill is discussed. At this stage, it is open to the House to refer the Bill to a Select Committee of the House or a Joint Committee of the two Houses or to circulate it for the purpose of eliciting opinion thereon or to straightaway take it into consideration.

If a Bill is referred to a Select/Joint Committee, the Committee considers the Bill clause-by-clause just as the House does. Amendments can be moved to the various clauses by members of the Committee. The Committee can also take evidence of associations, public bodies, or experts who are interested in the measure. After the Bill has thus been considered, the Committee submits its report to the House which considers the Bill again as reported by the Committee.

If a Bill is circulated for the purpose of eliciting public opinion thereon, such opinions are obtained through the Governments of the States and Union Territories. Opinions so received are laid on the Table of the House and the next motion in regard to the Bill must be for its reference to a Select/Joint Committee. It is not ordinarily permissible at this stage to move the motion for consideration of the Bill.

The **second stage** of the Second Reading consists of clause-by-clause consideration of the Bill as introduced or as reported by the Select/Joint Committee. Discussion takes place on each clause of the Bill and amendments to the clauses can be moved at this stage. Amendments to a clause which have been moved but not withdrawn are put to the vote of the House before the relevant clause is disposed of by the House. The amendments become part of the Bill if they are accepted by a majority of members present and voting. After the clauses, the Schedules if any, Clause 1, the Enacting Formula and the Long Title of the Bill have been adopted by the House, the Second Reading is deemed to be over.

Step 5 Third Reading

Thereafter, the member-in-charge can move that the Bill is passed. This stage is known as the Third Reading of the Bill.

At this stage, the debate is confined to arguments either in support or rejection of the Bill without referring to the details thereof further than that are absolutely necessary. Only formal, verbal, or consequential amendments are allowed to be moved at this stage. Money Bill can only be passed by the Lok Sabha.

In passing an ordinary Bill, a simple majority of members present and voting is necessary. But in the case of a Bill to amend the Constitution, a majority of the total membership of the House and a majority of not less than two-thirds of the members present and voting is required in each House of Parliament.

Step 6 Bill in the Other House

After the Bill is passed by one House, it is sent to the other House for concurrence with a message to that effect, and there also it goes through the stages described above, except the introduction stage.

TYPES OF BILLS

Following are the types of Bills that can be introduced in the parliament:

Ordinary Bills

Any Bill which is not a Constitution Amendment Bill or a Money Bill is classified as an Ordinary Bill. Ordinary Bills are of five types.

1. Original Bills (which embody new proposals, ideas, or policies)
2. Bills to replace Ordinances issued by the President
3. Consolidating Bills (which consolidate existing law on a particular subject)
4. Amending Bills (which modify, amend or revise existing Acts), and
5. Expiring Laws (Continuance) Bills (which authorise the continuance of an expiring Act).

Money and Financial Bills

A Bill is considered to be a Money Bill if it contains only provisions dealing with all or any of the following matters listed below.

1. The regulation of money borrowed by the Government of India or any guarantee given by the Government of India;
2. The custody of the Consolidated Fund of India or the Contingency Fund of India, the payment of moneys into or the withdrawal of moneys from any such Fund;
3. The imposition, abolition, remission, alteration, or regulation of any tax;
4. The appropriation of moneys out of the Consolidated Fund of India;
5. The Bill can also consider amendment of the law with respect to any financial obligations undertaken or to be undertaken by the Government of India;
6. The declaring of a new item to be expenditure charged on the Consolidated Fund of India. Also, if there is any increase in the amount of any such expenditure;
7. The receipt of money on account of the Consolidated Fund of India or the Public Account of India or the custody or the issue of such money or the audit of the accounts of the Union or of a State; or
8. Any matter incidental to any of the matters specified above.

A Financial Bill may contain other proposals in addition to these. For example, a Bill that contains a taxation clause, but does not deal solely with taxation is a Financial Bill.

If any question arises whether a Bill is a Money Bill or not, the decision of the Speaker of the House of the People thereon shall be final.

Constitution Amendment Bills

These Bills seek to amend the Constitution of India.

WHAT IS A FINANCE BILL?

The Finance Bill incorporates all the financial proposals of the Government for the following year. It is ordinarily introduced in the Lok Sabha every year, immediately after the Budget is presented. This Bill has to be considered and passed by the Parliament and assented to by the President within 75 days after its introduction.

How are the various types of Bills passed by the Parliament?

Article 107 refers to the provisions as to introduction and passing of Bills.

An Ordinary Bill may be introduced in Lok Sabha or Rajya Sabha. The Bill needs to be passed by both Houses by a majority of members present and voting. If it is passed by the House in which it was introduced, and rejected by the other House, the President may call a joint sitting of both the Houses. In this sitting, the decision to accept or reject a Bill is taken by the majority of the total number of members of both Houses present and voting.

A Money Bill can be introduced only in the Lok Sabha and requires the recommendation of the President. However, the Speaker of the House has the final authority to decide whether a Bill is a Money Bill or not. Money Bill cannot be introduced in Rajya Sabha nor can it be referred to a Joint Committee of Houses or be considered at a Joint Sitting of the two Houses. Once a Money Bill is passed in the Lok Sabha it is sent to the Rajya Sabha. The Rajya Sabha may not amend Money Bills but can recommend amendments.

A Money Bill should be returned by the Rajya Sabha to the Lok Sabha within 14 days or the Bill is deemed to have passed both Houses in the form it was originally passed by the Lok Sabha. The Lok Sabha has the discretion to accept or reject the recommended Amendments made by the Rajya Sabha.

A Constitution Amendment Bill may be introduced in either House or follow a process similar to an Ordinary Bill. A Constitution amendment Bill requires special majority.

ASSENT OF THE PRESIDENT

When a Bill is passed by both Houses, the Secretariat of the House which is last in possession of the Bill obtains the assent of the President as per Article 111. In the case of Money Bill or a Bill passed at a joint sitting of the Houses, the Lok Sabha Secretariat obtains assent of the President. The Bill becomes an Act only after the President has given his assent to it.

The President may give his/her assent or withhold his assent to a Bill. The President may also return the Bill (except a Money Bill) with his/her recommendations to the Houses for reconsideration, and if the Houses pass the Bill again with or without amendments the President cannot withhold his/her assent to the Bill.

The President, however, is bound to give his/her assent to a Constitution Amendment Bill passed by the Houses of Parliament with the requisite special majority and, where necessary, ratified by the States.

The President has three types of veto powers:

(i) Absolute Veto: The President may declare his assent to any Bill passed by the parliament or withold his assent to a Bill.

(ii) Suspensive veto: The President may return any Bill (other than Money Bill) for reconsideration by the parliament. If the Bill is passed again by both the houses, he is obligated to give his assent.

(iii) Pocket Veto: The President may neither sign the Bill nor send for reconsideration. It may lie on his table indefinitely and will not be enacted till then.

CONSIDERATION OF THE BILL AT A JOINT SITTING

Article 108 mentions, Joint sitting of both Houses in certain cases. If a Bill passed by one House is rejected by the other House, or, the Houses have finally disagreed as to the amendments to be made in the Bill, or more than six months elapse from the date of the receipt of the Bill by the other House without the Bill being passed by it, the President may call a joint sitting of the two Houses to resolve the deadlock.

If, at the joint sitting of the Houses, the Bill is passed by a majority of the total number of members of both the Houses present and voting, with the amendments, if any, accepted by them, the Bill is deemed to have been passed by both the Houses.

There cannot be a joint sitting of both Houses on a Constitution Amendment Bill.

FATE OF BILLS ON DISSOLUTION OF LOK SABHA

As per Article 107 following Bills lapse automatically on dissolution of Lok Sabha:

- All Bills that originated in Lok Sabha and are pending before Lok Sabha
- All Bills that originated in Lok Sabha and passed by it, but pending in Rajya Sabha
- All Bills that originated in Rajya Sabha and passed by Rajya Sabha but pending before Lok Sabha

Following Bills do not lapse on dissolution of Lok Sabha

- Bills originated in Rajya Sabha and pending before Rajya Sabha
- Bills passed by both houses of Parliament but waiting President's assent
- If President has called for a joint sitting to resolve deadlock, on a bill before Lok Sabha was dissolved

MOTIONS IN INDIAN PARLIAMENT

Apart from Bills, certain motions can also be introduced in the parliament. A motion is a proposal by a member of the house for its opinion/decision. The person making the motion (except privileged motion), known as the 'mover', must first be recognised by the chairman as being entitled to speak; this is known as 'obtaining the floor'.

As soon as the mover has obtained the floor; the mover States the motion, normally prefixed with the phrase "I move." Generally, if the motion has been proposed, consideration by the assembly occurs only if another member of the body immediately seconds the motion.

The various types of motions are:

1. **Privilege Motion:** The motion can be introduced by the opposition if a minister has misled the house by providing wrong information. The member of Indian legislatures, either the federal Parliament of India or the Vidhan Sabha and Vidhan Parishad in the States and territories, may raise a question involving a breach of privilege either of a member or of the Council or of a Committee with the consent of the Chairman.
2. **No-Confidence Motion:** This can be moved only in Lok Sabha and by the opposition of the house. It can be brought only against the Council of ministers and not against any individual minister. Unlike censure motion, a no-confidence motion does not require any specific ground. Once admitted in the House, it takes precedence over all the pending

business of the House. Generally, the PM answers the allegations after the members have spoken. If the motion is adopted by the House, the Council of Ministers is bound to resign.

3. **Censure Motion:** This motion can be moved only in Lok Sabha and by the opposition of the house. It can be moved against the ruling government or against any minister for the failure to act or seeking disapproval of their policy. No leave of the House is required for moving a censure motion but it must specify the charges against the government for which it is moved. If the censure motion is passed, the Council of ministers is bound to seek the confidence of the Lok Sabha as early as possible.
4. **Call-Attention Motion:** A member (after permission from Speaker) calls the attention of the minister to any matter of 'urgent public importance'. There is no Call-Attention motion in the Rajya Sabha. Instead there exists a motion called 'Motion for Papers'.
5. **Adjournment Motion:** Motion for an adjournment of the business of the House for the purpose of discussing a definite matter of urgent public importance may be made with the consent of the Speaker.
6. **Cut Motions:** The members of the Lok Sabha have a veto power to oppose a demand in the financial Bill discussed by the government. This is an effective tool to test the strength of the government. If a cut motion is adopted by the House and the government does not have the numbers, it is obliged to resign.

They are moved in the Lok Sabha only. They are part of the budgetary process which seeks to reduce the amounts for grants.

PARLIAMENTARY QUESTIONS

Question Hour is the first hour of a sitting session of India's Lok Sabha, devoted to questions that Members of Parliament raise about any aspect of administrative activity. The concerned Minister is obliged to answer to the Parliament, either orally or in writing, depending on the type of question raised. Questions are one of the ways Parliament can hold the Executive accountable.

The Right to ask questions was given to the legislators for the first time by the Act of 1892, and to ask supplementary questions in 1909. Any act of the Government can be made the subject of a question. Even though the question is directed to a particular minister, it is his office that is responsible for framing a response.

There are three types of Questions:

- **Starred Questions:** Starred questions refer to Questions that are distinguished by an asterisk mark. Members of Parliament have the option to raise the Supplementary Questions based on the replies to the starred Questions. These questions for which a notice period of minimum 10 days and maximum 21 days has been prescribed are asked during the question Hour on the fixed days allotted to the Ministry/Department. Starred Questions from Lok Sabha are printed on green paper and those of Rajya Sabha questions on pink paper.
- **Unstarred Questions:** Unstarred Questions do not carry asterisk mark and are answered in a written form. The notice period is the same as that for the starred Questions and these are also asked on the allotted days of the Department/Ministry during Question Hour. Lok Sabha Unstarred Questions are printed on white paper and those of Rajya

Sabha on yellow paper. The replies to the Unstarred Questions are laid on the Table of the House.

- **Short Notice Questions:** Short Notice Questions relate to a matter of urgent public importance and can be asked with a notice shorter than 10 days. These Questions are answered orally by the Minister concerned and Supplementary Questions can also be asked. However, a Short Notice Question can be asked only with the concurrence of the Minister. The Short Notice Questions from Lok Sabha are printed on pink white paper and those of Rajya Sabha on white paper.

Zero Hour is the period that follows the question hour and it starts at noon, while its duration is one hour. During the Zero Hour members raise matters of importance, especially those which cannot be delayed. Nobody knows which issue a member would raise during this hour.

As a result, questions so raised without prior notice result in avoidable loss of precious time of the House. It also obstructs the regular proceedings and business of the House.

PARLIAMENTARY COMMITTEES

The work done by the Parliament in modern times is not only varied in nature, but considerable in volume. The time at its disposal is limited. It cannot, therefore, give close consideration to all the legislative and other matters that come up before it. A good deal of its business is, therefore, transacted by what are called the **Parliamentary Committees.**

Parliamentary Committees are of two kinds:

1. Standing Committees
2. Ad hoc Committees

Standing Committees are appointed by each House of Parliament like the Business Advisory Committee, the Committee on Petitions, the Committee of Privileges, and the Rules Committee.

Ad hoc Committees are appointed for a specified purpose and they cease to exist when they finish the task assigned to them and submit a report. The principal Ad hoc Committees are the Select and Joint Committees on Bills. Others like the Railway Convention Committee, the Committees on the Draft Five Year Plans, and the Hindi Equivalents Committee were appointed for specific purposes.

Other Committees of special importance are those which act as Parliament's 'Watch Dogs' over the Executive. These are the Committees on Subordinate Legislation, the Committee on Government Assurances, the Committee on Estimates, the Committee on Public Accounts, the Committee on Public Undertakings, and the Departmentally Related Standing Committees (DRSCs).

The Committee on Estimates, the Committee on Public Accounts, the Committee on Public Undertakings, and DRSCs play an important role in exercising a check over governmental expenditure and policy formulation.

SELECT AND JOINT COMMITTEES

When a Bill comes up before a House for general discussion, it is open to that House to refer it to a Select Committee of the House or a Joint Committee of the two Houses.

A motion has to be moved and adopted to this effect in the House in which the Bill comes up for consideration. In case the motion adopted is for reference of the Bill to a Joint Committee, the decision is conveyed to the other House requesting them to nominate members of the other House to serve on the Committee.

The Select or Joint Committee considers the Bill clause by clause just as the two Houses do. Amendments can be moved to various clauses by members of the Committee.

The Committee can also take evidence of associations, public bodies, or experts who are interested in the Bill. After the Bill has thus been considered, the Committee submits its report to the House. Members who do not agree with the majority report may append their minutes of dissent to the report.

The composition and role of important committees is discussed below:

Committee on Estimates: Lok Sabha's Biggest Committee

This Committee consists of thirty members who are elected by the Lok Sabha every year from amongst its members. A Minister is not eligible for election to this Committee. The term of the Committee is one year.

The main function of the Committee on Estimates is to report what economies, improvements in organisation, efficiency, or administrative reform, consistent with the policy underlying the estimates, may be effected and to suggest alternative policies in order to bring about efficiency and economy in administration.

From time to time, the Committee selects such of the estimates pertaining to a Ministry or a group of Ministries or statutory and other Government bodies as may seem fit to the Committee. The Committee also examines matters of special interest which may arise or come to light in the course of its work or which are specifically referred to it by the House or the Speaker.

Committee on Public Accounts

This committee consists of 15 members elected by the Lok Sabha; 7 members of the Rajya Sabha are also associated with it. A Minister is not eligible for election to this Committee. The term of the Committee is one year.

The main duty of the Committee is to ascertain whether the money granted by Parliament has been spent by the Government "within the scope of the Demand". The Appropriation Accounts of the Government of India and the Audit Reports presented by the Comptroller and Auditor General mainly form the basis for the examination of the Committee. Cases involving losses, nugatory expenditure, and financial irregularities come in for severe criticism by the Committee. The Committee is not concerned with questions of policy. It is concerned only with the execution of the policy laid down by Parliament and its results.

Committee on Private Members' Bills and Resolutions

This Committee consists of 15 members and the Deputy Speaker is its Chairman when nominated as a member of the Committee. The Committee is nominated by the Speaker. The functions of the Committee are to allot time to Private Members' Bills and Resolutions, to examine Private

Members' Bills seeking to amend the Constitution before their introduction in Lok Sabha, to examine all Private Members' Bills after they are introduced and before they are taken up for consideration in the House, and to classify them according to their nature, urgency, and importance into two categories namely, category A and category B, and also to examine such Private Members Bills where the legislative competence of the House is challenged. The Committee, thus, performs the same function and acts in relation to Private Members' Bills and Resolutions as the Business Advisory Committee does in regard to Government Business. The Committee holds office for a term not exceeding one year.

Committee of Privileges

This Committee consists of 15 members nominated by the Speaker. The function is to examine every question involving breach of privilege of the House or of the members of any Committee thereof referred to it by the House or by the Speaker. It determines with reference to the facts of each case whether a breach of privilege is involved and makes suitable recommendations in its report.

Rules Committee

The Rules Committee consists of 15 members, including the Speaker who is the ex-officio Chairman of the Committee. The members are nominated by the Speaker.

The Committee considers matters of procedure and conduct of business in the House and recommends any amendments or additions to the Rules of Procedure and Conduct of Business in Lok Sabha that are considered necessary.

Committee on Petitions

The Committee consists of 15 members nominated by the Speaker. A Minister is not nominated to this Committee.

The function of the Committee is to consider and report on petitions presented to the House. Besides, it considers representations from individuals, associations, etc. on subjects which are not covered by the rules relating to petitions and gives directions for their disposal.

Committee on Subordinate Legislation

The Committee consists of 15 members nominated by the Speaker. A minister is not nominated to this Committee.

A Committee scrutinises and reports to the House on whether the powers to make regulations, rules, sub-rules, by-laws, etc. conferred by the Constitution or delegated by Parliament are being properly exercised by the Executive within the scope of such delegation.

Committee on Papers Laid on the Table

This Committee consists of 15 members nominated by the Speaker.

Its function is to examine all papers laid on the Table of the House by Ministers (other than those which fall within the purview of the Committee on Subordinate Legislation or any other Parliamentary Committee) and to report to the House

- Whether there has been compliance of the provisions of the Constitution, Act, rule, or regulation under which the paper has been laid
- Whether there has been any unreasonable delay in laying the paper
- If there has been such delay, whether a Statement explaining the reasons for delay has been laid on the Table of the House and whether those reasons are satisfactory
- Whether both the Hindi and English versions of the paper have been laid on the Table
- Whether a Statement explaining the reasons for not laying the Hindi version has been made and such reasons are satisfactory

It also reports on such other functions in respect of the papers laid on the Table as may be assigned to it by the Speaker from time to time.

Committee on Government Assurances

This Committee consists of 15 members nominated by the Speaker. A Minister is not nominated to this Committee.

While replying to Questions in the House or during discussions on Bills, Resolutions, Motions, etc., Ministers at times give assurances or undertakings either to consider a matter or to take action or to furnish the House further information later.

The functions of this Committee are to scrutinise the assurances, promises, undertakings, etc. given by Ministers from time to time and to report to Lok Sabha on the extent to which such assurances, etc. have been implemented and to see whether such implementation has taken place within the minimum time necessary for the purpose.

Committee on Absence of Members from the Sittings of the House

The Committee consists of 15 members who hold office for one year. The members are nominated by the Speaker.

This Committee considers all applications from members for leave of absence from the sittings of the House and examines every case where a member has been absent for a period of 60 days or more, without permission, from the sittings of the House.

In its report, it makes recommendations with respect to each case as to whether the absence should be condoned or leave applied granted or whether the circumstances of the case justify that the House should declare the seat of the member vacant.

Committee on the Welfare of Scheduled Castes and Scheduled Tribes

The Committee on the welfare of Scheduled Castes and Scheduled Tribes consists of 20 members elected by the Lok Sabha; 10 members of Rajya Sabha are also associated with it. The term of the Committee is one year. A Minister is not eligible for election to the Committee.

The main functions of the Committee are to consider all matters concerning the welfare of the Scheduled Castes and Scheduled Tribes, falling within the purview of the Union Government and the Union Territories, to consider reports submitted by the National Commission for Scheduled Castes and National Commission for Scheduled Tribes, and to examine the measures taken by the Union Government to secure due representation of the Scheduled Castes and Scheduled Tribes in services and posts in its control.

Joint Committee on Offices of Profit

This Committee consists of 15 members. Ten members are elected from Lok Sabha and five from Rajya Sabha. The Committee is constituted for the duration of each Lok Sabha.

The main functions of the Committee are to examine the composition and character of the Committees appointed by the Central and State Governments and to recommend what offices should disqualify and what offices should not disqualify a person for being chosen as, and for being, a member of either House of Parliament under Article 102 of the Constitution.

Committee on Public Undertakings

The Committee on Public Undertakings consists of 15 members elected by the Lok Sabha; 7 members of Rajya Sabha are also associated with it. A Minister is not eligible for election to this Committee. The term of the Committee is one year.

The functions of the Committee on Public Undertakings are:

(a) To examine the reports and accounts of Public Undertakings

(b) To examine the reports, if any, of the Comptroller and Auditor General on the Public Undertakings

(c) To examine in the context of the autonomy and efficiency of the Public Undertakings whether the affairs of the Public Undertakings are being managed in accordance with sound business principles and prudent commercial practices

Such other functions vested in the Committee on Public Accounts and the Committee on Estimates in relation to the Public Undertakings as are not covered by clauses (a), (b), and (c) above and as may be allotted to the Committee by the Speaker from time to time. The Committee does not, however, examine matters of major Government policy and matters of day-to-day administration of the Undertakings.

Committee on Empowerment of Women

This Committee came into being on 29 April, 1997 as a consequence of identical Resolutions adopted by both the Houses of Parliament on the occasion of the International Women's Day on 8 March, 1996.

The Committee consists of 30 members, 20 nominated by the Speaker, Lok Sabha from amongst the members of Lok Sabha and 10 nominated by the Chairman, Rajya Sabha from amongst the members of the Rajya Sabha. The term of the Committee is of one year.

The Committee has been primarily mandated with the task of reviewing and monitoring the measures taken by the Union Government in the direction of securing for women equality, status, and dignity in all matters.

The Committee would also suggest necessary correctives for improving the status/condition of women in respect of matters within the purview of the Union Government.

Another important function of the Committee is to examine the measures taken by the Union Government for comprehensive education and adequate representation of women in Legislative Bodies/services and other fields. The Committee may also consider the report of the National Commission for Women.

Railway Convention Committee

The Railway Convention Committee is an Ad hoc Committee. It consists of 18 members. Out of these, 12 members are from Lok Sabha nominated by the Speaker and 6 members are from Rajya Sabha nominated by the Chairman.

The main function of the Committee is to review the Rate of Dividend payable by the Railways undertaking to General Revenues as well as other ancillary matters in connection with the Railway Finance vis-a-vis the General Finance and make recommendations thereon.

Joint Committee on Salaries and Allowances of Members of Parliament

The Joint Committee on Salaries and Allowances of Members of Parliament constituted under the Salary, Allowances and Pension of Members of Parliament Act, 1954, apart from framing rules for regulating payment of salary, allowances, and pension of members also frames rules in respect of amenities like medical, housing, telephone, postal, constituency, and secretarial facilities.

Library Committee

The Library Committee consisting of members from both Houses, considers matters concerning the Library of Parliament. The Committee consists of 9 members, 6 from Lok Sabha and 3 from Rajya Sabha.

AD HOC COMMITTEES

Ad hoc Committees may be broadly classified under two heads:

- Committees which are constituted from time to time, either by the two Houses on a motion adopted in that behalf, or by the Speaker of the Lok Sabha or Chairman of the Rajya Sabha to inquire into and report on specific subjects (e.g., Committee on the Conduct of Certain Members during the President's Address, Committees on Draft Five-Year Plans, Joint Committee to suggest Facilities and Remuneration to Members of Parliament, Joint Parliamentary Committee on Installation of Portraits/Statues of National Leaders and Parliamentarians in Parliament House Complex)
- Select or Joint Committees on Bills which are appointed to consider and report on particular Bills. These Committees are distinguishable from the other Ad hoc Committees in as much as they are concerned with Bills and the procedure to be followed by them is laid down in the Rules of Procedure and the Directions by the Speaker of the Lok Sabha or Chairman of the Rajya Sabha.

OTHER COMMITTEES

The Lok Sabha has a Committee on Ethics, a Committee on Provision of Computers for Members of Parliament, Offices of Political Parties and Offices of the Lok Sabha Secretariat and a Committee on Member of Parliament Local Area Development Scheme.

DEPARTMENTALLY RELATED STANDING COMMITTEES

A full-fledged system of 17 Departmentally Related Standing Committees (DRSCs) came into being in April, 1993 covering under their jurisdiction all Central Ministries/Departments. The system was restructured in July, 2004 whereby the number of DRSCs was increased from 17 to 24 and the membership of each DRSC has been reduced from 45 to 31 members.

These restructured Committees are as under:

1. Committee on Commerce
2. Committee on Home Affairs
3. Committee on Human Resource Development
4. Committee on Industry
5. Committee on Science & Technology, Environment & Forests
6. Committee on Transport, Tourism and Culture
7. Committee on Health and Family Welfare
8. Committee on Personnel, Public Grievances, Law and Justice
9. Committee on Agriculture
10. Committee on Information Technology
11. Committee on Defence
12. Committee on Energy
13. Committee on External Affairs
14. Committee on Finance
15. Committee on Food, Consumer Affairs and Public Distribution
16. Committee on Labour
17. Committee on Petroleum & Natural Gas
18. Committee on Railways
19. Committee on Urban Development
20. Committee on Water Resources
21. Committee on Chemicals and Fertilizers
22. Committee on Rural Development
23. Committee on Coal and Steel
24. Committee on Social Justice and Empowerment

Out of the 24 Committees, 8 Committees (Sl. Nos. 1 to 8) are serviced by the Rajya Sabha Secretariat and 16 Committees (Sl. Nos. 9 to 24) by the Lok Sabha Secretariat.

Each of these Standing Committees consists of not more than 31 members–21 to be nominated by the Speaker from amongst the members of Lok Sabha and 10 to be nominated by the Chairman, Rajya Sabha from amongst the members of Rajya Sabha. A Minister is not eligible to be nominated to these Committees. The term of members of these Committees is one year.

With reference to the Ministries/Departments under their purview, the functions of these Committees are:

- Consideration of Demands.
- Examination of Bills referred to them by the Chairman, Rajya Sabha, or the Speaker, Lok Sabha, as the case may be.
- Consideration of Annual Reports.

- Consideration of national basic long term policy documents presented to the House and referred to the Committee by the Chairman, Rajya Sabha, or the Speaker, Lok Sabha, as the case may be.

The Departmentally Related Standing Committee System is a path-breaking endeavour of parliamentary surveillance over administration. With the emphasis of their functioning to concentrate on long-term plans, policies, and the philosophies guiding the working of the Executive, these Committees are in a very privileged position to provide necessary direction, guidance, and inputs for broad policy formulations and in the achievement of the long-term national perspective by the Executive.

JOINT PARLIAMENTARY COMMITTEE (JPC)

Joint Parliamentary Committee is one type of ad hoc Parliamentary Committee constituted by the Indian Parliament. The JPC is appointed to look, inquire into parliament matter or subject or fraud, or something which is important for the nation.

The JPC is constituted either through a motion adopted by one House and concurred by the other, or, through communication between the presiding officers of the two Houses.

The members are either elected by the Houses or nominated by the presiding officers. As in the case of other parliamentary committees, they are drawn from different groups. The strength of a JPC may vary. The Lok Sabha share is double than that of the Rajya Sabha.

Powers of JPC

A JPC can obtain evidence of experts, public bodies, associations, individuals, or interested parties suo motu or on requests made by them. If a witness fails to appear before a JPC in response to summons, his conduct constitutes contempt of the House.

The JPC can take oral and written evidence or call for documents in connection with a matter under its consideration. The proceedings of parliamentary committees are confidential.

Ministers are not generally called by the committees to give evidence. The government may withhold or decline to produce a document if it is considered prejudicial to the safety or interest of the State.

The Speaker has the final word on any dispute over calling for evidence against a person or production of a document.

Investigative JPCs

There have been **five** investigative JPCs so far:

- The **first** was instituted to inquire into the Bofors contract. The committee, headed by B. Shankaranand, held 50 sittings and gave its report on April 26, 1988. Opposition parties boycotted the committee on the ground that it was packed with Congress members. The JPC report was tabled in Parliament, but it was rejected by the Opposition.
- The **second** investigative JPC, headed by former Union Minister and senior Congress leader Ram Niwas Mirdha, was set up to probe Irregularities in Securities and Banking Transactions in the aftermath of the Harshad Mehta scandal. The recommendations of the JPC were neither accepted in full nor implemented.

- The **third** investigative JPC was assigned to probe the market scam. MP Lt Gen Prakash Mani Tripathi (retd) was named the chairman. The committee held 105 sittings and gave its report on December 19, 2002. The committees recommended sweeping changes in stock market regulations. However, many of these recommendations were diluted.
- The **fourth** JPC was set up in August 2003 to look into pesticide residues in soft drinks, fruit juice, and other beverages and to set safety standards. The committee, headed by Sharad Pawar, held 17 sittings and submitted its report to Parliament on February 4, 2004. The report confirmed that soft drinks did have pesticide residues and recommended stringent norms for drinking water.
- The **fifth** JPC was constituted in 2010 to probe 2G scam. It was headed by P.C. Chacko. Its recommendations were not unanimous.

FAQS ON JPC

What is a Joint Parliamentary Committee?

Considering the volume of work and limited time at its disposal, Parliament cannot precisely scrutinise all legislative and other matters that come before it. Hence, it appoints various committees responsible for the proper execution of various parliamentary businesses. These committees can be broadly classified as standing and ad hoc committees. Standing committees are appointed every year while ad hoc committees are constituted depending on the need. The Joint Parliamentary Committee (JPC) demanded by the opposition to probe the 2G scam was an ad hoc committee. Such committees are typically set up to enquire into and report on specific matters or subjects.

How is a JPC formed?

Such committees can be constituted either by a joint consensus of both houses when a motion is adopted in one and concurred in the other, or by consultation between the presiding officers of both houses. The number of members appointed on a committee is not fixed, but generally the members are appointed in such a way as to include the maximum number of parties or groups in the house. In a typical JPC, the Lok Sabha will have twice the number of members as the Rajya Sabha. These committees become *functus officio*, that is, they retain no authority after presentation of the report or conclusion of the assigned function.

How does a JPC Work?

Once formed, a JPC starts enquiring into the given matter by considering the terms of reference on the points for which it is constituted. For instance, the JPC constituted to inquire into the alleged presence of pesticides in soft drinks had two terms of reference–firstly, whether the findings of the Centre of Science and Environment were correct; and secondly, to suggest criteria for evolving suitable safety standards for the beverages industry. An investigation by the JPC requires consultation with experts, public bodies, and even interested parties. In technical matters, the JPC can also appoint consultants. Apart from this, the committee can also invite suggestions/ views from the general public on its terms of references. Although the proceedings of JPC are confidential, the chairman of the committee typically briefs the media from time to time about the discussions which take place during its sittings.

V. POWERS, PRIVILIGES, AND IMMUNITIES OF PARLIAMENT AND ITS MEMBERS

Article 105

(1) Subject to the provisions of this constitution and the rules and standing orders regulating the procedure of Parliament, there shall be freedom of speech in Parliament.

(2) No Member of Parliament shall be liable to any proceedings in any court in respect of anything said or any vote given by him in Parliament or any committee thereof, and no person shall be so liable in respect of the publication by or under the authority of either House of Parliament of any report, paper, votes, or proceedings.

(3) In other respects, the powers, privileges and immunities of each House of Parliament and of the members and the committees of each House, shall be such as many from time to time be defined by Parliament by law, until so defined, shall be those of that House and of its members and committees immediately before the coming into force of section 15 of the 44th Amendment ActAmendment Act, 1978. The amendment dropped the clause 'Privileges would be same as those of British House of Commons'.

(4) The provisions of clauses (1), (2), and (3) shall apply in relation to persons who by virtue of this constitution have the right to speak in, and otherwise to take part in the proceedings of, a House of Parliament or any committee thereof as they apply in relation to member of Parliament.

Immunities and Privileges: Houses of Parliament

Both Houses of Parliament have some immunities and privileges. The Speaker in the House of the People and the chairmen in the Council of States are the ultimate authority in the matter of enforcement.

(a) Right to exclude outsiders from its proceedings.

(b) Right to publish or exclude its proceedings.

(c) Right to punish individuals for contempt of Parliament.

(d) Right to regulate internal affairs of the House without interference from the courts.

(e) Right to punish members and outsiders for breach of its privileges; the punishment may be admonition, a reprimand, or imprisonment.

Privileges: Individual Members

Besides the privileges and immunities that the Houses of Parliament have, individual members of Parliament too have privileges and immunities.

(1) Freedom from being arrested in civil cases during the continuance of a meeting of the House or committee of which he is a member, and during a period of 40 days before and after such a meeting.

(2) Freedom of speech providing immunity from court action for anything said in the House, subject to rules of the House to maintain dignity if the House.

(3) A member enjoys freedom from being summoned, without the leave of the House to give evidence as a witness while parliament is in session. Reason, parliamentary work is paramount; others must wait.

(4) A member enjoys immunity from proceedings in any court in respect of publication by or under authority of either House of Parliament of any report, paper, votes or proceedings.

Article 361-A: Protection of Publication of Proceedings of Parliament and State Legislatures

No person shall be liable to any proceedings, civil or criminal, in any court in respect of the publication in a newspaper of a substantially true report of any proceedings of either House of Parliament or the Legislative Assembly; or, as the case may be, either House of Legislature of a state, unless the publication is proved to have been made with malice provided that nothing in this clause shall apply to the publication of any report of the proceedings of a secret sitting of either House of Parliament or the Legislative Assembly, or, as the case may be, either House of the legislature of the state.

(Inserted by 44th Amendment Sec 42, on 20/6/79)

Article 194

Article 194 deals with powers, privileges, etc. of the House of Legislatures and of the members and committees thereof. These are very same, similar as available under Article 105 to the House of Parliament and members and committees thereof.

Committee of Privileges

The functions of the committee are semi-judicial and it examines the cases of breach of privileges of the House and its members and recommends appropriate action.

Powers and Privileges

Powers and privileges of the Parliament are those which are being enjoyed by the Parliament ever since the commencement of the Constitution and also such of the unamended powers and privileges which the British Parliament had prior to 1950. It implies the old British Parliamentary powers and privileges are not absolute and they must be read in the context of the powers and privileges exercised by the Indian Parliament from 1950 up to date. It is seen that the Indian Parliament, though it is charged by the Constitution with power to enact a law on the parliamentary privileges, has not yet made any law on the subject.

'SEARCHLIGHT CASE': 1964

The Uttar Pradesh Legislative Assembly, in 1964, sentenced one Keshav Singh to imprisonment for the breach of privileges. Keshav Singh moved the High Court under Article 226 of the Constitution on grounds of fundamental rights (Article 21) and sought bail. The High Court granted him bail. Peeved, the Assembly ordered that Keshav Singh, his counsel, and the two judges who granted bail be produced in custody in the House. The judges moved the High Court at Allahabad and the full bench ordered stay of the execution of the resolution of the Assembly. The Assembly complied, but passed another resolution demanding that the judges be present in the House to offer an explanation. Independent India was witnessing a full blown contest of wits and wisdom.The President intervened and referred the case under Article 143 to the Supreme Court for opinion. The Supreme Court held out that even after powers and privileges are codified, they will be liable for judicial interpretation. In the instant case, Article 19 does not come in the way of exercise of freedom of speech inside legislature. Even if contempt of court is committed inside Parliament, courts can't interfere. The joke in the case was that Keshav Singh's counsel, one Mr. Solomon, was also ordered to be arrested. In history, Solomon is supposed to be "wise", state assembly thought otherwise!! of this Solomon.

Dissolution, Adjournment and Prorogation

The sitting of a house may be terminated by *dissolution*, *adjournment* or *prorogation*.

Rajya Sabha is a permanent body, so **dissolution** *applies only to Lok Sabha and it may happen in two ways:*

(i) By an exercise of the President's powers to dissolve the House if the Council of Ministers has lost the confidence of the House and advises the dissolution

(ii) On the expiry of the term

Adjournment is the end of a sitting of the House and it suspends the work of that sitting for some time. 'Sine die' adjournment is for an unspecified period. Adjournment is within the power of the Speaker of Lok Sabha and Chairman of Rajya Sabha.

Prorogation is done by the President and it terminates a session of the House. It does not end the life of the House but ends a session. In effect, dissolution brings the House of People to an end, paving way for fresh elections; adjournment simply postpones further transaction of business; prorogation terminates the session.

What happens to Bills?

Dissolution: All matters, including Bills lapse, but those Bills which originated in Rajya Sabha and are pending do not lapse.

Adjournment: There is no change in status of Bills and notices, since adjournment means mere postponement.

Prorogation: Bills do not lapse, but pending motions, notices and resolutions lapse (except for notices introducing Bills).

PARLIAMENTARY COMMITTEES

	Lok Sabha (No. of members)	Term	Rajya Sabha (No. of members)	Total members (LS & RS)	How they are represented
Committee of Estimates	30	One Year	×	30	Elected
Committee on Public undertakings	15	One Year	7	22	LS (Elected) RS (Associated)
Committee on Public Accounts	15	One Year	7	22	LS (Elected) RS (Associated)
Business Advisory Committee	15		×	15	Nominated by Speaker
Committee on Private Members bills	15	One Year	×	15	"
Rules Committee	15		×	15	"
Committee on Privileges	15		×	15	"
Committee on Petitions	15		×	15	"
Committee on Government Assurances	15		×	15	"
Committee on Absence of Members from the House	15		×	15	"
Joint Committee on office of Profit	10	Duration of LS	5	15	Elected
Committee on welfare of SC/ST	20	One Year	10	30	LS: Elected RS:Associated
Committee on empowerment of Women	20	One Year	10	30	Nominated

Money Bill *Vs* Finance Bill

Art 110(1): A money bill deals with items listed in Art 110(1) 'a' to 'g', whereas finance bill does not exclusively deal with these, all or any but contains some other provisions too.

110 (a) Imposition, abolition, remission, alteration or regulation of any tax.

(b) Regulation of borrowing money, giving guarantee by Government of India, amendment of law with respect to financial obligations by Government.

(c) Custody of consolidated or contingent fund of India.

(d) Appropriation of moneys out of consolidated fund.

(e) Declaring of any expenditure to be expenditure charged on the consolidated fund of India or increasing of the amount of such expenditure.

(f) Receipt of money on account of Consolidated Fund of India or public account of India or the custody of such money.

(g) Any matter incidental to any of the matters at (a) to (f) finance bill are of two types.

Art 117 (1): Finance Bills: These can be introduced only in Lok Sabha. These bill inter-alia contain provisions attracting article 110(1) a to f. Other restrictions of money bills don't apply but these bills can be introduced only after recommendation of the President.

Art 117 (3): Finance Bills: Such bills contain provisions which would on enactment involve expenditure from the consolidated fund of India. Such bills can be introduced in either house of Parliament but recommendation of President is essential.

Note: Constitution amendment bill is a constitution amendment bill, even if it attracts provisions of Art 110(1) a to g. Art 368 governs them in finality and totality.

Article 196 : Provisions as to Introduction and Passing of Bills

(1) Subject to the provisions of Articles 198 and 207 with respect to Money Bills and other financial Bills, a Bill may originate in either House of the Legislature of a State which has a Legislative Council.

(2) Subject to the provisions of Articles 197 and 198, a Bill shall not be deemed to have been passed by the House of the Legislature of a State having a Legislative Council unless it has been agreed to by both Houses, either without amendment or with such amendments only as are agreed to by both Houses.

(3) A Bill pending in the Legislature of a State shall not lapse by reason of the prorogation of the House or Houses thereof.

(4) A Bill pending in the Legislative Council of a State which has not been passed by the Legislative Assembly shall not lapse on the dissolution of the Assembly.

(5) A bill which is pending in the Legislative Assembly of a State, or which having been passed by the Legislative Assembly is pending in the Legislative Council, shall lapse on a dissolution of the Assembly.

State Legislatures

The Constitution has provided for State Legislatures which are organized on the same, similar basis as the Parliament with one notable difference that the legislative councils (upper houses) are not mandatory. Only seven states in the country have such councils.

Articles 168 to 212 in chapter 3 of part 6 of the Constitution cover the various provisions governing the powers, functioning and procedures of the State Legislatures. Like in Lok Sabha, there are provisions for the Speaker and Deputy Speaker (Article 178). Article 196 deals with introduction and passing of bills. Article 212 rules that Courts cannot inquire into the proceedings of the state legislatures.

State Legislatures are however restricted by the provisions of the Constitution which gives overriding power to the Parliament. (Articles 250, 251 and 254).

6

CHAPTER

Structure, Organisation and Functioning of Executive and The Judiciary

OVERVIEW

Besides the legislature, the Judiciary and the Executive are the two pillars on which the Constitution of India rests. The best of constitutions can come a cropper if these institutions are not allowed the space and freedom to work. How does the Indian Constitution ensure this, even while ensuring that the same institutions do not trod on others' territory? How is the Government organised and how do pressure groups and associations, both formal and informal, work in the system? What are the rules of the game and what games rule? Answers to these questions will reveal to what extent our democracy has matured.

THE EXECUTIVE

In our parliamentary democracy, the Executive is a vital organ, along with the Legislature and the Judiciary.The purpose of the Executive, as the name suggests, is `to execute'. Legislature makes the law and the Executive executes it in a manner with the means that the Judiciary finds agreeable and acceptable. Executive should interpret the Acts of Parliament as required, to work a plan and process, and particulars. In order to affect a clear understanding of intention behind the Act, parliament involves the Executive in framing rules and regulations to implement the Act. This pro-active stance is referred to as sub-ordinate legislation. The experience and skill of the Executive is used to fill in the gaps and details to implement the provisions of the proposed Act. In fact, often the help of the Executive is taken even at the stage of drafting the Act itself given the experience that the Executive possess. What is however of much importance is that the rules and regulations needed to implement the Act should neither overextend the provisions of the Act, nor fall short.

The Executive has, however, to keep in view two aspects always;

(a) **Anonymity of the Executive:** The Executive always works in the background and from the shadows; it does not claim to be the originator or the promoter of the Act. If there's success to be had, it's the due of the Government led by the party in power. If it is not successful, blame or at least a part of it could come to the Executive.

(b) **Neutrality of the Executive:** Parties may come, parties may go; governments may come, governments may go, the Executive goes on forever. Executive is neutral and natural; it is not committed to any party or posture. Executive should not align with any party in any manner to even remotely suggest compromise. During the Emergency period (1975-77), the Executive became over enthused to step forward to implement policies in a manner that clearly was 'excessive'; i.e., 'they became more loyal than the king.' The end of the emergency and following elections brought in a change of government. Then the Executive had a lot to answer for. Democracy abhors excesses, adores balance, sanity and neutrality. That is the strength of democracy, the joy of democracy, the essence of democracy, the fragrance of democracy.

MINISTRIES AND DEPARTMENTS OF THE GOVERNMENT

The Government of India is organised at the level of Ministry in the following manner:

1. Ministry of specific subject, say Agriculture, Home Affairs, Defence, Shipping, etc.
2. Within the Ministry there may be a Department, say Department of Agriculture and Cooperation, Department of Commerce, Defence Production, Science and Technology, etc. Not all Ministries have Departments.
3. Subordinate offices, which are field units, say Eastern Coalfields, Ordnance Factories, National Textile Corporation, Bhabha Atomic Research Centre.
4. Attached offices are offices attached to the Ministries. Attached offices have statistics, data, research papers, information, past records, etc. These offices prepare approach papers, analyse trends, etc.

Both sub-ordinate offices and attached offices have administrative and financial powers but are substantially under the concerned department. They have autonomy in their work spheres but are governed by the policies laid down by the concerned departments.

Article 77(3) of the Constitution of India empowers the President of India to make rules for transaction of the business of the government of India.

"The President shall make rules for the more convenient transaction of the business of the government of India and for the allocation among Ministries of the said business"

Government of India (Allocation of Business) Rules, 1961 came into effect specifying the ministries, departments, secretariat, and offices in which the work of the government will be carried out. These rules have been amended from time to time to meet the needs.

The structure, organisation, and system of Indian government is patterned after the British system; starting from filing system, ending with accountability to the Parliament. Transparency, accountability, traceability, delegation, hierarchy and timely delivery are some of its features. The system is time-tested and has rewards and reprimands for the performers and laggards respectively. If there's one major drawback, it is in-built job security for the majority of laggards and the dominance of routine work without innovation.In fact, the two `achievements' the Indian bureaucracy does not tire boasting are:

1) Desk Officer System
2) Single Window System

Desk Officer System is based on empowerment and disposal, where the lowest officer in the rung in administration is empowered with administrative and financial powers to dispose of all routine cases to his superiors. The Desk officer has the powers to procure all items necessary to run his office. Desk officer system has been a success as superiors need not be burdened with routine matters and the incumbent also feels immensely motivated. It's a marriage of convenience.

Single Window System is more organic and stimulating. All cases, especially from the public, are received at one window and processed, often at various levels, and replies/settlements are delivered from the same window. It saves a lot of hassles, time, and movement. The system has shown a lot of resilience and has found ready acceptance. Visitors earlier used to running from pillar to post, appointment to disappointment, find such a dispensation emotionally satisfying and increasingly pleasant. It is often not considered that the persons at the single window are the public face of the organisation and the interface between the public and the organisation. Single window system reduces 'discretion' element in the organisation and improves 'time bound' deliveries.

Successive Administrative Reforms Commissions (ARC)

ARC I (1969) and ARC II (2008) have painstakingly suggested ways and means to bring about reforms in administration. The 2nd ARC has stressed on automation and mechanisation of systems. Computerisation has helped in traceability, faster decision-making, organised and systematic filing, and above all evaluation of pros and cons in decision- making. Computerisation has also opened up access to files by the public bringing about a great deal of accountability. A single window system with a computer is like a dream come true. Mobile access adds to comfort, adds to versatility, adds to dynamism. This signifies end of queues, end of timeless wait, end of searches, end of hopelessness; all the veritable systems associated with the bureaucracy.

A corollary is paperless office-Nice to think of, comforting thought, and a feeling of achievement. It cuts costs, cuts time. Andhra Pradesh is the first state to declare 'paperless office' in its government; initial consternation among the uninitiated was that probably that government had run out of stationery!

Empowered Group of Ministries: EGOMs

This was a mechanism created by the previous UPA government involving concerned ministers with a set agenda to sort out issues. The idea was that if minsters are empowered, both administratively and financially, they can sit and sort issues of coordination and contract out. The plan was to bring the best of talent together. It worked well for a while:

(a) Ministries resolved differences in togetherness.
(b) Coordination and cooperation set the tone and tenor.

(c) In a group, the ministers could see the larger picture in perspective and appreciate concerns.

(d) Petty matters, bureaucratic wrangles got cleared.

However, the compulsions of coalition politics put a brake on its smooth functioning. Soon the empowered group of ministers were getting bogged down and they:

(1) Started protecting their turfs.

(2) Started passing the buck.

(3) Cared for authority, not responsibility.

(4) Started raising issues to divert, delay, digress, and derail and dilute too.

EGOM became stratified, problems multiplied overtime. None lamented its overdue departure. EGOM now belongs to the ages.

STRUCTURE, ORGANISATION, AND FUNCTIONING OF THE EXECUTIVE

The executive head of the Union is the President of India. Article 53 states, 'The executive power of the Union shall be vested in the President and shall be exercised by him directly or through officer subordinate to him in accordance with this constitution'. *The constitution has outlined the extent of executive power of the Union vide Article 73 which states,*

(1) subject to the provisions of this Constitution, the executive power of the Union shall extend.

(a) to the matters with respect to which parliament has power to make laws; and

(b) to the exercise of such rights, authority, and jurisdiction as are exercisable by the Government of India by virtue of any treaty or agreement.

(2) Until otherwise provided by parliament, a state and any officer or authority of a state may, notwithstanding anything in this article, continue to exercise in matters with respect to which parliament has power to make laws for that state such executive power or functions as the state or officer or authority thereof could exercise immediately before commencement of this constitution. Article 74 provides that, 'There shall be a Council of Ministers with the Prime Minister at the head to aid and advise the President who shall, in the exercise of his functions, act in accordance with such advice.

The 44th amendment in 1978 inserted that, 'Provided that the President may require the Council of Ministers to reconsider such advice, either generally or otherwise, and the President shall act in accordance with the advice tendered after reconsideration'.

(2) The question whether any, and if so what, advice was tendered by Minsters to the President shall not be inquired into in any court.

Article 75 : It has some critical provisions relating to Ministers

Article 75(1): The Prime Minster shall be appointed by the President and other Minsters shall be appointed by the President on the advice of the Prime Minister. The 91st amendment 2003 has restricted the total number of ministers, including the Prime Minister, in the Council of Ministers to not exceed fifteen percent of the total number of member of the House of the People (Lok Sabha).

Article 75(2): The ministers shall hold office during the pleasure of the President.

Article 75(3): The Council of Ministers shall be collectively responsible to the House of the People.

Article 75(5): A minster who for any period of six months is not a member of either House of Parliament shall at the expiration of that period cease to be a minister.

Article 77 of the Constitution lays down conduct of business of Government of India.

Article 77(1): All Executive actions of the Government of India shall be expressed to be taken in the name of the President.

Article 77(2): Orders and other instruments made and executed in the name of the President shall be authenticated in such manner as may be specified in rules to be made by the President, and the validity of an order or instrument which is authenticated shall not be called in question on the ground that it is not an order or instrument made or executed by the President.

Article 77(3): The President shall make rules for the more convenient transaction of the business of the Government of India, and for allocation among the ministers of the said business.

Article 78 : It states that the Prime Minister has a duty to communicate with the President. Article 78 stipulates that it shall be the duty of Prime Minister:

(a) to communicate to the President all decisions of the Council of Ministers relating to the administration of the affairs of the Union and proposals for legislation.

(b) to furnish such information relating to the administration of the affairs of the Union and proposal for legislation as the President may call for, and

(c) If the President so requires to submit for the consideration of the Council of Ministers any matter on which decision has been taken by a minister but which has not been considered by the Council.

As far as States are concerned, the Governors have similar powers;

Article 163: "There shall be a Council of Ministers with the Chief Minister at the head to aid and advice the Governor..."

Article 164: Other provisions as to ministers

(1) The chief Minister shall be appointed by the Governor and the other Ministers shall be appointed by the Governor on the advice of the Chief Minister, and the Ministers shall hold office during the pleasure of the Governor: Provided that in the State of Bihar, Madhya Pradesh and Orissa, there shall be a Minister in charge of tribal welfare who may in addition be in charge of the welfare of the Scheduled Castes and backward classes or any other work

(2) The Council of Ministers shall be collectively responsible to the Legislative Assembly of the State

(3) Before a Minister enters upon his office, the Governor shall administer so him the oaths of office and of secrecy according to the forms set out for the purpose in the Third Schedule

(4) A Minister who for any period of six consecutive months is not a member of the Legislature of the State shall at the expiration of that period cease to be a Minister

(5) The salaries and allowances of Ministers shall be such as the Legislature of the State may from time to time by law determine and, until the Legislature of the State so determines, shall be as specified in the Second Schedule.

Article 166: Conduct of Business of the State.

Article 167: Duties of Chief Minister as regards furnishing information to the Governor.

Structure

The Indian Executive is largely structured on the pattern of the British system; the notable features being:

(a) Neutrality of the Executive.

(b) Continuity of the civil servants despite change of governments.

(c) Anonymity of civil servants, with the political masters taking the responsibility for decisions.

(d) Careers open to talent.

(e) Governed by a set of rules and regulations.

(f) Protection of service through constitutional safeguards (Article 309, 311 in India)

As far as India is concerned, the Government of India Act 1935, created a set-up with a Central government and governments at the level of provinces; this has continued with the enactment of the constitution too. The quintessential matter in the structure is that the Executive is responsible to the Legislature and Judiciary. Legislature enacts laws based on the will and mandate of the people. This has to be put into action by a set of rules which are implemented by the Executive. In this, the Executive plays an important role in that it helps in framing the rules.

These rules should not be, so weak or ill-considered that they don't meet the very objectives of the acts or laws; nor should they be so strong or overriding that they go beyond the objectives of the Acts or laws.

It is here that 'Subordinate legislation' comes into reckoning; the lawmakers and the Executives come together to forge a workable, workmanlike working arrangement.

The President is the head of the state and the Prime Minister, the head of the government. The prime minister presides over cabinet meetings. A cabinet minister normally heads a ministry, unless he is without portfolio. A minister of state cannot attend a cabinet meet unless invited to. A deputy minister, who is below minister of state does not attend a cabinet meet.

Organisation

While it is fine to have a structure, the structure will remain a dead letter unless an organisation is there to make it function. A structure is like a skeletal shape, organisation gives it the muscles, veins, and blood. To begin with, there are cabinet committees which handle specific and specialised issues.

1. Cabinet Committee on Economic Affairs
2. Cabinet Committee of Defence
3. Cabinet Committee on Appointments.

In addition, there are cabinet committees on Parliamentary Affairs, Political Affairs etc. Ministries are headed by secretary rank officials and cabinet secretariat by the cabinet secretary where the chief secretary is at the state level.

Then there can be ad hoc committees to attend to specific issues; a committee was formed to sort out 'One rank one pension issue' which was hanging fire for years.

The expedient of cabinet committee serves dual purpose; one, it brings in expertise; two, it shapes collective decision-making. Above all, it gives the Prime Minister the relief that he needs.

Functions

The function of the Executive is to keep the government going. Basically, the Executive is there to fulfil the agenda of its political masters. Foremost, the Executive is there to take forward the 'Directive Principles of State Policy' as enshrined in the Constitution.

In other words, Executive is there for governance. The other functions include

(a) Defence of the country.

(b) Ensuring social justice.

(c) Promoting economic growth.

(d) Protecting the environment.

(e) Advancing social sector/services like Health, Education, and Human Resource Development.

(f) Promoting international goodwill

These functions are all discharged by individual ministries, charged with specific tasks, duties, and responsibilities.

MINISTRIES/DEPARTMENTS OF THE GOVERNMENT

The Government of India (GoI) consists of a number of ministries/departments, their number and character varying from time to time based on factors such as volume of work, priorities attached to certain subjects, etc.

List of the Ministries/Departments

1. Ministry of Agriculture and Farmers Welfare
   (i) Department of Agriculture, Co-operation and Farmers Welfare
   (ii) Department of Agricultural Research and Education
   (iii) Department of Animal Husbandry, Dairying and Fisheries
2. Ministry of Ayurveda, Yoga and Naturopathy, Unani, Siddha and Homoeopathy (AYUSH)
3. Ministry of Chemicals and Fertilizers
   (i) Department of Chemicals and Petro-Chemicals
   (ii) Department of Fertilizers
   (iii) Department of Pharmaceuticals
4. Ministry of Civil Aviation
5. Ministry of Coal

6. Ministry of Commerce and Industry
   (i) Department of Commerce
   (ii) Department of Industrial Policy and Promotion
7. Ministry of Communications
   (i) Department of Telecommunications
   (ii) Department of Posts
8. Ministry of Consumer Affairs, Food and Public Distribution
   (i) Department of Consumer Affairs
   (ii) Department of Food and Public Distribution
9. Ministry of Corporate Affairs
10. Ministry of Culture
11. Ministry of Defence
    (i) Department of Defence
    (ii) Department of Defence Production
    (iii) Department of Defence Research and Development
    (iv) Department of Ex-servicemen Welfare
12. Ministry of Development of North-Eastern Region
13. Ministry of Drinking Water and Sanitation
14. Ministry of Earth Sciences
15. Ministry of Electronics and InformationTechnology
16. Ministry of Environment, Forest and Climate Change
17. Ministry of External Affairs
18. Ministry of Finance
    (i) Department of Economic Affairs
    (ii) Department of Expenditure
    (iii) Department of Revenue
    (iv) Department of Investment and Public Asset Management (DIPAM)
    (v) Department of Financial Services
19. Ministry of Food Processing Industries
20. Ministry of Health and Family Welfare
    (i) Department of Health and Family Welfare
    (ii) Department of Health Research
21. Ministry of Heavy Industries and Public Enterprises
    (i) Department of Heavy Industries
    (ii) Department of Public Enterprises
22. Ministry of Home Affairs
    (i) Department of Internal Security
    (ii) Department of States

(iii) Department of Official Language
(iv) Department of Home
(v) Department of Jammu and Kashmir Affairs
(vi) Department of Border Management

23. Ministry of Human Resource Development
(i) Department of School Education and Literacy
(ii) Department of Higher Education

24. Ministry of Information and Broadcasting.

25. Ministry of Labour and Employment

26. Ministry of Law and Justice
(i) Department of Legal Affairs
(ii) Legislative Department
(iii) Department of Justice

27. Ministry of Micro, Small and Medium Enterprises

28. Ministry of Mines

29. Ministry of Minority Affairs

30. Ministry of New and Renewable Energy

31. Ministry of Panchayati Raj

32. Ministry of Parliamentary Affairs

33. Ministry of Personnel, Public Grievances and Pensions
(i) Department of Personnel and Training
(ii) Department of Administrative Reforms and Public Grievances
(iii) Department of Pensions and Pensioners'Welfare

34. Ministry of Petroleum and Natural Gas

35. Ministry of Planning

36. Ministry of Power

37. Ministry of Railways

38. Ministry of Road Transport and Highways

39. Ministry of Rural Development
(i) Department of Rural Development
(ii) Department of Land Resources

40. Ministry of Science and Technology
(i) Department of Science and Technology
(ii) Department of Scientific and Industrial Research
(iii) Department of Bio-technology

41. Ministry of Shipping

42. Ministry of Skill Development and Entrepreneurship

43. Ministry of Social Justice and Empowerment
    (i) Department of Social Justice and Empowerment
    (ii) Department of Empowerment of Persons with Disabilities
44. Ministry of Statistics and Programme Implementation
45. Ministry of Steel
46. Ministry of Textiles
47. Ministry of Tourism
48. Ministry of Tribal Affairs
49. Ministry of Urban Development
50. Ministry of Housing and Urban Poverty Alleviation
51. Ministry of Water Resources, River Development and Ganga Rejuvenation
52. Ministry of Women and Child Development
53. Ministry of Youth Affairs and Sports
    (i) Department of Youth Affairs
    (ii) Department of Sports

Independent Departments

1. Department of Atomic Energy
2. Department of Space

Apex/Independent Offices

1. NITI Aayog (National Institution for Transforming India)
2. Cabinet Secretariat
3. President's Secretariat
4. Prime Minister's Office

PROJECT MONITORING GROUP

Project Monitoring Group (PMG), is an institutional mechanism for resolving a variety of issues including fast tracking of approvals for setting up an expeditious commissioning of large Public, Private, and Public-Private Partnership (PPP) project. Project Monitoring Group (PMG) was set up in June 2013 under the cabinet secretariat. The PMG is presently functioning under Prime Minister's Office (PMO) since September 14, 2015.

Generally, following types of clearances/issues have been raised by the proponents of various projects for resolution and expeditious commissioning:

(a) **Issues Pertaining to Union Ministries :** (i) Environment, forest, and wildlife clearances; (ii) Eco-Sensitive Zone clearance; (iii) Tree cutting permission; (iv) Grant of working permission by Forest Department; (v) Approval for private railways siding construction; (vi) Industrial License Permission; (vii) Grant of right of way/right of use permission; and (viii) Shifting of utilities.

(b) **Issues pertaining to State Governments :** (i) Land acquisition issues such as government notifications/disbursement of compensation, transfer of title, and handing over of possession; (ii) Removal of encroachments; (iii) Relief and rehabilitation plan; (iv) Certificate under Forest Rights Act, diversion of forest land and compensation for afforestation; (v) Power and water supply connections/tariff; (vi) Consent to establish and operate from State Pollution Control Board; (vii) Transfer of Government land; (viii) Law and Order issues; and (ix) Right of way and right of use permissions.

PMG facilitates resolution of issues brought out by the Project Proponent through regular meetings involving Central and State Government officials as well as Project Proponents. So far 793 projects (anticipated investment of 15.31 lakh crore) have been resolved and issues in 106 projects (anticipated investment of 7.61 lakh crore) required no further action or intervention by PMG. As on August 1, 2016, 265 projects (anticipated investment of 10.81 lakh crore) with 614 issues are under consideration of PMG. Majority of the issues pointed out by the Investors/Project Proponents require intervention/expeditious action on the part of the state government. Hence, meetings are convened in the State capitals, where pending issues are reviewed with the concerned departments of the state government and Investors/Projects Proponents.

PUBLIC GRIEVANCES MECHANISM

The Directorate of Public Grievances (DPG) was set up in1988 to entertain grievances from the public after they failed to get satisfactory redress from the ministry/department concerned within a reasonable time. It is thus, an office of the last resort for redress of grievances relating to sectors in its purview. The sectors in DPG's purview are those with extensive public interface. Certain subjects are outside the purview of DPG.

Organisations under DPG's purview are: (i) Department of Posts, (ii) Department of Telecommunication, (iii) Ministry of Railways, (iv) Department of FinancialServices (Banking and Insurance), (v) National Small Savings Scheme: Department of Economic Affairs, (vi) Ministry of Urban Development (DDA, L&DO, CPWD), (vii) Ministry of Road Transport & Highways, (viii) Ministry of Shipping, Ministry of Civil Aviation, (ix) Regional Passport Authorities (MEA), (x) Ministry of Labour, (xi) Employees' Provident Fund Organisation, (xii) Employees' State Insurance Corporation-Hospitals and Dispensaries, (xiii) CGHS: Ministry of Health and Family Welfare, (xiv) Ministry of Petroleum & Natural Gas, Ministry of HRD, (xv) Central Universities, Kendriya Vidyalaya, (xvi) Navodaya Vidyalaya, (xvii) National Institute of Open Learning, (xviii) Central Board of Secondary Education, (xix) Ministry of Tourism & (xx) Ministry of Youth Affairs.

Subjects outside the purview of DPG are: (i) Policy matters, (ii) Matters that are sub judice (iii) Grievances disposed of at the level of the concerned Minister (iv) Service matters (except those relating to payment of terminal benefits) (v) Commercial contracts.

Grievance can be lodged with DPG through post, email, or by lodging the complaint online on the portal. The cases received offline are entered in the system and, thereafter, all cases are handled using Public Grievance Redress and Monitoring System (PGRAMS) application.

Each grievance is first scrutinised to see if it relates to a sector in DPG's purview. Those concerning the sectors outside the purview of the DPG are forwarded to the Department of Administrative Reforms and Public Grievances for appropriate disposal, under intimation to the complainants. The remaining grievances are then assessed to ascertain whether the issue involved is grave and whether the concerned ministry/department has been given an opportunity to redress the grievance. The grievances of a grave nature which are either long pending or where the redress is not forthcoming from concerned service organisation/ministry are taken up for detailed examination. These cases are followed upto a logical and reasonable conclusion. Other cases are transferred to the concerned ministry for appropriate action.

When DPG seeks comments, the department ororganisation is expected to examine the matter and give a reply within thirty days. After receipt of comments, DPG may, if considered necessary, seek further information to ensure that the grievance is dealt with in a fair and objective manner by the department or organisation and confirmation of satisfactory redress of the grievance is also sought from the complainant before closure.

To take an example, during 2015-16, 10357 grievances were received in DPG pertaining to sectors in its purview, out of which 595 cases were taken up taking the total number of taken up cases to 1372. Out of the 1372 taken up cases, 846 were disposed with 745 in favour of the complainant. Thus, approximately 88 per cent of the taken up cases were resolved. In addition, 1,782 grievances were transferred to the Department of Administrative Reforms and Public Grievances.

Grievance Redressal

The online system for grievance redress called the 'Centralized Public Grievance Redress and Monitoring System' (CPGRAMS) has been evolved since 2007.

Public grievance mechanism of PMO available on website www.pmindia.gov.in has been integrated with the pgportal.gov.in. Now, the grievances lodged to the PMO are being transferred to the Central Ministries/ Departments and State Governments and monitored through the online CPGRAMS which is part of the pg portal.

JUDICIARY

Structure, Organisation, and Functioning

'Justice should not only be done but seen to be done'.

... A popular saying.

Background

The Indian judicial system is unified and integrated, unlike the legislative and the executive which are divided between the Union and the States. As the apex court, we have the Supreme Court and the High Courts in the States. Both the Supreme Court as well as the High Courts has their own set, defined functions. The Supreme Court is the final interpreter and guardian of the constitution. It is also the guardian of the Fundamental rights. It is also the guardian of social revolution; the highest and final interpreter of general law, and the highest court of appeal in civil and criminal matters. With this exalted position comes the need for independence and safeguards. Constitution has accorded these through salaries from the Consolidated Fund away from executive execution, security of tenure, right to choose own staff, power of contempt proceedings, separation of judiciary from the executive, and no discussion on conduct of judges.

The power to issue writs for enforcement of Fundamental and other rights is a major tool to redress the wrong. Courts also have the right of judicial review. The commanding position that the judiciary holds is sine quo non for enforcing rule of law in the country.

Judiciary has 'procedure as established by law' and 'due process of law' to examine; the former signifying examination of law only from the point of view of the legislature, competence, and seeing that prescribed procedures have been followed; the latter where judiciary can examine the law itself not only from the view of competence but also the intention or motive behind the law. Public Interest Litigation or PIL, a form of judicial activism, is the tool for social transformation, a poor man's delight and a social crusader's door to delivery. Even so, courts are burdened with backlogs and workload is 'hair' splitting. A balance is needed between speed and creed.

'Justice delayed is Justice denied,

Justice hurried is Justice buried.'

Structure of Judiciary

The Constitution is the source of all authority, organisations, and functions relating to institutions created by it. India has a unified judiciary structure with the Supreme Court at the apex, High Courts below it, and subordinate courts further below; all three are separated from the executive and are independent. Courts in the country are an example of neutrality, integrity, and independence.

Article 124: Establishment and Constitution of Supreme Court:

There shall be a Supreme Court of India consisting of a Chief Justice of India and until Parliament by law prescribes a larger number, of not more than seven other judges (Now it is 30)

Article 214

There shall be a High Court for each State. (This has not been fully achieved).

Article 130: Seat of Supreme Court:

The Supreme Court shall sit in Delhi or in such other place or places, as the Chief Justice of India may, with the approval of the President, from time to time, appoint.

Article 216: Constitution of High Courts:

Every High Court shall consist of Chief Justice and such other judges as the President may from time to time deem it necessary to appoint.

Article 233 (i): Subordinate courts:

Appointment of persons to be, and the posting and promotion of, district judges in any state shall be made by the Governor of the state in consultation with the High Court exercising jurisdiction in relation to that state.

Control of High Court over subordinate judiciary is comprehensive, exclusive, and effective and it is to subserve a basic feature of the Constitution, i.e., independence of judiciary (*Parkash Singh Badal vs State of Punjab, 2007*).

The High Court has been vested with the power of superintendence of all courts and Tribunals within the state concerned.

In fact, the conference of Judges of Federal Court and Chief Justice of High Courts held in March 1948 recommended that there should be provisions in the constitution for ensuring independence of even the subordinate judiciary. The view was that so long as the subordinate judiciary, including district judges, have to depend on the provincial executive for their appointment, posting, promotion, and leave, they cannot remain free from influence of the party in power and cannot be expected to act impartially and independently in the discharge of their duties. The Drafting Committee found substance and merit in this to place them under the High Courts. It was to be a constitutional safeguard well worth its consideration.

Thus, the judiciary in the country is structured in a pattern with the Supreme Court at the apex, High Courts immediately subordinate, and District Courts and others Subordinate courts below the High Courts.

ORGANISATION

The Supreme Court, the High Courts, and the subordinate courts are all organised in a manner that they discharge their duties within a structure that ensures freedom, neutrality, and openness. For this purpose, the Constitution ensures safety and security of tenure, salary, and working conditions.

Supreme Court

Article 124(2):

Every judge of the Supreme Court shall be appointed by the President by warrant under his hand and seal after consultation with such of the judges of the Supreme Court and of the High Courts in States as the President may deem necessary for the purpose and shall hold office until he attains the age of sixty-five years:

[Provided that in the case of appointment of a judge other than the Chief Justice, the Chief Justice shall always be consulted.]

Article 124(3):

A person shall not be qualified for appointment as a judge of the Supreme Court unless he is a citizen of India and

a) Has been for at least five years a judge of a High Court or of two or more such courts in succession; or
b) Has been for at least ten years an advocate of a High Court or of two or more such courts in succession; or
c) Is in the opinion of the President, a distinguished jurist.

Article 124(4):

A judge of the Supreme Court shall not be removed from his office except by an order of the President passed after an address by each House of Parliament supported by a majority of the total membership of that House and by a majority of not less than two-thirds of the members of the House present and voting has been presented to the President in the same session for such removal on the ground of proved misbehaviour or incapacity.

Article 124(6):

Every person appointed to be a judge of the Supreme Court shall, before he enters upon his office, make and subscribe before the President, or some person appointed in that behalf by him, an oath or affirmation according to the form set out for the purpose in the Third Schedule.

Article 124(7):

No person who has held office as a judge of the Supreme Court shall plead or act in any Court of before any authority within the territory of India.

Article 125(1):

There shall be paid to the judges of Supreme Court such salaries, as may be determined by Parliament by law, and until provision in that behalf is so made, such salaries as are specified in the Second Schedule. (Salaries are paid out of Consolidated Fund of India to avoid dependence on the executive).

Article 129:

Supreme Court to be a court of record.

Article 141:

Law declared by Supreme Court to be binding on all courts.

Article 144:

Civil and judicial authorities to act in aid of the Supreme Court.

Article 145:

Rules of court subject to the provisions of any law made by Parliament, the Supreme Court may time to time, with the approval of the President, make rules for regulating generally the practice and procedure of the court.

Having covered the features of both structure and the organisation of the Supreme Court in outline, we now come to the substantial issue of functions. In both structure and organisation, the central issue is the constitutional position of the Supreme Court and the provisions, giving it the independence and freedom to stand to act. It is far removed from the executive to even remotely depend on it. Secondly, provisions give the Supreme Court the exalted position of independence so as to function in a fair, fearless manner.

Judiciary's role is not restricted to mere verdicts of right or wrong. It has a pivotal role in protecting Fundamental rights, advising the President if he chooses to be advised, acting as the arbiter, directing the executive and the legislature, decide as an appellate court, lay guidelines, look into Public Interest Litigation, and entertain writs. In extreme events, Supreme Court can issue notices for contempt in case its ruling or judgment is given a disinterested or disdainful look or a mixture of both. With a well thought structure and an organisation attuned to deliver, the Supreme Court is ideally placed to redress the balance, address the issues, and extend a worthy support to usher in a society that values equality, love, liberty, and cherishes social justice; all with rule of law and a conviction that 'truth alone' triumphs.

High Courts

High Courts are to be courts of record. Every High Court shall be a court of record and shall have all the powers of such a court including the power to punish for contempt of itself.

Appointment and conditions of the office of a judge of a High Court:

I. Every judge of a High Court shall be appointed by the President by warrant under his hand and seal after consultation with the Chief Justice of India, the Governor of the State, and, in case of appointment of a judge other than the Chief Justice of the High Court and shall hold office in the case of additional or acting Judge as provided in Article 224 and in any other case, until he attains the age of sixty two years.

II. A person shall not be qualified for appointment as a judge of a High Court unless he is a citizen of India and

(a) Has for at least ten years held a judicial office in the territory of India; or

(b) Has for at least ten years been an advocate of a High Court or of two or more such courts in succession.

Article 219:

Oath or affirmation by judges of High Courts.

Every person appointed to be a Judge of a High Court shall, before he enter upon his office, make and subscribe before the Governor of a state, or some person appointed in that behalf by him, an oath or affirmation according to the form set for the purpose in the Third Schedule.

Article 230:

Extension of jurisdiction of High Court to Union Territories.

Parliament may by law extend the jurisdiction of a High Court to or exclude the jurisdiction of a High Court from any Union territory.

FUNCTIONS AND JURISDICTION OF THE SUPREME COURT

The jurisdiction of the Supreme Court extends to:

a) Original Jurisdiction	Article 131
b) Appellate Jurisdiction	Article 132
c) Advisory Jurisdiction	Article 143
d) Writ Jurisdiction	Article 139
e) Revisory Jurisdiction	Article 137

(a) Original Jurisdiction

The original jurisdiction of the Supreme Court is purely federal in character, and it has the exclusive authority to decide any dispute involving a question of law or fact between:

a) The Government of India and any state.

b) The Government of India and any state or States on one side and one or more States on the other or

c) Between two or more States.

Exclusion

However, according to the Constitution (7th Amendment 1956) the original jurisdiction of the Supreme Court does not extend to a dispute if it arises out of any provision of a treaty, agreement, covenant, *sanad*, or other similar instrument which has entered into or executed before Jan 26th, 1950 and has been continued in operation after that or which has provisions that the said jurisdiction shall not extend to such dispute.

Supreme court's original jurisdiction barred

Article (b) 363	Bar to interference by courts in disputes arising out of certain treaties, agreements, etc.
Article (c) 262(2)	Complaints as to interference with inter-state water matters, referred to statutory tribunal mentioned Article 262(2).
Article (d) 280	Adjustment referred to the Finance Commission.
Article (e) 290	Adjustment of certain expenses between the Union and the States.
136(2) (f)	Armed Forces TribunalsTribunals.

Thus, it can be seen that the Supreme Court has original jurisdiction in all issues of law or fact, barring where there are specific enactments which provide for machinery or mechanisms or resolve disputes; example, agreements, treaties, or when statutory tribunals have been created by the constitution.

(b) Appellate Jurisdiction

Appellate jurisdiction of the Supreme Court is vast and varied; it is threefold.

(a) Constitutional. Article 136 (for special leave petition)

(b) Civil. Article133 (1)

(c) Criminal. Article 134.

Constitutional

In Constitutional matters, an appeal can go to the Supreme Court if the High Court certifies that the case involves a substantial question of law as to the interpretation of the constitution.

If the High Court refuses to give the certificate, the Supreme Court may grant 'Special Leave' (Article 136) for appeal if it is established that the case does involve such a question.

Civil Matters: Article133 (I)

Under Article 133(I), an appeal can go to the Supreme Court from any judgement, decree or final order in a civil proceedings of a High Court if it certifies:-

(a) That the case involves a substantial question of law of general importance; and

(b) That in the opinion of the High Court the said question needs to be decided by the Supreme Court.

No appeal in a civil matter lies to the Supreme Court as a matter of right; it lies only when the High Court issues a certificate on the above (a) conditions being fulfilled.

Criminal Matters: Article 134

Article 134 of the Constitution provides for the following provisions as to appeal in criminal matters.

(a) Article 134(I) of the constitutional provides for the following provisions as to appeal in criminal matters.

  (i) An appeal lies from any judgement, final order, or sentence of a High Court in a criminal proceeding if the High Court on appeal, reversed an order of acquittal of an accused person and sentenced him to death; or

  (ii) If the High Court has withdrawn for trial before itself, a case from lower court and in such a trial sentenced the accused to death; or

  (iii) If the High Court certifies that the case is fit for appeal to the Supreme Court.

  (iv) If the High Courts has on appeal reversed an order of acquittal for life or for a period not less than 10 years [as per Supreme Court (Enlargement of Criminal Appellate Jurisdiction, 1970 authorisation Supreme Court to hear appeals)].

  (v) The High Courts after withdrawal of a case from a Lower Court has sentenced the accused to imprisonment for life or for a period of not less than 10 years (as per 1970 enactment quoted at (iv) above).

(b) Article 134(2): Parliament may by law, confer on the Supreme Court any further powers to entertain and hear appeals from any judgement, final order, or sentence in a criminal proceeding of a High Court in the territory of India subject to such conditions and limitations as may be specified in such law.

(c) Advisory Jurisdiction

Article 143:

Article 143 provides for the President the power to consult Supreme Court for opinion.

(I) 'If at any time it appears to the President that a question of law or fact has arisen, or is likely to arise, which is of such nature and of such public importance that it is expedient to obtain the opinion of the Supreme Court upon it, he may refer the question to that court for consideration and the court, may, after such hearing as it thinks fit, report to the President its opinion thereon. It is not binding on the Supreme Court to give its opinion.

(II) The President may refer a dispute to the Supreme Court for opinion and the Supreme Court shall, after such hearing as it thinks fit, report to the President its opinion thereon.

So far, the Presidents have referred many questions, disputes to the Supreme Court for opinion. Further, the President is empowered to refer to the Supreme Court for its opinion, disputes arising out of any treaty entered into or executed before the commencement of the constitution. In such cases, it is obligatory for the court, under the Indian constitution, to give its opinion.

PRESIDENTIAL REFERENCES FOR OPINION OF SUPREME COURT (ARTICLE 143)

1. Delhi Laws Act 1951.
2. Kerala Education Bill 1958.
3. *Berubari Union case*. 1960.
4. Sea Customs Act 1963.
5. *Keshar Singh* case
   (Relating to the privileges of the legislature 1964).
6. President Election 1974.
7. Spl. Courts Bill in 1978.
8. J & K Resettlement Act 1982.
9. Cauvery Water Disputes Tribunal in 1992.
10. Ram Janmabhoomi Case 1993.
11. Consultative Process to be adopted by Chief Justice of India 1998.
12. Legislative competence of Centre-States on the subject of natural gas liquefied natural gas. 2001.
13. Constitutional Validity of the Election Commission decision on deferring the Gujarat elections. 2002.
14. Punjab termination of Agreements Act. 2004.
15. 2G Spectrum Case verdict and the mandatory auctioning of natural resources across all sectors. 2012.

The Supreme Court may give its opinion or deny; the President may accept that opinion or decline, it is well within their rights. The whole purpose is to extend the benefit of considered opinion. Only in the case, popularly known as the Babri Masjid case, the Supreme Court wanted to know from the government if its advice would be considered for acceptance, the government was non-committal and the exalted court, in a huff, closed the case shut. It was a case of what might have been; a path that was not traversed, a destination never reached.

(d) Writ Jurisdiction Article 32:

Article 32 confers jurisdiction on the Supreme Court to enforce Fundamental rights. Under Article 32, every individual has a right to move the Supreme Court directly by appropriate proceedings for the enforcement of their Fundamental rights. Without coming through a High Court, an individual can directly come to the Supreme Court. This gives an impression to writs as if they form part of original jurisdiction of Supreme Court; as original jurisdiction relates to federal issues, not individual freedoms. Supreme Court is empowered to issue writs of:

(a) *Habeas Corpus:* Produce the body
(b) *Mandamus:* Command issued to perform duty
(c) *Prohibition:* Higher court to lower court/tribunal to forbid exceeding jurisdiction
(d) *Certiorari:* To be certified, to be informed; by higher court to lower
(e) *Quo Warrants:* By what authority or warrant a public official is holding office. Writs can be used only against public officials.
(f) *Revisory Jurisdiction:* Under Article 147, the Supreme Court can revise its own judgement, order or direction.

All these, alone or in combination are used for protection of Fundamental Rights. This article (Art 32) is indeed a safety valve, used in hundreds of cases; even in emergencies. The Article has given lot of meaning and substance to individuals under oppression or suppression. High Courts, under Article 226, has similar provisions for usage of writs. There however, exists a significant difference between Article 32 with the Supreme Court and Article 226 with the High Courts. The jurisdiction to issue writs under Article 226 with High Courts is much larger that with the Supreme Court's under Article 32. Whereas Supreme Court can use Article 32 to issue writs for infringement of Fundamental rights only, the High Court can, under Article 226, issue writs for infringement of Fundamental rights but also ordinary legal rights. By this, the burden on Supreme Court is reduced substantially.

(e) Revisory Jurisdiction

High court exercises supervisory aka Revisory jurisdiction over trial courts of the state under article 227 of the Constitution.

Sometimes it happens that the Subordinate Courts exceed the jurisdiction vested in them; and go beyond their jurisdiction. Sometimes there occurs a gross irregularity in the working of the Subordinate Courts due to various reasons.

Whenever this comes to the notice of the High Court; then in both such cases the High Court can make any orders as it may seem fit.

This is the Revisory Jurisdiction of the High Court

The Supreme Court under Article 137 is empowered to review an judgment or order made by it with a view to remove any mistake or error that might have crept in the judgment or orders. This means that even though all the judgments and order passed by Supreme Court are binding an all courts of India, they are not binding on the Supreme Court.

INDEPENDENCE OF JUDICIARY

The Constitution has provisions to safeguard the judiciary in its functioning. The legislature and the executive, in their functions often outreach to come into confrontation with the judiciary. The judiciary too spreads its wings to create a flutter among the legislature and executive. The sixties and seventies saw the legislature and the judiciary issue challenges in Golaknath, Kesavananda Bharati cases over jurisdiction in Fundamental rights; issue was laid to rest with the amorphous doctrine of 'Basic Structure', a compromise of sorts, a conviction of mutual respect.

Article	Issue
Article 124 (4).	Security of tenure. Judges cannot be removed from service except by Parliament (2/3rds majority)
Article 125.	Fixed salaries, can't be varied or changed. Salaries charged to Consolidated Fund of India.
Article 135.	No curtailment of jurisdiction.
Article 50.	Separation of judiciary from the executive.
Article 146.	Freedom to appoint own staff.
Article 129.	Right to punish for contempt.
Article 124(7).	Judges prohibited from practice after retirement.
Article 142.	Enforcement of decrees and orders of Supreme Court and orders as to discovery etc.
Article 139 (A).	Supreme Court has been conferred with power to direct transfer of any civil or criminal case from one state to another high court.
Article 32, 136	Power of judicial review, writs, and Special Leave Petition are available.

SUPREMACY OF THE SUPREME COURT

Whatever is said by the Supreme Court turns into the law of the land. The guidelines for establishing blood banks came about. The Government has implemented the guidelines issued in relation to assaults on women in public places and also to control the students' indiscipline in colleges. But there is one important deviation, which relates to the Uniform Civil Code.

The Government has, contrary to the guideline,, enacted legislation which provides for maintenance of divorced Muslim women, if not by the husband, then by parents and relatives of the husband and also by Wakf Board.

Articles 124 to 147

A Narrative

The Supreme Court in India is the highest court in this land since the commencement of the Constitution. Before that, it was the Federal Court which was said to be the highest. Even earlier, the House of Lords in London called the Privy Council was the highest court.

The Supreme Court has original jurisdiction regarding all matters relating to the disputes between and among States, and has the appellate jurisdiction in civil and criminal matters and also such jurisdiction under what is called special leave procedure. The Supreme Court is also the appellate court over Central Industrial Tribunal and National Consumer Court. The jurisdiction which is exercisable by the Supreme Court under Article 32 read with Article 142 and the High Court under Article 226 is called Judicial Review. Under this, any person interested in any matter involving Fundamental rights and who is bona fide and who has no other expeditious, efficacious, or alternative remedy may approach the Supreme Court and the High Court either for redressal of the infringement of the Fundamental rights or to prevent their invasion. Public Interest Litigation (i.e., direct approach to the Supreme Court and the High Courts without the observance of the formalities and procedures in filing a petition) has allowed each and every citizen to approach directly by sending a mere letter to the Chief Justice or any other judge. If directed by the judge the office can number it as a regular petition and post the matter for hearing before the court. There are a few cases in which Judicial Review is barred. Article 136(2) (bar of interference in matters arising out of any Court or Tribunal relating to armed forces); and Article 227(4) (bar of interference in matters arising out of any court or tribunal relating to armed forces); Article 242(2) (disputes relating to waters of inter-States rivers); Article 243(0) (bar of interference in elections); Article 253(2) (bar of interference in the elections to panchayats and Municipalities); Article 329 (a) (bar of interference in election matters of parliament and Assemblies) are all held to be valid on the ground that they are relevant to achieve some specified purposes.

> The Special Leave Procedure has two aspects. Firstly the High Court, if it is satisfied that it is a fit case for appeal to Supreme Court, may directly permit the party to approach the Supreme Court in appeal. If the High Court refuses to grant such leave, the Supreme Court itself can grant leave to appeal notwithstanding the refusal of the High Court to certify the case as fit for appeal to Supreme Court.

The second angle is that the Supreme Court may directly grant leave to appeal against any final order of the High Court or any Court or Tribunal.

The judgements and orders of the Supreme Court are binding on all the Courts and authorities as well as all citizens throughout India. It can be said the law laid down by the Supreme Court shall be treated as the law of the land.

The appointment, transfer of Judges of the High Courts, and the appointment of the Judges of the Supreme Court has been a tricky question. The several procedures suggested like the Constitution of a collegium of Judges and the consultation with the Chief Justice of Supreme Court and the Chief Judge of the High Court have not proved to be foolproof. Till a special independent commission is constituted to recommend selection and transfer of Judges, the doubts about the propriety of their appointment and the transfer are likely to continue.

The Supreme Court is also the Court of Records. It means, it stores and preserves the essential records in each and every case. The suit/petition/appeal and the counters and the text of judgement are preserved. High Courts are, it is interesting to know, also Courts of Record and so also are all District Courts. The Court of Record word suggests that it is a Central Court and a permanent institution symbolic of its jurisdiction and powers. Therefore, every Court of Record has a power to punish any person for contempt. The Court of Record can be moved by any person and can also take up suo motu the issue of contempt occurring within its jurisdiction or in its presence or of any act done in violation of the orders of the Court. The punishment prescribed for contempt is six months imprisonment and/or imposition of fine which is limitless, or warning. Recently the Supreme Court punished one advocate by removing him from the rolls of the Bar Council. It is of interest, to know that to punish a person for contempt in any manner other than imprisonment, fine or warning, is not permissible, but the Supreme Court claims such power for debarring an advocate from practice under its jurisdiction available to it under Article 142.

The Supreme Court has power to review its own orders, but in one case it reviewed the orders made in another case by another Bench (while disposing of the case which was different from the case under review).

OTHER LEGAL MATTERS

Articles 214 to 232

A Narrative

One hears of one Governor for two or more States, but there can also be a High Court for more than one State and there can also be different High Court Benches in different areas of the State; Punjab and Haryana High Court is for the State of Punjab and also for the State of Haryana; Nagpur and Goa Benches of the Bombay High Court; so also the Bench of the Madras High Court at Madurai are the Benches of the High Court functioning within one State. While the common High Court for two States functions as an independent body, each State High Court's Benches which are within the State are mere branches of the same High Court.

The Chief Justice of the High Court can be called the administrative head of the work performed by the High Court. He constitutes Benches and allots workload. Any other judge or Bench of judges is not competent to tell the Registrar to post a particular case before him/them. Neither he has power to transfer the case pending before him to another judge, nor is he competent to transfer any case pending before any judge to himself or to any other judge. The Chief Justice can stay further hearing or transfer the case pending before any judge to himself or to any other judge. Unless the work is allotted, a judge suo motu cannot take up and dispose of any case. That is the reason why PILs through letters addressed to the judge are processed through office with the sanction of the Chief Justice.

The Chief Justice and other judges of the High Court are appointed by none other than the President. In appointing the Chief Justice of the High Court the President shall consult the Chief Justice of the Supreme Court and while appointing the other judges of the High Court the President shall consult the Chief Justice and some other judges of the concerned States also. The President can also transfer judges from one High Court to be a judge of another High Court. But the President shall consult the Chief Justice of all the High Courts concerned, i.e., the Court from which the judge is supposed to be transferred and the Chief Justice of the High Court to which the judge is supposed to be transferred. If the Chief Justice of a High Court is for any reason not able to function as Chief Justice for any reason, like, of his being appointed as Governor, the President may appoint any other judge of the High Court to function as Chief Justice. Similarly, if any judge is not able to function for any reason, say, that of his being appointed as in charge Chief Justice, the President may appoint any person qualified to be a High Court judge. The President can even appoint additional judges when necessary for a period of two years by increasing temporarily the strength of the High Court. Where services of any ad hoc judge becomes necessary, the Chief Justice of High Court can appoint with the consent of the President, a person who is a judge retired from the same High Court or any other High Court to enable him to clear the arrears of pending cases. No private individual or any other person, even the one who is qualified to be appointed as a judge can be appointed to post of ad hoc judge. A retired District judge or the judge Advocate of the Court Marshal cannot also be appointed as ad hoc judges.

The permanent High Court judge after retirement, is prohibited from practising as an advocate within the State in which he is a permanent judge, or before any court or authority within the jurisdiction of that High Court, but he can practise in the Supreme Court or in any other High Courts or authorities subordinate to them. But a person who remitted his office before he was made permanent judge can practise in such court or in any other court of tribunal in India including the Supreme Court.

The jurisdiction of the High Court under Articles 226 and 227 is known as judicial review just as a jurisdiction of Supreme Court under Article 32 read with Article 142 is called Judicial Review of the Supreme Court.

The jurisdiction under judicial review can be said to have no limits. Apart from entering the orders of administrative, executive, and judicial domains, judicial review can see any and every matter which affects the rights of citizens. In the case of human rights, the power of judicial review also covers the protection of the rights of the foreigners also. In particular, the judicial review empowers the High Court to issue writ of certiorari the issue of mandamus (i.e., the issue of injunctions both mandatory and prohibitory); writ of quo warranto (i.e., an order to the respondent to prove the authority under which he is performing his duties); and the writ of habeas corpus (i.e., production of the person whose whereabouts are not known). In case of certiorari, it has to be discussed as to how the impugned order is ultra vires. In the case of mandamus, it has to be explained fully as to how the applicant is entitled to injunction; in the case of quo warranto it has to be explained always as to how the authority alleged to occupy a public office is not entitled to hold that post. In the case of habeas corpus, it has to be always explained as to how the detention is illegal. It may be noted in this context that the contents of the application must conform to the prayers. Compulsorily, the applicant in all these cases has to declare that he has exhausted all the remedies, and that the remedy sought for is the only alternative and efficacious remedy, and that he is not simultaneously seeking relief in any other forum also. The applicant must be bona fide.

Articles 233 to 237

A Narrative

Subordinate Courts, it must be noted, include two classes of Courts. The District Courts presided by District Judges shall include Additional as well as Assistant District Judges and Session Judges.

These persons occupying the posts are selected and appointed directly by the High Court. The other class of courts are lower that of the District judge, i.e., the court of subordinate Judge, civil judge, and the court of magistrate. The persons occupying these posts are appointed by the government with the prior concurrence of the High Court. The disciplinary jurisdiction for all these officers resides with the High Court. Only after the High Court concludes enquiry and awards punishments, the governments makes appropriate orders. Regarding all other staff of the subordinate courts, it is the district judge who is both the appointing authority as well as the disciplinary authority. This scheme has been put into practice to protect the independence of judiciary. Separation of magistrates from the control of the District Collectors and making them subordinate to the District Court and the High Court is done for the purpose of preserving the independence of magistrates from the control of the District Collectors and police.

If a judicial officer is arrested, the fact should be notified at once to the District Judge concerned and the High Court. The police is not allowed keep him in police station. The police also can't record any statements from him and any *panchanama* can't be held except before another judicial officer of equal rank. The arrested judicial officers shall never be handcuffed nor shall he be produced before the public.

Articles 323-A and 323-B

A Narrative

As pendency of cases has reached massive proportions and also non-availability of the judges is a big problem and also with government being dragged to Court in all service matters, it is being echoed that separate tribunals may be constituted for all cases of grievances of the government employee. The difference between the trial before the tribunal and the trial before the Court is extremely wide. The Courts follow the detailed procedure and the tribunals follow a summary procedure. Both follow the principles of natural justice. Hence, while the Court follows scrupulously every step in the trial of suits, the tribunal is required to follow the principles of natural justice only. As a result, the latter follow procedure as would satisfy the requirements of natural justice. To supplement this power with the power to enforce attendance of witnesses and production of documents, the tribunals are normally invested with powers available under CPC. For shortening appeals and revisions, the orders of the tribunals are subjected to one appeal only to the Supreme Court, that too, under special leave jurisdiction.

The tribunals are armed with jurisdiction to punish any person or authority for violating the orders of the tribunals or failing to implement their orders. The power of the tribunal to punish persons for contempt is preserved. Once the matter falls within the jurisdiction of the tribunal, all such matters pending anywhere in India including Supreme Court stands transferred to the Tribunal and no Court in India is competent to entertain any suit. But this does not prevent the High Court and the Supreme Court to act under the Articles 226 and 227 and under Article 32 which in relation to jurisdiction is called judicial review. Under Article 323-B, the parliament and state legislatures can set up separate tribunals to deal with matters specified in that Article. All the rules relating to the jurisdiction of the tribunals will apply to tribunals constituted on those matters. In industrial tribunals and consumer tribunals, direct appeals also go to the Supreme Court.

Article 372

This Article lends the legal system in India a sense of continuity. It enunciates that all the laws existing as on the date and all the courts functioning as on the date will continue to be in force and function without any change. The expression 'laws in force' encompasses not only all the statutes, regulations, and rules, but also all that common laws including the personal laws of the different communities as well as all the accepted jurisprudential principles. What the President can do during the period of three years from the commencement of the Constitution is adaptation or modifications in the laws. That is, the President can change the names of the statutes and their application to the new situations. For any substantial matters (other than these formal modifications which are merely consequential, are required to be made), it is only the Parliament which can do so.

NJAC (NATIONAL JUDICIAL APPOINTMENTS COMMISSION)

The debate around the National Judicial Appointments Commission (NJAC) has often been emotive rather than dispassionate, with the discourse ranging from senior lawyer Ram Jethmalani calling it an "evil absurdity" to former attorney general Mukul Rohatgi pointing to judges who habitually turned up late in court as a reason to ditch the existing collegium system to select judges. The recent case of Calcutta High Court Judge Justice Karnan case who had been issued with an warrant from the Supreme Court is also a case in point.

The more complex reality is that this is easily one of the most difficult tasks the Supreme Court has faced in recent years. While the legal fraternity continues to be sharply divided over the matter of how to select the nation's senior judges, the SC's eventual decision will be a landmark, whatever it is.

Here's an easy guide to the issue:

What is the NJAC?

- The NJAC proposes to make the appointment of High Court and Supreme Court judges and Chief Justices more transparent. They will be selected by the commission, whose members will be drawn from the judiciary, legislative, and civil society.

How were judges appointed before?

- Until the NJAC came along, Articles 124 and 217 of the Constitution dealt with the appointment of judges of the higher judiciary.
- These Articles specifically said that judges would be appointed by the President of India after "consultation" with the Chief Justice of India (CJI) and other judges.
- The word "consultation" is significant, because in 1993, in the so-called Second Judges case, the SC decided that the CJI must agree to all judicial appointments–a concept known as "concurrence".
- This created the collegium system, wherein the three senior most Supreme Court judges decided on who would be a High Court or Supreme Court judge.

What will the NJAC do?

- It will replace the collegium.
- With the NJAC amendment, Articles 124 A, B, and C were added to the Constitution to make the NJAC valid.

- Articles 124 A and B define the NJAC, its members and their duties, while Article 124 C empowers Parliament to make laws in the future to regulate the procedure for the appointment of judges.

Who will be on the NJAC?

- The CJI will be chairperson
- The next two senior most Supreme Court judges
- The Law and Justice Minister; and
- Two eminent persons, to be selected by a committee comprising the CJI, Prime Minister, and Leader of the Opposition

Why is it not in action yet?

- The NJAC Bill 2014 that established the NJAC was introduced and passed by both Houses of Parliament with the Constitutional (99th Amendment) Bill 2014 in August 2015. The President gave his assent to the bill on 31 December 2014 and the Act was notified by the government on 13 April, 2015. However, by then the Act had been challenged in various public interest litigations in the Supreme Court.
- The NJAC hasn't yet taken up its mandate. The then CJI H.L. Dattu wrote to the Prime Minister on 25 April 2015, "I have to say that it is neither appropriate nor desirable to attend the meeting or be part of the NJAC till the Supreme Court decides its validity."
- On 15 July, 2015, both sides completed arguments in the NJAC matter and the Supreme Court has been working on writing its judgement since then.

The validity of Article 124 A, which basically did away with the collegium, replacing it with the NJAC, is the crux of the matter before the Supreme Court.

Arguments for validity of Article 124:

- The NJAC amended the Constitution, so the Second Judges Case that created the collegium is irrelevant because the Constitution is now different from what it was back then.
- The so-called "basic structure of the Constitution", whose primacy has been upheld by several SC judgements because it safeguards the separation of powers and the independence of the judiciary from the executive, remains intact under the NJAC, as the NJAC's chairperson is the CJI, who has an important role to play.
- Furthermore, the NJAC is good for democracy (which is also a basic feature of the Constitution) and requires that no organ of the State, including the judiciary, enjoys absolute freedom.
- Former Attorney General Mukul Rohatgi argued that to retain "public confidence", judicial appointments "must be seen both in the context of independence of the judiciary as also the need for checks and balances on it".

Arguments against validity of Article 124 A:

- The counter-argument is that Parliament made an unconstitutional amendment by introducing Article 124 A. In the second judges case a nine-judge bench laid down the primacy of the CJI as part of the basic structure of the Constitution and the 99th Amendment Act cannot simply violate this now.

Arguments for NJAC:

- Conventions are only a supplementary system of enforcement of the basic structure of the Constitution. Changing the convention of the collegium system does not change the basic structure if the independence of the judiciary is maintained.

Against NJAC:

a. The Second Judges Case decision gave the CJI the main power in appointments to ensure the independence of the judiciary, which has now become part of the basic structure of the Constitution.

b. Applying the English law doctrine of convention, the collegium system has already developed into a Constitutional convention and should not be tampered with.

In a landmark judgment, a seven member Constitutional Bench led by Justice Khehar rescinded the NJAC Bill in October 2015. It was unforeseen in the Indian judiciary when an amendment to Constitution under Article 368 and properly seconded by more than half of the state legislatures, even inked by the President, was invoked by the SC. For the present, the Collegium system continues with some consensus developing between the Executive and the Supreme Court on the matter of Memorandum of Procedure–a new method of filtering the names sent to the executive by the Collegium.

PRESSURE GROUPS

Pressure Groups: Formal or Informal Associations

As a term, 'pressure group' means a section of the public organised and active in the pursuit of some special interest, which its members are keen to promote. These groups bring pressure upon the Legislative and Executive to implement their demands. A pressure group seeks to influence governmental decisions without attempting to place its members in formal governmental capacities. Pressure groups are different from political parties in that they do not contest elections to capture political power. Pressure groups (or interest groups) are private associations formed to influence public policy.

The pressure groups provide a liaison between the people whom they represent and the administration. They act as a channel of communication through which the administration can inform the people of its policies and programmes and get a feedback on them as well. The groups keep their members informed of the rules and regulations of the government. Owing to their expertise, economic strength, and influence, they can also advise the government on matters like the extent of desirable regulation to be carried out. Pressure groups, however, become a problem when they represent narrow parochial interests and are intolerant of other interests. Then, not only are there unnecessary debates and violent clashes, but the interests of the society at large are also compromised.

The means used by pressure groups may be legitimate or illegitimate. Legitimate means include lobbying, electioneering, publicity and propaganda, petitions, public debates, and correspondence. Illegitimate methods include violence and corrupt practices–such as bribery to secure official favours. Strikes too are a means used by pressure groups, which may not always be legitimate.

The pressure groups that are most easily identified are those with formal organisations, such as labour unions, farm associations, and business and professional groups. This is a general case everywhere as also in India. In India, however, informal unorganised groups often play an important part in political decision-making too. Among these unorganised groups–variously labelled 'latent', 'potential', or 'non-associational' are cultural and ethnic groups, socio-economic classes, occupational groups with or without formal structures (peasants, workers, industrial managers, students, etc.), and such broad social categories as consumers. Informal groups seldom have political influence comparable to organised groups which have money, members and organisations to support their claims. Nevertheless, policy-makers, recognising the potential organisational and electoral strength of these informal groups, are likely to consider their interests even though they lack formal organisations and means of expression.

Pressure Groups in India

In India, each pressure group organises itself keeping in view certain interests. As resources are scarce, there are claims and counter-claims on these resources from different and competing sections of the society emerging as a pressure group. Pressure groups use party platforms to seek fulfilment of their interests. In India, pressure groups initially influenced negatively like preventing nationalisation of rice trade, increase in land tax, etc. But increasingly, pressure groups have come to have positive influence; they assist the government in forming rules. For example, the wheat policy of government framed in March 1974 was the outcome of positive efforts and support of the All-India Foodgrain Dealers Association.

In India, political parties always try to organise their own interest groups in various trades, professions, and industries. For example, the Congress Party has a Youth Congress, the Communist Party has a Student Federation of India, Rashtriya Swayamsewak Sangh (RSS) has the Akhil Bharatiya Vidhyarti Parishad , etc. Several Indian pressure groups have been formed for promoting the interests of certain castes and religious groups.

Pressure groups are temporary in nature which keep emerging and dissolving themselves after some time. Pressure groups in India function in a multi-party system environment, hence they try to maintain relations with all parties. They use both modern and traditional means. Modern methods adopted are lobbying, funding political parties, introducing a favourable person in the legislature and executive, etc. whereas, cultivating connections with bureaucratic officials, traditional loyalties, caste loyalties, religious loyalties, etc. were traditional methods.

Americans typically think of legislative lobbying as the major political activity of interest groups. However, lobbying represents only the tip of the iceberg of interest groups activities in

American politics. In Britain and France, the business and farm interests have close informal links with political parties. In the same manner, several of the major associations have close ties with political parties in India too. For example, Bhartiya Kisan Union, All India Trade Union Congress, Hind Mazdoor Parishad, etc., are among some of the most powerful in India, with interest in a broad spectrum of political issues. It should be emphasised that they are not the only important and powerful groups. Smaller groups with narrow interests to defend are often very influential in the shaping of policies that affect them.

Types of Pressure Groups in India

Following are some of the leading pressure groups in India:

Labour groups include (i) All India Trade Union Congress (AITUC)-CPI influenced, (ii) Indian National Trade Union Congress (INTUC)-affiliated to Congress (I), (iii) Hind Mazdoor Sabha-socialist influenced, (iv) United Trade Union Congress-CPI (Marxist Lenin), and (v) Hind Mazdoor Parishad-BJP influenced.

Business groups include (i) Federation of the Indian Chambers of Commerce and Industry (FICCI), (iii) Associated Chambers of Commerce (ASSOCHAM), (iv) All India Manufacturers' Organisation (AIMO), and (iv) Federation of All India Foodgrains Dealers Associations (FAIFDA).

Professional associations include (i) Bar Council of India, (ii) Indian Federation of Working Journalists, (iii) Indian Medical Association, and various others.

Agrarian groups include (i) All India Kisan Sammelan, (ii) All India Kisan Sabha–oldest and largest, (iii) Hind Kisan Panchayat, (iv) United Kisan Sabha, (v) Revolutionary Peasants Convention, (vi) Bharatiya Kisan Union, (vii) R.V. Sangham in Tamil Nadu, and (viii) Shetkari Sanghatana in Maharashtra.

Besides these, there are **cultural/religious organisations,** such as the Rashtriya Swayam Sevak Sangh, Vishwa Hindu Parishad, All India Conference of Indian Christians, Jamaat-e-Islami, Parsi Central Association; linguistic associations, such as Tamil Sangam, Hindi Sahitya Sammelan, Anjuman Taraqqi-i-Urdu; and ideology-based groups such as those fighting for environmental protection, civil rights, women's rights, etc.

There are also what are known **as anomic pressure groups**. When interest groups get alienated from the political system, they support a more or less spontaneous breakthrough into the political system in the form of riots, demonstrations, even assassinations. India is home to some such pressure groups–the Naxalites, the Jammu and Kashmir Liberation Front, All Assam Students' Union, and Dal Khalsa, to name a few.

Critical Analysis of Role of Pressure Groups in a Democracy

In democratic regimes, the power of interest groups raises important questions. When elected bodies pass broadly defined policies, and then bureaucrats and interest groups interpret and apply them; certain important policy-making powers are in the hands of not elected officials accountable to the voters, but anonymous group leaders and unaccountable bureaucrats. This situation often leads to the regulation of society and the economy by the very groups supposed to be the objects of regulation.

A second problem here is that much group activity takes place behind closed doors. Secret meetings facilitate negotiations and compromises between interest groups and government. Informal contacts between group spokesmen and government officials are not exposed to the public eye. Obviously, such secrecy is detrimental to democratic control by the public, since it is difficult or impossible for the voter to attribute to any individual or group the details of policies worked out in secret sessions.

A third problem is that, in India, some sections of the society are unable to participate in this process on an equal footing. The advantage lies with established and well-organised groups. Those elements of society that for a variety of reasons find it difficult to organise–the poor, ethnic minorities, the elderly, the young, consumers–find access to the decision-making process difficult or impossible. Access for such unorganised sections of society usually comes through public participants (generally bureaucrats) who have strong personal and professional links with the organised groups.

Finally, there is a question of the accuracy with which the spokesmen for pressure groups reflect the attitudes of their members. It is often alleged, and correctly, that union leaders do not accurately convey the political feelings of their members, and that employers' associations do not quite know the attitude of those they represent on any given issue.

Ultimately, pressure groups are likely to continue to be prominent participants in a much better fashion and in an organised manner in the democratic political process of India. Government in India needs the information pressure groups provide and their cooperation; and citizens here appear to believe that their government ought to consult groups affected by public policies. Group involvement in politics may also be seen as increasing the representative character and responsiveness of government by supplementing individual representation by legislators with the functional representation of specific interests by groups. Given the low levels of individual participation, group politics may be a means of making democracy work despite the inactivity of the masses. In the sense, pressure groups in India will serve as substitutes for individual participation

CONSTITUTIONAL BAR AS TO THE JURISDICTION OF COURTS		
(1)	Courts are barred to enquire into what advice the Ministry has tendered to the President	Art. 74
(2)	Authentication of the order made by President cannot be questioned in court	Art. 77
(3)	Validity of any action taking place in the Parliament cannot be questioned in any court and no officer of the Parliament including marshals is answerable to the court	Art. 122
(4)	No court can entertain any matter in which the Supreme Court is invested with special jurisdiction such as inter-state disputes and inter-state sharing of river waters etc.	Art. 131
(5)	Governor's order for dissolution of Assembly cannot be questioned in any court	Art. 163
(6)	Legislators are immune from the court's jurisdiction both in respect of actions done by them and the speeches delivered by them within the precincts of the Parliament/Legislatures	Art. 194 & Art. 361-A
(7)	Bar of jurisdiction of courts in election matters	Art. 343(O) & Art. 329
(8)	Bar of court's jurisdiction as regards claims arising out of breaches to fundamental rights during emergency	Art. 359
(9)	Courts cannot add or delete any community, such as Scheduled Castes, Scheduled Tribes, Backward Classes from the list published by the President	Art. 341 & Art. 342
(10)	President and Governors are not answerable to the court for anything done in exercise of their powers	Art. 361
(11)	Courts are barred from enquiring into the treaties entered into with the	Art. 363

High Court (Articles 221-235)

Article 221: Judges of each High Court shall be paid salaries as may be determined by the Parliament by law

Article 222: Transfer a Judge from one High Court to another; 99th amendment, 2014 is relevant

Article 225: Jurisdiction of existing High Courts would be the same as before the Constitution

Article 226: Power of High Courts to issue writs

Article 227: Power of superintendence over all courts by High Courts

Article 228: Transfer of certain cases to High Court

Article 229: Officers and servants and expenses of High Court

Article 230: Extension of jurisdiction of High Courts to Union Territories

Article 231: Establishment of a common High Court for two or more States

Article 233: Appointment of district judges

Article 235: Control over subordinate courts

S R Bommai Case : A Landmark Judgement

The *S R Bommai Vs Union of India* (1994) was a landmark judgement of the Supreme Court of India where the court addressed itself to the emergent issues relating to Art 356; its use and misuse.

Article 356 deals with the imposition of President's rule over a state with the administration being conducted by the Governor of the State. Always a thorny issue between the Centre and the States, the usage of the Article led many to decry its inclusion in the constitution.

Dr. Ambedkar said in the Constituent Assembly, 'I share the sentiments that such Article, will never be called into operation and they would remain a dead letter'. In actuality, the article saw rampant misuse to further political ends.

What was worse was that the trial of strength became a contest of sorts to woo the elected representatives. This naturally led to uncertainties and shady deals bringing the image of politicians down in the eyes of the people.

An end had to be put to the practice of parading and presenting of MLAs.

S R Bommai case judgement settled the issue once and for all. It ruled that the proper place for trial of strength is the floor of the house and voting should prevail.

Elected representatives may be taken to resorts but the last resort is the "floor test".

Did you know?

Indian constitution is built on the concept of 'Separation of Functions', not powers; all three wings; namely the Executive, the Legislature and the Judiciary are held in a fine balance of checks and balances. Now and then aberrations do take place with one wing zealously committing itself to excessive pitching; the Executive eclipsing the Legislature during the Emergency (1975-1977). Earlier, the legislature tried to pin the judiciary down with settlement coming through a truce in *Keshavananda Bharti Case (1973)*.

What is seen as 'Judicial Activism' is in fact a mode and a measure by the Judiciary to proactively step in to hold balance with a pre-emptive check. Beginning with the novel idea of 'Public Interest Litigation', the judiciary has moved to the noble idea of 'judicial activism' to address itself to rendering justice in socio-economic issues. The incontrovertible logic and reason is that the judiciary has to protect the rights of all; notably the weak and the downtrodden; if it didn't act, the balance of burden would increase to shift to it later. Take the case of 'sexual harassment of women at workplace'; the Supreme Court was compelled to lay down the guidelines in the *Vishaka case* (1978) after years of intransigence by the executive. In *Sunil Batra Vs Delhi Administration*, the Supreme Court judges actually visited the jails to see the conditions for themselves. In the field of environment protection, the Supreme Court has stepped in to bring both sanity and sensitivity; be it the Taj case or pollution of rivers or employment of children in hazardous industries. Cases of human dignity and rights have also seen the apex court come down heavily to protect the persecuted; the bonded labour or fake encounter cases show that.

Constitution of India

Model questions with answers

Q. Compare and contrast India's Preamble with that of USA and South Africa.

A. Each of the Preambles starts with 'we the people.' It means that the source of all authority to govern rests with the people of the country. All three Preambles contain the idea of justice. However, in the US Constitution, there is a statement for the formation of a Union. The South African Preamble makes a reference to the past, citing misery, and honouring those who suffered injustice. The South African Preamble asks to have an elected government. It also makes a reference to God, seeking blessings for the people. The Indian and US Preamble suggest citizens have freedom to follow any religion. Both the countries have no official religion.

Q. What is the purpose of India's Preamble?

A. The Preamble is the 'identity card of the Constitution,' according to well-known jurist Nani Palkiwala. Based on the "Objectives Resolution" of Jawaharlal Nehru, it is also said to be the preface of the Constitution.

- Begins with "We the people of India," meaning the Constitution is made by the people
- States the objectives and principles on which the Constitution establishes laws.
- Serves as a beacon for judiciary, for interpretation.
- Serves as a 'statement of purpose' for citizens of the country.
- Preamble is a telescope through which people view the government.

Q. What were the historical forces that led to the making of the Indian Constitution?

A. Many historical forces shaped the vision of a Constitution for India.

The French Revolution inspired the idea of liberty, and the American Revolution gave equality. The 1917 revolution in Russia ingrained social and economic equality.

Constitutions already 100 years old had made progress, after teething problems. The Indian Constitution took lessons from them when the country yearned for freedom and sovereignty.

Q. What are Constitutional conventions? How far are they found in our Constitution?

A. Constitutional conventions are unwritten practices which are not 'law' or 'legal rules.' They are more relevant for unwritten Constitutions. But India has Constitutional conventions, being brought into practice sometimes. For example, if a Prime Minister resigns and it is not clear which party enjoys majority, the President has to see whether a coalition can be formed or elections be ordered. Following Constitutional conventions, the President in 1979 invited Charan Singh to form the government.

Constitutional conventions give power to change policies, according to circumstances. But a caretaker government formed under such circumstances. can't take major financial decisions.

Q. What role did women play in the making of the Constitution?

A. In the newly formed Constituent Assembly of 1946, there were 299 members, of which 15 were women, who had significant role in drafting of India's Constitution. Among them were women freedom fighters, reformists, lawyers and suffragettes. There were many women who had gone to jail during the Dandi march.

Famous names included Sarjoini Naidu, Durgabai Deshmukh, Rajkumari Amrit Kaur, Vijayalakshmi Pandit, and Renuka Ray.

Hansa Jivraj Mehta played a role in abolition of *devadasi* system. She also fought for uniform civil code, incorporated under Directive Principles of State Policy.

Dakshayani Velayudhan was the only woman Dalit member. She fought to remove untouchability.

Sucheta Kriplani led the assembly by singing *Vande Mataram.*

Q. In some countries, Constitutions are not known to possess stability. Discuss how you rank India's Constitution, in terms of stability?

A. In the Soviet Union, there were 4 Constitutions in 74 years. New Constitutions came up in 1918, 1924, 1936 and 1971, in that country. After dismantling of the Russian Federation, yet another Constitution was adopted in 1993, by the Soviets. France had numerous Constitutions in last two centuries. After the French Revolution, a new Constitution was given in 1793 to the country. In fact, every time a new rule was established, a new Constitution was framed. As many as 5 Constitutions have been adopted by France till now.

India, after more than 50 years, has the same Constitution. It has been able to withstand all pulls and pressures. It also demonstrates that the Constitution makers had correctly foreseen various situations that would arise and incorporated measures to deal with them.

Q. The 42nd Amendment added the word "secular" in the Preamble, but the spirit of secularism has already been present in Constitution. Do you agree?

There are many Articles, which show the secular nature of Constitution, as envisaged by makers:

Article 14: Right to equality

Article 15 & 16: Non-discrimination

Article 19: Freedom of speech and expression

Article 27 & 28: Protection from religious taxes and religious instruction in state funded institutions

Article 29 & 30: Educational and cultural rights of minorities

Article 325: Equal ballots devoid of sectional preference

In cases like *Kesavananda Bharati*, the Supreme Court upheld that secularism is also the basic structure of Constitution, while in *S R Bommai case* (1992) it was said that removal of state governments for violation of secularism is valid. Of course, there are sections like Article 44 (uniform civil code) and Article 25(2)(a) which gives right to state to regulate or restrict any economic, financial, political or other secular activity which may be associated with religious practice. But it should be remembered that the 44th Amendment which struck down 42nd Amendment did not remove the word "secular" from the Preamble.

Q. The Supreme Court has held, in a recent case: "The right to privacy is not just a common law, not just a legal right..under the Constitution. It is a natural right inherent in every individual." Critically comment.

A. The Supreme Court has held right to privacy to be a fundamental right, by overruling verdicts given in *M.P.Sharma case* (1958) and *Kharak Singh case* (1961). Our body, home, thoughts, innermost feelings and identity are private. Article 12 of 1948 Universal Declaration of Human Rights says, "No one shall be subjected to arbitrary interference with his privacy, family, home or correspondence, nor to attacks upon his honor and reputation."Like all democratic societies, which follow this rule, India must also practise this right; the Court verdict seems to say.

A three-pronged test was adopted by the Court to declare right to privacy as a fundamental right:-

- One, encroachment of any Article 21,
- Two, legality in terms of a State objective and
- Third, a rational nexus between the object of invasion, and the means undertaken to achieve that object.

This ensures that dilution of right to privacy does not take place.

The Court said laws to seek restrict right to privacy must be just, fair and reasonable, but also 'serve some compelling state interest." How the new right to privacy will affect cases like Article 377 will depend on individual cases. Issues like criminal defamation may also be affected.

Q. In the context of a federal structure, what will be impact of GST on States? Discuss.

A. Goods and Services Tax (GST), the biggest tax reform since independence, attempts to simplify indirect tax regime and bring uniform taxation in the country, and act as economic unifier between Centre and States.

GST would have varied impact on the different States.

Criticism of GST as challenge to federalism:

GST subsumes State Value Added Tax/Sales Tax, Entertainment Tax (other than the tax levied by the local bodies), Central Sales Tax (levied by the Centre and collected by the States), Octroi and Entry tax, Purchase Tax, Luxury tax, Taxes on lottery, betting and gambling; and State cesses and surcharges in so far as they relate to supply of goods and services. State governments and local bodies will be affected.

Each state has its own socio-economic-political reasons to decide the type of tax to be levied. GST will take away the rights of states.

Without federal powers to decide taxes according to necessities, States will have to come with a begging bowl to the Centre, frequently.

Decision in GST council has to be taken by 75% votes, with the Centre having weightage of one third votes. It may undermine the aspiration of a few states.

GST will not hamper cooperative federalism:

GST has not prohibited States to create new taxes as such. Freedom exists for States to gain revenue from innovative taxation.

A 5 year compensation provision exists, in case of any losses, to fill the revenue gap of the States to some extent.

There is 2/3rd representation to States in the GST council.

As per the finance commission recommendations, state has all the discretionary authority to spend 42% tax revenue as decided by the sharing mechanism.

The GST would do away with the existing complicated tax-levy system and one common national market evolve. In the long term, GST is expected to create more revenues for states.

Q. The 42nd Amendment is known as mini Constitution. Examine this statement.

A. The 42nd Amendment is the most controversial amendment in the Indian Constitution. The amendment had four purposes:

- Exclude the courts entirely from election disputes
- Strengthen Central government vis a vis the State governments
- Give maximum protection to social revolutionary legislations from judicial challenges
- Tame the judiciary making it difficult for courts to interfere in parliamentary policy related to money matters

The 42nd Amendment amended the Preamble of the Constitution, 40 articles and Seventh Schedule and added 14 new Articles and 2 Parts to the Constitution. A complete Act in itself, the amendment was extensive in nature and character. Hence it is famously known as the "mini Constitution."

Q. Compare and contrast the powers of Lt. Governor of Delhi and Lt. Governor of Puducherry.

A. Although all the Union Territories belong to one category, there is no uniformity in their administrative system.

Similarities:

Both Puducherry (in 1963) and Delhi (in 1992) were provided with a legislative assembly and a council of ministers headed by the Chief Minister.

The Lieutenant Governor (LG) can act in his/her discretion in the matter of lawmaking, even though the Council of Ministers advises him/her. The LG, claiming that the matter is urgent can take immediate action. For eg, the LG of Puducherry cancelled the Puducherry Government's circular on social media use.

Prior sanction of the LG is required for certain legislative proposals (Section 22, 23 of Govt Act, 1963) in both UTs

Differences

Administrative powers of Lt Governor of Delhi are wider and broader compared to his/her counterpart in Puducherry. For eg, Delhi LG's executive domain extends over public order, police and land, under consultation with CM (Art.239AA).

Considering the importance of Delhi, LG of Delhi is vested with higher authority over elected representatives and ministers. For example, former LG of Delhi Najeeb Jung cancelled appointment of 15 Delhi government lawyers appointed by the State Government. He also cancelled appointment of DERC chief.

Delhi being the national capital is a more sensitive area. Hence, the Centre indirectly exerts more control over the state through the LG than over Puducherry.

Q. The Finance Bill, 2017 attempts to rationalise functioning of multiple tribunals. What are the implications?

A. The Finance Bill, 2017 strives to rationalise tribunals through merger mode. For example, merger of Competition Appellate Tribunal with the National Company Law Tribunal, merger of the Cyber Law Appellate Tribunal with the Telecom Disputes Settlement Appellate Tribunal, etc.

The aim is to streamline functioning by reducing structural complexity. The benefits are better performance, efficiency in adjudication, and reduction in delays. Preventing overlapping of functions is a big advantage. For example, Competition Appellate Tribunal (COMPAT) will be merged with the National Company Law Appellate Tribunal. Since both deal with similar matters, it will immensely help in cases where a single transaction is overseen by both, e.g. Idea-Vodafone merger.

The danger however, is that separation of powers will be affected, as a direct control of the Central government over the existing tribunals is not an ideal situation. The winding up of adjudicatory tribunals through the tool of a money bill sets an ominous precedent.

Q. Though India has incorporated many features of the British system, there are significant differences between the two electoral systems. Comment on this statement.

A. India follows largely the British political system, yet there are differences in their election processes.

Differences

In India, Election Commission of India (ECI) decides the dates for elections, whereas in the UK, the date is always decided by the prime minister, giving the ruling party a political advantage. In 2011, therefore, the system was changed to a fixed date election – May 7, every five years. No clarity, however, what happens to this date if mid-term election takes place.

In the UK, campaigning is much cheaper, confined to door to door visits by candidates or agents, and TV debates. Paid political advertising on TV and radio is not permitted – whereas Paid news is rampant in India. There is a cap on election expenditure of both candidates and parties in the UK, whereas in India, it extends only to the candidates.

India uses electronic voting machines (EVMs) since 1998, while the demand for electronic voting in the UK has never been very audible.

The UK is the only country in the world where no identity proof is required. No photo on the electoral rolls. No marking of fingers. There are no party agents in the booth to verify the voter's identity. There is no police near polling stations, whereas in India, a booth has to be secured like a fort.

In Britain, poll day is not a holiday. To enable working class persons to vote, the voting hours are long – 7 am to 10 pm. They normally vote either early in the morning or late evening.

Both countries follow the First-Past-The-Post (FPTP) system of election, where a candidate getting the highest number of votes is declared elected. In the UK, controversy snowballed to the extent that a referendum was held in 2011, though it failed with 68 to 32 per cent vote (with a low turnout of 42 per cent). In India, demand for replacing FPTP with Proportional Representation has become louder after the 2014 general election, when a party (the BSP) with the third largest vote share in the country ended up with zero share in parliamentary seats.

Regarding logistics and management of elections in the UK, in 2010 and 2015, there were complaints about postal ballots and some polling stations, even in London, falling short of ballot papers before the polls ended a situation unthinkable in India. Indian election management can claim to be really fool-proof.

Q. What are the drawbacks of the Inter-State Water Disputes Act? Critically examine the new Act, which is proposed by government.

A. Interstate River Water Disputes Act – 1956 (IRWD Act) was first enacted on 28th August, 1956 to resolve the water disputes that would arise in the use, control and distribution of an interstate river or river valley.

The Article 262 of the Constitution of India deals with adjudication of water disputes.

Drawbacks of Interstate Water Dispute Act, 1956:

Delays are on account of no time limit for adjudication by a Tribunal, no upper age limit for the Chairman or the Members, work getting stalled due to occurrence of any vacancy and no time limit for publishing the report of the Tribunal.

- Only three out of eight Tribunals have given awards accepted by the States, while Tribunals like Cauvery and Ravi Beas have been in existence for over 26 and 30 years respectively without any award.
- The River Boards Act 1956, which is supposed to facilitate inter-state collaboration over water resource development, remained a 'dead letter' since its enactment.
- Surface water is controlled by Central Water Commission (CWC) and ground water by Central Ground Water Board of India (CGWB). Both bodies work independently and there is no common forum for common discussion with state governments on water management.

The Inter-State River Water Disputes (Amendment) Bill, 2017 proposes to streamline the adjudication of disputes regarding rivers and make present legal and institutional architecture strong.

Features of the proposed bill:

- The Bill proposes a Single Standing Tribunal (with multiple benches) instead of the existing multiple tribunals, which shall consist of one Chairperson, one Vice-Chairperson and not more than six other Members.
- While the term of office of the Chairperson is five years or till he attains the age of 70 years, whichever is earlier, the term of office of Vice Chairperson and other member of tribunal shall be co-terminus with the adjudication of the water dispute.
- The Bill also provides for the appointment of Assessors to provide technical support to the tribunal. They shall be appointed from amongst experts serving in the Central Water Engineering Service not below the rank of chief engineer.
- The total time period for adjudication of disputes has been fixed at maximum of four and half years. The decision of the Tribunal shall be final and binding with no requirement of publication in the official gazette.
- The Bill proposes to introduce mechanism to resolve the disputes amicably by negotiations, through a Dispute Resolution Committee (DRC) to be established by the Central Government consisting of relevant experts, before such dispute is referred to the tribunal.
- The Bill provides for transparent data collection system at the national level for each river basin and for this purpose, an agency to maintain data-bank and information system shall be appointed or authorised by the Central Government.

Q. Supreme Court's collegium system has attracted controversy. Are recent steps taken by Supreme Court to douse the fires, enough?

A. Supreme Court of India s collegium system appoints judges to the nation s constitutional courts. The apex court evolved judicial independence to mean that no other branch of the State – including the legislature and the executive – would have any say in appointment of judges and hence created the collegium system in force since 1993.

Recently, the Supreme Court quashed the 99th amendment to the Constitution and National Judicial Appointment Commission. Now has agreed on implementing the Memorandum of Procedure (MoP) for appointments, uploading collegium decisions on website etc

The move is praiseworthy, but still not enough. Supreme Court must take necessary steps to make the collegium system more appealing, transparent.

- Make collegium's deliberations publicly available
- Annual reporting of vacancies, appointments, number of candidates interviewed and the time taken for appointments etc; are equally important.
- All this requires data management skills, administrative and logistical capacity, for which a secretariat needed, to ensure that appointments calendar and processes are strictly followed, records are maintained and placed in public domain on time.

Q. What is judicial performance index?

A. The NITI Aayog has proposed a judicial performance index in a bid to fix the justice system that is in 'dire need of reform.' It can reduce delays and bring in outsourcing of non-core functions of the police to private agencies or other government departments.

- It would help High Courts and their chief justices keep track of the performance and processes at district courts and subordinate levels for reducing delay, which can be 'the first step' in judicial system reforms.
- The index will entail fixing of 'non-mandatory time frames for different types of cases to benchmark when a case has been delayed.' It would include certain progress on process steps already approved by High Courts and such an annual evaluation should give judges 'a sense of where they are failing and what they need to fix.'
- Since the subordinate judiciary is largely within the domain of High Courts, this could also spur competitive reform of the judiciary

Policing

- The think tank has asked the Home Ministry to create a task force to identify 'non-core functions' that can be outsourced to private agents or government departments reducing the workload of police.
- Functions like serving court summons and antecedents and address verification for passport applications or job verifications can be outsourced.

India's police to population ratio should reach the United Nations norms of 222 per lakh population (current level 137), over the next seven years.

Q. What are the issues involved in Section 35A of the Indian Constitution?

A. Article 35A empowers the Jammu and Kashmir state's legislature to define "permanent residents" of the state and provide special rights and privileges to them.

It covers issues like employment, property, scholarships, settling in state.

It is legally wrong as the said Article added without presenting to Parliament under Article 368

Issues that Strengthen Arguments against Article 35A

- Indian residents don't have same rights & privileges as permanent residents
- Non-residents can't buy properties, get local jobs or vote in local elections
- Women marrying non-permanent residents can't give children PCR status and land
- Children of non-state subjects can't get admission to state colleges
- Free hand to the state government and politicians to discriminate between citizens on unfair basis and give preferential treatment to some by trampling over others,

Arguments in Support of Article 35A:

- Nagaland and Mizoram too have Article 371A and Article 371G respectively
- Protects legislation passed by the J&K legislature relating to benefits to Permanent Residents from challenge on the ground of violation of Fundamental Rights

Conclusion: Central government has moral responsibility to protect citizens

Q. Law of conducting floor tests is ambiguous, causing abuse and misuse. Elucidate.

A. Article 356 of the Indian Constitution under states that if the governor of a state feels that the state machinery has broken down, he can request the President of India to take direct control of the State which is termed as President's Rule.

State judiciary felt that governments at the Centre were misusing their power to bring down "unfriendly" state governments and imposing President's rule according to whims.

Post the *S. R. Bommai v. Union of India case*, the Supreme Court of India decided to stop the misuse of Article 356 to prevent the Centre from bearing down on the State. Thus, came into the affect the Floor Test. The Supreme Court decided that the constitutional machinery would be tested on the floor of the Legislative Assembly of the State (by votes) and not as per the whims of the governor.

The issue over confidence on floor comes to forefront in Arunachal Pradesh, Tamil Nadu and Uttarakhand. In all the three cases there were differences and ambiguity over the role played by various constitutional and political institutions.

Ambiguities in law linked with floor test :

No provision clarifies role of the governor in case of disqualification or in case of decision to be taken about floor test. This discretionary power of the governor has resulted in misuse.

The interpretation of Article 356 by the Speaker of the House is one of the controversial issues.

Many times an administrative breakdown is shown as a political one, forcing the manipulated floor test that waste the time of government machinery.

To be specific, the SC laid down the following principles:

- The majority enjoyed by the Council of Ministers shall be tested on the floor of the House.
- Centre should give a warning to the state and a time period of one week to reply.
- The court cannot question the advice tendered by the CMs to the President but it can question the material behind the satisfaction of the President. *Hence, Judicial Review will involve three questions only:*
- Is there any material behind the proclamation?
- Is the material relevant?
- Was there any mala fide use of power?

If there is improper use of Art. 356 then the court will provide remedy.

Under Article 356(3) limitations exist on the President's powers. Hence, the President shall not take any irreversible action until the proclamation is approved by the Parliament i.e. he shall not dissolve the assembly.

Art.356 is justified only when there is a breakdown of constitutional machinery and not administrative machinery.

These guidelines are generally not followed leading to the misuse and ambiguity in floor test provision in our Constitution.

Q. Should every Bill, introduced in Lok Sabha and Rajya Sabha be referred to a Standing Committee? Discuss.

A. A Standing committee is a committee consisting of members of Parliament. A Standing Committee's work is voluminous and complex.

Arguments for referring bill to Select Committee

- Legislators can't scrutinize everything on the floor of the House
- Efficiency and expertise increases when handled by experts
- MPs are briefed on the whole gamut of govt activity – defence, finance, external affairs, industry, agriculture
- Standing Committees oversee executive and scrutinize govt expenditure
- The data they generate can serve as a huge reservoir of information

Arguments against referring bill to Select Committee

- Amendment bills to alter existing Acts have to be passed urgently to handle specific situations
- Money Bills- Finance Bill, Appropriation Bill are never referred as they have to be passed in specific time frame
- MPs more busy with constituency
- Committee chairman has little power, presiding officer has dominating influence

Steps to Improve & Reform Standing committees:

- Have mechanism to assess performance regularly
- Call specialist advisers
- Speaker and Chairman must meet committee atleast twice in 2 months
- All Bills except those urgent be referred to them
- Elicit public views, where possible

Q. Discuss issues pertaining to salaries of legislators in India.

A. The average monthly salary of a member of Parliament (MP) in India is Rs. 2.7 lakh. MPs are also entitled to other perks, including free housing, limited free water, electricity, telephone facilities and medical treatment. However, this is not reflected in the expenses paid out every month by the Lok Sabha.

Salaries of MLA are decided by the respective states. There is wide variation in MLA salaries across state assemblies. An MLA in Maharashtra earns Rs. 75000 and MLAs of Karnataka earn approx. Rs. 95 000 per month. MLAs also get similar facilities like MPs – daily allowance, constituency allowance, office expenses allowance, provisions for accommodation, travel etc.

Issues involved:

- Hikes in salaries are proposed, without any formula or rationale, while there is a strict timeline regarding when salary of a government official will be revised.
- Salaries and perks for MPs are decided by a Joint Parliamentary Committee consisting of members of both Houses of Parliament. All proposals are usually approved, without any delay, as there is all-party consensus.
- No independent external agencies exist, regarding salaries of legislators in India. In other advanced democracies such as the U.K. and Australia, MPs salaries are decided by an autonomous body called the Independent Parliamentary Standards Authority and the Remuneration Tribunal (set up by the Remuneration Tribunal Act, 1973), respectively.

- Allowances should be in proportion to services that they have rendered, but in past two decades, Parliament has seen less than 50% of Bills being scrutinised by parliamentary committees.
- Parliamentary representatives have hiked their own fiscal compensation by 1,250% over the last two decades.

Q. If more districts are created, would it become ideal for decentralisation ?

A. Decentralisation means a plan to redistribute authority, responsibility and financial resources for providing public services among different levels of government.

Creating more districts is done to provide smooth and effective public services delivery to people. Often other factors like geographical area, population etc; are also taken into account. However the state governments' thinking has not paid off as intended.

Decentralised planning is meant to think of districts – and nothing below. The administrative machinery below the district level in usually neglected in the process.

In 1950s, government development programmes were carried through community development blocks (CD blocks), under the overall charge of a BDO (block development officer). There was also the tehsildar/talukdar and the intermediate-level panchayat, variously referred to as the mandal, taluka or block panchayat or panchayat samiti below district level. The BDO, MP and MlA were all members of panchayat samiti.

Decentralised planning is meant to start from below and "below" doesn't mean the district. Gram panchayats/gram sabhas are supposed to have several "planning" functions. There is no direct link between the executive and the elected in the gram panchayat.

Even at district level the process of decentralisation is fraught with many problems. Once there is a new district, barring time-lags, there will also be a new zila parishad (ZP), through the relevant state election commission. There are various entities involved in a district's development – the district collector/district magistrate/district commissioner, the DRDA, the MP, multiple MLAs and ZPs. Unless they work in unison, a lot of resources, not just financial, will be lost. Planning must be participatory.

Q. What is the role of UPSC in strengthening democracy?

A. The UPSC is expected to maintain meritocracy in democratic India. It selects candidates by merit to strengthen democratic values; as good administrators will implement ideal policies, practise implementation, ensure low corruption and empathise with the poor. Bureaucrats selected through such processes are expected to truly represent society.

The UPSC functions to uphold democratic values

- Upholds values of merit and calibre through a rigorous selection process of officers to the Indian bureaucracy
- Provide vital data and information about functioning of Indian civil services to government and other agencies
- Lends advisory functions to the government of the day in order to ensure high standards of civil services in terms of education, moral values
- Provides key inputs toward reforms in civil services to match current trends and needs

- Plays vital role in overall development of sensitive, ethical, efficient civil services in India

The role of UPSC has been of great significance in functioning and strengthening of Indian democracy. For vibrant and dynamic democracy, more autonomy and powers according to changing times can be attempted. However, UPSC has no control or regulatory role over state service commissions.

Practice Questions

1) What are the unique features of the Rajya Sabha that differentiates it from the Lok Sabha?
2) Woman's reservation of seats issue has not made much headway. What are the reasons for this? Discuss.
3) The concept of 'Basic Structure' was thought of to end the confrontation between legislature and the judiciary. Discuss.
4) 'One man, one vote', gave us equality in political arena but economic emancipation is still a far cry. Do you agree?
5) Which features of the Government of India Act, 1935 have found their way into the constitution? Elaborate.
6) 'Right to Property' has undergone significant changes from 1950 onwards. Elaborate.
7) Which article of the constitution gives it a bias towards the Union? Explain.
8) Justice Venkatachaliah commission suggested some changes. Discuss some of these.
9) President of India should be elected directly and not in the manner done now. Give your views.
10) What changes, if any, can be thought of in the Seventh Schedule to give the states more powers and functions? Give example, if in agreement.
11) What are the main recommendations of Justice Punchhi Commission? How is it different from earlier similar commissions/committees? Discuss.
12) What has been the experience with Joint Parliamentary Committees? Do party affiliations matter? Elaborate.
13) Indian Constitution is often called a bag of borrowings, what can be said to refute this? Elucidate.
14) MPLAD funds are often criticized on grounds that they are not spent fully or spent wrongly. Do you agree? Give your views.
15) Stalling the proceedings of Parliament is shown to be a democratic right. Critically evaluate this statement.
16) Evaluate the functioning of statutory bodies citing the example of any one such body.
17) In the issue of office of profit, trace out the developments and weigh the pros and cons of disqualification of AAP MLAs.
18) What are the provisions of Schedule 5 and 6? Have they helped in development agenda?
19) Comment on the role and functions of JPC. Do the JPCs rise above party politics?
20) What is the purpose of legislative councils and utility in today's context? Comment.

PART II

Polity

The Representation of The People Act (RPA)

OVERVIEW

Democracy is a government of the people, by the people, for the people and elected by the will of the people. The Representation of the People Act is the mechanism that ensures all this in a peaceful and organised manner. It sets the rules of the game, and over the years with the benefit of experience, the nation has excelled itself in sustaining the democratic process.

SALIENT FEATURES OF REPRESENTATION OF THE PEOPLE ACT

In order to understand and appreciate the salient features of Representation of the People Act, it is essential that the context and perspective are seen. This Act was first enacted in 1950 and subsequent to that has undergone modifications. The constitution has provisions for conduct of elections and has envisaged machinery to ensure polls in a fair and free manner. *The following aspects become important in our understanding of where the Representation of the People Act began and how it stands today.*

(a) Constitutional provisions of RPA.
(b) Evolution of Representation of the People Act over the years.
(c) The Indian Electroal System.

CONSTITUTIONAL PROVISIONS OF RPA: PART XV

Art. 324:

Superintendence, Direction, and Control of Elections to be Vested in an Election Commission

(1) The superintendence, direction and control of the preparation of the electoral rolls for,

and to the conduct of, all elections to Parliament and to the Legislature of every state and of elections to the offices of President and Vice-President held under this constitution shall be vested in a Commission (referred to as Election Commission).

(2) The Election Commission shall consist of the Chief Election Commissioner and such number of other Election Commissioners, if any, as the President may from time to time appoint. The appointment of the Chief Election Commissioner and the other Election Commissioners shall be subject to any law made on behalf of the Parliament by the President.

(3) When any other Election Commissioner is so appointed, the Chief Election Commissioner shall act as the chairman of the Election Commission.

(4) Before each general election to the House of the People and to the legislative assembly of each state, and before the first general election and thereafter before each biennial election to the legislative council of each state having such council, the President may also appoint after consultation with the Election Commission such Regional Commissioners as he may consider necessary to assist the Election Commission in the performance of the functions conferred on the Commission by clause (1).

(5) Subject to the provisions of any law made by the Parliament, the conditions of service and tenure of office of the Election Commissioners and the regional commissioner shall be such as the President may by rule determine:

[Provided that the Chief Election Commissioner shall not be removed from the office except in like manner and on like grounds as a judge of the Supreme Court and the condition of service of the Chief Election Commissioner shall not be varied to his disadvantage after his appointment.

Further provided that any other Election Commissioner or a regional commissioner shall not be removed from office except on the recommendation of the Chief Election Commissioner.]

(6) The President or the Governor of a state, shall, when so requested by the Election Commission, make available to the Election Commission or to a regional commissioner such staff as may be necessary for the discharge of the functions conferred on the Election Commission by clause (1).

Art. 325:

No Person to be Ineligible for Inclusion in, or Claim to be Included in a Special Electoral Roll on Grounds of Religion, Race, Caste, or Sex

There shall be one general electoral roll for every territorial constituency for election to either House of Parliament or to the House or either House of Legislature of a state and no person shall be ineligible for inclusion in any such roll or claim to be included in any special electoral roll for any such constituency on grounds only of religion, race, caste, sex, or any of them.

Art. 326:

Elections to the House of People and to the Legislative Assemblies of States to be on the Basis of Adult Suffrage

The elections to the House of the People and to the Legislative Assembly of every state shall be on the basis of adult suffrage; that is to say, every person who is a citizen of India and who is not less than (eighteen years) of age on such date may be fixed in that behalf by or under any law made by appropriate legislature and is not otherwise disqualified under this constitution or any law made by the appropriate legislature on the ground of non-residence, unsoundness of mind, crime, corrupt or illegal practice, shall be entitled to be registered as a voter at any such election.

Note:- Substituted to 18 years from 20 years by sixty-first amendment w.e.f 28.3.1989.

Art. 327:

Power of Parliament to make Provisions with Respect to Elections to Legislature

Subject to the provisions of this constitution, Parliament may from time to time by law make provision with respect to all matters relating to, or in connection with, election to either House of Parliament or to the House or either House of Legislature of a state including the preparations of electoral rolls, delimitation of constituencies, and all other matters necessary for securing the due constitution of such House or Houses.

Art.328:

Power of Legislature of a State to make Provision with Respect to Elections to such Legislature

Subject to the provisions of this constitution and in so far as provision in that behalf is not made by Parliament, the Legislature of a state may from time to time by law make provisions with respect to all matters relating to, or in connections with, the elections to the House or either House of Legislature of the state including the preparation of electoral rolls and all other matters necessary for securing the due constitution of such House or Houses.

Art. 329:

Bar to Interference by Courts in Electoral Matters

(a) The validity of any law relating to delimitation of constituencies or the allotment of seats to such constituencies, made or purporting to be made under Art. 327 and Art. 328 shall not be called in question in any court.

(b) No election to either House of Parliament or either House of the legislature of a state, shall be called in question except by an election petition presented to such authority and in such manner as may be provided for by or under any law made by the appropriate legislature.

PART XV of the Constitution deals with Articles on Elections

Comment

The Election Commission has come to occupy a pivotal role in our democracy; even to the extent that free and fair elections are part of the basic structure of our constitution and the role of the Election Commission is vital in it. From the time the first general elections took place in 1952 to now, the role of Election Commission has always been appreciated, even applauded. Conduct of elections has grown more complex, more challenging, and more exasperating. Rising usage of money power, criminalisation, regionalism, naxalism, and a whole host of local problems have made the whole process intensely perplexing. The Election commission has kept pace with all these to be ahead and inventive. Electronic voting machines, quick counting, and declaration of results on a scale never thought possible are some of the achievements.. Even an advanced country like Britain had paper ballots in the recently conducted Referendum on European Union Exit. Deployment of forces across the country, ensuring posting of neutral officials, settling electoral disputes, and fair counting of votes; all in an environment of freedom and fairness is a tribute to the high standards set by the commission. Educating the voters, asking them to vote without fear or favour, sending observers, liaison with state governments, arranging for re-poll, and setting election aside are some of the onerous tasks the commission is conducting with aplomb. The steady increase in the numbers of the electorate, increased percentage of voting, diverse base of voters, and resort to violence are also some of the issues that the commission has now to contend with. Elections are being contested with vigour and vehemence; more and more issues are coming to the fore. For the detractors, those who feel that the choice among the candidates is indeed no choice, the commission has made an abundantly graceful offering: NOTA meaning 'none of the above'. Notwithstanding all this, there are some issues always. Candidates in a multi-party democracy in an era of coalition politics have their own compulsions of alliances and associations; this often leads to confrontations. Mass illiteracy of villages is another issue. Back in 1952 when the elections were over, the authorities were casting away all the ballot boxes when the election commissioners ran from place to place to preserve them for the next election. It was visionary, as it was also precautionary; laced with faith and conviction that democracy had come to stay. Not a one-time tryst.

EVOLUTION OF RPA ACT

In pursuance of the constitutional provisions in Part XV, the Parliament, from time to time, has enacted laws for the smooth and satisfactory functioning of the commission as also conduct of elections.

Acts

1950: Representation of People Act 1950

(Allocation of seats in Parliament, State Legislature, delimitation of Constituencies, voter's qualifications, and electoral rolls).

1951: Representation of People Act 1951

(Administrative machinery for conducting elections, by-elections, political parties' registration, disputes, corrupt practices, offences, and disqualification of members).

1952: Presidential and Vice-Presidential Elections Act 1952

(An Act to regulate certain matters relating to or connected with elections to the offices of President and Vice-President of India.)

2002: The Delimitation Act 2002

(Delimitation and reservation of constituencies).

Rules/Orders

1950: Prohibition of Simultaneous Membership Rules, 1950.
1960: Registration of Electors Rules, 1960
1961: Conduct of Election Rules, 1961
1968: Election symbols Reservation and Order, 1968.

Constitutional Amendments Regarding Defections

The 10th Schedule introduced through the 52nd amendment of 1985 was included in the constitution to curb 'defections.' This Act, however, laid that one-third of members leaving the party was not defection but merger. The 91st constitution amendment of 2003 removed this provision; so now at least two-thirds of the members of a party have to be in favour of a 'merger' for it to have validity in the eyes of the law. 'Aya Rams and Gaya Rams' have made things for themselves a bit difficult: their pastime is now past time.

THE INDIAN ELECTORAL SYSTEM

(i) It is based on geographical representation;
(ii) There are only single-member territorial constituencies and no functional or plural constituencies; and
(iii) Each territorial constituency elects a single representative by a simple majority vote.

However, indirect election system exists in the election of members of the Upper Houses.

All disputes regarding elections are decided by the High Courts. High Court decisions can be appealed against in the Supreme Court which is the final arbiter. Article 323B inserted by the 42nd Amendment conferred power on the appropriate legislature to set up a tribunal for adjudication of election disputes. So far, no such tribunal has been set up.

The Election Commission

For the conduct of free and fair elections, the Constitution provides for an independent body in the form of the Election Commission (Article 324).

Composition

The Election Commission consists of the Chief Election Commissioner and such other commissioners as the President may from time to time determine. The Constitution does not specify the strength of the members of the Election Commission and leaves it to be determined by the President. The Election Commission remained a single-member body from 1950 till October 1989. Its strength was increased by adding two deputy Election Commissioners in 1989 by Presidential notification. The reason was that there would be a huge increase in workload as a result of the voting age being lowered to 18 years. The National Front government, however, abolished the posts and reverted to the old position in 1990. In 1993, the commission was again made a three-member body and by an ordinance the two Election Commissioners were given the same status as the Chief Election Commissioner. The ordinance was later replaced by the Chief Election Commissioner and Other Election Commissioners (Conditions of Service) Amendment Act, 1994. The Act was given retrospective effect from October 1993. (In the *T.N. Seshan vs Union of India case,* 1995, a five-judge bench of the Supreme Court unanimously upheld the validity of the act equating the status, power, and authority of all members of the Election Commission including the Chief Election Commissioner.) The commission is required to act as a body, taking decisions by majority or unanimously. So, if the Chief Election Commissioner differs from the other members, he may be overruled.

Under Article 324, regional commissioners may be appointed by the President at the time of general elections, after consultation with the Chief Election Commissioner. According to the Constitution, in a multi-member Election Commission, the Chief Election Commissioner will act as the chairman of the commission. The Constitution does not specify the qualifications of the members of the Election Commission and the President is free to appoint anyone to this office. The President determines the tenure and conditions of service of members of the Election Commission and the regional commissioners. They get the same salary and allowances as those of a Supreme Court judge.

Term and Independence

The term of the Chief Election Commissioner and other members of the Election Commission is not fixed by the Constitution. The Election Commissioners hold office for six years or until they attain the age of 65 years, whichever is earlier. They may resign at any time. They can also be removed before the end of their term as prescribed by the Constitution.

The independence of the Election Commission has been sought to be ensured by the Constitution so that it may carry out its functions impartially. The Chief Election Commissioner cannot be removed from office except in the manner and on the grounds that a judge of the Supreme Court can be removed from office. An Election Commissioner or a regional commissioner shall not be removed from office except on the recommendation of the Chief Election Commissioner.

Their salaries and allowances and service conditions cannot be changed to their disadvantage during their tenure of office. However, Election Commissioners have not been debarred from appointments under the government after their retirement.

Functions

The Election Commission performs administrative and advisory as well as quasi-judicial functions.

(i) It registers voters and prepares and revises electoral rolls for the elections to Parliament as well as the State Legislatures.

(ii) It supervises, directs, and controls elections of the President, Vice-President, Parliament, and State Legislatures.

(iii) It lays down general rules for elections and issues notification of dates and schedules of elections and scrutinises and ensures security of nomination papers.

(iv) It determines the code of conduct to be observed by the parties and the candidates at the time of the elections.

(v) It allots symbols and accords recognition to political parties.

(vi) Any association or body of individual citizens of India calling itself a political party shall make an application to the Election Commission for its registration as a political party, as per the RPA, 1951. After considering all the particulars, the Election Commission decides either to register the association or body as a political party or not. It decides whether the party is a national or a state party. It acts as a court in settling disputes related to the grant of recognition and election symbols to political parties.

(vii) It tenders advice to the President and governors on questions relating to disqualification of members of Parliament and State Legislatures. As per the Representation of the People Act, 1951, if the Election Commission considers it necessary or proper to make an inquiry, and the commission is satisfied that it cannot come to a decisive opinion on the matter which is being inquired into, the commission shall have, for the purposes of such inquiry, assume the powers of a civil court in respect of the following matters, namely: (a) summoning and enforcing the attendance of any person and examining him on oath; (b) requiring the discovery and production of any document or other materials object producible as evidence; (c) receiving evidence on affidavits; (d) requisitioning any public record or a copy thereof from any court or office; and (e) issuing commissions for the examination of witnesses or documents.

(viii) It postpones or countermands elections for specific reasons.

(ix) It appoints election offices for inquiring into the disputes arising out of or in connection with the election arrangements.

(x) On the basis of the past performance of a recognised political party, it allocates equitable sharing of time on the cable television network and other electronic media in such manner as may be prescribed to display or propagate any election matter or to address the public in connection with an election.

Deputy Election Commissioners drawn from the civil services are appointed by the Election Commission on tenure basis to assist it in its functions. Other civil servants are posted in the secretariat of the commission to carry out the work.

Conduct of Elections

Administrative Machinery

The Representation of the People Act, 1951 gives details on the administrative machinery for the election.

The functions of the Election Commission may be delegated by the Election Commission to be performed also by a deputy Election Commissioner or by the secretary to the Election Commission. Subject to the superintendence, direction, and control of the Election Commission, the chief electoral officer of each state is to supervise the conduct of all elections in the state under the Representation of the People Act, 1951. Subject to the superintendence, direction, and control of the chief electoral officer, the district election officer coordinates and supervises all work in the district or in the area within his jurisdiction in connection with the conduct of all elections to Parliament and the legislature of the state. The district election officer also performs such other functions as may be entrusted to him by the Election Commission and the chief electoral officer.

The Election Commission may nominate observers (general/election expenditure) who must be officers of government to watch the conduct of election or elections in a constituency or a group of constituencies and to perform such other functions as may be entrusted to them by the Election Commission.

For every constituency, for every election to the State Legislature, the Election Commission shall, in consultation with the state government, designate or nominate a returning officer who must be an officer of government or of a local authority. It is the general duty of the returning officer at any election to do all such acts and things as may be necessary for effectually conducting the election in the manner provided by the RPA and rules or orders made under it. (In the case of Union Territories, the returning officer appoints the presiding officers and polling officers.)

The district election officer appoints a presiding officer for each polling station and such polling officer or officers as he thinks necessary. The regional commissioner or the chief electoral officer of the state makes available to any returning officer such staff as may be necessary for performance of any duties in connection with an election. It is the general duty of the presiding officer at a polling station to keep order and to see that the poll is fair. It is the duty of the polling officers at a polling station to assist the presiding officer.

Electoral Procedure

The Election Commission decides the schedule of election to Parliament or the State Legislature, taking into account the recommendations of the government concerned. The Election Commission generally announces the schedule at a press conference, but the election process starts only with the notification by the President or the Governor.

As per the Representation of the People Act, 1951, the President shall, by one or more notifications published in the *Gazette of India* on such date or dates as may be recommended by the Election Commission, call upon all Parliamentary constituencies to elect members in accordance with the provisions of the RPA, 1951 and of the rules and orders made there under.

However, RPA, 1951 stipulates that where a general election is held otherwise than on the dissolution of the existing House of the People, no such notification shall be issued at any time earlier than six months prior to the date on which the duration of that house would expire.

The governor or administrator, as the case may be, calls upon all assembly constituencies in the state to elect members to a state legislative assembly. The governor calls upon the members of the legislative assembly of the state and all the council constituencies concerned to elect members to a state legislative council in the biennial election.

After the notification for election is issued, the Election Commission declares the last date for making nominations, the date for the scrutiny of nominations, the last date for withdrawal of candidates, the date or dates on which poll has to be taken, and the date before which the election shall be completed.

The returning officer gives public notice of the intended election inviting nomination of candidates and specifying the place for the nomination papers to be delivered.

Any person may be nominated as a candidate if he is qualified to be elected under statutes. *The Representation of the People Act, 1951 gives the qualifications and disqualifications of candidates in an election. These have been considered in their relevant contexts in the chapters on Union Executive, Union Parliament, and State Legislatures. A few points are recalled here.*

- According to the Act, a person shall not be qualified to be chosen as a representative of any state or union territory in the Council of States unless he is an elector for a Parliamentary constituency in India.
- A person shall not be qualified to be chosen to fill a seat in the legislative assembly of a state unless he is an elector for any assembly constituency in that state.
- A person shall not be qualified to be a member in the legislative council of a state to be filled by election unless he is an elector for any assembly constituency in that state. In case of nomination by the governor he needs to be an ordinary resident in the state.

The Election Commission decides the schedule of election to Parliament or the State Legislature, taking into account the recommendations of the government concerned. The Election Commission generally announces the schedule at a press conference, but the election process starts only with the notification by the President or the Governor.

The Act deals with disqualifications for membership of Parliament and State Legislatures on the basis of conviction in an offence under the laws listed in the act, such as, the Protection of Civil Rights Act, 1955, the Foreign Exchange (Regulation) Act, the Narcotic Drugs and Psychotropic Substances Act, the Narcotic Drugs and Psychotropic Substances Act, the Prevention of Corruption Act, and the Prevention of Terrorism Act.

A person convicted under these Acts is disqualified: (i) for a period of six years plus fine only; (ii) in case of imprisonment, for the period of imprisonment plus a further period of six years since his release.

Since August 1, 1996, by the Representation of the People (Amendment) Act, 1996, any conviction for an offence of insulting the Indian National Flag or the Constitution of India or offence of preventing the singing of the National Anthem under the prevention of Insults to National Honour Act, 1971 shall entail disqualification for contesting elections to Parliament and State Legislatures for a period of six years from the date of such conviction.

A candidate either in person or by his proposers needs to deliver to the returning officer at a place specified a nomination paper completed in the prescribed form within the prescribed time limit. The RPA, 1951, amended in 1996 provides that the nomination of a candidate in a Parliamentary or assembly constituency should be subscribed by ten electors of the constituency as proposers, if the candidate has not been set up by a recognised national or state party. In the case of a candidate set up by a recognised party, only one proposer is required.

For the purpose of listing of names of candidates, candidates shall be classified as (a) candidates of recognised political parties, (b) candidates of registered, unrecognised political parties, and (c) other (independent) candidates. While the candidate has to be a voter in the country, the proposers must be voters in the constituency in which the candidate is contesting.

A person is not to be nominated as a candidate for election in more than two constituencies of Parliament or state assembly or legislative council of a state in case of general election (whether or not held simultaneously from all respective constituencies). Similar restrictions will apply for biennial elections and bye-elections to the Council of States and state legislative councils.

A candidate, apart from other information, has to furnish the information as to whether he is accused of any offence punishable with imprisonment for two years or more in a pending case in which a charge has been framed by the court of competent jurisdiction.

A candidate needs to deposit a stipulated sum of money in the case of an election; if a candidate has been nominated by more than one nomination paper for election in the same constituency, not more than one deposit shall be required of him.

Any candidate may withdraw his candidature by a notice in writing.

A candidate at an election may appoint in the prescribed manner any one person to be his election agent and notice of the appointment is to be given to the returning officer.

The RPA, 1951, amended in 1996 provides that the nomination of a candidate in a Parliamentary or assembly constituency should be subscribed by ten electors of the constituency as proposers, if the candidate has not been set up by a recognised national or state party. In the case of a candidate set up by a recognised party, only one proposer is required.

A contesting candidate or his election agent may appoint one or more persons to be present as his counting agent or agents at the counting of votes, and notice of the appointment is to be given to the returning officer. Previously, the election was countermanded on the death of a contesting candidate. Now, no election will be countermanded on the death of a contesting candidate. If the deceased candidate, however, was set up by a recognised national or state party, the party concerned will be given an option to nominate another candidate within seven days of the issue of a notice to that effect to the party concerned by the Election Commission.

The state government makes requisitions of premises, vehicles, etc. for the purpose of election on the payment of compensation.

A candidate in person has to make and subscribe an oath or affirmation after presenting his nomination papers; this can be done before an officer authorised by the Election Commissioner. Normally, this officer is the returning officer or the assistant returning officer for the constituency. However, in special cases, the following arrangements are made. If the candidate is in prison or under preventive detention, he makes the oath to the prison superintendent or commandant of the detention camp; the oath can be administered by the medical superintendent of the hospital or doctor attending the candidate if he happens to be sick and confined to bed; if he/she is abroad, a candidate can make the oath before the Indian ambassador or high commissioner or consular official authorised for such a task.

After the period of nominations is over, the returning officer scrutinises the nomination papers, and any serious defect in them may lead to their rejection. After scrutiny, two days are allowed for withdrawal of candidature. The list of candidates is then finalised by the returning officers and symbols allotted to the parties and independent candidates. Reserved symbols are granted to the recognised parties and 'free symbols' to the others.

A period of not less than 14 days from the last date for withdrawal of nominations is allowed for campaigning. Limits have been prescribed for the election expenses of candidates at rates for each state depending on the number of voters in the constituencies. However, the election expenditure of political parties on behalf of candidates is not included in this amount. The campaign has to end in a constituency 48 hours before the close of poll. The Election Commission evolves a model code of conduct from time to time and the political leaders are expected to follow it while campaigning.

The Representation of the People Act provides that no person has right to vote if he/she is not entered in the electoral roll of the constituency. No person can vote in a general election in more than one constituency of the same class. No person can vote in any election in the same constituency more than once. No person shall vote in any election if he/she is confined in a prison, whether under a sentence of imprisonment or transportation or otherwise, or is in the lawful custody of the police. However, this provision does not apply to a person subjected to preventive detention under any law for the time being in force.

Votes are counted by, or under the supervision and direction of, the returning officer, and each contesting candidate, his election agent, and his counting agents have a right to be present at the time of counting.

Previously, the election was countermanded on the death of a contesting candidate. Now, no election will be countermanded on the death of a contesting candidate. If the deceased candidate, however, was set up by a recognised national or state party, the party concerned will be given an option to nominate another candidate within seven days of the issue of a notice to that effect to the party concerned by the Election Commission.

If, after the counting of the votes is completed, an equality of votes is found to exist between any candidates, and the addition of one vote will entitle any of those candidates to be declared elected, the returning officer shall forthwith decide between those candidates by lot, and proceed as if the candidate on whom the lot falls had received an additional vote.

When the counting of the votes is completed, the returning officer declares the name of the winning candidate.

As soon as may be, after the result of an election has been declared, the returning officer reports the result to the appropriate authority and the Election Commission, and in the case of an election to a house of Parliament or of the legislature of a state, also to the secretary of that house. The appropriate authority publishes in the Official Gazette the declarations containing the names of the elected candidates. The date on which a candidate is declared elected by the returning officer is the date of election of that candidate.

If a candidate is chosen as a member of both the houses and he has not taken his seat in either house, he may, by notice in writing delivered to the secretary to the Election Commission, intimate in which of the Houses he wishes to serve. In default of such intimation within the stipulated period, his seat in the upper house shall, at the expiration of that period, become vacant.

If a person is elected to more than one seat in either house of Parliament or in either house of the legislature of a state, then, unless within the prescribed time he resigns one of the seats, both seats shall become vacant.

The deposit of a candidate is forfeited if at an election where a poll has been taken, the candidate is not elected and the number of valid votes polled by him does not exceed one-sixth of the total number of valid votes polled by all the candidates or in the case of election of more than one member at the election, one-sixth of the total number of valid votes so polled divided by the number of members to be elected.

Declaration of Assets and Liabilities

Every elected candidate for a House of Parliament, within ninety days from the date on which he makes and subscribes an oath or affirmation for taking his seat in either house of Parliament, furnishes the information relating to

(i) The movable and immovable property of which he, his spouse, and his dependent children are jointly or severally owners or beneficiaries;

(ii) His liabilities to any public financial institution; and

(iii) His liabilities to the central government or the state government–to the Chairman of the Council of States or the Speaker to the House of the People, as the case may be.

Account of Election Expenses

Regarding the elections to the House of the People and to the legislative assembly of a state, every candidate at an election shall keep a separate and correct account of all expenditure in connection with the election incurred or authorised by him by his election agent between the date on which he has been nominated and the date of declaration of the result, both dates inclusive. The candidate within thirty days from the date of election of the candidate needs to lodge with the district election officer the account of his election expenses.

Corrupt Practices and Electoral Offences

Corrupt Practices

The following practices are considered as corrupt practices as per the Representation of the People Act, 1951.

1. "Bribery" which is (a) any gift, offer or promise by a candidate or his agent or by any other person with the consent of a candidate or his election agent of any gratification, to any person whomsoever, with the object, directly or indirectly, of inducing a person to stand or not to stand as, or to withdraw or not to withdraw from being a candidate at an election; or an elector to vote or refrain from voting at an election, or as a reward to (i) a person for having so stood or not stood, or for having withdrawn or not having withdrawn his candidature; or (ii) an elector for having voted or refrained from voting; (b) the receipt of, or agreement to receive, any gratification, whether as a motive or a reward- by a person for standing or not standing as, or for withdrawing or not withdrawing from being, a candidate; or by any person whomsoever for himself or any other person for voting or refraining from voting, or inducing or attempting to induce any elector to vote or refrain from voting, or any candidate to withdraw or not to withdraw his candidature.

2. Undue influence, which is any direct or indirect interference or attempt to interfere on the part of the candidate or his agent or of any other person with the consent of the candidate or his election agent, with the free exercise of any electoral right.
3. The appeal by a candidate or his agent or by any other person with the consent of a candidate or his election agent to vote or refrain from voting for any person on the ground of his religion, race, caste, community or language or the use of, or appeal to religious symbols or the use of, or appeal to, national symbols, such as the national flag or the national emblem, for the furtherance of the prospects of the election of that candidate or for prejudicially affecting the election of any candidate.
4. The promotion of, or attempt to promote, feelings of enmity or hatred between different classes of the citizens of India on grounds of religion, race, caste, community, or language.
5. The propagation of the practice or the commission of *sati* or its glorification.
6. The publication of any statement of fact which is false, and which he either believes to be false or does not believe to be true, in relation to the personal character or conduct of any candidate, or in relation to the candidate, or withdrawal, of any candidate, being a statement reasonably calculated to prejudice the prospects of that candidate's election.
7. The hiring or procuring, whether on payment or otherwise, of any vehicle or vessel.
8. The incurring or authorising of expenditure in contravention of this Act.
9. The obtaining or procuring or abetting or attempting to obtain or procure by a candidate any assistance (other than the giving of vote) for the furtherance of the prospects of that candidate's election, from any person in the service of the government.

Electoral Offences

The Representation of the People Act, 1951 lists the following as electoral offences:

(i) Promoting enmity between classes in connection with election on ground of religion race, caste, community, or language;
(ii) If a candidate fails to furnish information, or gives false information, or conceals any information required under law;
(iii) Conducting public meetings during the period of forty-eight hours before the election;
(iv) Causing disturbances at election meetings;
(v) Printing pamphlets, posters, etc. which do not bear on its face the name or address of the printer and the publisher;
(vi) Violation of maintenance of secrecy of voting by any officer, clerk, agent, or other person who performs any duty in connection with voting processes;
(vii) Any act (other than the giving of vote) for furtherance of the prospects of the election of a candidate by a district election officer or a returning officer, or an assistant returning officer, or a presiding or polling officer, or an officer or clerk appointed for conduct of election;
(viii) Canvassing in or near polling station on the poll dates;
(ix) Disorderly conduct in or near polling stations;
(x) Misconduct at the polling station;

(xi) Failure to observe procedure for voting;

(xii) Illegal hiring or procuring of conveyance at elections;

(xiii) Breaches of official duty in connection with election;

(xiv) Acting of a government servant as election agent, polling agent, or counting agent of a candidate;

(xv) Going to or near a polling station with arms defined in Arms Act, 1959;

(xvi) Attempt to take a ballot paper out of a polling station;

(xvii) Selling, giving, or distributing liquor on polling day;

Other offences are committed when a person engages in acts like:

(a) Fraudulently defacing or fraudulently destroying any nomination paper; or

(b) Fraudulently defacing, destroying, or removing any list, notice, or other document affixed by or under the authority of a returning officer; or

(c) Fraudulently defacing or fraudulently destroying any ballot paper or the official mark on any ballot paper or any declaration of identity or official envelope used in connection with voting by postal ballot; or

(d) Without due authority supplying any ballot paper to any person or receiving any ballot paper from any person or is in possession of any ballot paper; or

(e) Fraudulently putting into any ballot box anything other than the ballot paper which he is authorised by law to put in; or

(f) without due authority destroying, taking, opening, or otherwise interfering with any ballot box or ballot papers then in use for the purposes of the election; or

(g) Fraudulently or without due authority attempting to do any of the foregoing acts or wilfully aiding or abetting the doing of any such acts.

Disputes Regarding Elections

High Courts of respective constituencies have jurisdiction to try an election petition. An election may be called in question only by an election petition to the high court presented within forty-five days from the date of election of the returned candidate.

At the conclusion of the trial of an election petition, the high court may make an order:

(a) Dismissing the election petition; or

(b) Declaring the election of all or any of the returned candidates to be void; or

(c) Declaring the election of all or any of the returned candidates to be void and the petitioner or any other candidate to have been duly elected.

An election may be declared void if the high court is of the opinion that:

(a) On the date of his election a returned candidate was not qualified, or was disqualified, to be chosen to fill the seat;

(b) Any corrupt practice has been committed by a returned candidate or his election agent or by any other person with the consent of a returned candidate or his election agent; or

(c) Any nomination has been improperly rejected; or

(d) The result of the election, in so far as it concerns a returned candidate, has been materially affected, (i) by the improper acceptance or any nomination, or (ii) by any corrupt practice committed in the interests of the returned candidate by an agent other than his election agent, or (iii) by the improper reception, refusal, or rejection of any vote or the reception of any vote which is void, or (iv) by any non-compliance with the provisions of the Constitution or of this Act or of any rules or orders made under this Act.

The high court may declare a candidate other than the returned candidate duly elected and the election of the returned candidate to be void if the court is of the opinion that:

(a) In fact the petitioner or other candidate received a majority of the valid votes; or

(b) But for the votes obtained by the returned candidate by corrupt practices the petitioner or other candidate would have obtained a majority of the valid votes. Regarding any decision of the high court concerning election petition, an appeal can be made to the Supreme Court within a period of thirty days from the date of the order of the high court or any question of law or fact.

Amendments to Electoral Laws

Voting Age Lowered

The Constitution (Sixty-first Amendment) Act, 1988 amended Article 326 by substituting the words 'eighteen years' for 'twenty one years'. This came into force on March 28, 1989. Consequent to this, amendments were also made in the Representation of the People Act, 1950 and the Representation of the People Act, 1951. Voting age is thus 18 years. This has been done to give a voice to the youth of this country and help them participate in the political process.

Increase in Number of Proposers and Security Deposit

The Representation of the People (Amendment) Act of 1988 increased the number of proposers for Rajya Sabha and state legislative council candidates to 10 per cent of the electors of the constituency or 10 such electors. Again, in an amendment to the RPA in 1996, the nomination of a candidate in a Parliamentary or assembly constituency was fixed to be subscribed by ten electors of the constituency as proposers, if the candidate was not set up by a recognised national or state party. In the case of a candidate set up by a recognised party, only one proposer is required.

The Presidential and Vice-Presidential Elections (Amendment) Act, 1997 increased the number of proposers and seconders for contesting election to the office of the President of India to fifty each in place of ten; number of electors as proposers and seconders for contesting the Vice-Presidential election was increased to 20 each in place of five. The amount of security deposit was increased to Rs.15,000 in place of Rs. 2,500 for contesting election to the offices of President and Vice-President.

The increase in proposers is meant to discourage non-serious candidates. By the Representation of the People (Amendment) Act 2009, the amount of security deposit to be paid by candidates to the Lok Sabha and state assembly elections was increased. This again, was a measure to check non-serious candidates.

Introduction of Electronic Voting Machines

The Representation of the People Act, 1951 was amended to facilitate use of electronic voting machines (EVMs) in elections from 1989. EVMs were first used in November 1998 in various constituencies in the State elections of Rajasthan, Madhya Pradesh, and Delhi. The entire State Assembly elections in Goa in June 1999 were held with EVMs.

Now EVMs are used on an all-India basis.

The use of EVMs reduces the use of paper, and they are, thus, eco-friendly. It is cost-effective, reducing the cost of printing–only one ballot paper is required for every polling station.

Where booth-capturing is concerned, its impact can be controlled with the EVMs, if not eliminated altogether. The presiding officer or one of the polling officers can always press the close button in EVMs. Then, it will not be possible to record any vote.

The microchip used in EVMs is sealed at the time of import. It cannot be opened and no rewriting of programme can be done by anyone without damaging the chip. There is, therefore, absolutely no chance of programming the EVMs in a particular way to select any particular candidate or political party. Nor is it possible to vote more than once. As soon as a particular button on the balloting unit is pressed, the vote is recorded for that particular candidate and the machine gets locked.

There are no invalid votes under the system of voting under EVMs. To this extent, the choice of the electorate will be more correctly reflected when EVMs are used.

Yet another advantage is that, in case one EVM goes out of order there is no need to start the poll from the beginning; the duty officer in charge of about 10 polling stations carry spare EVMs, and can replace the EVM which has gone out of order.

Meeting the Challenge of Booth Capturing

Section 58A has been inserted in the Representation of the People Act, 1951 by Act 1 of 1989 providing for adjournment of poll or countermanding of elections because of booth capturing. Booth capturing has been defined in Section 135A of the Representation of the People Act, 1951. It includes among other things: (a) seizure of a polling station or a place fixed for poll by any person or persons, making polling authorities surrender ballot papers or voting machines, and doing of any other act which affects orderly conduct of elections; (b) taking possession of polling station or a place fixed for poll by any person or persons and allowing only his or their own supporters to exercise their franchise and preventing others from voting; (c) threatening any elector and preventing him from going to the polling station or a place fixed for poll to cast his vote; (d) seizure of a place for counting of votes by any person or persons, making counting authorities surrender ballot papers or voting machines and doing of anything which affects orderly counting of votes, and (e) doing, by any person in the service of government, of all or any of aforesaid activities or aiding or conniving at any such activity in furtherance of election prospects of a candidate.

Section 135A provides penalty for booth capturing which shall be imprisonment along with fine.

Listing Names of Candidates

The amendment to the RPA, 1951 in 1996 stipulated candidates, who are to be classified as (a) candidates of recognised political parties, (b) candidates of registered, unrecognised political parties, and (c) other (independent) candidates. Their names in the list of contesting candidates and in the ballot papers needs to appear separately in the above order and in each category they are to be arranged in alphabetical order. This is meant to help voters to identify the contestants easily.

Restriction to Two Constituencies

A candidate is now not eligible to contest election from more than two Parliamentary or assembly constituencies at a general election or at the bye-elections which are held simultaneously. Similar restrictions apply for biennial elections and bye-elections to the council of states and state legislative councils.

Death of a Candidate not to Affect Election

Previously, the election was countermanded on the death of a contesting candidate. But after the 1996 amendment to the RPA, 1951, no election will be countermanded on the death of a contesting candidate. If the deceased candidate, however, was set up by a recognised national or state party, the party concerned will be given an option to nominate another candidate within seven days of the issue of a notice to that effect by the party concerned to the Election Commission. This ensures that time and the costly preparation for elections are not wasted.

By-elections Within Stipulated Time

Bye-elections to any house of Parliament or a State Legislature have to be held within six months of occurrence of the vacancy in the house. However, this stipulation will not apply where the remainder of the term of the member whose vacancy is to be filled is less than one year or where the Election Commission, in consultation with the central government, certifies that it is difficult to hold the bye-election within the said period.

Arms and Liquor Banned near Polling Area

Going armed with any kind of arms as defined in the Arms Act, 1959 within the neighbourhood of a polling station was made a cognisable offence punishable with imprisonment up to two years or with fine or with both in the 1996 amendment. Arms found in possession of the offender are liable to confiscation and licence granted in relation to such arms would also be revoked. These provisions, however, do not apply in the case of returning officer, presiding officer, any police officer, or any other person appointed to maintain peace and order at the polling station.

No liquor or other intoxicants are to be sold, given, or distributed at any shop, eating place, hotel, or any other place, whether public or private, within a polling area during the period of 48 hours ending with the hour fixed for the conclusion of poll. Any person contravening the law shall be punished with imprisonment up to six months or with fine up to Rs. 2,000 or with both.

Requirement by Candidates to Declare Assets and Criminal Antecedents, etc.

In a far-reaching order in 2003, the Election Commission issued guidelines requiring every candidate in Parliamentary and state polls to file an affidavit at the time of his/her nomination, furnishing information on whether he/she has been convicted, acquitted, or discharged in any criminal offence in the past; whether he/she has even been imprisoned; whether he/she has a case pending against him/her in an offence punishable with imprisonment for two years or more, and in which charges were framed and cognisance was taken by a court prior to six months of filing nomination, and details of the case; details of the movable and immovable assets owned by the candidate and his/her spouse and dependents; his/her liabilities/dues to public financial institutions and government dues; and his/her educational qualifications.

Changes in Rajya Sabha Elections

Domicile requirement has been removed. Also, the open ballot system has been introduced, the purpose being to weed out cross-voting and the use of money power to induce electors to vote for particular candidates. These steps were taken in 2003 by amending the Representation of the People Act.

Restrictions on Exit Polls

Restrictions were made on exit polls in 2009 by inserting the clauses 126A and 126B in the Representation of the People Act, 1951. No person is to conduct any exit poll and publish and publicise by means of the print or electronic media or disseminate in any other manner, whatsoever, the result of any exit poll during such period, as might be notified by the Election Commission in this regard.

All Officials in Corrupt Practice Net

The 2009 amendment to RPA provides for the inclusion of all officials (government or non-government service) appointed or deputed to the Election Commission with regard to the conduct of elections within the scope of the corrupt practice act if they indulge in assisting a candidate for furthering his/her prospects in the election.

Concessions Towards Election Expenses

An amendment of the Election and other related laws in 2003, was made when it was declared that the travel expenses of campaign leaders of political parties need not be included in the election expenses of a candidate.

Political parties, by the same amendment, are entitled to accept any amount as contribution from anyone or any company (though not a government company); however, a contribution exceeding Rs. 20,000 has to be reported to the Election Commission if claim to relief from income tax is sought. The contributing company is entitled to income tax exemption on the contribution.

The government is expected to make available to all candidates of recognised political parties, free of cost, copies of the electoral rolls, and other prescribed material.

Appeal Against Electoral Registration Officer's Order Within District

As per the amendments of 2009, appeal against the order of the Electoral Registration Officer (during continuous updation of the electoral roll) under the Representation of the People Act, 1950 would now lie with the district magistrate (DM), additional district magistrate (ADM), executive magistrate, or district collector. A further appeal against the order of DM or collector would now lie before the chief electoral officer of the state.

Postal Ballot

The Representation of the People (Amendment) Act, 1999 provided for voting through postal ballot by certain classes of people. These classes can be notified by the Election Commission in consultation with the government. Persons of such notified classes cannot vote in any other manner at elections in their constituencies.

Disqualification Case to be submitted Within Specified Time

The Representation of People's (Amendment) Act of 2009 simplified the procedure for the disqualification of a person found guilty of corrupt practices. A three-month limit is now provided for the authority concerned to submit a case of a person found guilty of corrupt practice to the President who may then decide on the disqualification.

Citizens of India Living Abroad get Voting Rights

The Representation of the People (Amendment) Act, 2010, which amends the Representation of the People Act, 1950, confers voting rights on citizens of India who are absent from their place or ordinary residence in India owing to their employment, education, or otherwise outside India (whether temporarily or not).

Vote Through Proxy

Service voters belonging to the armed forces and members belonging to a force to which the Army Act applies were given the facility to opt to vote through proxy under the amendment in 2003 of the Election Laws and the Conduct of Elections (Amendment) Rules, 2003. Such a voter has to appoint a proxy in the prescribed format and intimate the returning officer of the constituency to the effect.

NATIONAL PARTIES AND STATE PARTIES

The Election Commission registers the political parties so that they participate in elections. The commission grants them recognition on the basis of their poll performance as national or state parties under the Election Symbols (Reservation and Allotment) Order, 1968. Those that are neither national nor state parties are known as registered unrecognised parties.

The Election Commission promulgated the Election Symbols (Reservation and Allotment) Order, 1968 on August 31, 1968, in exercise of its powers under Article 324 of the Constitution and the Conduct of Elections Rules, 1961.

The commission has, from time to time, keeping in view the changes in the political scenario in the country, brought about amendments to the symbols order. In 1977, in a major amendment, the commission recognised the importance of the role being played by state parties in the country's democratic structure and sought to give, as far as possible, the usage of symbols on an exclusive basis, all over the country, for all state parties.

In 2000, the commission, brought in amendments based on the following five principles, which, in its view, should govern the polity in the country.

(i) Legislative presence is a must for recognition as a national or state party.

(ii) For a national party, it must be the legislative presence in the Lok Sabha, and, for a state party, the legislative presence must be reflected in the state assembly.

(iii) In any election, a party can set up a candidate only from amongst its own members.

(iv) A party, that loses its recognition, shall not lose its symbol immediately, but shall be given the facility to use that symbol for some time to try and retrieve its status. (However, the grant of use of symbol does not mean the extension of other facilities to it, as are available to recognised parties, such as, free time on electronic media, free supply of copies of electoral rolls, etc.)

(v) Recognition should be given to a party only on the basis of its own performance in elections and not because it is a splinter group of some other recognised party.

The revised criteria for recognition are not to be applied to the detriment of any of the existing recognised national and state parties.

Criteria for a National Party

As of 2013, a party is considered national if (i) it secures at least six per cent of the valid votes polled in any four or more states, at a general election to the Lok Sabha or to the state legislative assembly; and in addition, it wins at least four seats in the Lok Sabha from any state or states; or (ii) It wins at least two per cent seats in the Lok Sabha (i.e., 11 seats in the existing house having 543 members), and these members are elected from at least three different states; or (iii) It is recognised as a state party in four states.

Criteria for a State Party

As of 2013, a political party entitled to be recognised as a state party, if

(i) it ensures at least six per cent of the valid votes polled in the state at a general election to the legislative assembly of the state concerned, and in addition, it wins at least two seats in the legislative assembly of the state concerned; or

(ii) it wins at least three per cent of the total number of seats in the legislative assembly of the state, or at least three seats in the assembly, whichever is more; or

(iii) it secures six per cent of the valid votes polled in the state in a general election to the Lok Sabha from that state, and in addition it wins one state in the Lok Sabha from the state concerned; or

(iv) it wins one seat in the Lok Sabha for every 25 seats or any fraction thereof allotted to the state at a general election to the Lok Sabha from the state concerned; or

(v) it secures eight per cent or more of the total valid votes polled in the state in a general election to the Lok Sabha or legislative assembly of the state, even if it fails to win any seat.

[The last provision was added after the Election Commission amended Election Symbols (Reservations and Allotment) Order 1968 and issued a new order in September 2011.]

In all the above cases, 'state' includes the National Capital Territory of Delhi and the Union Territory of Puducherry.

Convicted Lawmakers

The Supreme Court of India held section 8(4) of Representation of People Act 1951 as void being unconstitutional in *Lily Thomas Vs Union of India Case*.

It was held that under Article 102(1)(e) and 191(1)(e) of the constitution, competence does not exist to provide different grounds for disqualification for a person to be chosen as a member of legislature and sitting member of legislature (These Articles provide different yardsticks for persons; the existing members and those seeking to be).

Furthermore, the Supreme Court held:

Article 101(3) and 190 (3) mandates that the seat of a member will become vacant automatically and immediately on disqualification.

Therefore, deferring the date of disqualification is unconstitutional and void.

The court however held further that the judgement will not apply to sitting members of parliament and state legislatures who had been using the provisions.

In effect, this judgement has brought automatic disqualification as against the previous system where convicted law makers would go in for appeal and await the outcome. Convicted lawmakers will not face law first.

'Office of Profit'....Oop(s).

The term 'Office of Profit' has its origins from the English Parliament of the times of around the time of the civil war of the 17th century. The king and the Parliament were at loggerheads; many of the Parliamentarians often were not available to attend the sessions owing to being in employment in service of the king. A bar was put on such persons to being members of the Parliament.

Indian constitution too addressed the issue through Article 102(1)(a) and 191 (1)(a). Between the two of them it held that 'who holds the office of profit under the government is disqualified from being chosen a member of Parliament or state legislative assembly'.

If pecuniary gain isn't present, it is not an office of profit. *Gobinda Basu Vs Shankari Prasad Ghosh (1964), Maulana Abdul Shakoor Vs Rikhab Chand (1958)* cases laid down the basic conditions to determine if someone is holding an office of profit.

Article 102(2) makes it obligatory on the part of the President to act according to Election Commission's opinion. Jaya Bachchan and Jayalalitha's cases are relevant examples of such instances of those holding 'offices of profit'. Main consideration is remuneration in cash.

Did you know?

The Supreme Court of India held section 8(4) of Representation of People Act 1951 as void being unconstitutional in *Lily Thomas Vs Union of India Case.*

It was held that under Article 102(1)(e) and 191(1)(e) of the constitution, competence does not exist to provide different grounds for disqualification for a person to be chosen as a member of legislature and sitting member of legislature (These Articles provide different yardsticks for persons; the existing members and those seeking to be).

Furthermore, the Supreme Court held:

Article 101(3) and 190 (3) mandates that the seat of a member will become vacant automatically and immediately on disqualification.

Therefore, deferring the date of disqualification is unconstitutional and void.

The court however held further that the judgement will not apply to sitting members of parliament and state legislatures who had been using the provisions.

In effect, this judgement has brought automatic disqualification as against the previous system where convicted law makers would go in for appeal and await the outcome.

8

CHAPTER

Appointments to Various Constitutional Posts, Bodies–Powers, Functions and Responsibilities

OVERVIEW

Constitutional bodies are like watchdogs that keep a watch on various institutions related to polity and governance. Sanctified by the Constitution, these bodies have posts that are also granted constitutional status. This makes both the bodies as well as the posts independent of the executive, supported by the legislature, and sustained by the judiciary. What are the functions and responsibilities of such constitutional bodies and how are the posts therein filled? This is indeed a vital issue and this chapter provides valuable insights.

INTRODUCTION

The chapters on 'Polity' (8-11) are best understood when tackled together. There are linkages which when seen in the larger perspective becomes easy to relate.

Policies are made by governments in the context of political, economic, social and other compulsions. These in turn are unfolded and extended through various schemes and plans. Once the schemes are announced, the implementation stage takes over. However, the best of plans fail in implementation if their original design is faulty or flawed. Moreover, even good plans come a cropper if the policies are not implemented properly

During the implementation stage, there are many factors that matter viz, technology, transparency, accountability, time schedule, ethics, etc. There are also social and environmental issues that need to be considered. A case in point is the relentless drive for industrialisation bringing pressure on landholders.

Another issue is the impact of infrastructure development on the environment. For example, the highways development plan will result in cutting down of trees.

In the development process, essentially, besides the government, who are the other stakeholders? What of NGOs, SHGs, charities, donors, various groups and associations, etc.? Everything can't be left to the government; there has to be mobilisation, motivation, and meaning. This can happen only when the policies, plans, and processes are not only manifestly seen, but believed by the stakeholders to be of merit and use for them.

Governments come under compulsion both internally as well as externally to evolve policies which could be short-term as also long-term. Compulsions could be economic, political, or social. Demographic changes compel evolving of policies. In the country today, 40 per cent of the population is below 20 years of age, making our country one of the youngest in the world. Policy makers have to keep this reality in view while evolving policies. Similarly, the life expectancy is rising giving policy makers anxious moments to find policies to sustain them. Gender ratio is another consideration.

It is an interesting fact that India has always had major changes taking place after every twenty years; the following will illustrate the point.

2013–2014: General Elections brought in a new government with a decisive shift in policies.

1995–1996: 73rd /74th amendments brought in devolution of powers to the grassroot level with Panchayats and Municipalities.

1991 Forced by circumstances, the country goes in for economic liberalisation and a decisive break from the socialistic model of development.

1975–1976: Internal Emergency at the Centre, country saw loss of freedom but gain in order.

1955–56: Second Five Year Plan, push for massive industrialisation.

1935–1936: Government of India Act, a giant stride in our constitutional development.

1919: Montague–Chelmsford Act; 1915–1916 were years of war: hence no major shift.

1899: Curzon's reformist zeal engages India. In fact, the British East India company too laid the seeds of 20 year reviews.

1773: Regulating Act of Warren Hastings.

1793: Cornwallis's Act of permanent settlement.

1813: Review of the Act; charter reviewed.

1833: Charter Act revised, reviewed.

1853: Charter Act reviewed; East India bit the bullet and was consigned to oblivion.

1858: Queen's proclamation signalling end of the Company rule.

1877–78: Viceroy's Lytton's Delhi Durbar. India reeled under famine.

1898–99: Curzon arrives in India to give the decisive push, the divisive prod, and the determined pace to wake all up. India would never be the same again.

May be it was the British who laid the system of review after every twenty years in our psyche or system that we have imbibed it so meticulously.

POWERS, FUNCTIONS, AND RESPONSIBILITIES OF VARIOUS CONSTITUTIONAL BODIES

The Indian Constitution permits creation of some bodies through its own mechanisms and procedures to discharge set obligations, without the slightest of dependence, fear, or favour or consideration from the executive. Such bodies draw their sustenance from the Constitution, substance from the Parliament, and sustainability from the systems in place guaranteeing their independence, neutrality, and vitality. These constitutional bodies owe their existence to given Articles of the constitution.

They maintain their neutrality and independence because of the provisions as under:

(a) They draw their salaries for officials and expenses for office from the Consolidated Fund which is not under the executive but with the House of elected representatives, Lok Sabha, or State Legislature.

(b) Removal of constitutional body heads is like removal of Supreme Court judges; removal on account of misbehaviour can be decided only by the Supreme Court.

(c) Rights and powers of constitutional bodies are mentioned in the constitution itself and executive cannot change it.

Article	Constitutional Body
280.	Finance Commission.
315-323.	Union Public Service Commission, State Public Service Commission.
324.	Election Commission.
338.	National Commission for Scheduled Castes.
338A.	National Commission for Scheduled Tribes.

Constitutional bodies submit their annual reports to the President who, in turn, causes them to be laid on the table of the Parliament which proceeds to discuss, debate, and decide.

APPOINTMENT TO VARIOUS CONSTITUTIONAL POSTS

The Constitution of India provides for various constitutional posts which are created to further the cause of constitutional governance in the country. These posts are safeguards for ensuring that the provisions of the constitution are in place, in force, and in acceptance.

The Constitution, by itself, ensures that these post holders are independent and have the mandate to function. This is ensured by:

(a) The provisions in the constitution itself that they are not dependent on the executive for their salary and other allowances. They are paid from the Consolidated Fund of India which is with the Parliament to vote and account for.

(b) In order that these constitutional post holders do not come under executive whims, fancy, or caprice, they are given constitutional protection for removal from the posts.

(c) They are, in the ultimate analysis, accountable to the legislature; the will of the people, who are supreme.

What are the constitutional posts and how does the constitution deal with them? The major ones are given below:

1. The President
2. The Vice-President
3. Judges of Supreme Court, High Court.
4. The Prime Minister and the Council of Ministers.
5. The Governors.
6. The Chief Minister and the Ministers.
7. The Speaker of Lok Sabha, the Deputy Chairman of Lok Sabha; as also Deputy Speaker of Lok Sabha.

Note: *Cabinet Secretary and Chief Secretary are civil post holders, not constitutional post holders.*

The following are the other important constitutional post holders.

1. Comptroller and Auditor General (Art. 148–151)
2. Attorney General (Art. 76, 88)

   It may be of interest to note that although the constitution provides for the post of Attorney General, he is to hold office during the pleasure of the President (Art. 76(4)); just the same way Advocate General is to hold the office in the state during the pleasure of the Governor. (Art. 165(3))

   Comptroller and Auditor General is there for the Union as also the States, and for any other authority or body as prescribed by the Parliament.

COMPTROLLER AND AUDITOR GENERAL (CAG)

The word 'Comptroller' means 'the person who computes and calculates accounts such as income and expenditure' and the expression 'Auditor General' means, the principal person who inspects and checks the accounts.

Two capacities are invested in one person. The Comptroller and Auditor General has jurisdiction to go into the nature of expenses and its applications and reasonableness with the provision made in the budget and also as to the truth and correctness of the entries made in the account. Reports of the Comptroller and the Auditor General are given to the President and through him to the Parliament. In the case of the accounts of the State, they are submitted to the Governor and through him before the State Legislature. His post is a Constitutional appointment directly made by the President. He can be removed only by impeachment. While submitting reports of the Comptroller and Auditor General to the Parliament, the President also encloses the report of the Government called Action Taken Report. This Report deals with all objections and recommendations made by the Comptroller and Auditor General. Parliament can issue directions to the Government on the manner in which the recommendations and objections should be complied. Though the appointment is made by the President, the pay and allowance of the Comptroller and Auditor General is fixed by the Parliament. While doing so the pay and allowances of the staff of the Comptroller and Auditor General are also fixed.

Art. 148 :

(1) There shall be a Comptroller and Auditor General of India who shall be appointed by the President by warrant under his hand and seal and shall only be removed from office in like manner and on like grounds as a judge of the Supreme Court.

(2) Every person appointed to be the Comptroller and Auditor General of India, shall before he enters his office, make and subscribe before the President, or some person appointed in that behalf by him, an oath or affirmation according to the form set out for the purpose in the Third Schedule.

(3) The salaries and other conditions of service of the Comptroller and Auditor General shall be such as may be determined by Parliament by law and, until they are so determined, shall be specified in the Second Schedule.

[Provided that neither the salary of a Comptroller and Auditor General nor his rights in respect of leave of absence, pension, or age of retirement shall be varied to his disadvantage after his appointment.]

(4) The Comptroller and Auditor General shall not be eligible for further office either under Government of India or under the Government of any state after he has ceased to hold his office.

(5) Subject to the provisions of the constitution and of any law made by Parliament, the conditions of service of persons serving in the India Audit and Accounts Department and the administrative powers of the Comptroller and Auditor General shall be such as may be prescribed by rules made by the President after consultations with the Comptroller and Auditor General.

(6) The administrative expenses of the office of Comptroller and Auditor General shall be charged upon the Consolidated Fund of India (including all salaries, allowances, and pensions payable to or in respect of persons serving in that office)

Art. 149:

Duties and Powers of the Comptroller and Auditor General

"Comptroller" means an official in charge of public finance.

The Comptroller and Auditor General shall perform such duties and exercise such powers in relation to the accounts of the Union and the States and of any other authority or body as may be prescribed by on under any law made by Parliament and until provisions in that behalf is so made shall perform such duties and exercise such powers in relation to the accounts of the Union and of States as were conferred on or exercisable by the Auditor General of India before commencement of this constitution in relation to the accounts of the Dominion of India and of the Provinces respectively.

Art. 150:

Form of Accounts of the Union and of the States

The accounts of the Union and of the States shall be kept in such form as the President may on the advice of the Comptroller and Auditor General of India prescribe.

Art. 151:

Auditor Reports

(1) The reports of the Comptroller and Auditor General of India relating to the accounts of the Union shall be submitted to the President who shall cause them to be laid before each House of Parliament.

(2) The reports of the Comptroller and Auditor General of India relating to the accounts of a state shall be submitted to the Governor of the state, who shall cause them to be laid before the legislature of the state.

ATTORNEY GENERAL AND ADVOCATE GENERAL

Attorney General of India occupies dual posts, being the advisor to the Union on legal matters and also the advocate for the Union. Nobody else can carry out these functions. In fact, nobody can be appointed even temporarily to carry out his functions. The Attorney General can concede the points, which according to his conscience are reasonable and correct, even though they are opposed to the opinion of the Government. If he does not agree with the views of the Government he must resign and not continue to drum his views. That's why the Attorney General offers to resign from his post whenever the Government alters after each election. The Attorney General carries out and discharges functions as the President may order. He has to appear before the Commissions and Tribunals such as inter-State river water tribunals on behalf of the Union; He can even appear for any State Government on its behalf in which the Union is not a party. The Attorney General is entitled to private practice but can't argue against the Union Government when appointed by the State Government. He can while appearing for private parties oppose the State Government. Attorney General is the empowered authority to sanction applications of private parties in contempt matters. Only in the case where he himself does not prefer to file a contempt application, he shall permit private parties to file contempt applications. The Attorney General, if so requested, may even address the Parliament and participate in discussions. However, he is not entitled to vote on any issue. If requested, he can also participate in the discussions of Parliamentary Committees.

Art. 76:

Attorney General of India

(1) The President shall appoint a person who is qualified to be appointed as Judge of the Supreme Court to be Attorney General for India.

(2) It shall be the duty of the Attorney General to give advice to the Government of India upon such legal matters, and to perform such other duties of a legal character, as may from time to time be referred or assigned to him by the President and to discharge the function conferred on him by or under this constitution or any other law for the time being in force.

(3) In the performance of his duties the Attorney General shall have right of audience in all courts in the territories of India.

(4) The Attorney General shall hold the office during the pleasure of the President and shall receive such remuneration as the President may determine.

Art. 165:

Advocate General for the State

(1) The Governor of each state shall appoint a person who is qualified to be appointed as Judge of a High Court to be Advocate General for the State.

(2) It shall be the duty of the Advocate General to give advice to the Government of the State upon such legal matters, and to perform such other duties of a legal character, or may time to time be referred or assigned to him by the Governor, and to discharge the functions conferred on him by or under this constitution or any other law for the time being in force.

(3) The Advocate General shall hold office during the pleasure of the Governor, and shall receive such remuneration as the Governor may determine.

Note : Solicitor General, Additional Solicitor General are not constitutional posts.

Art. 350B:

Special Officer for Linguistic Minorities

1) There shall be a special officer for linguistic minorities to be appointed by the President

2) It shall be the duty of the Special Officer to investigate all matters relating to the safeguards provided for linguistic minorities under this Constitution and report to the President upon those matters at such intervals as the President may direct and the President shall cause all such reports to be laid before each House of Parliament and sent to the governments of the States concerned. Article 350 provides for any language to be used by every person to redress his grievances.

Article 350-A provides that it shall be the endeavour of every State government to provide facilities for instruction in mother tongue for the children belonging to minority groups.

ROLE OF CONTROLLER GENERAL OF ACCOUNTS (CGA)

In recent times the Controller General is seen to be entering the matters of policy. 2G Spectrum is an example and allegations of corruption were also taken up by him. Both the matters are outside the jurisdiction of the Controller. He is mainly and substantially concerned only with accounting–whether the expenditure is duly supported by records and whether the expenditure is within the budget provision. There are also several issues involved in sanctioning a project and the method under which the project shall be executed. Tenders can be granted only when the tender fulfils the qualifications required. Such fulfilment may be prior to the grant of tender or after the tender is proposed to be granted. The bidders who win the tender are granted time to fulfill certain terms after which they qualify for acceptance of the tender. The Controller has no jurisdiction to interfere or comment upon all these issues.

COMMISSIONS

Public Service Commission

Articles 315 to 323

Why is the Public Service Commission set up? It selects public servants who would help the Government to carry on the administration successfully. Only such persons are selected:

(1) who have the attitude to receive the advices to which he is exposed; and

(2) who are found to be dedicated to serve the subject to which he is attached.

In other words a public servant should be liberal, educated and trained in all subjects of human endeavour. The Public Service Commission holds two written examinations and an interview. The first test is called Preliminary and the second written test is called Mains. The Public Service Commission can be consulted for purpose of recruiting public servants for the Union. A Public Service Commission can also be appointed for each State and if so desired by the States, a common Public Service Commission may be appointed for two or more States. Union Public Service Commission may also serve the needs of any State or States, if requested. The Parliament has also power to appoint joint Public Service Commission for two or more States.

The Chairman and members of Public Service Commission can hold office till they reach the retirement age of 65 years in the case of Union Public Service Commission and till they reach the age of 62 in case of State Public Service Commission. The members of the Public Service Commission are appointed for a fixed period of six years and after they retire they may be reappointed to the post when they have not reached the age of their retirement. A special procedure for removal of the members of the Public Service Commission exists. Only when the charge of misbehaviour is held proved by the Supreme Court, the President or the Governor may remove the member of the Public Service Commission. The only ground on which a member of the Public Service Commission can be removed is misbehaviour and nothing else. Misbehaviour means functioning as Commissioner and indulging in such actions which demeans his status. In one case where a member of Public Service Commission slapped another openly, his conduct was held to be a conduct below his status and he was removed.

Besides selection of candidates for appointments, the Commission has responsibility to provide advice to the Government on these matters:

(1) methods of recruitment;

(2) methods of selection, promotion, and transfer of employees from one place to another;

(3) on all disciplinary matters affecting the person serving under the government;

(4) on all claims raised by the employees for reimbursement of the costs incurred by them in defending themselves in Court cases filed against them;

(5) on claims for pension arising out of any injuries sustained by the employee during the course of his service;

(6) on any other matter which the President or the Governor may require the Commission for advice.

But, the government is not bound to act by the advice of the Commission and any decision taken by the government on any of the above matters without seeking the advice of the Commission will not in any case render the action of the government invalid.

The advertisements published by the Commission should and ought to be followed by the Commission in all respects but if the Government changes any rule and terms of the advertisement, the Commission must cancel the earlier advertisement and issue a fresh advertisement. If any person who is qualified to be appointed as per the rules but his eligibility is not included in the advertisement, the advertisement only prevails. But, if any qualification mentioned in the advertisement is subsequently omitted under the rule, such omission will not render the rights of the candidate to be considered as per the original advertisement.

Election Commission

Articles 324 to 329-A

Our Constitution has given prominence to elections. Elections are based on the principle of Universal Adult Franchise. The conduct of the elections to Parliament and State Legislatures is entrusted to the Election Commission which is entrusted with full powers of superintendence, control, and direction of elections. The expression 'superintendence, control, and direction of elections' is given widest possible meaning and it implies full freedom to that authority not only from the executive but also from judiciary. The executive directly complies with all requests from the Election Commission and judiciary is restrained from interfering with the work of the electoral body. The Election Commission is entitled to the services of all such persons it may choose for helping in the conduct of elections. But, the Election Commission is not entitled to the services of persons engaged in private establishments. The role of the Election Commission in preparation of electoral rolls, choosing the election stations, and organising elections is full and absolute. Election Commission holds power to lay down a Code of Conduct for the candidates and take action against violators by censuring them on matters which are not offences and prosecuting candidates in matters which are offences. The Election Commission has the power to ask the Government to transfer any officer engaged in election duties and take also disciplinary action against those officers who violate the directions of the Election Commission. The Election Commission has power to ban pre-polls, exit polls, and surveys, if it is of the opinion that such publication may affect the free choice of the voters. It is the Election Commission which always announces the programme of elections. While making the announcement, it is not compulsory for the Election Commission to hold elections within six months of the dissolution of the House if it is premature. When Andhra Pradesh Chief Minister Chandrababu Naidu wanted the Election Commission to hold elections immediately after he got the Assembly dissolved, the Election Commission refused his request but held them later after more than six months along with General Elections which were then impending. For operation of the Code of Conduct and for the embargo on the interference of the Courts with the election process, the prohibited period comes into operation not with the date when the Election Commission announces the programme of election, but with the notification for the election issued by the President calling upon the electors to choose the legislators.

THE FINANCE COMMISSION

Article 280:

(1) The President shall, within two years from the commencement of this Constitution and thereafter at the expiration of every fifth year or at such earlier time as the President

considers necessary, by order constitute a Finance Commission which shall consist of a Chairman and four other members to be appointed by the President.

(2) Parliament may by law determine the qualifications which shall be requisite for appointment as members of the Commission and the manner in which they shall be selected.

(3) It shall be the duty of the Commission to make recommendations to the President as to:

(a) the distribution between the Union and the States of the net proceeds of taxes which are to be, or may be, divide between them under this Chapter and the allocation between the States of the respective shares of such proceeds;

(b) the principles which should govern the grants-in-aid of the revenues of the States out of the Consolidated Fund of India;

(c) the measures needed to augment the Consolidated Fund of a State to supplement the resources of the Panchayats in the State on the basis of the recommendations made by the Finance Commission of the State;

(d) the measures needed to augment the Consolidated Fund of a State to supplement the resources of the Municipalities in the State on the basis of the recommendations made by the Finance Commission of the State;

(e) any other matter referred to the Commission by the President in the interests of sound finance.

(4) The Commission shall determine their procedure and shall have such powers in the performance of their functions as Parliament may by law confer on them.

Article 281:

Recommendations of the Finance Commission

The President shall cause every recommendation made by the Finance Commission under the provisions of this Constitution together with an explanatory memorandum as to the action taken thereon to be laid before each House of Parliament.

Article 338:

National Commission for Scheduled Castes

(1) There shall be a Commission for the Scheduled Castes to be known as the National Commission for the Scheduled Castes.

(2) Subject to the provisions of any law made in this behalf by Parliament, the Commission shall consist of a Chairperson, Vice-Chairperson, and three other Members and the conditions of service and tenure of office of the Chairperson, Vice-Chairperson, and other Members so appointed shall be such as the President may by rule determine.

(3) The Chairperson, Vice-Chairperson, and other Members of the Commission shall be appointed by the President by warrant under his hand and seal.

(4) The Commission shall have the power to regulate its own procedure.

(5) It shall be the duty of the Commission:

(a) to investigate and monitor all matters relating to the safeguards provided for the Scheduled Castes under this Constitution or under any other law for the time being in force or under any order of the Government and to evaluate the working of such safeguards;

(b) to inquire into specific complaints with respect to the deprivation of rights and safeguards of the Scheduled Castes;

(c) to participate and advise on the planning process of socio-economic development of the Scheduled Castes and to evaluate the progress of their development under the Union and any State;

(d) to present to the President, annually and at such other times as the Commission may deem fit, reports upon the working of those safeguards;

(e) to make in such reports recommendations as to the measures that should be taken by the Union or any State for the effective implementation of those safeguards and other measures for the protection, welfare, and socio-economic development of the Scheduled Castes; and

(f) to discharge such other functions in relation to the protection, welfare, and development and advancement of the Scheduled Castes as the President may, subject to the provisions of any law made by Parliament, by rule specify.

(6) The President shall cause all such reports to be laid before each House of Parliament along with a memorandum explaining the action taken or proposed to be taken on the recommendations relating to the Union and the reasons for the non-acceptance, if any, of any of such recommendations.

(7) Where any such report, or any part thereof, relates to any matter with which any State Government is concerned, a copy of such reports shall be forwarded to the Governor of the State who shall cause it to be laid before the Legislature of the State along with a memorandum explaining the action taken or proposed to be taken on the recommendations relating to the State and the reasons for the non-acceptance, if any, of any of such recommendations.

(8) The Commission shall, while investigating any matter referred to in sub-clause (a) or inquiring into any complaint referred to in sub-clause (b) of clause (5), have all the powers of a civil court trying a suit and in particular in respect of the following matters, namely:

(a) summoning and enforcing the attendance of any person from any part of India and examining him on oath;

(b) requiring the discovery and production of any document;

(c) receiving evidence on affidavits;

(d) requisitioning any public record or copy thereof from any court or office;

(e) issuing commissions for the examination of witnesses and documents;

(f) dealing with any other matter which the President may, by rule, determine.

(9) The Union and every State Government shall consult the Commission on all major policy matters affecting Scheduled Castes.

(10) In this Article, references to the Scheduled Castes shall be construed as including references to such other backward classes as the President may, on receipt of the report of a Commission appointed under clause (1) of Article 340, by order specify and also to the Anglo-Indian community.

Article 338A:

National Commission for Scheduled Tribes

(1) There shall be a Commission for the Scheduled Tribes to be known as the National Commission for the Scheduled Tribes.

(2) Subject to the provisions of any law made in this behalf by Parliament, the Commission shall consist of a Chairperson, Vice-Chairperson, and three other Members and the conditions of service and tenure of office of the Chairperson, Vice-Chairperson, and other Members so appointed shall be such as the President may by rule determine.

(3) The Chairperson, Vice-Chairperson, and other Members of the Commission shall be appointed by the President by warrant under his hand and seal.

(4) The Commission shall have the power to regulate its own procedure.

(5) It shall be the duty of the Commission:

(a) to investigate and monitor all matters relating to the safeguards provided for the Scheduled Tribes under this Constitution or under any other law for the time being in force or under any order of the Government and to evaluate the working of such safeguards;

(b) to inquire into specific complaints with respect to the deprivation of rights and safeguards of the Scheduled Tribes;

(c) to participate and advise on the planning process of socio-economic development of the Scheduled Tribes and to evaluate the progress of their development under the Union and any State;

(d) to present to the President, annually and at such other times as the Commission may deem fit, reports upon the working of those safeguards;

(e) to make in such reports recommendations as to the measures that should be taken by the Union or any State for the effective implementation of those safeguards and other measures for the protection, welfare, and socio-economic development of the Scheduled Tribes; and

(f) to discharge such other functions in relation to the protection, welfare, and development and advancement of the Scheduled Tribes as the President may, subject to the provisions of any law made by Parliament, by rule specify.

(6) The President shall cause all such reports to be laid before each House of Parliament along with a memorandum explaining the action taken or proposed to be taken on the recommendations relating to the Union and the reasons for the non-acceptance, if any, of any of such recommendations.

(7) Where any such report, or any part thereof, relates to any matter with which any State Government is concerned, a copy of such report shall be forwarded to the Governor of the State who shall cause it to be laid before the Legislature of the State along with a memorandum explaining the action taken or proposed to be taken on the recommendations relating to the State and the reasons for the non-acceptance, if any, of any of such recommendations.

(8) The Commission shall, while investigating any matter referred to in sub-clause (a) or inquiring into any complaint referred to in sub-clause (b) of clause (5), have all the powers of a civil court trying a suit and in particular in respect of the following matters, namely:

(a) summoning and enforcing the attendance of any person from any part of India and examining him on oath;

(b) requiring the discovery and production of any document;

(c) receiving evidence on affidavits;

(d) requisitioning any public record or copy thereof from any court or office;

(e) issuing commissions for the examination of witnesses and documents;

(f) dealing with any other matter which the President may, by rule, determine.

(9) The Union and every State Government shall consult the Commission on all major policy matters affecting Scheduled Tribes.

Article 339:

Control of the Union over the Administration of Scheduled Areas and the Welfare of Schedule Tribes

(1) The President may at any time and shall, at the expiration of ten years from the commencement of this Constitution by order appoint a Commission to report on the administration of the Scheduled Areas and the welfare of the Scheduled Tribes in the States.

The order may define the composition, powers, and procedure of the Commission and may contain such incidental or ancillary provisions as the President may consider necessary or desirable.

(2) The executive power of the Union shall extend to the giving of directions to [a State] as to the drawing up and execution of schemes specified in the direction to be essential for the welfare of the Scheduled Tribes in the State.

Article 340:

Appointment of a Commission to Investigate the Conditions of Backward Classes

(1) The President may by order appoint a Commission consisting of such persons as he thinks fit to investigate the conditions of socially and educationally backward classes within the territory of India and the difficulties under which they labour and to make recommendations as to the steps that should be taken by the Union or any State to remove such difficulties and to improve their condition and as to the grants that should be made for the purpose by the Union or any State and the conditions subject to which such grants should be made, and the order appointing such Commission shall define the procedure to be followed by the Commission.

(2) A Commission so appointed shall investigate the matters referred to them and present to the President a report setting out the facts as found by them and making such recommendations as they think proper.

(3) The President shall cause a copy of the report so presented together with a memorandum explaining the action taken thereon to be laid before each House of Parliament.

PUBLIC SERVICE COMMISSION

Two or more States may agree that there shall be one Public Service Commission for that group of States, and if a resolution to that effect is passed by the House or, where there are two Houses, by each House of the Legislature of each of those States, Parliament may by law provide for the appointment of a Joint State Public Service Commission (referred to in this Chapter as Joint Commission) to serve the needs of those States.

Any such law as aforesaid may contain such incidental and consequential provisions as may be necessary or desirable for giving effect to the purposes of the law.

The Public Service Commission for the Union, if requested so to do by the Governor of a State, may, with the approval of the President, agree to serve all or any of the needs of the State.

References in this Constitution to the Union Public Service Commission or a State Public Service Commission shall, unless the context otherwise requires, be construed as references to the Commission serving the needs of the Union or, as the case may be, the State as respects the particular matter in question.

Article 316:

Appointment and Term of Office of Members

(1) The Chairman and other members of a Public Service Commission shall be appointed, in the case of the Union Commission or a Joint Commission, by the President, and in the case of a State Commission, by the Governor of the State:

[Provided that as nearly as more than one-half of the members of every Public Service Commission shall be persons who at the dates of their respective appointments have held office for at least ten years either under the Government of India or under the Government of a State, and in computing the said period of ten years any period before the commencement of this Constitution during which a person has held office under the Crown in India or under the Government of an Indian State shall be included.]

[(1-A) If the office of the Chairman of the Commission becomes vacant or if any such Chairman is by reason of absence or for any other reason unable to perform the duties of his office, those duties shall, until some person appointed under clause (1) to the vacant office has entered on the duties thereof or, as the case may be, until the Chairman has resumed his duties, be performed by such one of the other members of the Commission as the President, in the case of the Union Commission or a Joint Commission, and the Governor of the State in the case of a State Commission, may appoint for the purpose.]

(2) A member of a Public Service Commission shall hold office for a term of six years from the date on which he enters upon his office or until he attains, in the case of the Union Commission, the age of sixty-five years, and in the case of a State Commission or a Joint Commission, the age of [sixty-two years], whichever is earlier:

[Provided that

(a) a member of a Public Service Commission may, by writing under his hand addressed, in the case of the Union Commission or a Joint Commission, to the President, and in the case of a State Commission, to the Governor of the State, resign his office;

(b) a member of a Public Service Commission may be removed from his office in the manner provided in clause (1) or clause (3) of Article 317.]

(3) A person who holds office as a member of a Public Service Commission shall, on the expiration of his term of office, be ineligible for re-appointment to that office.

Article 317:

Removal and Suspension of Member of a Public Service Commission

(1) Subject to the provisions of clause (3), the Chairman or any other member of a Public Service Commission shall only be removed from his office by order of the President on the ground of misbehavior after the Supreme Court, on reference being made to it by the President, has, on inquiry held in accordance with the procedure prescribed in that behalf under Article 145, reported that the Chairman or such other member, as the case may be, ought on any such ground to be removed.

(2) The President, in the case of the Union Commission or a Joint Commission, and the Governor in the case of a State Commission, may suspend from office the Chairman or any other member of the Commission in respect of whom a reference has been made to the Supreme Court under clause (1) until the President has passed orders on receipt of the report of the Supreme Court on such reference.

(3) Notwithstanding anything in clause (1), the President may by order remove from office the Chairman or any other member of a Public Service Commission if the Chairman or such other member, as the case maybe:

(a) is adjudged an insolvent; or

(b) engages during his term of office in any paid employment outside the duties of his office; or

(c) is, in the opinion of the President, unfit to continue in office by reason of infirmity of mind or body.

(4) If the Chairman or any other member of a Public Service Commission is or becomes in any way concerned or interested in any contract or agreement made by or on behalf of the Government of India or the Government of a State or participates in any way in the profit thereof or in any benefit or emolument arising therefrom otherwise than as a member and in common with the other members of an incorporated company, he shall, for the purposes of clause (1), be deemed to be guilty of misbehaviour.

It is a cardinal point that no opportunity of hearing needs be given for suspension of member of Public Service Commission at the stage of reference by President or Governor. In fact, principles of service law are also not applicable. It is available when the matter is actually decided by Supreme Court, for example, writ of certiorari not maintainable *(Ramkumar Kashyap vs Union of India)*

Article 318:

Power to make Regulations as to Conditions of Service of Members and Staff of the Commission

In the case of the Union Commission or a Joint Commission, the President and, in the case of a State Commission, the Governor of the State may by regulations:

(a) determine the number of members of the Commission and their conditions of service; and

(b) make provision with respect to the number of members of the staff of the Commission and their conditions of service:

[Provided that the conditions of service of a member of a Public Service Commission, shall not be varied to his disadvantage after his appointment.]

Article 319:

Prohibition as to the Holding of Offices by Members of Commission on Ceasing to be Such Members

On ceasing to hold office:

(a) the Chairman of the Union Public Service Commission shall be ineligible for further employment either under the Government of India or under the Government of a State;

(b) the Chairman of a State Public Service Commission shall be eligible for appointment as the Chairman or any other member of the Union Public Service Commission or as the Chairman of any other State Public Service Commission, but not for any other employment either under the Government of India or under the Government of a State;

(c) a member other than the Chairman of the Union Public Service Commission shall be eligible for appointment as the Chairman of the Union Public Service Commission, or as the Chairman of a State Public Service Commission, but not for any other employment either under the Government of India or under the Government of a State;

(d) a member other than the Chairman of a State Public Service Commission shall be eligible for appointment as the Chairman or any other member of the Union Public Service Commission or as the Chairman of that or any other State Public Service Commission, but not for any other employment either under the Government of India or under the Government of a State.

Article 320:

Functions of Public Service Commission

(1) It shall be the duty of the Union and the State Public Service Commissions to conduct examinations for appointments to the services of the Union and the services of the State respectively.

(2) It shall also be the duty of the Union Public Service Commission, if requested by any two or more States to do so, to assist those States in framing and operating schemes of joint recruitment for any services for which candidates possessing special qualifications are required.

(3) The Union Public Service Commission or the State Public Service Commission, as the case may be, shall be consulted:

(a) on all matters relating to methods of recruitment to civil services and for civil posts;

(b) on the principles to be followed in making appointments to civil services and posts and in making promotions and transfers from one service to another and on the suitability of candidates for such appointments, promotions, or transfers;

(c) on all disciplinary matters affecting a person serving under the Government of India or the Government of a State in a civil capacity, including memorials or petitions relating to such matters;

(d) on any claim by or in respect of a person who is serving or has served under the Government of India or the Government of a State or under the Crown in India or under the Government of an Indian State, in a civil capacity, that any costs incurred by him in defending legal proceedings instituted against him in respect of acts done or purporting to be done in the execution of his duty should be paid out of the Consolidated Fund of India, or, as the case may be, out of the Consolidated Fund of the State;

(e) on any claim for the award of a pension in respect of injuries sustained by a person while serving under the Government of India or the Government of a State or under the Crown in India or under the Government of an Indian State, in a civil capacity, and any question as to the amount of any such award, and it shall be the duty of a Public Service Commission to advise on any matter so referred to them and on any other matter which the President, or, as the case may be, the Governor of the State, may refer to them:

[Provided that the President as respects the All India Services and also as respects other services and posts in connection with the affairs of the Union, and the Governor, as respects other services and posts in connection with the affairs of a State, may make regulations specifying the matters in which either generally, or in any particular class of case or in any particular circumstances, it shall not be necessary for a Public Service Commission to be consulted.]

(4) Nothing in clause (3) shall require a Public Service Commission to be consulted as respects the manner in which any provision referred to in clause (4) of Article 16 may be made or as respects the manner in which effect may be given to the provisions of Article 335.

(5) All regulations made under the proviso to clause (3) by the President or the Governor of a State shall be laid for not less than fourteen days before each House of Parliament or the House or each House of the Legislature of the State, as the case may be, as soon as possible after they are made, and shall be subject to such modifications, whether by way of repeal or amendment, as both Houses of Parliament or the House or both Houses of the Legislature of the State may make during the session in which they are so laid.

Article 321:

Power to Extend Functions of Public Service Commission

An Act made by Parliament or, as the case maybe, the Legislature of a State may provide for the exercise of additional functions by the Union Public Service Commission or the State Public Service Commission as respects the services of the Union or the State and also as respects the services of any local authority or other body corporate constituted by law or of any public institution.

Article 322:

Expenses of Public Service Commission

The expenses of the Union or a State Public Service Commission, including any salaries, allowances and pensions payable to or in respect of the members or staff of the Commission, shall be charged on the Consolidated Fund of India or, as the case may be, the Consolidated Fund of the State.

Article 323:

Reports of Public Service Commissions

(1) It shall be the duty of the Union Commission to present annually to the President a report as to the work done by the Commission and on receipt of such report the President shall cause a copy thereof together with a memorandum explaining, as respects the cases, if any, where the advice of the Commission was not accepted, the reasons for such non-acceptance to be laid before each House of Parliament.

(2) It shall be the duty of a State Commission to present annually to the Governor of the State a report as to the work done by the Commission, and it shall be the duty of a Joint Commission to present annually to the Governor of each of the States the needs of which are served by the Joint Commission a report as to the work done by the Commission in relation to that State, and in either case the Governor, shall, on receipt of such report, cause a copy thereof together with a memorandum explaining, as respects the cases, if any, where the advice of the Commission was not accepted, the reasons for such non-acceptance to be laid before the Legislature of the State.

TRIBUNALS

Article 323-A:

Administrative Tribunals

(1) Parliament may, by law, provide for the adjudication or trial by administrative tribunals of disputes and complaints with respect to recruitment and conditions of service of persons appointed to public services and posts in connection with the affairs of the Union or of any State or of any local or other authority within the territory of India or under the control of the Government of India or of any corporation owned or controlled by the Government.

(2) A law made under clause (1) may:

(a) provide for the establishment of an administrative tribunal for the Union and a separate administrative tribunal for each State or for two or more States;

(b) specify the jurisdiction, powers (including the power to punish for contempt), and authority which may be exercised by each of the said tribunals;

(c) provide for the procedure (including provisions as to limitation and rules of evidence) to be followed by the said tribunals;

(d) exclude the jurisdiction of all courts, except the jurisdiction of the Supreme Court under Article 136, with respect to the disputes or complaints referred to in clause (1);

(e) provide for the transfer to each such administrative tribunal of any cases pending before any court or other authority immediately before the establishment of such tribunal as would have been within the jurisdiction of such tribunal if the causes of action on which such suits or proceedings are based had arisen after such establishment;

(f) repeal or amend any order made by the President under clause (3) of Article 371D;

(g) contain such supplemental, incidental, and consequential provisions (including provisions as to fees) as Parliament may deem necessary for the effective functioning of, and for the speedy disposal of cases by, and the enforcement of the orders of such tribunals.

(3) The provisions of this Article shall have effect notwithstanding anything in any other provision of this Constitution or in any other law for the time being in force.

Article 323-B:

Tribunals for Other Matters

(1) The appropriate Legislature may, by law, provide for the adjudication or trial by tribunals of any disputes, complaints, or offences with respect to all or any of the matters specified in clause (2) with respect t o which such Legislature has power to make laws.

(2) The matters referred to in clause (1) are the following, namely:

(a) levy, assessment, collection, and enforcement of any tax;

(b) foreign exchange, import, and export across customs frontiers;

(c) industrial and labour disputes;

(d) land reforms by way of acquisition by the State of any estate as defined in Article 31A or of any rights therein or the extinguishment or modification of any such rights or by way of ceiling on agricultural land or in any other way;

(e) ceiling on urban property;

(f) elections to either House of Parliament or the House or either House of the Legislature of a State, but excluding the matters referred to in Article 329 and Article 329A;

(g) production, procurement, supply, and distribution of foodstuffs (including edible oilseeds and oils) and such other goods as the President may, by public notification, declare to be essential goods for the purpose of this Article and control of prices of such goods;

(h) rent, its regulation and control, and tenancy issues including the right, title, and interest of landlords and tenants;

(i) offences against laws with respect to any of the matters specified in sub-clauses (a) to (j) and fees in respect of any of those matters;

(j) any matter incidental to any of the matters specified in sub-clauses (a) to (i)

(3) A law made under clause (1) may:

(a) provide for the establishment of a hierarchy of tribunals;

(b) specify the jurisdiction, powers (including the power to punish for contempt), and authority which may be exercised by each of the said tribunals;

(c) provide for the procedure (including provisions as to limitation and rules of evidence) to be followed by the said tribunals;

(d) exclude the jurisdiction of all courts, except the jurisdiction of the Supreme Court under Article 136, with respect to all or any of the matters falling within the jurisdiction of the said tribunals;

(e) provide for the transfer to each such tribunal of any cases pending before any court or any other authority immediately before the establishment of such tribunal as would have been within the jurisdiction of such tribunal if the causes of action on which such suits or proceedings are based had arisen after such establishment;

(f) contain such supplemental, incidental, and consequential provisions (including provisions as to fees) as the appropriate Legislature may deem necessary for the effective functioning of, and for the speedy disposal of cases by, and the enforcement of the orders of, such tribunals.

(4) The provisions of this Article have effect notwithstanding anything in any other provision of this Constitution or in any other law for the time being in force.

[Explanation: In this Article, "appropriate Legislature", in relation to any matter, means Parliament or, as the case may be, a State Legislature competent to make laws with respect to such matter in accordance with the provisions of Part XI.]

National Commission for Backward Classes.

Did you know?

The Lok Sabha passed the 123rd amendment Bill, 2017 which seeks to give constitutional status to National Commission for Backward Classes. *The Bill seeks to bring in the following:*

(a) A new Article 338 B to be inserted.

(b) A new Article 342-A will empower the President to notify the list of socially and educationally backward classes of state/U.T. Parliament will exclude or include the classes from the central list.

With this Bill, the long standing demand to place the National Commission for Backward Classes at par with National Commissions for SC and ST is finally becoming a reality as far as placing on constitutional status is concerned.

National Commission for SC/ST was created in 1987 and it was given Constitutional status by passage of 65th amendment Bill Act 1990 leading to the creation of National Commission of SC/ST in 1992.

The NCSCST was split into two commissions, as National Commission for SC and National Commission for ST by inserting Article 338A. National Commission for SC was mandated to look after the grievance of Backward Classes too.

The Supreme Court, in the *Indira Sawhney Case*, directed the government to create a permanent body to examine and recommend the inclusion and exclusion of various Backward Classes for protection and promotion. Parliament passed in 1993 the National Commission for Backward Classes Act giving it a Statutory status. The Rajya Sabha has to pass it for the President to clear it.

9

CHAPTER

Statutory, Regulatory and Various Quasi-Judicial Bodies

OVERVIEW

For good governancet the Executive needs to function effectively. This can best happen only when it has statutory/constitutional bodies created to meet and serve its needs. Statutory/constitutional bodies created by the legislature, regulatory bodies to regulate the set functions in the sectors, and quasi-judicial bodies dispensing judicial functions in a limited way, are some of the options. Notwithstanding their standing, these bodies are ultimately subject to judicial scrutiny except where by law provided otherwise; rare but nevertheless there. Most of these bodies are in the economic and social sectors.

STATUTORY BODY

A statutory body is created by an act of the legislature. It is established to carry out specific functions that government considers could be performed more effectively outside a conventional departmental structure.

Features and issues surrounding statutory bodies are:

(a) Statutory bodies are subject to varying degrees of ministerial control as specified in the enabling legislation.

(b) Statutory bodies can be abolished by acts of Parliament with a simple majority.

(c) Statutory bodies have a certain level of independence but the government is still responsible to ensure that taxpayers' monies are well spent; prudently, timely, effectively, and lawfully. Independence for best results, working with earnestness for best efforts, and decision-making for best comprehension of situation: all to give the taxpayers the best deal, best shot, and best way forward.

(d) Statutory bodies are governed by their own enabling legislation, as also general common laws across all statutory bodies.

(d) Statutory bodies are governed by their own enabling legislation, as also general common laws across all statutory bodies.

Some important statutory bodies :

1) **National Commission for Women**: Established in January 1992 under the provisions of the Indian Constitution, as defined in the 1990 National Commission for Women Act 1990.
2) **National Commission for Protection of Child Rights**: The National Commission for Protection of Child Rights (NCPCR) established by an Act of Parliament, the Commission for Protection of Child Rights Act in December 2005, amended in 2006.
3) **National Commission for Backward Classes**: National Commission for Backward ClassesisundertheMinistryofSocialJusticeandEmpowermentestablishedon14August 1993.
4) **National Commission for Minorities**: The Union Government set up the National Commission for Minorities (NCM) under the National Commission for Minorities Act, 1992. Six religious communities, viz; Muslims, Christians, Sikhs, Buddhists, Zoroastrians (Parsis) and Jains have been notified in Gazette of India as minority communities by the Union Government all over India.
5) **Central Commission for Disabled Persons: 1995**.

The list is illustrative but could be more. It is revealed that in all these cases, the general understanding is that issues and problems to be handled could be handled more effectively, impartially, and with sensitivity by independent bodies, rather than by rule-bound government departments already burdened with responsibilities. Such statutory bodies give a fair, fresh, and farsighted look, given the measure of authority they are vested with by the enabling statute.

Statutory bodies are no doubt accountable but they can independently put their point of view across without fear or favour. Such views cannot be ignored even while law takes its own course.

REGULATORY BODIES

A regulatory body is a public authority responsible for exercising autonomous authority over some area of human activity in a regulatory or supervisory capacity. The operating word is 'regulation'.

Important features are:

(1) Regulatory bodies are generally set up to enforce standards and safety, or to oversee use of public goods and regulate commerce.

(2) Regulatory bodies are normally a part of the executive branch of the government, or they have the statutory authority to discharge their functions with approval from the legislative branch.

(3) There exists a case or cause for independent regulatory bodies due to complexity of tasks that call for expertise and immediate implementation. Political interference has to be avoided and a whole lot of issues and developments have to be handled in a consummate or integrated manner.

Independent regulatory bodies carry out audits, checks, and give interim reports for course correction.

Regulatory bodies are like watchdogs; they can bark, bite, and chase too. These bodies ultimately are there for public good, to ensure that there exists a level playing field for all, to ensure that smart practices are curtailed, and to see that there's always a road ahead for the law abiding. These bodies are not a check; they are like referees to punish the infringements. *A list of regulatory bodies is provided here:*

(1) Insurance Regulatory and Development Authority; 1999 (IRDA)
(2) Securities and Exchange Board of India; 1992 (SEBI)
(3) Telecom Regulatory Authority of India; 1997 (TRAI)
(4) Central Pollution Board; 1974 (CPB)
(5) Directorate General of Civil Aviation (DGCA)
(6) University Grants Commission, 1956 (UGC)
(7) Competition Commission of India, 2002 (CCI)

It is abundantly clear that regulatory bodies frame their rules and establish rule of law, justice, and fair play. It's worth nothing that in a milieu of fast changing technology, social base, expectations, government policies, and means of communications, the environment for business also changes. In such a situation, need for regulation arises. Without regulation, notionally all will be equal, but some will be more equal (in Orwellian aside). Regulation is for common good, common goal, and common governance. Without regulation there could be monopolies, cartels and syndicates. Every country has 'regulators'; in fact, in form and in effect. However, decisions of the regulators can be held to question, legally or administratively or both. India's experience is ample testimony to this.

QUASI-JUDICIAL BODIES

Quasi-judicial bodies are organisations having powers akin to courts of law. They can adjudicate and impose penalties, either on a person or an organisation.

Some of the features are:

(1) Quasi-judicial bodies reduce the burden on courts of law. These bodies, acting on the principles of natural justice, are fast, fair, and free. However, an aggrieved person or organisation can appeal to higher law courts.
(2) Quasi-judicial bodies act within a set domain of pre-determined set of rules and have prescribed powers for penalties, depending on the nature, degree, and extent of the offence committed.

Quasi-judicial bodies may exist independently as organisations or may function within an organisation.

A list of quasi-judicial bodies is provided here:

(1) Railway Claims Tribunal, 1987.
(2) Press Council of India, 1978.
(3) National Green Tribunal, 2010.
(4) Income Tax Appellate Tribunal, 1941.

(5) Cyber Appellate Tribunal, 2000.

(6) Customs, Excise and Service Tax Appellate Tribunal, 1982.

(7) Telecom Disputes Settlement and Appellate Tribunal, 2000.

The general underlying fact is that decisions are taken by the concerned government departments and these may be appealed against. The need to give a fair hearing based on principles of equity and natural justice is paramount for the credibility of the government. A quasi-judicial body with members having administrative experience and expertise and members having sound technical knowledge and understanding can redress the wrongs, if any. Similarly, a quasi-judicial body with a chairman and members having knowledge of law, like in the case of National Green Tribunal, can effectively render justice.

Quasi-judicial bodies are not courts of law, nor can they use the provisions of Civil Procedure Code (CPC), but they ensure delivery of justice as per principles of natural justice. They follow the enacted law, they follow the rules, they look for infringements, and they go by basic principles of justice and fair play.

These bodies, statutory, regulatory and quasi-judicial have varied functions to meet specific needs. In the beginning, the need was felt for statutory bodies to address issues of basic needs of citizens and rights. Regulatory bodies came in later as the size of the economy expanded and the paramount need was to regulate resources, check malpractices and bring in order to ensure equitable systems. Quasi-judicial bodies became inevitable to reduce the burden on courts and the government.

The bodies can be divided along following lines:

(a) Rights related bodies

(b) Finance and Industry related bodies

(c) Administration related bodies

(d) Environment related bodies

(e) Agriculture related bodies

(f) Enterprise related bodies

(g) Education related bodies

(h) Medical field related bodies

(i) Welfare oriented bodies

Both central and state governments have powers to appoint such like bodies. These bodies do not have constitutional status.

10

CHAPTER

Government Policies & Interventions For Development

OVERVIEW

Government lays down policies in some critical areas for overall development. What are these areas and what are these policies? Also, what are the issues arising out of their design and implementation? To address these issues, the Constitution lays down the broad direction, the legislature and the executive ensure the delivery of these policies. The legislature, the executive and the judiciary ensure that the ends are met by the means; methodically, meaningfully, and measurably. The end goal is inclusive growth through exclusive policies.

GOVERNMENT POLICIES AND INTERVENTIONS FOR DEVELOPMENT IN VARIOUS STAGES

'*There is nothing I fear more than waking up without a program that will help me bring a little happiness to those with no resources, those who are poor, illiterate, and ridden with terminal disease.*'

– Nelson Mandela (Former President of South Africa and once a long-time prisoner)

In all probability, Mandela slept better as a prisoner than as the President. As a prisoner, he was confined in space and time; he knew he could not break free. As a President he was free, but everyday he had to break free in the space of his mind, and the time was not his; this also he knew. What was agitating him? –Policies or programmes, as he put it.

What in essence are government policies? Every government, whether democratic, capitalistic, socialist, dictatorship or monarchy or even a combination of these has to have policies. Policies are a road map based on available resources and generally has a time frame as well.

Policies may be long-term or short-term; top-down or bottom to top; may be general or specific; may have a financial element or may not; may show immediate tangible benefits or may not, but all policies are intended with some action and some results. How do these policies come to happen? Let us look at the Indian scenario. There certainly has never been any dearth of plans, policies, or programmes in this country.

CONSTITUTIONAL PROVISIONS

Article 246:

Formal Division of Powers

This article deals with the formal division of powers between the Union and the federated units (States). In a sense, this Article establishes India as a federal state in the most comprehensive way.

The Constitution of India has essentially followed the Canadian pattern of distribution of powers. In the Canadian pattern, there are three lists and the residuary powers rest with the Parliament. Matters of national importance have been incorporated into the Union List, on which the Parliament has exclusive powers to make laws. Matters of local importance have been put under the State List on which the State Legislature has been given exclusive powers to make laws. On matters mentioned in the Concurrent List, both the Parliament and State Legislatures have concurrent jurisdiction with a provision that in case of conflict between the law made by Parliament and the State Legislature, the law made by the former will prevail.

Laws made consistent with the aforementioned provisions are supported by plans, policies, and rules. Laws made by Parliament or State Legislatures have constitutional authority and backing. In the very first instance, all government policies have to be consistent with the provisions of Article 246, whether by the Parliament or the State Legislatures.

POLICIES

Policies are made owing to a variety of reasons. Society is dynamic and change is the only constant; changes call for policies to meet the needs: both expected and the unexpected.

The Directive Principles of State Policy (DPSP) :

Articles 36–51 lay down the broad principles for the state (both the Union and the States) to follow for the welfare of its citizens. It is in this context that policies are evolved. DPSP are not justiciable in courts for enforcement, but they are justifiable even to the remarkable extent that they can prevail upon fundamental rights.

Why is a policy needed? Plain and simple: it gives a road map, shows a commitment for action, conforms to a pattern, and indicates likely benefits and beneficiaries. Policies put issues in perspective, matters in straitjacket, and adhere to principles of transparency and accountability. *Generally, policies have some of the following features.*

Features of Policies

(a) **For whom is the policy meant:** Scope, applicability.

(b) **Objectives:** What it seeks to achieve? Goals.

(c) **Key issues:** What are the major issues?

(d) **Expectations:** What the policy is not about, to whom it is not applicable

(e) **Strategies:** Priorities.
(f) **Seeks:** Both qualitative and quantitative targets.
(g) **Identifies:** Target groups.
(h) **Sets out:** If institutions are needed to set up to implement the policy.
(i) **Time frame:** For how many years a policy will be valid.
(j) **Logistics:** What is needed... men, money, machines, means, methods, markets.

PLANNING

In management, it is taught that major elements are planning, directing, organising, coordinating, control, and costing. Due weightage is given to each of these elements depending on the nature of project. Of course, underlying factors also include quality control and customer satisfaction. In policies to be unfolded also, all these elements are important. Some policies need a lot of planning, some lot of organising, some need effective control, and some coordination. Even so, these elements are not exclusive of others, rather are in consonance.

The Indian Scene

After Independence, the country having been duly impressed by the Soviet model of five year plans, embarked upon a similar path here. Plans were evolved duly outlining policies for their success.

Public sector was given a commanding presence and private sector a secondary preference. Initial plans worked for growth, subsequent ones on self-reliance, later on, plans were on poverty reduction, structural changes, and inclusiveness. These plans had a modicum of success, but it must be conceded however that odds were many and mighty.

Plan	Period	Policy Objective
I	1951-56	Increase in rate of investment
II	1956-61	Rapid industrialisation
III	1961-65, 66	Increase national income by 30%
IV	1969-74	Improving the lot of the poor
V	1974-79	Bring down inflation after 1973 oil crisis
VI	1980-85	Removal of poverty
VII	1985-90	Growth, modernisation, self-reliance, and social justice
	1990-92	Years of oil and turmoil, Gulf war, and disputed Babri masjid structure. Planning took a beating, and so did policies.
VIII	1992-97	Launched after structural reforms. Growth with discipline, reforms a success.
IX	1997-2002	Total emphasis on social welfare and basic minimum services.
X	2002-2007	Creation of jobs, tackling poverty, and revitalising agriculture
XI	2007-2012	Strategy for inclusive growth
XII	2012-	Broad-based improvement in the economic and social condition of people

Reforms in Policies

All these Plans in turn involved policies to achieve the set goals. Industrial policies were first conceived in 1948, followed up with major ones in 1956, then in 80s, followed by the 1991 reforms, etc. Industrial policy resolution from 1948 onwards gave a commanding presence to the public sector and considerably less role to the private sector. Globalisation drive ensured that by 1991 India too would remove the shackles on the private sector. Liberalisation, Privatisation, and Globalisation (LPG) became the battle cry.

Education, largely a state subject with select Union presence, has seen many a policy statement from the Union, not to speak of state governments' own initiatives to stir the pot. Many Committees, Commissions, missions, study groups, etc. have, from time to time, contributed to evolving policies to confront the situation. This too, after the British themselves kept the pot boiling during their rule. Parliament too has been active with the enactment of various Acts. No doubt, education has expanded in the country, but quality remains agonisingly suspect; and our world ranking is distant and dismal. We had national education policy in 1968, then 1986, and then 1992. Surprisingly, till 2000 there was no policy on agriculture. Agriculture being a state subject and land reforms and taxation being touchy subjects, no central policy was evolved. During the British period, famines were rampant and as a policy, 'famine code' was in operation. After Independence the country has improved the food situation. The problem today is not starvation but malnutrition and distribution of foodgrains.

'Paddy and poverty go together,' said a former Prime Minister. Had agriculture been paid attention along with other reforms, left-wing extremism would have been controlled. 7th (seventh) plan onwards, greater emphasis has been placed on social sector leading to evolution of many policies.

Surprisingly, till 2000 there was no policy on agriculture. Agriculture being a state subject and land reforms and taxation being touchy subjects, no central policy was evolved. During the British period, famines were rampant and as a policy, 'famine code' was in operation. After Independence the country has improved the food situation. The problem today is not starvation but malnutrition and distribution of foodgrains.

Two other factors changed the landscape further. Globalisation brought forth pressure for better communication. This meant that telecom policy had to change. Emergence of service sector similarly called for change in policies too, covering banking policies. Environmental concerns moved to the centre stage and as a result many policies had to be evolved. All in all, the country witnessed a flurry of activities with numerous policies being unfolded.

Enlightened public opinion, excited social media, and engaging media, both print and electronic, kept the pressure on for the government to act. Judiciary too started intervening on occasions to push the State to act. International developments too set the ball rolling for more and more policies to be unfolded. Governments had to evolve policies for foreign investment. The second wave of development after 1991 reforms brought in the private sector as a major player. Many new policies had to be announced to meet the emergent situations. Enactment of

Right to Information Act further intensified the need to put in policies to streamline the government working. Bureaucracy too rose to the occasion and evolved many policies for governance, notably in the field of social welfare. Even so, notwithstanding the penchant for policies, the country does not hold a glittering record of many outstanding policies; some of them had to be abandoned mid-way.

Characteristics of Policies

What are the characteristics of a policy? All policies have some common features. Briefly,

(a) Policy should spell out clearly for whom it is meant and what are its objectives.
(b) Policy should be realistic spelling out quantifiable targets.
(c) Policy should have a time frame and not open-ended.
(d) Policy should connect with process and must identify stakeholders.
(e) Policy should be well researched, tested, and flexible.
(f) Policy should have control points for evaluation and must be supported by a feedback system.
(g) Policy should address itself to aims, missions, and objectives to involve all stakeholders rather than focus on process.
(h) Policy should be need-based and rooted in reality; copying policies successful elsewhere is not a good prescription as each country has its own situations.
(i) It is often a good idea to have SWOT analysis done before the policy is implemented. SWOT stands for Strengths, Weaknesses, Opportunities, and Threats.
(j) Ad hoc, short-term, emergent plans should be exceptions rather than the rule for a policy to succeed.
(k) Tendency to evolve sub-plans, by-plans, and part-plans should be avoided as it makes one lose focus on the core plan and policy.
(l) Publicity for incoming policies should be made in advance so that everyone becomes aware and gets involved.
(m) Policies should be supported by appropriate, adequate, and accurate funding system and funds should be released when due. Sometimes, audit arrives before accounts are ready to release funds! In short, policies are all fine as pious declarations of intent, faith, and altruism but reality should be reckoned with. Sometimes, policies are unfolded to showcase action or intention to act; sometimes by the bureaucracy to protect its turf, sometimes by government departments to garner funds; sometimes to publicise; sometimes to find work for idle bureaucracy; sometimes to show to the whole world that we too can act; sometimes under compulsion to implement an Act or to implement a court judgement; sometimes as a result of the whims, fancy or fear of those in power; sometimes to replace an old policy; and sometimes out of patriotism. It is always, sometimes.

WHITHER POLICIES, WHETHER POLICIES, WEATHER POLICIES: THE INDIAN EXPERIENCE

Whither Government

There's some truth in stating that India has retained the same structure that the British evolved for us over two centuries. The Government of India Act, 1935, formed the bedrock on which our constitution has rested. Consequently, the policies evolved by our British masters still service – we have made no efforts either to mend or end. Our police systems and system of policies has remained unaltered from its modest but menacing beginning in 1861. Our forest policies, similarly, are rooted in tradition, history, and history of tradition. If at all we have made any changes under compulsion of environmental laws, we have only aggravated the problem of rights of the indigenous people. In mining also, colonial policies have been followed but owing to greed and graft in mining allotment issues, Supreme Court has stepped in to draw the lines. We never had any policy on Agriculture till fifty three years after independence in 2000; and we say agriculture is the mainstay of our economy. The 2000 policy on agriculture also has mainly stayed put for want of systematic implementation. Our policy on rivers, if at all existing, is in all possibility the same as handed down to us by the British. In fact, the colonial masters proposed Ganga-Cauvery link in 1897! Our municipalities and local government models date back to the colonial era. Although people's participation is a reality after 73/74 amendments, structure remains the same. In substance, the withered British policies have weathered the change. Yet, the country calls for a change. One of the institutions which can call the shots for a change is the bureaucracy, itself steeped in British traditions and totems. Its policies draw sustenance from the British era precedents. The other institution which can step in to bring about the change is the judiciary, but it itself is a throwback to the colonial era; it can hardly be expected to lead the charge, although now and then the judges do call for a change.

Whether Government

Whether we do need policies at all is a question heard more in whispers than whoops. It has been our experience that whenever the government comes across a problem, it brings in more bureaucracy and more controls. Secondly, the country steadily moved from 'commanding height of bureaucracy' to release of its shackles at least in the economy. The 1991 reforms, though modest and moderate, gave the right impetus. Policies are the happy hunting ground of bureaucracy and the breeding ground of ineptness. Industrial policies, education policies, textile policies, infrastructure policies, and food policies are all examples of bureaucratic misplaced ideas. This needed to be revisited, revised, and reinvented, each time with self-congratulatory messages. On the contrary, wherever bureaucracy has, by accident or by design or both, remained aloof, progress is in evidence. Examples of space technology, even agriculture, energy, and other fields readily testify to this. The issue is, do we need policies only for policing? It has been suggested that the Government could lay the policy down and implement it through Public-

Private Partnership, (PPP). It is an option where none exist. Mahbub ul Haq, the originator of United Nations Human Development Report said, 'the basic purpose of development is to engage people's choices.' Choice is a splendid, liberal, open, and engaging word. It opens up new vistas. Indian economy, fettered by choice, gave us the world of licenses, controls, permits, quotes, queues, shortages, slippages, quality starved, and unsafe products. The moot point was policy-making was beyond reproach. As for choice, Henry Ford the fabled car maker once said, ' You can have any colour you want, so long as it is black.' He manufactured only black colour cars, swept away by choice once it was available to the public. For us, when in 1991 the famous LPG (Liberalisation, Privatisation, and Globalisation) came not by choice but by circumstance, many in the bureaucracy said, 'LPG can be best handled if it is PLUG (Policy Laid Under Government)'. Thankfully, the plug was pulled off.

Weather Government

Post-independence the accent was on weather conditions of monsoon. Economy was still largely dependent on agriculture that was dependent on monsoon. The two sectors, agriculture (to a larger extent) and manufacturing (to a lesser extent) employed the workforce. After 1990, services covering IT, banking, tourism, education, healthcare, insurance took up space. It not only gave the country valuable foreign exchange but also gave sizeable employment. Policy-making shifted to this sector. International regulations also compelled the governments to evolve many policies to either confirm or conform. Banking sector is one example; policies to conform to Basel norms. Policies to help IT sector grow by way of concessions is another instance. The entire SEZ (Special Economic Zone) policy is yet another example. Relook at education and health policies, one more instance. Its policies of Green Revolution bore the fruit. This unsung story of success took the world by surprise as much as it did the country. It succeeded because of involvement of everyone, though handled by the government.

Focus of Policies

What is expected of the Government today, what should engage its attention, where should the focus of it policies be? Briefly :

(a) Government should evolve policies for development of infrastructure, the engine of growth.

(b) Create an environment of trust and faith for participation by all to foster economic development on sustainable basis.

(c) Support those in need with inclusive growth by imparting skills.

(d) Take active measures in the area of social development with access to basic minimum services for all.

(e) Government should regulate the social sector, not rule. 'Growth with inclusiveness, development without exclusiveness,' should be the motto of the Government.

GOVERNMENT INTERVENTION FOR DEVELOPMENT IN VARIOUS SECTORS

This topic has to be addressed with the following issues in mind:

(a) Why and where Government intervention is needed?

(b) Which are the various sectors where such intervention is needed?

(c) What is meant by 'development' in the context?

At the very outset, it has to be understood that intervention are in the content and context of government policies as distinct from government plans. Policies are in the domain of macro issues and plans flow from the policies. At times, policies themselves flow from Acts of the Parliament. Any policy changes, if they happen to impinge or affect the Act itself, have to be brought before the Parliament for necessary amendments. Such instances are few are far between.

Most of the policies are, however es evolved by the government for its working. If these policies are implemented, interventions are required at times. Society is dynamic, changes are frequent, and expectations are not static. Our constitution itself has been amended on more than a hundred occasions. Interventions, therefore become inescapable and inevitable.

Need for Interventions

(1) Due to international spotlight and emphasis on environmental issues, India had to put in place environmental acts, rules, and safeguards to keep pace with other countries. India's civil-nuclear deal with the United States called for intervention in our nuclear policy. Our policy of non-alignment itself has undergone changes from passive disengagement to active engagement, particularly after the collapse of the Soviet Union.

(2) Capacity creation is a major issue for policy intervention. If existing policies are coming in the way of planning for some agreed to capacities, policies have to be changed through intervention. 'Open skies' is an example to substantiate this. With our national carrier Air India and Indian Airlines tagged by an unruly workforce, lack of capacity, instantly forgettable service, cancellations, delays, pilots a law unto themselves, unabashed VIP racism etc, to mention a few afflictions, a change through intervention was always on the cards. 'The Maharaja' had his privy purse snatched away when India opened up the skies for private airlines in a big way.

In the armament industry, the policy intervention option had to be exercised. India started importing in a big way to meet its needs. Private sector in the country was eyeing the pie but the government preferred the foreign capitalists. Over the years the government realised that indigenisation does not mean in-house production by its captive units alone, but collaboration with others in the country. Interventions have seen the private sector show its might publicly. It is a win-win situation. Now the private sector can even collaborate with foreign players.

(3) Change in technology is a strong, potent factor for intervention in policy for change. When typewriters were introduced, workforce protested against labour saving devices; when computers came long, protests too came along. Protests apart, it called for change of policies. IT act became necessary, piracy became an issue, computer security became important and urgent, data transmission too came under focus. Government had to intervene urgently to change the policies all over the country. Later, applications of items like Aadhar card become a useful reality.

(4) Awareness levels are increasing day by day. This also calls for policy intervention. An outstanding case in point is the policy to introduce the 'Right to Information.' Government today has to be transparent and accountable; it cannot hide behind files or indulge in filibustering. 'Secret,' 'confidential', and 'classified' are all terms which are not feared or respected now. Due to RTI, the government has had to change policies to bring in transparency and accountability.

(5) Change in product also calls for government intervention in policies. When plastic replaced jute, policies had to be brought in to protect jute, yet promote plastic. Arrival of electronics also necessitated change of policies. Policy changes take place on account of many considerations, notably environmental safety, security, etc.

(6) Demographic change is perhaps the most important and significant aspect. 1921 was the year when demographic change took place with explosion in population; today we have a situation where the demographic explosion is of a different kind. With forty (40%) percentage of our population below the age of twenty, we are the youngest nation in the world. This creates challenges in policy changes and interventions. Three sectors are at once affected: health, education and human resource, and housing. In health, policy interventions have to address the issue of much needed infrastructure, quality healthcare, chronic diseases, and epidemics. National Health Policy, 2017 is aimed at redressal of these issues. The task is daunting. Education, likewise, is in urgent need of attention. National Education Policy of 1968 and 1986 and have not sorted the issue out. Today, the challenge is to meet the need to find education for all, quality being the prime consideration. Higher education must match the best in the world. Infrastructure is the main bottleneck.

Both health and education are state subjects predominantly, policies of states therefore matter too. Human resource policies need significant measures; skill development is the issue. All policies on human resource must find urgent implementation as the numbers (of jobless) are growing.

Housing policies too are considerable significant. Government policy of 'Houses for all by 2022' is definitely inspiring.

In short, compelling demographic changes call for suitable policy interventions. Gender equality in the context is very significant too.

(7) Public opinion too is an important aspect calling for policy intervention. This opinion can be built over the years through relentless campaign by those who value it or it can be harnessed when suddenly bursting forth. Campaign over the years concerning pollution of our rivers, including the Ganges, forced the government to act. Delhi's shocking gangrape and killing of an innocent girl led to spontaneous outburst to force the government to intervene. Law was changed, Nirbhaya fund was created; cases continue, fund remains untouched. Policy intervention was sudden, not planned.

Media has a positive role to play in mobilising public opinion. Campaigns by the media have led to policy intervention. Governments have had to change their policy of rehabilitation of those dispossessed.

(8) Judiciary has, in the recent years, taken to activism and rightly so. Government has bowed to judicial intervention to change the policies. Auction of natural resources, like coal is one such example. Ending crony capitalism in spectrum auction is another. Open and transparent mining policy is the result of judicial intervention. For years, government slept over the issue of harassment of women at the workplace. The Supreme Court finally issued the guidelines. Now the policy is in force.

Similarly, the government was indifferent to the issue of regulating blood banks in the country.

The Supreme Court finally issued the guidelines which form the policy now.

(9) Research scholars and academia too very often lead in policy interventions. Based on their study and analysis, they have the advantage of the total perspective.

(10) Adversity is the best teacher. Crises trigger changes like nothing else. It is not to suggest that one must wait for the crisis to envelop and engulf us before the act, rather that understanding the crisis brings everyone together. 1991 reforms were preceded by severe Balance of Payment crisis; modernisation of our army began in earnest after the 1962 Chinese aggression and put us in good stead in 1965 when Pakistan took its second chance. Green Revolution happened because of US President L.B. Johnson's orders to delay food shipments to India. Our country developed the super computer after the West denied such a facility. The point is that crises led to change in policies and suitable interventions had to be thought of. Necessity, for once, was the mother of interventions.

ISSUES ARISING OUT OF DESIGN AND IMPLEMENTATION OF POLICIES

Policies are designed with best of intention and care for implementation, yet they fail. How does this happen? Is the policy to blame or does it lie elsewhere? India has seen the policy covering the 'green revolution' succeed beyond expectations and also seen policies covering 'family planning' fail beyond comprehension. Policies governing space technology have succeeded beyond belief but policies surrounding indigenisation of arms and ammunition fail beyond relief. Social welfare measures in one state are worth showcasing, and in others, a dismal failure.

Are the policies faulty or the implementation is so? The issue has been debated for decades and yet no consensus has emerged. The fact remains that no one perfect prescription is there, it all depends on facts and circumstances. The Green Revolution which succeeded in Punjab and Haryana made no significant impact in Uttar Pradesh and coercion adopted in family planning found some success.

Issues Related to Design of Policies

(1) Creating awareness of policies among stakeholders is important for the design to succeed.

(2) Policy designs fail if they are worked on at with a pre-conceived notion. Objectivity is much needed.

(3) All relevant factors have to be taken into account. Sometimes, even a small factor can become critical to create damage.

(4) If the assessment itself is wrong, consequent design of the policy will be wrong. More time and attention has to be given to assessment for need of a policy rather than rushing into designing.

(5) A common pitfall is the top man syndrome, i.e going by the view of topmost man in the hierarchy. No doubt his or her support is important, but a collective wisdom must also be relied upon.

(6) Tweaking designs or specifications is also common. Lack of transparency permits such practices. With the coming of RTI, such cases are on the decline.

(7) Borrowing designs is common. 'Why reinvent the wheel' is a common refrain. But such practices do not help always, as individual conditions differ. Sometimes, borrowing can be very costly and time-consuming.

(8) No trial or test runs. With the aid and assistance of technology and software, it is very easy to do trial runs and test runs and do course correction, if needed.

(9) Experts and their world. It's good to have expertise aiding in the design of policies quite often experts are parachuted into the system. With their presence, others tend to either withdraw or become silent. The situation has to be objectively handled.

(10) Casual approach is always a casualty: Quite often in the design of policies, critical issues like land acquisition, skilled manpower, and automation versus manual arrangements are ignored; these create major problems later.

(11) Environmental and safety concerns are vital in the design of any policy. These issues along with security matters are moving to the centre stage.

Implementation Issues

(1) Lack of infrastructure: Howsoever good be the design of a policy, without proper and adequate infrastructure it is bound to be a failure. Quite often infrastructure is taken for granted and this proves very costly.

(2) Lack of involvement is suicidal for any policy. In the hierarchy-bound bureaucracy, if the higher management shows lack of involvement, it becomes viral. Everyone has to be involved at each stage. Periodic reviews are one way of showing involvement.

(3) Interference can be equally disastrous. It saps the energies of all those involved. Many a time works get halted due to interference or fear of interference or both.

(4) Change of regimes: In India this has a solid bearing on implementation as the incoming powers run down the previous regime. Quite often wrangling takes place even over symbols, names, signboards, even foundation stones.

'What is there in a name? Fame, all the same.'

(5) Funds are not released or not released on time.

Funds are the lifeline and cutting them off or slowing down their release can choke the implementation. Momentum is lost when funds don't reach.

(6) Shortage of manpower is often a vital issue: skilled manpower is not available causing shutdowns and delays.

(7) Faulty design: The policy itself has faults in its design; such a policy cannot be implemented.

(8) Fear of failure: In implementation sometimes there is a fear of failure. In such instances the progress is very slow.

(9) Lack of standards or standard operating procedures (SOPs): Implementation in such cases is left to ad hocism or improvisation. This can be a stifling factor.

(10) Feedback or control system is either poor or lacking: This is very significant as course corrections when and where needed, can be put in place. Without feedback or control points the implementations is left to fate.

(11) Inappropriate software: This is more common than one thinks. In the name of cost-cutting, cheaper software is used leading to more costs later on. Sometimes, common software is prescribed which doesn't handle local variations.

(12) No alternate plans are there while implementing policies; result is vacuum or paralysis.

(13) Implementation fails also when only one authority controls all the decision-making process and that authority cannot be approached readily. Delegation is the key.

(14) Time and cost overruns sounds familiar. Such overruns run over implementation. The escalated costs are audit's delight and government's nightmare.

(15) Sometimes, the policy itself becomes redundant; in such cases implementations is pointless.

NITI Aayog

NITI Aayog (National Institution for transformation of India) is the vital functional cog between policies and the process, between precepts and pursuit, between thoughts and treading, between anxious and actions. It is envisaged to be a catalyst to the development process; nurturing an overall enabling environment, through a holistic approach to development going beyond the limited sphere of the public sector and Government of India. It is to built on the foundation of : an empowered role of states as equal partners in national developments; underlying the principle of cooperative federalism. A knowledge hub of internal as well as external resources; serving as a repository of good governance best practices, and a think tank offering domain knowledge as well as strategic expertise to all levels of government. A collaborative platform facilitating implementation; by monitoring progress, plugging gaps and bringing together various ministries at the centre and the states in the joint pursuit of development goals.

With such broad based strategies NITI Aayog could well have been called 'National Initiative for Transformation of India, instead of an 'Institution.'

Objectives:

(1) To evolve a shared vision of national development priorities, sectors, strategies with the active involvement of states in the light of national objectives.

(2) To foster cooperative federalism through structured support initiatives and mechanism with the states on continuous basis, recognising that strong states make a strong nation.

(3) To ensure, on areas that are specially referred to it, that the interests of national security are incorporated in economic strategy and policy.

(4) To pay special attention to the sections of our society that may be at risk of not benefitting adequately from economic progress.

(5) To design strategic and long term policy and programme frameworks and initiatives and monitor their progress and their efficacy.

(6) To create a Knowledge, innovation and entrepreneurial support system through a collaborative community of national and international experts, practioners and other partners.

(7) To offer a platform for resolution of intersectoral and inter departmental issues in order to accelerate implementation of development agenda.

(8) To undertake other activities as may be necessary in order to further the execution of National Development agenda and objective mentioned above.

Niti Aayog has consciously shifted focus from planning to policy, giving the centre and the states the operational drive to put this policy in to process.

In the context of evaluating development process, two issues emerge:

(a) Education

(b) Enthusiasm and commitment.

Did you know?

PURA (Provision of Urban Amenities in Rural Areas) is a concept given by APJ Kalam; essentially a strategy for rural development through provision of infrastructure and services to create economic opportunities away from the cities. The scheme envisages provision of rural infrastructure alongside economic regeneration. The immediate purpose is to provide basic amenities to people in remote areas. Expectation is also there that the private sector would bring in its expertise and efficiency in providing basic services.

PURA would also ensure that the influx to the cities would stop and that provision of urban amenities in rural areas would energise the local youth. The immediate focus is connectivity. Physical connectivity by providing roads; electronic connectivity by providing communication network; and knowledge connectivity by providing technical and professional institutions is the need of the hour.

Ministry of Rural Development has launched this scheme. Asian Development Bank and Department of Economic Affairs are supporting this scheme. Panchayats and private sector are also stakeholders in this unique scheme of convergence, construction and cooperation. PURA is a plan undertaken for rapid advancement.

Development Processes and Development Industry–Role of NGOs, SHGs and other Stakeholders

OVERVIEW

The days of 'Mai Baap Sarkar' seem to be over, done and dusted with. Today's government seeking inclusive growth has to have the willingness to engage its citizens through various bodies and institutions as partners in prosperity and partners till posterity.

INTRODUCTION

Development planning and interventions are no doubt important for they lay the road map and course corrections. Even so, it is development process and engagement of people that matter more at times. Best of pans and pursuits do not either deliver or do not deliver that much as desired without the processes being put in place.

What does the process involve? Enthusiasm, for one, is a must. 'Nothing great was ever done without enthusiasm', said Emerson, the American writer and essayist. Enthusiasm can neither be demanded nor decided; it is voluntary and be visible. Development processes must be enthusiastically supported by all the stakeholders. One way to bring this about is engagement. Involvement or engagement is often infectious. Another way is to identify the beneficiaries and work for them. Nothing is more significant than showing good intent and purpose. Yet another way is to show case and concern by showing the whole process how beneficial or benign it is. Fear of unknown is never to be either ignored or belittled. It is also quite a common practice to work on a small group of people with a development process and showcase the ultimate benefits to the larger segment of people for acceptance.

The very best of plans and interventions do not succeed for the simple reason that process does not take off. It is not the fault of the plan but the process that cannot get it going. Sometimes it becomes obvious straightaway, other occasions it does not.

What makes process so enigmatic, why there's an element of uncertainty about it?

Two issues highlight the significant points.

Two issues highlight the significant points.

(1) Development Process must be compatible with other elements in the environment.

(2) The Stakeholders must be taken on board and suitably involved.

The first point revolves round compatibility between the plans and the processes. If the plan needs support of software and if the software is either too complicated or cumbersome, the results are bound to go awry. Similarly, if the plans are based on technology that is not compatible with delivery system there's bound to be uncertainty and ambiguity.

Some plans are based on many factors and in t eh event if these factors do not match or materialise they are bound to fail.

If the development processes become unwieldy or disorganised, would it be correct to blame the plans?

It is here that the significance of development industry becomes relevant. Development industry refers to various organisations which play a vital rôle in promoting success of development processes. These organisations in the non-government sector are extremely useful to the processes for a number of reasons:

1) They are endowed with domain knowledge and specialisation.
2) They are acceptable to the society and are trusted to deliver.
3) They have the requisite means and the infrastructure to deliver.
4) They are self-driven and motivated.
5) They are free from bureaucratic red tapism and procedural wrangles.
6) They can reach the stakeholders and the beneficiaries at once.
7) They can deliver at a much lower cost and in time.

These organisations are NGOs, Self-Help Groups, Donors, Cooperatives, Philanthropists, Stakeholders, Associations, Institutions etc.

Policies and governance mean nothing unless they are turned into concrete plans and processes to achieve tangible results. For example, a policy statement that 'doubling the farmers' income in next five years' remains empty rhetoric unless concrete plans are in place, like providing loans, making available seeds, subsidies, fertilisers, marketing arrangements etc, and all these are monitored through dedicated men and technology.

Along the way, irrigation facilities, mechanisms, and multi-cropping are also critical factors. Then there are three factors, say X, Y, and Z; which are imponderables.

X factor: Farmers have to be motivated, educated, and trained.

Y factor: Acre yield has to increase as also the total area.

Z factor: The increase in crop yield should not lead to prices crashing, yield rotting, and farmer going bankrupt.

Above all, the middleman has to be handled. All this needs planning and implementation through processes.

As for plans, we have come a long way. Starting from the First plan to Twelfth plan now, the country has seen growth, crisis, management, social justice, ... everything.

An interesting parallel can be found in the world of Management. Systematised, organised management began with emphasis on production and more output (Taylor, Fayol). In our case, we had our First, Second, and Third Five Year plans; World War II brought emphasis on systems, operations research (OR), and mathematical model. From the Fourth Plan through to the Seventh

Plan we stressed on systems approach; post war management schools adopted case study methods.By 1960s, management as a discipline began looking at the human element (McGregor, Likert). The Eighth Plan grappled with structural changes but the Ninth Plan dealt with Basic Minimum Services, Tenth Plan with poverty and employment and Eleventh Plan with Inclusive development and social justice. Management meanwhile moved to strategic management, corporate management, missions, and visions. We moved to NITI Aayog (National Institution for Transforming India). The Twelfth Plan took the lessons from NITI (our version of strategic management).

NITI Aayog is envisaged to be a catalyst to the development process; nurturing an overall enabling environment through a holistic approach to development and going beyond the limited sphere of the public sector and government. It is built on the foundation of an empowered role of states as equal partners in national developments thereby underlying the principle of cooperative federalism. It is meant to serve as a repository of good governance best practices, and a think tank offering domain knowledge as well as strategic expertise to all levels of government It is also meant to serve as a collaborative platform facilitating implementation by monitoring progress, plugging gaps, and bringing together various ministries at the Centre and the States in the joint pursuit of developmental goals.

With such broad based strategies, NITI Aayog could well have been called 'National Initiative for Transformation of India', instead of an 'Institution.'

OBJECTIVES OF NITI AAYOG

(1) To evolve a shared vision of national development priorities, sectors, and strategies with the active involvement of States in the light of national objectives.

(2) To foster cooperative federalism through structured support initiatives and mechanism with the states on continuous basis, recognising that strong states make a strong nation.

(3) To ensure, on areas that are specially referred to it, that the interests of national security are incorporated in economic strategy and policy.

(4) To pay special attention to the sections of our society that may be at risk of not benefitting adequately from economic progress.

(5) To design strategic and long-term policy and programme frameworks and initiatives and monitor their progress and their efficacy.

(6) To create a knowledge, innovation, and entrepreneurial support system through a collaborative community of national and international experts, practitioners, and other partners.

(7) To offer a platform for resolution of inter-sectoral and interdepartmental issues in order to accelerate implementation of development agenda.

(8) To undertake other activities as may be necessary in order to further the execution of National Development agenda and objectives mentioned above.

Niti Aayog has consciously shifted focus from planning to policy, giving the Centre and the States the operational drive to put this policy in to process.

In the context of evaluating development process, two issues emerge:

(a) Education

(b) Enthusiasm and commitment

Educating all the stakeholders is the key. Quite often good policies fail for want of education. Bureaucracy, in particular, needs to be alerted and educated about the policy and its process of implementation.

ROLE OF NGOs, SHGs, DONORS

What role do NGOs, SHGs, various groups, and associations, donors, charities, institutional and other stakeholders play in the development process and development industry?

What has been their contribution over the years and what mechanisms or regulations are there to ensure their free and fair functioning? Do these institutions need to be controlled or regulated at all?

Broadly, there are some issues which are common to all these institutions; these quintessentially show too why these arrangements are needed.

We can categorise briefly as follows:

A. Non Governmental Organisations (NGOs), Self Help Groups (SHGs), Associations

B. Donors and Charities

C. Institutional and Other Stakeholders

What are the common and considered features? Firstly, the government cannot and must not try to enter all areas of development; it gives the feel of a totalitarian regime. The role of the government is to ensure that justice, equality and welfare reach to all always. The means do not matter.

Why is it then better to involve non-governmental agencies in spreading welfare measures?

(a) There usually exists a fear of the unknown while dealing with the government; it is the result of the might of the state machinery.

(b) There's always the issue of delays, dilemmas and dithering as far as the government is concerned. Red tape and red herrings are well known. People are wary of it.

(c) Corruption and casualness are also strong factors as far as dealing with the government is concerned. Many people do not want to get involved in such a mess or methods.

(d) Government often presents an aloof, hostile, indifferent and diffident face, given the attitude of bureaucracy. It does not inspire any confidence.

(e) It is often the case that the government has its own priorities and all cases cannot be given the same share or status.

(f) There's a limit to the resources that the government has at its disposal; it simply cannot handle everything.

(g) It is admittedly a fact that government departments lack in specialisation and given this position, specialised NGOs, SHGs and others can be of great help.

All things considered, it is the one factor of 'motivation' that makes all the difference. NGOs, SHGs and others bring to the table their commitment and involvement that sets them apart. Their zest and zeal makes the big difference enthusing everyone.

CHARITABLE ORGANISATIONS AND TRUSTS

A charitable organisation, being of non-profit nature is motivated by philanthropic goals. It pursues charitable, educational, religious or other types of activities for the common public interest. A Charitable Trust has also same goals but consists of Trusts and has to be approved by the Income Tax Department (ITD). They are eligible for exemption from the payment of tax. Also, the donors who make donations to such trusts also clinch exemptions from their own taxable income.

SELF HELP GROUPS (SHGs)

SHGs are informal associations who join together for ways to improve their living conditions. They help build social approval among the poor, especially women. The groups stand as a collective guarantee system for members who borrow from organised sources. Naturally, Self-Help Groups have become the most successful mechanism for delivery of micro-finance services, like deposits, loans, money transfer and even insurance to the poorest of poor.

COOPERATIVES

A cooperative is an autonomous association of persons who, willingly cooperate for mutual social, economic and cultural benfit. However, these organisations might be non-profit or profit seeking. The most famous example of cooperatives in India is Amul (Anad Milk Union Limited.

NGOs

A **Non-Governmental Organisation** (NGO) is an organisation that is neither a part of government nor a traditional profit-seeking business. Common citizens establish them, but NGOs may be funded by governments, foundations, businesses or private persons. Some may back off from formal funding altogether and are run by volunteers. NGOs are highly varied in nature, take part in different activities and emerge in different forms in any part of the globe.

NGOs of India

The nomenclature NGO became popular in India in the 1980s, but the voluntary work has an older tradition. NGOs command respect because first, the father of the nation Mahatma Gandhi was an active participant; and second, because India holds tradition of honouring those who have made some sacrifice in helping people.

A developing country needs organisation and action. While performing services, governments cannot deal effectively with unorganised individuals. One important instrument is the Non-Governmental Organisation (NGO). It provides services for the underprivileged while the government devotes only a minimal fraction of resources to social welfare programmes. Of course, roles and shapes differ from place to place in India.

DIFFERENCE BETWEEN VOLUNTARY AGENCIES, NGOs AND NON-OFFICIAL AGENCIES

Earlier voluntary organisations, devoted time and money for serving the needy. Now, they also on specific jobs given by welfare organisations. They are neither on the board, nor on the committees of the voluntary agencies, but they utilise their leisure time to asssist the voluntary agencies in their day to day work.

A Non-Government Organisation (NGO), on the other hand, is an organisation, which whether its members are paid or unpaid, is started and governed by its own members without any external control. The action is local. In many cases, one individual may be doing all the work, but in the present age, this effort is being channelised through agencies and institutions.

An NGO benefits from group thinking, helps in pooling resources and efforts of many individuals for the utilisation of the community's resources, all on democratic basis. Under the category of NGOs, apart from voluntary agencies, there may be some non-official agencies. These may be sponsored by the government. They organise welfare services and development work in areas, which lack them. Example: All India Women's Conference, Indian Red Cross Society etc.

National Policy on the Voluntary Sector 2007

The National Policy on the voluntary sector has two aims: one, to provide an enabling environment for the voluntary sector and two, make it accountable. The objective is voluntary organisations can play own constructive role in development activities effectively.

The main objectives of the policy include

- Creating an enabling environment for Voluntary Organisations (VOs) that not only stimulates their effectiveness, but also protects their identity and safeguards their autonomy.
- Enabling VOs to legitimately mobilise the necessary financial resources from India and abroad.
- Identifying systems by which the government may work together with the voluntary sector.
- Encouraging VOs to adopt transparent and accountable systems of governance and management.

In the policy, the section 'Establishing Enabling Environment' will examine the feasibility of enacting a simple and liberal process to register societies, trusts and non-profit companies. Under 'Partnership in Development', three instruments of partnership between the Government and the voluntary sector have been elaborated upon. In the section `Strengthening the Voluntary Sector', there is a commitment to encourage independent philanthropic institutions to provide financial assistance to deserving VOs.

CITIZEN PARTICIPATION

The most important role of NGOs is to stimulate active participation of the citizens. The matters may concern them and the community they represent. These agencies build linkage between the official programmes and the beneficiaries. NGOs rope in beneficiaries in decision-making, implementation, monitoring and evaluation of the programmes, through specific activities, NGOs come close to the beneficiaries, educate and train them on their problems, show how to resolve them and empower on how to remove imoediments.

HELPING GOVERNMENT EFFORTS

A laudable fact is that even after 40 years of planned development, the government looks up to these agencies for help in the implementation of various programmes of social welfare, rural development. However, the NGOs do so without compromising on strategies, policies and methods adopted by the government. They are independent to devise own strategies and methods. They even come up with low-cost techniques, simple methods and improvisation.

BRIDLING GOVERNMENT ACTIONS

The NGOs point the legislative loopholes in social legislation, and make sure that legislations like the Minimum Wages Act, the Abolition of Bonded Labour Act, the Protection of Civil Rights Act, Land Ceiling legislation etc are being properly applied and implemented.

They are the eyes and ears of people and take the voice of the citizens to planners and policy-makers.

They have highlighted the legislative loopholes built into the land ceiling legislation, exposing how a whole troop of party functionaries got their ownership/tenancy rights registered. They have helped the informal tenants in regularisation of village records. Benami transfers of surplus lands have been brought to the fore by them.

NGOs AND RELATIONSHIP WITH GOVERNMENT

The role of NGOs in development and governmental initiatives are as follows

- Strengthening social sector policy implementation through proper follow-through of policies, monitoring, social audit, capacity building, mobilising the resources and knowledge base etc.
- Enabling NGOs to legitimately mobilise necessary financial resource from India and abroad.
- Adopt transparent accountable system of governance and management for voltintary orgitinsalions.
- Making people aware about the government policies and programmes and their rights through mass awareness compaigns.
- Helping people in rehabilitation after the natural disaster and calamities.
- Suporting poverty alleviation programme, housing, sanitation, education health, women empowerment and their rights, child labour, water , rights for tribal people, removing caste based stigma and discrimination, leprosy eradication programme etc
- Gram Sree Mela (GSM) through NGOs for providing an opportunity to rural producers to sell their products directly to major markets.

NGOs AND THEIR PROBLEMS

Little financial resources, mismanagement of funds

One of the severemost problems of the NGOs is lack of financial resources. They depend upon grants and contributions, but most of them find it a hard task to get regular grants from the government and raise funds from the business community. Also the problem exists regarding proper use of funds. Here there is lack of trust between the government and these agencies.

Outreach and concentration

There has been a preponderance of NGOs / voluntary organisations, in the country but none has a nationwide outreach or network reaching every State and UT and certainly not, to every district, block or village in the country. The government, hence can't totally depend upon these agencies.

No coordination

Coordination among the voluntary agencies themselves represents some problems. These are as follows:

- Overlapping of efforts in certain areas;
- Because of the myriad number of voluntary agencies and the political patronage to some, it is often difficult to make them stand on a common forum;
- They do not like to pool or share own resources with other agencies; and,
- Muutual jealousies among the voluntary agencies can make coordination really difficult.

Mutual distrust

Except for the coordination between NGOs and the Ministry of Social Welfare, there is mutual distrust with other ministries/departments, rendering joint planning and delivery of goods and services impossible. Health, Education, Rural Development Departments, both at the Union and State levels, feel these agencies as unwelcome intruders into their terrain.

A number of governmental agencies interfere in the working of the non-governmental agencies. Some government agencies even join the dominant political party in the state in obstructing the work of the voluntary agencies.

Obstacles by bureaucrats

The bureaucracy in general seems to be averse to NGOs. They would not like a truly voluntary sector to emerge and grow in India. Only so-called voluntary agencies which are agents of the local oligarchy and/or the bureaucracy are promoted. They are a conduit for the misappropriation of funds.

Lack of trained and dedicated workers

Shortage of trained and committed workers has been the paramount problem of not only India but all countries. Poor salaries, inadequate security, weak personnel practices and competing job opportunities in industry and business are cited as the major causes for the shortage of dedicated workers.

Several organisations have built up huge structures, many of them are lying unused for the purposes for which they were built. Many of them have developed cracks. It is not the 'funds' which are most essential, what is needed is honest devoted workers. High principles of service must be retained by men and women with a zeal for service, empathy for the needy.

FOREIGN FUNDING OF NGOs

Changes in FCRA

Recently, the Central Government has taken action against a few NGOs including Greenpeace International, Avaaz and others for violations of rules under foreign contribution act. It was also alleged that many of these NGOs are hindering the developmental projects of the government. The government has, of late, brought about a few changes in rules governing foreign funding of NGOs under the Foreign Contribution (Regulation) Act (FCRA):

- All FCRA services including applications for registration, prior permission and renewal of registration are to bemade online.
- Bank will have to report to FCRA department within 48 hours of any transactions in respect of receipt and utilisation of any foreign contribution.
- To make the receipt and utilisation of foreign contribution by associations transparent, associations are required to place the annual returns and such data quarterly on their website or website as prescribed by the Central Government.
- The condition of submission of certificate from Chartered Accountant and audited accounts with Annual Return is removed in respect of associations who do not receive foreign contribution in a financial year.

Impact

- The new changes usher in more transparency in the foreign funding process and make the NGOs really accountable.
- Provision of online service of FCRA makes the process of registration and prior permission easier and faster. This cuts down the bureaucratic red tape.
- Reduces complexities like muliplicity of forms, physical copies of tax returns
- It removes the present rule of compulsory filling of auditor's report for every NGO, irrespective of whether or not they have received any foreign donations.
- Some of the provisions such as reporting by banks looks more stringent.

NGOs have been witnessing greater scrutiny over the past year and have been at the receiving end of the arbitrary use of the FCRA. It is hoped the new rules will make the honest NGOs comfortable.

SELF-HELP GROUPS (SHGs)

The cardinal functions of a Self-Help Groups (SHGs) are as follows:

- To stimulate and motivate members to save.
- To incentivise a collective plan for generation of additional income and
- To act as a conduit for formal banking services to reach members.

Impact of SHGs

Self-Help Groups (SHGs) have taken up the challenge of poverty alleviation in rural India. A growing number of poor people (mostly women) in various parts of India are members of SHGs and take part in savings and credit, as well as in other activities (income generation, natural resources management, literacy, child care and nutrition etc). The savings and credit function is the most prominent element and offers a chance to create some control over capital, albeit, in very small amounts. Problems do arise with design, development and introduction of programmes to promote income generating activities for generating sufficient, sustainable and regular income.

SHGs in India

1950s

The first SHG was started in Gujarat (1954), when the **Textile Labour Association of Ahemdabad** formed a women's wing for organising the women belonging to mill worker families, to train them in primary skills like sewing, knitting, embroidery, typesetting and stenography etc.

1970s

In 1972, SHGs became more systematised, when **Self Employed Women's Association (SEWA)** was formed as a trade union under the leadership of Ela Bhatt. She organised women workers such as hawkers, vendors, home based operators like weavers, papad makers, small producers like cattle-rearers etc with the salient objectives of:

(a) increasing their income and assets;

(b) enhancing their food and nutritional standards and;

(c) increasing their organisational and leadership strength.

The real intention was to organise women for full employment.

1980s

In the 1980s, MYRADA, a Karnataka based non-governmental organisation, promoted several locally formed groups to enable members secure credit collectively and use that alongwith their own savings for activities, providing them economically gainful employment.

Small group formations at the local level started in Tamil Nadu and Kerala through the **Tamil Nadu Women in Agriculture Programme** (TANWA) 1986, Participatory Poverty Reduction Programme of Kerala, (Kudumbashree) 1995 and Tamil Nadu Women's Development Project (TNWDP) 1989. A firm footing ensued for SHG movement in these States.

Today, around 44% of total bank-linked SHGs of the country are in the four southern States of Andhra Pradesh, Tamil Nadu, Karnataka and Kerala.

The SHG-Bank linkage programme was initiated as a Test Project in 1989 when NABARD, the Apex Rural Development Bank in the country, sanctioned 10 lakhs to MYRADA as seed money assistance for forming credit management groups. Ministry of Rural Development also provided financial support to PRADAN, to establish SHGs in some rural pockets of Rajasthan.

1990s and Onwards

On the basis of all these experiences, a full-fledged project involving a partnership among SHGs, banks and NGOs was launched by NABARD in 1992.

In 1995, the RBI streamlined the credit delivery procedure by launching a set of guidelines to commercial banks. It enabled SHGs to open bank accounts. The scheme was further strengthened by a standing commitment given by NABARD to provide refinance and promotional support to banks for credit disbursement under the SHG-Bank Linkage Programme.

In the starting years, the progress was slow; around 33000 groups could be credit-linked during the period 1992-99. But, thereafter the programme grew rapidly and the number of SHGs financed increased to more than 7 lakhs in 2010. Cumulatively, 33 million poor households in the country have been able to gain access to micro-finance from the formal banking system.

Strengths of SHGs

In the context of poverty prevailing in the country and the overall quantum of the fund flow available under various anti-poverty programmes of the government, the size of the SHG movement is modest.

SHGs strength can be seen as under:

- Establishes gender equality through economic empowerment of women as well as inculcating leadership skills among them.
- Promotes social justice by strengthening the voice of economically vulnerable sections.
- Encourages smooth credit flow in remote rural areas.
- Promotes poor households' access to formal banking system.
- It not only creates thrift among members, but also encourages oneness among all. The need for keeping the records and accounting indirectly promote the literacy among them.
- Strong social movement against ill practices of society becomes possible
- The micro finance facility offered to and by SHGs has reduced money lenders role.
- Peer pressure ensures timely repayment and replaces the collateral for the bank loan .
- SHG performs the role of collective bank and enterprise and ensures access to loan with a lower rate of interest to start micro unit enterprises.
- SHG has better local area understanding and can be developed even at remote places.

Weaknesses of SHGs

- Selecting members from heterogeneous community in Indian society is not easy.
- There is apathy among rural banks to provide funds to SHGs keeping in view their failures to repay bank loans in time.
- Lack of knowledge and proper orientation among SHG members to take up suitable and profitable livelihood options.
- Lack of awareness among SHG members regarding their own community resources, often leave them with limited option of income generation activities.
- The products developed by SHG face certain drawbacks such as quality as provided by corporate counterparts, scale of operation, finance, skills and marketability.

- Prevention of small cottage industries to micro-enterprises status, because of lack of regular business and secured revenue.

Challenges of SHGs

- Dominance of patriarchal mentality across rural societies prevent women from participating in SHGs.
- Inability of SHG group members to explore innovative options for livelihood opportunity.

Remedies of SHGs

- Integrated approach is a must for meeting overall credit needs in terms of backward linkages with technology and forward linkages with processing and marketing organisation.
- Simplification of process in loans to SHGs.
- A separate SHG monitoring cell must be created in every state with direct links with district and block level monitoring system.

DONORS

Donors are those who give donations by way of charity to a cause or concern . These donors may be organizations or individuals or governmental or non-governmental organizations. These donors help out in development work, socio-economic upliftment. They come forward even in emergencies.

Donors want their names to be publicized and appreciated. It is also fact that not all donations come without strings attached.

Example :

a) Of foreign countries: SWISSAID, USAID, Canadian International Devleopment Agency (CIDA) etc;

b) Private: Aga Khan Foundation, Sir Ratan Tata Trust, OXFAM etc;

CHARITIES

Charities are historical and are non-profit organisations. Originally rooted in religion and linked with missionaries, they are now profoundly secular and predominantly social. Charitable institutions may work for social upliftment or educational advancement or for health care.

The government of India has acknowledged their efforts and has given various concessions, notable tax relief on donations to charitable institutions

Examples : HelpAge, Sampradaan, Save The Girl Foundation, Plan India, Pratham

INSTITUTIONAL AND OTHER STAKEHOLDERS

International institutions play a very significant role in the development process. World Bank and its affiliated bodies are engaged in many projects. Similarly ,

United Nations related bodies like UNDP and UNCTAD are also contributing. ADB, Asian Development Bank, Japan International Cooperation Agency and OECD (Organisation of Economic Cooperation and Development) are also playing an important role.

In India, besides the banks, cooperative societies are very well spread to assist in development in various areas. The Constitutional Amendment , 97th of 2011brought in lot of changes to bring accountability and stability to cooperatives. Administrative Reforms Commission (2nd) too has recommended changes to help improve functioning of cooperatives.

FINANCIAL INCLUSIONS

Government of India became aware of the problems surrounding lack of access to fiancés by Self-Help Groups and others. In 2007, it appointed a committee under the chairmanship of Dr.C.Rangarajan, ex-Governor, RBI to study the issue of financial inclusion.

The Committee identified four reasons for lack of financial inclusion:

1. Inability to provide collateral security
2. Inadequate reach of institutions
3. Poor credit absorbtion capacity
4. Weak community network

Problems were seen to be most acute in north-east. A total of 256 districts in the country suffer from credit stress.

Malegam Committee on micro-finance institutions

Yezdi Malegam headed a committee that was constituted to study the issue of micro-finance. The panel submitted a report in 201. The main recommendations was to constitute Non-Banking Finance Companies (NBFC) as NBFC-MFS. These companies would provide financial services to low income borrowers with loans on unsecured basis.

There should be three components in the policing of the loan:

a. A processing fee not exceeding one per cent of the gross loan amount
b. The interest charge
c. The insurance premium:-Actual cost of insurance to be charged; no administrative costs

Mudra Bank

In 2015-16 budget, micro unit development and refinance agency scheme was announced to attend to loan needs of small business. The bank would be responsible for developing and refinancing all Micro Finance Institutions which are in the business of lending to micro/small business and entities engaged in manufacturing/trading and service activities.

Polity

Model questions with answers

Q. Can exit poll results be published online? What are other rules regarding these polls? How are they different from opinion polls?

A. No, exit polls results cannot be published online. FIRs were filed in Uttar Pradesh against the editor of a leading regional daily and the head of the surveying agency after they let publish the results of an exit poll online.

An exit poll is a post-election survey conducted immediately after people have cast their votes. Exit poll results cannot be published till the last round of elections is over. It covers even other states when polls are being held in more than one. The Election Commission has banned exit polls from the time the poll begins till half-an-hour after the polling ends.

An opinion poll is a pre-election survey to gather voters' views on a range of election-related issues. Results of any opinion poll or any other poll survey in any electronic media is prohibited during the period 48 hours, including the hour fixed for conclusion of voting in each of the phases in connection with the elections.

Q. Write a note on voter-verifiable paper audit trail (VVPAT) machine. Critically examine merits and demerits for 2019 Lok Sabha elections.

A. The voter-verifiable paper audit trail (VVPAT) machine allows voters to identify, whether their vote has gone to the intended candidate. Attached to electronic voting machine, it is a verification printer. When the voter presses the EVM, the VVPAT generates a paper slip, called "ballot slip." It contains name, serial number and symbol of chosen candidate. The voter can see this slip through a screened window, where it stays for seven seconds and then it automatically gets cut and falls into a sealed drop box.

The plus point is that voter can challenge his cast vote, on basis of paper receipt, for the first time. The advantages are:

- The voter will know that his vote has gone to his candidate
- The grouse of political parties that polls were not fair, would come to an end
- The VVPAT machine would also ensure that EVMs are not tampered with
- Cross-checking with paper slip would add another shield of accountability in system
- The Election Commission would be regarded with trust

But, as 16 lakh VVPAT machines would be required, funds have to be released urgently. Secondly, massive paper quantities would be wasted on the verification trail. As EVMs have notably reduced electoral frauds and rigging, it would be a practical move to have VVPAT machines only as a back-up.

Q. Should recall election be introduced in our country?

A. In ancient Athens, people could recall those whom they had elected, before their term ended. This system has been favoured in contemporary times by some people. A written request can be made by a specific number of voters to remove those who are not discharging duties properly. The recall system gives real power to people and they don't have to suffer under an irresponsible leader. It checks arbitrariness among elected representatives and corruption is effectively thrown out. If the citizens' expectations are not met with, the elected representatives may be asked to step down.

However, the recall system may put a brake on legislators' powers to take decisions as they will fear decisions going awry. Those who win elections may be pushed out, and others may gain power. As by-elections would be required every time a legislator is recalled, the amount of money spent would reach mind-boggling proportions. Recall may be used against women and disadvantaged sections of society, as shown in past. Unless there are checks and balances, recall seems an idea whose time has not yet come.

Q. What are the challenges faced by Election Commission and what are the mechanisms it has adapted to counter them?

A. The Election Commission of India is an autonomous constitutional authority responsible for administering election processes in the country.

Procedural Challenges

Diversity in India exists due to varied topography, beliefs, languages, sensibilities, aspirations, and living standards. In this situation, to conduct a free and fair election is always a challenge.

EC ropes in workforce from different wings of government, deploying maximum security forces for ensuring free and fair elections.

The fact that there are nearly 81.4 cr eligible voters shows the sheer size of electorate. Poor infrastructure and hard terrain pose accessibility challenges. Naxal affected areas and vulnerable polling stations pose security threats.

EC has devised a model code of conduct (MCC) and also issued guidelines to be observed during campaigning. But the rapid growth of social media, which has massive potential for interaction and propaganda has made it practically impossible for the EC to regulate it.

Structural Challenges

The tenure of Election commissioner is not fixed. So, it is not independent of government's intervention.

The election process expenditure of the Chief election commissioner is not charged on the Consolidated Fund of India, making it prone to allegations. It doesn't even have separate staff for conducting election process and has to be dependent on various government departments.

In recent times, many political parties have challenged the EC by allegations of EVM tampering. The EC has handled it well by throwing open challenge to any political party or expert to hack or crack EVMs code.

The EC can only disqualify a candidate if money expenditure is not shown in his accounts. Tackling black money is outside the purview of EC.

As a solution, the EC has recommended the govt. to amend RPA and make it an offence. It has also suggested to include new clause 58 (B) to empower itself to cancel poll in case of proof of use of muscle power.

Q. Comment on NOTA voting patterns in India.

A. None of The Above or NOTA, allows the voter to indicate disapproval of all candidates in an election. However NOTA in India does not provide for a 'right to reject'. The candidate with the maximum votes wins the election irrespective of the number of NOTA votes polled.

NOTA polling figures are still small. On an average, the maximum NOTA vote share has not crossed 2.02% of the total votes polled in any election cycle.

NOTA button made its debut in the 2013 Assembly elections held in four States – Chhattisgarh, Mizoram, Rajasthan and Madhya Pradesh and the former Union Territory, Delhi, where NOTA constituted 1.85% of the total votes polled. The average NOTA vote share dropped to 0.95% in the 2014 Assembly elections held in eight States.

Bihar saw 2.49% of NOTA votes, which remains the highest NOTA votes polled so far in any State in Assembly elections.

Analysis of NOTA voting patterns

- NOTA takes place where there is corruption and excessive crime. For example, Bihar has high NOTA, as it is a means of dissent; campaigning of youth took place for NOTA in Tamil Nadu elections.
- In states like Kerala, women campaigned for NOTA, in case there were no women candidates in a constituency.
- Direct contest between major political parties causes more voters to use NOTA as there is lack of alternative candidates.

Yet, NOTA will become meaningful only if it becomes a 'right to reject' rather than merely being a showpiece to express resentment.

Q. Is Finance Commission really acting as arbitrator between Union and State governments?

A. Article 280 of the constitution mandates the President of India to constitute Finance Commission every fifth year. The constitutional intent behind the Finance Commission is to uphold principle of federalism in financial matters.

FINANCE COMMISSION recommends formulae for distribution of Net proceeds of Central taxes between Centre and States and for distribution of State's share of Central taxes among themselves. It moots suggestions regarding grants-in -aid to States and tells how States should augment their respective constitutional funds in the interest of local government resources.

ROLE AS ARBITRATOR

The finance commission has a constitutional obligation to act as an arbitrator between the Centre and States because of its quasi-judicial character.

It tries to devolve funds according to the needs of state: population; area; demographic changes; forest cover and not on basis of one-size-fits-to-all. But some states complain that the formula used for devolution treats the States on unequal grounds.

The 14th FC also hiked percentage under disbursal i.e 42% [highest leap ever]. *But there are points of dispute:*

Reduction of the horizontal devolution percentage which significantly affects states like TN, Odisha, etc.

Additional burden of funding priority sectors such as health and education fall on the state where central support has reduced

Devolution of performance-based funds to local bodies will be discretion of Centre now

Focus on development of backward regions without resolving debt burden reduction.

However, the finance commission's position is constitutionally lopsided towards the Centre because only Central Government can decide its terms of reference. Hence Centre gets leverage to put forth its own view of States' fiscal situation.

To sum up, with the Planning Commission being replaced by the NITI Aayog now, the Finance Commission's mandate should be revisited. Giving it permanency will further strengthen its position in the realm of financial federalism.

Q. As the Supreme Court has criticised the appointments by Tamil Nadu Public Service Commission, critically analyse the situation and suggest ways to make such institutions transparent.

A. A standing order by Madras High Court has quashed the appointment of 11 Tamil Nadu Public Service Commission members and directed the State government to make a fresh selection of TNPSC members after a "meaningful and deliberative process".

The Second ARC report has, in this matter, highlighted several structural flaws:

- The ascribed based appointments, instead of prescribed (merit based) appointments in constitutional bodies, act more like retirement home.
- Constitutional bodies are plagued by class, caste, regional interest which overpower in various aspects.
- Fictitious bodies are also known to exist. For example Himachal Pradesh for over a decade had fictitious zonal planning committee.
- The constitutional bodies lack powers, as for example, State Human Rights Commissions are regarded as toothless tigers. Centralisation of power with chief minister office makes bodies inconsequential.
- State public commission mindlessly copies UPSC.

Suggested Measures:

- Merit based selection must be implemented and educational qualifications like university degree must be a must for state public commission.
- Consultation with parent body at Centre would ensure inculcation of the best practices in central bodies.
- Yearly report regarding the performance and evaluation must be laid out and, if possible, in public domain.
- Proceedings can be made digital and RTI queries answered.
- Strength of the board must be fixed, to eliminate extraneous appointments and outsiders have to be appointed for political neutrality.
- All state PSCs must have a laid down procedure for recruitment and imposed penalty for deviating from it.

Thus, autonomy must be given regarding functions, functionaries and funds.

Q. One-size-fit-all approach must go, in centrally sponsored schemes. Comment.

A. Centrally Sponsored Schemes (CSS) are special purpose grants or loans extended by Central government to States, with the aim to motivate them to implement programmes that help attain national goals.

There is criticism of CSS, as under:

- CSS dictate the Centre's agenda and priorities, which may not be important for states
- CSS offer little flexibility to States
- A universal CSS package may not suit all, as needs of States are different
- Many CSS offer only partial support from Centre, which places burden on states

- As government structure is changing to citizen-centric pattern, the same schemes can't be applied to all. Need-based solutions are necessary.

Q. Is National Company Law Tribunal a worthy successor to the Company Law Board? Elucidate.

A. The National Company Law Tribunal would provide a single forum for all company law and corporate matters. It would reduce the burden on High Courts too. All pending matters with HCs and Company Law Board are now transferred to NCLT. It would also unlock distressed corporate assets as it would take over liquidation process, now being performed by official liquidator attached to high courts.

But some drawbacks exist. For example, recruitment of NCLT officers was frozen after the Madras Bar Association filed a writ petition in Supreme Court.

Tribunalisation should be avoided and executive and technical members should not be dominant in a quasi-judicial body. The National Company Law Tribunal should be headed by a retired high court judge, who and other members should be appointed by a committee headed by Chief Justice of India. If these points are kept in mind, the NCLT would be a worthy successor to Company Law Board.

Q. Outdated regulations continue to remain in statute books leading to slack enforcement, corruption and unethical practices. Due to this, objectives of legislation are not met. Critically analyse.

A. According to the 20th Law Commission findings, there are 1145 regulations and laws which are outdated. Some don't have relevance like Hindu Widow Remarriage Act, but exist in law books. The tendency to over-regulate with a huge number of regulations is counterproductive. The Juvenile Act allows heinous crimes to take place, under the guise of minor age provision. The Santhanam Committee and the first and second ARC had all been entrusted with reviewing the problem of outdated laws.

Government agencies should have a single window agency within organisations, so that delays are minimized and citizens are not inconvenienced. Information and communications technology can provide service in faster, more efficient and transparent way. A web-enabled single window interface can be provided for all government organizations. Simplifying transactions, reducing discretion and effective supervision are all necessary.

Q, India has mounting foodgrain stocks and endemic mass hunger. Comment on this dichotomy.

A. The PDS scheme, which involves distribution of essential commodities to a large number of people is a major instrument of the government's policy for ensuring availability of foodgrains to the poor and needy people and ensuring food security in country. The deficiencies of PDS system are:

- Poor identification of beneficiaries
- PDS is not cost-effective, as its operations are too costly, due to wasteful movements of foodgrains and high storage losses.
- FCI warehouses have a lot of grains, but they don't get distributed fast enough, leading to spoilage
- Leakage of grains owing to the black market occurs and beneficiaries get poor quality of foodgrains

Q. What are the implications of proposed amendment to Ancient Monuments and Archaeological Sites and Remains Act, 1958 which would remove the security net around our nationally protected monuments?

A. The Amendment to section 20A of Ancient Monuments and Archaeological Sites and Remains Act, removes the security net of 100 meters and would allow any department or office of the Central Government to carry out public works in the prohibited area after obtaining permission from the Central Government.

The 2013 report of the Comptroller and Auditor General (CAG) noted that of the 1,655 monuments surveyed, 546 of them were encroached.

In 2010, the Archaeological Survey of India (ASI) stated its staff strength did not permit the deployment of even a single person on a regular full-time basis at more than 2,500 of its monuments.

Monuments are endangered structures and vulnerable to human interference. Zoning around monuments is necessary to prevent monuments from defacement.

Implications

Ministry of Culture would approve the projects of the ministry of Road and Surface Transport for creating structures. There are possibilities that the MoC would act as only as facilitator of such projects and not offer protection to monuments.

The rise in structures around the monuments and increase in public movement could lead to vandalism and defacement of the existing structures.

The beauty and aesthetic looks of the monuments would suffer due to the rise in structures in the immediate vicinity of the monuments.

Thousands of other historical monuments are not protected by the ASI nor are there security nets. The proposed amendment would give impetus to the encroachment on such unprotected and vulnerable monuments.

The other side:

The new amendment is proposed with the view of de-congesting crowded places and offering better transport and communication facilities.

The establishment of commercial structures around the monuments could generate the resources for ASI which could be used in better protection of the monument itself.

Q. A robust grievance redressal mechanism is necessary to provide safeguards to disadvantaged sections. In the light of this, analyse the shortcomings of National Commission for Women.

A. The National Commission for Women is a statutory body, which safeguards the rights of women. However, there are many overlapping sections, which create confusion and lead to shifting of responsibility. For example, National Human Rights Commission and National Commission for SCs, STs have similar duties. The ARC had suggested combining of decentralized nodes of human rights agencies, so that a strong decentralized arrangement could be provided with sufficient expertise. Specialists and infrastructure linkages are limited with the NCW and this is an area of concern. Use of information technology must be increased.

Q. NGOs need institutional and legal reform. At same time, their societal, development and professional work can't be ignored. Comment.

A. There are nearly 31 lakh non-governmental organizations (NGOs) in the country and only 8%–10% file their accounts with the registrar of societies. Even the Supreme Court went on to say that NGOs get "mind-boggling" funds and it has become a "major problem," implying that these funds were "unaccounted" for.

Due to absence of systematic record, the assessment of their voluntary work is difficult.

No clear framework for accounting and tracking the source of their funding exists.

However the NGOs have played critical role in socio-economic spheres in India. Some of the prominent functions of the NGOs are mentioned here-

- They have ears to the ground, which makes them suitable for the proper implementation of government's welfare schemes.

- NGOs have been accelerating development activities by taking up specific issues like poverty alleviation, child rights, caste stigma and discriminations, women rights, child labour, rural development, water and sanitation, environmental issues etc.,
- In the last two decades, NGOs have become proactive in education, health etc; NGOs have played a crucial role in sending the school dropouts back to school especially in rural areas.

Also the NGOs' health sector development programs like leprosy eradication program and programs on eliminating TB, malaria and improving water and sanitation facilities have met with huge success.

The real success of NGOs is their achievement in influencing government to bring out various development-oriented policies and laws like Right to Information, Integrated child development scheme (ICDS), Integrated child Protection Scheme (ICPS), MNREGA, Juvenile justice, Nirmal gram initiative, Rastriya swasthya bhima yogna (RSBY), various policies on women development, forest and environment development, anti-trafficking, people with disability etc.

Along with Panchayats, NGOs have played important role in strengthening grass-root democracy in rural areas.

A modernised legal and institutional framework for non govt organisations is the need of hour to reward those who are truly serving the society.

Practice Questions

1) Foreign contribution received by NGOs in the country is a matter of concern but excessive control and checks can lead to hurting the genuine work being done by them. Give your views.
2) Give an account of the work being done by SHGs for women's upliftment.
3) Philanthropy is another name for self-promotion and advancement of family name. Do you agree or not?
4) Many policies and plans of the government are excellent in their concept and design but fail to deliver. What could be the reasons?
5) What is the role of judiciary in policy making? Discuss.

PART III

Social Justice

12
CHAPTER

Welfare Schemes For The Vulnerable

OVERVIEW

Inclusive growth means growth for all, irrespective of their status. Yet, the society has many who are vulnerable and are devoid of the means to survive. The reasons could be many; historical, economic, social, etc. The government has a duty to look after their interests through welfare schemes. Economic and social marginalisation is the issue. Such schemes need to be monitored to ensure that the intended beneficiaries are reached. It is said, not without basis, that the holes in the schemes are sometimes so big that a truck can pass through.

"On the 26th of January, 1950 we are going to enter into a life of contradictions. In politics, we will have equality, and in social and economic life, we will have inequality. In politics we will be recognizing the principle of one man one vote and one vote one value. In our social and economic life, we shall, by reason of our social and economic structure, continue to deny the principle of one man one value. How long shall we continue to live this life of contradictions? How long shall we continue to deny equality in our social and economic life?"

–Dr. B.R. Ambedkar

VULNERABLE SECTIONS OF THE POPULATION

Let us now turn our attention to the vulnerable sections of the society, who are they? Essentially, those who are marginalised, sidelined, and excluded; either economically or socially or both.

Who then are the vulnerable who are the objects of the plans, policies and pursuits of the state?

They are in essence those who need care and compassion. To list them:

(1) Those below the poverty line (BPL)
(2) Women, girl child.
(3) Children
(4) Old and infirm
(5) Scheduled Castes, Scheduled Tribes
(6) Physically challenged
(7) Minorities
(8) Other Backward Castes (OBCs)
(9) Vagrants, beggars, migrants
(10) Drug addicts, lunatics

It is the duty of the state to ensure some form of protection to these who are vulnerable. Constitutional provisions are fair and fine, but they can be frail and fickle if not backed by appropriate, adequate, and accurate legislation.

Welfare related matters are covered in the Seventh Schedule, in the Concurrent list, meaning thereby that both the Union as well as the State can legislate (Article 246) However, the legislation by the Union will prevail (Art. 246).

CONSTITUTIONAL PROVISIONS FOR VULNERABLE SECTIONS OF THE SOCIETY

To analyse and examine these compelling issues, one must, out of necessity and need, begin from the Constitution. What does the Constitution hold for the vulnerable sections of the society? As we have seen, the Constitution has a promise of equality for all politically; each person one vote. What of social and economic life? It was the considered view of the men who mattered that political equality would usher in an era of social and economic emancipation. Political freedom would lead to social and economic fulfilment.

The Constitution, for its part, certainly has provisions for the welfare of all and provisions for welfare of the underprivileged, socially and economically backward, and also the vulnerable. Constitution only lays the broad framework within which the goals have to be set through plans and policies in the domain of the governments, both at the Centre as well as the States.

In our Constitution we have Fundamental Rights ensuring citizen equality and expectations there to protect and promote the socially deprived like Scheduled Castes and tribes. Alongside we have Directive Principles of State Policy, historically fair and eternally noble articles to advance the cause of all in a welfare state.

Fundamental Rights

FUNDAMENTAL RIGHTS	
Article	**Rights**
14	Equality before law.
15	Prohibition of discrimination on grounds of religion, race, caste, sex, or place of birth.

16	Equality of opportunity in matters of employment.
16(4)	Provide for reservation in appointments or posts in favour of any backward class of citizens which, in the opinion of the state, is not adequately represented in the services under the state.
16(4)(A) by (77th) amendment (1995) Act	Provision for reservation in promotion to Scheduled Castes and Scheduled Tribes. 85th amendment Act, 2001 permitted promotions with consequential seniority in government service.
335	Acknowledges claims of Scheduled Castes and Scheduled Tribes while making appointments to posts and services, consistent with the maintenance of efficiency of administration, even with relaxed standards.
17	Abolishes untouchability

Note: Article 17 (dealing with Untouchability) was adopted by the Constituent Assembly with wildest enthusiasm and unprecedented cheers). It abolished a historic absurdity; a shame on humanity. Later, Civil Rights Act, 1955 was passed providing for penalties for such practices.

All these rights, available to all, may be called positive rights subject to provisions made for betterment of deprived classes.

Directive Principles of State Policy

Directive Principles of State Policy (Article 36 to 51 in Part IV of the Constitution) enumerate the measures the state (both Union and States) is desired to take for the welfare of citizen, including the oppressed, depressed, and the vulnerable sections of the society. These principles are justifiable but not justiciable; they can't be enforced through a court of law like the Fundamental Rights.

DIRECTIVE PRINCIPLES OF STATE POLICY

Article	Principle
38	State to secure a social order for the promotion of welfare of the people.
39	Certain principles of policy to be followed by the state.
39A	Equal justice and free legal aid
41	Right to work, to education, and to public assistance in some cases.
42	Provision of just and humane conditions of work and maternity relief.
43	Living wage, conditions of work ensuring a decent standard of life, etc. for workers.
45	Provision for free and compulsory education for children substituted by 86th (Eighty sixth) amendment Act 2002.
46	Promotion of educational and economic interests of Scheduled Castes and Scheduled Tribes and other weaker sections.
47	Duty of the state to raise the level of nutrition and the standard of living and to improve public health.

Directive Principles enjoin noble thoughts, lofty ideals, pious intent, and philanthropic outlook for the welfare of the poor, India's living dead, Gandhiji's 'Daridranarayana', the subjects of Christian charity, and the veritable last men in the line.

MECHANISMS, LAWS, INSTITUTIONS, AND BODIES CONSTITUTED FOR THE PROTECTION AND BETTERMENT OF VULNERABLE SECTIONS

What are the mechanisms, laws, institutions, and bodies in existence for the welfare of vulnerable sections? The Parliament, through the aid and assistance of the Constitution, provides the mechanism for enacting suitable laws. Sometimes the Parliament creates institutions too; the Government too creates institutions and bodies for the welfare of its citizens. Broadly, there are four pillars upon whom the mechanism rests. First is the Parliament along with State Legislature, second is the judiciary, third is the executive, and last is the media, alongside NGOs/SHGs/, etc.

The Legislature, largely through its members, enacts legislation for the welfare of citizens.

In this, the ruling party or parties have decidedly a significant role. As part of their manifesto and programmes, legislation is pushed forward. In the event of delays, digression, deviations, dilly-dallying, or division, pressure is mounted on the government to deliver. A case in point is the women's reservation bill which most parties, without reservation, are not wholly in favour. The issue of sexual harassment of women at the workplace lingered on for a decade till the Supreme Court intervened decisively.

Executive itself too is often guilty of slackened pace in the matter of welfare. Often in implementation, lack of sensitivity is the cause more often than not. Role of the executive is twofold; implementation and evaluation, tempered by transparency and accountability.

Judiciary is another important player in the whole gamut of mechanism; judicial activism and Public Interest Litigation are becoming increasingly vital. Legislative lethargy or executive ennui are often the subject matter of judicial scrutiny and censure.

Media too is an important element in the whole mechanism. Both the electronic and print media are active in highlighting cases of apathy and abuse. Examples abound; be it about child labour or unfair wages for women, or lack of drinking water, or drug abuse or corruption in government, etc. the role of media is increasing steadily.

NGOs/trade unions/stakeholders/self-help groups, etc. are also becoming increasingly active. It is a fact that everything can't be left to the government, others too have to move in, and state may step in with help and assistance, given the resources it has. It is therefore clear that mechanisms are a dynamic, distinct and detailed process which works on interplay of forces.

Acts Relating to Women and Children

The Ministry of Women & Child Development is in charge of the administration of the following Acts relating to women and children: (a) The Immoral Traffic (Prevention) Act, 1956 (as amended in 1986), (b) The Indecent Representation of Women (Prevention) Act, 1986 (60 of 1986), (c) The Dowry Prohibition Act, 1961 as amended in 1986, (d) The Commission of Sati (Prevention) Act, 1987 (3 of 1988), (e) The Prohibition of Child Marriage Act, 2006 (notified in January 2007), (f) Protection of Women from Domestic Violence Act, 2005, (g) National Commission for Women Act, 1990, (h) Infant Milk Substitutes, Feeding Bottles and Infant food (Regulation of Production, Supply and Distribution) Act, 1992 (41 of 1992), (i) Commission for Protection of Child Rights

Act, 2005, and (j) Juvenile Justice (Care and Protection of Children) Act, 2000, (k) The Protection of Children from Sexual Offences (POCSO) Act and POCSO Rules, 2012 and (l) Sexual Harassment of Women at Workplace (Prevention, Prohibition and Redressal), 2012.

The Juvenile Justice (Care & Protection of Children), Amendment Bill was passed in Parliament in August, 2011. The Ministry's mandate primarily includes formulation of plans, policies, and programmes for women and children; enactment and amendment of legislations related to them; and overall guidance and coordination of efforts of governmental and non-governmental organisations working in the field of women and child development.

Food and Nutrition Board

Food and Nutrition Board in the Ministry of Women and Child Development is involved in policy-making, strategy development, as well as identifying innovative measures for the improvement of the nutritional status of the people of our country. It also focuses on improving the dietary habits of the people through nutrition education and extension; promotion of low cost, locally available foods; conservation of fruits and vegetables through home-scale processing; and training of health functionaries in nutrition.

The National Nutrition Policy was formulated in 1993, and as a follow up the National Plan of Action was developed in 1995. The National Plan of Action has identified the different sectors in the government for taking up coordinated action to combat malnutrition. Programmes are undertaken to train master trainers such as medical officers/nursing officers, child development project officers/supervisors, and principals of schools implementing mid-day meal scheme, as well as the field level functionaries. Nutrition awareness programmes for the community, home-scale preservation of fruits and vegetables programmes which also promotes skill development in the adolescent girls and women are organised. Demonstrations for promotion of low cost nutritious recipes are held to facilitate adoption of means to achieve better nutrition. Linkages with the Integrated Child Development Services (ICDS) for better quality of supplementary nutrition, health, and nutrition education are maintained. For promotion of infant and young child feeding practices, focus on appropriate feeding and implementation of the Infant Milk Substituties (IMS) Act are undertaken.

POLICIES, BOARDS, COMMISSIONS, AND INITIATIVES FOR EMPOWERMENT OF WOMEN

National Policy for Empowerment of Women

In 2001, the National Policy for Empowerment of Women (NPEW) was formulated as the blueprint for the future, with the goal of bringing about the advancement, development, and empowerment of women. The NPEW laid down detailed prescriptions to address discrimination against women, strengthen existing institutions which includes the legal system, provide better access to health care and other services, equal opportunities for women's participation in decision-making, and mainstreaming gender concerns in the development process, etc. The policies/programmes of the Government are all directed towards achieving inclusive growth with special focus on women, in line with the objective of the National Policy for Empowerment of Women.

Schemes for Women

Rajiv Gandhi Scheme for Empowerment of Adolescent Girls (RGSEAG): Sabla

Sabla was introduced in the year 2010–11 and is operational in 205 selected districts on a pilot basis. It aims at all-round development of adolescent girls (AGs) of 11–18 years (with a focus on all out-of-school AGs). Sabla is being implemented through the state governments/UTs with 100 per cent financial assistance from the Central Government for all inputs other than nutrition provision for which 50 per cent Central assistance to states is provided. Anganwadi Centre (AWC) is the focal point for the delivery of the services. The scheme has two major components nutrition and non-nutrition. Nutrition is being given in the form of take home ration or hot cooked meal for 11–14 years out of school girls and 14–18 years for all AGs (out of school and in school girls). In the non-nutrition component, out of school adolescent girls of 11–18 years are being provided IFA supplementation, health check-up and referral services, nutrition and health education.

Indira Gandhi Matritva Sahyog Yojana (IGMSY)

A conditional cash transfer scheme for pregnant and lactating women was introduced in October, 2010 to contribute to better enabling environment by providing cash incentives for improved health and nutrition to pregnant and nursing mothers. The scheme attempts to partly compensate for wage loss to pregnant and lactating women both prior to and after delivery of the child. The beneficiaries are paid Rs. 4000/- in three instalments per Pregnant & Lactating woman between the second trimester and till the child attains the age of 6 months on fulfiling specific conditions related to maternal and child health.

Women Empowerment and Livelihood Programme in Mid-Gangetic Plains: "Priyadarshini"

The Ministry is administering a pilot project titled Women's Empowerment and Livelihood Programme in the Mid-Gangetic Plains "Priyadarshini" in 13 blocks spread over five districts in Uttar Pradesh and two in Bihar. The project is assisted by International Fund for Agricultural Development (IFAD). It aims at holistic empowerment (economic and social) of vulnerable groups of women and adolescent girls in the project area through formation of women's self-help groups (SHGs) and promotion of improved livelihood opportunities. Though the focus of the project is on livelihood enhancement, the beneficiaries will be empowerment to address their political, legal, and health problems through rigorous capacity building.

National Bank for Agriculture and Rural Development (NABARD) is the lead programme agency for the implementation.

Ujjawala

Launched in 2009, 'Ujjawala' is a comprehensive scheme for prevention of trafficking, with five specific components; (i) prevention, which includes formation of community vigilance groups/ adolescents groups, awareness and sensitisation of important functionaries like policy, community leaders, and preparation of awareness generation materials, holding workshops, etc.; (ii) rescue, for safe withdrawal of the victim from the place of exploitation.; (iii) rehabilitation, which includes providing safe shelter for victims with basic amenities such as food, clothing, counselling, medical care, legal aid, vocational training, and income generation activities, etc.; (iv) reintegration, for restoring the victim into the family/community (if she so desires) and the accompanying costs; (v) repatriation, to provide support to cross-border victims for their safe repatriation to their country of origin.

Beti Bachao, Beti Padhao

In the backdrop of a trend of declining sex ratio in the age group up to five years, the Government has introduced a new scheme called *Beti Bachao, Beti Padhao* with the twin aims of not only improving the adverse sex ratio, but also to ensure that girls are educated. With an initial corpus of Rs. 100 crore, it will help in generating awareness and improve the efficiency of delivery of welfare services meant for women. The important activities that would be undertaken under the *Beti Padhao Abhiyan* are as under: activate School Management Committees (SMCs) to ensure universal enrolment of girls; Balika Manch in schools; construction of girl's toilets; make dysfunctional toilets functional; completion of Kasturba Gandhi Bal Vidyalayas; sustained campaign to re-enroll dropout girls in secondary schools; and construction of girls hostels for secondary and senior secondary level.

The overall goal of the *Beti Bachao, Beti Padhao* (BBBP) scheme is to celebrate the girl child and enable her education.

The objectives of the scheme are as under:

- Prevent gender biased sex selective elimination
- Ensure survival and protection of the girl child.
- Ensure education of the girl child.

Mass communication campaigns on *Beti Bachao Beti Padhao* aims at ensuring girls are born, nurtured, and educated without discrimination to become empowered citizens of this country.

Sukanya Samriddhi Account

Along with the *Beti Bachao, Beti Padhao scheme*, the government has also launched the "Sukanya Samriddhi Account" programme. Despite being a small savings scheme, the Sukanya Samriddhi Account has the potential to have a phenomenal impact on the lives and self-esteem of young girls in the country. The scheme aims to ensure a bright future for the girl children by facilitating their education and marriage expenses.

Under the scheme, a parent or legal guardian can open an account in the name of the girl child until she attains the age of ten years. As per the government notification on the Scheme, the account can be opened in any post office branch and designated public sector bank. The rate of interest for the scheme is an attractive 9.2 per cent which will be compounded annually.

Stree-Shakti Puraskar

As a recognition of achievements of individual women in the field of social development, the government has instituted six national awards known as 'Stree Shakti Puraskar'. These awards carry a cash prize of Rs. 3 lakh and a citation in the name of eminent women personalities from

Indian history, who are famous for their personal courage and integrity: Devi Ahilyabai Holkar, Kannagi, Mata Jijabai, Rani Gaidenliu Zeliang, Rani Lakshmibai, and Rani Rudrama Devi.

Rashtriya Mahila Kosh

Rashtriya Mahila Kosh (RMK) extends microfinance to the needy and poor women in the informal sector through a client-friendly, no collateral system and in a hassle-free manner for livelihood activities, housing, micro-enterprises, etc., for their socio-economic upliftment. RMK has pioneered an alternate credit delivery mechanism in the country by advancing micro-credit to the self-help groups (SHGs) of poor women through a diverse range of intermediary organisations working at the grassroot level such as NGOs, women federations, co-operatives, and urban women cooperative banks. In order to remove the uneven presence of micro-credit in the country which is witnessed mostly in North-Eastern region due to the poor presence of banking network, lack of infrastructure, and awareness, RMK has formulated a client-friendly credit package for the N-E region by relaxing its credit norms to meet the needs of the women. RMK believes in women empowerment through microfinancing.

Gender Budgeting Initiatives

Gender budgeting is a powerful tool for achieving gender mainstreaming so as to ensure that benefits of development reach women as much as men. It is not an accounting exercise but an ongoing process of keeping a gender perspective in policy/programme formulation, its implementation, and review. To institutionalise gender budgeting in the country, the setting up of Gender Budgeting Cells (GBCs) in all ministries/departments was mandated by the Ministry of Finance in 2005. The Ministry of Women and Child Development (MWCD) as the nodal agency for gender budgeting has been undertaking several initiatives for taking it forward at the national and state levels. One of the key areas has been advocating setting up of GBCs in all ministries/ departments, strengthening internal and external capacities, and building expertise of GBCs to undertake gender mainstreaming of policies/schemes/programmes.

National Mission for Empowerment of Women

National Mission for Empowerment of Women (NMEW), a Centrally Sponsored Scheme (CSS), was launched by the government in 2010 with a view to empower women holistically. The Mission aims to achieve empowerment of women by securing intersectoral convergence of schemes/programmes of different ministries/departments of Government of India as well as state governments. It has the mandate to strengthen and facilitate the process of coordinating all the women's welfare and socio-economic development programmes.

The model is aimed at convergent implementation of programmes intended for welfare and development of women. The model would include introduction of convergence cum facilitation centres at the district (few urban agglomerations), tehsils/ward and village/area levels.

National Commission for Women

The National Commission for Women (NCW) was constituted in January, 1991 as a statutory body at the national level in pursuance of The National Commission for Women Act, 1990 desire to safeguard the interests of women. It has a wide mandate covering almost all aspects of women's development, viz., to investigate and examine the legal safeguards provided for women under the Constitution and other laws and recommend to Government measures for their effective implementation; review the existing provisions of the Constitution and other laws affecting women and recommended amendments to meet any lacunae, inadequacies, or shortcomings in such laws; look into complaints and take suo motu notice of matters relating to deprivation of women's rights etc., and take up the issues with appropriate authorities; take up studies/research on issues of relevance to women, participate and advise in the planning process for socio-economic development of women, evaluate the progress made thereof, inspect jails, remand homes, etc. where women are kept under custody, and seek remedial action wherever necessary. National Commission for women had taken up the review of the MTP Act, 1971 and Immoral Trafficking (Prevention) Act, 1956 with a view to examine whether the existing provisions of the Act require any amendments. The recommendations have been forwarded to the Government. The Commission was designated as the coordinating agency at the National level for dealing with issues pertaining to NRI marriages. NRI Cell of NCW deals with complaints received from deserted women in India and abroad due to cross country marriages wherein there is any deprivation of women's rights or any issue involving grave injustice to women.

POLICIES, INSTITUTES, INITIATIVES, AND SCHEMES FOR WELFARE OF CHILDREN

National Policy for Children

The Government adopted a new National Policy for Children (NPC) in April, 2013. The new policy reaffirms the government's commitment to the realisation of the rights of all children in the country. It recognises every person below the age of eighteen years as a child. The policy recognises childhood as an integral part of life with a value of its own, and a long-term, sustainable, multisectoral, integrated, and inclusive approach is necessary for the harmonious development and protection of children. The policy lays down the guiding principles that must be respected by the national, state, and local government in their actions and initiatives affecting children. Some of the key guiding principles are the right of every child to life, survival, development, education, protection and participation, equal rights for all children without discrimination. It considers the best interest of the child as a primary concern in all actions and decisions affecting children, and family environment as the most conducive for all-round development of children.

The policy has identified survival, health, nutrition, education, development, protection, and participation as the undeniable rights of every child, and has also declared these as key priority areas.

The Protection of Children from Sexual Offences Act, 2012

To deal with child abuse cases, the Government has brought in a special law "The Protection of Children from Sexual Offences Act, 2012".

The Act defines a 'child' as any person below eighteen years of age. Being gender neutral, this definition provides equal protection to both the male and the female child. The Act provides for stringent punishments, which have been graded as per the gravity of the offence. The punishments range from simple to rigorous imprisonment of varying periods. There is also a provision for fine, which is to be decided by the Court. An offence is treated as 'aggravated' when committed by a person in a position of trust or authority of child such as a member of security forces, police officer, public servant, etc. The Act provides for the establishment of special courts for trial of offences under the Act, keeping the best interest of the child as of paramount importance, at every stage of the judicial process.

The National Commission for the Protection of Child Rights (NCPCR) and State Commissions for the Protections of Child Rights (SCPCRs) have been made the designated authority to monitor the implementation of the Act.

National Commission for Protection of Child Rights

The National Commission for Protection of Child Rights Act (NCPCR), 2005 was notified in January, 2006. A National Commission for Protection of Child Rights was set up in March, 2007 in accordance with the provisions of the Act for proper enforcement of children's rights and effective implementation of laws and programmes relating to children. Its mission is to project, promote, and defend child rights in India. Its mandate is to ensure that all laws, policies, programmes, practices, and administrative structure in the country are in consonance with the child rights perspective as enshrined in the Constitution of India and also the UN Convention on the Rights of the Child (CRC). Under the provisions of the Act, state commissions have been set up in Assam, Bihar, Chhattisgarh, Delhi, Goa, Karnataka, Madhya Pradesh, Maharashtra, Manipur, Odisha, Punjab, Rajasthan, Sikkim, Tamil Nadu, Uttarakhand, West Bengal, and Nagaland. The Rights of Child to Free and Compulsory Education Act, 2009 came into force in April, 2010. The NCPCR along with the state commissions has a specific role for the implementation of the Act. The Protection of Children from Sexual Offences Act, 2012 (POCSO) came into force on November 14, 2012. This comprehensive piece of legislation provides protection to all children under the age of 18 years from offences of sexual assault, sexual harassment, and pornography and overcomes the lacunae in the different sections of IPC and more important, does not distinguish between adult and child victims. The SCPCRs have also been entrusted with the task of monitoring the implementation of the Protection of Children from Sexual offences (POCSO) Rules, 2012.

National Institute of Public Cooperation and Child Development

National Institute of Public Cooperation and Child Development (NIPCCD), an autonomous organisation under the aegis of the Ministry of Women and Child Development, is a premier organisation devoted to promotion of voluntary action and research, training, and documentation in the overall domain of women and child development.

The objectives of the institute are to: develop and promote voluntary action in social development; take a comprehensive view of child development and to promote relevant need-based programmes in pursuance of the National Policy for Children; national policy for empowerment of coordination between governmental and voluntary action in social development; evolve framework and perspective for organising programmes related to women and children through governmental and voluntary efforts; and establish liaison with international and regional agencies, research institutions, universities, and technical bodies engaged in activities similar to those of the institute.

Schemes for Children

Rajiv Gandhi National Creche Scheme

Rajiv Gandhi National Creche Scheme provides daycare facilities to the children in the age group of 0–6 years from families with monthly income of less than Rs. 12,000/-. In addition to being a safe space for the children, the creches provide services as supplementary nutrition, pre-school education, and emergency health care, etc. The scheme is presently being implemented through the Central Social Welfare Board (CSWB), Indian Council for Child Welfare (ICCW).

Integrated Child Protection Scheme (ICPS)

Ministry of Women and Child Development is implementing this comprehensive centrally sponsored scheme since 2009–10 through the state government/UT administrations on a predefined cost-sharing financial pattern. The objectives of the scheme are to contribute to the improvement in the well-being of children in difficult circumstances, as well as reduction of vulnerabilities to situation and actions that lead to abuse, neglect, exploitation, abandonment, and separation of children from parents. ICPS provides preventive, statutory care, and rehabilitation services to children who are in need of care and protection and children in conflict with law as defined under the Juvenile Justice (Care and Protection of Children) Act, 2000 and its Amendment Act, 2006 and any other vulnerable children. It provides financial support to state governments/UT administrations for running services for children either themselves or through suitable NGOs.

Integrated Child Development Services

Integrated Child Development Services (ICDS) scheme is one of the flagship programmes of the government and represents one of the world's largest and unique programmes for early childhood development. The programme aims at addressing health, nutrition, and the development needs of young children, and pregnant and nursing mothers. The National Institute of Public cooperation and Child Development (NIPCCD) has been functioning as an apex institution for training of the ICDS functionaries since 1975. As a nodal resource agency, the Institute has also been entrusted with the responsibility of training and capacity building of functionaries at the national and regional level, under the Integrated Child Protection Scheme (ICPS). The Institute had finalised syllabi for functionaries under ICPS in collaboration with UNICEF and training manuals have been prepared for various stakeholders for effective child protection, as envisaged under the legal framework. The current thrust areas which relate to child development are maternal and child health and nutrition, early childhood care and education, childhood disability, positive mental health in children, and child care support service. Several programmes have been designed for various groups of clientele, namely, representatives of NGOs, parents, teachers, and officers of various government departments.

WELFARE OF PERSONS WITH DISABILITIES

Section 2 (t) of The Persons with Disabilities (Equal Opportunities, Protection of Rights and Full

Participation) Act, 1995, (also referred to as PwD Act, 1995) defines "Person with Disability" as a person suffering from not less than 40 per cent of any disability as certified by a medical authority. The disability being (a) blindness (b) low vision (c) leprosy cured (d) hearing impairment (e) locomotor disability (f) mental illness (g) mental retardation (h) autism (i) cerebral palsy, or (j) a combination of any two or more of (g), (h), and (i) (Section 2 (i) of the PwD Act, 1995 read along with Section 2(j) of The National Trust for Welfare of Persons with Autism, Cerebral Palsy, Mental Retardation and Multiple Disabilities Act, 1999).

In order to give focussed attention to different policy issues and meaningful thrust to the activities aimed at welfare and empowerment of the Persons with Disabilities, a separate Department of Disability Affairs was carved out of the Ministry of Social Justice and Empowerment in May, 2012. The Department acts as a Nodal Agency for matters pertaining to disability and Persons with Disabilities and affects closer coordination among different stakeholders: related Central ministries, state/UT governments, NGOs, etc. in matters pertaining to disability.

According to Census 2011, there are 2.68 crore persons with disabilities in the country (who constitute 2.21 per cent of the total population). Out of the total population of persons with disabilities, about 1.50 crore are men and 1.18 crore are women. These include persons with visual, hearing, speech and locomotors disabilities, mental illness, mental retardation, multiple disabilities, and other disabilities.

Relevant Constitutional Provisions Regarding the Disabled

The Constitution of India through its Preamble, inter-alia seeks to secure to all its citizens; justice, social, economic, and political; liberty of thought, expression, belief, faith and worship; equality of status and of opportunity. Part III of the Constitution provides for a set of six Fundamental Rights to all the citizens (and in a few cases to non-citizens also). These include, Right to Equality; Right to Freedom; Right against Exploitation; Right to Freedom of Religion; Cultural and Educational Rights, and Right to Constitutional Remedies. All these rights are also available to the Persons with Disabilities even though no specific mention of such persons appear in this Part of the Constitution.

The Directive Principles of State Policy have been incorporated in Part IV of the Constitution. Even though non-justiciable, these have been declared as fundamental in the governance of the country. These principles are intended to be the imperative basis of State policy. These are really in the nature of instructions issued to future legislatures and executives for their guidance. Article 41: Right to work, to education and to public assistance in certain cases, provides: "The State shall, within the limits of its economic capacity and development, make effective provision for securing the right to work, to education and to public assistance in case of unemployment, old age, sickness and disablement, and in other cases of undeserved want. Besides, the Eleventh Schedule to Article 243-G and Twelfth Schedule to Article 243-W, which pertain to the powers and responsibilities of the Panchayats and Municipalities respectively with respect to implementation of schemes for economic development and social justice, include welfare and safeguarding the interests of Persons with Disabilities among other weaker sections of the society.

The following legislations govern different aspects of disability and welfare & empowerment of the Persons with Disabilities:

1. The Rehabilitation Council of India Act, 1992.
2. The Persons with Disabilities (Equal Opportunities, Protection of Rights and Full Participation) Act, 1995; and
3. The National Trust for the welfare of Persons with Autism, Cerebral Palsy, Mental Retardation and Multiple Disabilities Act, 1999.

Department of Empowerment of Persons with Disabilities (DEPwD), has formulated the accessible India Campaign (*Sugamya Bharat Abhiyan*), as a nation-wide campaign for achieving universal accessibility for PwDs. The campaign targets three separate verticals for achieving universal accessibilities, namely the built-up environment, transportation ecosystem, and information and communication ecosystem. The campaign has ambitious targets with defined timelines and will use IT and social media for spreading awareness about the campaign and seeking commitment/engagement of various stakeholders.

Welfare Measures for the Disabled

Mental Health Act

Mental illness has been recognised as one of the disabilities under The Persons with Disabilities (Equal Opportunities, Protection of Rights and Full Participation) Act, 1995. The treatment and care of the mentally ill persons are governed by The Mental Health Act, 1987. The Act is administered by the Ministry of Health and Family Welfare.

Persons with Disabilities Act

A comprehensive law, namely, The Persons with Disabilities (Equal Opportunities, Protection of Rights and Full Participation) Act, 1995 was enacted and enforced in February, 1996. The law deals with both prevention and promotion aspects of the rehabilitation such as education, employment and vocational training, creation of barrier-free environment, provision of rehabilitation services for persons with disabilities, institutional services, and supportive social security measures like unemployment allowance and grievance redressal machinery both at the Central and state Level.

National Trust for the Welfare of Persons with Autism, Cerebral Palsy, Mental Retardation, and Multiple Disabilities

The National Trust is a statutory body under "The National Trust for the Welfare of Persons with Autism, Cerebral Palsy, Mental Retardation and Multiple Disabilities Act, 1999". The main objectives of the Trust are to enable and empower persons with these disabilities to live independently as fully as possible, to extend support to registered organisations providing need-based services, and to evolve procedure for appointment of legal guardians for persons with disabilities requiring such protection.

Office of the Chief Commissioner for Persons with Disabilities

The Chief Commissioner is an important statutory functionary, appointed under Section 57 of The Persons with Disabilities (Equal Opportunities, Protection of Rights and Full Participation) Act, 1995. The functions and duties of the Chief Commissioner include coordinating the work of State Commissioners for persons with disabilities, monitoring of utilisation of funds disbursed by the

Central Government, taking steps to safeguard rights and facilities made available to persons with disabilities, and also to look into complaints with respect to deprivation of rights of persons with disabilities. The Chief Commissioner can also take suo motu notice of non-implementation of any rule, law, etc. meant for persons with disabilities and is vested with the powers of a civil court relating to summoning of witness, discovery, requisitioning, and production of any document, etc.

Rehabilitation Council

The Rehabilitation Council of India is a statutory body set up under the Rehabilitation Council of India Act, 1992. The Council is responsible for regulating the training policies and programmes for various categories of professionals in the area of rehabilitation and special education. Its functions include: (i) standardisation and regulation of training courses at different levels in all the training institutions throughout the country, (ii) recognition of institutions/universities running training courses in the area of rehabilitation of the disabled within and outside the country on a reciprocal basis, (iii) promotion of research in rehabilitation and special education, (iv) maintenance of a Central Rehabilitation Register for professionals possessing the recognised rehabilitation qualifications in the area of rehabilitation, and (v) encouragement of Continuing Rehabilitation Education Programmes in collaboration with organisations working in the area of disability.

National Institutes for the Disabled

In order to effectively deal with the multi-dimensional problem of the disabled population, the following National Institutes/apex level Institutes have been set-up in each major area of disability; (i) National Institute for the Visually Handicapped, Dehradun, (ii) National Institute for Orthopedically Handicapped, Kolkata, (iii) Ali Yavar Jung National Institute for the Hearing Handicapped, Mumbai, (iv) National Institute for the Mentally Handicapped, Secunderabad, (v) National Institute of Rehabilitation Training and Research, Cuttack, (vi) Institute for the Physically Handicapped, New Delhi, and (vii) National Institute for Empowerment of Persons with Multiple Disabilities, Chennai. These institutes are mainly responsible for conducting innovative researches, organising training programmes for manpower development, and deliver services in the country.

ALIMCO

The Artificial Limbs Manufacturing Corporation of India (ALIMCO), Kanpur is a public sector body, engaged in manufacturing of aids and appliances for persons with disabilities. The products manufactured by the Corporation conform to ISI standards approved by the Bureau of Indian Standards. Marketing of products is done through Regional Marketing Centres at Kolkata, Mumbai, Chennai, Bhubaneshwar, and Delhi and also through National Institutes and voluntary organisations.

CRCs

Five Composite Regional Centres (CRCs) for the Persons with Disabilities are located at Srinagar, Lucknow, Bhopal, Sundernagar, and Guwahati. These centres conduct training programmes to prepare professionals in the field of rehabilitation as well as provide rehabilitation services to the disabled. Four Regional Rehabilitation Centres for Spinal Injuries and other Orthopaedic Disabilities at Mohali, Cuttack, Jabalpur, and Bareilly are providing services for basic management and follow-up of the spinally injured so as to make the affected persons functionally independent.

Economic Development of the Disabled

The National Handicapped Finance and Development Corporation (NHFDC) is an apex-level financial institution for extending credit facilities to persons with disabilities for their economic development. Funds assistance is disbursed through the channelising agencies authorised by the State Governments/UT Administrations and Non-Governmental Organisations. It also extends loans for pursuing education at graduate and higher levels. Besides, it assists in the upgradation of technical and entrepreneurial skills to enable beneficiaries to manage their production units efficiently.

Under the scheme for Assistance to Disabled Persons for Purchase/Fitting of AIDs and Appliances assistance is given for procuring durable, sophisticated, and scientifically manufactured standard aids and appliances that can promote their physical, social, and psychological rehabilitation by reducing the impact of disability and enhance their economic potential. The scheme is implemented through agencies like voluntary organisations, national institutes under the Ministry, ALIMCO, Zilla Panchayats, DRDAs, etc. The implementing agencies are provided grant-in-aid for purchase, fabrication, and distribution of aids and appliances. The scheme also includes under its ambit medical/surgical correction and intervention that may be essential prior to fitment of aids and appliances.

WELFARE OF WEAKER SECTIONS: SCHEDULED CASTES AND SCHEDULED TRIBES

Statutory Framework for SCs and STs

The Constitution contains several provisions in the nature of safeguards for the Scheduled Castes and Scheduled Tribes. The following two Acts specifically aim at curbing (i) untouchability and (ii) atrocities against SCs and STs, and are therefore very important for the Scheduled Castes and Scheduled Tribes:-

(i) The Protection of Civil Rights Act, 1955, and

(ii) The Scheduled Castes and the Scheduled Tribes (Preventions of Atrocities) Act, 1989.

Protection of Civil Rights

In pursuance of Article 17 of the Constitution of India, The Untouchability (Offences) Act, 1955 was enacted and notified in May, 1955. Subsequently, it was amended and renamed in the year 1976 as The Protection of Civil Rights Act, 1955. Rules under this Act, viz., The Protection of Civil Rights Rules, 1977 were notified in 1977. The Act extends to the whole of India and provides punishment for the practice of untouchability. It is implemented by the respective state governments and union territory administrations.

Scheduled Castes and the Scheduled Tribes (Preventions of Atrocities) Act

The Scheduled Castes and the Scheduled Tribes (Prevention of Atrocities) Act, 1989 (The PoA Act) came into force with effect from 1990. This legislation aims at preventing commission of offences by persons other than Scheduled Castes and Scheduled Tribes against Scheduled Castes and Scheduled Tribes.

Comprehensive Rules under this Act, titled "Scheduled Castes and the Scheduled Tribes

(Prevention of Atrocities) Rules, 1995" were notified in the year 1995, which, inter-alia, provide norms for relief and rehabilitation. These Rules had not been amended thereafter.

Scheduled Castes and Scheduled Tribes (Prevention of Atrocities) Amendment Act, 2015

Despite the deterrent provisions made in the PoA Act, continuing atrocities against the members of Scheduled Castes (SCs) and Scheduled Tribes (STs) has been a cause of concern. High incidence of occurrences of offences against members of SCs and STs also indicated that the deterrent effect of the PoA Act was not adequately felt by the accused. It was, therefore, considered appropriate to strengthen the Act and make the relevant provisions of the Act more effective. Based on the consultation process with all the stakeholders, amendments in the PoA Act were proposed to broadly cover five areas.

National Commission for Scheduled Castes and Scheduled Tribes

The National Commission for Scheduled Castes and Scheduled Tribes which was set up under Article 383 of the Constitution in 1990 was bifurcated into two Commissions namely, National Commission for Scheduled Castes and National Commission for Scheduled Tribes after the 89th Constitutional (Amendment) Act, 2003.

The National Commission for Scheduled Castes: NCSC

The National Commission for Schedule Castes is responsible for monitoring the safeguards provided for Scheduled Castes and also to review issues concerning their welfare.

Functions of the NCSC as enumerated in the Article 338(5) of the Constitution are:-(a) to investigate and monitor all matters relating to the safeguards provided for the Scheduled Castes under the Constitution or under any other law for the time being in force or under any order of the government and to evaluate the working of such safeguards; (b) to inquire into specific complaints with respect to the deprivation of rights and safeguards of the Scheduled Castes; (c) to participate and advise on the planning process of socio-economic development of the Scheduled Castes and to evaluate the progress of their development under the Union and any State; (d) to present to the President, annually and at such other times as the Commission may deem fit, reports upon the working of those safeguards; (e) to make in such reports, recommendations as to the measures that should be taken by the Union or any State for the effective implementation of those safeguards and other measures for the protection, welfare, and socio-economic development of the Scheduled Castes; and (f) to discharge such other functions in relation to the protection, welfare, and development and advancement of the Scheduled Castes as the President may, subject to the provisions of any law made by Parliament, by rule specify.

National Commission for Scheduled Tribes: NCST

In addition to the Office of the Commissioner for Scheduled Caste and Scheduled Tribes created in 1950 for effective implementation of various safeguards provided in the Constitution for the SCs & STs and various other protective legislations, a multi-member Commission for SCs and

STs was set up in 1978. In 1992, these two organisations were replaced by a statutory multi-member National Commission for Scheduled Castes and Scheduled Tribes. However, since the needs and problems of Scheduled Tribes and the solutions required were quite different from those of Scheduled Castes, a special approach for tribal development and independent machinery to safeguard the rights of Scheduled Tribes was considered necessary. Accordingly, a separate National Commission for Scheduled Tribes (NCST) was set up with effect from 19th February, 2004 by amending Article 338 and inserting a new Article 338A in the Constitution, through the Constitution (Eighty-ninth Amendment) Act, 2003.

DEVELOPMENT OF SCHEDULED TRIBES

The Ministry of Tribal Affairs was set up in 1999 after the bifurcation of Ministry of Social Justice and Empowerment with the objective of providing more focussed approach on the integrated socio-economic development of the Scheduled Tribes (STs), the most underprivileged of the society, in a coordinated and planned manner.

Scheduled Areas and Tribal Areas

Scheduled Tribes live in contiguous areas unlike other communities. It is, therefore, much simpler to have an area approach for development activities and also regulatory provisions to protect their interests. In order to protect the interests of Scheduled Tribes with regard to land alienation and other social factors, provisions of the "Fifth Schedule" and "Sixth Schedule" have been enshrined in the Constitution.

The Fifth Schedule under Article 244(1) of Constitution defines "Scheduled Areas" as such areas as the President may by Order declare to be Scheduled Areas after consultation with the Governor of the state. The Sixth Schedule under Article 244(2) of the Constitution relates to those areas in the states of Assam, Meghalaya, Tripura, and Mizoram which are declared as "Tribal Areas" and provides for District Councils and/or Regional Councils for such Areas. These Councils have been conferred with wide ranging legislative, judicial, and executive powers.

WELFARE OF OTHER BACKWARD CLASSES

The Second Backward Classes Commission (commonly known as Mandal Commission), constituted under Article 340, submitted its Report in 1980. In the light of this report, the Government of India provided 27 per cent reservation in Central Government posts for persons belonging to the Socially and Economically Backward Classes, (also referred to as "Other Backward Classes" or OBCs). Several writ petitions were disposed of by the Supreme Court in 1992, commonly known as the *Indra Sawhney case*. In this judgement, the Court upheld 27 per cent reservation for OBCs in civil posts and services under the Union of India, subject to exclusion of the "Creamy Layer". The Government of India in 1993 reserved 27 per cent of vacancies in civil posts and services under the Central Government, to be filled through direct recruitment in favour of the Other Backward Classes (OBCs). With the amendment of Article 15 of the Constitution in January, 2006 and the enactment of the Central Educational Institutions (Reservation in Admissions) Act in January, 2007, listing of other backward classes has become relevant for admission in Central Educational Institutions also. Under this Act, OBC students are entitled to 27 per cent reservation in Central Educational Institutions in a phased manner, over a period of three years commencing from the academic session 2008"09. The National Commission for Backward Classes (NCBC) was set up in August, 1993 as per the provision of the National Commission for Backward Classes Act, 1993.

SOCIAL DEFENCE

In the areas of Social Defence, the Ministry is committed towards welfare of older persons and rehabilitation of drug addicts and alcoholics. *The programmes for the targeted groups are as follows:*

National Policy for Older Persons

The National Policy for Older Persons (NPOP) was announced in January, 1999, with the primary objective viz., to encourage individuals to make provision for their own as well as their spouse's old age; to encourage families to take care of their older family members; to enable and support voluntary and non-governmental organisations to supplement the care provided by the family; to provide care and protection to the vulnerable elderly people, to provide health care facility to the elderly; to promote research and training facilities to train geriatric caregivers and organisers of services for the elderly; and to create awareness regarding elderly persons to develop them into fully independent citizens.

National Council for Older Persons

The Government has reconstituted National Council for Older Persons (NCOP) to advise and aid the Government on developing policies and programmes for older persons. It provides feedback to the Government on the implementation of the National Policy on Older Persons and the specific initiatives for older persons. The NCOP is the highest body to advise and coordinate with the Government in the formulation and implementation of policy and programmes for the welfare of the aged. Under Integrated Programme for Older Persons, financial assistance up to 90 per cent of the project cost is provided to NGOs for establishing and maintaining old age homes and daycare centres.

Prevention and Rehabilitation of Drug Addicts/Alcoholics

Under the Scheme, grant-in-aid to the extent of 90 per cent (95 per cent in North East States, J & K, and Sikkim) of the expenditure is provided to voluntary organisations for rehabilitation of drug addicts and alcoholics. Assistance to Voluntary Organisation for Social Defence Services provides for undertaking programmes for the rehabilitation of various social segments at risk, not currently covered under the existing schemes of the Ministry. In particular, the scheme provides for Pilot Projects in unchartered areas in which the Ministry may like to formulate independent programmes in due course. A number of programmes are being supported for rehabilitation of children of sex workers. Initiatives have also been taken to support projects for rehabilitation of widows and for providing counselling and support to traumatised children and women, particularly those who have been victims of physical violence and sexual abuse.

WELFARE MEASURES FOR THE MINORITIES

Six religious communities, viz., Muslims, Christians, Sikhs, Buddhists, Zoroastrians (Parsis), and Jains have been notified as minorities as per provisions under the National Commission for Minorities (NCM) Act, 1992. The Government has taken the following measures for the welfare of Minorities: The Ministry of Minority Affairs was created in January 2006 to ensure a focussed approach to the issues relating to the minorities and to play a pivotal role in the overall policy planning, coordination, evaluation, and review of the regulatory and development programme for the benefit of the minority communities. The Ministry is also responsible for the administration and implementation of the: (i) National Commission for Minorities Act, 1992; (ii) Wakf Act, 1995, and (iii) Durgah Khwaja Saheb Act, 1955. In a short period of time, not only the Ministry has been made fully functional but concerted efforts have been made to streamline the ongoing programmes/schemes and to launch innovative and effective schemes/programmes for the welfare of minority communities.

Commissions for Minorities

National Commission for Minorities

The Minorities Commission which was set up in January, 1978 by a Resolution issued by Ministry of Home Affairs became a statutory body with the enactment of The National Commission for Minorities Act, 1992 and was renamed as the National Commission for Minorities. The first statutory National Commission was set up on May 17, 1993. The NCM Act, 1992 was amended in 1995 which provided for a Vice Chairperson in the Commission. With the 1995 amendment, the Commission's composition was expanded to 7 members (including a Chairperson and a Vice Chairperson). The provision under Section 3(2) of the Act stipulates that five members including the Chairpersons shall be from amongst the minority communities.

State Commission for Minorities

Thirteen state governments namely Andhra Pradesh, Assam, Bihar, Chhattisgarh, Government of NCT of Delhi, Jharkhand, Karnataka, Maharashtra, Madhya Pradesh, Rajasthan, Uttar Pradesh, Tamil Nadu, and West Bengal have set up statutory commissions for minorities. Manipur and Uttarakhand have set up non-statutory commissions.

National Commission for Religious and Linguistic Minorities

The Government of India has been seized of the welfare needs of socially and economically backward sections among religious and linguistic minorities.

Central Wakf Council

A Wakf is a permanent dedication of movable or immovable properties for purposes recognised by the Muslim Law as religious, pious, or charitable. Apart from these religious aspects, the

Wakfs are also instruments of social and economic upliftment. Administration of Central Legislation for Wakfs is the responsibility of the Ministry of Social Justice and Empowerment. For the purpose of advising the Central Government on matters relating to working of the State Wakf Boards and the proper administration of the Wakfs in the country, the Central Wakf Council was established as a statutory body by the Central Government in December, 1964, under Section 8A of the Wakf Act, 1954 (now read as Sub-Sec(1) of the Section 9 of Wakf Act, 1995). The present Council has been reconstituted in March, 2005. The Union Minister in charge of Wakf is the Chairperson of the Council. The Central Wakf Council is also playing a vital role in the development of the society by way of implementing Development of Urban Wakf Properties and Educational Development Programmes.

Durgah Khwaja Saheb Act

It is an Act to make provision for the proper administration of Dargah and Endowment of the Dargah Khwaja Moin-ud-din Chishti (R.A.). Under this Central Act, the administration, control and management of the Dargah endowment has been vested in a representative committee known as the Dargah Committee appointed by the Central Government. The Dargah of Khwaja Moin-ud-din Chishti at Ajmer in Rajasthan is a Waqf of international fame. The Dargah is being administered under the Dargah Khwaja Saheb Act, 1955.

WELFARE SCHEMES FOR THE VULNERABLE SECTIONS BY THE STATES

In our federal structure, the state governments too have a role. As is known, the Directive Principles of the state policy outline the constitutional direction for the welfare orientation; the state governments also follow these. Besides these, the constitution has demarcated as per the provisions of article 246, areas where the state governments have exclusive powers to make laws and also with the centre in concurrent list items (both in the Seventh Schedule).

The welfare schemes by the state government for the vulnerable sections of the society cover girl child, women, SCs and STs, old and infirm, physically challenged, destitutes among others. The schemes are in the area of health, education and human resource development. As is also known, some of the schemes of the Union Government are jointly funded and implemented by the state governments. MGNREGA (Mahatma Gandhi National Rural Employment Guarantee Act) is one such scheme; this scheme is driven by work need rather than amount being sanctioned and spent on areas explored.

State Governments are placed in a definite and decidedly clear position as far as welfare needs are concerned as they are closer to the ground realities. The local self government institutions, like panchayats and municipalities, are very useful in this regard.

Schemes

On 28 November 2001, the Supreme Court of India passed a mandate saying, 'We direct the state Governments / Union Territories to implement the Mid Day Meal scheme by providing every child in every government and government assisted primary school with a prepared mid day meal.'

The Akshaya Patra Foundation of Karnataka was the first agency to start this scheme in 2000 in Karnataka. The pioneering move by the Government of Karnataka to make NGOs the implementing arm of the Government has been one of the major reasons for the success in reaching the programmes' goals.

The Government of West Bengal got the United Nations award for its scheme, 'Kanyashree Prakalpa' for promoting education among girls. The Government of Madhya Pradesh got the United Nations special Public Service Award for its 'Public Service Delivery System' Act which imposes fines on government service officers for delay in replying or disposing queries. This act has been replicated in total 14 states.

Uttar Pradesh Government had reduced duty on stamp paper by one percent for women for purchase of land. Bihar has 'free bicycles' scheme for students.

States do not have adequate resources. They expect the Finance Commission to see their cases sympathetically. The 14th Finance Commission increased the share of states by ten percent. The Central Government, at once, passed on many schemes being funded by it to the states causing hue and cry.

One of the major causes of concern is the lack of infrastructure with the states. Leakages and corruption too are common. Notwithstanding this, states like Kerala, MP, West Bengal, Tripura, Telangana, Karnataka have done well on social issues. States like Haryana, Bihar, UP, Odisha, have not shown that much of progress as was expected.

Overall, it must however be admitted that there are many indices of evaluation and some states have done well on some indices, others on many others, Really progress would be in evidence when a state does well on all indices. It cannot also be denied that economic progress is a sine qua non for social upliftment, mostly; social norms do create hindrance though.

13

CHAPTER

Health, Education and Human Resources

OVERVIEW

Vital sectors of health, education, and human resource are of the essence in orerall economic development. If these sectors are taken good care of, there is real economic progress. A healthy, skilled, and educated workforce is an asset to the society, and such a workforce can meet the social prejudices also head on. With this initiative we create our tomorrow today. A nation is known for its progress through its prowess to create educated, skilled, and healthy humans. It is an investment, not an indulgence.

INTRODUCTION

Issues relating to development and management of social sector/services relating to Health, Education and Human Resources.

Before we analyse the topic in details, it is well worth considering some indices and facts, to set the scene. These aspects will not only reveal how these sector namely, Health, Education and Human Resource are performing, but also how they have been addressed.

	Item	health	education	human resource
1.	Rank	143/188 (Countries)	92/145 (Countries)	131/188 (HDI report 2016) (Countries)
2.	Constitutional Provisions	State list (Sl No. 6)	Concurrent list subject to Sl No. 63-64, 65-66	Concurrent list

As may be seen, the Directive principles of state policy meant for advancement of welfare of citizens has provisions for Health, Education and Human Resources in the constitution. Although these provisions have been there, yet the progress has been dismal.

The reasons are not far to seek:

(i) Health, Education and Human Resource are predominantly with the state and they view it as infringement if the Union decides to push its considered stance. Years back, in education, some states opposed the Navodya schools as elitist. In health sector too, the opposition of some states to civil service (Medical) Rules is well known. Some training schemes under Human Resources Development do no find favour with some states. Even so, there are certain aspects which the states welcome: setting up of AIIMS-like institutions in the health sector; IITs, IIMs in the education sector; MGNREGS (Mahatma Gandhi National Rural Employment Guarantee Scheme) in the human resources sector. Overall, states jealously guard their autonomy and Union's interference is not welcome.

(ii) With different states pursuing their own policies, there is no uniformity and consequently differing yardsticks for performance evaluation. In some states, education sector is in a veritable mess, some states have their health sector in shambles.

(iii) Health, Education particularly and Human Resource to an extent are highly unionised in almost all the states. Agitations are rampant, there's no dearth of issues: national or international. Political compulsions preclude any possibility of clean up. In such a situation, making these sectors competitive and quality ranked is a dream only.

(iv) On health and education sector even the doctors and teachers call for strikes, agitation. How can there be discipline? Quite often the courts have had to intervene.

(v) India ranks nowhere in education, health and human resource index. Even war torn countries like Syria, Iraq fare better. In Asia too our position is bad, behind Sri Lanka, Bangladesh in human resource index. Quality of our healthcare, education is 'survival class.' We complain of 'brain drain' when inside the country most of the 'brains are in the drain.' Over the years we have put in many health policies and education policies; they hardly made an impact.

(vi) Bureaucracy has spread its tentacles in all these sectors. With this stranglehold, it has stymied these sectors. Sheer numbers have crippled education and health sectors. Infrastructure lags behind, posts remain unfilled, litigation shadows everything, equipments are in short supply, corruption and malpractices rule. Lower rung employees and contract labour call the shots in some states. Medicare is a nightmare, educare is a simple scare.

(vii) The picture is not complete. There's a huge private sector presence, notably in education and health. At one end of the spectrum, they are equipped to cater to the elite and at the other to fleece the not so rich. Barring few, most of the private players look for profits. Contrast these with the missionary and charitable institutions, facts will shock.

(viii) Some states have emotive issues. Some of the Union schemes in human resource sector have part state funding but the scheme is known as a centre scheme. Reason enough for virulent debate, hostility and non-cooperation. In such instances the intended beneficiaries suffer even as brownie points are collected.

(ix) How often we see old schemes being repackaged, how often we see schemes being renamed, how often we see the same scheme being inaugurated again. A party comes to power and launches a plan naming it after one of its icons; the party loses power, the other party grabs power and promptly renames the same said schemes after one of its own icons. Nothing changes except a coat of paint. A little matter of difference between tweedeldum and tweedeldee. 'Little Alice wanted to find out.'

(x) Finally, we have the issue of recognition of educational institutions, medical colleges, hospitals. A huge bureaucratic jungle with its own rules. These are verily self-inflicted wounds; unrecognised institutions thrive anyway. Be that as it may, the issue is that there is an elephant in the room, it has to be acknowledged.

Having set the scene, we now come to the main issue; development and management in these three core sectors of health, education and human resource. In all three sectors, the pattern will be as outlined here. It is not intended to go into miniscule details or irrelevant matters, what is planned is that overall picture is drawn with due and diligent focus on relevant issues. All the three sectors are large and expanding, they have issues for the future as well.

RIGHT TO HEALTH AND THE INDIAN CONSTITUTION

Right to health is not included directly as a Fundamental Right in the Indian Constitution. What the Constitution makers imposed is duty on the state to ensure social and economic justice. Part IV of the Indian Constitution is Directive Principles of State Policy (DPSP), which imposed duties on the States. If only we see those provisions, then we find that some of them are directly or indirectly related with Public Health. The Constitution of India does not provide for the Right to Health as a Fundamental Right.

The Constitution directs the state to take measures to improve healthcare of the people. Thus, the Preamble to the Constitution of India, inter alia, seeks to secure for all its citizens justice–social and economic. It provides a framework for the achievement of the object as laid down in the Preamble. The Preamble has been amplified and elaborated in the Directive Principles of State Policy (**DPSP**).

DPSP and Health

Article 38 of the Indian Constitution imposes liability on the state that states will secure a social order for the promotion of welfare of the people. But without public health we cannot achieve it. It means that without public health, welfare of people is impossible. Article 39 (e) relates with workers to protect their health. Article 41 imposes a duty on the state to provide public assistance, basically for those who are sick and disabled. Article 42 makes provision to protect the health of infants and mothers by maternity benefit.

In India, the Directive Principles of State Policy (DPSP) under Article 47 consider it the primary duty of the state to improve public health, securing of justice, humane conditions of work, and extension of sickness, old age, disablement, and maternity benefit are also contemplated. Further, state's duty includes prohibition on consumption of intoxicating drinks and drugs as they are injurious to health. Article 48A ensures that state shall endeavour to protect and impose a pollution free environment for good health.

Panchayat, Municipality, and Health

Not only the state, panchayats and municipalities are also liable to improve and protect public health.

Article 243G says state that "the legislature of a state may endow the panchayats with necessary power and authority in relation to matters listed in the Eleventh Schedule."

Fundamental Rights and Health

The DPSP are only directives to the state. This is non-justiciable. No person can claim for non-fulfiling these directives. But the Supreme Court has brought the right to health under the purview of Article 21. In 1995, the Supreme Court held that right to health and medical care is a fundamental right covered by Article 21 since health is essential for making the life for workmen meaningful and purposeful and compatible with personal dignity. The state has an obligation under Article 21 to safeguard the right to life of every person, preservation of human life being of paramount importance. The Supreme Court has in the case of *Parmanand Katara vs Union of India*, held that whether the patient be an innocent person or be a criminal liable to punishment under the law, it is the obligation of those who are in charge of the health of the community to preserve life so that the innocent may be protected and the guilty may be punished.

The Supreme Court, while examining the issue of Constitutional right to healthcare under Article 21, Article 41, and Article 47 of the Constitution of India in *State of Punjab vs Ram Lubhaya Bagga vs the Supreme Court*, in *Paschim Banga Khet Mazdoor Samiti and others vs State of West Bengal and another*, while widening the scope of Article 21 and the government responsibility to provide medical aid to every person in the country, held that in a welfare state, the primary duty of the government is to secure the welfare of the people.

HEALTH POLICY

The National health policy (NHP) of 2002 guides the strategy adopted by the Government for the health sector. The NHP 2002 evolved from the National Health policy of 1983. Guidance was provided by the Bhore Committee Report (1946) wherein the main underlying principles for future health development of the country, inter alia, included that 'No individual should fail to secure adequate medical care because of inability to pay for it. In view of the complexity of modern medical practice, the health services should provide, when fully developed all the consultant, laboratory, and institutional facilities necessary for proper diagnosis and treatment.'

The National health policy, 2002 framework envisages accelerated achievement of public health goals in the backdrop of the socio-economic circumstances prevailing in the country. Some of the salient aspect of the NHP 2002, inter alia, include: making good the deficiencies in availability of health facilities, narrowing the gap between various states, the gap across the rural-urban divide in attainment of health goals, and reducing the uneven access to and benefits from the public health system between the better endowed and the more vulnerable sections of the society.

Accordingly, consistent with the primacy given to equality, emphasis has been provided for expanding and improving the primary health facilities. Emphasis has been laid on the implementation of public health programs through local self-governments.

It also envisages setting up of an organised urban primary care structure, a network of decentralized mental health services, and upgrading the physical infrastructure of Mental Health institutions. It visualizes an information, education, and communication policy which maximizes the dissemination of information to those population groups which cannot be effectively approached by using only the mass media and giving priority to school health programs with an aim at imparting preventive health education apart from providing regular health check-ups and promotion of health seeking behaviour among children.

The Union Ministry of Health and Family Welfare is instrumental and responsible for implementation of various programmes on the national scale in the areas of health and family welfare, prevention and control of major communicable diseases, and promotion of traditional and indigenous systems of medicines. The Ministry also assists states in preventing and controlling the spread of seasonal disease outbreaks and epidemics through technical assistance. Expenditure is incurred by Ministry of Health and Family Welfare either directly under central schemes or by way of grants-in-aids to the autonomous/statutory bodies, etc., and NGOs.

In addition to the centrally sponsored family welfare programmes, the Ministry is implementing several World Bank assisted programmes for control of AIDS, malaria, and tuberculosis in designated areas. Besides, state health systems and developments projects with World Bank assistance are under implementation in various states. The projects are implemented by the respective state governments. The Department of Health and Family Welfare only facilitates the state in availing of external assistance. All these schemes aim at fulfiling the national commitment to improve access to Primary Healthcare (PHC) facilities keeping in view the needs of rural areas and where the incidence of disease is high.

NATIONAL HEALTH MISSION

The National Health Mission (NHM) has its two sub-missions, the National Rural Health Mission (NRHM) and the National Urban Health Mission (NUHM). The NHM envisages universal access to equitable, affordable, and quality healthcare services that are accountable and responsive to people's needs. The main programmatic components include health system strengthening in rural and urban areas, Reproductive-Maternal-Newborn child and Adolescent Health (RMNCH+A), and control of communicable and non-communicable diseases.

There has been a significant improvement in creation of new facilities and infrastructure, though adequate staffing of these facilities by qualified health personnel remains a problem. Availability of drugs has improved at all levels and the robust logistic arrangements for procurement and storage of these drugs are being put in place. An important achievement of NHM has been a considerable reduction in out-of-pocket expenses from 72 per cent to 60 per cent.

Recently, new initiatives have been launched under NHM. *Rashtriya Bal Swasthya Karyakram* (RBSL) was launched to provide comprehensive healthcare and improve the quality of life of children through early detection of birth defects, diseases, deficiencies, and development delays including disability. Another initiative, viz., *Rashtriya Kishore Swasthya Karyakram* (RKSK) was launched to comprehensively address the health needs of the 253 million adolescents, who account for over 21 per cent of the country's population, by bringing in several new dimensions like mental health, nutrition, substance misuse, injuries and violence, and non-communicable diseases. The programme has introduced community-based interventions through peer educators and is underpinned by collaborations with other ministries and state governments and knowledge partners, coupled with operational research. In addition to these initiatives, the Weekly Iron Folic Acid supplementation (WIFS) programme was launched to address adolescent anaemia where under supervision, Iron-Folic Acid (IFA) tablets are given to adolescent population between 10–19 years of age in both rural and urban areas throughout the country. NUHM, a sub-mission under the NHM, caters to the healthcare needs of the urban population with the focus on urban poor and is aimed at reducing out-of-pocket expenses for treatment. NHM is a step towards realizing the objective of Universal Health Coverage (UHC) in the country.

National Urban Health Mission

The National Urban Health Mission (NUHM) seeks to improve the health status of the urban population, particularly urban poor and other vulnerable sections by facilitating their access to quality primary healthcare. NUHM would cover all state capitals, district headquarters, and other cities/towns with a population of 50,000 and above in a phased manner. Cities and towns with population below 50,000 will continue to be covered under The National Rural Health Mission (NRHM).

Major Initiatives Under NRHM/NUHM

Janani Suraksha Yojana

Janani Suraksha Yojana (JSY) aims to reduce maternal mortality among pregnant women by encouraging them to deliver in government health facilities. Under the scheme, cash assistance is provided to eligible pregnant women for giving birth in a government health facility. Since the inception of NRHM, 8.55 crore women have benefitted under this scheme.

Janani Shishu Suraksha Karyakram

Launched on June 01, 2011, JSSK entitles all pregnant women delivering in public health institutions to absolutely free and no expense delivering, including caesarean section. This marks a shift to an entitlement-based approach. The free entitlement include free drugs and consumables, free diagnostics, free diet during stay in the health institutions, free provisions of blood, free transport from home to health institution, between health institutions in case of referrals and drop back home, and exemption from all kinds of user charges. Similar entitlements are available for all sick infants (up to 1 year of age) accessing public health institutions. All states and union territories are implementing this scheme.

ASHA

More than 9.15 lakh Accredited Social Health Activists (ASHAs) are in place across the country and serve as facilitators, mobilizers, and providers of community level care. ASHA is the first port of call in the community especially for marginalized sections of the populations, with a focus on women and children. Since 2013, when the National Urban Health Mission was launched, ASHAs are being selected in urban areas as well. Several evaluations and successive Common Review Missions show that the ASHA has been a key figure in contributing to the positive outcomes of increases in institutional delivery, immunisation, active role in disease control programmes (malaria, kala-azar, and lymphatic filariasis, in particular) and improved breastfeeding and nutrition practices. The majority of states have in place an active training and support system for the ASHA to ensure continuing training, on site field mentoring and performances monitoring.

Rogi Kalyan Samiti

Rogi Kalyan Samiti/Hospital Management Society is a simple yet effective management structure. This committee is a registered society whose members act as trustees to manage the affairs of the hospital and is responsible for upkeep of the facilities and ensure provision of better facilities to the patients in the hospital. Financial assistance is provided to these committees through untied fund to undertake activities for patient welfare.

OTHER INITIATIVES FOR HEALTH AND FAMILY WELFARE

Jansankhya Sthirata Kosh

Jansankhya Sthirata Kosh (JSK) also known as National Population Stabilisation Fund is an autonomous body under the Ministry of Health and Family Welfare, constituted on the recommendations of the National Commission of population. It was established in 2003 as an autonomous society under the MoHFW and was reconstituted in 2005 with the addition of a General Body. Its mandate is to promote and undertake schemes, programmes, projects, and initiatives to meet the unmet need for contraception, and reproductive and child health. It is aimed at achieving population stabilisation at a level consistent with the needs of sustainable economic growth, social development, and environment protection by 2045.

Family Planning Programme

With its historic initiation in 1952, the family planning programme has undergone transformation in terms of policy and actual programme implementation. There has been a gradual shift from clinical approach to the reproductive child health approach and further, the National Population Policy 2000, brought a holistic and a target free approach which helped in reduction of fertility. The target free approach is now reflected in the state project implementations plans based on community needs assessment.

Presently, the expected level of achievement is estimated for each state by the indicators reflecting the community needs like contraceptive usage, parity, unmet need, and existing fertility. Over the years, the programme has been expanded to reach every nook and corner of the country and has penetrated into PHCs and SCs in rural areas, Urban Family Welfare Centres, and Postpartum Centres in the urban areas. Technological advances, improved quality, and coverage for healthcare have resulted in a rapid fall in the Crude Birth Rate (CBR) and growth rate.

The objectives, strategies, and activities of the Family Planning Division are designed and operated towards achieving the family welfare goals and objectives stated in various policy documents (NPP: National population policy 2000; NHP: National Health Policy 2002 and NHRM: National Rural Health Mission) and to honour the commitments of the Government of India (including ICPD: International Conference on Population and Development; MDG: Millennium Development Goals; FP2020 Summit, and others).

Causes of Child Mortality in India

The major causes of child mortality in India (as per WHO, 2012) are–neonatal causes (53 per cent), pneumonia (15 per cent), diarrhoeal diseases (12 per cent), measles (3 per cent), and others (17 per cent). Besides these, malnutrition is a contributory factor in 33 per cent child deaths.

Child Health Programmes

Rashtriya Bal Swasthya Karyakram (RBSK)

Rashtriya Bal Swasthya Karyakram has been launched to provide child health screening and early interventions services by expanding the reach of mobile health teams at the block level. These teams will also carry out screening of all the children in the age group 0–6 years enrolled at Anganwadi Centres at least twice a year. RBSK covers 30 common health conditions. States/UTs may incorporate a few more conditions based on high prevalence/endemicity. An estimated 27 crore children in the age group of zero to eighteen (0–18) years are expected to be covered in a phased manner.

Rashtriya Kishore Swasthya Karyakram

This initiative was launched in January, 2014 to reach out to 253 million adolescents in the country in their own spaces and introduce peer-led interventions at the community level, supported by augmentation of facility based services. This initiative broadens the focus of the adolescent health programme beyond reproductive and sexual health and brings in focus on life skills, nutrition, injuries, and violence (including gender-based violence), non-communicable diseases, mental health, and substance misuse.

INDIAN COUNCIL OF MEDICAL RESEARCH

The Indian Council of Medical Research (ICMR), New Delhi, working under the Department of Health Research (DHR), ministry of Health and Family Welfare, Government of India, is the apex body in the country for the formulation, coordination, promotion, and conduct of biomedical research. In the context of the changing public health scene, the balancing of research efforts between different competing as well as emerging fields, especially when resources are severely limited, is a challenging problem encountered in the management of medical research, particularly in a country like India. In addition to tackling the prevailing health problems being faced by our populations, in recent years the research has been intensified progressively on emerging health problems. Strengthening of research capabilities as well as definite and robust research strategy are recognised as vital tools for conduct of successful research and the ICMR has strived hard to adopt new strategies from time to time as per need of the situation. For the fulfilment of its goals, the strategies adopted by ICMR includes careful selection of thrust areas as per the national needs, with further refinement in the light of past experiences, undertaking studies to enlarge the scientific basis of preventive medicine and health promotion, development of simplified, cost-effective and mass applicable tests which are specific and accurate for early and definitive recognition of diseases/health problems, establishment of close and effective linkages with social and behavioural scientists, and active pursuance of problem-oriented and problem-solving research.

The ICMR discharges its primary function of promoting biomedical research through intramural as well as extramural research. Apart from 32 permanent research institutes/centres, ICMR has several regional centres, research units, and field stations spread across the country.

ICMR's Flagship Programmes which include Tribal Health Research Forum and Vector Borne Diseases Science Forum continued to work for the health problems of the tribal populations as well as studies on the control of Malaria, Filariasis, Japanese Encephalitis, Kala-azar, Dengue, and Chikungunya.

ICMR continues to support, coordinate, and monitor extramural research in different biomedical subjects, viz., anatomy, anthropology, haematology, and human genetics through Task Force Projects, adhoc schemes, and fellowships in various research institutions, medical colleges, and universities of the country.

ICMR coordinates international collaborations in biomedical research between India and other countries as well as with national and international agencies such as Ministry of Science and Technology, Indian and foreign missions and WHO, etc.

INDIAN SYSTEMS OF MEDICINE AND HOMEOPATHY

Department of Indian systems of Medicine and Homeopathy was created in March,1995 and renamed as Department of Ayurveda, Yoga and Naturopathy, Unani, Siddha and Homeopathy (AYUSH) in November, 2003. It was elevated to the status of Ministry of AYUSH with a view to providing focused attention to development of education and research in Ayurveda, Yoga, Naturopathy, Unani, Siddha, and Homeopathy systems. The Ministry continued to lay emphasis on up gradation of AYUSH educational standards, quality control and standardisation of drugs, improving the availability of medicinal plant material, research and development, and awareness generation about the efficacy of the systems domestically and internationally. Sowa-Rigpa (Tibetan system of medicine) is the recent addition to the existing family of AYUSH systems.

Ayurveda, Siddha, Unani, and Homoeopathy drugs are covered under the purview of Drugs and Cosmetics Act, 1940. Since most of the medicines of AYUSH sector are made from medicinal plant materials, the Ministry has set up a National Medicinal Plants Board to promote cultivation of medicinal plants and ensure sustained supply of quality raw material. A separate National Policy on India Systems of Medicine and Homoeopathy is in place since 2002.

Healthcare

Drug Quality Control

The Drug Control Cell (DCC) in the Ministry of AYUSH deals with regulatory and quality control matters of Ayurveda, Siddha, Unani, and Homeopathy drugs including amendment in the regulations, introduction of new regulations, and examination of other drugs related issues. The Cell is made up of Technical Officers and it also administers the Centrally Sponsored Scheme for Quality Control of AYUSH drugs and coordinates with the State Licensing Authorities to achieve uniform administration of the Act, approval of drug testing laboratories and for drugs related matters. The DCC provides secretarial support to the two statuary bodies–Ayurveda, Siddha, Unani Drugs Technical Advisory Board (ASUDTAB) and Ayurveda, Siddha, Unani

Drugs Consultative Committee (ASUDCC), which are set up under the provisions of Drugs and Cosmetics Act, 1940. A collaborative mechanism is in place with Central Drugs Standard Control Organisations (CDSCO) for WHO GMP (Good Manufacturing Practice) certifications scheme and any other export and import related matters of ASU (Ayurveda, Siddha, Unani) Drugs.

STATUTORY REGULATORY COUNCILS, INSTITUTES, AND BOARDS

Central Council of Indian Medicine, New Delhi

The Central Council of Indian Medicine is a statutory body constituted under the Indian Medicine Central Council Act, 1970. The Central Council of Indian Medicine with the previous sanction of the Central Government as required under Section 36 of the Indian Medicine Central Council Act, 1970 and after obtaining the comments of the State Governments as required under Section 22 of the said Act has prescribed courses for Under-graduate and Post-graduate education in Ayurveda, Unani, Siddha, and Sowa-Rigpa through the Regulations. The Central Council has prescribed 19 Regulations to achieve the goal of the Central Council.

National Institutes

At present, national institutes to promote the Indian System of Medicine are: National Institute of Ayurveda, Jaipur; National Institute of Homoeopathy, Kolkata; National Institute of Unani Medicine, Bengaluru; National Institute of Siddha, Chennai; Moraji Desai National Institute of Yoga, New Delhi; Rashtriya Ayurveda Vidyapeeth, New Delhi; and National Institute of Naturopathy, Pune.

National Medicinal Plants Board

National Medicinal Plants Board (NMPB) is an apex national body which coordinates all matters relating to medicinal plants in the country. The Board which was established in November 2000, acts as advisory body to the concerned ministries, departments, and agencies in strategic planning of medicinal plants related initiatives and to plan and provide financial support to programmes relating to conservation, cultivation, and also all-round development of medicinal plants sector. The NMPB is presently implementing two schemes namely Central Sector Scheme for 'Conservation, Development and Sustainable Management of Medicinal Plants' and centrally sponsored scheme of National Mission on Medicinal Plants.

INTERNATIONAL COOPERATION

World Health Organisation (WHO) is one of the main UN agencies collaborating, in the Health Sector, with the Ministry of Health & Family Welfare, Government of India and providing technical support. Activities under WHO are funded through two sources–The Country budget, which comes out of contributions made by member countries and Extra Budgetary Resources which comes from (a) donations from various sources for general or specific aspects of health, and (b) funds routed through the WHO to countries by other member countries or institutes/ agencies. India is the largest beneficiary of the country budget within the South East Asia Region. The budget is operated on a biennium basis, calendar year-wise.

HEALTH SECTOR IN INDIA: THE WAY WE ARE

The health sector in India is at the crossroads. This is partly due to an interesting relationship between development and health, which is known as the Preston Curve. In 1975, Samuel Preston showed that if the health of nations as measured by life expectancy is plotted against the wealth of nations as measured by GDP per capital, then up to a point, there is a sharp increase in life expectancy for even the modest increase in GDP per capita. Then the curve suddenly flattens out–and after this point, large increases in public health expenditure are required for modest increase in life expectancy (Deaton 2013).

In the 2010 version of the Preston Curve, India today is at or near the bend on the curve, and this has major implications for policy. At the bend in the curve, the past problems of reproductive and child health and of communicable disease persist, but new problems have got added on. If public investment in healthcare does not increase, private investment would, but there is no certainty that this would lead to better health outcomes. If public investment increases, a choice has to be made between deploying it to strengthen public health systems and purchasing care from the private sector. If the case is the latter, then one needs to be ready to impose a strong regulatory regime and also increase public expenditure far above the 2.5 per cent of GDP that the current national health policy draft calls for (*Sundararaman*, *Muraleedharan*, and *Mukhopadhyay 2016*).

Progress in Reproductive and Child Health

In earlier decades, a major proportion of deaths were related to deaths in the young child–most of this happening below the age of 5. Pregnancy related deaths were also high. Both of these have decreased sharply, partly because the number of deaths per live birth has decreased greatly and partly because with fertility control, the number of children or pregnant women has itself declined sharply.

There are many reasons why India has been successful in achieving such a reduction. One important reason is the focussed attention on the reduction of infant and maternal mortality over the last 25 years. First, we had the child survival and safe motherhood programme in the early nineties, and then the reproductive and child health programmes in the late nineties and early part of the last decade. Then, until 2005, there was a revised and much more successful (Reproductive Child Health) RCH-II programme, and this time it integrated with the National Rural Health Mission. Despite the adverse impact of the financial crisis and structural adjustment programmes in the nineties, these project ensured that the RCH programme was relatively better protected from the crisis.

It is important to note that these achievements were made without comparable improvements in sanitation or in child nutrition–two of the most important social determinants of health–where Indian levels of achievements lag far behind the global averages. However, what is clear is that these reductions in child and maternal survival had to be achieved by the health sector in the face of continuing adverse social determinants.

On the positive side, on two social determinants, India did some serious catching up with global standards. One was the supply of safe drinking water where over 94 per cent of hamlets are now covered and the other is women's literacy where the latest census reveal that 65.04 per cent of females are literate now (Census 2011).

The achieving of improved female literacy is closely linked to the great ongoing demographic transition. Decadal population growth rates are now falling and most states have now achieved a crude birth rate compatible with population stabilisation. Growth rates would continue to be high for some more years–due to what is known as the population momentum. This refers to the fact that there would be many more women now entering and passing through the reproductive age due to past high fertility rates–and therefore more children continue to be born, even though the small family norm has been achieved.

This is not to state that the challenges in reproductive and child health are over. There are still close to 46,500 maternal deaths and about 1.5 million deaths of children under 5 deaths each year, which is a high proportion of global maternal and child deaths. Quality and safety of healthcare is an issue.

Mixed Progress with Communicable Diseases

The impact of NRHM and the previous two decades of public health systems interventions on the control of communicable disease is mixed. One programme that did relatively well was the National Aids Control Programme (NACP). A systematic campaign that addressed both preventive and curative aspects and that grounded itself on good quality health information and estimates was able to cap—and to a fair extent, reverse the epidemic. The single success against polio is another great achievements of this period. Less remarked about—but equally impressive, is the major reduction in leprosy—reducing the prevalence of the disease to below the threshold which defines elimination.

Progress in vector control is mixed. Filaria has decreased dramatically and new cases of elephantiasis are negligible. Malaria has also seen significant declines and with a range of new tools becoming available, a confidence is gathering to transit to a malaria elimination programme. Kala-azar is an anachronism. It should have been eliminated by now. However, it festers in some deep pockets in a few villages of two to three states. About 20,000 cases annually occur across four states—but the majority are from Bihar. Meanwhile, new vector borne diseases have emerged—notably dengue and chikungunya. The good news is that deaths, both in absolute numbers and as a proportion of all deaths, and even of all cases have declined, and even of all cases have declined significantly. Most deaths due to infectious disease are due to diarrhoea and respiratory infections, especially in children and a number of other germs that do not have the same epidemic potential—but have significant prevalence.

Rise of Non-Communicable Diseases: A Public Health Challenge

The major and increasing proportion of mortality is due to non-communicable diseases (NCDS) which now account for over 60 per cent of all deaths and due to injuries which account for almost 12 per cent of all deaths (WHO 2014). The probability of dying during the most productive years (ages 30–70) from one of the four main NCDs is estimated to be as high as 26 per cent.

So, in addition to having serious persistent problems with infectious diseases, India finds itself challenged by a very high and rising prevalence and premature deaths due to non-communicable disease—even as compared to most developed and developing nations. In injuries per lakhs population also, India does very poorly.

The Challenge of Addressing NCDs in India

But there is another major difference between India's ability to address non-communicable diseases and its ability to address infections and reproductive and child health. The requirements in terms of financial and human resources and managements of care is much higher. More important, due to having consciously excluding these diseases from all governments' provision of primary healthcare for over two decades, even the perception of how to address these problems at the primary healthcare is low. Most conservations about primary care get limited to Imfant Mortality Rate (IMR), Maternal Mortality Rate (MMR), immunisation rates, and family planning. The system is not even geared to conceptually see these diseases as primarily part of a primary and not tertiary care mandate.

One must also note the contrast between communicable diseases and non-communicable disease with respect to risk factors. India's slow progress in communicable diseases is due to lack of significant gains in poverty, nutrition, and sanitation–in all of which we are doing much poorer than the developed world and even many developing nations. But when it comes to major risk factors for NCD–whether it is overweight and obesity, physical inactivity, alcohol, or smoking–these risk factors are far more prevalent in the developed world. Why then does India have much higher prevalence rates of the disease? The answer lies not only in identifying the pathways through which social determinants play out with respect to NCDs in the developing world, but also in complete absence of primary healthcare that addresses these diseases. Private sector has no doubt expanded to fill these gaps but market forces largely promote curative and preferably tertiary care. Market driven growth is unable to meaningfully address the needs of primary and secondary prevention and it falls on the government to take up this role.

The government has initiated a National Disease Control Programme against non-communicable diseases but these are far from universal. In non-communicable diseases, except in sporadic instances, such a clear strategy for universal access to care has yet to be implemented.

Part of the problem in building a strategy against NCDs, is that the list of non-communicable diseases is long, and it is not easy to construct multiple vertical programmes the way the major communicable diseases were addressed. To be effective with non-communicable diseases, horizontal integration is mandatory. It would be quite impractical to expect separate clinicians and support staff for each NCD, or even for all NCDs together.

STRENGTHENING HEALTH SYSTEMS UNDER DIFFERENT PLANS AND TIME PERIODS

Health System under the 11th Five Year Plan

The main vehicle of health systems strengthening was the National Rural Health Mission, now with integration of the National Urban Health Mission now renamed as the National Health Mission. Though health is a state subject, it was clear that a central push, both in financing and ideas was needed to break the logjam and get states moving onto strengthening their health systems. To respect the federal nature, states were required to draw up their annual project implementation plans, which would be sanctioned under a joint centre-state coordination committee. Though, over time the rules got more and more rigid, states had considerable flexibility in drawing up their plans.

One of the innovations that most states opted for was the creation of a workface of close to 900,000 community health volunteers, the ASHAs. They made a major contribution to bringing public health services closer to the community, and increasing its utilisation and in health education. Another important National Health Mission (NHM) contribution was the addition of over 178,000 health workers to a public system that had depleted its workforce to sub-critical levels over a long period of neglect in the nineties. The NHM deployed over 18,000 ambulances for free emergency response and patient transport services.

Health Systems in the 12th Plan Period

From 2012 onwards, the increase in funding did not keep pace with requirements and this was the time when the neediest states were developing the institutional capacity to absorb the funds. The lack of increase in financing was attributed to inefficiencies in fund utilisations, poor governance, and leakages that gave NHM a bad name in some policy circles. In 2013, the National Urban Health Mission was approved, but even this did not lead to any significant increase in central funds.

All nations successfully moving towards universal healthcare irrespective of their road maps share one common feature namely adequate number of well skilled and salaried health workers in the frontline. If the systems are based on purchasing care from the private sector, then it is likely that they are spending far more, not less, on salaries.

HEALTHCARE INDUSTRY AND INCREASING IMPOVERISHMENT DUE TO HEALTHCARE COSTS

Further, the National Health Policy 2015, draft notes that "the failure of public investment in health to cover the entire spectrum of healthcare needs is reflected best in the worsening situation in terms of costs of care and impoverishment due to healthcare costs." As the burden of diseases shifted to non-communicable diseases and as these were not covered by public health systems, except perhaps in the highly overcrowded government medical college hospitals, people had to shift to private healthcare. The shift is most pronounced in urban areas and for chronic illnesses. The immediate impact of this shift–which occurs even in relatively well performing states like Kerala and Tamil Nadu–is a huge rise in out-of-pocket expenditures for healthcare.

This shift was also a cause and consequence of a rapid growth of private sector in healthcare as in industry. Whereas private healthcare had largely consisted of one-doctor clinics or small nursing homes where owners were the investors and managers and there were little differences between top managements salaries and profits, a new type of private healthcare which is based on funds from investors whose main concern is maximizing return on investment gained ground. This private healthcare industry grows at almost 15 per cent CAGR which is twice the growth rate of the service sector and about thrice the overall national growth rate.

Government Financed Insurance Programmes

An important measure that the government has introduced is publicly financed health insurance schemes that cover the costs of hospitalisation of the poor. The major central government scheme in this regard is the *Rashtriya Swasthya Bima Yojana* which largely addresses secondary care. In addition, eight or more states have introduced insurance programmes that cover tertiary care needs.

Engaging the Private Sector

Given the size of the private sector there is of course an urgent need to engage with it and ensure that it contributes to public health goals. Insurance is, of course, one of the best ways of doing so. All nations that have a health system based on purchasing healthcare from private providers have an extensive regulatory regime in place.

Beyond insurance and regulation, there are other ways of guiding the growth of private sector. Grievance redressal mechanisms for private sector could help. So also would provisions of training and updating skills for the small providers and nursing homes. There is a need to persist, intensify, and expand the efforts that were initiated under the National Health Mission, if we have to sustain the progress that the Mission achieved. In particular, we need to focus such expansion both in urban primary care and in the four large states.

In strengthening public health systems, the challenge is of expanding the workforce, increasing investments, and the quality of governance so that the challenges of non-communicable diseases can be addressed without compromising the fragile advance we have made in RCH and communicable disease control.

EDUCATION

The Indian Constitution has certain provisions regarding education.

Art. 21A:

The State shall provide free and compulsory education to all children of the age of six to fourteen years in such manner as the State may, by law, determine. (Eighty-sixth Amendment Act, 2002)

Art. 41:

Right to work, to education and to public assistance in certain cases.

The State shall, within the limits of its economic capacity and development, make effective provision for securing the right to work, to education and to public assistance in cases of unemployment, old age, sickness and disablement, and in other cases of undeserved want.

Art. 45:

Provision for free and compulsory education for children.

(1) The State shall endeavour to provide, within a period of ten years from the commencement of this Constitution, for free and compulsory education for all children until they complete the age of fourteen years.

(2) The State shall endeavour to provide early childhood care and education for all children until they complete the age of six years. (Eighty-sixth Amendment Act, 2002).

Art. 46:

Promotion of educational and economic interests of Scheduled Castes, Scheduled Tribes and other weaker sections.

The State shall promote with special care the educational and economic interests of the weaker sections of the people, and, in particular, of the Scheduled Castes and the Scheduled Tribes, and shall protect them from social injustice and all forms of exploitation.

Education of Minorities

Art. 29:

Protection of interest of minorities.

(1) Any section of the citizens residing in the territory of India any part there of having a distinct language, script or culture of its own shall have the right to conserve the same.

(2) No citizen shall be denied admission into any educational institution maintained by the State or receiving aid out of State funds on grounds only of religion, race, caste, language or any of them.

Art. 30:

Right of minorities to establish and administer educational institutions.

(1) All minorities, whether based on religion or language, shall have the right to establish and administer educational institutions of their choice.

(1A) In making any law providing for the compulsory acquisition of any property of an educational institution established and administered by a minority, referred to in clause (1), the state shall ensure that the amount fixed by or determined under such law for the acquisition of such property is such as would not restrict or abrogate the right guaranteed under that clause.

(2) The State shall not, in granting aid to educational institutions, discriminate against any educational institution on the ground that it is under the management of a minority, whether based on religion or language.

Art. 350A:

Facilities for instruction in mother-tongue at primary stage.

It shall be the endeavour of every State and of every local authority within the State to provide adequate facilities for instruction in the mother-tongue at the primary stage of education to children belonging to linguistic minority groups; and the President may issue such directions to any State as he considers necessary or proper for securing the provision of such facilities.

INITIATIVES IN THE EDUCATION SECTOR

National Education Policy

India, on the eve of Independence, had a very low level of literacy rate in the society. Thus, since Independence, the Indian Government sponsored a variety of programmes to address the problems of illiteracy in both rural and urban India.

The first Minister of Education, in independent India, Maulana Abul Kalam Azad envisaged strong Central Government control over education and a uniform educational system in India. The Union Government established the University Grants Commission (UGC)(1948–49) and the Secondary Education Commission (1952–53) to develop proposals to modernise the Indian Education System. In 1961, the Union Government formed the National Council of Educational Research and Training (NCERT) as an autonomous organisation to advise both the Union and State Governments on education policies.

Sarva Shiksha Abhiyan (SSA)

SSA is an Indian government programme aimed at the universalisation of elementary education 'in a time bound manner', as mandated by the 86th Amendment to the Constitution of India making free and compulsory education to children of ages 6–14 a Fundamental Right. As an intervention programme, SSA has been operational since 2000–2001. The expenditure on the programme was shared by the Central Government (85%) and the State Governments (15%). The central share was funded by the number of external Agencies, including the World Bank, Department for International Development (DFID), UK and UNICEF. Its goals were to:

- open new schools in areas which do not have them and expand existing schools infrastructures and maintenance.
- address inadequate teacher numbers and provide training for existing teachers.
- provide quality elementary education including life skills with special focus on the education of girls and children with special needs as well as computer education.

Padhe Bharat Badhe Bharat

Padhe Bharat Badhe Bharat is a nationwide sub-programme under the Sarva Shiksha Abhiyan (SSA). *It is planned in a twin track approach:*

- to improve language development by creating an enduring interest in reading and writing with comprehension.
- to create a natural and positive interest in mathematics relating to the physical and social world.

The two tracks of *Padhe Bharat Badhe Bharat* are:

1. Early reading and writing with comprehension
2. Early mathematics

The main objective is to enable children to become motivated, independent and engaged readers and writers, and possessing sustainable and lasting reading and writing skills. It also aims at achieving learning levels appropriate to the class of study and to associate reading and writing with the experience of joy and real-life situations.

National Programmes for Education of Girls at Elementary Level (NPEGEL)

NPEGEL is a focussed intervention of Government of India, to reach the 'Hardest to Reach' girls, especially those not in school. Launched in July 2003, it is an important component of SSA, which provides additional support for enhancing girl's education over and above the investments for girl's education through normal SSA interventions. The programme provides for development of a 'model school' in every cluster with more intense community mobilisation and supervision of girls enrolment in schools. Gender sensitisation of teachers, development of gender-sensitive learning materials and provision of need-based incentives like escorts, stationery, workbooks, and uniforms are some of the features under the programme.

National Literacy Mission (NLM)

NLM was set up by the Government of India on 5th May, 1988 with an aim to eradicate illiteracy in the country by imparting functional literacy to non-literates. Thus, National Literacy Mission was established not only to make everybody just self-reliant in reading, writing, and arithmetic; but also to make them aware of development issues affecting the society. The target group of NLM is people between 15 and 35 years. National Literacy Mission works under the guidance of National Literacy Mission Authority, an independent wing of Ministry of Human Resources and Development.

NLM has two flagship programmes: Total Literacy Programmes and Post Literacy Programme through which it gives shape to its aims. But with the revitalisation of National Literacy Mission Programme on 10th September, 1999 both the campaigns have come under one single project 'Literacy Campaigns and Operation Restoration'.

Undertaking literacy campaigns across various districts of the country, NLM releases funds for each district.

Rashtriya Uchchatar Shiksha Abhiyan (RUSA)

- The scheme will increase the GER (Gross Enrolment Ratio) from 18% to 30%.
- Funding will be through the state Council of Higher Education. The funding by the centre will be up to 90% and it will be available to even private institutions based on certain norms.
- The scheme emphasises to promote reforms in the state higher education system by creating a facilitating institutional structure for planning and monitoring at the state level.
- It will help to promote autonomy in state universities and include governance in the institutions.
- It will ensure academic examination reforms in the Higher Education Institutions.
- It will enable conversion of some of the universities into research universities at par with the best in the world.

The project will be implemented through HRD Ministry with matching contribution from the State Government and UTs.

Scheme for Infrastructure Development in Minority Institutes (IDMI)

IDMI has been operationalised to augment Infrastructure in Private Aided/Unaided Minority Schools/Institutions in order to enhance quality of education to minority children.

The salient features of IDMI scheme are:

(1) The scheme would facilitate education of minorities by augmenting and strengthening school infrastructure in minority institutions in order to expand facilities for formal education to children of minority communities.

(2) The scheme will cover the entire country but, preference will be given to minority institutions (private aided/unaided schools) located in district, blocks, and towns having a minority population above 20%.

(3) The scheme will inter alia encourage educational facilities for girls, children with special needs, and those who are most deprived educationally, amongst minorities.

National Mission on Teachers and Teaching

The National Mission on Teachers and Teaching is envisaged to address comprehensively all issues related to teachers, teaching, teacher preparation, and professional development. The mission would focus in a holistic manner dealing with the whole sector of education without fragmenting the programmes based on levels and sectors as school, higher, technical, etc. This is a Central Sector Scheme with all-India coverage. The main objective of the programme is to ensure a coordinated approach so as to holistically address the various shortcomings relating to teaching and teachers across the educational spectrum ranging from school education to higher education, including technical education, using the best international practices for excellence.

EDUCATION AND TWELFTH FIVE-YEAR PLAN STRATEGY

The six core principles and strategy for the Twelfth Plan are as follows.

(i) All stages of education need to be viewed in an integrated manner, through the perspective of lifelong learning and education.

(ii) Strengthening the quality of teaching – learning processes requires comprehensive and concerted large-scale efforts with simultaneous attention towards how these processes translate into better outcomes.

(iii) Motivation, capacity, and accountability of teachers for improving learning outcomes at all levels must be focussed upon.

(iv) Governance of educational institution requires an institutional focus on quality based on principles of autonomy and accountability and performance; this may require re-defining the recruitment criteria, eligibility of teachers, and merit-based processes of recruitment in these institutions.

(v) Within a common national legal and policy framework, innovations and diversity of approaches will be encouraged in matters of curricula, teaching systems, and community engagement in order to respond to the diversity of learner groups, regional/social contexts, and various stages/forms of institutional and human development in the educational sector.

(vi) It is necessary to strengthen the monitoring and accountability mechanisms of stakeholders in school education including community and parents as envisaged under the RTE Act.

Higher Education and Twelfth Plan

The Twelfth Plan aims on achieving the 'Three Es'–expansion, equity, and excellence. First, the emphasis will be on quality, as further expansion without quality improvement would be counterproductive for the future of India. Second, there will be an effort to diversify higher education opportunities, not only to meet the needs of employers, but also to offer a wide range of path to success for the youth. India must develop world-class research universities as well as have sophisticated teaching institutions to impart key vocational and generic skills in a timely manner to cope with the rapidly changing labour market needs. Third, this excellence in diversity will be implemented through governance reforms, to enable institutions to have the autonomy to develop distinctive strengths, while being held accountable for ensuring quality. Hence, there will be a holistic approach to the issues of expansion, equity, and excellence.

ISSUES AND CHALLENGES IN THE EDUCATION SECTOR

Low Performance

India's performance is lower compared to other emerging economies. The county's mean years of schooling at 5.12 years is well below the other emerging market economies such as China (8.17 years) and Brazil (7.54 years), and significantly below the average for all developing countries (7.09 years).

Imbalanced Pupil–Teacher Ratio (PTR)

While PTR has improved, there remains imbalance in their development. There has been a substantial increase in the availability of teachers at elementary level during the past few years and if all the teacher posts sanctioned under both Sarva Shiksha Abhiyan (SSA) and State Budgets are filled, the Pupil–Teacher Ratio (PTR) at the National level will almost be 27:1. The challenge, however lies in correcting the imbalance in teacher deployment.

Untrained Teachers

Another serious challenge is the presence of teachers without professional qualifications, approved by the National Council of Teacher Education (NCTE), as is required under the RTE Act. There are about 81 lakh untrained teachers in the country with four States–Bihar, Uttar Pradesh, Jharkhand, and West Bengal accounting for 72% of them.

Out-Of-School Children (OOSC) Level

Another issue is that the children from marginalised social categories continue to remain out of school in spite of different initiatives. While there has been a decline in the percentage of Out-of-School Children (OOSC) across gender and social categories, Muslim, SC, and ST children need greater and focussed attention. The number of OOSC who are physically or mentally challenged remains a cause for concern.

Steep Dropout Rate

The sharp drop-off in enrolment at the middle school level and the increasing enrolment gap from elementary to Higher Secondary suggests that the gains at the elementary level have not yet impacted the school sector as a whole. Disadvantaged groups are worse off with the dropout rates for SCs and STs higher than the national average.

Very Low Student Attendance Rates

While enrolment levels at the elementary level are generally high, there is considerable variation across states in the percentage of enrolled students who are attending schools on any given day during the school year. Of particular concern is that some of the most educationally backward States (UP, Bihar, Madhya Pradesh, and Jharkhand) have the lowest student attendance rates (below 60%).

Schools Lacking in Necessary Infrastructure

Under SSA, the country has seen massive infrastructure development at the school level. Apart from opening over 3 lakh new schools, SSA has also provided basic facilities in existing schools. There are still a large number of schools which do not have the minimum facilities.

Very Poor Learning Outcomes

The biggest concern in elementary education, however, is poor level of student learning, both scholastic and co-scholastic/non-cognitive. Evidence suggests that learning outcomes for children in Indian schools are far below corresponding class levels in other countries, and that the learning trajectories for children who remain in school are almost flat.

Weak teaching processes and transactions between teachers and learners that are neither child-friendly and non-adoption of child-centred approach to curriculum are at the root cause of poor quality.

Improving learning outcomes is crucial for inclusive growth and therefore, major focus of the Twelfth Plan will be on measuring and improving learning outcomes for all children, with a clear recognition that increasing inputs (number of schools, classrooms, teachers, and so on) will by themselves not be enough to ensure quality education for all children.

RIGHT TO EDUCATION

The Constitution (86th Amendment) Act, 2002, inserted Article 21A in the Constitution which provides for free and compulsory education of all children in the age group of 6–14 years as a Fundamental Right in such manner as the state may, by law, determine. In order to put in place a suitable legislation as envisaged under Article 21A, The Right of Children to Free and Compulsory Education (RTE) Act 2009 was passed by Parliament in August 2009. The RTE Act, inter alia, seeks to provide that every child has a right to be provided full time elementary education of satisfactory and equitable quality in formal school which satisfies certain essential norms and standards.

The Constitution (Eighty-sixth amendment) Act, 2002 and the Right to Children to Free and Compulsory Education Act, 2009 have come into force w.e.f. 1 April, 2010. The RTE Act provides children in the 6–14 age group, a legal entitlement to free and compulsory education. It has considerable implications for the implementation strategies of SSA. Steps have been taken to harmonise the vision, strategy, and norms under SSA with the RTE mandate.

Education of Scheduled Castes and Scheduled Tribes

Constitutional Provisions: Article 46 of the Constitution

Articles 330, 332, 335, 338 to 342, and the entire Fifth and Sixth Schedules of the Constitution deal with special provisions for implementation of the objectives set forth in Article 46. These provisions need to be fully utilised for the benefit of the weaker sections in our society.

AUTONOMOUS BODIES, COUNCILS, INSTITUTES, AND COMMISSIONS TO PROMOTE EDUCATION IN INDIA

Central Board of Secondary Education

Set up in 1929, the second oldest Board of the country, Central Board of Secondary Education is an autonomous body working under the aegis of the Ministry of Human Resource Development. The main objectives of the CBSE include: affiliating institutions in and outside the country, conduct annual examinations at the end of class X and XII, conducting entrance examinations to professional courses for admission into medical and engineering colleges, updating and designing curriculum, and empowering the teachers and heads of institutions.

The Board conducts various examinations viz. Senior School Certificate Examination (Class XII), Secondary School Examination (Class X), All India Pre-Medical/Pre-Dental Entrance Examination, all India Engineering Entrance Examination, and Jawahar Navodaya Vidyalaya Selection Test.

National Institute of Open Schooling (NIOS)

Initiated as a project in 1979 under the Central Board of Secondary Education, the Open Schooling Programmes have now taken shape as an independent system of education in India. The NIOS, with international recognition and presence, provides access to sustainable and learner-centric quality school education, skill upgrading and training through open and distance learning, and ensures convergence of Open Schooling organisations, resulting in an inclusive learning society, human resource development, national integration, and global understanding.

NIOS works through its five departments and two units at headquarters and 11 regional centres located at Hyderabad, Pune, Kolkata, Guwahati, Chandigarh, Delhi, Allahabad, Patna, Jaipur, Kochi, and Bhopal. Three sub centres of the regional centres of NIOS have been set up at Bhubaneswar, Dehradun, and Darbhanga. The institute provides opportunities to interested learners by making available various courses/programmes through open and distance learning mode.

NCRI

The National Council of Rural Institutes (NCRI) was set up in 1995 as an autonomous organisation fully funded by the central government to promote rural higher education on the lines of Mahatma

Gandhi's revolutionary vision. It encourages voluntary agencies in accordance with Gandhian philosophy of education in promoting research as a tool of social and rural development.

AIU

The Association of Indian Universities (AIU) is the nodal agency for granting academic equivalence to degrees awarded by the accredited foreign universities and institutions for the purpose of admission to higher academic courses. It acts as a bureau of information exchange in higher education.

National Council of Educational Research and Training (NCERT)

Established in 1961, the National Council of Educational Research and Training (NCERT) is an apex resource organisation of Government of India in the field of school education. It is an autonomous organisation registered under Societies Registration Act to advise and assess the Ministry of Human Resource Development, Government of India and Departments of Education in states/union territories in formulation and implementation of policies and major programmes in the field of education, particularly for qualitative improvement of School Education. NCERT undertakes programmes related to research, development, training, extension, international cooperation, publication, and dissemination of educational information. Besides, NCERT acts as a major agency for implementing the bilateral cultural exchange programmes with other countries.

University Grants Commission

The University Grants Commission (UCG) which came into existence on 28 December 1953 became a statutory organisation by an Act of Parliament in 1956. It is a national body for the coordination, determination, and maintenance of standards of University education. It serves as a coordinating body between the Union and State governments and the Institutions of higher learning. It also acts as an advisory body to these governments and institutions on issues relating to higher education. The commission consists of the chairman, vice chairman, and 10 other members appointed by the Government of India. The executive head is the secretary.

AUTONOMOUS RESEARCH ORGANISATIONS

The Indian Council of Historical Research (ICHR), New Delhi, set up in 1972, reviews the progress of historical research and encourages scientific writing of history. It operates research projects, oversees financial research projects by individual scholars, awards fellowships, and undertakes publication and translation work.

The Indian Council of Philosophical Research (ICPR), functioning from 1977 with offices in New Delhi and Lucknow, reviews the progress, sponsors or assists projects and programmes of research in philosophy, and gives financial assistance to institutions and individuals to conduct research in philosophy and allied disciplines. The Indian Institute of Advanced Study (IIAS), Shimla set up in 1965 is a residential centre for advanced research in Humanities and Social

Sciences and Natural Sciences. It is a community of scholars engaged in exploring new frontiers of knowledge aimed at conceptual development and offering interdisciplinary perspectives on questions of contemporary relevance.

The Indian Council of Social Science Research (ICSSR), New Delhi, is an autonomous body for promoting and coordinating social science research. Its main functions are to review the progress of Social Science Research, give advice on research activities in government or outside, sponsor research programmes, and give grants to institutions and individuals for research in social sciences.

OTHER TYPES OF EDUCATION

Distance Education: Indira Gandhi National Open University

The Indira Gandhi National Open University (IGNOU) established in September 1985, is responsible for the promotion of Open University and distance education system in the educational pattern of the country and for coordination and determination of standards in such a system. The major objectives of the university include widening access to higher education to larger segments of the population, organising programmes of continuing education, and initiating special programmes of higher education for specific target groups like women, physically challenged and people living in backward regions and hilly areas such as the north-east and those predominantly inhabited by tribals and scheduled castes.

Technical Education

The technical education system in the country covers courses in engineering, technology, management, architecture, pharmacy, etc. The technical education system in the country can be broadly classified into three categories: central government funded Institutions, state government/ state-funded institutions, and self-financed institutions.

The Ministry of Human Resource Development caters to programmes at undergraduate, postgraduate, and research levels. The technical education system at the central level comprises of, among others, the following:

1. The All India Council for Technical Education (AICTE), which is a statutory body for proper planning and coordinated development of the technical education system
2. Fifteen Indian Institutes of Technology (IITs)
3. Seven Indian Institute of Management (IIMs)
4. One Indian Institute of Science (IISc), Bengaluru
5. Five Indian Institutes of Science Education and Research and
6. Twenty National Institutes of Technology (NITs) (converted from RECs with 100 per cent central funding). Initiatives have been taken to promote research and education in basic sciences in the country. On the recommendation of the Scientific Advisory Council to the Prime Minister, the Indian Institutes of Science Education and Research have been approved at Pune and Kolkata. These will combine education in basic sciences at undergraduate and postgraduate level, with world-class research facilities.

HUMAN RESOURCE DEVELOPMENT (HRD)

Human resource development (HRD) means enhancement of human capacity at work by means of investment in human capital.

Importance

Human capital means people can act as capital assets. An improvement in the mental capability, skill, and physical capacity of the people constitutes an increase in the human capital because this enables the human factor to produce more. Two types of expenditure can be called as investment in human capital. One is expenditure on education, i.e., general education and technical training; the other is expenditure on the provision of healthcare services like hospitals, medicines, etc.

As a general rule of economies, for optimum utilisation of existing physical capital, investment in human resources on capital is essential because technical, professional, and administrative people are required to make effective use of material resources. The basic objective behind development of human resources is to increase the productivity of labour. Productivity of labour can be raised either by increasing use of capital intensive tools and machines, or by imparting education, both technical and non-technical, to the labourers for skill-generation.

National Policy on Skill Development

A National Policy on Skill Development has been formulated by the Ministry of Labour and Employment. The objective is to create a workforce empowered with improved skills, knowledge, and internationally recognised qualifications to gain access to decent employment and ensure India's competitiveness in the dynamic global labour market. It aims at increase in productivity of workforce both in the organised and unorganised sectors, seeking increased participation of youth, woman, disabled, and other disadvantaged sections and to synergise efforts of various sectors and reform the present system.

At present, the capacity of skill development in India is around 3.1 million persons per year. India has set a target of creating 500 million skilled workers by 2022. Thus, there is a need for increasing capacity and capability of skill development programs. Skill development initiatives support employment generation, economic growth, and social development process. Skill development policy will be an integral part of comprehensive economic labour and social policies and programmes. A framework for better coordination between various stakeholders–Ministries, States, and Industry, etc. will be established. It will promote excellence and will meet the requirements of the knowledge economy.

Mission

National Skill Development initiative will empower all individuals through improved skills, knowledge, nationally and internationally recognised qualifications, to gain access to decent employment and ensure India's competitiveness in the global market.

Aims

(1) The aim of skill development in the country is to support achieving rapid and inclusive growth through enhancing individuals' employability (wage/self employment) and ability to adapt to changing technologies and labour market demands.

(2) Improving productivity and living standards of the people.

(3) Strengthening competitiveness of the country.

(4) Attracting investment in skill development.

Objectives

The objectives of the national policy on skill development are to:

(1) Create opportunities for all to acquire skills throughout life, and specially for youth, women, and disadvantaged groups.

(2) Promote commitment by all stakeholders to own skill development initiatives.

(3) Develop a high-quality skilled workforce/entrepreneurs relevant to current and emerging employment market needs.

(4) Enable the establishment of flexible delivery mechanisms that respond to the characteristics of a wide range of needs of stakeholders.

(5) Enable effective coordination between different Ministries, the centre and the states, and public and private providers.

Scope

The coverage of the national policy on skill development includes the following:

(1) Institution-based skill development including ITIs/ITCs/Vocational schools/technical schools/polytechnics/professional colleges, etc.

(2) Learning initiative of sectoral skill development organised by different ministries/ departments.

(3) Formal and informal apprenticeships and other types of training enterprises.

(4) Training for self employment/entrepreneurial development.

(5) Adult learning, retraining of retired or retiring employees, and lifelong learning.

(6) Non-formal training, including training by civic society organisations.

(7) E-learning, web-based learning, and distance learning.

Challenges

The challenges facing India with respect to HRD are to universalise secondary education and provide the right to education to all children, achieve full literacy for adults, upscale higher and technical education, and expand opportunities for vocational training. The government is also faced with the challenges of drawing of inclusive plans to bridge regional, social, gender, and economic disparities which would provide equality of opportunity as well as a productive and meaningful life for all. There is also the challenge of ensuring availability of funds for achieving upgradation and strengthening of education infrastructure required to meet the desired objectives.

In order to meet the challenges in the field of HRD, special schemes have been drawn up by the Government of India to focus on specific segments of the education system, by promoting the participation of the private sector. The objectives of government policy are sought to be achieved through formulation of annual plans and long-term and medium-term plans, along with milestones and target dates. It also involves coordination with related institutions and dovetailing the development plan with plans of other sectors so as to achieve the national goals and objectives including HRD. Public investment is being suitably supplemented by encouraging private investment, directly as well as through PPPs.

SKILL DEVELOPMENT

Skill India

Skill India is an initiative of the Government of India which has been launched to empower the youth of the country with skill sets which make them more employable and more productive in their work environment. India is a country today with 65 per cent of its youth in the working age group. If ever there exists a way to reap this demographic advantage, it has to be through skill development of the youth so that they add not only to their personal growth but to the country's economic growth as well. Skill India offers courses across 40 sectors in the country which are aligned to the standards recognised by both, the industry and the government under the National Skill Qualification Framework. The courses help a person focus on practical delivery of work and help him enhance his technical expertise so that he is ready on Day One of his job and companies do not have to invest in training him for his job profile.

For the first time in 68 years of India's Independence, a Ministry for Skill Development and Entrepreneurship (MSDE) has been formed to focus on enhancing employability of the youth through skill development. Some reforms and policy interventions are possible because of skill ecosystem in the country which is reinvigorating and re-energising the country's workforce and is preparing the youth for job and growth opportunities in the international market. The flagship scheme, Pradhan Mantri Kaushal Vikas Yojana (PMKVY) alone has seen close to 20 lakh people getting skilled and prepared for a new successful future.

National Skill Development Mission

The National Skill Development Mission has been developed to create convergence across sectors and states in terms of skill training activities. Further, to achieve the vision of 'skilled India', the National Skill Development Mission would not only consolidate and coordinate skilling efforts, but also expedite decision-making across sectors to achieve skilling at scale with speed and standards. It will be implemented through a streamlined institutional mechanism driven by Ministry of Skill Development and Entrepreneurship.

National Policy on Skill Development and Entrepreneurship

The Ministry is an integral part of the government policy on "Sabka Saath, Sabka Vikas" and has fixed its commitment to overall human resource development to take advantage of the demographic profile of the country's population in the coming years. Developing a comprehensive and holistic policy document is an integral part of the process. This requires a fresh look at the already existing National Policy on Skill Development (NPSD). The objective of the National Policy on Skill Development and Entrepreneurship, 2015 will be to meet the challenge of scaling with speed and standard (quality). It will aim to provide an umbrella framework to all skilling activities being carried out within the country, to align them to common standards, and link the scaling with demand centres. In addition to laying down the objectives and expected outcomes, the effort will also be to identify the various institutional frameworks which can act as vehicles to reach the expected outcome. The national policy will also provide clarity and coherence on how skill development efforts across the country can be aligned within the existing institutional arrangements. This policy will link skill development to improve employability and productivity.

Deen Dayal Upadhyaya Grameen Kaushalya Yojana

The *Deen Dayal Upadhyaya Grameen Kaushalya Yojana* (DDU-GKY) is the flagship placement linked skill training programme under the Ministry. Announced in 2014, DDU-GKY is a critical component of the National Skill Development Policy, and has an ambitious agenda, to benchmark wage placement-linked skill programmes to global standard and requirements. The ultimate aim is to convert India's demographic surplus into demographic dividend by developing rural India into a globally preferred source of skilled labour. As a result, the scheme will also benefit more than 55 million poor rural youth who are ready-to-be-skilled, by providing sustainable employment. In this way the scheme is expected to play a crucial role in generational poverty alleviation.

DDU-GKY is a pioneer in standards-led delivery of skilling in India, the first to notify standard operating procedures for training, and the first to introduce IT Solutions for skilling, including mandatory tablets for trainees, Aadhar-linked biometric information for attendance, and geo-tagged time-stamped record of training centres and classes. DDU-GKY has its roots in the *Swarnjayanti Gram Swarozgar Yojana* (SGSY), which was formed by the restructuring of the Integrated Rural Development Programme (IRDP) in 1999, allotting a 15 per cent education component for special projects.

Key features of DDU-GKY

DDU-GKY follows the three tier implementation architecture in PPP mode, with the national unit responsible for policy, the state unit looking after investments, implementation, and monitoring controls.

(i) The focus of these programmes is on the rural youth from poor families, in the age group of 15 to 35 years. Full social inclusion of candidates is insured by the mandatory coverage of socially disadvantaged groups–50 per cent allocation to SC/ST groups, 15 per cent to minorities, 33 per cent for women, and 3 per cent for persons with disabilities.

(ii) Regional inclusion of candidates is enabled through a special sub-scheme for the youth of Jammu and Kashmir called *Himayat*; a special initiative for the rural youth of poor families in 27 most-affected Left-Wing Extremist (LWE) districts across nine States, called *Roshni* and 10 per cent of DDU-GKY's capital investment is reserved for projects from Northeast region.

(iii) The programme promotes *Make in India*, through pro-active partnership with industry through multi-pronged engagement–champion employer policy, captive employer policy, and industrial internship policy.

CHAPTER 14

Issues Relating to Poverty and Hunger

OVERVIEW

Poverty and hunger are as old as the hills. 'Blessed are the poor' for they shall inherit the earth (though not its minerals), we are forever told. More likely, these poor will inherit the earth, sooner or later, but underneath it: bemoaned, blessed, and buried. The poor can wait, poverty won't; the hungry can wait, hunger can't. Governments of the day are busy with committees, commissions, and conventions to estimate poverty.. The truth is 'paddy and poverty' go together.

'To the poor, God can only appear in the form of bread' ***M.K. Gandhi***

'I brought food to the hungry, and people called me a saint.
'I asked why people were hungry; and people called me a communist'.

Dom Helder Camara
Brazilian Archbishop

POVERTY

Introduction

Poverty and hunger are inseparable twins. To understand them, one has to feel them. To write about poverty, expand on figures, and evolve a philosophy is for most part an invitation to debate, discussion, and digression. It all tends to lead to shifting, intractable, interwoven arguments; controversies that lead to more controversies, figures to more figures, philosophies to more philosophies, committees to study poverty and hunger for more figures; absolute poverty, relative poverty, and comparative poverty. The game is endless and rules are mindless.

In the end, statistics and more statistics.

Even so, poverty has many dimensions, and they can be felt, assuaged, and shared. Human dimension has triggered the desire for action to an extent.

D.F. Karaka, in his book, 'I have shed my tears', narrates an instance of a tribal during British times, who, having killed his wife and her paramour in a fit of rage, surrenders to the law and is sentenced to death. The British superintendent of police at Bastar, Central India, before carrying out the sentence, seeks to know if the convict on death row had any last wish. 'Yes, a bowl of fish curry, I am told it is very delicious', was the demand. Having got his wish fulfiled the convicted man rushed at it, only to leave half the curry. 'Was it not tasty?' The police official sought to know. 'Very much so, but my ten year old son is waiting outside. He, like me, will be so very poor too that he too cannot ever hope to have it. Please give the rest of the fish curry to him'. This is the human dimension of poverty.

Eugene O'Neill in 'Fog' puts it across so well. 'The child was diseased at birth, stricken with a hereditary ill that only vital men are able to shake it off. I mean poverty, the most deadly and prevalent of all diseases.'

DIFFERENT DIMENSIONS OF POVERTY

Social Dimension

What is the social dimension of poverty? A whole society afflicted with poverty, a whole society having to struggle to eke out a living, a whole society looking at today with dread of a tomorrow, a whole society too tired, even to dream of a miracle of a manna from the sky.

Social dimensions of poverty draw a thin red line, separating the haves from the have-nots, hunger from anger, and a revolt from a revolution.

'The Grapes of Wrath' by John Steinbeck was published in 1939, and instantly provoked a storm of controversy. It was denounced as obscene by many prominent men of the day. It was attacked with equal violence on political grounds, and the book's central message, an appeal to the 'haves' to behave with common humanity to the 'have-nots', was misinterpreted as a deliberate attempt to stir up class warfare, to incite the working class to rise against the owing class. 'The Grapes of Wrath' was not only provocative but provoking too. It is a cry for social justice and it is in the social dimension that action takes place; social justice is the focus of all attention. Governments act to deliver to reduce the gaps, the inequities, and the imbalances. Social transformation, not only in terms of wealth redistribution, but also breaking down barriers of social order, becomes an urgent call. Social justice must not only be manifestly seen to be given, future but it must also take roots for the generations to view it as natural and noble.

Economic Dimension

The economic dimension is riddled with systems and scenarios to define, devise, and deliver mechanisms for alleviating poverty. How to measure property, how to identify the poor, how to reach the poor, how to uplift the poor, and how always to put in place a system which will not be 'poor' in performance are questions that arise. Do we focus on creation of wealth and then distribute, or do we simultaneously attend to the elimination of social inequality. Economists are divided: The Bhagwatis versus the Amartya Sens of the world.

India still bears the burden of poverty despite tall claims to the contrary. Centuries of despair, destitution, and denial have reduced our country to be a land of the downtrodden. Predominantly, an agrarian economy, the country is monsoon dependent; failure of rains leads to ruin. Paddy and the poor co-exist. Life and food are inseparable.

'From food are born all creatures that live on earth; afterwards they live on food.

And when they die they return to food.' **'Upanishads'**

Colonial Dimension

Two centuries of colonial rule in India gave a new impetus to re-engage us in addressing the broader aspects of poverty. Economic sequestration by Britain to serve its economic interests led to our ruin. In England, the Industrial Revolution began in the latter part of the 18th century. This was made possible not only by the invention of steam power applied to industry, but by the fact that England, through its political power, had been progressively destroying Indian industries in favour of its own manufacturers. All the raw material was taken from India and products finished in England were shipped to India in a ready market here. We paid for our own enslavement.

Deprived of their industry, progressively more and more of the growing population of India had to rely for all its requirements on their income from land. Nearly 75 per cent of them were engaged in agriculture. The size of the farm holdings went on diminishing, till most of them became uneconomic. The agriculturist in India was without work for at least three months in the year. The landless whose number was ever on the increase could find work only in the sowing and reaping seasons. This unemployment and underemployment was the cause of India's poverty, with all its attendant ills such as low vitality, shortened span of life, ignorance, squalor, and disease.

Political Dimension

No doubt, some progress and prosperity came to major cities, but the vast hinterland remained tied to poverty, to paucity, and to pestilence. Famines were regular visitors as were shortages and epidemics. India continued to live in the past, paying for the present, and uncertain about future. Even so, the realisation was dawning that only science and technology could lead the country forward. The future lay in application of science and technology to eradicat poverty, fight disease, combat famines, challenge ignorance, and make life rich, meaningful and comfortable. But this needed planning, this needed discipline, and above all, this needed devotion, dedication and determination. Then came freedom ... at last and our tryst with destiny. Dr. Ambedkar and Nehru in tandem they produced a system of governance and a method of implementation—the Constitution and a government to go by it. Rule of law was now laws of the land, landed and landless were equal, politically. Dr. Ambedkar outlined political freedom, equality, system of checks and balances, and flexibility. Constitution gave Fundamental Rights to citizens, Directive Principles for citizens welfare, courts as sentinels, Parliament as law-making body, and a whole set of enactments to govern Centre State relations.

A unique, dynamic document was crafted to respect diversity, democracy, and devolution of powers. The Constitution gave political emancipation through equality. Its cherished goal was to act as a guide for uplifting the teeming millions in grinding poverty, but the noble intentions to an extent, went awry as Dr. Ambedkar was to lament: "we built a temple for God to come in and reside, but before the God could be installed, if the devil had taken possession of it, what else could we do except destroy the temple". Dr. Ambedkar realised the importance of economic upliftment in the fight against poverty. He looked ahead, far too ahead.

On the 26th of January, 1950 we are going to enter into a life of contradictions. In politics, we will have equality, and in social and economic life, we will have inequality. In politics we will be recognising the principle of one man one vote, and one vote one value. In our social and economic life, we shall, by reason of our social and economic structure, continue to deny the principle of one man one value. How long shall we continue to live this life of contradictions? How long shall we continue to deny equality in our social and economic life?

Dr. Ambedkar, above summed up our historical contradictions well: a nation in turmoil and turmoil in a nation!

POVERTY AND THE PLANERA

Prime Minister Nehru, enamoured by Soviet-style planning and socialistic ideals, set about to combat stubborn poverty, bring about social justice, challenge hunger, and improve standards of living, among India's millions. This was a daunting, defying, and disconcerting task, by any reckoning.

Five-Year Plans, fashioned after the Soviet Russia model, were adopted. The First and Second Plans looked hard at infrastructure, and growth rate. The Third Plan looked at both, but was overwhelmed by wars with China, Pakistan, and a crippling drought. The Fourth Plan harnessed itself to 'Garibi Hatao' (Remove Poverty) but Bangladesh war interfered; plan failed, nay, flopped.

The Fifth Plan stressed on poverty eradication and was moderately successful in other areas, but there was no significant decline in poverty. The Sixth Plan resumed the battle with poverty and new schemes like Integrated Rural Development Programme (IRDP) and Minimum Needs Programme were launched. It was a successful Plan with good results; private sector was given recognition for the first time. Seventh Plan saw the launch of 'Jawahar Rojgâr Yojna', an employment generation scheme on a large scale. The Eighth Plan shifted gears, changed track, and expounded on reforms: Liberalisation, Privatisation and Globalisation. Pradhan Mantri Rojgar Yojna (PMRY) for employment avenues was launched. The Ninth Plan launched 'Growth with social justice and equity,' a push toward agricultural, rural development; the twin areas of poverty syndrome. Plan floundered against recession in the international economy and the Gulf War. The Tenth Plan addressed itself to removal of regional disparities–commendable achievement of creditable goals. The Plan looked at state-led support for welfare schemes. Social sector outlays increased significantly.

Henry Ford, the car maker, once said famously,' All I want to engage is a pair of hands, unfortunately a head comes attached to it.' Government of India, until the Ninth Plan, emphasised on employment, employment, and employment... as a panacea to all evils, including poverty. Welfare of women, children, sanitation, drinking water, housing, electrification, and healthcare were issues alright, but employment also had to be taken care of. Over the years, extremism grew manifold and the pair of hands took to violence and terror. Red corridor appeared and the Government woke up. Social sector now engaged itself to combating, comforting, and compensating.

Meanwhile 'the central and state governments began cultivating the poor–part politics, part realpolitik. Subsidies, waiver of loans, plans for drinking water, child care, empowerment of women, and care for destitute now took centre stage. Meanwhile, the 11th Plan unfolded strategies for 'social inclusiveness' with measurable and quantifiable objectives. Given the experience of the past plans, emphasis now shifted to improving delivery mechanisms and plugging the loopholes and elimination of that historic Indian invention the 'middleman'.

'It is well-known what a middleman is: he bamboozles one party and plunders the other.'

Benjamin Franklin

The government of India is now set to use technology to reach out to the beneficiaries to choke corruption prevalent in welfare benefits. Aadhaar card, Jan Dhan Yojana, Aadhar and mobile technology (JAM) form a trinity to plug the loopholes and gaps to stop leakages. Results are already showing. Time is ripe for the country to move away from the traditional paternal 'sarkar' towards a vibrant social democracy that thrives on innovation. What causes poverty? How did India tackle this problem historically? Famines and shortages are not unknown to the country. Partly man-made, partly infested by nature, famines have always ravaged the country. Akbar's reign, huge famine during 1877–78 when Viceroy Lytton was occupied heralding 'Durbar', turn of the century famine around 1890–are all examples of nature casting fury. In 1943–44, wartime famine rampaging Bengal was man-made. Burma being overrun by the Japanese, cut off the rice supply and ships and barges being diverted for the war effort accentuated the crisis. Millions perished, more than those who died in the war. The Governor of Bengal, Sir Frederick Burrows, who was ailing and sick, made impassioned pleas, 'Get out of Bengal, famine is looming large. We have no resources, we are helpless. Get out of Bengal.'

CAUSES OF POVERTY

What then causes poverty? One obviously thinks of Malthus. Thomas Robert Malthus, in 1798, postulated, 'population growth will always tend to outrun the food supply and the betterment of humankind is impossible without stern limits on reproduction.' Happily, Malthus has been proven wrong but growth is a possible cause of poverty. There are other causes too, as in the case of India.

(a) Low productivity in agriculture: Rain dependent, small land holdings, lack of technology, lack of capital, good seeds, traditional methods, sole bread earner, illiteracy, and bad soil are all factors causing emergence of conditions for grinding poverty.

(b) The rate of economic development in India has been low compared to developed nations leading to a aperennial state of poverty.

(c) Underemployment and disguised unemployment, as also under-utilisation of human resources have led to low productivity in the agricultural sector. It has led ultimately to decline in the standard of lives of farmers.

(d) Inflation and price rise have led to more misery for the poor. Unemployed are increasing in numbers as job opportunities are dwindling.

(e) Capital formation depends on capital and entrepreneurship and once they are in short supply, growth gives way to stagnation. Result is poverty.

(f) Social tensions halts progress with outmoded traditions and beliefs. After independence, politics has preceded economics. Political interests are paramount, and poverty alleviation and unemployment took a back seat.

POVERTY AND THE UN-BRITISH RULE

Dadabhai Naoroji in his celebrated book, 'Poverty and the Un-British rule in India' brought out the significant causal factors which impoverished India. British rule had successfully ended one set of systems and governance, but failed to implant another to mitigate the hardships inflicted by their own system. R. C. Dutta's work 'Economic History of India' powerfully affected Gandhiji to tears, as recorded by him in *Hind Swaraj*.

Millions famished, while millions feasted.

Throughout the period of British rule, most Indians always lived on the verge of starvation. The poverty of the people found its culmination in a series of famines which ravaged all parts of India in the second half of the nineteenth century. Uttar Pradesh, 1860–61: 2 lakh lives, 1865–66: Orissa, Bengal, Bihar, Madras: 20 lakh lives. 1868–70: western UP, Bombay Punjab: 14 lakh lives, 1876–78, Lytton's viceregal years (Lytton was busy attending Dances and Derbys) – Madras, Mysore, Hyderabad, West UP, Maharashtra, and Punjab: totally 75 lakh lives, a third of the country, 1896–97: 45 lakh perished, and 1899–1900: 25 lakh. Lord Curzon improved the famine code, worked energetically, divided Bengal for administrative convenience and political conviction, woke up the nation, and left the country. Some writers hold that India's economic backwardness and poverty are not due to niggardliness of nature, they are man-made. Resources of the country are abundant and capable of yielding, but foreign rule and exploitation of a backward agrarian and industrial economic structure, led to its historic outcome of next to nothing. India presents a paradox; poor people living in a rich country; its tryst with density and destitution. Industrial revolution began in Britain around 1750s; Indian regimentation with Plassey in 1757. Britain subordinated the Indian economy to its economy and determined the basic social trends in India according to her needs. The result was stagnation of India's agriculture and industries, exploitation of its peasants and workers by the zamindars, landlords, princes, moneylenders, merchants, capitalists and the foreign government and its officials, and the spread of poverty, disease, and starvation.

Article 43 Minimum Wage, Factories Act for Workers

According to Article 43 of the Constitution: The state shall endeavour to secure, by suitable legislation or economic organisation or in any other way, to all workers, agricultural, industrial, or otherwise, work, a living wage, conditions of work ensuring a decent standard of life and full enjoyment of leisure and social and cultural opportunities, and in particular, the State shall endeavour to promote cottage industries on individual or cooperative basis in rural areas.

The Minimum Wages Act, Payment of wages Act, and Factories Act are examples of such endeavour to improve standards of life, of enjoyment, of leisure, and of human dignity.

Article 47: Duty of the State to Raise the Level of Nutrition and the Standard of Living and to Improve Public Health

According to this Article, the state shall regard the raising of the level of nutrition and the standard of living of its people and the improvement of public health as among its primary duties and, in particular, the state shall endeavour to bring about prohibition of consumption except for medicinal purposes of intoxicating drinks and drugs which are injurious to health.

POVERTY AND AGRICULTURE GROWTH

Till 1980s, policy makers in the country were focussed on self-sufficiency in food as a priority, but then shifted their attention to making plans to generate additional income in rural areas to combat poverty. It marked action in the following areas:

(a) Improving the position of small, marginal farmers.
(b) Extension of productivity revolution to non-irrigated areas.

Additionally, anti-poverty programmes were also launched to meet the needs of those not benefitting from agricultural growth. This strategy worked well to register growth in agricultural Gross Domestic Product. Coupled with reforms in the non-agricultural sector, the Gross Domestic Product recorded 5.8 per cent growth compared to a measly 3 per cent in 1970s, derisively referred to as 'Hindu rate of growth' by economists of note.

1990s began with a bang and the Balance of Payments crisis; it necessitated structural reforms and changes. By 1993–94, the results were showing a steady, steely growth of 6.8 per cent for three years. Agricultural growth declined even as industrial and service sectors prospered. In the Ninth Plan period (1997–2002), agricultural growth fell to 2 per cent while overall growth stood at 5.5 per cent. The trend of dropping agricultural growth continued in the tenth plan period (2002–2007).

Slow growth in agriculture is the cause of distress and depression among the farmers. Uncertainty has added to reduced risk-taking and stagnation in agriculture is leading to poverty and hunger.

Increase in agricultural productivity and incomes can instantly alleviate poverty; this is possible with state intervention through

(a) Increased investment in irrigation
(b) Better management of existing irrigation facilities
(c) Improved variety of seeds being used
(d) Availability of finance
(e) Making available transport
(f) Marketing infrastructure
(g) Insurance and pest control
(h) Diversification of agriculture
(i) Minimum support price and subsidies

A vibrant, modern, and growing agriculture can help manufacture and service sector grow too, with increased demands. Poverty can disappear at once too. Even with a modest growth in agriculture, a sizeable reduction in poverty levels has been witnessed. It is recorded that incidence of poverty fell from 36 per cent in 1993–94 to 26 per cent in 2000, although there are those who doubt not the fall, but the figures.

Answer to India's poverty lies in application of science and technology to agriculture and mechanisation of our farms, pursuit of Green Revolution, further improved techniques, less wastage, better marketing, public distribution, and above all diversification. The growth of cash crops to eliminate imports of oil seeds, etc. will enhance incomes in the farm sector. Multi-pronged strategies are required: only a crisis can wake us up!

PL 480: WAKE UP CALL ?

1966–67 saw widespread failures of rains, shortages and the spectre of acute food crisis. Orissa was in distress, with famine-like conditions. The country had just about started recovering from Pakistan aggression of 1965. United states had offered a humiliating agreement, called Public Law 480, to agree to supply wheat and rice to India. Given the compulsions, it was agreed to Lyndon Johnson was the President of US when suddenly supplies became erratic and then stopped. None had a clue as to the reason behind this. Meanwhile the country was perilously close to starvation. Prime Minister Indira Gandhi was anxiously making inquiries and finally she got confidential information that the President had not authorised shipments, although ships were all set to sail. Informal checks revealed that the President felt 'Indians could do better than seek mercy or beg. Intelligent people, but they should find their own solutions, lazy lot.' Enter the Green Revolution, exit the era of shortages; enter food surplus, food security, self-pride, exit PL 480.

POVERTY: ESTIMATION

India is home to millions living in penury and object poverty. Poverty is so natural that it has come to be accepted as so very common. From times immemorial, countless rulers have tried to combat poverty, tried to ameliorate the conditions, find space to accommodate, create systems to engage people in work, and opened themselves to charity, all having desultory plans to have a moment of success and fleeting moment of glory. Poverty remained defiant, destined, and devouring. It kept going on and on and on.

After Independence, the country resumed its tryst with poverty. Planning Commission set about its task to lifting the poor above a line, fatuously called, Poverty Line; that was their line of action.

Poverty Line

It is the income or consumption expenditure level that is considered to represent the minimum desirable level of living in a society for all its citizens. This minimum level may be defined in absolute or relative terms. Absolute Poverty Line is often defined as the threshold income that just meets food expenditure corresponding to minimum energy needs of an average person and makes a small allowance for non-food expenditure. Energy is related to intake of calories.

1993: Expert committee headed by Prof. D.T. Lakdawala submitted its recommendations for assessing and estimating poverty. The methodology adopted was called to question holding that advancement in the economy was ignored.

2009: Prof. Suresh Tendulkar, appointed to head a committee in 2005, submitted the report. This committee made substantial changes in the methodology for adjusting Poverty Line to price changes. Planning Commission adopted these recommendations and National Sample Survey Organisation (NSSO) survey for 2009–10, applied Tendulkar committee recommendations. Criticism inevitably followed that like Lakhdawala committee's recommendations, Poverty Line was set too low. Point-wise, the following issues emerged:

(a) Poverty declined during 2004–05 to 2009–10, and without doubt it was a cause of joy and celebration. NSSO survey takes into accounts all types of households; single, medium, large, and then squeezes to per capita income, thus it is neither accurate about family income, nor household-wise.

(b) Tendulkar Committee recorded that in rural areas, poverty levels have declined at the lower levels.

Several representations were made indicating that Poverty Line set by the Tendulkar Committee was low. Planning Commission set up another committee, headed by C. Rangarajan to review the methodology adopted by Tendulkar Committee for estimating poverty.

Rangarajan Committee Recommendations

(a) The Poverty Line should be based on certain normative levels of adequate nourishment including clothing, house rent, conveyance, and education, and behaviourally determined level of other non-food expenses.

(b) The committee computed the average requirement of calories, proteins, and fats based on Indian Council for Medical Research (ICMR) norms differentiated by age, gender, and activity for all India rural and urban regions to derive the normative levels of nourishment.

(c) The protein and fat requirements have been estimated on the same lines as for energy. These requirements are 48 gms and 28 gms per capita per day, respectively, in rural areas and 50 gms and 26 gms per capita per day in urban areas.

(d) The new Poverty Line thus worked out to monthly per capita consumption expenditure of Rs. 972 in rural areas and Rs. 1407 in urban areas in 2011–12.

New Criteria for Different Committees

The pivotal issue is that the Tendulkar Committee moved away from mere calorie intake to a broader set of factors like education, health, and clothing besides food – a life in dignity, not merely digits of calories. In September 2009, the Government's rural development ministry appointed committee, headed by N.C. Saxena, submitted its report on rural poverty. This committee recommended the concept of automatic inclusions and automatic exclusions.

Automatic Exclusions: (from BPL)

(a) Families having three or four wheeler vehicles.

(b) Families who own doubled the land of district average of agricultural land per agricultural household, if partially or wholly irrigated.

(c) Income tax payers

(d) Families that have a person drawing a salary of Rs. 10000 per month.

(e) Families that have at least one mechanized farm equipment.

Broadly, N.C. Saxena Committee has taken economic criteria for exclusions and social criteria for inclusions.

Automatic Inclusions

(a) Designated primitive tribal groups.

(b) Designated most discriminated against SC groups, called maha dalits.

(c) Single women headed households.

(d) Households with disabled as breadwinner.

(e) Destitute households living on alms.

(f) Household headed by a minor.

(g) Households with bonded labourer as member.

The Committee does away with intake of calories, as protein consumption had been going down; especially cereals. The whole exercise in estimation of poverty is fraught with uncertainties and unease. On the one hand, there is the issue with the methodology and on the other, the application of methodology to figures compiled by NSSO – a marriage of convenience, not conviction. Then there's always the cry, a howl that the Poverty Line is set low, in fact, too low. Committees supersede committees, the poor watch, they wait, and they wane. And the Game goes on.

'Remember the poor, it costs nothing'

Josh Billings

TYPES OF POVERTY

Poverty has two aspects: (a) Absolute Poverty and (b) Relative Poverty. Absolute Poverty is expressed in terms of the Poverty Line. It represents a situation in which the consumption or income level of people is less than some minimum level necessary to meet basic needs as per the national standards. Relative Poverty reflects the extent of inequality. It is expressed in the form of comparisons of the levels of income, nutrition, or consumption expenditure of the poor vis-à-vis the rich in the society.

YOJANAS... PLANS... PLAN YOJANAS

Back in early 1970s, a couple of tourists from a centrally planned economy country were fascinated by the imposing building block called 'Yojana Bhavan' in New Delhi and were prompt to delight, 'Is this where Yoga, the ancient Indian art, is practised?'. 'Yes, we are doing 'asanas' to pull some scheme for the nations ubiquitous poor', chuckled the guide.

Plans, plans, plans..more plans. Old plans, new packages. Old wine new bottles, new wine, old bottles, only bottles, no wine. Never: no wine, no bottles.

Government of India from 1952 onwards has set itself onerously to the task of combating poverty. At one level, we had the political one-upmanship, with emotive, charged slogans like 'Garibi Hatao', at another we had serious logistic exercise defining poverty, deifying the poor, and determining the poorest. Broadly, the schemes have revolved around three basic themes:

a) Employment generation.
b) Poverty alleviation.
c) Social upliftment.

Later, a more consummate script emerged of social inclusiveness. A narrative to integrate, a package for the poor leading to a distinctly better life.

Employment Generation Schemes.

There are two types of programmes under this scheme. One is to train persons for employability and the other to provide employment assistance. Schemes are implemented by the States with assistance from the Centre. Given the experience, increased understanding of the dimension of the problem of unemployment, and given the maturity attained in implementing projects, the employment assistance programmes have come to find increased acceptance among the beneficiaries. Loopholes having been plugged, pilferages stopped, and quality work improved, the schemes are adding value. The National Rural Employment Guarantee Act (NREGA), for one, has found itself to be a game changer.

Over the years, following initiatives have been taken.

1. Jawahar Rojgar Yojna launched during the Seventh Plan (1989): Employment assistance in rural areas.
2. Employment Assistance Scheme (EAS) launched in Oct 2, 1993 (Merged with Jawahar Rojgar Yojana in 1996): Employment assistance in rural areas.

3. Integrated Rural Development Programme (IRDP) launched in 1980 (Meant for those below Poverty Line): Employment Assistance Scheme.
4. National Food for Work Programme: 100 days' employment to able-bodied rural folk.
5. National Rural Employment Guarantee Programme (NREGP): 100% centrally sponsored, with conditions same as that of National Food for Work Programme.

Mahatma Gandhi National Rural Employment Guarantee (MGNREGA) Act

MGNREGA Act was a landmark legislation heralding 100 days of guaranteed wage employment in a financial year. It has the following features:

1. Rights based framework
2. Time-bound guarantee
3. Labour intensive work.
4. Decentralised planning
5. Women empowerment
6. Work-site facilities
7. Transparency and accountability
8. Funding

With MGNREGA, the country has stepped into a framework of institutional set up with dedicated lines of work and plans. The scheme, having the force of an act of the Parliament, is spread across the country and has found rapid acceptance among beneficiaries. State Governments and local panchayats are increasingly using this scheme for developmental works, like roads, sanitation, health centres, etc. Overall, MGNREGA has provided the impetus to rural development in a manner of inclusive growth.

POVERTY ALLEVIATION

While employment assistance to the able-bodied is fine, it is poignant to keep in mind others who are not covered by these conditions namely, destitutes, aged, infirm, women, children, weak, and the incapable. Some regions in the country are resource-starved, with lack of facilities and skills, and are historically neglected. To add to this, they are inaccessible and remote. Hence, the Government has brought out programmes for alleviation of poverty.

1995: National Social Assistance Programme: To assist people living below Poverty Line.

1999: Annapurna Yojana: 10 kg foodgrains to senior citizens not getting pension.

2000: Antyodaya Yojna: Food security for the poor.

2001: Shiksha Sahyog Yojana: Education of children below Poverty Line.

Poverty alleviation schemes have, by and large, met their objectives. Some state governments have launched their own programmes too.

Social Upliftment

In a country torn asunder by social strife, historic inequalities, caste considerations, class confrontations, regional imbalances, economic disparities, religious regimentation, and prevailing illiteracy, the case for social upliftment needs no debate.

'India is the nearest example of prevailing anarchy', said J.K. Galbraith, former US Ambassador to India. Prevailing anarchy is on account of social dissensions. Not to ignore is another factor namely, condition of women in the country and their empowerment. Caste system has cast itself in our mould, our psyche, our thinking, our living, our liking, and our very existence.

Some social upliftment initiatives of the Government:

(a) *Beti Bachao, Beti Padhao*: Seeks to address gender imbalance and discrimination. Launched from Haryana.

(b) *Vande Mataram Scheme*: 2004. Maternity care, check up. Public–Private Partnership initiative.

(c) *Swajaldhara*: 2002. Drinking water supply to all villages.

(d) *Pradhan Mantri Gram Sadak Yojana*: 2004. Scheme for labourers of unorganised sector providing family pension, insurance, and medical assistance.

Recent Schemes of the Social Sector

1. *Atal Pension Yojana*: For unorganised sector. Fixed minimum pension of Rs. 1,000, 2,000, 3,000, 4,000, or 5,000 per month, beginning at the age of 60. having joined between the age of 18 and 40, commensurate with contribution.
2. *Pradhan Mantri Jeevan Jyoti Bima Yojana*: Premium Rs. 330 per month. Renewable one year life cover of Rs. 2 lakhs. Age group 18 to 50 years.
3. *Pradhan Mantri Suraksha Bima Yojana*: Premium Rs. 12 per annum per subscriber. Accident death-cum-disability cover of Rs. 2 lakhs. Age group 18–70 years.

Additionally, the Government has lots of schemes for housing, health, and welfare.

'Miles to go before we sleep'.

NREGA Scheme

Projects under NREGA are now spread over 661 districts of the country, Altogether, 6858 blocks have been covered by the scheme that aim to provide a minimum level of income and a minimum number of working days to the rural poor. Nearly 27.85 crore people have been the beneficiaries of the scheme.

NATIONAL FOOD SECURITY ACT, 2013

National Food Security Act, 2013, a landmark legislation, provides for food and nutritional security besides the right to receive adequate quantity of foodgrains at affordable prices to the people.

State-wise coverage will be determined by the Central government. The work of identification of eligible household is left to the States/Union territories, which may frame their own criteria or use social, economic, and caste census data, if they so desire.

The Central Government will provide funds to the states/union territories in case of short supply of foodgrains from central pool. In case of non-supply of foodgrains or meals to entitled persons, the concerned state/union territory governments will be required to provide such food security allowance as may be prescribed by the Central government to the beneficiaries.

There is special focus on nutritional support to women and children. Pregnant women and lactating mothers, besides being entitled to nutritional meals as per the prescribed nutritional norms will also receive maternity benefit of Rs.. 6000. Children in the age group of 6–14 (6 months–14 years) will be entitled to take home ration or hot cooked food as per prescribed norms.

The Act contains provisions for reforms in Public Distribution System (PDS) through doorstep delivery of foodgrains, application of IT, and leveraging Aadhaar in order to identify beneficiaries for effective implementation of the provisions of the Act. States will get assistance for intra-state transportation and handling of foodgrains.

Chhattisgarh, Tamil Nadu, and Madhya Pradesh have implemented the scheme well.

The scheme has supporters who laud its noble intent and national extent; they cite the examples of subsidies being given to industry. Economists like Amartya Sen and Dreze are all for food security and critics too are vocal. Good monsoon, good output presents no crisis but failure of monsoon, El-Nino, shortages can bring crisis to the doorstep. A slip between promise and performance can be dangerous for credibility.

Critics focus that malnutrition, and not hunger is the issue although they all concede that poverty is a stubborn enemy and hunger, a silent killer. Critics feel malnutrition is worse than poverty or hunger as it carries a frail body and a feckless mind.

Identification of beneficiaries is another gargantuan task although Aadhar is solving it to some extent. Add to this the danger of people getting used to doles, subsidies, and easy access to food. Farmers will start taking easy recourse to production of wheat, rice, coarse grains for enjoying benefits of minimum support price: cash crops will crash. A balanced approach is the need of the hour.

MALNUTRITION

'Although there is improvement in child nutrition over the last decade, one in three children is still stunted'

NFHS-4

Bihar, Madhya Pradesh, and Meghalaya present a dismal picture with 40% children stunted, according to National Family Health Survey – 4 (NFHS-4) for 2015-16 covering 13 states and 2 union territories.

Compared with NH-3 (2005-06) there's improvement all-round.

(a) Under 5 years of age-**stunting**	Decline from 42% to 37%
(b) Under 5 years of age-**wasted**	Decline from 48% to 22%
(c) Under 5 years of age-**underweight**	Decline from 39% to 34%

Integrated Child Development Services (ICDS) scheme was introduced in 1975. A central scheme, it has the following objectives:

i. To improve the nutritional and health status of children below the age of six years and pregnant lactating mothers.

ii. To lay the foundation for proper psychological, physical, and social dropouts.

iii. To reduce the incidents of mortality, morbidity, malnutrition, and school dropouts.

iv. To achieve effective coordination among various departments to promote child development.

v. To enhance the capability of the mother to look after the health and nutritional needs of the child through proper health and nutrition education.

The scheme has had a fair degree of acceptance and success.

HUNGER

'The rich swell up with pride, the poor from hunger'

Sholom Aleichem
(Russian writer)

It is said as an anecdote that during the revolution in France in 1789 out of ten people, nine died out of starvation, and one due to overeating. Hunger is a silent killer.

In global hunger index, India stands at position 55 out of 76 nations; below Nepal, hardly a case for cheer. In human development index, India ranks at 135 out of 188 countries; below Sri Lanka. In multi-dimensional poverty index, it ranks at 73 out of 103, which is lower than Bangladesh. While the size of the country significantly brings multi-faceted problems, issue remains that hunger index is disconcerting. China has proved a point in effectively tackling poverty, hunger, and human development.

With the passage of National Food security Act, (if its implementation doesn't throw up glitches, snags, and slacks) the country can address itself to the issue of hunger. People's participation holds the key. Voluntary agencies, self-help groups, social organisations must be initiated in the process.

Examples set by some states of success stories must be emulated, not envied. Similarly, due recognition must be given to individual initiatives. Notably, the media must cover such stories to sensitise people. Government's efforts to extend employment assistance are, no doubt, laudable; its efforts in advancing measures for alleviating poverty and social distress are equally commendable. Community services must be encouraged to ensure that none goes hungry in the neighborhood. Sensitisation is the issue.

An example can be given of C.F. Andrews, an Englishman who was more Indian than Indians. 'Mother, give me only rice and that too not much. I am told people in India eat rice and are very poor. When I grow up I will go to that country and work among the poor. Please let me get used to eating rice now onwards,' an eight-year-old C.F. Andrews had exhorted his mother. He was later known as Deenbandhu who dedicated his life to the service of the poor in India.

Did you know?

The richest 1% in India own 73% of the wealth generated in the country last year. In the past 12 months, the wealth of the group increased by Rs. 20, 913 billion-equivalent to the Union Budget in 2017-18. 67 crore Indians who comprise the poorer half of the population saw 1% increase in their wealth. India added 17 new billionaires last year, raising their number to 101.

In rural India, it will take 941 years for a minimum wage worker to earn what the top paid executive at a leading Indian government firm earns in a year.

– Oxfam report

Did you know?

According to the Rangarajan Committee, one snapshot is that out of every ten Indians, three are poor. How poor? If living in rural India, earnings would have to be less than Rs. 32/- per person per day and Rs. 47/- per person per day if living in urban areas. These figures would translate to an amount spent in urban areas to Rs. 7035/- per month for a family of five and Rs. 4860/- per month for a family of five in rural areas. Per se, it doesn't look bad and why?

(i) Rangarajan Committee is talking of a family of five. Expenses in a family of five would be common for rent, fuel, electricity, cooking.

Thus allowing for a margin:

(ii) When Rs. 7035 is getting divided by 5 and then by 30, it is coming down to a drastically low figure of Rs. 47/- per person per day.

(iii) Global figures on principles of purchase pay parity are $ 2.00 per person per day as against $ 2.4 per person per day arrived at by Rangarajan. This is comfortably comparable.

(iv) Spending Rs. 7035/- per month would safely mean some income above this for savings etc. Rangarajan committee has taken the outgo figure only. In India with prevalent joint family set up, some incomes would be pooled and some payments shared. This would ease the burden.

All in all, Rangarajan has assessed India's poor to be 37.0 crores; up from 27 crores visualised by Tendulkar Committee. The poor can only hope and pray that calculations should not be "poor".

Social Justice

Model questions with answers

Q. India has been climbing up the per capita income ladder while slipping down the slope of social indicators. Discuss.

A. India's rapid growth in the last decade has been a remarkable achievement. The living standards of top 20 per cent of population have improved, the middle class has moved forward, but the conditions of the really poor and downtrodden continues to be in abysmal state. Their conditions of living have progressed, but at an excruciatingly slow rate. There has been a slowdown in growth of real agricultural wages – 5% in 1980s, 2% in 1990s and virtually zero in 2000s. After 2006, when NREGA came, the wages somewhat perked up a little, especially for women. For casual or unskilled workers, the growth has been very slow. Between 1993-94 to 2009-10, the average per capita expenditure was 1% in rural and 2% in urban areas according to the National Sample Survey.

Q. Comment on the importance and potential of Niti Aayog promoted open innovation workspaces in high schools.

A. The National Institution for Transforming India (NITI) Aayog, the government policy think-tank has thought of open innovation workspaces in high school or 'Atal tinkering labs' as a part of Atal Innovation Mission (AIM), which provides a platform for high school students to build an inventor temperament.

The objective is promotion of world-class innovation hubs and other self-employment activities, particularly in technology driven areas. The core functions are:

- Entrepreneurship promotion through self-employment and talent utilisation, wherein innovators would be supported and mentored to become successful entrepreneurs
- Platform where innovative ideas would be generated in Atal Tinkering Labs
- Atal Incubation Centers
- Scale up support to established incubators.

This concept relies on the premise that innovators are not born, but they can be created from the ground-up, by following a systematic approach, which is about defining the problem to be solved, ideating, brainstorming, creating prototypes, testing solutions and finally making changes as per user feedback.

These labs will make youth acquire required know-how to get jobs in international market. Finally, this scheme is in synergy with the Make in India program and Skill India mission.

Q. Write a note on RTE (Right To Education) Act, its successes and failures.

A. The Right to Education Act (RTE), enacted on August 4, 2009 describes the modalities of the importance of free and compulsory education for children between 6 and 14 in India under Article 21A of the Indian Constitution.

The right is a joint responsibility of the state and the Centre to provide free and compulsory education. It means that ' All children between the ages of 6 and 14 shall have the right to free and compulsory elementary education at a neighborhood school.'

Success of RTE

- In the last six years, the Right to Education Act has shown promising developments. The government's budget for the Sarva Shiksha Abhiyan, the main vehicle for the Act's implementation, has increased substantially from ? 12,825 crores in 2009-10 to ?22,500 crore in 2016-17.
- 5 lakh schools have been opened in the last decade and 99% of India's rural population now has a primary school within a one kilometer radius. A survey in 2014 reported that 84.4% schools now served the mid-day meals, 48.2% schools had proper and functioning toilets for girls and 73% schools had available drinking water.

Yet a critical appraisal of the functioning of Right to Education reveals that large gaps exist in its implementation. India has the largest number of out-of-school children in the world, which is more than the out of school children in whole of sub-Saharan Africa.

Shortcomings of the implementation of the RTE:

- Abilities in reading, writing and other comprehensive skills are deteriorating among children between the ages of 6 and 14.
- The flow of public funds has focused on developing school infrastructure, not teacher training. An Oxfam India policy report in March 2015 indicated that over 5 lakh sanctioned teachers' post were lying vacant and more than 6.6 lakh in-service teachers were un-trained.
- Around 37% of primary schools were found to be non-conformant with the prescribed national pupil – teacher ratio (PTR) norm of 30:1. Moreover, around 10% of schools across the country remain single teacher schools.

Despite these shortcomings, the Act offers a first step towards an educational system in India that provides access, equity and inclusion for all children.

Q. What is role of National Council for Teacher Education (NCTE) in improving quality of teacher education and training?

A. The National Council for Teacher Education (NCTE), established in 1993 is the all-powerful regulatory body for teacher education system in the country.

To fulfil the national commitment to education for all, India began a massive expansion of its schooling system in the late 1980s and early 1990s. This demanded a proportionate increase in the number of teachers. The NCTE was set up in this period, with a view to achieving planned and coordinated development of the teacher education system.

NCTE Functions:

It shall be the duty of the Council to take all such steps as it may think fit for ensuring planned and co-ordinated development of teacher education and for the determination and maintenance of standards for teacher education and for the purposes of performing its functions under this Act, the Council may:

- Undertake surveys and studies relating to various aspects of teacher education and publish the result thereof;
- Make recommendations to the Central and State Government, Universities, University Grants Commission and recognised institutions in the matter of preparation of suitable plans and programmes in the field of teacher education;
- Co-ordinate and monitor teacher education and its development in the country;
- Lay down guidelines in respect of minimum qualifications for a person to be employed as a teacher in schools or in recognised institutions;
- Lay down norms for any specified category of courses or trainings in teacher education, including the minimum eligibility criteria for admission thereof, and the method of selection of candidates, duration of the course, course contents and mode of curriculum;
- Lay down guidelines for compliance by recognised institutions, for starting new courses or training, and for providing physical and instructional facilities, staffing pattern and staff qualification;
- Lay down standards in respect of examinations leading to teacher education qualifications, criteria for admission to such examinations and schemes of courses or training;
- Promote and conduct innovation and research in various areas of teacher education and disseminate the results thereof.

Q. Critically evaluate merits and demerits of National Health Policy (2017).

A. India recently released National Health Policy (NHP) 2017, which has immense potential to tackle the major health problems of the country.

MERITS:

Aspires to improve spending from current 1.6% to 2.5% of GDP by 2025.

Provision of Health card to families for basic medications in primary health centres (PHCs)

Involvement of the private sector for secondary & tertiary health sectors.

Upgradation of district hospitals & expansion of institutional capacity

State based public health management cadre will be established.

New courses will be included in medical education.

Target based elimination of HIV, TB etc

Focus on male sterilization

AYUSH will be integrated into research component of health systems.

DEMERITS:

No provision for medical tourism.

The NHP has not spoken about proper regulation & licensing of private sector.

Joint operation of private & public sector is must to reduce expenditure. But NHP is silent on this.

Barely any focus on skill development of nurses.

The provision of 'Health as a right' in the previous policy has been done away with

Thus, the merits far outweigh the demerits. The NHP must be pursued in earnest.

Q. Why is there urgent need to control Japanese encephalitis?

A. Japanese encephalitis was recognised in 1955 for the first time as a potentially life-threatening and rare disease causing "acute inflammation" of the brain.

It spread to Tamil Nadu, West Bengal, Uttar Pradesh, Assam, Bihar, Manipur, Andhra Pradesh, Goa, Pondicherry and Karnataka, Uttar Pradesh and Bihar. The two states, which have seen the most number of encephalitis cases in recent years are UP and Bihar. By 2014, at least 550 cases of deaths due to encephalitis were reported in the country.

Thus encephalitis needs to be targeted on priority with dedicated state measures. Following are some of the measures that need to be taken on priority basis.

- Mass awareness and door-to-door campaigns in severely affected districts about the causes of the disease and ways of prevention should be a priority.
- A study specific to Gorakhpur had suggested a possibility of faecal-oral transmission of the virus by contaminated drinking water. Sanitation, mosquito control, prevention of open defecation, and ensuring clean drinking water can help prevent an outbreak.
- The State governments need to allot maximum funds to those districts most affected by encephalitis. More infrastructures are required in states like UP and Bihar where the prevalence rate is high.
- Encephalitis vaccine has been included in the Universal Immunisation Programme (UIP) since 2011. It has helped to reduce the prevalence rate among the children. Encephalitis is a predictable disaster. Its transmission intensifies during the rainy season, during the pre-harvest period in paddy-cultivating regions, and in flood-prone districts. Thus, careful measures taken by States will surely improve the present condition and help in towards eliminating the disease completely.

Q. What is Nutrition Atlas?

A. The Nutrition Atlas provides information and data on nutritional status of population groups at national and state levels, along with an overview of nutrition-related deficiencies, disorders and prevalence levels in various parts of the country.

In addition, it provides information on nutrients, nutrient rich foods, nutritional deficiency disorders and a host of other topics.

The portal also includes information on nutrition rich foods and nutri guide for various nutrients, minerals, essential amino-acids, fatty acids, dietary fibers and proteins, along with their biochemical cut-offs, recommended dietary allowances, signs and symptoms and dietary sources.

The nutrition atlas will help to implement preventive healthcare by targeting the right areas and right population groups.

The huge information will help in analysing the eating habits of various demographic groups in different areas of the country.

It makes use of publicly available data sources like reports of National Nutrition Monitoring Bureau, National Family Health Survey, World Health Organisation and other public databases. The dashboard of the portal acts like an information management tool, helping the user track data on under nutrition, overweight, obesity and communicable and non-communicable diseases.

Q. What measures do you suggest, to end problem of farmer suicides?

A. Farmer suicides account for 11.2% of all suicides in India. According to National Crime Records Bureau, 80 per cent of farmers killed themselves because of bankruptcy or debts after taking loans from banks and registered microfinance institutions.

How government can prevent these suicides-

Special agricultural zones-just like industrial zones-are essential. Here farming and farming related activities can be promoted and sustained with government help

Awareness about crops to be taken in particular soil types, best rotation practices, fertilisers to be used etc. must be spread by government and other private agencies.

As increasing unpredictable nature of weather has caused havoc, insurance is to be provided to all types of crops. Recently launched Pradhan Mantri Krishi Sinchai Yojana is step in right direction.

Water management is important as only 43% of the farm land is irrigated. Drip irrigation can be practiced. Inter-state cooperation on water resources must ensue. Maharashtra government's *Jalyukta Shiwar Yojana* is commendable.

Farmers, particularly the small and marginalized farmers should not depend solely on agriculture. Co-occupations like dairy, poultry, fishing, horticulture etc. must be promoted.

Better prices for produce are necessary. APMC acts must be reformed to check middlemen. Recent e-NAM scheme has potential to provide good prices for the agricultural produce. e-NAM (National Agriculture Market) is a pan-India electronic trading portal launched by Ministry of Agriculture & Farmers' Welfare, Govt of India, to facilitate farmers, traders, buyers, exporters and processors with a common platform for trading commodities. It currently links 250 APMCs (Agriculture Produce Marketing Committees) from across 10 states. 69 commodities including staple food grains, vegetables and fruits are currently listed in its list of commodities available for trade.

Integrated Pest Management can be done as in Vietnam through no- spray policy.

Development of weather and disease resistant seeds must be encouraged.

Systematic Rice Intensification (SRI), precision farming solutions may help farmers to produce more with less.

Contract farming must be promoted along with formation of custom hiring centres,

Deployment of Early Warning Systems: Farmers will not take unsustainable loans if drought like situation is predicted well in advance and they can switch over to less water-intensive crops like pulses

Farmer centric policies: With the help of NABARD & local bodies, prepare a list of highly indebted farmers in the region for counseling, interest subvention scheme.

Universal Health Coverage must be set afoot to reduce expenditure of farmers on health issues.

Q. Analyse the changes made by the Union government to child and women welfare schemes in last three years.

A. **The positives**

The *Beti Bachao Beti Padhao* scheme has promoted the concept of gender equality and ensured the welfare and development of the girl child.

Sukanya Samriddhi Yojana is a saving deposit scheme meant exclusively for girl child and is meant to meet the education and marriage expenses of girl child.

The improved implementation of the POCSO (Protection of Children from Sexual Offences) Act, and the new system of online complaints in a hassle-free manner, is being regarded as a child-friendly measure adopted by the government.

The recent amendments to Maternity Benefits Act, 1961, increasing the maternity leave period for working women from 12 to 26 weeks, facilitating maternity leave for adopting mothers, and providing crèches in workplaces, are indeed welcome steps.

The negatives

The government has cut the budget allocation of Integrated Child Development Scheme (ICDS) by 50% in 2015-16, with funds being even short for giving salaries of anganwadi workers.

Like ICDS, the midday meal scheme was slashed by 36

Government is planning to phase out Janani Suraksha Yojana, a scheme of conditional cash transfers aimed at promoting institutional deliveries.

Q. In the context of Forest Rights Act, elucidate the problems of tribal population.

A. Forest Rights Act (FRA) recognises the right of tribals to live in the forest land under the individual or common occupation for habitation or for self-cultivation for livelihood, and also grants several other rights to ensure their control over forest resources.

The Act also provides for diversion of forest land for public utility facilities managed by the government, such as schools, dispensaries, fair price shops, electricity and telecommunication lines, water tanks, etc. with the recommendation of Gram Sabhas.

Challenges in implementation of FRA

- A series of legislation viz, amendments to the Mines and Minerals (Development and Regulation) Act, the Compensatory Afforestation Fund Act and a host of amendments to the Rules to the FRA undermine the rights and protection given to tribals in the FRA, including the condition of "free informed consent" from gram sabhas for any government plans to remove tribals from the forests and for resettlement or rehabilitation package.

- The process of documenting communities' claims under the FRA is intensive – rough maps of community and individual claims are prepared by Gram Sabhas. These are then verified on the ground with annotated evidence.
- There is a reluctance of the forest bureaucracy to give up control. Collective claims – Community Forest Resource (CFR) rights are ignored. To date, the total amount of land where rights have been recognised under the FRA is just 3.13 million hectares, mostly under claims for individual occupancy rights.
- In almost all States, instead of Gram Sabhas, the Forest Department has either appropriated or been given effective control over the FRA's rights recognition process.

Forest Rights Act can be a powerful instrument to protect the rights of tribal communities if we strengthen the nodal tribal departments and provide clear instructions to the State and district administration.

Q. What are the problems in aiding Particularly Vulnerable Tribal Groups (PVTGs) in India?

A. In 1973, the **Dhebar Commission** created Primitive Tribal Groups (PTGs) as a separate category, who are less developed among the tribal population. They were later renamed as PVTGs.

- The highest number of PVTGs are found in Odisha (13) followed by Andhra Pradesh (12). All the four tribal groups in Andaman and one in Nicobar Islands are PVTGs.
- Surveys showing data on demographic and socio-economic status of the PVTGs contain repetitions and overlapping data. Some PVTGs are distributed in more than one State and are recognized multiple times like Birhors spread in 4 States.
- There are regional and State-specific variations in welfare schemes for PVTGs. For example, while Odisha has exclusive micro-projects for the PVTGs, there are none such for the PVTGs in Gujarat. Sometimes micro projects extend only to some blocks of district and not others.
- They are physically isolated, have no written language and still have primitive social institutions.

Q. Spell out the recommendations of NITI Aayog task force on eliminating poverty.

A. The NITI Aayog's task force on poverty elimination has made suggestions, as under:

- Sweeping changes have been recommended in MGNREGA scheme. It has been mooted that its funds should be used to pay for labour on private farms, also.
- Modest cash transfer should be given for 5 poorest families in village
- In peak season, farmers can hire MGNREGA labour by paying 75% of wages, while balance can be given from MGNREGA funds
- With Aadhar knowledge, volume of beneficiaries can be known, so that new schemes for cash transfer are easily made

Q. What are UN's Sustainable Development Goals (SDG) regarding poverty and hunger? Are there difficulties in India's path ?

A. The UN's Sustainable Development Goals (SDG) have laid down 17 goals, which have to be accomplished in 15 years. One of the goals is elimination of poverty and another is elimination of hunger. The SDG seeks that number of poor people should come down by half and food insecurity be removed from globe. India has agreed to SDG, but the difficulties are many:

- Lack of data is the biggest problem
- The SDG is silent about funding by developed countries. It is estimated $66 billion would be required for poverty alone. From where would funds come?
- There has always been difficulty in reaching consensus among countries. For example, there is no agreement on food security till now.
- Climate change is a factor, which has not been accounted for in SDG, which makes prediction of food security a tough task.
- The goals are too many. It is said only 10 goals should have been laid down.

Q. What is the difference between Severe Acute Malnutrition (SAM) and Severe Chronic Malnutrition (SCM) ?

A. Severe Acute Malnutrition (SAM) is a condition prevalent in children, which carries high mortality risk. It is found in Africa and other countries. The causes of SAM are drought, crop failure, civil wars etc; The child needs therapeutic feeding and also medical inputs. Severe Chronic Malnutrition (SCM) is a less serious condition, but a continual affliction. The children show stunted growth. This malnutrition is prevalent in India. The Rapid Survey on Children (2103-14) showed that 29.4% children, below age of 3, in India are underweight, 15% are wasted (low weight for height) and 38.7% are stunted (low height for age), which show that SCM is existent in country. The causes of SCM are chronic food insecurity, latent poverty, poor feeding and protracted morbidity. They need quality local diet, pediatric care and private and public investment resources planning. The children are hungry, though not sick.

Q. Just providing resources is not enough. There should be capacity building too, if poverty is to be really eradicated. Comment.

A. Provision of lakhs of crores to rural India is not enough, unless there is capability to devise ways to effectively use such resources. The panchayats, for example, have neither technical facility nor trained labour force if they want to set up a water harvesting project or food processing plant. The capacity building for setting up roads, sanitation and water supply is not there. The extension service for educating farmers is scarce. Geo tagging inspection by district officials can detect whether insurance is reaching beneficiaries. Digital literacy is essential for telemedicine and agrimarkets. Hence, unless effective utilization of resources takes place, funds won't be much of a help.

Q. In our country droughts are a recurrent feature. Suggest measures to fight drought.

A. To combat drought, several steps can be taken, as under:

- Micro irrigation should be adopted, not flood irrigation
- Check dams and farm ponds have to be built
- Afforestation holds ground water under surface and reduces evaporation
- Cloud seeding can be done
- Organic farming must be taken up

Q. What is hidden hunger? Enumerate.

A. Hidden hunger is a form of under nutrition, where the intake of vitamins and minerals like zinc, iodine and iron is too low to sustain health of a person. Poor diet, infection, disease and low intake during lactation and poor intake by mothers-to-be are causes for hidden hunger. Poor health is seen and death may also occur. Till a child is 2 years, the problem of hidden hunger has to be particularly taken care of. Eating staple cereals like rice and wheat only also cause hidden hunger.

The solutions are fortification, where vitamin A is added to sugar, vitamin B to wheat flour but fortified food must be cheap. Fortification can also be done, during plant breeding. For example, zinc rice, iron beans and vitamin A maize can be grown.

Practice Questions

1) Elaborate the features of the National Rural Health Mission?
2) What are the policies and plans the government has for the aged groups in the society? Outline.
3) Employment generation alone is the best and only viable tool to combat poverty. Discuss with examples from the initiatives taken by the government.
4) Outline some of the initiatives taken by state government for the upliftment of the Girl Child?
5) What are the features of new national health policy? How is it different from the previous ones?

PART IV

Governance

15

CHAPTER

Aspects of Governance

OVERVIEW

Government should always look for a 'PAT'; not the self-congratulary one that it cares for, but 'Performance (P) with Accountability (A) and Transparency (T). This can best be achieved with the aid, assistance, and application of technology. A defined and dedicated citizen's charter and detailed and dispensing e-technology can usher in an era of successful governance. Systems would be the interface between the man and the machine; systems that discern, disseminate, and deliver: all with speed, accuracy, and impartiality. A dream come true? No, a true dream come through.

There is good government when those who are near are made happy and when those who are far are attracted.

Confucius

Good governance is perhaps the single most important factor in eradicating poverty and promoting development.

Kofi Annan, Former UN Secretary General

IMPORTANT ASPECTS OF GOVERNANCE

Benito Mussolini grabbed power in Italy in the early part of the previous century and soon promised 'good governance'; by itself a remarkable offer in ailing, anarchic Italy. It was taken to be a hoax, even a well-intended prank, and few believed it. Soon the trains started arriving on time and astounded Italians started looking up the timetable. Much else also was accomplished, the world sat up and took notice, notably the Germans. For good governance to be a reality, do you need a superman, a demi-god ? No. Even a 'Part Recipe' can usher in total 'good governance'.

'PART RECIPE'

P. Participatory.

A. Accountable.

R. Responsive.

T. Transparent.

R. Rule of law.

E. Efficient and Effective.

C. Consensus.

I. Inclusive.

P. Predictable.

E. Equitable.

These are the elements of 'good governance', not all of them are visible, nor are they all spread in equal measure. Accountability and transparency stand out, and they form the bedrock of good governance.

Participation is a must, it makes everyone a stakeholder. Participation in decision-making, implementing plans and policies, raising issues, carrying the message forward, and building consensus are vital for robust and good governance. The 73rd/74th amendment to the Constitution ushered in 'Panchyati Raj', an experiment to bring governance to the grassroots. It found acceptance, even if slowly.

Today, participation is enthusiastic, intense, and meaningful.

Accountability is at the heart of good governance. Without it, governance can lapse into irregularities, corruption, and bias. Before the country got its freedom, the British were not too keen to be accountable, least to us. We now have a system of checks and balances, and ultimate accountability to the legislature and the judiciary.

The 73rd/74th amendment to the Constitution ushered in 'Panchyati Raj', an experiment to bring governance to the grassroots. It found acceptance, even if slowly.

Responsive governance is best served when it is responsive to the needs of the people. It is seen often that governments which are not responsive face the wrath of the people. The oft quoted example is of the Congress government at the Centre in 1977 losing power all too suddenly after nearly two years of emergency. It had become insensitive to the crying need of a crying population; the ragtag-condition government which replaced it came with a bang and left with a whimper. Transparency is the key to governance. Without transparency, governance is like 'Hamlet' without Prince of Denmark or 'Bhagavad Gita' without Lord Krishna. Right to information is at the base of transparency. Governance can't be a cloak and dagger operation: it has to be open, visible, and understandable. Both accountability and transparency will be dealt with at length.

The rule of law to us in the country is not so readily understandable because it is there with us. The Constitution has ensured that without the rule of law, the country would be face to face with anarchy, jungle raj, and disorder. Today, everyone accepts the Supreme Court as Supreme, its verdict is final. In our minds the tussle between the Parliament and Supreme Court in late 70s is still fresh. Judicial review was ultimately accepted. Without a well laid out 'rule of law', no foreign businessman will come here.

Efficiency and effectiveness are essential to governance. Efficiency is doing things rightly and effectiveness is doing right things, says Shiv Khera. Governance embraces both, rightly and doing it the right way. Mussolini found only these two elements as key to governance; he soon dragged his country to war. We in India faced a dismal power situation, leading to shortages, power cuts, and drop in output. But, with an efficient turnaround, we are now well served, we are not power starved. Examples abound, we are a nation on the move.

Consensus is essential to good governance. Meeting of minds is a key prerequisite for acceptance and implementation of plans and policies. Sometimes it takes months and even years to build consensus. Our Constitution evolved through consensus. The present government at the centre had to withdraw its land bill for want of consensus. GST bill got delayed for want of consensus but ultimately found it when even die-hard sceptical opponents who termed it as 'God Sent Trouble' (GST) pulled their lot with the government. Government run by consensus is every government's dream; it ensures better implementation.

Inclusiveness is not a fad or a fancy or a force. It is an imperative need. Carrying everyone along is inclusiveness. After independence, we launched into our Five-Year Plans laying stress on development but this development created stress. The gulf between the 'haves' and 'have-nots' increased; disparities led to rise of left-wing extremism (LWE). By the Sixth plan onwards, social justice found increasing acceptance. Eleventh plan firmly endorsed it further. We are racing against time having been timed against the race till 1980s. We look to catch up with China which is no mean task.

Predictable...? Yes, governance needs to be predictable. Flip-flops, frequent change of policies, plans, and the policy of *predictable to be unpredictable* do not advance the cause of governance. The 'Junta' government from 1977–1980 was predictably dangerous and dangerously predictable too; one of its Cabinet ministers, for a while, sat in a park to break the tradition set by his predecessors to sit in air-conditioned offices. Rain gods were not amused, they drove him back to office, sans air-conditioning. Who says governance is dull, drab, and despairing?

Equitable means fair and just. Governance without equitable ideals is like Mephistopheles selling his soul to the devil. Mussolini's Italy, Hitler's Germany, and Stalin's Soviet Russia were never believers in equitable systems; they were totalitarians.

Thus, we have seen 'Part Recipe' for good governance'. But then, as they say, excess of spices make any recipe unpalatable. What harm can 'SPICE' do? Let's look at the acronym.

S....Selectivity.

P....Population.

I....Ignorance.

C....Corruption.

E....Exclusions.

Selectivity is harmful for governance as it amounts to favouritism despite lack of merit. Favours bestowed selectivily create dissent and distrust, We have examples galore in the country of such cases; scams pointing to allegations in coal, 2G, 3G, Commonwealth games, and other cases are examples of selectivity. The entire system of license, permit and quota raj of 50s to 90s was an institutionalised version of selectivity. It bode evil for governance. 'All are equal but some are more equal', is the Orwellian prescription in Communist countries. Population is another retarding factor. With growing population, benefits get evened out; more and more resources have to be created to keep governance in place. India suffers in comparison, by contrast. Countries of western Europe and Scandinavia show best results in governance evaluation whereas India languishes at the bottom. China however emerges with better results but then the reports emerging from that country have to be taken at face value, given the state control. Ignorance can strike at the roots of governance. With an illiterate, ignorant, and ill-informed population, governance becomes doubly difficult. Often the schemes meant for such classes of people are misunderstood and ignored. Misuse of 'Jan Dhan' scheme in the wake of demonetisation is a recent, live example where gullible, ignorant people passed on their account details to the scheming, crafty rich, having ill-gotten wealth.

Corruption can finish off any governance and many a governance. We often hear of cases corruption in welfare schemes too: NREGA, Housing scams (Adarsh, etc.), and PDS irregularities are all examples of abounding cases. Some cynics say, 'You can take India out of corruption but not corruption out of India'. A very damning, uncharitable view totally unfair to the country's toiling millions.

Exclusions, often the bane of politics, is another issue eating into the vitals of governance. Quite often, some segments of the society are left out from the schemes and it does not augur well for the society or governance. The extreme backward and poor find themselves left out in India, given the indisputable fact that they have no political clout.

ROLE OF TECHNOLOGY IN GOVERNANCE

Governance today needs technology to reach out to the poor. For this it needs systems which have to be flexible to accommodate changing needs, accuracy to instil confidence and acceptance, safe systems which won't break down and will generate results on time. Only technology can ensure this. In fact, technology reduces interaction among men, thus reducing corrupt practices, delays, discretion and discrimination. Technology is neutral, and mercifully noiseless too. Governance has considerably expanded due to technology.

India's manufacturing and service sectors are driven by technology. The challenge now is to extend it toother sectors. The task is daunting and the challenges are demanding. *The benefits IT can offer to governance are listed here:*

1) Openness and transparency.
2) Alerting and educating citizens.
3) Empowerment of citizens through knowledge
4) Timely and trustworthy deliveries.
5) 24/7/365 service mechanism without manual intervention
6) Delivery of services at lower cost
7) Offers linkage between the administration and the citizens.
8) Effective mode and medium for grievance redressal.
9) Useful in monitoring performance.

The world is a village now; well connected, well served and well advanced.

The challenge however is to bring to fore technology to advance transparency and accountability.

Transparency and Accountability

Transparency is both a journey as well as a destination. Accountability is a destination, pure and simple.

The Eleventh Plan document highlighted six aspects of desired good governance:

1. Free, fair, and timely elections in all spheres of political authority
2. Transparency and accountability of all institutions of the state to its citizens
3. Efficient and effective delivery of public services
4. Effective devolution of authority, resources, and capabilities to panchyati raj institutions and municipalities
5. Rule of law where legal rights are clear and understood; legal compliance and enforcement of those rights is time-bound and swift
6. Needs and interests of hitherto excluded sections included with dignity

As may be clearly seen, transparency and accountability feature very prominently in the priorities but India's record in transparency is still very dismal. As per Transparency International, the country ranked 79th among 176 countries. However, given the size of our country, the diversity, division, and dynamics, it could well be argued that the ranking is manifestly unfair and unjust. Illiteracy and ignorance also contribute to lack of awareness of systems, schemes, and services available in an open manner. Comparing India with a small country with minimal population is not the right prescription.

Transparency in administration is built on a number of factors; in the absence of these, securing transparency is well neigh impossible:

1. Empowerment of local bodies with decentralised delivery. If everything is concentrated in Delhi, 'Delhi will remain far'.
2. Effective and speedy public grievance redressal system%justice should not only be done but seen to be done.
3. Right to Information–citizens must know, should know, always on time.
4. Accountability–the system should have inbuilt accountability. Citizens should not runn from pillar to post, nor the officials. Things must be in place–everything in place and a place for everything.
5. Ethics must govern in the system, duty should be equated with divinity. It must take roots in belief and practice. Slogans and oaths hardly ever translate to actual practices.
6. Laws, rules, procedures, and systems must be reviewed from time to time to be in tune with the aspirations and expectations of people. In many parts of the country, British-era forms are still in usage!
7. Technology is the most useful component in ushering in transparency. Citizens can access information and be better armed. Railway reservation system is a case in point. Gone are the days of dependence on counter clerks, always ready to counter you.
8. Notwithstanding all these, the corrupt should be tracked and corruption should be tackled.

Finally the system should have time bound clearances; it knocks the bottom out of the system of corruption.

Technology and transparency go best together heralding an era of openness with swiftness; an era of transparency within time schedule.

E-GOVERNANCES

CONCEPT

E-governance is the application of information and communication technologies to transform the efficiency, effectiveness, transparency, and accountability of informational and transactional exchanges within government, between government and government agencies of national, state, municipal, and local levels, citizen and businesses, and to empower citizens through access and use of information.

The rise of e-governance has been one of the most striking repercussions of the mindboggling use of the Web. Global shifts towards increased deployment of IT by governments emerged in the nineties, with the advent of the World Wide Web. The technology as well as e-governance initiatives have come a long way since then. With the increase in Internet and mobile connections, the citizens are learning to exploit their new mode of access in wide ranging ways. They have started expecting more and more information and services online from governments and corporate organisations to further their professional and personal lives, thus creating abundant evidence that the new "e-citizenship" is taking hold.

The initial introduction of e-governance in India started in the early 80s with an emphasis on computerising applications for defence services, economic planning, national census, elections, tax collections, etc. However, from the early 90s, e-governance has taken on a broader dimension, using IT for wider sectoral applications with a policy emphasis on reaching out to rural areas and taking in greater inputs from NGOs and the private sector. While the emphasis was initially on automation and computerisation, the later forays began to encompass connectivity, networking, setting up systems for processing information, and delivering services. The implementation of the National e-Governance plan (NeGP) in May 2006 was with the vision of making all government services accessible to the common man in his/her locality through common service delivery outlets to ensure efficiency, transparency, and reliability of such services at affordable costs.

The effective use of Information and Communications Technology (ICT) services in the Government has greatly enhanced existing efficiencies, driven down communication costs, and increased transparency in the functioning of various departments. It has also given citizens an easy access to tangible benefits, be it through simple applications such as online form filling, bill sourcing and payments, or complex applications like distance education and tele-medicine.

Some of the steps in e-governance that have been taken by the Government in the recent past are discussed in this section.

PAHAL (Pratyaksh Hanstantrit Labh)

The (Pratyaksh Hanstantrit Labh) PAHAL (Direct Benefit Transfer of LPG) DBTL ambitious scheme was earlier launched on June 1, 2013 by the previous UPA government with the objective of giving cash subsidy on cooking gas and it covered 291 districts. The present NDA government has comprehensively examined the PAHAL scheme and after reviewing the problems faced by the consumers, it modified the prior scheme and relaunched it in 54 districts on November 15, 2014 to cover 2.5 crore households. The second phase of this revised scheme started on January 1, 2015 to cover all the districts of the country. Under the previous scheme, it was mandatory to have the Aadhar number. For all consumers who did not have the Aadhar Card, it meant that they could not avail of the subsidy.

In the modified scheme, consumers who wished to join the scheme would have to either link their Aadhar number with their bank account and their LPG consumer number, and if they did not possess Aadhar number, they would have to link their bank account directly with their 17 digits LPG consumer ID. Once a consumer joins the scheme, he would get the cylinders at market price and would receive LPG subsidy directly in his bank account.

Currently, over 6.5 crore consumers, i.e., 43 per cent have already joined the scheme and will receive subsidy in their bank account.

DBTL is designed to ensure that the benefit meant for the genuine domestic customer reaches them directly and is not diverted. By this process, the public money would be saved.

DIGITAL INDIA

The Digital India initiative is a renewed push to address the delays plaguing flagship programs that focus on universal broadcast access and mobile connectivity. Direct spending via public-sector organisations like BSNL, Railtel, and PGCIL will be limited, but significant indirect demand will result from many more of the 68 per cent of India's population that lives in rural areas coming online.

The vision of Digital India programme aims at inclusive growth in areas of electronic services, products, manufacturing and job opportunities, etc. It is centered on three key areas:

1) Digital infrastructure as a utility to every citizen;
2) Governance and services on demand; and
3) Digital empowerment of citizens;

This programme has been envisaged and coordinated by the Department of Electronics and Information Technology (DeitY) in collaboration with various Central Ministries/Departments and state Governments. The Prime Minister is the Chairman of Monitoring Committee on Digital India activities which carefully monitors the Digital India initiative. All the existing and ongoing e-Governance initiatives have been revamped to align them with the principles of Digital India.

Digital India is composed of many phases, but the largest phase is last mile connectivity. While government is looking to connect all the gram panchayats (GPs) and common service centres through fibre optics, that's not the only thing that they need.

Government is now looking for entrepreneurs who could set up ISPs in rural areas to reach the last mile connectivity goal. Once small businesses start getting ISP licences, it will further accelerate the process. It will take a couple of years to reach that stage. An ISP provides Internet services leveraging digital infrastructure such as fibre optic networks.

Key Projects of Digital India

Several projects/products have already been launched or ready to be launched as follows:

1) The Government of India has undertaken an initiative namely BharatNet, a high speed digital highway to connect all 2.5 lakh gram panchayats of the country. This would be the world's largest rural broadband connectivity projects using optical fibre.
2) MyGov.in has been implemented as a platform for citizen engagement in governance, through a "Discuss", "Do", and "Disseminate" approach. The mobile App for MyGov would bring these features to users on a mobile phone.
3) Digital Locker system aims to minimise the usage of physical documents and enable sharing of e-documents across agencies. The sharing of the e-documents will be done through registered repositories thereby ensuring the authenticity of the documents online.
4) DeitY has undertaken an initiative namely Digitize India Platform for large-scale digitisation of records in the country that would facilitate efficient delivery of services to the citizens.
5) The online registration system under the e-Hospital application has been introduced. This application provides important services such as online registration, payment of fees and appointments, online diagnostic reports, enquiring availability of blood online, etc.
6) eSign framework would allow citizens to digitally sign a document online using Aadhar authentication.
7) Swachh Bharat Mission Mobile app would be used by people and Government organisations for achieving the goals of Swachh Bharat Mission.
8) BSNL has introduced Next Generation Network to replace 30 years old exchanges, which is an IP based technology to manage all types of services like voice, data, multimedia/ video, and other types of packet switched communication services.
9) BSNL has undertaken large-scale deployment of Wi-Fi hotspots throughout the country. The user can latch on to the BSNL Wi-Fi network through their mobile devices
10) National Scholarships Portal is a one-stop solution for end-to-end scholarship process right from submission of student application, verification, sanction, and disbursal tothe end beneficiary for all the scholarships provided by the Government of India.
11) To deliver citizen services electronically and improve the way citizens and authorities transact with each other, it is imperative to have ubiquitous connectivity. The government also realises this need as reflected by including 'broadband highways' as one of the pillars of Digital India. While connectivity is one criterion, enabling and providing technologies to facilitate delivery of services to citizens forms the other.

POLICY INITIATIVES IN E-GOVERNANCE

Policy initiatives have also been undertaken in the e-Governance domain like e-Kranti Framework, policy on Adoption of Open Source Software for Government of India, Framework for Adoption of Open Source Software in e-Governance Systems, policy on Open Application Programming Interfaces for Government of India, E-mail policy of Government of India, policy on Use of IT

Resources of Government of India, policy on Collaborative Application Development by Opening the source Code of Government Applications, and Application Development & Re-Engineering Guidelines for Cloud Ready Applications.

1) BPO policy has been approved to create BPO centres in different North Eastern states and also in smaller/mofussil towns of other states.
2) Electronics Development Fund (EDF) policy aims to promote Innovation, R&D, and Product Development and to a create a resource pool of IP within the country to create a self-system of Venture Funds.
3) National Centre for Flexible Electronics (NCFLexE) is an initiative of the Government of India to promote research and innovation in the emerging area of Flexible Electronics.
4) Centre of Excellence on Internet of Things (loT) is a joint initiative of Department of Electronics & Information Technology (DeitY), ERNET, and NASSCOM.

E-GOVERNANCE

ANALYSIS

E-governance reforms have been able to serve as a powerful platform for improving India's anti-poverty programs. Interventions like this may help the poor lead healthy and productive lives. The task now is to determine how to leverage this platform to maximise its impact on India's poorest. The merits and demerits of Direct Benefit Transfer (DBT) are mixture of hopes and assumptions, but DBT is in good spirit and will definitely benefit all stakeholders, i.e., government, beneficiaries, and private institutions. It will ensure right to economic equality by making every beneficiary gets his share on time.

While e-governance is often thought of in terms of online or internet-based governance, there are that many non-internet electronic governance technologies can be used in this context. Some non-internet forms include telephone, fax, PDA, SMS text messaging, MMS, wireless networks and services, Bluetooth, CCTV, tracking systems, RFID, biometric identification, road traffic management and regulatory enforcement, identity cards, smart cards and other Near Field Communication applications, polling station technology (non-online e-voting for instance), and TV and radio-based delivery of government services.

Objectives

One of the main objectives of e-governance is to promote citizen participation in the decision-making process and make governments more accountable. It enables active citizens' involvement by informing the citizens, representing the citizens and encouraging the citizens to vote, and by consulting the citizens and encouraging participation of the citizens in governance. It is convenient and cost-effective for businesses, and the public benefits by getting easy access to latest information without spending too much of time, energy and money to get it.

More broadly, e-governance is about transforming the nature of society from industrial to informative, and enhancing people's capabilities for socio-economic development.

Blogging and interactive surveys will allow politicians and public servants to note and understand the perspectives of the people they represent on any given issue. Chat rooms can place citizens in real-time contact with elected officials and their offices or provide them with the means to replace them by allowing their interaction directly with public servants. This allows voters to have a direct impact and influence on their government. Government transparency will give insight to the public on how decisions are made and elected officials or public servants can be held accountable for their actions. The public could become a direct and prominent influence in government/legislature to some degree. E-governance helps voters better decide whom to vote for in the future or how to help the public servants become more productive. A government could theoretically move towards a true democracy with the proper application of e- governance.

APPLICATION AND SUCCESSES

E-governance in India steadily evolved from computerisation of government departments to initiatives that encapsulate the finer points of governance, such as citizen centricity, service orientation, and transparency. The National e-Governance Plan (NeGP) of the Indian government launched in June 2006, seeks to lay the foundation and provide the impetus for long-term growth of e-governance within the country.

The National e-Governance Plan, takes a holistic view of e-Governance initiatives across the country, integrating them into a collective vision, a shared cause. Around this idea, a massive countrywide infrastructure reaching down to the remotest of villages is evolving and large-scale digitisation of records is taking place to enable easy, reliable access over the Internet. The ultimate objective is to bring public services closer home to citizens, as articulated in the NeGP vision statement.

The National e-Governance Plan (NeGP) of the Indian government launched in June 2006, seeks to lay the foundation and provide the impetus for long-term growth of e-governance within the country.

NeGP comprises 8 core and support components and 31 Mission Mode Projects (MMPs) encompassing eleven central MMPs, thirteen state MMPs and seven integrated MMPs. MMPs are owned and spearheaded by the various line ministries concerned. State governments are responsible for implementing state sector MMPs, under the overall guidance of respective line ministries in cases where central assistance is also required.

Under Central government's initiatives, the main thrust for e-governance was provided by the launching of NICNET in 1987–the national satellite-based computer network. This was followed by the launch of the District Information System of the National Informatics Centre (DISNIC) programme to computerise all district offices in the country for which free hardware and software was offered to the state governments. NICNET was extended via the state capitals to all district headquarters by 1990. In the ensuing years, with ongoing computerisation, teleconnectivity and Internet connectivity established a large number of e-governance initiatives, both at the Union and State levels.

Under state governments' initiatives, several steps have been taken to promote e-governance and states have drawn up a roadmap for IT implementation and delivery of services to the citizens online. The applications that have been implemented are targeted towards providing

G2C (Government to Citizen), G2B (Government to Business), and Government to Government (G2G) services with emphasis on use of local language.

States have MMPs on agriculture, commercial taxes, e-district, employment exchange, land records, municipalities, gram panchayats, police, road transport, treasuries, etc. Apart from MMPs, the states have other e-governance initiatives.

Implementation of NeGP

For the implementation of NeGP, the government is creating the common and support infrastructure through projects such as State Wide Area Networks (SWANs), State Data Centres (SDCs), Common Services Centres (CSCs), and National Service Delivery Gateway/State Service Delivery Gateways (NSDG/SSDGs).

The State Wide Area Networks (SWANs) scheme was approved by the central government. Under the scheme, technical and financial assistance is being provided to the states/union territories for establishing SWANs to connect all state/union territories headquarters up to the block level via district/sub-divisional headquarters in a vertical hierarchical structure with a minimum bandwidh capacity of 2 Mbps per link.

The Common Service Centres (CSCs) scheme established 100,000 + Internet enabled centres in rural areas to be implemented in a Public"Private Partnership (PPP) mode. The CSC scheme is envisaged to be a bottom-up model for delivery of content, services, information, and knowledge that can allow like-minded public and private enterprises–through a collaborative framework-to integrate their goals of profit as well as social objectives, into a sustainable business model for achieving rapid socio-economic change in rural India.

The Business to citizen/consumer or B2C services like e-learning, financial services, telecom-mobile charging/DTH recharge, utility services, employment services, railway ticketing, matrimony services, UTI-Pan Card processing. etc., are being offered/identified through the CSCs.

E-Panchayat

To improve the quality of governance of the Panchayati Raj Institutions, the Ministry of Panchayati Raj, Government of India has initiated the e-governance scheme known as e-Panchayats. E-Panchayat aims to cover all information requirements of the village panchayat, both from the staff angle and the citizens' angle. E-Panchayat strives at equipping rural folk with updated information. Data on gram panchayats can be easily obtained through Internet, and computerisation of comprehensive data incorporated seen.

To address all core aspects of panchayats' functioning such as planning, monitoring, budgeting, accounting, and social audit, the Ministry of Panchayati Raj has taken the full responsibility to manage the operations from a central station which has been set up in Delhi.

E-governance Projects

Many e-governance projects are under various stages of development and deployment in India: *Bhoomi* (land record management in Karnataka), *Akshaya* (IT literacy and local entrepreneurship in Kerala), *Khajane* (treasury network in Karnataka), *Gyandoot* (ICT to boost village level entrepreneurship in Madhya Pradesh), *e-Seva* (single window access to many government services in Andhra Pradesh), SARI (sustainable access in rural India in Tamil Nadu), and Honey-bee Network (knowledge centres for local knowledge in Gujarat). It is estimated that India has the largest number of pilot projects in e-governance today, and some of them have won awards like the Stockholm Challenge Award.

Some of the e-Governance projects are discussed below.

The Bhoomi project, an online delivery of land records in Karnataka, demonstrates the benefit of making government records more open so that citizens are empowered to challenge arbitrary action. It also illustrates how automation can be used to take discretion away from civil servants at operating levels. Nearly 20 million records of land ownership of 6.7 million farmers in the state have already been computerised.

Under the Interstate Computerised Check Post Project in Gujarat, ten check posts on interstate highways entering the state of Gujarat in India were computerised with the objective of tightening the inspection of incoming trucks for overloading and validity of documents. The essential components of computerisation were: a video camera to capture registration numbers of incoming vehicles; electronic weigh bridge for weighing truck to determine overload; and creation of a database of trucks to retrieve.

Aarogyam is a unique community based reproductive and child health related service delivery programme in the state of Uttar Pradesh based on an end-to-end usage of information and communication technology tools.

E-Sanchar integrates mobile telephony with information technology for generating voice calls for the timely transfer of information to rural citizens, specifically target groups including the elderly, physically challenged, and widowed persons. The project provides quick and efficient dissemination of information to citizens through database driven automated voice calls. This is to address the problems of deprived citizens, informing them of the government's interest and mission to adhere to the principle of SMART Governance.

Some Examples of E-governance

Some of the best programmes practised on transparency and accountability through e-governance in India are:

- Aarogyam: ICT based digital health mapping programme;
- Citizen Report Cards: Public Affairs Centre, Bengaluru;
- Community Scorecards of Government Schemes;
- Computerisation of Paddy Procurement under PDS in Chhattisgarh;
- Computerised Electricity Bill Collection and Online Remittance System;
- eSLA Monitoring System; Geo-informatics for Forest Rights;
- Grievance redressal over-the-phone;
- Husk Power Systems: Electrifying Rural Bihar;
- Implementing the Forest Rights Act in Madhya Pradesh;

- Improving transparency through e-Housing;
- Integrated Taxpayer Data Management System (ITDMS);
- Maha-e-Biz: Single Window Clearance Portal;
- Nirmithi kendra-Post-disaster housing; Odisha Disaster Rapid Action Force;
- Online Scholarship Monitoring System;
- Power Reforms, Government of Rajasthan;
- Re-inventing Targeted Public Distribution System in Gujarat;
- RTI Central Monitoring Mechanism;
- Sulekha-Decentralised Planning;
- Transparent Chennai: Maps, Data and Insights;

MODELS OF E-GOVERNANCE

E-governance can be classified under different models depending upon the kind of interactions involved and the agencies involved in the interaction. The primary delivery models of e-governance can be divided into the following: Government-to-Citizen or Government-to-Consumer (G2C), Citizens-to-Government (C2G), Government-to-business (G2B), Government-to-Government (G2G), Government-to- Employees (G2E), and Government-to-NGO (G2N).

The G2C model involves interaction of the government with the citizens to provide them information and different services. Websites publish information including procedures about government services. For instance, the citizens can simply download application forms for services like filling of tax returns and licence renewal. Government departments present many facilities and services at one place through Internet portals. Citizens can submit applications and even make payments online. The G2C model is applicable to education, medicine, transport, and other sectors.

In the C2G model, citizens give information on themselves, including their preferences, complaints, and suggestions to the government by making use of electronic devices (e-voting, for instance). This is an important component of e-democracy.

The G2G model involves connecting of different departments through network within the government for speedy communication between the government departments which would reduce time, expenses, and resources. Where the office management is computerised, that is, involving the personnel, accounting, office manuals, procedures and other activities, there is quicker and accurate processing of tasks, low handling costs, and reduced labour costs.

The government interacts with private and civil society actors to provide information and services in the G2B and G2N models.

BENEFITS OF E-GOVERNANCE

E-governance is convenient and cost-effective for governments, citizens, and businesses. The public benefits by getting easy access to the most current information available without having to spend time, energy, and money to get it.

E-government helps simplify processes and makes access to government information more easily accessible for public sector agencies and citizens. Procedures and processes for routine government services are simplified. E-democracy is simple and e-democracy services can reduce costs.

The anticipated benefits of e-government include efficiency, improved services, better accessibility of public services, and more transparency and accountability.

E-governance promotes efficiency in administration in different ways.

Transparency and Reduction in Corruption

The speedy and efficient dissemination of information for access by all citizens ensures transparency. It empowers citizens to ensure accountability and the administration is thwarted from indulging in corrupt practices. E-governance encourages openness, rules out administrative delays, ensures efficiency of administrators, and forces the government to be vigilant. Display of information on the Internet, for instance, reduces the tendency of the officials to manipulate information and misuse resources. People then become more trusting of the government. As the interactions are openly done, the officials have to be accountable and cannot mislead the people. E-governance promotes citizens' participation in shaping policies and improving the service delivery. Citizens can debate public policies before their enactment. Peoples' participation means ensuring greater transparency in actions and decisions.

Speed, Easy Accessibility and Efficiency

E-governance allows citizens to interact with computers to achieve objectives at any time and at any location, thus eliminating the necessity for physical travel to government offices. Improved accounting and record keeping has been possible through computerisation, and information and forms can be easily accessed. On the administrative side, information can now be stored in databases. Individuals with disabilities no longer have to be mobile to reach the government, they can participate in governance seated in the comfort of their own homes.

Environmental Benefits

Proponents of e-governance services point out that online government services would lessen the need for hard copy forms. Pressure from environmentalist groups, the media, and the public have forced some governments and organisations to rely on e-governance to reduce wasteful use of paper.

SCOPE OF E-GOVERNANCE

There are virtually innumerable fields where scope of e-Governance lies. Some of the most prominent fields are as follows.

E-Citizen

Under e-citizen, integrated service centres will be created. The purpose of these centres will be to take over the various customer services in due course. It will offer services like issue of certificates, ration cards, passports, payment of bills and taxes, etc.

mean that all citizens are in a position to access the information and services. E-governance involves use of computers, as well as wireless networks, CCTV, tracking systems, TV, and radio among other things. For countries that are developing and without a large amount of material resources at their disposal, acquiring many of these technologies would be a problem. Also, it requires some level of computer literacy.

False Sense of Transparency and Accountability

Online governmental transparency has been seen as dubious because it is maintained by the governments themselves. Information can be added or removed from the public domain (the Internet) with or without public notice. For example, after the terrorist attack on the World Trade Centre in New York City (September 11, 2001), the federal officials in the US removed a large amount of government information from its websites in the name of national security.

CONDITIONS NECESSARY FOR SUCCESS OF E-GOVERNANCE

For success of e-governance in developing countries, there is a need for adequate infrastructure particularly in rural and backward regions. There is a need for 'e-readiness' for promoting effective e-governance. E-readiness is defined by the World Economic Forum Consultation Report as the ability of the ICT networks to effectively adapt itself to the social and economic advancement which can be achieved by building up infrastructure and making leaders of government, business, and civil society more 'aware' of the benefits of e-governance.

E-governance can be promoted by establishing infrastructure and engaging in rural-centric e-government projects. Non-availability of adequate skilled human resources and lack of an appropriate strategy hinder use of ICT in governance.

There is a need for new laws and regulations to ensure accountability and supply of quality goods and services by the public and private sectors in e-governance. The discretionary powers need to be restricted and procedures have to be simplified. Regulations should ensure constitution of single windows for quick disposal of cases. Legislative regulations need to cover electronic signatures, electronic archiving, data matching and protection, cyber crimes, and intellectual property rights.

Socially relevant technologies and integrated management is necessary to ensure ICTs are used to deliver the full range of services in governance. For instance, the data has to be updated in local languages (the e-governance project should be in the local language and the project software has to be developed in the local language); standardisation is necessary in areas like encoding; data dictionaries are needed; procedural and legal changes in the decision and delivery-making processes are needed, and public–private partnerships have to be encouraged.

CITIZEN'S/CLIENT'S CHARTER: CONCEPT

The Citizen's /Client's Charter is a written declaration by a Government department that highlights the standards of service delivery that it subscribes to, availability of choice for consumers, avenues for grievance redress, and other related information. In other words, it is a set of commitments made by a department regarding the standards of service which it delivers.

Though not enforceable in a court of law, the Citizen's /Client's Charter is intended to empower citizens so that they can demand committed standards of service and avail remedies in case of non-compliance by service provider organisations. The basic thrust of the Citizen's/Client's Charter is to render public services citizen centric by making them demand driven rather than supply driven.

Citizens

Citizens are individuals, groups of individuals (companies, trusts, associations, unions, etc.) and the common public at large. They are outside the government and are generally referred to as external clients. Being outside the government machinery, the general presumption is that they do not have sufficient knowledge of the government's internal processes. Therefore, the onus is on the service provider to ensure that citizens are well aware of the service standards and the expectations from service recipients. It cannot be presumed that all citizens are literate or understand the official language, and it may be necessary to communicate with them in the local language also.

Clients

Clients could be government agencies and government employees availing services from another government agency. Services here will exclude administrative control activities, references, and opinions to be provided on policy-related matters which cannot be disposed-off within pre-defined time norms. Clients are part of the government and are generally referred to as internal clients. Being part of the government machinery, the general presumption is that clients have sufficient knowledge of the government's internal processes. Therefore, the onus of ensuring that clients who are also part of the government are well aware of the service standards and the expectations from service recipients is equally divided between the service provider and the service recipient. It is presumed that all clients are literate and communicating with them in the official language of the service provider agency is sufficient.

Note: The Charter prepared by the department may be either called a Citizen's Charter or a Client's Charter depending on whether the organisation is serving an internal or external client. It can be called 'Citizen's/Client's Charter' in case the service recipients are a combination of the two.

More on Citizen's Charter

Citizen's charter is a document which represents a systematic effort to focus on the commitment of an organisation towards its citizens in respect of standard of services, information, choice and consultation, non-discrimination and accessibility, grievance redressal, courtesy, and value for money. It includes expectations of the organisation from the citizens as well for fulfiling the commitment of the organisation. The term 'citizen' in the citizen's charter implies the clients or customers whose interests and values are addressed by the citizen's charter. It includes not only the citizens but also all the stakeholders, namely, customers, clients, users, beneficiaries, ministries or departments, or organisations and state governments.

Citizen's charter is a device that aims at improving public service by making those who provide the services accountable and responsive to the users. According to Arvind K. Sharma "The concept of citizen's charter espouses, quintessentially, the idea of citizen's entitlements vis-a-vis the government: entitlement to easy, unhassled access to public services, to services of stipulated quality and specifications, to efficient and courteous delivery of services, to a transparent conduct on the part of the service-provider, and so forth. At the level of application, this conceptualisation manifests itself in a range of measures, which by compelling a minimum level of performance from the service-provider conduces towards a higher level of user-satisfaction. In this sense, the citizen's charters address multiple concerns."This is done by letting people know the mandate of the ministry/department/organisation concerned, how one can get in touch with its officials, what to expect to by way of services, and how to seek a remedy if something goes wrong. The citizen's charter does not by itself create new legal rights, but it surely helps in enforcing existing rights.

Development of Citizen's Charter in the United Kingdom

The development of the citizen's charter can be traced to several initiatives taken by the British Prime Minister Margaret Thatcher to make public servants accountable and responsive to the people. These included compulsory competitive tendering, privatisation of public utilities, internal marketing especially in health services, the Next Step Agencies Programme and financial management initiatives. The Next Step Agencies Programme allowed for a distinction between the policy-making role of the government and its executive functions. Many governmental agencies were converted into Next Step Agencies. It was aimed to follow the agencies' full functional autonomy and to make them accountable to meet their targets. The financial management initiatives included strategic plans for all units, developing accurate income and cost accounting, and clear performance targets along with a system of sanctions and rewards.

Continuing the process of administrative reforms, John Major, on July 22, 1991, launched a political initiative called the citizen's charter. It aimed to improve public services in the UK by making administration accountable and citizen friendly, ensuring transparency and the right to information, taking measures to cleanse and motivate the civil services, and adopting a stakeholder approach. Major's 'programme for a decade' covered the activities of a range of public sector bodies, including the police, the health service, schools, local authorities, and public and private utility companies. It promised better quality for consumers through the publication of service standards, the right of redress, performance monitoring, penalties for public services, and tighter regulation of privatised utilities. Published charters set out the standards of service that consumers could expect and, in some cases, the compensation that could be claimed if performance was deficient. 'Charter marks' were awarded to the most successful providers of services. The guiding principle of charter marks, borrowed from the private sector, was that 'the customer was king'.

In preparing the chart, the organisation must first clearly describe its activities and the service it provides to the people.

The charter standards should be simple. They should be framed from the perspective of the users. The quality of service provided must be mentioned along with the time limit for providing a service. The standards must be realistic and must not raise expectations or be of such a high level that the users cannot abide by them. The standards should be measurable; they should be such that they can be monitored by the agency and the users. The standards should cover all users.

CITIZEN'S CHARTER INITIATIVES IN INDIA

There has been an attempt to introduce citizen's charters in a phased manner to make public services more efficient, clean, accountable, and people-friendly in India.

In mid-1997, the conference of chief ministers stated that governments at the Union and State level should work together to improve the performance of functionaries and provide an accountable and people-friendly government. It agreed that government departments and agencies with a public interface should introduce citizen's charters which would publicise standards of performance and ensure quality of services, provide access to information for citizens, provide complaints procedures that are simple, result in time-bound citizen grievance redressal, and independent scrutiny of performance of the organisation/department. Task forces were then established by state governments, with the help of field agencies and user groups' representatives, for the purpose. It was recommended that, to begin with, a few services should be taken up for implementation of citizen's charters. A core group under the chairmanship of secretary (personnel) was then established to monitor the progress of the initiatives taken by the ministries and their field agencies. State governments have since issued citizen's charters for departments and organisations in areas like municipal services, healthcare, electricity, education, and police.

The concept of citizen's charters has strengthened over the years. However, the problem is that though the physical features of the system–the client entitlements, the service standards, the timeframes, the grievance redressal mechanism and so on–are in place, the conditions for the system's success have not been met. For instance, there is the absence of a sensitised bureaucracy that would be a willing partner in setting up a client-led delivery system and lack of well trained functionaries who can take quick decisions and keep to the deadlines mentioned in the citizen's charters.

LIMITATIONS OF CITIZEN'S CHARTERS

The citizen's charter, though an effective way of ensuring clean and efficient public services, has some shortcomings.

The citizen's charter is based on the assumption that the consumer is always right. Sometimes the emphasis on the rights and needs of the individual consumer may come at the cost of the interest of the community. It may be noted that the responsibilities of the citizens are not mentioned in the charter.

There is no adequate mechanism to enforce the provisions of the citizen's charter. Moreover, it would succeed only if the complaint redressal system is effective.

The quality of service provided has suffered owing to tensions between the limited resources of the public sector and the desire to maintain quality especially with increasing privatisation and decrease in public sector investments. This has been seen in the operation of the citizen's charter scheme in Britain. Though the Citizen's Charter Unit in the central government has been providing general guidance and involving local people in preparing and implementing the charter, the system still has its shortcomings.

Charterism essentially concerns making the bureaucracy deliver services of specified volume and quality. As Arvind K. Sharma notes, "Declaration of the provider-obligations and acknowledgement of the user-entitlements invests the initiative with the power to make things happen. But because these are not backed by legal sanctions, the citizen's charters can at best exert a moral pressure upon the bureau officials. That notwithstanding, these would exercise, upon public systems, a pervasive disciplining influence, via their stringent codes...and stress on information sharing."

Public management has ultimately to do with maintaining a cost-effective system to ensure that public resources are devoted to achieving specified outcomes. The citizen's charters are a means to ensure that the public bureaucracies remain relevant by keeping them focussed on achieving intended results.

FORMAT OF CITIZEN'S CHARTER

The Citizen's Charter for a Ministry/Department should contain the following nine sections:

i. Cover page
ii. Vision
iii. Mission
iv. Service standards
v. Grievance redress mechanism
vi. Stakeholders/Clients
vii. Responsibility centres
viii. Indicative expectations from service recipients
ix. Month and Year for next review of the Charter

In what follows, each section is described briefly.

i. Cover page

To ensure instant recognition and user-friendliness, it is important that all Citizen's/Client's Charters have a uniform cover page as given below:

ii. Vision

This should be consistent with the Vision in the Results-Framework document.

iii. Mission

This should be consistent with the Mission in the Results-Framework document as well as Departmental strategy.

iv. Service standards

The information in this section should be presented in the following format.

* Main services include services that are being provided on a regular basis to the Ministry/Department's service recipients. Departmental services rendered occasionally

under exceptional or extraordinary circumstances should not be a part of Main services. These services should also have supporting grievance redress processes.

* Timelines are the most common form of service standard.

v. Grievance redress mechanism

Concluding remarks on Charter format

The formats above are the standard format for the Citizen's Charter for printing and dissemination by all central ministries/departments. It is imperative that the Citizen's Charter be kept user-friendly as well as concise.

SERVICE DELIVERY

Concept of Service Delivery Capability

The common meaning of 'capability' is the 'the ability to do something'. 'Service delivery capability' means the capability of an organisation to deliver services as per standards promised in the Charter. Capability of an organisation also means its ability and capacity expressed in terms of use of its Resources. Resources available with an organisation include the following:

1) Human resources: their number, quality, skills, and experience,
2) Physical and material resources: equipment, machinery, building, furniture, and fixtures,
3) Financial resources: ready finance, access to sources for additional finance when needed,
4) Information resources: pool of knowledge, database, and
5) Intangible assets: process designs, image and goodwill, patents, etc.

Organisations need to build new capabilities and upgrade existing ones, in order to ensure that they are able to fulfil the purpose for which they have been set up. In general, when organisations are created, they have limited resources at their disposal, and one of the activities that they must do is to find ways and means to access additional resources to improve their performances over time. With changes in the external environment of an organisation, new methods to acquire new resources have to be tried out. Over a period of time, organisations that are not able to deliver high quality services, due to limitations on their current resources, must find out legitimate ways to augment their resources, so that they can deliver. This brings us to the issue of how to define 'high quality service' or 'service quality'.

Service Quality and its Measurement

The word 'Quality' is generally associated with tangible products that can be measured in terms of quality of its physical attributes such as (i) dimensions, (ii) angles, (iii) weight, (iv) power (v) hardness, (vi) tensile strength, (vii) colour, and many other physical characteristics. Understanding the aspects of 'Quality' in the context of services is comparatively more difficult, as there are no measurable physical or tangible attributes. Even where they exist, they may not be directly affecting the essential nature of services. Therefore, Quality in services is about 'What really matters to the service recipient.' Although this is the case with both goods and services, it acquires a special significance in the context of public service delivery in general, and service delivery under the Sevottam framework, in particular.

There are several methods already developed to measure quality of service. For measuring and certifying quality of service delivery by public service organisations, a special standard has been created by Bureau of Indian Standards, called Indian Standard 15700:2005. The Standard defines:

i. 'Public Service Organisation as 'An organisation which provides service (s) to public at large and/or whose activities influence public interest. Example: Government ministries and departments, Regulatory bodies, public utility service providers, etc.

ii. 'Quality' as 'Degree to which a set of inherent characteristics fulfils requirement'.

Parameters for Quality in Public Service Delivery

In the implementation of Sevottam framework, three main areas have been found as the most common causes of inability to deliver services as per standards included in the Charter, and/or to meet expectations of service recipient citizen/clients. These are:

i. Absence of or incorrect understanding of citizen/ client expectations,

ii. Lack of motivation and training of employees, involved in the service delivery, and

iii. Non-availability of adequate infrastructure for service delivery.

Under Sevottam, it is the responsibility of ministry/department/organisation to examine its current position in respect of the three parameters and work towards bridging the existing gaps observed therein. For example, if the staff dealing with service recipients is not trained to deliver services as per standards in the Charter, the organisation has to arrange for the required training, either internally or externally, and also have a system of induction training for those who join the organisation later on from time to time.

LOKPAL AND LOKAYUKTA

Liberal democracies have a strong, element of welfare in the system besides just political rights. As more and more activities in the socio-economic field are taken up by government and the civil services, a complexity has developed in the system, and many discretionary powers are enjoyed by politicians as well as civil servants. This has led to an increase in power and a concomitant abuse of power by authorities. Citizens suffer at the hands of administrators. They are forced to pay bribes, and face harassment, delays, and inefficiency in service. Citizens' grievances against the administration have to be addressed and redressed. Different redressal systems have been in practice, especially in democracies. The ombudsman system is one such.

The term 'ombudsman' is derived from an old norse word that means 'representative'. Today, this term is used for an official usually appointed by the government or by parliament. He or she is charged with representing people's interests by looking into complaints and grievances of citizens. The modern use of the term began in Sweden, with the Swedish Parliamentary Ombudsman instituted by the Instrument of Government of 1809, to protect the rights of citizens. An ombudsman examines complaints from outside the erring state institution, thus avoiding the conflicts of interest inherent in self-policing. The Parliamentary Ombudsman is the institution that the Scandinavian countries (such as, Finland, Norway, and Denmark, besides Sweden) subsequently moulded into its contemporary form, and which subsequently has been adopted by many other countries.

Many countries around the world have the office of the ombudsman. These include Sweden, Finland, Denmark, the Netherlands, Austria, New Zealand, Burkina Faso, and the UK. They are called by different names in different countries, such as the 'people's advocate' or 'public defender of rights', and so on.

The basic idea of Lokpal and Lokayukta in India is borrowed from the concept of the ombudsman.

Recommendations for Lokpal in India

Several commissions have examined the need for a Lokpal and suggested ways to make it effective, without violating constitutional principles. They include: the first Administrative Reforms Commission (ARC) of 1966; the National Commission to Review the Working of the Constitution (NCRWC) of 2002 also called the Venkatachaliah Commission, and the second Administrative Reforms Commission of 2007.

The first ARC under Moraji Desai's chairmanship submitted a special interim report, 'Problems of Redressal of Citizens' Grievances' in 1966. It recommended that there should be two independent authorities to redress grievances: (1) the Lokpal, to deal with complaints against the administrative acts of ministers and secretaries of government at the Centre and the state; and (2) the Lokayukta in each state and at the Centre, which would deal with complaints against the administrative acts of other officials. The Lokpal should be independent of the executive, legislature, and judiciary. The Lokpal may either act on the complaints made by an affected citizen or on his/her own cognition.

The NCRWC recommended that the Lokpal should be a constitutional authority and that the Constitution should be amended to include a provision making it obligatory for state governments to set up Lokayuktas, but the office of the Prime Minister should be kept out of its purview to maintain the autonomy and privilege of the office. It suggested that a Member of Parliament could be prosecuted after the investigating agency received prior sanction from a committee constituted by the President.

The second ARC headed by M.Veerappa Moily, in its fourth report titled, 'Ethics in Governance' called for an urgent legislation on the subject as well as constitutional status for the institution of Lokpal. It recommended a Rashtriya Lokayukta at the central level.

The second ARC was in favour of including ministers, chief ministers, and Members of Parliament. However, it wanted to keep the Prime Minister outside the ambit of the Lokpal. The ARC also recommended that a reasonable time limit for investigation of different types of cases should be fixed.

All these committees felt that the judiciary should be kept out of the ambit of the Lokpal, unlike in Sweden where the judiciary is within the purview of the institution of Ombudsman.

The second ARC also recommended that the Lokpal should be empowered to supervise the prosecution of corruption-related cases. It recommended that prior sanction need not be required in cases where public servants have been "trapped red-handed or in cases of possessing assets disproportionate to their known sources of income".

Attempts at Introducing Lokpal Bill

A bill to create a Lokpal was introduced in the Lok Sabha by the government under Indira Gandhi, first in 1968 (which lapsed with the dissolution of Lok Sabha in 1969) and then in 1971, which also lapsed due to dissolution of the Lok Sabha.

In 1977, the Janata Party government brought its own Lokpal Bill, and this was the first time that the Prime Minister was brought under its ambit. The short-lived post- Emergency government fell and the bill lapsed once again.

Another bill came in 1985 and this time it was Rajiv Gandhi who was the Prime Minister. The Prime Minister's office was kept out of the Lokpal's ambit along with offices of the Speaker of Lok Sabha, Chief Justice of India, and other Supreme Court judges. The bill was withdrawn because there was no agreement on many of the key issues, including that of the Prime Minister being in or out of the Lokpal's ambit.

In the wake of the Bofors controversy, which involved allegations against Rajiv Gandhi himself, the office of the Prime Minister was back in the Lokpal ambit in the 1989 version of the bill brought in by the V.P. Singh government. This too lapsed. There were bills for the Lokpal in 1996 under the United Front government under Deve Gowda and then in 1998 under the BJP-led coalition government headed by A.B. Vajpayee. Both lapsed.

In 2001, the NDA government headed by A.B. Vajpayee introduced another Lokpal Bill in the Lok Sabha. In the 2001 bill, the Prime Minister and members of Parliament were brought under the Lokpal following the Supreme Court judgement in 1998 in the P.V. Narasimha Rao case where it was declared that MPs were public servants. The bill, however, lapsed due to dissolution of the 13th Lok Sabha.

Agitations by civil society groups led by Anna Hazare practically forced the UPA government in 2011 to set up a committee under the then union finance minister, Pranab Mukherjee, to draft a bill for the setting up of a Lokpal. By July-end, a draft had been approved by the government to be introduced in the monsoon session of the Lok Sabha. However, the bill met with much opposition.

The Lokpal and Lokayukta Act, 2013

The Lokpal and Lokayukta Act, 2013 provides for the establishment of Lokpal for the Union and Lokayuktas for States to inquire into allegations of corruption against public functionaries.

The Act was passed in accordance with the Constitution of India to establish a democratic republic to ensure justice for all, to implement the United Nations Convention Against Corruption ratified by India, and to fulfil the government's commitment to clean and responsive governance through bodies which contain and punish acts of corruption. The Act shall apply to the whole of India and to public servants in and outside India.

According to the Act, autonomous and independent bodies shall have powers of superintendence and direction for holding a preliminary inquiry, causing an investigation to be made, and prosecution of offences in respect of complaints under any law for the prevention of corruption. The Act provides a uniform vigilance and anti-corruption road map for the nation, both at the Centre and the states. The Act institutionalises the separation of investigation from prosecution, thereby removing conflict of interest as well as increasing the scope for professionalism and specialisation.

The salient features of the Act are as follows:

1. The Lokpal will consist of a chairperson and a maximum of eight members, of which 50 per cent shall be judicial members. Fifty per cent members of the Lokpal shall be from among the SCs, STs, OBCs, minorities, and women.
2. The five-member selection committee will comprise the Prime Minister, the Lok Sabha Speaker, the Leader of the Opposition in the Lok Sabha, and the Chief Justice of India. A fifth member of the selection committee for selection of Lokpal under the category of "eminent jurist" may be nominated by the President on the basis of the recommendation of the first four members of the selection committee.
3. The Lokpal's jurisdiction will cover all categories of public servants and members of Parliament. All entities (NGOs) receiving donations in excess of Rs. 10 lakh per year from foreign sources in the context of the Foreign Contribution Regulation Act (FCRA) will be under the jurisdiction of Lokpal. Bodies creating endowments for performing religious or charitable functions will be excluded from the purview of the Lokpal.
4. Before taking a decision on filing a chargesheet in a case upon consideration of the investigation report, the Lokpal may authorise its own prosecution wing or the investigating agency concerned to initiate prosecution in special courts.
5. For independence of the CBI, a directorate of prosecution will be formed. Appointment of the director of prosecution will be on the recommendation of the Central Vigilance Commissioner. The director of prosecution will have a fixed tenure of two years like the CBI chief.
6. Transfer of officers of CBI investigating cases referred to by the Lokpal will be only with the approval of the Lokpal that will also have superintendence over the CBI in relation to Lokpal-referred cases.
7. A government servant will get a hearing before a decision is taken by the Lokpal.
8. The Prime Minister will be under the purview of the Lokpal provided that the Lokpal shall not inquire into any matter involved in, or arising from or connected with, any such allegation of corruption against the Prime Minister, (i) in so far as it relates to international relations, external and internal security, public order, atomic energy and space; and (ii) unless a full bench of the Lokpal consisting of its chairperson and all Members considers the initiation of inquiry and at least two-thirds of its members approves of such inquiry. Inquiry against the Prime Minister has to be held in-camera and approved by two-thirds of the full bench of the Lokpal.
9. The judiciary is completely excluded from the ambit of the Lokpal.
10. Members of Parliament are excluded from the purview of the Lokpal in respect of their votes and speeches in Parliament.
11. Inquiry has to be completed within 60 days and the investigation has to be completed within six months. The Lokpal shall order an investigation only after hearing the public servant.
12. The law provides for imprisonment up to one year and a fine upto Rs. 1 lakh for false and frivolous complaints. Public servants can face imprisonment upto 7 years. Criminal misconduct and habitual abetment of corruption can attract jail terms of upto 10 years.

13. The central government would send this law to the states as a model legislation; states have to set up Lokayuktas through a state law within 365 days. However, states have the freedom to determine the nature and type of the Lokayukta.
14. Lokpal can initiate prosecution through the prosecution wing before the special court trial to be completed within two years.
15. All expenses regarding the Lokpal institution would be charged on the Consolidated Fund of India as charged expenditure.
16. The Lokpal is to be the final appellate authority on all decisions by public authorities relating to provision of public services and redressal of grievances concerning findings of corruption. The Lokpal is to have power of superintendence and direction over any investigation agency including the CBI with regard to cases referred to them.
17. The act seeks to make necessary consequential amendments in the Commissions of Inquiry Act, 1952, the Prevention of Corruption Act, 1988, the Code of Criminal Procedure, 1973, the Central Vigilance Commission Act, 2003, and the Delhi Special Police Establishment Act, 1946.

Inclusion of Prime Minister in Rashtriya Lokayukta's Ambit

The second ARC proposed to keep the Prime Minister out of the scope of the Rashtriya Lokayukta, as scrutiny by extra-parliamentary authorities is likely to undermine parliament's supremacy. The inclusion of the Prime Minister's post in the Lokayukta's scrutiny has been favoured in the past only by a minority among the political class with some Prime Ministers (such as Vajpayee and Manmohan Singh), also endorsing the idea. As Soli Sorabjee observes, the proposal to exclude the Prime Minister generated intense debate when the Lokpal legislation was formerly under consideration. The National Commission to Review the Working of the Constitution favoured the exclusion of the Prime Minister for the reason that he should not be exposed to the risks of well-orchestrated and well-planned attempts to malign his image and weaken his position on which the functioning of government depends.

RIGHT TO INFORMATION

Right to Information and Right to Service Act are important tools to secure transparency and accountability in India. Following a nationwide campaign led by grassroots and civil society organisations, the government passed a landmark Right to Information Act in 2005. Social activist Aruna Roy has described India's RTI Act as "the most fundamental law this country has seen as it can be used from the local panchayat to Parliament, from a non-descript village to posh Delhi, and from ration shops to the 2G scam". 'Right to information' laws, or 'sunshine' laws as they are commonly called, grant citizens the legal right to access information held by their governments, bringing much-needed transparency in the otherwise opaque functioning of the government.

A 2009 study estimates that in the Act's first three years alone, close to two million RTI requests were filed in different parts of the country. Case studies and media reports show that RTI is being used to redress individual grievances, access entitlements such as ration cards and pensions, investigate government policies and decisions, and to expose corruption and misuse of government resources. In addition to such initiatives, the law is increasingly being used to tackle high profile corruption. Much of the information regarding corruption in the allocation of tenders and contracts for 2010 Commonwealth Games was unearthed using RTI.

Right to public services legislations guarantee time-bound delivery of services for various public services rendered by the government to citizens and provide mechanism for punishing the errant public servant who is deficient in providing the service stipulated under the statute. They are meant to reduce corruption among the government officials and to increase transparency and public accountability. Madhya Pradesh was the first state in India to enact Right to Service Act on August 18, 2010 and Bihar, the second to enact this on July 25, 2012.

Apart from Madhya Pradesh and Bihar, several other states have passed or notified to the right to service legislations. They are Punjab, Uttarakhand, Delhi, Jharkhand, Himachal Pradesh, Rajasthan, Uttar Pradesh, Kerala, Karnataka, Chhattisgarh, Jammu and Kashmir, Odisha, Assam, and Gujarat. The central government has also proposed a Citizen's Charter and Grievance Redressal Bill, 2011.

Other good governance practices, apart from RTI Act and right to service legislations, to install transparency and accountability in administration are: public records of operations and finance; human resource management system; crime and criminal tracking network system; and integrated workflow and document management system.

It is imperative that administration is subject to the rule of law with an inbuilt system of accountability. There is considerable frustration particularly among the weaker sections of the society about apathy, irresponsive behaviour, and lack of accountability of public servants. Growing corruption in administration with a strong nexus with vested interest like politicians, criminals, business class, and some bureaucrats has weakened the body structure of Indian administration.

Transparency and accountability in the modern world are best facilitated by e-governance programmes as the scope for human manipulation is reduced when services are computerised. (Refer to the section on e-governance for some of the best programmes of this sort.)

Concept and Importance of RTI

The Right to Freedom of Speech and Opinion is meaningless when others are prevented from listening or knowing (access to information). So, in the sense, this also means the Right to have access to other's views and opinions. It is for this interpretation that the Right to Information (RTI) as a Fundamental Right emerges under Article 19(1) (a).

Need for RTI

Strong grounds have been advanced for the promotion of RTI.

1. Availability of this Right makes for the empowerment of the people who would otherwise be ignorant about the processes of governance.
2. The Right to Information, by removing unnecessary secrecy surrounding the decision-making process in government makes the citizens 'co-sharers' in public policy-making and administration. This helps improve the quality of overall government at the cutting edge level. It becomes much more authentic and people-centric when people participate directly and observe first-hand how the government functions in reality.

3. People's Right to Information brings about a major change in the 'quality' of government by making it really public. People's easy access to information about governmental operations as a matter of 'Right' makes these operations open and transparent. It ensures accountability and responsibility to people's needs and demands.
4. The Right to Information creates conditions for 'open governance' which are the foundations of democracy. By contrast, secrecy in governmental functioning tends to promote corruption, and misuse or abuse of public authority.
5. The Right to information is an investment in people's trust in government which is the basis of democratic governance.
6. Educating citizens about influence on local government is the product of openness affording access to government departments and documents and thus enabling citizens to acquire knowledge about the goings on in the government.
7. RTI is an ongoing process, not a one-time effort; it creates an environment of transparency and accountability.

THE RIGHT TO INFORMATION ACT, 2005

Right to Information Act was enacted by the UPA regime. The new Act affirms that 'democracy requires an informed citizenry and transparency of information which are vital to its functioning and also to contain corruption and to hold Governments and their instrumentalities accountable to the governed'.

The objective, as stated in the Act, is 'to provide for setting out the practical regime of Right to Information for citizens to secure access to information under the control of public authorities, in order to promote transparency and accountability in the working of every public authority'.

With the coming into force of the new Act of 2005, the earlier Act of 2002 has been repealed.

Features of the RTI Act

The RTI Act (Clause 3) provides that 'subject to the provisions of this Act, all citizens shall have the Right to Information'. The Act has defined the two terms–information and authority–very widely.

'Information means any material in any form including records, documents, memos, e-mails, opinions, advices, press releases, order, circulars, contracts, reports, papers, logbooks, samples, modes, data material kept in any electronic form, and information relating to any private body which can be accessed by public authority under any other law for the time being in force.

The term 'record' includes any document, manuscript any file; any microfilm, microfiche, and facsimile copy of a document; any reproduction of image and images embodied in such microfilm (whether enlarged or not); and any other material produced by devices including the computer.

'Right to information' means the right to information accessible under this Act which is held by or under the control of any public authority and includes the right to inspection of work, documents, records; taking notes, extracts or certified copies of documents or records; taking certified samples of material; and obtaining information through electronic mode as through diskettes, floppies, tapes, video cassettes, or through printouts where such information is stored in a computer or in any other device.

Only 'citizens' can request information from a 'public authority'. 'Public Authority' has been defined as any authority or body or institution of self-government established are constituted (a) by or under the Constitution, (b) by any other law made by Parliament, (c) by any other law made by State legislature, and (d) by notification issued or made by the appropriate government, and includes any (i) body owned, controlled, or substantially financed, (ii) non-government organisation substantially financed, directly or indirectly, by funds provided by the appropriate government.

It covers a wide spectrum of bodies and officials from the central government, the state governments, Panchayati Raj Institutions (PRIs), and non-governmental organisation (NGOs).

The Act provides for the constitution of a Central Information Commission with a Chief Information Commissioner and up to 10 Central Information Commissioners (CICs)

A similar set-up is envisaged for the State Information Commissions (SICs).

THE RIGHT TO INFORMATION: ISSUES OF CONCERN

The RTI Act, prima facie, surely marks a major step forward toward openness and transparency in governance. But there are many challenges that this Act has to face in the course of its implementation.

1. The bureaucratic culture of 'secrecy' is not easy to change. Structurally, procedurally, and behaviourally, bureaucracy in India has to prepare itself to accept 'openness' as criterion of good governance. The colonial mindset still prevails.
2. People in India, in many places; suffer from a variety of 'bondages'. The social bondages be it of caste, religion, or anything stand in the way of enjoyment of the Rights which are enshrined in the Constitution or provided in any statute. Thus, 'social freedom' through education and popular movements is the key to real assertion of any popular right.
3. Often in the past, it has so happened that a liberating and progressing legislation (e.g., abolishing child marriage or sati, for instance) will be actually internalised by the society only when appropriate 'people preparedness' will be taking place through liberating social movements. The example of Mazdoor Kisan Shakti Sangathan (MKSS) in Rajasthan is a case in point in the context. The success of RTI Act will ultimately depend on people's understanding of its real worth in day-to-day living.
4. 'Right to Information' of the citizens means the right of the citizens to share information that is with the government regarding all its actions (though exceptions may have to be made in matters relating to public order and security of the country). Most of the constitutions of the world do not mention right to information as a specific right of the people. The Constitution of South Africa is one exception.

INTERNATIONAL ORGANISATIONS AND THEIR STAND ON THE NEED FOR RTI

The United Nations has from the very beginning spoken for the freedom of information as a part of human rights. According to the UN General Assembly's Resolution 59(1) adopted in December 14, 1946 at the 65th Plenary Meeting, "Freedom of Information is a fundamental human right and the touchstone for all freedoms to which the United Nation is consecrated."

Article 19 of the Universal Declaration of Human Rights states, "Everyone has the right to freedom of opinion and expression; this right includes freedom to hold opinions without interference and to seek, receive, and impact information and ideas through any media and regardless of frontiers."

In recent times, the UN and its donor agencies have continually pressurised developing countries for making governance open and accountable to strengthen democracy.

The World Bank has stressed on people's right to information from public institutions and their right to participate in developmental policies and projects that have a bearing on their lives. So its Disclosure Policy ensures release of information on the institutions' policies and operations in time. It has emphasised on the Global Transparency Initiatives' 'Transparency Charter for International Financial Institution' to reveal its commitment to greater accountability and better governance. Contract and revenue transparency has been stressed in order to set up an environment conducive for civil society and media to monitor revenue-generating projects throughout implementation.

The United Nations Development Programme (UNDP) has recognised the right to information as fundamental for an open and democratic society, besides being a crucial means of fighting the challenges of poverty and promoting human development.

RIGHT TO INFORMATION ACT: ORIGIN AND PROGRESS

In India, the need to empower people and strengthen democracy by ensuring people's right to information has been seen as paramount by civil society groups and the Supreme Court. NGOs like the Lok Satta, People's Union for Civil Liberties and Association for Democratic Reforms have demanded electoral reforms and freedom of information.

History of RTI Act

The Supreme Court of India, in 1975 recognised the Right to Information as implied in the right to freedom of speech and expression [Article 19(1)] and right to life [Article 21] of the Constitution of India. In 1981 it stated that people can play a constructive role in democracy only when there is "an open government where there is full access information in regard to the functioning of the government". *(S. P. Gupta vs Union of India).*

Later, during the period (1994"96), the Fifth Central Pay Commission stressed on easy and speedy access to information and need for openness in government. It called for a Right to Information Act "somewhat on the lines of Canada and the United Kingdom".

In 1997, the Government of India established a working Group on Right to Information and Promotion of Open and Transparent Government, keeping in view the need for a full-fledged Right to Information Act to make government open and responsive. The working group made a draft bill that held that disclosure of information should be the rule, there should be well-defined exemptions, and there should be an independent mechanism for adjudicating disputes that may arise between citizens and public authorities. Later, at the Conference of Chief Ministers in May 1997, a statement was issued on the subject along with an Action Plan for Effective and Responsive Government at the Central and State levels.

The Freedom of Information bill, 2000 was introduced by the government but it could not be pushed through. Later, the Freedom of Information Act was passed, in 2002. It provided for an accountable government and the freedom to secure information from the central and state public authorities. But the Act could not be enforced as it was not notified and values had not been framed. The Right to Information (RTI) Act was finally enacted and it came into force on October 12, 2005, after the repeal of the Freedom of Information Act, 2002.

RTI: ANALYSIS AND COMMENTS

The RTI Act has received overall appreciation as it is expected to make government functioning more transparent and change the lay person's relationship with the government. However, it is not free from flaws.

For one, the State Information Commissions (SICs) are to be financed by the states, many of which may not have the resources to set up the commission. The RTI Act does not specify how much money has been allocated for setting up the mechanisms that the legislation will require.

The major challenge that lies ahead is in formulating rules that will deal with the nuts and bolts of the legislation. These rules will have to look at processes relating to the receipt of request, selection and training of staff, developing user-friendly manuals to demystify and publicise information, and providing special legal status for information that is accessed.

16

CHAPTER

Role of Civil Services in a Democracy

OVERVIEW

Democracy and the civil services go together because they herald a system that delivers seamlessly and 'facelessly'. Civil service with its systems, procedures, and conventions and Democracy with its voice, versatility, and variability provide to citizens the best environment for development, growth, and sustenance. What we need to know are the rules of the game. How adaptable is civil service in India and how adoptable is democracy in India. Both the journey and the destination are fascinating.

INTRODUCTION

Hardly a month into our independence, the country was aflame with riots; Delhi was on the boil and everyday fresh stories of mayhem were bringing gloom, panic, and despair. India's Home Minister, Sardar Patel lay afflicted with a crushing back pain, when a group of civil servants walked in, an emergent situation needing attention at once. The leader of the group, an ICS (Indian Civil Service) officer opened, 'Sir, if you permit me, if I am kindly allowed with your kind permission and indulgence and due consideration. If I am allowed to make a submission with your permission.' 'Listen,' Patel advised, 'Government does not pay you for thousand rupees a month to take my permission to do your job. As a civil servant, you are expected to give your views, advice, and arguments. You are expected to guide me and for that you don't need my permission. If I like your advice, I'll take it, but you are expected to use your judgment, present your arguments, and submit your knowledge and show your wisdom.' This incident brings forth succinctly, some aspects of civil servant – politician relations in the context of working in a democracy:

i. There's a master–servant relationship between the elected representatives, the politicians, and the career-oriented civil servants.
ii. Civil servants are expected to use their experience, expertise, knowledge, and information, along with judgment to advise the representatives of the people, Ministers or elected representatives.
iii. The politician, representative of the people, will use his discretion to take the proffered advice: it may be accepted or rejected, either in part or full; or kept in limbo, if the politician dithers.
iv. Responsibility rests with the elected for the consequences of the decision, they being answerable to the people.

BASIC FEATURES OF CIVIL SERVICES

Historically, the relationship between the elected representatives and the civil servants has evolved over the years with the underlying principle of change with continuity. Civil servants are expected to offer the bedrock of continuity, and elected representatives, the essence of change. Civil servants are expected to conform to rules, regulations, and regimentation, the elected representatives to aspirations, anxieties, and altruism.

Civil servants work within a structured environment and elected representatives structure the environment. Over the years, civil servants have worked with principles of integrity, neutrality, anonymity, and civility; the elected representatives with eventuality, personality, and finality. The relationship between the two could be of synergy, lethargy, or leverage or dependence, independence, or interdependence–yet interdependence is preferred but we do have on occasions, a Tom and Jerry varient too.

> Civil servants are expected to conform to rules, regulations, and regimentation, the elected representatives to aspirations, anxieties, and altruism.

Even so, the dominant feature is that civil service has a set of rules to go by. Rules governing code, conduct do's and don'ts, precedents, expectations, powers, limitations, discretions, appeals, time frames, and above all, a sense of credibility exist to guide the civil servants.

Peter Drucker, the management doyen said, that in history two institutions succeeded over centuries without a parallel, the Roman Catholic Church and the Indian Civil Service. Both had a hierarchy and everyone in the service knew his role, function, and authority. A Pope in the Vatican could control all the Catholics and a meagre 500 + civil servants from the ICS, the whole of India. The secret was obedience, obeisance, and obligation. Organisations have existed for centuries, and services are the lifeline of any organisation. The acronym 'COACH' signifies it all: 'C' for communication, 'A' for Authority, 'O' for Organisation, 'C' for Control, and 'H' for hierarchy. 'COACH' is essential for any organisation to flourish and excel. The ancient Chinese, Indians, Greeks, Romans all had vast, well-run organisations. These organisations, under imperial rule, had set defined services of civil service with marked rules of hierarchy, authority, control, organisations and communication. Ancient Chinese civil service with code of conduct, India under the Mauryas, Guptas, Sultans, Mughals, Cholas, and Pallavas–all had a patently well organised civil service. Rules of existence, execution, and essence were all well-defined and understood. Basically, the service was crafted and created to execute the will of the ruler/emperor. France was the country to talk of 'Liberty, Equality, and Fraternity.' United States stressed on 'Liberty', Soviet Russia on 'Equality', and India always welcomed 'Fraternisation among people.' All these countries proceeded with the evolution of their systems. French during the French revolution derided Bureaucracy, the word having evolved from the Bureau table where four persons sat to dispense administration. United States evolved a system where with the exit of a President all the civil servants resigned, allowing for the incoming President to choose or re-appoint civil servants new or afresh. Soviet Union brought in the concept of committed civil servants: committed to the communist party, comrades' partisan policy, India grappled with a monolith, the Indian Civil Service (ICS), the heaven born, twice born, always blessed, Mai-Baap Sarkar. The ICS, also called the "Steel Frame", held the people in a tight frame of awe, respect, fear, and fancy. ICS was a broomstick, the British employed in India to confront, contain, and cleanse . Starting with Clive, who was amazed at his own moderation in relation to others in corruption, to Lord Cornwallis who despised, distrusted, and doubted coming of Indians to high posts in services, Dalhousie, Lytton, Ripon, and Curzon who, in various forms, tinkered or tampered with the service to further their colonial interest, Indian civil service remained a redoubtable force. Its critics called it a 'Law and Order' machinery, more articulate with expression, 'Neither Indian, nor civil nor service.' Yet, Indian civil service left a legacy: a wealth of experience, a storehouse of knowledge, a system of tradition, an example of integrity, and also a belief that success and achievement are there to be had, if you willed. The ICS ended as it began, neither with a bang, nor a whimper.

Elsewhere in Europe, in Germany, a notable thinker emerged, Max Weber. He firmly started advancing the case for Bureaucracy as the best form of Governance–Career open to talents, merit in a system of governance administered by set, defined rules and regulations, with reward or retribution as outcomes for duty or dereliction, output as measure for satisfaction–and bureaucracy soon emerged as the best, viable option. Soviet Union, United States, Britain, and France all opened up to it. Civil services became the lifeblood running through the system, and bureaucracy began to deliver. What then are the characteristics and functions of a civil servant? What constitutes the basic features of civil service, as rooted in the civil servant ? It is of essence to note that although all civil servants cannot be expected to be behaving, responding, and thinking alike, yet a common basic understanding of how to behave, respond, and think is not exceptional but desirable.

CHARACTERISTICS OF CIVIL SERVANTS

A civil servant has to:

(a) **Be full of integrity:** He should be seen to be a person of impeccable integrity. Without integrity, he is like a pack of cards that can be shuffled at will, for a bill, or for a till.

(b) **Be neutral in his dealings:** Not only neutral but seen to be manifestly neutral in his dealings. He can't run with the hare and hunt with the hounds. If he does that, the hunt will haunt and run will cramp. A civil servant should present himself in a manner desirable, not despicable. His neutrality is his asset, a bank balance. Partisan or side taking attitude can give small gains but in the long run, only pains.

(c) **Work in strict anonymity:** A civil servant must work from the shadows. He is like a lion but under the throne of elected representatives. He is to guide, advice, inform, intimate, implement, course-correct, give options, but never take the centre stage, upstage, or stage games.

(d) **Flexible:** A civil servants needs to be accommodative, flexible, understanding, rule- bound, and ramrod straight. Inflexibility is often confused with authority and discipline.

(e) **Emotional maturity:** Civil servants cannot afford to become panicky, unsure of themselves in the face of conflicting forces, doubtful of their principles when challenged, or amenable to influence. Civil servants should act with self-confidence, take decisions on rational basis, and think clearly.

(f) **Civil servant must be intelligent:** Civil servants should be intelligent enough to separate grain from the chaff but never chaff at anyone purely to poke fun, it can rebound.

(g) **Motivation:** Civil servants should be driven by self-motivation. Motivation gathers together all efforts to action and action to goals.

FUNCTIONS OF A CIVIL SERVANT

A civil servant has multifarious functions: Briefly he has executive functions, quasi-legislative, quasi-judicial, and public relation functions. Civil servants need to develop skills to meet the expectations of milieu of every generation.

(a) **Implementation:** Implementation of the policies of the government, even if he personally disagrees. It is a broad-based function involving many tasks, some routine, some not. This may involve stage-by-stage implementation.

(b) **Quasi-legislative:** Making rules and regulations where authorised by the legislature. Legislature enacts the law, delegates the function of making rules that are required to implement the provisions of the act, to civil servants.

(c) **Quasi-judicial:** There are many functions that have a judicial or legal component. Civil servants have to discharge these functions keeping in view the judicial visage. These functions are delegated to civil services by the legislature from the functions belonging to the judiciary. Adjudication should be through the administrative angle. Examples could be of arbitration, dispute between parties, levying of taxes, adjudication as appellate authorities, etc.

(d) **Image or makeover:** Presenting the government plans, policies, explaining the perspective, helping image makeover for the Government are also part of functions of civil servants. Quite often, as the civil servants have made or drafted the policy, they are in a better position to explain them.

(d) **Participate in decision-making:** Civil servants are often participating in decision-making in evolving policies, or their implementation or their review of implementation. They are accountable for their role and often some constitutional body or the other carries out annual audit or examination. While participating in decision-making, civil servants express themselves freely and for this, they are often welcomed. Functioning through committees, commissions, and confabulations is becoming more popular and acceptable as responsibility gets diffused while expertise gets the deserved nod.

ROLE OF CIVIL SERVANTS

Civil services is the name given to the collectivity of officers of the government. The term 'civil services' denotes the non-military wing of the government service. The civil services is a hierarchical organisation and bureaucracy is an essential character of the civil services.

In a democratic political system, the party with the mandate of majority of the people gets the controlling authority to govern; it is the politicians who have to fulfil people's demands and aspirations; they reflect the nation's will.

Parliament debates, resolves, and enacts laws; the cabinet initiates policies and legislation. These are roles of the politicians but Parliament cannot enforce the laws; the cabinet cannot carry out or implement them. It is the civil services that implements the policies that the political masters (who are the people's representatives) present to them in the form of laws and regulations.

The civil services is the instrument of the political executive to put policy decided by the political executive into effect. This is the ideal theoretical position, but in practice this type of balance often does not hold. To some extent, the higher echelons of civil services are also involved in the process of policy formulation. They supply information to their political masters and often suggest alternatives based on their expertise and experience.

The bureaucrats have no primacy and no supremacy in determining such macro-level national policies.

Though not the policy-makers, civil servants have the duty to tender professional advice and render assistance, as may be needed from time to time, to the political policy makers in defining and refining the policies. They play, most certainly, the significant crucial role in implementing such policies and taking decisions within the overall framework of such policies.

The subordination of civil services to elected representatives who act as law-makers and policy-setters forms a precondition of democratic politics.

Thus, a fundamental ethical duty of civil servants in pluralist parliamentary democracies is to subordinate themselves to political authority. They owe a duty of loyalty to the duly elected or appointed political masters, however transient they may be. In the same vein, they would have to show a spirit of neutrality and discretion in their official capacity as members of the administrative infrastructure of the state with regard to partisan politics, besides controlling their own personal preferences in the performance of their duties and responsibilities.

PROVISIONS IN THE INDIAN CONSITUTION REGARDING CIVIL SERVICES

The constitution of India has provisions to regulate and safeguard civil servants for their recruitment, conditions of service, tenure and dismissal, removal or reduction in rank. These provisions are a check on arbitrary use of power and excesses; allowing civil servants to work in the comfort of feeling that they are secure from any unilateral, arbitrary, biased, illogical, whimsical, haughty, emotive, rash decisions or judgements. Rule of law is of essence and justice, fairplay always of consequence. If civil servants err, they too could be held accountable, but again by the rule of law.

Constitution provides a level playing field, equitable norms and always a domain of positive certainty. It prescribes checks and balances, with fine consideration for checks on balances too.

Balance to regulate must also not go on overdrive, else checks suffer. The availability of avenues or options for civil servants to redress their grievances through court of law is a balance but over enthusiasm on part of courts could end up in an overdrive.

PART XIV

Services under the Union and the states:

Chapter I (CONSTITUTION)

SERVICES

Art. 309: Recruitment and conditions of service persons serving the union or a state. Subject to the provisions of this constitution, Acts of the appropriate Legislature may regulate the recruitment, and condition of service of persons appointed, to public service and posts in connection with the affairs of the Union or of any state.

Art. 310: Tenure of office of persons serving the union or a state

(1) Except as expressly provided by this constitution, every person who is a member of a defence service, or of a civil service of the union or of an all. India service or holds any post connected with defence or any civil post under the union, holds office during the pleasure of the President, and every person who is a member of a civil service of a state or holds and post under a state holds office during the pleasure of the Governor of the state.

(2) Notwithstanding that a person holding a civil post under the union or a state holds office during the pleasure of the President or, as the case may be, of the Governor of the state, any contract under which a person, not being a member of a defence service, or of an all India service or of a civil service of the union or a state is appointed under the constitution to hold such a post may, if the President or the Governor as the case may be, deems it necessary in order to secure the services of a person having special qualifications, provided for the payment to him of compensation, if before the expiration of an agreed period that post is abolished, if or he is, for reasons not connected with any misconduct on his part, required to vacate that post.

Art. 311: Dismissal, removal or reduction in rank of persons employed in civil capacities under the union or a state.

(1) No person who is a member of a civil service of the union or on all India service or a civil service of a state or holds a civil post under the union or a state shall be dismissed or removed by an authority subordinate to that by which he was appointed.

(2) No such person as aforesaid shall be dismissed or removed or reduced in rank except after an inquiry in which he has been informed of the charges against him and given a reasonable opportunity of being heard in respect of those charges.

All these three articles, 309-310-311, from the backbone of civil service's functioning. Art 309 defines the nature and dimension of their initiation. Art 310 outlines that civil servants function under the doctrine of pleasure; pleasure conveying acceptance and limits of tolerance, displeasure signifying unease or unacceptability. Art 311, provides both safeguards as well as predominance of principles of natural justice; an official can't be dismissed, removed by any authority subordinate to that by which he was appointed (safeguard) and no such person can be dismissed, removed or reduced in rank except after an inquiry where he is informed of the charges against him and reasonable opportunity of being heard (Natural Justice).

These articles give civil servants a whiff of freedom, an air of certainty and a feel of self-belief. Had these been not there, civil servants would have been subject to order, authority, direction, decision and determination - not rooted in law. Civil servants would be subject to pleasure but vicarious one, their tenure uncertain and recourse to natural justice denied. If these articles were not there, it would back to middle ages, back to despotism, back to games without rules, back to authority without responsibility.

Articles 323- A provides: Parliament may, by law, provide for the adjudication or trial by administrative tribunals of disputes and complaints with respect to recruitment and conditions of service of persons appointed to public services and posts in connection with the affairs of the union or of any state or of any local or other authority with in the territory of India or under the control of the Government of India or of any corporation owned or controlled by the Government. Today we have Central Administrative Tribunals, with a chairman and a member, dispensing justice reducing the burden on high courts, largely.

CIVIL SERVANTS : NEW PASTURES

An emerging trend, discernable lately, is the growing desire among civil servants to join politics, to start afresh. The wealth of experience, width of exposure and world of expertise, doubtless gives them a ready advantage. Politics is not new field for them given the time they spend working with elected representatives. While many join politics after retirement, it is the serving civil servants, who resign their plum jobs to join politics that raise curiosity. We already have sizeable number of cases of nominations to the upper house from civil servants, mostly retired, yet the rising numbers willing to face the rough and tumble of politics is indeed a surprise.

No doubt it is a happy trend as politics needs entry of qualified, experienced persons who have seen the other side of the fence. Among civil servants there exist many specialists, professionals and very competent personnel who can enrich and enliven the political arena. Moreover, these civil servants may strike a harmonious chord with the serving civil servants and understand their issues much better. Another marked advantage could be the experience of civil servants evolving policies in as much as they can visualize what is possible within the realm and what is not. Like what time frames can be realistic, what not. Civil servant turned politicians can bring a degree of freshness that politics needs, or it would be derisively said, as usual, that politics is all talk. Track record of civil servants is therefore important. As you may have guessed it, politicians have only "sound track record."

Governance

Model questions with answers

Q. Discuss the salient features of National Land Records Modernisation Programme (NLRMP), under e-governance and its benefits.

A. The main features of National Land Records Modernisation Programme (NLRMP) are:

- Data entry of all records
- Digitization of maps
- Interconnectivity between revenue offices
- Use of GPS
- Modern record room/land records management

Benefits

- Real time records will be available to citizens
- Property owners will have free access to records from their websites
- PPP mode of service and free accessibility will reduce interface between citizens and government functionaries
- Abolition of stamp papers
- Conclusive title will reduce litigation
- Certificates on land data will be available to people through computers

Q. Drones should be made an essential part of policing in urban metropolises. Do you agree?

A. Drones are unmanned aerial vehicles fitted with high-definition cameras. As there are not enough police personnel doing quality surveillance, drones can be utilised.

Traffic violators can be hauled up, as exact location of violations can be mapped by drones. Thermal sensors can aid in catching suspected and hiding criminals. Videos and pictures can be sent at once to police headquarters. These would also verify known criminals in records. Riot –affected areas can be also surveyed and suspect persons who instigate trouble can be rounded up. Delhi police used drones to keep watch in riot-affected Trilokpuri. Search for missing persons during fairs can be done through this highly developed technology. But police may misuse drones to spy on whoever they want, like RTI activists. There should be regulation for judicious and legitimate use of drones.

Q. The government is thinking of bringing transparency in administration, through TORA. What is it ? Analyse.

A. After the Economic Survey suggested introduction of TORA (Transparency of Rules Act), the government is thinking of bringing in a new law to ensure transparency of rules.

Need for TORA

- It is not easy for ordinary citizens to navigate the multitude of rules, regulations, forms, taxes and procedures which are further updated and changed as per the requirement.
- All this causes inefficiency, and delay. It is also an important source of corruption and endless litigation.
- The '**Three Year Agenda**' by NITI Aayog also talks about the need for creation of a repository of all existing Centre and State laws, rules and regulations.

Features of TORA

The proposed legislation would have the following three elements.

- It would make it mandatory for all departments to place before every citizen every rule, regulation, form and other requirement on its website (preferably in English, Hindi and regional language). Once a department is declared "TORA-compliant", any rule that is not explicitly on the website would be deemed not to apply.
- It will further specify that all laws, rules and regulations need to be presented as updated and as a unified whole at all times.
- The websites should clearly state the date and time when each change is made. Laws would normally be applicable after the rule has been posted to give citizens a reasonable time to comply. The officials cannot retrospectively change the rules.

Significance

All the three features are crucial for addressing issues like lack of awareness, delay and corruption.

The proposed law is solely concerned about the ease of finding out these varied rules and regulations that the citizens are expected to know about. It will also support the Digital India initiative.

Once a department has shifted to the platform, it can be deemed "TORA-compliant" and citizens can be sure that the information is authentic and updated.

Q. What is PRAGATI?

A. PRAGATI stands for Pro-Active Governance and Timely Implementation, which is a new multipurpose platform set up by the Union government to address grievances of people, monitor and review important programmes and projects of Central and State governments. It is a three-tier system, where the Prime Minister's Office (PMO), union secretaries and state secretaries work together. It uses three technologies– digital data usage, video conferencing and geo-spatial technology– for quicker monitoring of projects and redressal of grievances. It shows cooperative federalism at best, as chief secretaries and state secretaries sit together and discuss issues. The PM takes personal interest in such meetings where visuals and data are presented, by union secretaries. Chief Secretaries and other secretaries get three days to answer questions.

Q. What is the new 360-degree rating system for bureaucrats?

A. The novel 360-degree rating system for bureaucrats is one of the major administrative reforms by the government. It is a new multi-source feedback system for performance appraisal of bureaucrats, started by the current government for future postings. The system seeks to look beyond the ratings received in appraisal reports written by the bureaucrats' bosses. It relies on feedback of juniors and colleagues for an all-round view.

Criticism of the rating system

According to the Second Administrative Reforms Commission, in the context of India, strong hierarchical structures exist. Therefore, for historical and social reasons it may not be possible to introduce this system unless concerns of integrity and transparency are addressed. The rating system is not apt. The Commission also feels that the 360-degree approach does not have any statutory backing, or supported by any Act.

Advantages of 360-degree system

Improves credibility of performance appraisal as it reduces bureaucrat's zone of maneuverability such as lobbying the minister concerned for a job in his department, or even other senior bureaucrats in key positions.

- It provides feedback from all angles and bring to table differing opinions and perspectives.
- It positively impacts the work culture of an organisation.

Q. What is meant by 'Minimum government, maximum governance?'Has this been practised? Elaborate.

A. The present Indian government is elected with the slogan of 'Minimum government, Maximum governance'. A citizen friendly and accountable administration is the focus of such type of government.

Minimum government, as practised by Margaret Thatcher or Ronald Reagan, means a complete retreat of the state from spheres of economic activity.

But in the Indian context it means state should retreat from spheres where it plays an obviously counterproductive role, like over-regulation, overspending, etc leading to ballooning fiscal deficit, particularly due to careless populism, crowding out the productive private sector.

On the other hand, the state cannot retreat altogether, especially in a developing country like India. It has to be more efficient in providing security/law and order or the provision of public facilities like sanitation, primary education and primary healthcare or in the building of critical infrastructure like roads, ports and railways, all areas where private sector cannot be fully entrusted with the task.

During the last three years, the government is encouraging participation of private players through initiatives like Public-Private Partnership (PPP) particularly in infrastructural projects, labour reforms, making provisions for ease of doing business (single window clearance), increased FDI in different sectors etc.

The Union government has rationalised the Centrally Sponsored Schemes, abolished Planning Commission which adopted 'top-down' and 'One Size Fits All' approach, increased the devolution of revenue to the states to 42% of the total revenue collection of the union government and increased the proactive roles of the state in nation building. For the first time, States have a say in Union policy – subcommittees of CMs have studied Skill India, Swachh Bharat, centrally sponsored schemes and digital payments. On land and labour, which are in the concurrent list, the Union government is encouraging States to legislate liberal laws. NITI Aayog is providing model land-leasing laws. There is now a ranking of States on the Ease of Doing Business. There will soon be indices for health, education and water outcomes. Union government's role is limited to conceptualizing the indices and monitoring their integrity and, of course, sharing best practices and model laws. The rest is in the domain of the States.

Q. The Supreme Court has recently said that safe custody, storage space and surveillance for seized drugs should be given by states. Critically examine.

A. The problem of seized drugs disappearing or appearing in recirculation has assumed massive proportions. Many drugs like hashish, heroin and ganja are again coming back into market, despite seizures. The drugs are again consumed by old and new addicts. The reasons for this sorry state of affairs are:

- the drugs are stored in police malkhanas
- there is no record of safe custody or destruction of seized drugs
- the drugs are kept for analysis purposes for many years
- for court cases, the drugs are claimed to be kept for evidentiary value

When seized drugs are kept for years together, they are stolen or disappear. Many times, drugs have been known to vanish from police malkhanas. The problem has become so serious and acute that the Supreme Court has asked Solicitor General to consult officers about this menace.

Q. Discuss implementation and performance of Right to Information Act.

A. The Right to Information Act empowers people with information so that the citizens can use the info to assert their rights and check government apathy, misuse and indifference.

But, many areas are still outside the ambit of the Act. For example, law enforcement agencies are not covered. The judiciary and legislature are hardly under the scope of the Act. The Official Secrets Act restricts the functioning of the Act, as matters related to security and integrity are taboo. For example, files relating to Subhash Chandra Bose were not released for many long ears. There is no deadline set from government departments to give information.

Public interest litigation in courts has been successfully used by practitioners of Right to Information Act in our country.

The government departments give information, but in a highly mysterious language and technical verbose words. Information is not fully automated. Yet, it can't be denied, Right to Information Act is a tool to check excessive use of power.

Q. Civil servants are not equipped with sufficient knowledge and information about their posting. Comment.

A. A civil servant posted in telecom department must have knowledge about spectrum, wavelength, pricing policy and health hazards. To enter into contracts with private entities, a civil servant must know the service rules and laws. Thus, the civil servants must have a broad understanding of both ground realities and technical nitty-gritties. Their general training does not impart technical prowess and field knowledge. The ARC and Hota Committee had recommended that domain specialization in form of diploma training should be given to civil service officers.

Q. What are the new changes made in Prevention Of Corruption Act (PCA), 1988 ?

The Union Cabinet has given approval to amend the Prevention of Corruption Act, 1988 through the Prevention of Corruption (Amendment) Bill, 2013.

Proposed Amendments

The proposed amendments would fill in perceived gaps in the domestic anti-corruption law and also help in meeting the country's obligations under the United Nations Convention Against Corruption (UNCAC) more effectively.

FEATURES

- Provides for more stringent punishment for offences of bribery both for the bribe giver and the bribe taker.
- Penal provisions enhanced from minimum 6 months to 3 years and from maximum 5 years to 7 years. The seven year imprisonment brings corruption to the heinous crime category.
- To contain illegal benefits from profits of corruption, the powers of attachment are proposed to be conferred upon the trial Court (Special Judge) instead of the District Court.
- The provision for containing inducement of public servants to commercial entities is being added to check corruption.
- Providing for issue of guidelines for commercial organizations to prevent persons associated with them from bribing a public servant.
- The average trial period of cases under the Act in the last 4 years has been above 8 years. It is proposed to ensure speedy trial by providing a trial completion within 2 years.
- Non-monetary gratification has been covered within the definition of the word gratification.
- By way of explanation 2 to Section 7(2), the obligation of a public servant has been explicitly delineated such that the public servant deters from violating a statutory duty or any set of rules, government policies, executive instructions and procedures

Q. Are PILs losing their relevance? Discuss.

A. Public Interest Litigations (PILs), which were originally initiated for taking up the cause of the poor and marginalised sections of society, have, over the years changed. In a recent case, the Chief Justice of Supreme Court castigated the NGO, which filed a PIL for becoming a "proxy litigant" and using the PIL as a front for "settling corporate rivalry and personal vendetta." The original purpose of protecting fundamental rights of disadvantaged and under-privileged seems to have been lost. At present, PILs are being filed for collective rights also. In PIL, the law is more flexible, the judge expands functions to become an ombudsman and monitor. Hence, PILs are filed to gain advantage by interested parties. The judge is forced nowadays to ask whether the PIL has been verified or scrutinised, to avoid frivolous PILs.

Q. The Supreme Court was meant to be a constitutional court. But it is finding that it is unable to devote time to constitutional issues. Examine the problems and suggest solutions.

A. The Supreme Court finds itself dealing with landlord tenant cases, whereas it was primarily meant to deal with constitutional cases. In the early years after independence, it was handling 15% constitutional cases, but now 0.12% constitutional cases only are being attended. There are many reasons. In 2016, the backlog of cases in the Supreme Court was 59,468, which means there is little time for constitutional cases hearing. Mundane cases arrive for judgments. The solutions are:

- there should be cassation benches in the four major metros of the country namely New Delhi, Mumbai, Kolkata and Chennai
- a national court of appeal can be set up, which can handle cases, after high court hearing. This court can settle mundane cases. But there is no legislative sanction for such a court .
- Two constitutional benches can be set up to hear cases every week
- the e-court project of Supreme Court should be implemented so that cases are settled fast
- single chamber judges should hear cases where there is no substantial question of law

Q. What is UBIN ?

A. Unique Business Identification Number is a new project of Department of Industrial Policy and Promotions. It allows budding entrepreneurs to start business without delay. Previously, one had to approach registrar of companies for identification number, then get PAN from income tax department, or go to indirect tax office, get formalities done at import and export departments and procure labour identification number from labour department. But with UBIN, all these separate formalities have been done away with.

Q. Does having women on board promote corporate governance?

A. The Companies Act, 2013 and SEBI guidelines have made it compulsory to have one woman director on corporate board. In countries of Europe, 25% women are on companies boards. Here, the easy way is taken out y having one woman from promoter family on board. Having women on company board means a lot of improvement in a way the firm works. Women take responsibilities seriously, fewer risks are taken, there is orderliness in boardroom, efforts for consensus are made, and they are respectful towards office management. In fact, there should be two women on board. One of them, at least, should be an independent director.

Q. What are the views of the Supreme Court (SC) on precondition of "sanction" for prosecution of a public servant under Section 19 of Prevention of Corruption Act? Have these opinions impacted the fight against corruption?

A. The conflicting views of the Supreme Court on the precondition of "sanction" for prosecution of a public servant under Section 19 of the Prevention of Corruption (PC) Act, 1988 have allowed unscrupulous public servants to stifle criminal investigation.

Section 19 of the PC Act states: "No court shall take cognizance of an offence... alleged to have been committed by a public servant except with the previous sanction."

The provision aims to balance two competing interests.

One is the need to ensure that an honest public servant is not hounded in the performance of his or her duties by frivolous complaints.

The other is that investigation into an allegation of crime isn't stifled at the threshold due to the power wielded by a public servant.

SC Views in favour of Section 19

Validity of Section: In *Manzoor Ali Khan vs Union of India (2015) and Subramanian Swamy (2014)* case it was held that the provision for sanction of prosecution in a corruption case is not unconstitutional, as mere possibility of abuse cannot be a ground to declare a provision unconstitutional, but executive needs to expedite the sanction process.

It has healthy objective of protecting an innocent public servant against unwarranted and mala fide prosecution *(Aiyappa vs Anil Kumar (2013)* and *Narayana Swamy vs State (2016)* cases)

Counter-View

- In *Subramanian Swamy vs Union of India 2014) case*, the SC held Section 6A of the Delhi Special Police Establishment Act, which required prior sanction for investigation as invalid (Similar views in *Rajasthan vs Raj Kumar-1998* and *R.R. Chari vs. State-1951*).
- Undermines core constitutional values of justice, equality, liberty and fraternity, as status of offender is not relevant during investigation of crime.
- By imposing a restriction on investigation by police at preliminary level itself, it subverts judicial process
- Protection to dishonest and corrupt politicians and government officials even after proof of their involvement has been found is known to have taken place. Eg. Captain Satish Verma (96) for arbitrarily allocating petrol pumps.
- Subjugation of constitutional and judicial provisions occurs as there is violation of Art. 14 (Equality before law) and restraining powers imposed on court to punish the culprit.
- Not in line with the provisions under the Lokpal and Lokayukta Act, 2013
- High-ranked officials can pressurise the police for not registering an FIR and threaten the victim, and courts would remain powerless to initiate any action.
- Instill fear among citizens regarding informing about crime

A relook at Section 19 is therefore essential. It needs to be reworked. There is need to protect a public servant against mala fide prosecution but where a lot of contrary evidence exists, he must be punished for the sake of probity in public life.

Q. If there is lateral entry of specialists into the civil service how should their training be imparted?

A. There have been demands to include specialists from outside the government into the administration, as governance is changing and private sector is entering the economy in a big way.

A specialist can bring knowledge, best practices, efficiency and a different look towards administration. But he may lack ground experience, personnel management, breadth and the dynamism required. A combination where some generalisation is imparted into specialist officers and some specialisation into generalist officers would strengthen the system.

Thus lateral entry into civil services should be accompanied by changes in career progression and specialized training for the directly recruited professionals.

- Acclimatize the new entrants to work environment in the public institutions.
- There must be short duration courses to give in-depth knowledge of all facets of administration.
- Lateral entrants must be trained to understand the lacunas of the public institutions. Training should help them to take bold decisions to check policy paralysis.
- Once officers are allocated specialist positions, they should be afforded opportunities through training.
- They should be allowed to work in a non-governmental organization for a few years, irrespective of their area of specialization.

Q. Can blockchain system create a transparent and accountable system of government? Critically examine.

A. Blockchain, the underlying technology behind Bitcoin and other cryptocurrencies, has the potential to optimize India's fight against corruption.

Mr. X wants to send money to Mr. Y. The transactions get represented online as a 'block.' All parties get to know about it. They approve the transaction. The block is added to chain, which provides a transparent record of transactions. The money, then moves from Mr. X to Mr. Y.

Thus, a blockchain is an anonymous online ledger that uses data structure to simplify transactions. A bank's ledger is connected to a centralized network. However, a blockchain is anonymous, protecting the identities of users.

A more honest government is created, as a public blockchain records all information and transactions on the decentralized database permanently, publicly, and most importantly, securely. By allowing governments to track the movement of government funds, blockchain can hold state and local actors accountable for any misappropriation.

Blockchain also aids in bypassing the middleman entirely. For example, in conjunction with biometric registration data for authentication, citizens can pay for food. With Aadhaar cards, adopting blockchain could pave the way for a digital economy.

Practice Questions

1) Transparency and accountability are fine in promoting good governance but how can they be effective in the context of mass illiteracy? Comment.
2) Explain the concept and significance of e- governance.
3) What is National e-Governance Plan (NeGP)?
4) What are the challenges before the Indian bureaucracy in the modern context to deliver and excel?
5) Right to Information (RTI) is being misused and is not serving the purpose for which it was intended. Do you agree?

PART V

International Relations

17
CHAPTER

India and Its Neighbourhood

OVERVIEW

'Love Thy Neighbour', says the Bible. Well, the love could be one-sided, often as it is. India has Pakistan and China as its immediate neighbours, even if we have not chosen them. Both of them are competitive, combative and conniving, to put it mildly. We have Sri Lanka, Nepal, Bhutan, Bangladesh and Afghanistan, in the neighbourhood– to some extent cooperative and considerate. India has now launched a proactive Look East policy to enlist the support of countries like Myanmar, Cambodia, Vietnam, Indonesia, Singapore etc. How best we handle our neighbours, both immediate and those in the neighbourhood is the primary issue. It is a challenge as also an opportunity. But then in diplomacy, there are no permanent friends or enemies, only permanent interests. Can we ignore permanency of interests?

FOREWORD

The topics covered in Paper II of Civil Services (Mains) exam, so far, have understandable linkages as among Constitution, Governance, Polity, and Social Justice. Constitution has provisions and a road map for Governance, Polity, and Social Justice; similarly, Governance has clear association with Polity and Social Justice; Polity and Social Justice are also interlinked. What of International Relations? How does it find its presence here? Obviously, there's no direct linkage. Even so, for the country to showcase itself in the international arena, it goes without saying that it should have a strong, acceptable, and robust foreign policy. International relations is all about projecting and protecting the country's interest and getting reciprocity for the same. The topics covered here are India and its neighbourhood relations, relations with the developed and developing countries, bilateral, regional and global groupings impinging on the country's interests, and lastly the international institutions, agencies, etc. Essentially, it is all about how the country is positioned and placed vis-a-vis globally. To study these aspects, understanding the historical background is a must. International relations is a complex, evolving, dynamic process based on strategies and national interests. It is not mere coverage of events, meets, talks, and signing of treaties.

The matrix evolved here is simple, dynamic, and interlinked. In this chapter, India and its neighbourhood, the historical background of the country's past, has been traced to bring it to the present. Countries who are our neighbours and those in the neighbourhood have been covered.

India's equation with both the developed and the developing countries is around issues of national interest: A,B,C,D, and E: A- Agriculture (Economy), B-Balance of Trade (Trade) , C-Climate (Environment), D- Defence (Strategies), and E-Energy (Raw material).

Bilateral and regional treaties are covered outlining India's areas of thrust. A section on 'India and the world: A paradigm shift' adds to stimulate the interest. Details of international institutions are given with their organisational framework. The subject has been attended to keeping with the objective of meeting the requirement of the syllabus.

INTRODUCTION

'You can choose your friends, not your neighbours

Atal Bihari Vajpayee, former Indian Prime Minister

Two ex-Presidents of the United States were being briefed about the emerging scenarios in the Indian Ocean when they got interested about the islands, Andaman and Nicobar, and when informed of these being with India, they looked incredulous. 'What? Assets the British created for India? These islands are closer to Myanmar, Indonesia than India,' exclaimed one of them. To understand India's foreign policy and appreciate it in the context of its neighbourhood, it is imperative that we first look at what the British left us as a legacy and tradition.

During the nineteenth century, after the British Crown took over the administration of India in 1858, the dominant obsession was the 'Great Game'– the struggle to contain Russian, Persian and Afghan influence in India's northern areas. The fixation with Afghanistan after an inglorious exit following the debacle in 1840–41 occupied most plans. The Afghans proved tough opponents,, standing up to the British in 1877, 1920, etc. Russia extended silently, steadily; but never clashed with the British. Persia under Nadir Shah in 1739 had attacked northern India and ravaged it. The British were wary of them and they always counted the Persian threat as real. China, after the overthrow of the Manchu dynasty, emerged as a republic under Sun Yat-sen in 1911. But China was not a serious factor then. Back in 1842, British India launched the 'Opium War' against China to close its consumption and the Chinese resented. In 1914, the British had under the command of Mc Mahon, drawn the demarcating line between India and Tibet; the Chinese would repudiate this in course of time. Burma remained under British control until 1934, as was Ceylon (now Sri Lanka) until 1948.

During the Second World War (1939–45), Japan overran most of Asia with the British getting beaten, as also the French and the Dutch. Following the defeat of Japan in China by the communists under Mao and the nationalists under Chiang Kai-shek, China relapsed into civil war till 1949 when finally, the communists emerged victorious. The French and the Dutch in

Vietnam and Indonesia, behaved like the famed Bourbons who 'learnt nothing and forget nothing' and tried to come back to reassert. It was an invitation to doom, doomsday being not far.

India emerged battered and bruised, but still the 'head was held high and the mind without fear.' India now launched into the international arena with support to other countries under colonial rule. In Africa and Asia, India provided leadership for liberation from foreign rule.

Apartheid

1949 saw the election in South Africa bringing a harsh white minority rule, heralding 'apartheid' regime; a system based on racial segregation and economic sequestration. Soon, Rhodesia (now Zimbabwe) followed suit. India, given the experience Gandhi had in South Africa, drew inspiration from him and fought bitterly in all international bodies against apartheid. Mandela became an inspiration, a legend, and a liberator.

NAM

India, under Nehru, began in earnest to launch the 'Non-Aligned Movement' or NAM. 'Non-aligned' meant not to support either the Soviet led bloc or the United States led bloc. Malice towards none, charity towards all; lot of advice was given by India charitably. Egypt, Yugoslavia, and India steered the Non-Aligned Movement with a modicum of success, though.

UN

India used the United Nations and in particular the General Assembly to further the cause and prospects of democracies in the world. As a non-aligned bloc, India, in the UN, was able to dispense matters with equanimity, poise and positivity. From time to time, the UN General Assembly with the democratic principle of one country, one vote, becomes a happy, famed stage for countries to stand and be counted.

Panchsheel

India also embarked on the lofty 'Panchsheel', a doctrine of 'Live and let live'; non-interference, respect for sovereignty, peace, and prosperity. At Bandag in 1955, Indonesia hosted the conference where China also participated. India emptied its heart out: Panchsheel, five principles to command, govern, and lead us to light. Unfortunately, only India stood by it, the Chinese found more in 'Punch, Kill' to satiate. India soon found to its discomfiture that in the world of 'real-politic', might is right and words have no meaning. Tibet, the autonomous region under the Chinese suzerainty was now coming under direct Chinese control. Dalai Lama, the spiritual head of Tibetans fled to India and sought asylum. It was given and the Chinese were incensed. They saw it as interference in their internal matters: violation of principles of 'Panchsheel'! Soon border disputes surfaced, so did acrimony, distrust, and disrespect. In 1962, the Chinese launched an unprovoked assault, catching India unprepared. India reaped a bitter harvest; disaster, defeat, and desolation. Very curiously, the Chinese timed their aggression with the Cuban missile crisis and unilaterally declared ceasefire, the moment the Cuban missile crisis was over. It was India's moment of reckoning: despair in defeat. India soon shook it off and looked ahead afresh. World was changing, a new harsh world was emerging.

Domino Theory

The United States found a new cause and concern: 'Domino Theory'-in effect, if one country falls to communism, rest would follow soon. A paranoid US rushed to war with Vietnam and Cambodia to contain the spread of communism. India condemned, criticised, and called for a halt. The United States was not amused. A world 'safe for democracy' was the US narrative. India had its tryst with destiny too–wars of 1965 and 1971 inflicted by Pakistan. In both these wars, India emerged a victor. In the 1971 Pakistan war, the Soviet Union stood beside India with a 20 year treaty of mutual help and cooperation in the event of aggression. Bangladesh was a reality. India had a new neighbour, a new reality. Another reality: Pakistan emerged leaner, meaner, capricious, and envious.

Events That Shaped History

The seventies saw four momentous events and the world would never be the same again.

1. First, the United States limped away battered and bruised from Vietnam—a case of David slaying Goliath. It was a painful knock for 'Uncle Sam', that he would not be forgetting it in a hurry.
2. Second, in 1973, aided by the Soviets, Egypt launched a surprise attack on Israel. Syrians joined a little later and it was called the 'Yom Kippur War', as it coincided with the Jewish festival of remembrance of the dead. The surprise element gave Egypt some success initially, but soon Israel outflanked the Egyptian army. The Soviet Union refused help and Egypt sued for peace. India got a rude jolt as oil prices shot up incredibly. Inflation hit India hard.
3. Thirdly, India exploded its own nuclear device in May 1974. The political fallout was much bigger than the nuclear blast. The United States led a call for a ban on India. India has not signed the nuclear non-proliferation treaty as it discriminated the nuclear 'haves' from nuclear 'have-nots'. India has of course signed the Outer Space Ban Treaty in 1963. India going nuclear was a harsh reality and the world had to accept that, not with a bang, but with a whimper.
4. Fourthly, one cannot keep the Soviet Union out of action for a long time. It was itching for action, waiting for its 'Vietnam': it got it in 1979. The Soviet Union invaded Afghanistan and stayed there for ten long years. India's muted protest was not liked by the Afghans. The United States, with Pakistan as its ally, entered into a proxy war with the Russians. Pakistan trained the Afghan freedom fighters and the Russians bled. By 1990, the Soviet Union itself started disintegrating and soon it was a new reality; a new world with a single super power, the United States of America. In 1990, Iraqi forces, under Saddam Hussein, invaded Kuwait and United States joined the action against Iraq in its 'Bush War'. Iraqi forces were hardly a match to the highly technically superior US forces. India condemned the aggression by Iraq but stopped short of disapproving the United States action.

By 1999, that traditional foe, Pakistan was ready for contest again this time, a perfidious round of action at Kargil, only to retreat with ignominy. In the previous year, 1998, both India and Pakistan went for nuclear tests successfully, but Kargil was a traditional fight with a traditional foe. China and Pakistan are constants in the denominator in India's equation of variables in foreign policy. It is disconcerting that these two countries, one sitting across high mountains and the other across rivers have a liking for each other. Pakistan generously gave China territory from occupied Kashmir to China, who started making all-weather roads to link the two countries. In 1985, India moved fast and occupied the Siachen glacier to thwart future encroachments, a proactive approach against a hyperactive foe.

In September 11, 2001, the United States faced a nameless, fameless and shameless enemy namely terrorism (trans-continental terrorism). The loss of lives, prestige, security, safety, Twin Towers, all combined, made the attacks reminiscent of 'Pearl Harbour'. Now terrorism took the centre stage; Bush Jr vowed revenge. He declared war on Afghanistan, where the architect of 9/11 attacks, Bin Laden was hiding and subsequently, Iraq, where Saddam Hussein was still ruling. India supported action on Afghanistan but demurred on the attack on Iraq. India suffered in silence the economic impact through uncertainty in oil prices and supplies. The United States sank deep into Middle East mire; ISIS was born as a reaction.

To study the case of India and its neighbourhood, given the background as outlined above, one must look at each of the countries in the region and their ties with India. Alongside, one must look at issues of importance like environment, nuclear energy, security, communications, and above all economic considerations. Geo-politics has changed over the years; countries have changed their outlook and priorities.

Bilateral, regional, and multi-lateral engagements and treaties are also important. India, given its strategic location finds itself in a unique position. Today, economic considerations outweigh political considerations. The Bank is more crucial that an artillery or battle tank piece.

INDIA's FOREIGN POLICY: AN OVERVIEW

1947–1962 Nehru Years : India realised that joining either of the blocs would result in a compromise of national interest and would compromise the values that shaped our freedom struggle. Preference was to build a stronger neighbourhood bordering India. Indus Water treaty with Pakistan was a happy outcome; Chinese aggression blew the lights out of Nehruvian outreach of trust. India led the movement for independence of African nations from foreign rule. Non-alignment was a creed with Nehru in a harsh bi-polar world of arms, armaments, and ammunition.

1966–1985 Indira Gandhi Years : Perfidious attack by China woke us up with clear understanding of geo-politics. Mrs. Gandhi re-affirmed her faith in non-alignment, yet moved with alacrity to visit both the US and USSR. Developments in Pakistan in 1971 resulting in a constitutional crisis broke all prospects of a living, lasting solution and forced India to engage for settlement. Crowning glory was the Indo-Soviet treaty and crowning achievement was creation of Bangladesh. India was emerging from the shadows of non-alignment. The world was beginning to listen, and nuclear explosions of 1974 made them listen with eyes wide open. 'Pokhran' was the crowning moment of the nation.

1985–1990 Rajiv Gandhi Years : During this period, India signed a treaty with Pakistan, agreeing not to attack each other's nuclear installations. India got drawn into Sri Lanka's Tamil conflict and set up India's Peace Keeping Force (IPKF), which soon got embroiled in conflict with LTTE, an extremist Tamil outfit. Out of office, on re-run for return, Rajiv Gandhi lost his life to Tamil assassins. The period marked cautions progression. India got Siachen glacier under control.

1990–1997 P.V. Narasimha Rao Years : Country grappled with crisis of confidence, economic downturn, and ensuring radical reforms.

Subsequent Period : Inder Kumar Gujral reached out to neighbours with transparent sincerity and bubbling enthusiasm. It was well received as 'Gujral' doctrine. Vajpayee arrived on the scene with three successive underground nuclear tests, promptly reciprocated by Pakistan. Vajpayee assured that India would not be the first to use nuclear weapons but only in self-defence. Manmohan Singh kept the peace process on. Mumbai 2008 attacks reopened painful wounds; how to reason with ransom, peace with provocation, assurance with aggression?

POLITICS: BALD OR BOLD

Parliament took up Chinese aggression for debate and discussion. Post 1962 debacle, country seethed with anger; hurt by the humiliation, and benumbed by harsh reality of retreat. Blame game started, accusations filled the air. Prime Minister Nehru listened with rising impatience. Clearly for him, it was time for introspection, not inquisition. Pacifist at heart, he yearned for peace, peace at all costs. Suddenly he exploded, 'Aksai Chin... a barren piece of land... nothing grows there. Not even a blade of grass has grown there...' Mahavir Tyagi, a member of Nehru's own party screamed, 'Sir, look at my head; here also nothing has grown for years... should I cut it off?" Nehru, himself balding, puffed in sullen anger. Clearly it was showing 'time' for Nehru and his band of bland politics. Non-aligned nations were truly non-aligned in the India-China rivalry. Panchsheel with 'glory to god' and 'greatness to nation' culminated with New Delhi's elite diplomatic enclave roads being named, 'Nyay Marg, Niti Marg', etc. Small irony that these roads led to the Chinese and Pakistani embassies! Nehruvian pomposity was set to end, so was the make-believe world of 'Panchsheel' and the like. Nehru's tryst with destiny was over; it was time to come into the open.

PANCHSHEEL

..... Ruled our hearts, not heads...

Lofty idealism, purity of thought, a universal declaration of mankind, actualisation of moralistic values, and principles above penchant, all formed the bedrock of Panchsheel. In reality, it was looking for perfection in an imperfect world–looking for a needle in a haystack where each hay was as sharp as a needle. Panchsheel glorified human purity, existence in a world which was crass materialistic and full of avarice.

The Five Principles are:

(a) Mutual respect for each other's territorial integrity and sovereignty.

(b) Mutual non-aggression.

(c) Mutual non-interference in each other's internal affairs.

(d) Equality and mutual benefit.

(e) Peaceful co-existence.

If these principles are followed by all, the world would be a much better place to live; such principles can thrive only among equals. Countries with equal power will signify 'Balance of Terror' rather than 'Balance of Power'. But then, as they say, equality is among equals! China soon showed what they thought of 'Panchsheel' by declaring the Indo-China war in 1962.

OUR NEIGHBOURHOOD...IMPASSE OR WAY OUT?

"In diplomacy there are no permanent friends, no permanent foes, only permanent interests."

MBBS.....PIN, defines as an acronym the state or stage of India's immediate neighbourhood:

M... Myanmar
B... Bangladesh
B... Bhutan
S... Sri Lanka
P... Pakistan
I... India
N... Nepal

This leaves China, Afghanistan, Iran, Maldives, Gulf (UAE) countries, and Seychelles out to yet define the neighbourhood.

Again as an acronym.

SCAM...IOUT
S...Seychelles
C...China
A...Afghanistan
M...Maldives
I...Iran
O...Ocean, Indian Ocean.
U...UAE
T...Thailand

India's neighbourhood is dynamic, populous, engaging, diverse, and distraught. We have a variety of regimes namely communist countries, democracies, single party rule, kingdoms, sheikdoms, and fledgling guided democracies. Apart from unity in diversity, these countries have historic ties, cultural affirmations, social affinity, and economic alignments among themselves. Religion also is an incisive factor.

Blessed with a 'place in the Sun', these countries are rich in solar energy. These countries have resources in minerals and materials that can sustain them, oil in abundance, rivers plenty, flora and fauna, and marine wealth too.

A huge population is no doubt a challenge, but an opportunity too for a country like India. India is a young nation with 40 per cent of its age population below 20 years, unlike countries in Europe or China which have ageing populations. India has a workforce which is reasonality skilled, sizeable, and seeking to serve.

Even so, the main challenges before these countries are:

(a) **Environment:** Sustain the environment
(b) **Energy:** Find energy resources, preferably renewable.
(c) **Equitable distribution:** Justice for all, wealth redistribution.
(d) **Education:** Educated, employable population.
(e) **Egalitarian society:** All men are equal, some are not 'more equal'; a just fair and free society.

Earnestness also begins with 'E', and that is required to find solutions to problems, not problems to solutions. Countries must engage, evolve, and adduce to emerge winners.

India, given its size and historic background can provide leadership. 'CBM'(confidence building measures) are needed in the event of uncertainty, 'MBM' (mutual benefit measures) where bilateral engagements benefit both, 'SBM' (several benefits measures) where common denominator benefits all: decisions involving environment, economic issues, etc. Opportunities are many, challenges too, but if benefits outweigh losses, countries will resolve to respond. Reason must score over repudiation.

TALE OF THREE STATES

Independence saw three states, all princely states, in a quandary–Junagarh with a Muslim Nawab with majority population of Hindus, Hyderabad with a Muslim ruler with majority Hindu population with aggressive Muslim influence in pockets, and Jammu and Kashmir with a Hindu ruler having Muslim majority in the valley, Hindu majority in Jammu, and Buddhist majority in Ladakh. Dilemma was: to join India or Pakistan? Junagarh went for a referendum, obtaining 99.06 per cent vote for union with India. The Nawab packed off his wives and dogs that he loved, in a plane to Karachi, offloaded quite a few wives to accommodate more dogs, and Karachi airport reception party fled in panic seeing exuberant canine rush and howling. In Hyderabad, the Nizam found himself in a jam, siding with Muslim extremists, called Razakars, led by one Qasim Rizvi. The Nizam wanted independence, no desire to join either India or Pakistan. Conditions were getting hopeless with Razakars unleashing terror, maiming, and killing at will. Sardar Patel, then home minister, ordered a police action, called Operation Polo which soon but paid all pretenses to independence. The Nizam was allowed a privy purse, and a ceremonial purse, and a ceremonial existence; an anachronism in democratic India. A relic was retained, a relation restored, and a pledge redeemed. Hari Singh, ruler of Kashmir was in no hurry (pun intended). By October 1947, Pakistan-backed irregulars had overrun Baramulla, and now Srinagar was within sights. There was no force to stop the marauders and India could not act till the ruler, Hari Singh signed the treaty of accession to India. Rape and rapine kept the aggressors engaged in a convent in Baramulla for three days. Pro Indian forces moved in and thwarted the aggression when the Nehru Government took the case and cause to the United Nations. UN moved in to declare truce–2/5 part of Kashmir lay with Pak supported troops. Pakistan demanded referendum along the lines of Junagarh. India stood by the periodic elections to the assembly with high percentage of cast votes as proof of accession to India. Added prop was special provisions in the Constitution, Art. 370. Simla agreement in 1972 held that all disputes between India and Pakistan have to be resolved bilaterally.

ISSUES BETWEEN CHINA AND INDIA

Chinese have a tradition of building walls, great walls where their interests are affected. History is witness to this, and it shows in their policies, though not in their inscrutable mask-like faces.

An average Chinese prefers 'Bicycle' to 'Buddhism', pragmatism decidedly rules their choices. Chinese showed such predilection, when Deng Xiaoping, diminutive and definitive, succeeded Mao to dismantle the ideological apparatus to launch his brand of 'real politik' in 1979. 'It does not matter whether the cat is black or white, so long it catches mice', quipped Deng. China has not looked back, cats in China are domesticated, not state-owned.

i. **Border Dispute :** Tibet, an autonomous region, under Chinese overall suzerainty lies between India and China. India always accepted the position. In 1954, India signed a trade treaty with Tibet without, unfortunately, resolving border issues (Chinese dispute regarding India's hold on Arunachal Pradesh and Aksai Chin in Ladakh, notably). Border talks have been on since 1981, though not in the public domain. Both countries have resolved to skirt the border issue, skip the disagreements, and scan other issues to increase the areas of agreement. Pakistan has its finger in the pie: it has handed over parts of occupied Kashmir to China, thereby rubbing India hard on India's claim to whole of Kashmir, and adding to India's disputes with China.

ii. **String of Pearls :** China is seemingly encircling India in a string of pearls. Gwadar port, at the mouth of Persian Gulf in Pakistan, is with China, a container shipping facility is at Chittagong in Bangladesh, and Hambantota Port in Sri Lanka and facilities in Myanmar are also with Chinese interests. Strategically and commercially, they pose a formidable threat although China downplays, calling it 'measures for economic gains and security of 'sea lines'. Chinese see these as facilities for import of raw material and oil from Africa and the Middle East.

iii. **One Belt, One Road (OBOR) :** It consists of a network of rail routes, overland highways, oil and gas pipelines, and other infrastructural projects stretching from Xi'an in central China through central Asia and Russia with:

(i) One artery crossing Kazakhstan and

(ii) Other through Mongolia

both linking with Trans-Siberian railway going on to Moscow, Rotterdam, and Venice. This displays China's thirst and thrust for overland link with Eurasia, Asia, and Europe—a modern version of an ancient route (Silk Route) and a tribute to Marco Polo.

India's interest is the Bangladesh, China, India and Myanmar (BCIM) corridor, connecting Yunnan in China, Myanmar, Bangladesh, and eastern India. India is apprehensive, uncertain, and split in doubts. OBOR is a reality. Prudence dictates that India supports it rather than flex muscles and waste resources in competition. Cooperation, not confrontation, collaboration, not countering, and calculation not cynicism, seems to be more prudent.

iv. **United Nations Reforms :** China is opposed to an extended, larger UN Security Council. India had fought for China's entry into UN and Security Council. China has not voiced any views about UN reforms; it is too pleased always to support Pakistan. On the

Nuclear Supply Group (NSG) issue also, it has shown marked interest in furthering Pakistan's claim. China's role in the UN is big, to India's discomfiture, but as UN itself is becoming seemingly redundant, India's distress is less. USA and Russia have shown how they can circumvent the UN. China had sorted out Taiwan and Hong Kong issues.

v. **South-China Sea :** China has warned India to keep off the South China Sea even as India along with Japan tried to take a toehold. The Chinese Navy established extensive presence to deter others.

vi. **Support to insurgency in North-East :** India has a cause for concern regarding the extension of support to insurgency in Nagaland, Mizoram, etc. by China. China cities Tibet and support by India to voices of dissent in tibet. A low intensity issue of simmering discord between the two countries; not heart-breaking but heartburning.

vii. **Economic imbalance :** India's trade with China shows imbalance; main concern is Yuan (Chinese currency) which hurts India's exports, chiefly base metals. Two-way India–China trade has been static for three years; it remains frozen at US $70 billion.

Overall, India–China relations are stable, suspicions are less, but not the way India wants. Both countries are competing for resources and energy security as also influencing and enhancing linkages with South and South-East Asian countries.

viii. **Dam on the Chinese side :** India has expressed strong concern over the dam being built by the Chinese over the river Brahmaputra on the Chinese side. In the ecologically and environmentally fragile Himalayan range (considered very unstable), the dam presents a great threat to India. The twin dangers of storing huge amounts of water and release of water, when in excess, expose lower Indian plains to floods, devastation, and destruction. The Chinese are in denial, defiance, and disagreement. India is seeking assurances and China is downplaying.

PROJECT MAUSAM

On the backdrop of growing Chinese naval activity in the Indian Ocean region, which India considers its zone of supremacy, the government has launched Project Mausam. It is believed to rival the Chinese Maritime Silk Road (MSR) initiative. The project which is still in the evolving phase, is being worked on to focus an ancient trade and cultural linkages, and emphasise on future maritime cooperation in the Indian Ocean region, stretching on from Southeast Asia to East Africa with the central location being India. The name 'Mausam' which in Arabic means 'monsoon' has been chosen, given its considerable meaning and substance in ancient maritime trade which always factored seasonal monsoon winds. Although conceived in relation to the need to counter Chinese moves in the Indian Ocean, unless the maritime countries find relevance in modern day context, the project will not take off to desired levels of expectations.

RELATIONS BETWEEN INDIA AND ITS IMMEDIATE NEIGHBOURS

Pakistan

Kashmir remains the dispute, discord, and disenchantment factor between India and Pakistan. The 1947-48, 1965, 1971, and 1999 wars between the two countries show the extent of animosity.

Yet there's been an agreement or two, which has succeeded between the countries. The Indus Water Treaty of 1960 about sharing water is one. Clause I of the treaty gave India full right to utilise the water of three eastern rivers Sutlej, Beas, and Ravi. Clause II of the treaty allows western rivers' Indus, Jhelum, and Chenab waters to flow to Pakistan, for some limited use like domestic use: agriculture, hydro-electric run up, non-consumptive use, etc. Baglihar dam on the Chenab by India is being held to be disputing the clause of 1960 treaty by Pakistan. Kishanganga project is also being objected to by Pakistan as violation of 1960 treaty.

Terrorism is another main issue between India and Pakistan. India has suffered repeatedly due to insurgent groups in Pakistan being patronised. Now and then, Pakistan also gets stung by these groups. A former Pakistani President called these terrorists as the country's 'assets'.

Both India and Pakistan are nuclear powers and are competing to enter NSG (Nuclear Supply Group), with US supporting India's case and China supporting Pakistan's claim. India has been given the privilege agreement by US, separating civil, military, and nuclear basis. Pakistan wanted a similar agreement but was denied.

Pakistan has extended the Gwadar Port facility to China; India has tied up with Iran for developing Chabahar port to engage Afghanistan also. In the TAPI (Tajikistan, Afghanistan, Pakistan, India) gas pipeline covering Pakistan's Baluchistan area also, Pakistan is delaying and dilly dallying.

Similarly, in 'SAARC' also, India is feeling increasingly choked by Pakistan. Bay of Bengal Initiative for Multi-Sectoral Technical and Economic Cooperation (BIMSTEC) is more to India's comfort. Pakistan signed the Simla agreement in 1972 to amicably and peacefully solve all outstanding issues bilaterally, but it still chooses to raise the Kashmir issue at all forums including the UN.

Back in 1965, India agreed to UK arbitration to resolve Rann of Kutch dispute, and although the award went against India, it was still accepted in the interest of lasting, long interest of 'friendship'.

If you have a friend like Pakistan, what for do you need enemies?

China

Napoleon when once asked about China said, 'Ah, that's a dragon, now sleeping. Let it sleep'. Two centuries later, the dragon is spitting fire. India and China have a shared history of culture and tradition, trade and travel, and religion and relics. Buddhism went to China from India, silk come to India from China, travellers came to India from China, and explorers went to China from India. The list could be endless. During the Second World War, Dr. Kotnis and his medical team earned the enduring respect and gratitude of the Chinese. India stood by China against Japanese aggression. India was the first non-communist country to give recognition to the Chinese government under communist party. India championed the entry of China into the United Nations too.

China took the border dispute with India, in three sectors–North, Central, and East, to new levels of acrimony and agitation. It refuses to acknowledge India's control of eastern sector, what is now Arunachal Pradesh. India formally took Sikkim into the Indian union, notwithstanding the Chinese protestation (1975). In the northern sector, Ladakh, Aksai Chin is the area of discord.

In 1962, the Chinese launched an unprovoked attack, occupied large areas, and then unilaterally withdrew to an extent. India's stand is to vacate the aggression and then talk; Chinese stand is– land taken is ours and accept the reality and justification. It's a deadlock but both countries are progressing well in mutual trade with the Chinese having a hefty trade surplus. India and China are cooperating in many areas internationally on environmental issues. There is a lot of convergence. At WTO (World Trade Organisation), both India and China are seeing eye to eye, though developed countries are calling for tooth for tooth. Daggers are drawn, but all countries of the world are now well integrated into the WTO regime; dissent yes, destabilisation no.

The Chinese economy is roughly nine times larger than India's. Both countries are looking for FDI (Foreign Direct Investment), with the Chinese having a distinct advantage of a regimented, control oriented government, but rising wages are a threat. Good infrastructure, disciplined workforce, lack of unionism and good service support through insurance, and banking are other favourable factors in China's favour. India presents a veritable option of 'do it, if you will' option. Skilled workforce, English speaking population, availability of raw materials, and entrepreneurship are good takeaways, but infrastructure, services, local factors, political will, and interference are bottlenecks, but not life-threatening. Investment friendly, yes; but overtly seeking; no. Work culture is an issue too, but it is an unknown variable, one can extract results beyond belief or one can sink into a morass beyond relief. The people are enigmatic, they can excel or they can exit.

Sri Lanka

India and Sri Lanka have a shared past and a common cultural and ethnic bonding. The Tamil issue which dogged the eighties and nineties, now stand muted with the elimination of LTTE. It snarled up the India–Sri Lanka relations and interventions of IPKF (Indian Peace Keeping Force) proved futile.

Sri Lanka's recent hobnobbing with China with the lease of Hambantota port to China, and moves by the present government to ease relations with India show up the subtle dimensions of Sri Lanka's policy.

The issue of fishermen and refugees from Sri Lanka are also spots of inconvenience and occasional clashes.

Myanmar

India and Myanmar are bound by common historical, cultural and religious ties. Myanmar's strategic location, long border, and proximity to India's north-east make it a very important partner. It is critical to India's 'Act East Policy'.

In 1948, Burma (as Myanmar was then known), saw the overthrow of U Nu's civilian government by the army. The army rule shut the country down to opt for isolation. India got all the cooperation in hunting down insurgency. With the restoration of democracy, Myanmar is completing a painful transition.

Myanmar offers connectivity to ASEAN countries and a great scope for development of India's north-east. India has started a direct shipping service to Myanmar.

Bhutan

Bhutan has huge importance to India, given its potential for hydro-electric projects with a win-win situation for both countries–India getting electricity and Bhutan revenue. Flood control in India also gets an impetus. China too has been converging on Bhutan. The kingdom has an emperor who has coined the index of measure for progress, the 'happiness index'. Being member of SAARC and BBIN (Bangladesh, Bhutan, India, Nepal) Bhutan presents an example of regional, localised combination for economic growth and development.

Bangladesh

Bangladesh has a long border with India and consequential problems. Some of the problems are a legacy of history, some appeared later. Problem of enclaves and islands dates back to pre-independence. The Farraka Barrage and sharing of water later on, shelter to insurgents, and armed groups is also an issue, particularly ULFA groups.

Bangladesh, an active member of SAARC, Bangladesh, Bhutan, India, Nepal (BBIN), and BIMSTEC has a vital role to play in India's foreign policy. China has got involved in preparing and developing Container Shipment Services at Chittagong.

Teesta Water sharing issues is still not fully resolved, but Bangladesh has met all its commitments, as always.

Land corridor issue has been resolved as also the thorny Enclaves' issues.

Iran

US and Iran have ended the hostility and signed agreements covering a whole host of issues. With the lifting of the nuclear ban, Iran is now free to trade. India has extended help to Iran to build the Chabahar port issue, along with Afghanistan. Cooperation with Iran is paramount to India's policy as the country's energy needs are mounting.

Afghanistan

India needs an Afghanistan that is free, progressive, and friendly. A stable Afghanistan is in India's interest. The country is still embroiled in terror, Taliban, and turmoil. India has invested in Afghanistan's future such as its new parliament building, in a major dam (Salma Dam), and in its infrastructure. TAPI pipeline also has Indian and Afghan participation. Pakistan (across the Durand line), too, is watching and waiting, even as Afghanistan is settling down to democracy and stability.

UAE

The United Arab Emirates (UAE) has emerged as one of our strongest trading partner, supplier of oil, etc. A large ethnic population from India is another happy outcome leading to sizeable remittances. It is also the gateway to the Arab world. UAE now ranks as India's 3rd largest trading partner.

Maldives

An island in the Indian Ocean, Maldives has a large number of people of Indian origin. The country has historic ties with India. Its location is strategic and critical. Environmental crisis is looming large and the future is full of challenges.

NEW FACETS TO OUR FOREIGN POLICY

The present Indian Government has brought in a fresh impetus and dynamism to its foreign policy. Robert Walpole, the first person to be credited with the designation 'Prime Minister', is famous for his quip, 'Let sleeping dogs lie'. India's foreign policy did, in the past, have a policy in tune with Walpole's thinking. Years later, the country adopted a policy of 'Reaction and response.' Now the policy is 'proactive'; let us explore opportunities, grab them when they come, or incubate and reach them when ready. Tomorrow is here today, let's not bide for time, instead bid for time, and buy the time. If we are ready today, we are first tomorrow. If we can fathom today, we can conquer tomorrow.

India's concerns are energy needs, environmental safeguards, and safety and security of our sea lines and air space. Elimination of terrorism and growth of tolerance, development, and progress in an environment of sustainable order are other issues.

Days of 'Gunboat' diplomacy are over. Today's diplomacy runs on principles of economic dominance and political convergence. Nations are tied to the world order operating with democratic ideals and expectations. The operating theme is 'interdependence'; operating style is 'cooperation'. WTO (World Trade Organisation), IMF (International Monetary Fund), IBRD (International Bank for Reconstruction and Development), UNDP (United Nations Development Programme), EU (European Union), etc; matter more for countries, more than anything else.

INDIAN OCEAN: COUNTRIES AND ISSUES

Mauritius : Mauritius is an important country for India to count on. With a large ethnic population of Indian origin and similar outlook to issues as India, Mauritius has stood by India on many issues. With shared culture and history, Mauritius has many traditions that have roots in India. Often the preferred destination for Bollywood's foreign locale shooting, Mauritius is also a tax haven. India is renegotiating for a more rational, reasonable, and resolute treaty to replace the existing one which is a conduit for money transfer. Mauritius is important to India to facilitate growing trade with Africa. India has set up a listening post in nearby Madagascar, first of its type outside India and is setting up coastal surveillance radar network system in Mauritius. Pirates in the Indian Ocean are a live threat and India has suffered due to Somali pirates in the past. Mauritius has a very useful and crucial location in our sea lanes and choke points.

Seychelles : India recognises the commanding, strategic location of Seychelles islands in its neighbourhood. Recently, India set up eight coastal surveillance radar systems in Seychelles. These systems will be integrated with Indian's coastal monitoring network gradually.

REGIONAL TREATIES: PATH TO PROGRESS

Of particular interest and significance are initiatives made by countries to come together to further their own individual interests, be it economic or security or sharing of knowledge or resources or social and cultural agendas or environment protection or even purely academic pursuits. Unlike multi-lateral treaties, regional treaties are less complicated and governed by less intricate arrangements. There is better understanding and commonality of interests, and such arrangements are attended to with deeper understanding and commitment. Regional treaties, world over, have shown easy implementation to deliver results.

Given the dynamics of Cold War, it was well neigh impossible to forge regional ties in the fifties and sixties, except under the two super powers' patronage. The Seventies saw the Arab world come under the banner of OPEC (Organisation of the Petroleum Exporting Countries) and handle oil prices and crisis to its member countries' interests. Of course, Non-Aligned Movement was also there but it never advanced to any meaningful outcome as treaties or arrangements.

Countries in South and South-East Asia started working towards regional agreements and arrangements to produce outstanding results. The growth story of these economies in Singapore, Malaysia, Thailand, Philippines, South Korea, Taiwan, and Hong Kong caught the imagination of the world. Economics was the focus and growth was the benchmark.

ASEAN

ASEAN stands for Association of Southeast Asian Nations comprising of Indonesia, Malaysia, Philippines, Singapore, Thailand, Brunei, Vietnam, Laos, Myanmar, and Cambodia.

ASEAN has two wings : The East Asia summit and the ASEAN Regional Forum. India attended the meet of the forum in 1994 and presently the Government of India is coming closer to ASEAN after years of Wait and Watch policy. In the 2018 Republic Day function, the chief guests were the heads of the above mentioned ASEAN countries. It sent a powerful message to the region that India is proactively engaged in developing stable and durable relationships with its south east Asian neighbours.

SAARC

South Asian Association for Regional Cooperation (SAARC) is an economic and political organisation of eight countries in southern Asia and includes three states with observer status. It was established on December 8, 1985. SAARC now has eight members namely India, Pakistan, Bangladesh, Sri Lanka, Nepal, Maldives, Bhutan, and Afghanistan.

In 1993, SAARC countries signed an agreement to gradually lower tariff within the region. In 2002, SAARC countries devised SAFTA (South Asia Free Trade Area) which created a framework for the establishment of a free trade area covering 1.4 billion people. Under this agreement, SAARC countries have brought their duties down to 20 per cent in 2007. India is now proposing to launch a satellite for covering SAARC countries to share knowledge and help resolve communication issues.

However, India is finding Pakistan a stumbling block in many of the initiatives. SAARC has more problems than solutions.

BIMSTEC

Bay of Bengal Initiative for Multi-Sectoral Technical and Economic Cooperation (BIMSTEC), an organisation with countries from South and South-east Asia was launched in 1997. Initially it had India, Bangladesh, Sri Lanka, and Thailand as its members. Myanmar joined in December 1997. Nepal and Bhutan joined in 2003. It was christened BIMSTEC in July 2004.

It focusses on fourteen priority sectors, some of them being trade, investment, communication and transport, environments and disaster management, counter-terrorism and transnational crimes, energy, cultural cooperation, and people to people contact. India's North East region lies at the cusp of BIMSTEC.

Benefits of BIMSTEC

BIMSTEC offers some unique benefits :

i. It is purely an economic configuration. Politically, the countries in BIMSTEC are not divergent like India and Pakistan in SAARC. There are a few issues between India and Bangladesh but they are not insurmountable such as Teesta waters, infiltration into India, and insurgents taking shelter in Bangladesh.

ii. Free trade agreement: This remains elusive among BIMSTEC over the last ten years, as countries are more keen on free trading of accusations. India's concerns are textiles and four wheelers from Thailand.

iii. Infrastructural bottlenecks and their linkages: India's northeast lags behind in infrastructural arrangements.

iv. Institution problems in manufacture and service sectors: Problem lies in job creation.

v. LDCs Concerns: Least Developed Countries (LDCs) are not happy about compensation over revenue loss; they want their items under negative list as a protection. Tourism offers a huge potential for job growth.

BIMSTEC has a huge potential for growth and expansion given the convergence of interests among member countries. Connectivity and communication is the problem, not confluence of efforts. BIMSTEC make can use of science and technology to gather momentum and magnitude.

INDIA AND THE WORLD: A PARADIGM SHIFT

India's Neighbourhood

Afghanistan

President Ashraf Ghani's maiden state visit to India and PM Modi's visit to Afghanistan underscored the longstanding, growing, and deep bilateral ties between the two countries. They were further strengthened with PM and President Ghani jointly dedicating the Afghan Parliament building to the Afghan nation, constructed with Indian cooperation, and provision of Mi-25 helicopters by India for strengthening Afghanistan's defensive capabilities.

Bangladesh

India's close relations with Bangladesh were further strengthened through various initiatives. It is notable that in the last few years, there has been progress on issues that have eluded solution for decades. Both the countries have worked closely to strengthen bilateral cooperation on all issues including settlement of land boundary issues, security, infrastructure development, cooperation in power, trade and investments, connectivity, sub-regional cooperation, and people-to-people exchange. The two nations jointly inaugurated through video conferencing the second cross border transmission line between India and Bangladesh to supply 100 MW of power from Palatana power plant in Tripura to Bangladesh and international bandwidth for leasing 10 Gbps for broadband internet from Bangladesh to Tripura.

Bhutan

India and Bhutan share close and friendly relations characterised by mutual trust and understanding. The recent years saw sustained progress in all areas of cooperation, including hydropower, transport, communication, infrastructure, health, education, culture, IT industry, and agriculture. The momentum of the bilateral ties was carried forward by high level visits and interactions.

China

India and China agree that their simultaneous re-emergence as two major powers in the region and the world offers a momentous opportunity for realisation of the Asian century. Both countries agree to pursue their respective national developmental goals and security interests in a mutually supportive manner and in a spirit of mutual respect and sensitivity to each other's concerns, interests, and aspirations.

Closer developmental partnership, which is at the core of India-China bilateral relations received a further boost with the signing of an unprecedented 24 agreements/MoUs in areas including railways, trade and commerce, science and technology, space, and people-to-people exchanges along with 26 commercial/business agreements amounting to US $22 billion. Nothwithstanding the issues arising out of the Doklam imbroglio, both India and China are cautiously moving forward to normalise ties.

Myanmar

Relations between India and Myanmar are multi-faceted and rooted in shared historical, ethnic, and cultural ties. Bilateral cooperation between India and Myanmar is aimed at promotion of inclusive growth and development and to contribute to peace, prosperity, and stability in the two countries and in the region.

India-Myanmar relations were further strengthened through exchange of high level visits and setting up of institutionalised mechanisms to carry forward our cooperation in various sectors. Of particular significance was the visit to India of the Myanmar Foreign Minister for the first meeting of the newly established India Myanmar Joint Consultative Commission, intended to promote all-round development of relations in promising areas for cooperation covering security and defence, trade and investment, development partnership activities, global and multilateral issues, etc.

Nepal

India-Nepal friendship and cooperation has been characterised by open borders, extensive people-to-people ties, and multi-faceted socio-economic interaction. India continues to support Nepal in its transition to a prosperous, peaceful, stable, and democratic country. Several agreements were signed including MoU on utilisation of USD 250 million grant component of India's assistance package for post-earthquake reconstruction assistance in four sectors, i.e., housing, health, education, and cultural heritage; MoU on strengthening of road infrastructure in the Terai, and Letters of Exchange on rail transport. The two Prime Ministers inaugurated the Muzaffarpur Dhalkebar power transmission line. The third meeting of Pancheshwar Development Authority was held in Kathmandu in March, 2016.

Pakistan

The period 2015–16 was marked by high-level engagements, both formal and informal, focussed on normalising relations between the two countries paving the way towards a meaningful dialogue. A beginning was made in the form of an agreement of the two countries on a new Comprehensive Bilateral Dialogue to address all outstanding issues through peaceful means. Nevertheless, cross-border terrorism, ceasefire violations, and infiltration across the Line of Control (LoC) and International Border (IB) remain our core concerns.

Indian Ocean Region

Recent years have seen a concerted focus by India on securing her interests in the Indian Ocean region. The direction was set with Prime Minister Modi's visits to Seychelles, Mauritius, and Sri Lanka. The process was given form through the creation of a separate division in MEA in January 2016 for the Indian Ocean region bringing together relationships with key countries in the region such as Sri Lanka, Maldives, Seychelles, Mauritius, and the structured Trilateral Maritime Security Dialogue (between India, Sri Lanka, and Maldives) to address geostrategic security, economic and developmental interests in the Indian Ocean region. India's approach to the future track of the Indian Ocean Rim Association (IORA) was also made integral to this approach.

Sri Lanka

India-Sri Lanka relations have undergone a significant and qualitative shift during the last couple of years. Bilateral relations reached a new high with a number of high level visits. Sri Lankan Prime Minister Ranil Wickremesinghe paid an official visit to India. This was his first overseas visit after the Parliamentary elections. The President of Sri Lanka, also made a working visit to India. Around that time, India extended help and relief to Sri Lanka which was battling torrential rains and landslides that caused significant devastation and loss of life. India's relationship with Sri Lanka has been progressing in keeping with the "neighbourhood first" principle. Since 2005, the Government of India has committed Rs. 2,300 crore as grant assistance and Rs. 12,900 crore under lines of credit for the rehabilitation of internally displaced persons and reconstruction of infrastructure in the northern and eastern provinces of Sri Lanka. India's flagship project of assistance to Sri Lanka namely, the Housing Project, with an overall commitment of over Rs. 1,372 crore in grants, is progressing well and completion of second phase is expected shortly. Projects completed include the Mahatma Gandhi International Centre in Matale, Language Labs in Ampura, Matara, Badulla, and Jaffna, and a 200-bed ward complex in Vavuniya. Bilateral cooperation has continued to expand in various areas particularly, defence, economic, education, agriculture, development partnership, culture, and people-to-people exchanges. Bilateral trade and investment continued to grow, spurred by growth in both economies. Trade between the two countries has grown rapidly to rise to US $7.45 billion. In the investment field, India is one of the major foreign investors in Sri Lanka's largest trading partner globally, while Sri Lanka is India's second largest trading partner in the SAARC. India continued to be the largest source of tourist arrivals into Sri Lanka.

Maldives

The 50th anniversary of establishment of India-Maldives diplomatic relations has been celebrated. External Affairs Minister Sushama Swaraj visited Maldives for the 5th India-Maldives Joint Commission, where discussions were held on bilateral and regional issues of mutual interest. Six MoUs/agreements were signed to further strengthen our robust bilateral relationship. Bilateral defence and security co-operation broadened and deepened further into several areas including defence, hardware, and capacity building. It also included monthly EEZ surveillance by Indian Navy ships and aircraft, holding of EKUVERIN 2015, a joint Indian Army-MNDF Marine Corps training exercise in Thiruvananthapuram, the participation by India, Sri Lanka and Maldives in the second Table Top Exercise (TTEX-15), handing over of Phase-I of the Composite Training Centre for Maldives National Defence Force (MNDF) Which is a project funded by India.

Mauritius

India and Mauritius enjoy close political, economic, cultural, and diaspora linkages. 70 per cent of the population of Mauritius is of Indian origin. Mauritius is a hub for financial services and has emerged as the largest route for FDI into India. Mauritius is also an important jurisdiction for Indian investments into Africa. India-Mauritius trade is nearly US $2 billion. There is a close defence partnership on issues of maritime security. The India-Mauritius partnership further intensified and broadened in scope. The Indian naval and coast guard ships visited Mauritius to undertake joint surveillance and patrolling of the Exclusive Economic Zone (EEZ), in addition to conducting hydrographic surveys.

Seychelles

As part of India-Seychelles partnership, development partnership, capacity building programmes, maritime security cooperation, and cultural exchanges was held in the recent past. Blue economy, climate change, renewable energy, tourism, and health are the emerging areas of focus. 10 per cent of the population of Seychelles is of Indian origin. In the field of development assistance, India provided a grant of US $4.3 million for procurement of public transportation buses, medicines, ICT equipment, and educational items. To facilitate people-to-people contacts and travel, Seychelles has been included in the e-tourist visa scheme of the Government of India. A Bilateral Air Services agreement has also been signed. The period also witnessed further deepening of the strategic India-Seychelles defence and security cooperation, focusing in particular on maritime safety and surveillance of the extensive Exclusive Economic Zone of Seychelles.

South East Asia and the Asia-Pacific

Australia

Australia is emerging as an important partner in different sectors including development of mineral resources, science and technology, education and skills, and water resources management. The bilateral Civil Nuclear Cooperation Agreement was announced in November 2015. This enables Australian companies to commence uranium exports to India. Defence cooperation received a strong boost through the first ever bilateral maritime exercise AUSINDEX that was conducted in the Bay of Bengal. The Indian community in Australia continues to grow in size and importance. Australian universities have attracted almost 50, 000 students from India. India is now regarded as the largest source of skilled migrants to Australia.

Brunei Darussalam

Bilateral relations with Brunei Darussalam continue to be very close and friendly and Brunei remained Country Coordinator for India in ASEAN. Yearly visits took place between the two countries including from the National Defence College of India, ISRO, and Deputy Minister of Culture, Youth and Sports of Brunei. Since 2012, officers from Indian Armed Forces have regularly attended the Royal Brunei Armed Forces Command Staff Course at Staff College, Brunei.

Cambodia

Bilateral relations between India and Cambodia remain cordial, friendly, and continue to grow stronger. India and Cambodia have close civilisational and cultural links from ancient times which continue till today. A Memorandum of Understanding on Tourism Cooperation and an agreement on Indian Grant Assistance for implementation of Quick Impact Projects under Mekong Ganga Cooperation initiative have been signed. The first and second phases of conservation and restoration work of Ta Prohm Temple were completed successfully by the Archaeological Survey of India.

Indonesia

The recent years witnessed many high-level political engagements that have helped in reinvigorating our relationship and has provided the necessary momentum to the bilateral relations. India-Indonesia Defence Cooperation witnessed significant qualitative and quantitative enhancement. India's trade with Indonesia was US $11 billion which included import of commodities worth US $8.9 billion and export of US $2.1 billion worth goods.

Lao PDR

There is a continued upward trend in bilateral relations with Lao PDR. Infrastructure projects in areas of irrigation systems, power transmission, capacity building, human resources, cultural cooperation in restoration of heritage monuments, and regular high level visits were focus of cooperation. Added to this were 100–150 scholarships given to Laos students and technical personnel for undergoing training programmes and regular courses of study in India under various schemes.

Malaysia

Bilateral relations with Malaysia, marked by traditional friendship and cordiality, have continued to progress and expand. Prime Minister Modi undertook an official visit to Malaysia. Earlier, PM Modi participated in the 13th ASEAN-India Summit and 10th East Asia Summit held in Kuala Lumpur. The PM inaugurated the Torana Gate in Brickfields, Kuala Lumpur, which was a gift from India.

New Zealand

Then President of India Pranab Mukherjee visited New Zealand in 2016 where several agreements were signed during the visit. India's relations with New Zealand continue to progress in various fields such as economic, scientific, cultural, people-to-people contact, and coordination on regional and issues of global importance.

The Philippines

India-Philippines partnership continues to strengthen. The 3rd edition of the bi-annual Joint Commission on Bilateral Cooperation, the highest institutionalised bilateral mechanism, was held in New Delhi. The defence cooperation continued to strengthen with the visit of *INS Sahyadri* on a goodwill visit to Manila. Trade relations between the two countries remained steady at US $1.8 billion, despite global downturn, with a positive trade balance in India's favour. Indian investment in the Philippines has been characterised by the presence of a large number of major Indian IT and pharma firms that continue to do well in the IT-enabled services and the generics sector respectively. A new trend of Indian investment is now visible in sectors such as infrastructure, automobiles, renewable energy and agriculture.

Singapore

Defence cooperation between India and Singapore was strengthened by the signing of the enhanced Defence Cooperation Agreement. Further, the Technical Agreement on sharing White Shipping Information between the Indian Navy and the Republic of Singapore Navy has been operationalised. Besides, there were regular exchanges between the three services and the defence establishments of India and Singapore. Both the nations have close economic and commercial ties which has shown some declining trends during recent times (17 per cent decline in the volume of bilateral trade). The total bilateral trade was US $8.6 billion with Indian export accounting for US $4.2 billion. The outward Indian FDI to Singapore increased, with Singapore being one of the most favoured destinations for Indian investments abroad. Recently, Indian investments in Singapore have reached US $2.18 billion. Singapore is the second largest source of FDI for India, the total in figures from April 2000 to September 2015 being US $38.9 billion.

Thailand

India's relationship with Thailand continues to deepen and strengthen with the exchange of high-level visits and enhanced interactions at all levels. Bilateral trade was US $6.18 billion. The first meeting of the Joint Task Force (JTF) on Maritime Cooperation and Legal and Judicial Cooperation was held in New Delhi. Four meetings of Transport Ministry Officials of India, Myanmar, and Thailand on the finalisation of Motor Vehicles Agreement of the Trilateral Highway were held. Around 1 million Indian tourists visited Thailand and over 100,000 Thai tourists visited India. Both the countries agreed to enhance cooperation in the maritime domain, counter terrorism, cyber security, etc. Dual entry e-tourist visas to facilitate Thai pilgrims travel to cities in India and Nepal were announced. It was decided to celebrate 2017 as the 70th anniversary of establishment of diplomatic relations between the two countries.

Vietnam

The Strategic Partnership between India and Vietnam has been consolidated further. Economic cooperation was accorded strategic priority, even as efforts continued to implement decisions taken at the highest level, encompassing all areas of the bilateral comprehensive cooperation. A Joint Vision Statement for 2015–2020 on Defence Cooperation and a MoU on cooperation between the Coast Guards of the two countries was signed. Bilateral trade between India and Vietnam has seen continuous growth over the past few years. India is now among the top ten trading partners of Vietnam. Both sides agreed on a new trade target of US $15 billion by 2020. Bilateral defence relation is broadening and deepening into all the areas of defence co-operation including defence production. Vietnam has, over the years, been a large recipient of training programmes under Indian Technical and Economic Cooperation (ITEC) programme.

East Asia

East Asia forms part of India's extended neighbourhood. Cultural, trade, and people-to-people contacts with the region go back several centuries. Shared values and traditions of peaceful co-existence, pluralism, and peace symbolised by Buddhism have provided the glue to this engagement. India's rising political and security stature and its readiness to play a more active role in international relations combined with a growing economic clout is powering closer integration between India and East Asia.

A peaceful and stable East Asia is integral to India's economic development. A substantial volume of India's trade is with the countries of this region. It is important that there is an agreement on the principles of international law and peaceful settlement of disputes; freedom of navigation and overflight; and unimpeded lawful commerce governing the affairs of this region.

Democratic People's Republic of Korea

Diplomatic relations between India and the Democratic People's Republic of Korea (DPRK) were established in the recent past. Relations between India and DPRK are cordial India maintains an embassy in Pyongang and North Korea has an embassy in New Delhi. The visit of the Foreign Minister to India took place, the first at the Foreign Minister level from DPRK to India. Bilateral trade is around $ 500 million annually and is mostly food exports.

Japan

India-Japan relations have witnessed a gradual transformation in recent years and reflect a broad convergence of their long-term political, economic, and strategic goals. PM Modi's visit to Japan, which was his first overseas visit outside the neighbourhood, prepared the ground for a qualitative shift in bilateral relations which elevated the bilateral relationship to a "Special Strategic and Global Partnership". This was further reinforced by the Japanese PM's visit to India, which resulted in Japan agreeing to provide funding for a slew of key infrastructure projects along with agreements in defence cooperation and civil nuclear energy. The two sides also signed an agreement to implement high speed railways in India.

Japan and India are committed to leverage the synergy between India's "Act East" policy and Japan's "Partnership for Quality Infrastructure" to develop and strengthen reliable, sustainable, and resilient infrastructures that augment connectivity within India and between India and other countries in the region. Japanese Official Development Assistance (ODA's) contribution to the building of social and physical infrastructure in India was acknowledged. The total commitment of Japanese ODA yen loan to India may reach around 400 billion yen, the highest ever provided to India.

Indian ships *Satpura*, *Sahyadri*, *Shakti*, and *Kirch* participated in the 20th edition of Exercise Malabar 2016 with the US Navy and Japan Maritime Self Defence Force (JMSDF) in Japan with harbour phase at Sasebo in June 2016 and the sea phase in the Pacific Ocean in June 2016. The exercise was aimed at increasing interoperability amongst the three navies and developing common understanding of procedures of maritime security operations.

Mongolia

India and Mongolia, share a common Buddhist legacy, and have a history of cultural exchanges spanning centuries. India and Mongolia elevated their bilateral relationship to a strategic partnership and identified a host of new areas of bilateral cooperation including development of equal and mutually beneficial trade, investments, and economic cooperation, which is balanced, sustainable, and leads to prosperity in both countries.

Republic of Korea

Recently, the sixtieth anniversary of establishment of diplomatic relations between the two countries was celebrated. Bilateral relations between India and Republic of Korea (RoK) are increasingly becoming multifaceted, spurred by a significant convergence of economic, political, and security interests. The year 2016 saw adding of new substance, speed, and content in the partnership in a wide range of areas including foreign affairs, defence, trade and investment, science and technology, culture and people-to-people exchanges, and regional cooperation, to take the bilateral relations to a qualitatively higher level. India views the RoK as vital to its "Act East" policy, and the RoK and India recognise the value of the bilateral partnership and its contribution to bringing peace, stability, and security in the Asia Pacific Region.

Eurasia

Relations with Russia remain a central pillar of India's foreign policy. Enhancing India's special and privileged strategic partnership with Russia is a key focus with as many as three visits at Head of State/Government level from India to Russia. The then President Pranab Mukherjee participated in the 70th anniversary commemoration of victory in World War II in Moscow. Prime Minister Modi visited Russia twice–for the 7th BRICS Summit and SCO Summit in Ufa, Russia and for the 16th India-Russia Annual Summit in Moscow. India's engagement with its Central Asian partners gained significant momentum with the historic visit by Prime Minister Modi to all five Central Asian countries namely Uzbekistan, Kazakhstan, Turkmenistan, Kyrgyz Republic, and Tajikistan. Relations with Belarus, Ukraine, and the South Caucasus (Armenia, Azerbaijan, Georgia) also continue to develop well.

Russian Federation

In recent years, high-level visits as well as ministerial and official interactions in diverse formats contributed to a significant strengthening and deepening of India-Russia relations in diverse fields. Over 25 bilateral agreements and MoUs covering cooperation in areas such as defence, civil nuclear cooperation, education, science and technology, hydrocarbons, railways, solar energy, visa simplification, ayurveda, satellite navigation, heavy engineering, and supercomputing have been signed. During the 16th Annual Summit, particular focus was given to enhance trade and economic ties as a strong pillar of the strategic partnership. A wide-ranging joint statement 'Shared Trust, New Horizons' was also issued, which fully reflects the diversity and dynamism in India-Russia relations.

In addition to considerable progress on bilateral relations, India and Russia maintained close consultations on regional and global issues. Russia reaffirmed its strong support for India's candidature for a permanent seat in a reformed UN Security Council, multilateral export control regimes, as well as other plurilateral frameworks such as the Shanghai Cooperation Organisation. India and Russia also continued their close cooperation in the framework of Russia's chairmanship of BRICS.

Several measures to promote bilateral trade and investment were implemented, including simplification of visa regime for businessmen, signing of protocol on pre-arrival exchange of information ("Green Corridor"), setting up of a Special Notified Zone for trade in rough diamonds, and market access for agricultural exports. Significant investments, particularly in the hydrocarbons sector in both countries, were also announced.

Ukraine and South Caucasus

India's relations with Ukraine continued to develop. Ties with Armenia, Georgia, and Azerbaijan were consolidated through active cultural and business exchanges.

Central Asia

The visit of Prime Minister Modi to all the five Central Asian countries, i.e., Kazakhstan, Kyrgyz Republic, Tajikistan, Turkmenistan, and Uzbekistan raised the profile of our bilateral relationship with these countries and the region as a whole to an unprecedented high. Visits and interactions at ministerial and senior official level further consolidated relations with these countries located in India's extended neighbourhood. India continued its significant contributions to capacity building and human resources development in the region. A total of 22 agreements in different fields were signed with the five Central Asian countries.

Gulf and West Asia

India enjoys close historical ties with the countries of the Gulf region, which are cemented in age old civilisation links and strong people-to-people contact. This friendly relationship was further strengthened this year by regular exchange of high-level visits. The Gulf region is India's largest trading partner region with bilateral trade over US $97 billion. The region also continues to be a major supplier of crude oil and LNG to India, and accounts for over 50 per cent of India's crude oil imports and over 70 per cent of India's natural gas imports and thus remains vital to India's energy security needs. Among India's top six oil sourcing countries, four are from the Gulf region namely, Saudi Arabia, Iraq, UAE, and Kuwait. The Gulf countries also host an eight million strong Indian expatriate community which contributes to the development of the host countries and forms an organic link between India and the Gulf states.

The continued fragile security situation in Iraq resulting out of ISIS attacks launched in June 2014 has remained a matter of deep concern for India. Despite the volatile security situation there, India continues to maintain its Mission in Baghdad to engage closely with the Government of Iraq and also a control room in Erbil, Kurdistan to provide consular assistance to Indian nationals.

India sees Islamic Republic of Iran as an important country in India's immediate 'economic and security space'. Interactions between the leadership and senior ministers of the two countries provided thrust to the bilateral relations in 2015, including the economic sphere. India had welcomed the signing of Joint Comprehensive Plan of Action (JCPOA) between Iran and P5+1 in July 2015. (The P5+1 refers to the UN Security Council's five permanent members (the P5); namely China, France, Russia, the United Kingdom, and the United States; plus Germany. The P5+1 is often referred to as the E3+3 by European countries.)

The announcement of the Implementation Day, as agreed in the JCPOA, is a victory for patient diplomacy and dialogue. This will open a new chapter of peace and prosperity for friendly people of Islamic Republic of Iran and the neighbouring regions. There have been regular bilateral interactions and high level consultations including meeting between PM and President of Iran in Ufa, Russia. Minister of Road Transport, Highways and Shipping visited Iran for the Inter-Governmental MoU on Chabahar Port.

After the talks, the two leaders witnessed signing of twelve cooperation documents. The India-Iran-Afghanistan Trilateral Agreement on Establishing Chabahar Transport and Transit Corridors was signed and an India-Iran Joint Statement titled "Civilisational Connect, Contemporary Context" was also issued during the visit.

The close, multifaceted, and friendly relations between India and Kuwait were further cemented during the year. India has consistently been among the top ten trading partners of Kuwait and Kuwait has been a reliable supplier of crude oil and LPG to India and meets about 6 per cent of our energy needs. The Indian community of over 800,000 is the largest expatriate community in Kuwait. Regarding bilateral ties with Lebanon, the focus continued on academic and cultural relations.

Oman is India's maritime neighbour and bilateral historical relations with the country have evolved into a strategic partnership. The recent times have marked the Diamond Jubilee of establishment of diplomatic relations between India and Oman and to commemorate the 60th anniversary, a series of cultural events were organised.

India and Saudi Arabia enjoy cordial and friendly relations reflecting the centuries old economic and socio-cultural ties. Saudi Arabia hosts nearly 3 million Indian expatriates, the largest Indian passport holding community outside India. The two countries have made steady progress in political, economic, defence, and security cooperation. The two sides regularly exchange high level visits and remain engaged at various levels. During Haj, around 136,000 Indians visited the Kingdom to perform Haj.

The multi-faceted engagement between India and Qatar further intensified during this period. PM Modi paid an official visit to the State of Qatar, Doha wherein regional and international issues of mutual interest were discussed and 7 MoUs/agreements were signed.

In the ongoing crisis in Syria, India continues to maintain its consistent position of peaceful resolution of conflicts. India has called upon all sides to the Syrian conflict to abjure violence so that conducive conditions can be created for an inclusive political dialogue leading to a comprehensive political solution, taking into account the legitimate aspirations of the Syrian people. India has maintained that there can be no military solution to this conflict.

The traditionally close and friendly relations between India and UAE were further cemented by exchange of high-level visits during this period. Prime Minister Modi paid a visit to UAE and this historic visit of the Prime Minister taking place after a gap of 34 years brought a paradigm shift in our relations with UAE, elevating the relationship to a comprehensive strategic partnership. Shortly after the PM's visit, Crown Prince of Abu Dhabi paid a visit to India and several MoUs were signed during the visit.

India and Yemen enjoy a long history of close and historical people-to-people contacts. Due to the deterioration of political and security situation in Yemen, the Government of India, in coordination with the Indian Missions in Sana and Addis Ababa, undertook a massive evacuation exercise 'Operation Raahat' in April 2015. A total number of 6,710 persons, including 4,748 Indians and 1,962 foreign nationals of 48 countries were assisted in evacuation by air and sea routes from Sana's airport and Aden, Al Hudaydah and Al Mukalla ports.

India and Israel

Israeli Prime Minister Benjamin Netanyahu visit to India in January 2018 underlined the extent to which Indo-Israel ties had strengthened over the past few decades. There is now domestic consensus in India that strong ties with Israel are essential for Indian national security interests.

From India's recognition of Israel in 1950 to the early 1990s, the relationship remained informal in nature. India's opposition to official diplomatic relations with Israel stemmed from both domestic and foreign considerations. Indian politicians feared losing the Muslim vote if relations were normalised with Israel. India's stake in the Middle East was also high given the large number of its its citizens working in Arab States of the Persian Gulf, who were helping India maintain its foreign-exchange reserves. India's domestic need for energy was another reason for the lack of normalisation of ties with Israel, in terms of safeguarding the flow of oil from Arab nations. But Prime Minister Narendra Modi deserves credit for investing personally in this relationship and for finally de-hyphenating India's relationship with Israel from Palestine. This was an important move, as for decades, even as Israel stood with India in times of crises, Indian political leadership was shy of reciprocating. Everything was done behind the scenes which was not sustainable in the long run. Modi has made it clear that bilateral relationships should stand on their own merit.

Today, the relationship is moving beyond just defense. Netanyahu's visit largely focused on economic and high-end technology cooperation as well as boosting people-to-people linkages through cinema and tourism. Israel's technological prowess remains unmatched in areas as diverse as waste management and reprocessing, desalination, agriculture, waste water recycling, health, biotechnology, and nanotechnology. This is something that India is looking to tap into.

But Prime Minister Narendra Modi deserves credit for investing personally in this relationship and for finally de-hyphenating India's relationship with Israel from Palestine. This was an important move, as for decades, even as Israel stood with India in times of crises, Indian political leadership was shy of reciprocating. Everything was done behind the scenes which was not sustainable in the long run. Modi has made it clear that bilateral relationships should stand on their own merit.

India-Israel economic cooperation is still below potential, but the two sides are now re-evaluating it. But, in the meantime, India-Israel counterterrorism cooperation is quite robust and has been scaled up gradually over the last few years through a joint working group on terrorism. Intelligence-sharing in this realm has been the most important element of this partnership. Israel is helping India improve border management along the India-Pakistan border given Israel's experience in dealing with cross-border infiltration and terrorism. Cybersecurity cooperation is also expanding, with cybersecurity academies being set up in India by an Israeli company, Vital Intelligence Group.

For Israel, Iran is the most significant national security threat. But it is a sign of the growing maturity of India-Israel relations that Israel has not made Indo-Iranian ties central to its engagement with India. There is a recognition in Israel that India's ties with Iran are longstanding and should be viewed in the wider regional context, where India is trying to develop regional connectivity via Iran to Central Asia.

Also, like most countries, Israel is also adjusting to a world where China's influence is getting stronger. Its ties with China have been growing at a time when it is reaching out to non-Western powers in a big way. The breadth and depth of India-Israel ties is no match as of now for the Sino-Israeli one, which is largely driven by trade and commerce. In this context, India is prioritizing economic and trade ties with Israel. India is Israel's 10th largest trading partner. After the establishment of diplomatic relations between the two countries in 1992, civilian bilateral trade has grown to about $5 billion per year.

Over the last 25 years, bilateral trade between the two countries has increased from $200 million to more than $4 billion (excluding defence) in 2016-17. Still, given India's large market and huge consumer base, the numbers are low compared to India's economic relations with other countries.

Currently, India is the largest arms buyer from Israel; trade is to the tune of approximately $600 million.

If defence ties keep increasing at the same rate, Israel may replace Russia as India's largest arms supplier. In 2016, India signed the biggest weapons deal in Israeli defence history, which is nearly $2 billion. This mega deal will provide India with an advanced defence system of medium-range surface-to-air missiles, launchers and communications technology.

Africa

The year 2015 marked a very special and a historic year in India-Africa partnership that saw unprecedented interaction at the leadership level. India hosted the Third India Africa Forum Summit in New Delhi with all 54 African countries, with whom India has diplomatic relations, participating in the Summit with a record 41 African countries participating at the level of Heads of State/Government.

The 70th anniversary year of the establishment of the United Nations saw two important world conferences take place in Africa namely, the Third International Conference on Financing for Development (Addis Ababa) and the WTO Ministerial Conference in Nairobi in December. India cooperated closely with the African partners on issues of 2030 Agenda for Sustainable Development that was adopted by the UN General Assembly and on finalisation of the post 2020 Agreement on Climate Change that was finalised at the COP 21 of the UNFCCC in Paris. The adoption of the Agenda 2063 by the African Union took place.

The India-Africa engagement intensified the focus on the strengthening of the business linkages of trade and investment and the political interaction that is based on the unique south-south cooperation comprising the multifaceted development partnership that includes education and capacity building, cooperation in agriculture, energy, technology, infrastructure, and healthcare among others. The partnership also focussed on emerging issues of cooperation in the areas of blue economy, counter-terrorism, and maritime security. Longstanding diaspora linkages form an important aspect of India-Africa ties. The West African region is home to Africa's largest population and fastest growing economies with largest proven reserves of energy resources. Over the past 10 years, many of the economies within the region have been outpacing economies anywhere else in the world, and this booming economic growth has helped create the fastest-growing middle class in the world.

A growing population and abundance of natural resources ensure that West Africa offers tremendous investment and economic opportunities for states and businesses alike. Prior to 2000, the combined Gross Domestic Product (GDP) for this region was estimated to be less than

$250 billion. Yet, within the space of a decade, GDP had more than doubled to approximately $565 billion. Of fundamental importance to economic growth have been a host of economic and political reforms that have stimulated new business opportunities across West Africa. Indeed, the growth in GDP has been mirrored by a substantial rise in Foreign Direct Investment (FDI). Since the mid-1990s, West Africa has seen the historic shift from military regimes to constitutional rule, cessation of civil wars in several countries, and renewed regional economic integration.

The West African region is home to Africa's largest population and fastest growing economies with largest proven reserves of energy resources. Over the past 10 years, many of the economies within the region have been outpacing economies anywhere else in the world, and this booming economic growth has helped create the fastest-growing middle class in the world.

The West Africa region continues to gain strategic importance for India. India's bilateral trade with the region has been following a rising trend and currently stands at around US $31 billion, having increased 15 times since 2003. India sources about 18 per cent of its crude oil requirements from this region. Capacity building, skills development, and strengthening of physical and social infrastructure have remained at the centre of India's expanding development partnership with the region. India has continued to lend its active support to international efforts aimed at restoration of constitutional order, peace, security, and stability in the region. Indian troops are involved in several peace keeping operations in countries in West Africa. The Third India Africa Forum Summit provided an opportunity for renewed high level contacts with leaders of West Africa.

Europe and the European Union

Outreach to West has remained a key focus where high-level visits were instrumental in establishing robust roadmaps for enhanced partnerships with these important countries in priority areas of mutual interest.

India-France relations received a boost with the highly successful visit of Prime Minister Modi to France. The Prime Minister of India and French President met again in Paris at the Leaders' Event of the 21st Session of the Conference of the Parties to the United Nations Framework Convention on Climate Change (COP 21) in Paris and jointly launched the International Solar Alliance (ISA). The President of France visited India as the Chief Guest of India's 67th Republic Day. With this, France became the country with the most number of invitations (five) as the Chief Guest on India's Republic Day. The visit saw concrete progress in bilateral cooperation in the defence, civil, and nuclear and space sectors which are the tripod of our Strategic Partnership with France.

New emergent areas of counter-terrorism, maritime security, and renewable energy were added to the strategic agenda.

Prime Minister Modi paid an official visit to Germany to inaugurate the Hannover Messe 2015 where India participated as the Partner Country.

India's rising profile forged a deeper strategic partnership in areas such as nuclear power, defence, cyber security, counter-terrorism, maritime security, and organised crime; and India's flagship development projects through fund raising, Smart Cities, Clean India, Skill India, and Clean Energy projected our interest to enhance ties.

India continued to share close and cordial relations with the countries in Central Europe. The bilateral relations strengthened through a constant exchange of visits, business interactions, and cultural exchanges. A special focus during the year was on holding seminars and other such fora to disseminate information about Government of India's policies and flagship projects particularly, *Make in India*, *Digital India*, *Clean Ganga*, *Skill India*, etc. The second edition of India-Central Europe Business Forum was held in Bengaluru, wherein official and business representatives from 18 countries from Central Europe participated. Poland was the partner country in the Forum this year. The first ever International Day of Yoga was also marked by a number of simultaneous yoga classes, lectures and demonstrations in a number of cities throughout the region.

The Americas

Canada

India-Canada bilateral relations have seen a transformation in recent years which is underpinned by shared values of democracy, pluralism, expanding economic engagement, regular high-level interactions, and long standing people-to-people ties. The relationship witnessed a new momentum with the visit of the Prime Minister to Canada and the elevation of bilateral relationship to a strategic partnership. India will continue to engage with the newly elected government in Canada. Canada is home to over 1.2 million Persons of Indian Origin (PIO) who comprise more than 3 per cent of the country's population. In order to expand people-to-people ties, during his visit to Canada, the Prime Minister announced the Electronic Travel Authorisation for Canadian nationals. Long-term visa of ten years for the Canadian nationals was also announced.

Energy has been a primary area of our focus, considering that Canada is an 'energy superpower' with one of the world's largest resources of uranium, natural gas, oil, coal, minerals, and advanced technologies in hydrocarbons, mining, renewable energy, and nuclear energy. In the hydrocarbon sector, Indian Oil has acquired 10 per cent participating interest in Pacific North West PNW LNG Project, British Columbia. During the visit of the Prime Minister to Canada, Department of Atomic Energy and M/S CAMECO Inc., Canada signed an agreement for supply of 3000 metric tonnes of uranium ore concentrate to India in 2015–2020. The first shipment of uranium arrived in India. Bilateral trade amounted to US $4.48 billion. The cumulative Indian FDI was US $789.6 million in India. To spur bilateral trade and economic ties, both sides are actively negotiating CEPA (Comprehensive Economic Partnership Agreement) and BIPPA (Bilateral Investment Promotion and Protection Agreement).

United States of America

Prime Minister Modi visited the US and the trip was aimed at consolidation of progress made in various areas and to intensify cooperation for the future. There were significant and concrete outcomes in key areas of cooperation such as civil nuclear clean energy defence and security; politico-strategic engagement; economy, and people-to-people ties. A number of documents were also signed/finalised in the run up to the visit. India-US bilateral relations have developed into extensive bilateral strategic and global partnership, based on shared democratic values and increasing convergence of interests on bilateral, regional, and global issues. The Prime Minister's second visit to the US was aimed at harnessing the US capital and technology and in strengthening existing investment and technology partnerships with the US industry across a range of diversified areas, especially renewable energy; digital economy, innovation, and manufacturing. There were major exchanges at political and functional levels in various sectors, including in trade and economy, health, energy, science and technology, homeland security, counter-terrorism, climate change, and others, which culminated in the first Strategic and Commercial Dialogue. There was also renewed interest on both sides to strengthen bilateral economic engagement. There was robust defence engagement with greater focus on co-development and co-production under the defence technology and trade initiative. Reciprocal visits at the Defence Minister's level this year put the cooperation on a firm footing with the signing of 10 year 'Framework for the India-US Defence Relationship'.

India-US trade and commercial engagement continued to expand with healthy growth in trade (in goods and services), investment, and technology partnerships. During 2014–15, Indian goods exports to the US amounted to US $42.45 billion which accounted for 13.67 per cent of India's global exports. Indian imports amounted to US $21.82 billion which accounted for 4.87 per cent of India's total import over the same period. The trade surplus of US $20.63 billion is in favour of India. The US is India's second largest trading partner in goods. FDI from the US has increased from $806 million in 2013–14 to $1.8 billion in 2014–15 marking an increase of 126 per cent making it the 6th largest investor in India.

Latin America and Caribbean Countries

Argentina

There has always existed a lot of warmth and mutual respect in bilateral relations between India and Argentina. The relationship between the two countries continued to grow in substance through high-level visits and increased trade and tourism. Two important developments in India and Argentina's bilateral commercial relations strengthened bilateral trade relations namely, (i) Presidential Amendment of Annexe II to include India in the list of countries for pharma imports in Argentina and (ii) India's issuance of phytosanitary clearance on exports of Argentine apples, pears and quinces.

Bolivia

India and Bolivia relations continued to be friendly and intensified particularly after conclusion of the first Foreign Office Consultation. Bilateral trade between the two countries substantially increased due to the visit of trade delegations.

Brazil

On the bilateral front, relations have been very important and productive, particularly after the visit of the Indian Prime Minister Modi. The global drop in commodity prices and the economic recession affected Brazil's overall trade as also our bilateral trade which is approximately US $6.63 billion with Indian exports at US $3.73 billion and Brazilian exports at US $2.9 billion, giving India a trade surplus of US $828 million.

Chile

India and Chile continue to enjoy excellent relations. The bilateral trade between India and Chile reached US $1,636.46 million with Indian exports at US $404.44 million and imports from Chile at US $1,232.02 million.

Colombia

India-Colombia relations continue to grow. Due to fall in crude oil, the bilateral trade between the two countries was affected. Colombia's exports to India accounted for US $909,72 mn, a fall of 7.15 per cent mainly due to fall in export of crude oil and its price.

Ecuador

Bilateral relations with Ecuador continue to be cordial and strong. Bilateral trade also continued to grow.

Guyana

Bilateral relations between India and Guyana continue to grow. President Pranab Mukherjee paid a state visit to India, where he attended the Pravasi Bharatiya Divas as its Chief Guest and was conferred with the Pravasi Bharatiya Samman Award.

Mexico

India's relations with Mexico received a boost when Prime Minister Modi paid a working visit to Mexico, with the objective to continue the dialogue held by the two leaders on the margins of the 70th regular session of the United Nations General Assembly. The Foreign Minister of Mexico visited India and held bilateral discussions with his counterpart. They undertook a comprehensive review of the entire gamut of bilateral relations including political, commercial, trade, financial, technical, and other areas to further broaden and strengthen cooperation. They also discussed important regional and international issues of mutual interest. The 65th anniversary of the establishment of diplomatic relations between the two countries has taken place. Growth in bilateral trade has been impressive in recent years. In Mexico's total global exports, India ranks 8th whereas India is Mexico's 14th largest partner in global market. The total bilateral trade in 2014 was recorded as US $6.4 billion. Mexican investments in India too are on the rise.

Peru

As always, bilateral relations between the two countries have been cordial. India's exports were US $819.858 million while imports amounted to US $590.395 million.

Venezuela

India and Venezuala have been maintaining cordial relations. Venezuala has emerged as India's 3rd largest supplier of crude oil. India imported oil worth US $12 billion. Bilateral trade touched US $12.3 billion in 2014"15, a steep jump from US $6.6 billion in 2011.

Honduras

The bilateral relations between India and Honduras were strengthened with the conclusion of first Foreign Office Consultations (FOC) between India and Honduras.

Nicaragua

India-Nicaragua bilateral relations strengthened with the holding of the first India-Nicaragua Foreign Office Consultation. Both sides committed to strengthen relations in the political, economic, commercial, and consular area. Bilateral trade registered at US $92 million marginal increase.

Barbados

Barbados and India enjoy close and cordial relations and interact actively in the UN, Commonwealth, and NAM. The first ever Foreign Office Consultations between India and Barbados was held in Bridgetown in Barbados. India and Barbados have signed the Air Services Agreement for facilitation of travel arrangements for the citizens and the possibility of direct air connectivity and chartered flight operations between the two countries. The electronic travel authorisation system (eTVA) for Barbadians has already been implemented.

MEETS, SUMMITS, ASSOCIATIONS, & ORGANISATIONS

Association of Southeast Asian Nations (ASEAN)

The India-ASEAN Strategic Partnership has acquired new momentum following the enunciation of the "Act-East Policy" by PM Modi at the 12th ASEAN-India Summit and 9th East Asia Summits at Na Pyi Taw, Myanmar. ASEAN is the anchor of India's Act East Policy and India has continued to deepen its political, security, defence, and economic ties with ASEAN member states, including by establishing an Indian Mission to ASEAN. It has also proactively engaged with the various ASEAN-centric fora for shaping the evolving regional architecture, notably the East Asia Summit (EAS), ASEAN Regional Forum (ARF), ASEAN Defence Ministers' Meeting Plus (ADMM+)

and Expanded ASEAN Maritime Forum (EAMF). With the entry into force of the ASEAN-India Free Trade Area, India looks forward to greater integration with ASEAN and the wider Asia-Pacific. In 2017, ASEAN and India observed the 25th anniversary of Dialogue Relations, 15 years of Summit -level interaction, and 5 years of strategic partnership by undertaking a wide range of commemorative activities.

East Asia Summit

The Prime Minister, Narendra Modi, participated in the 10th East Asia Summit (EAS) in Kuala Lumpur. He shared India's perspectives on regional and global issues such as terrorism, maritime security, etc. with his counterparts, while reiterating India's support for strengthening of the East Asia Summit.

A conference to popularise the International North-South Transport Corridor (INSTC) route in Mumbai was also held. Customs officials of India, Russia, and Azerbaijan also met in Astrakhan, Russia.

Turkmenistan-Afghanistan-Pakistan-India (TAPI) Gas Pipeline Project

The Vice President of India attended the ground-breaking ceremony of the Turkmenistan-Afghanistan-Pakistan-India (TAPI) Gas Pipeline Project held in Mary, in Turkmenistan along with President of Turkmenistan and Afghanistan and the Prime Minister of Pakistan. The Cabinet approved India's accession to the Ashgabat Agreement. The transit agreement provides for a transit corridor between Uzbekistan, Turkmenistan, Iran, and Oman before reaching the Persian Gulf. India's membership bid now awaits the approval of the original parties to the Agreement. India was invited to join Ashgabat Agreement during the visit of the Prime Minister to Turkmenistan.

Shanghai Cooperation Organisation

The year heralded a new phase in India's relations with the Shanghai Cooperation Organisation (SCO). During its Council of Heads of State Meeting in Ufa, Russia, the SCO announced its decision to initiate India's membership. Prime Minister Modi addressed the SCO Plenary Session. Representatives from India attended various SCO meetings during the year including the health, interior, justice, trade and commerce ministerial meetings, and the meeting of SCO Prosecutors General. India signed the Memorandum of Obligation with the Organisation at the Council of Heads of States Summit held in Tashkent, Uzbekistan. This initiated India's membership process of SCO, which will be followed by timely accession to various documents under the SCO framework.

18

CHAPTER

Bilateral, Regional and Global Groups and India

OVERVIEW

No nation can ignore permanency of interests. India is no exception. We have therefore bilateral, regional, and global treaties through groupings to promote our cause and interests; economic, political, cultural, etc. 'Country first, countrymen next, and country cousins last' often rules the policy. It is always an interesting thought 'how we got here'; our 'tryst with destiny'. What lies ahead and where?

INTRODUCTION

This topic regarding bilateral, regional, and global groupings involving India and affecting the country's interests is interesting, intriguing, and intricate. Simply outlining bilateral, regional, and global groupings on the one hand, and narrating agreements involving India and/or affecting her interests would at best be like a notification. It serves no the purpose except meeting the need only in a perfunctory manner.

Hans J. Morgenthau, in his world famous book '*Politics Among Nations*,' has analysed how nations shape their policies and what has happened in history over the last two centuries. Why do countries go for bilateral, regional, and global groupings? Countries have some common themes and basic interests.

1) Political interests.
2) Economic interests.
3) Strategic interests.
4) Social, cultural interests.
5) Historic compulsions.

Let's examine them one by one.

Basic Interests

(1) Political interests : Political interests are paramount. Nations do not want to get isolated. Pacts and treaties are important; the intent may be aggressive or passive. France was isolated in 1870 by Prussia under Bismarck and then defeated in a battle. This changed the political equations in Europe, leading ultimately to the First World War (1914–1918). Pakistan's aggressive designs with China compelled India to have pacts with other countries to offset this. The India-Soviet Pact of 1971 for twenty years is another instance of an enduring political pact.

(2) Economic interests : Economic interests are of supreme importance. Nations want to expand, extend, and excel in their trade. As is known, no nation has all the facilities, so trading is inescapable. A country like Japan has hardly any oil or other raw materials, it has to import them. Similarly, India has a huge dependence on West Asian countries for oil. India is short in nickel, copper, etc. as also uranium. Such are the compulsions; nations have to go in for treaties.

(3) Strategic interests : Strategic interests also predominate. Nations often have strategic considerations that shape their policies. Such considerations push nations to go in for treaties. Examples of this could be protecting sea lanes, usage of port facilities of the other nations, and pre-empting other nations from reaching there. India's treaties with Maldives, Nepal, Sri Lanka are all examples of this. Strategic interests are often for security reasons. For example, India has strategic ties with Israel for arms and agricultural technologies.

(4) Social/cultural interests : Social/, cultural interests are another set of interests which form the basis of ties and treaties. India's ties with Nepal, Bangladesh, Bhutanand Bhutan is a fine example of this.

Existence of such basis helps in forging ties or treaties.

(5) Historic compulsions : Historic compulsions are not rare. Many a nation goes for such consideration in outlining their policies. India's ties with Britain through the Common Wealth comity of nations are the result of historical compulsions: it's a bond that bridges the gap. Britain and United states are tied historically, historically; they fought the two World Wars together. Portugal and Brazil are linked similarly.

FACTORS GOVERNING POLITICAL RELATIONS

Basically, politics among nations are governed by three factors:

A. National power.

B. Problems of international peace.

C. Position of The international scenario.

National Power

National power, in essence, means the elements that constitute a nation's power. All nations do not have all the elements favourably placed. It is interesting that many nations possess considerable power even with a few elements they are positively blessed with. Some elements of national power are as given below:

(a) Geography.

(b) Natural capacity.

(c) Industrial capacity.

(d) Military preparedness.

(e) Population.

(f) Morale.

(g) Quality of diplomacy, and government

India scores adequately well on most of the points but her unsustainable population and lack of industrial capacity brings her down. Two hundred years back, Britain with its navy shone very well in military preparedness. Germany before the First World War excelled in many area but the quality of its diplomacy and government was poor–beyond belief and, beyond relief. China today scores well on most points, but is now seen as a threat to the sovereignty of nations.

Problems of International Peace

International peace is always a factor; without peace there can be no trade or treaties. 'Peace is dependent on many factors but essentially it is indivisible', as M. Litvinov, Soviet Foreign Minister put it in 1939 before Nazi-Soviet pact. Before we look at it, it is well worth pointing that national power has limitations too. National power is limited by:

(1) Balance of Power : Power among nations

(2) International Morality : Rights and Wrong.

(3) International Law : Existing Laws.

The International Scenario

National power is also limited by culture and tradition; some nations do not have the desire to further their national power for aggression. Switzerland, Tibet, and Denmark are examples of this. India too is peace-loving. Peaceful living and international peace is factored in by the following:

1) Limitation–example, disarmament.

2) Transformation–example, the efforts of United Nations, etc.

3) Accommodation–example, diplomacy.

DIFFERENT PHASES IN THE WORLD

The world has seen all three factors at work. Today's world has reached a stage of end to limitations phase. Countries like North Korea and China are going ahead with armaments. The transformation stage through UN, etc. has reached an abrupt end. Accommodation through diplomacy is still on, although rules of the game are changing.

International schemes have undergone a sea change. We can broadly state that the old balance of power has given way to new balance of power. In our analysis, the world has seen the following phases.

(i) 1871–1914 : Phase of Division. Germany and France remained hostile, leading to division between triple alliance (Austria-Hungary, Italy , Turkey and Germany) and triple entente (France, Britain, and Russia)

(ii) 1914–1945 : Phase of Disruption: Two World Wars.

(iii) 1945–1990 : Phase of Deterrence: Cold War between US block and USSSR block.

(iv) 1990–2001 : Phase of Dominance: Disintegration of Soviet Union and dominance by United States.

(v) 2001–Present, Phase of Dissent : Narrow nationalism and dissent between Middle East countries and the US block, growth of China as a superpower.

Given this background, nations go for bilateral treaties, regional treaties and global groupings. Considerations are predominantly economic or political; a few are based on strategic interests too.

India has bilateral agreements with most of the nations. However, to fully understand the issues in perspective it is essential to appreciate the following factors.

FACTORS INFLUENCING BILATERAL TIES AND TREATIES.

Political

Issues involved here include peace and cooperation treaties, extradition issues, terrorism related matters, security, cyber crimes, fugitives, non-interference in each other's matters, and respecting each others sovereignty. Panchsheel, in essence, marked quintessentially such treaties' basic tenets.

India's treaty with Pakistan in 1972 known as the 'Simla Agreement' is one such example.

Economic

While economic ties have expanded the world over, political arrangements have shrunk. Economic ties relate to trade, balance of trade, aid and assistance, investments, collaborations, most favoured nation status, tariffs, and banking transactions. The emergence of world order under the World Trade Organisations (WTO) obviously has resolved many issues. Even so, bilateral trade through arrangements of treaties still remains patently a strong issue. India has good working relations with almost all countries of the world. The moot point is what is that which nations can offer to each other to foster economic ties. Years back, UAE was hardly a dominant player for India's economic scenario but today, it is so. Presently, India is also looking to the east to expand its economic footprints even as China is aggressively reaching to Africa and Central Asia. India is seeking Iran out with Port facilities at Chahbahar to reach Central Asia through Afghanistan while China is perched in Gawadar port in Pakistan for similar pursuits.

Historic

Historical factors are another set of issues that make ties and treaties easy. Australia and Britain look justifiably proud in such associations. New Zealand and Britain too bond. India also cannot overlook its British association, notwithstanding two centuries of rule, repression, and regression. History beckons, historical associations beseech, and historic events bestir ourselves to advance. India and Indonesia, Cambodia, Afghanistan, Iran, and Mongolia have historic ties. Sometimes historic ties are rooted in religion, like with Buddhism for India and its neighbours. India and China share a history of culture, trade, and religion; ancient Silk Route is testimony to that. Bhutan and India are linked historically.

BASIS OF REGIONAL TIES AND TREATIES

What is the basis of regional ties or treaties? Mutual interests apart, there are compulsions. What are the mutual interests and what are the compulsions?

For years, India was dependent upon Russia (the then Soviet Union) for import of arms, but today the United States, France, Israel, Italy, and Belgium are emerging as partners. For oil, India has treaties with Saudi Arabia, UAE, Iran, etc. while Iraq and Libya have fallen behind due to strife and turmoil. For some years in the Middle East, oil and turmoil have gone together. Strategic interests sometimes override all other considerations. For the sake of peace and security under political interests, and prosperity and sustenance under economic interests, nations give strategic interests the prime thrust. Britain considered holding India as its strategic asset even though economically it was proving a difficult choice; after the Second World War, the harsh realisation dawned on Britain to set the ball rolling for our freedom. India, with two hostile neighbours in Pakistan and China, has an inescapable need to befriend other countries in the region. India has strategic ties with Nepal, Bhutan, Bangladesh, Afghanistan, and Sri Lanka. In such situations, it is often the case that ties have to be maintained at any cost. Both Sri Lanka and Bangladesh have seen ties with India go down, albeit not for long in the past. Aggressive Chinese outreach through economic aid and assistance is a cause for concern, even though India has genuine concern for causes that are worthy of intervention. Assistance to Nepal in the wake of earthquakes, supply of drinking water to Maldives, etc. is a case in point. Strategic interests are always there, a good part of the nineteenth century saw the 'Great Game' being played in the vastness of Central Asia and vastness of the Himalayas between Britain and Russia, with India as the 'Prize'. Today, India has a strategic interest in advancing its pursuit in keeping sea lanes safe for economic interests.

'Struing of Pearls,' by China is seen by India as encirclement–One Belt, One Road by China with Pakistan help through occupied Kashmir. Social and cultural interests are other factors in the matter of bilateral ties and treaties, nations cannot escape it. Often social and cultural ties act as a bonding factor. India too has this issue of social and cultural factors. Churchill during the Second World War cleverly used the bonding factor of 'Anglo-Saxon' ties. "What kind of people we Anglo-Saxons are, Germany thinks?', caught the imagination of the Americans. Russia came to the aid of Serbia in the First World War, driven by slave brotherhood appeal. Nepal, Sri Lanka, Bhutan, Maldives, and Myanmar bond with India, given the social and cultural affinity.

These then are the various underlying issues that attend bilateral issues. Bilateralism does not mean negation of regionalism, rather it enhances it. Regional ties, treaties, and groupings generally are for political and economic interests. Peace pacts, treaties acknowledging regional issues, and agreements covering general principles of association form the essence of political treaties. NATO, CENTO, and SEATO were all formed for advancing regional security efforts; CENTO, and SEATO have fallen by the wayside to pass into the limbo of history, NATO lived on and with the exit of threat of communism, it stands without a cause, but with a case. US is giving a rethink on its funding. SAARC is another fine example of regional aspirations, BIMSTEC is yet another.

BILATERAL, REGIONAL AND GLOBAL TIES

We have covered bilateral ties of India with other countries with dominant issues being economic. Bilateral ties, generally, focus on security, trade, tourism, infrastructure and movement of people. As it is commonly believed and understood , bilateral issues do not permit interference by other countries and, hence, it is preferred mode of sorting outstanding matters of interest. India sees "Kashmir's issue" as a bilateral matter and doesn't want third party involvement.

REGIONAL GROUPINGS

Geographic or political or economic or social or environmental compulsions dictate formation of regional groupings. We have seen the SAARC, BIMSTEC being two such examples.

European Union (EU0), ASEAN (Association of South EAST Asian Nations), SCO (Shanghai Cooperation Organisation), APEC (Asia Pacific Economic Cooperation) – India's interests are affected by these regional groupings, particularly with it's Look East policy. As a growing market, India interests these regional groupings. China remains a factor in so far as it competes with India. These regional groupings are predominantly economic oriented and political underpinnings do not influence that much. Problem, however, is one of perception as many of these countries see India as an uncertain choice, given it's red tapism and bureaucratic tangles and wrangles. Indian tariffs and trade tiffs too figure high.

ASEAN, no doubt, is the best known example of regional cooperation based on trust and tolerance. It gives ASEAN great strength too that major shopping lines pass through this region. India's growing strength and opportunities make it an alternative destination, particularly, after the country has shed off it's inhibitions dealing with free trade countries.

GLOBAL GROUPINGS

Here are those groupings which transcend geographical barriers with countries coming together due to mutuality of interests and multiplicity of common concerns. BRICS (Brazil, Russia, India, China and South Africa) was first conceived in 2009 with Brazil, Russia, India and China; South Africa joined in 2011. G-20 (established in 1999) has 19 countries and the European Union. It is a body of developed and emerging economies, accounting for 90 per cent of global economy and two-thirds of world population. Brics has come a long way but sheer geographical distances make meaningful cooperation a messy issue, although initiatives like setting up of a new development bank, think tank council are welcome moves.

G-20 is a group of advanced countries and emerging economies that was set up in 1999; India is the only participant from SAARC countries. In G-20, India us driven by the need to bring in greater inclusivity un the financial system and to seek avoidance of protectionist tendencies. Adequate flow of finances to developing and emerging economies too is a n urgent issue on India's agenda.

Indian Ocean Rim Association (IOR-ARC) is an international organization comprising coastal states bordering Indian Ocean. Priority areas identified by it are: Maritime safety and security, trade and investment facilitation, fisheries management, disaster risk reduction, academic and science and technology competition, tourism and cultural exchange.

India's perspective on Regional and Global Treaties

Regional Treaties: India's position is piquant; it is obviously to contend with China with all it's economic and political might. Pakistan is an irritant, as always. Regional issues have trade, energy, security, environment, infrastructure and tourism as the major concerns. Free trade doesn't work to India's advantage, given domestic compulsions. Infrastructure in India's north-east is weak. China's CPEC policy and it's close links with Pakistan to exploit Pak occupied Kashmir is a major concern. China 's domination of sea lanes too is a major concern.

Regional treaties are also hamstrung by lack of resources to back them up. Political instability and severe competition make the scenario even more complicated. Tax matters are another irritant. It cannot be denied also that notwithstanding emerging complementaries between India and the regional players, India's performance and commitment to time schedules is tardy and deficient. Chahbahar Port in Iran is an example.

INTERNATIONAL TREATIES AND INDIA

India is indeed one of the fastest growing economies in the world and is considered an attractive destination. It has vast resources and rich in human resources as well. It, therefore, seeks agreements that are favourable to it's development. It is India's interests to pursue international agreements that promote financial inclusion and upgradation of systems.

India has lot of concern about environmental issues that usually are addressed through international meetings and treaties. Rio declaration, Cartegna protocol on bio-diversity, Agenda 21, Ramsar convention are all examples of this.

Similarly, India is vocal about agreements on security and terrorism; it has signed all the protocols and agreements against hijacking etc; Likewise, it has deep interest in patents and Intellectual Property Rights too. There have been disputes between United States and India on drug patent issues for long.

Atomic Energy and nuclear materials are another field in which India has issues; Nuclear supply Group (NSG) is a burning issue. India has had no success so far, given Chinese opposition.

19

CHAPTER

Developed and Developing Countries and India

OVERVIEW

The world is expanding economically but narrowing politically. Sooner or later politics will dominate economics. Both the developed and developing countries are at crossroads. India is poised to grow; it has need of FDI, technology, and systems from the developed countries. It can offer skilled workforce, manufacture base, and software support. To the developing countries India can offer technology, assistance, and services. The point however is globalisation and integration. With Brexit, President Trump's protectionist America, a disunited Europe and an ambitious China, globalisation has been replaced by protectionism and narrow nationalism. The only hope lies in somehow activating international institutions and hoping that they act as a bridge between countries and interest groups.

INTRODUCTION

This chapter is about the effect on India's interests and Indian diaspora, due to the policies and politics of developed and developing countries. There always has been a debate between the haves and have nots, between the developed and the developing, between the north and the south, and between G-7 and G-77 countries. India finds itself as a country of paradoxes. It is indeed is a fast developing country with vast underdevelopment; a country launching space missions to probe the Mars, while its masses languish in grinding poverty. A country of contrasts : of unbelievable riches and inexplicable poverty. Where does India stand in relation to developed and developing countries? To appreciate the full position, first we need to understand and evaluate certain underlying factors and certain harsh realities. Foremost, where does India stand in terms of its exports and imports. The Table provided here gives an indicative position of the country's exports and imports.

INDIA'S EXPORTS AND IMPORTS (2014–15)

No.	Share of	Imports	Exports
1.	Plantation	0.59	0.24
2.	Agri and Agri products	9.18	5.37
3.	Marine products	1.92	0.02
4.	Ores and Minerals	0.72	5.35
5.	Leather and Leather manufactures	2.15	0.26
6.	Gems and Jewellery	14.6	15.22
7.	Sports goods	0.09	0.05
8.	Chemicals and Related items	12.17	9.91
9.	Plastic and Rubber articles	2.46	3.61
10.	Stone, Plaster, Cement, Mica, Glass, Ceramic, Asbestos	1.46	0.64
11.	Paper and related products	0.9	1.84
12.	Base metals	7.28	6.46
13.	Medical and surgical	10.61	1.08
14.	Electronic items	2.1	10.43
15.	Machinery	7.15	8.12
16.	Office equipment	0.03	0.03
17.	Transport equipment	8.1	3.22
18.	Project goods	0.01	0.07
19.	Textiles and Allied items	13.64	1.39
20.	Petroleum crude and products	12.2	23.05
21.	Others (handicrafts, packaging material, etc.)	2.65	3.04
	Total	100.00	100.00

Source : *India Year Book 2017*

It emerges clearly that imports exceed exports, giving us an adverse balance of trade. The country has a dependence on others for oil (energy) imports, and exports revolve round traditional items like textiles. The country does well to import gold, gems, jewellery, and work on it to export it. We export chemicals and related products more than we import them.

However, our share of the world market on the whole for all the items is very low. In this context, a matrix showing the position of India in relation to Developed Countries here and to Developing Countries later in the chapter can set the scene for further elaboration.

Developed Countries and India					
(I)	**Developed Countries** • *What they want from us*		(II)	**India** • *What it wants from them*	
	1.	Software		1.	Arms
	2.	Satellite launches		2.	Technology
	3.	Medical tourism		3.	FDI, FII
	4.	Skilled labour		4.	Tourism
	5.	Textiles		5.	Immigration
	6.	Chemicals		6.	Nuclear fuel
(III)	**Developed Countries** • *What they want to give developing countries*		(IV)	**India** • *What it wants to give to developed countries*	
	1.	Patented medicines		1.	Manufacturing base
	2.	Consumer goods		2.	Raw materials
	3.	Retail FDI		3.	Vast expanding markets
	4.	Insurance opening		4.	Investment in infrastructure
	5.	Wines, beverages		5.	Modernisation of agriculture
	6.	Defence items		6.	Expansion of services sector

The above matrix shows where India stands, but it does not tell the whole story. *There are many irritants between the developed countries and India. To briefly bring out :*

(1) Environment : Developed countries have, in their own way polluted the environment, and now demand that India should pay for the damage it is causing. India has adopted the western model of development and seeks a larger role from the developed countries. India and China are vociferous and united on this. The Paris COP 21 went a long way with a benevolent Obama joining the issue favourably. Change of situation in the US has brought Trump who feels India and China are literally pay nothing for the damage they cause to the environment. US had stayed aloof from Kyoto protocols as had Russia initially. The Copenhagen Meet saw the developed nations pull one back to strengthen their case. USA is now back to usage of coal in a big way to push for employment in that country. India made big promises for hefty cuts in CO_2 emissions at Paris COP 21 but the situation has changed with US backtracking. 'Political Warming' is more a reality than global warming.

Churchill and Gandhiji never agreed on many issues, yet both were right in their own ways; one in his haughty means and the other in his humble manner. Churchill said, 'Americans always do the right thing after trying everything else.'

Gandhiji said in 1928, 'God forbid that India should ever take to industrialism after the manner of the West. The economic imperialism of a single tiny island Kingdom (UK) is today keeping the world in chains. If the entire nation of 300 million took to similar economic exploitation it would strip the world bare like locusts.'

(2) **Subsidies :** Subsidies to farmers in India are a sore point between India and the developed countries. India has to continue with subsidies to sustain the farmers who are living at subsistence level. The developed world, led by the US, quotes the WTO regimentation; India argues back showing cash subsides given by the US to its farmers. Arguments go on and on. The US cites the case India has put up for 'Window scheme' under which WTO allows for import of food stuffs (essentially for sub-Saharan countries with no food output), and cries foul. India also cries fouls stating that it too has shortages and vagaries of monsoon. Debate is on, so is the acrimony.

(3) **Drugs and Patents :** Drugs and patent issues defy amicable settlement. Developed countries want to cover and recover their research expenses. India looks to its poor who need these drugs. Research by Indian companies has been challenged by the developed countries but as with the Ranbaxy case, India has won the day in court battle. India is now moving over to a regime of 'generic' names which will give more unease to the developed world.

(4) **Immigration and Visas :** This also is an issue. India has an embarrassment of riches; the developed countries have a situation of ageing population and declining birth rates. India has emerged as the youngest country in the world but visas and immigration issues remains a sore point. Recent decisions of US are exacerbating the situation with restriction of work permits, and H-1B visas.

(5) **Labour reforms :** Labour reforms, or the lack of it, in India stings the developed countries; they want to enter the Indian scenario with a culture of 'hire and fire' but Indian compulsions do not envisage that. The country is more used to 'hire and perspire.' Yet, it must be said that India itself is moving towards 'contract labour' regime.

(6) **Indian bureaucracy :** Another sore point is the Indian bureaucracy–a heritage product of 'ancient-regime'; creaky and cynical. For once, we can sympathise with the developed countries. Edwin Montague of 'Montague-Chelmsford' reforms fame once said, 'Indian bureaucracy : too much wood, too much iron, too much of the same think, too much inflexible, too much absolute... too much rule bound, too much.......too much.' He should have known, after all he was the Secretary of State for India and spent two months in India.

(7) **Administration Policy :** Developed countries have a 'business-military administration' nexus which finds ways and means to sell arms and ammunition. Repeated arming of Pakistan has only worsened the scenario for India. 'Arm Pakistan, harm India' is the motto. It is said that when Iran–Iraq war lasted seven years, both sides were being armed by the developed countries. Good economics, good politics.

. Besides the aforementioned, developed countries use imposed quality standards to deny and deprive the developing countries. Quality standards, both in manufacturing and agriculture, insist on series of steps which are time-consuming and costly too. Insistence on avoidance of child labour as with Mirzapur carpets is another sore point.

Investments through FII (Foreign Institutional Investor) is another issue. When the markets in the United States dipped, investors flocked to India but when the situation improved back home they withdrew at once. European countries, save Germany, however were not part of this as they were wrestling with PIGS (Portugal, Ireland, Greece, and Spain) countries.

'Dumping' is a sore point between the developed countries and India; both sides accuse each other.

In the World Trade organisation (WTO) regime, such cases are being sorted out with mutual consent.

EFFECT OF POLITICS AND POLICIES OF DEVELOPED COUNTRIES ON INDIA'S INTERESTS

Politics dictate the policies that countries follow. Politics that the developed countries follow in relation to India set the tone for policies that are followed in the context. Policies are the means and politics the end.

What then are the underlying objectives of politics of developed nations, agreeing that self-interest guides them?

Politics

(1) Resources are scarce and should not be used up; without benefit to the developed world.
(2) Technologies developed by us should be restricted.
(3) Patents in drugs are ours; research was costly, we need to be paid back.
(4) Our development model suits us fine, others must not emulate us if not beneficial to them.
(5) Old, obsolete technologies could be spared.
(6) Polluting industries must move out of our countries.

Policies

(1) Follow policies that will restrict usage of scarce resources. US put an embargo on sale of oil by Iran for years; it affected India among others.
(2) Developed countries deprive others of technologies developed by them through policies, through practice. India was denied access to super computers and missle technology : both were developed by India, the denial by US not with standing.
(3) Developed countries have fleeced the patients in developing countries in the matter of usage of patented research medicines. India responded by research and won court case challenges. Ranbaxy, Dr. Reddy's lab cases are fresh in our minds. In many cases the companies from the developed countries withdrew their patented medicines.
(4) Developed countries, where it suits them, spend heavily to advertise so that developing countries emulate them and become dependent. Cosmetics, consumer goods, life style persona are some ready examples. Mobiles, body sprays, clothes, cars etc are instant examples of this.

(5) Old, obsolete technologies are parcelled out at once and given to developing countries. Birlas took from Italy whole plant for manufacture of 'Ambassador' car which ruled our roads for decades. Developed countries want to get rid of old and obsolete technologies, profitably.

(6) China has taken lots of polluting industries from the developed countries 'for a few dollars more' in its kitty. At what cost, at whose cost? India is now vying for such 'mannas'. Our western coast is all full of huge scrap being dumped by developed countries.

Here again, the matrix does not bring out the very many irritants that stand in the way between India and the developing countries.

(1) Arms and ammunition : Many developing countries are keen to buy very many items from India but Indian government does not encourage that for fear of the said items falling in wrong hands. Hamid Karzai, the previous Afghan President made repeated visits to India to get some sophisticated arms but was denied.

(2) Many developing countries bargain hard with India, citing China. It becomes difficult to match the Chinese. Nepal and Sri Lanka have been approached by the Chinese often. Bangladesh too has been in touch with the Chinese. China has made rapid headway in Africa leaving India far behind. Some African countries initially supported India in NSG (Nuclear supplier Group) but the arm twisting by China saw reversal of stand. Namibia is one example.

(3) Double Taxation Avoidance Agreement (DTAA) is another irritant between many developing countries and India. Mauritius was being used as a conduit for unhealthy bank transactions till India moved in to snap it.

INDIA AND THE DEVELOPING COUNTRIES

Developing countries face both challenges as well as opportunities today; challenges in that they have to develop against all odds in a competitive, combative and constricted world; opportunity in that they have, in most cases, advantages such as strategic location, gifted with raw materials, available population and scope for advancement. The present world order based on democratic principles and equality of opportunity affords lots of opportunities for progress. Yet, it is not so very easy or convenient.

Developing countries face critical choices. Capital is scarce and dependence on developed countries is increasing. Conditions for loans from International Monetary Fund (IMF) are humiliating, as India itself discovered in the eighties. International Bank for Reconstruction and Development (IBRD) is more accommodating in comparison, but condition-oriented nevertheless.

These countries need technology which the developed countries are unwilling to part with. Obsolete and redundant technologies however are handed over with enthusiasm. More often than not, the developing countries don't even need them. Case in point is promotion of labour saving devices which the highly populated developing countries don't even need.

Globalisation has led to massive disruption in developing countries following shut down of local, non-competitive industries. Instance of this can be our own much vaunted television industry which was simply blown away by foreign brands like LG, Samsung etc. Another example could be of our well protected 'Ambassador car' which has bowed out. Examples abound, instances haunt.

Many of the developing countries were colonies of the developed countries, which exploited them for years, draining off all their wealth. Today, these ex-colonies are not sustainable; they somehow still seek the old associations and connections. Even so, some of these countries possess valuable raw materials which they leverage for survival. Colonialism has changed spots, today the economic exploitation does not envisage actual occupation and rule; rather it is done through companies, capital, banks and conferences; it is tele-colonialism.

India, itself as an ex-colony, has gone through these stages. A resurgent India with a marked upswing in economy, expanding market, technological advancement and economies of scale is poised for further progress and growth. In this, the country has enormous opportunities to deal with other developing countries. The catch however is that China too is trying for the same space. The following matrix shows the emerging position.

Developing Countries And India

(I)	**Developing Countries**		**(II)**	**India**	
	• *What they want from India*			• *What India wants from Developing Countries*	
	1.	Technology		1.	Energy and oil
	2.	Engineering goods		2.	Raw materials
	3.	Manpower support and training		3.	Some foodstuffs
	4.	Medicines and drugs		4.	Increased trade
	5.	Communication networks		5.	Immigration
	6.	Arms and ammunition		6.	Tourism
(III)	**Developing Countries**		**(IV)**	**India**	
	• *What they want to give to India*			• *What India wants to give Developing Countries*	
	1.	Turnkey infrastructure projects		1.	Education cooperation
	2.	Raw materials		2.	Tourism facilities
	3.	Joint ventures		3.	Skilled manpower
	4.	Oil prospecting		4.	Textiles, leather goods
	5.	Agri products		5.	Transportation
	6.	Port facilities		6.	Agricultural foodstuffs

Predictably, not presumably, the given matrix does not reveal the full picture or position. There are many factors which compound the complexity. Developing countries are waiting with open arms to receive India, not that India is extending its arms to reach one and all. Issues rooted in history, heritage, hangovers, and hopes are vital too.

All developing countries are not similarly placed. They have their unique features too. Almost all the African countries have come under the colonial rule of European countries like Britain, France, Belgium, Portugal, Holland, and Germany; after independence following the

Second World War they still look to their erstwhile masters (except Germany which lost their possessions after First World War). The ties are, though not strong, relevant. For aid, loans, and technology, many of these countries look for support from the European countries. The model for development too is borrowed from them.

India has to contend with China which has made deep inroads into Africa. Chinese capital, technology, expertise, and experience are a major issue. As a country, China is both feared and favoured, India does not have that fervour or flavour.

As for Asia, the developing countries can be categorised into two parts. First are the so called 'Tiger economies' of 80s like South Korea, Singapore, Malaysia, Hong Kong, etc. which following a model of commerce using shipping, banking, and insurance, recorded spectacular growth but have since slowed down. Second are the tiger cub countries like Thailand, Philippines, Laos, Vietnam, Kampuchea (Cambodia), and Indonesia which are now showing signs of progress. From the first set of countries, India has a chance to learn and earn. South Korea is one country with technology and tradition for collaboration and India is already on to it. The second set of countries offer great prospects for advancing trade and development. Japan has a major presence and has to be rightfully acknowledged. Instead of competing, Japan is the only major country which has not endorsed China's OBOR (One Belt and One Road) project besides India.

South America presents two fold problems; one is the distance and the other domination. India is disadvantaged due to distance. United States has a dominant position there. Monroe doctrine of 1823 declares South America to be under US influence. Even so, Brazil has shown its willingness to cooperate; it is an active member of BRICS. (A wag called them CRIBS countries as they always crib too).

Central Asian Republics (CARs) have enormous potential with huge reserves of gas and minerals. But the terrain is difficult to reach; India is collaborating with Iran with port facilities at Chabahar to link via road through Afghanistan to these republics. Potential and prospect are beckoning but task is daunting. Pakistan is building its Gwadar port 78 miles away with Chinese assistance, India has a task cut out for itself.

Countries which are in Europe, those which were part of the erstwhile Soviet Union like Poland, Hungary, Rumania, Bulgaria, Czech republic, Slovakia, Slovenia, etc. and those in western Europe like Portugal, Spain, Greece, Ireland, etc.–both blocs are at varying stages of development. India has trade agreements with all. India needs engineering goods from these countries and has IT related services to offer. The issue is that European Union covers most of these countries and others are under Russian influence. Hence a balancing act is needed.

An important and interesting aspect of India's relations with developing countries is that in the global slowdown of the economy, India remains one of the bright spots with its economy showing both continuous as well as continual growth. This is in contrast to even China whose economy is slowing down, although it must be said that that country's economy size is huge.

On the other hand, India is still an enigma. A country of contrasts, a country rooted in tradition, and a country with culture, but not work culture. Laws, licenses, litigation, are part of our lexicon on work culture. Many countries and investors find it hard to reconcile to it.

Another interesting aspect that the matrix does not reveal is that developing countries are both our competitors as well as our collaborators. For example, Sri Lanka competes with India in tea, while it collaborates in shipping, Malaysia competes in agri products but collaborates in travel, and China competes with US on many issues but collaborates with it at WTO meets and environmental meets. The list goes on.

Most significantly, all the developing countries are coming under one banner or the other. In the UN General Assembly, under the democratic principles 'one member, one vote,' the developing countries are a force to reckon with. UN agencies like UNDP (United Nations Development Programme) and, ECOSOC (Economic and Social Council) have taken the mantle of development and progress. The unified and integrated approach is bringing forth synergy and satisfaction. There are other specialised UN agencies like UNICEF, UNHCR, UNIDO, and UNEP– all are active in their respective fields. The world order based on Bretton Woods dispensation (1944) with IMF and IBRD ruling the roost, failed to bridge the gap between the developed and the developing. Consequently, the need was felt for a new world order based on dignity, distribution, and direction. What emerged was a challenge by itself.

The new world order in effect was 'Globalisation', an order based on breaking barriers to trade, recognising Intellectual Property Rights (IPR), and jurisdiction of a court for justice. Globalisation, in its wake, did away with tariffs, bilateral quota agreements, and other discriminatory, restrictive trade practices including subsidies, for once. It also ushered in an era of competition, quality standards, choice of option, and uniformity in banking practices. World became one, and all countries chose to join. Developing countries counted the benefits even as they courted disasters too; one by one local industries caved in. India too was no exception. The skills had to be upgraded to meet international challenges of quality and precision. Sadly, in many of the developing countries, there was no mechanism or social net to absorb such shocks. Demand of globalisation brought forth another disaster; the inevitability of mechanisation and automation: consequence, loss of more jobs. But economies moved on ahead. Jobless growth was the outcry. Private sector took full advantage. Globalisation has come to stay.

POLITICS AND POLICIES OF DEVELOPING COUNTRIES VERSUS INDIA

Politics

(1) Get the best of each bargain.

(2) Leverage position in terms of using geographical position, and critical endowed raw materials.

(3) Join with other developing countries in various bodies, or create a block of likeminded countries.

(4) Create an environment for safety and security.

(5) Go for indigenisation using appropriate technologies, not accorded technologies.

(6) Fight for rights in areas of trade, environment, security, and development.

Policies

(1) Not to reinvent the wheel, not to start from the beginning; take advantage of experience of other countries.

(2) Use the advantage of location and available critical raw materials to leverage bargaining power. Middle East countries use oil as a bargaining chip, and so do Nigeria, as also Iran.

(3) Use all forms of platforms like G-80, BRICS, SAARC, ASEAN, SCO, etc. to argue and advance your case and cause.

(4) Go for bilateral, regional, and global agreements for safety and security. Each country has its own compulsions.

(5) Developing countries need money and technologies. The need for development is paramount; use of appropriate and adequate technologies is a must. Joint ventures, collaborations, and agreements are an option. Multinationals have to be allowed with caution and control. Many developing countries have been trampled upon by multinationals.

(6) For developing countries, fighting poverty, getting employment, social security, growth, and development are the areas of focus. Following the Western model of development is neither the option nor the answer. These countries adopt policies seeking concessions in trade, consolidation in rights, and consideration for position.

Years back, some African countries had to choose between creating facilities for drinking water or set up television in their capital; they chose the latter upon insistence from their former colonial masters. India went for extensive industrialisation creating need for mining, requirement of industrial usage water, uprooting the poor from their lands, buying machinery using scarce foreign exchange, building roads for transportation, training manpower for production, creating power facilities, and finding markets for consumption. They forgot the people they displaced initially. This is the story of all developing countries. The upshot is that they need collaboration to do this, India is more than willing.

INDIAN DIASPORA

India has a significant and sizeable advantage in the matter that a large number of its people are settled outside. The 'Indian Diaspora' as it is called has established itself well in many diverse and distinct fields. They not only serve the country as its true 'Ambassadors' but also effectively help its economy with remittances.

It stands to the country's advantage to cultivate this 'Diaspora'; to take advantage of their skills and strengths; to seek their support in investment; to enlist their help in sorting out issues in the countries of their residence and to get their support in upgradation of systems and technology.

Indian Diaspora is vast and varied, ranging from skilled workforce, to businessmen to engineers and doctors to space and nuclear experts. Their dedication and determination makes them highly sought for. It cannot be denied either that they are usually available for lower wages and lesser comforts.

A huge number of Indian students go abroad for studies and ultimately settle there. It is a matter of immense advantage to the recipient countries too as a talented pool of workforce becomes available to them without any investment.

It comes as no surprise to see names of countrymen excelling various fields and occupying high positions.

Indian Diaspora offers a huge market for our products; the popularity of our entertainment offers is a testimony to that. Equally popular are out jewelleries and traditional items. Our craze for gold is well known and the results of export are greatly beneficial to us in our balance of payments. It cannot be denied either that our real estate business in the country is getting huge fillip due to the countrymen residing abroad who are investing here.

Yet, it must also be kept in mind that there are problems galore as far as Indian Diaspora is concerned. India cannot ignore them or their plight. So long the economies of the countries where the diaspora is resident are doing well, there indeed are no issues. But come recession, come regression, come retardation problems shoot up.

The recent events of strife and resultant turmoil in middle east has sprung lot of dislocation and uprooting. Egypt, Syria, Yemen, Libya are all fresh examples. Countries like Saudi Arabia and Iran are also in some despair or dilemma; they are putting restrictions on immigration.

Economies of European countries too are not doing well to continue accommodating more immigrants.

Government of India has now a full-fledged Ministry for Overseas Indian Affairs and it has a job at hand to ensure welfare of all countrymen resident abroad.

Indian diaspora has some expectations from the government:

- Proper environment and hassle-free VISA on arrival in India
- Regular intimation of statutory requirements to avoid confusion
- Safe and secure environment for investment
- Government's help and intervention in case of overseas labourers from India

The government wants the diaspora to help in health, education and human resource segments. Swachh Bharat campaign and tourism are other areas where help is needed

January 9th is observed as "Pravasi Bharatiya Divas" every year, commemorating the arrival of Gandhiji in India in 1915, from South Africa.

20

CHAPTER

International Organisations

OVERVIEW

The present world order has the United Nations (UN) with its numerous agencies, International Monetary Fund, and International Bank for Reconstruction and Development (World Bank) to steer the order. Besides these, regional institutions like ASEAN, SCO, etc. are also there in an aggressive way. India is part of all these in an appropriate way. GATT held lot of promise, now it holds lots of prescription. All said and done, the world order is well served by its institutions, even as international co-operation is searching for a new impetus.

UNITED NATIONS

"The UN wasn't created to take mankind into paradise, but rather, to save humanity from hell."

- Dag Hammarskjold

2nd UN Secretary General (1953-1961)

United Nations, which came into existence on October 24, 1945 in the aftermath of the Second World War has had a chequered existence with some notable achievements and some not. The world of 2018 is much different from the world of 1945; today the United Nations has to look through the prism of globalization whereas back in 1945 it had to contend with a bipolar world. Today's challenges are 'policies'; back in 1945 the challenge was 'policing'; today's world challenge is 'economic integration,' back in 1945, it was 'political stabilization.'

Purposes of United Nations (Article 1)

1. To maintain peace and security
2. To develop friendly relations among nations based on respect for the principles of equal rights and self-determination of people
3. To cooperate in solving international economic, social, cultural, humanitarian problems and in promoting respect for human rights and fundamental freedoms
4. To be a centre for harmonizing the actions of nations in attaining these common ends

Principles on which UN acts

1. The organization is based on the principle of sovereign equality of all its members
2. All members are to fulfill in good faith all their charter obligations
3. Member nations are to settle their international disputes by peaceful means and without endangering international peace, security and justice
4. They are to refrain from the threat or use of force against any other state
5. All members shall refrain in their international relations from the threat of force or use of force against the territorial integrity or political independence of any state or in any manner inconsistent with the purposes of the UN
6. All members shall give the UN every assistance in any action it takes in accordance with the present charter and shall refrain from giving assistance to any state against which the UN is taking preventive or enforcement action.
7. The organization shall ensure that states which are not members of the UN act in accordance with these principles so far as may be necessary for the maintenance of international peace and security.
8. Nothing contained in the present charter shall authorize the UN to interfere in matters which are essentially within the domestic jurisdiction of any state.

United Nations has 193 members; South Sudan is the latest. Six languages, mainly Arabic, Chinese, English, French, Russian and Spanish are recognized.

It has six principal organs (Article 2):

1. General Assembly2. Security Council 3.Economic and Social Council 4.Trusteeship Council (now defunct) 5. International Court of Justice (Hague) 6. Secretariat

United States contributes 22 per cent of its budget, followed by Japan 10.83 per cent. India contributes 0.66 per cent.

A. General Assembly :

UN General Assembly works on the democratic principle, One country, One vote. It means that if United States has one vote, so too, say, South Sudan or Papua New Guinea have. The UN General Assembly is mainly concerned with establishment of peace and security. It discusses all such issues except those with the Security Council. It operates through six main committees:

1. Disarmament and International Security Committee
2. Economic and Financial Committee
3. Social, Humanitarian and Cultural Committee
4. Special Political and Decolonisation Committee
5. Administration and Budgetary Committee
6. Legal Committee

Presidency of UN General Assembly rotates each year among five groups of states: Asian, African, Eastern European, Latin American and Caribbean, Western European.

Special sessions are also called either at the behest of Security Council or majority of members or one member with others concurring.

B. Security Council:

It is the organ of the UN charged with specific responsibility of maintenance of peace and security. It can call upon the armed forces and other facilities of the members for assistance. It investigates a dispute and suggests ways of settling it. It can suggest use of military force, as a last resort.

Approval of permanent members os necessary in every case of decision; negative vote is called "veto." The council also makes recommendations to General Assembly on the appointment of the Secretary General and also with General Assembly elects the judges of the International Court of Justice.

India has been striving for a seat on the Security Council as a permanent member but is running into hurdles of China 'veto.' A sizeable chunk of humanity with excellent credentials for peace is, thus, left out.

C. Economic and Social Council (ECOSOC):

It is the apex body of UN charged with directing and supervising economic and social matters. UN recognizes that economic and social issues need stability for peace and security. ECOSOC works with many autonomous and specialist bodies like:

i) UNCTAD:United Nations Conference on Trade and Development
ii) UNDP: United nations Development Programme
iii) United Nations Environment Programme (UNEP)
iv) UNICEF, UNCHR, UNCHS, UNIDO & many more

Regional economic commissions have also been appointed to assist ECOSOC.

International Court of Justice

The International Court of Justice shall be the principle judicial organ of the United Nations. It shall function in accordance with the annexed Statute, which is based upon the Statute of the Permanent Court of International Justice and forms an integral part of the present Charter.

The Secretariat

Article 97

The Secretariat shall comprise a Secretary-General and such staff as the Organization may require. The Secretary-General shall be appointed by the General Assembly upon the recommendation of the Security Council. He shall be the chief administrative officer of the Organization.

INTERNATIONAL MONETARY FUND: INTRODUCTION

A landmark in the history of world economic co-operation is the creation of the International Monetary Fund, briefly called IMF. The IMF began its operations in March, 1947.

The fundamental object of the IMF was the avoidance of competitive devaluation and exchange control that charaterised the era of 1930s. It was set up to administer a 'code of fair practice', in the field of foreign exchange and to make short-term loans to members experiencing temporary deficits in their balance of payments, to enable them to meet these payments without resorting to devaluation or exchange control, while at the same time following international policies to maintain domestic income and employment at high levels. *Thus, basically there are three general objectives of the IMF:*

(i) the elimination or reduction of existing exchange controls,

(ii) the establishment and maintenance of currency convertibility with stable exchange rates, and

(iii) the widest extension of multi-lateral trade and payments.

In essence, the Fund is an attempt to achieve the external or international advantages of gold standard system without subjecting nations to its internal disadvantages, and at the same time maintaining the internal advantages of paper standard while bypassing its external disadvantages.

The following are the major functions of the IMF:

1. It functions as a short-term credit institution.
2. It is a reservoir of the currencies of all the member countries from which a borrower nation can borrow the currency of other nations.
3. It is a sort of lending institution in foreign exchange. However, it grants loans for financing current transactions only and not capital transactions.
4. It provides a machinery for the orderly adjustments of exchange rates.
5. It also provides a machinery for altering sometimes the par value, of the currency of a member country. In this way, it tries to provide for an orderly adjustment of exchange rates, which will improve the long-term balance of payments position of member countries.
6. It also provides a machinery for international consultations.

In short, the Fund contributes to the promotion and maintenance of high levels of employment and real income and to the development of the productive resources of all member nations.

The Fund is an autonomous organisation affiliated to the UN. IMF's constitution represents a departure in the formation of an international organisation. It is financed by the participating countries, with each country's contribution fixed in terms of quotas according to the relative importance of its prevailing national income and international trade. Thus, the quota assigned to a country is determined by its contribution to the capital of the Fund. The quotas of all the countries taken together constitute the total financial resources of the Fund. Contributed quota of a country determines its borrowing rights and voting strength. India being one of the largest quota-holders (600 million dollars) has the honour of having a permanent seat on the Board of Executive Directors. Each member nation of the IMF is required to subscribe its quota partly in gold and partly in its own currency. Specifically, a member nation must contribute gold equal to 25 per cent of its quota or 10 per cent of its gold stock and US dollar holdings, whichever is less. The portion of subscription paid in a nation's own currency is generally paid in the form of deposit balance in favour of the IMF held in the nation's central bank. Thus, the Fund gets a pool of foreign currencies to lend, which together with gold enables it to acquire additional amounts of currencies whenever its initial supply of some currencies becomes depleted.

IMF may be described as a bank of central banks of different countries, because it collects the resource of the various central banks in the same way in which a country's central bank collects cash reserves of all the commercial banks, and assists them in times of emergency. However, while a central bank can control the credit policy of its member banks, the Fund cannot control the domestic economic and monetary policies of member nations. It only seeks to maintain a multiple payments system through an orderly adjustment of the exchange rates.

The lending operations of the Fund technically take the form of sale of currency. Any member nation running short of foreign currency may buy the required currency from the Fund, paying for it in its own currency. Since each member contributes gold to the extent of 25 per cent of its quota, the Fund freely permits a member to draw up to the amount of its gold contribution. Additional drawings are permitted only after certain careful and strict scrutinies.

The Fund has also laid down provisions relating to exchange stability. At the same time, the Fund started functioning, members were required to declare the par values of their currencies in terms of gold as a common denominator or in terms of the US dollar. Thus, under IMF arrangements, gold retains its role in determining the relative values of currencies of different nations. And once the par values of different currencies are fixed, it is quite easy to determine the exchange rate between any two member nations. IMF may be described as a bank of central banks of different countries, because it collects the resource of the various central banks in the same way in which a country's central bank collects cash reserves of all the commercial banks, and assists them in times of emergency. However, while a central bank can control the credit policy of its member banks, the Fund cannot control the domestic economic and monetary policies of member nations. It only seeks to maintain a multiple payments system through an orderly adjustment of the exchange rates.

Achievements of the IMF

(1) It provided an excellent machinery for consultations in international monetary affairs. It serves as an excellent forum for discussions, practically on a day-to-day basis of the economic, fiscal, and financial policies of member countries with particular reference to their balance of payments impact. The Fund has created a feeling among the member countries that their economic problems are not their exclusive concern but of the whole intenational society.

(2) The Fund has contributed in certain ways to the expansion of world trade. By providing credit facilities to member countries, the IMF has reduced the need for their imposing import and exchange control, and assists the deficit countries to meet their temporary disequilibriumin payments. It also works for facilitating multi-lateral payments and trade, promoting the international trade as a whole.

(3) Another fundamental object of the IMF is to promote exchange stability. The measure of exchange stability that the world has witnessed in the IMF is remarkably superior to what was seen during inter-war period of Gold Standard regime. Under IMF arrangements, stable exchange rates do not imply rigid exchange rates. IMF's object is to combine the merit of stability with flexibility in exchange management. It aims at avoiding competitive exchange depreciations by wanting the members to declare the par values of their currencies fixed in terms of gold or the US dollar. However, it allows for an orderly adjustment of the exchange rates when this is needed for correcting a fundamental disequilibrium in a country's balance of payments.

(4) Moreover, the Fund has been particularly interested in the newly developing countries of the world and has been liberally assisting them to have a healthy balance of payments and to maintain monetary. stability at home. In recent years, however, underdeveloped countries have started looking to the Fund to assist them in their economic development programmes also. Furthermore, most of the new members who have acquired independence recently are facing difficult problems in organising their monetary, fiscal, and exchange systems, so they need a solid basis for their economic growth.

The Fund has been already providing technical assistance to its members in this respect, but now its activity is substantially widened to meet this challenge. In many of these countries, the Fund's experts have assisted in the formulation of appropriate monetary, fiscal, and exchange policies in the implementation of stabilisation programmes.

SPECIAL DRAWING RIGHTS

The post-war international monetary system may be characterized as the "currency reserve standard," wherein the US dollar has been serving as a reserve asset as good as gold, at least, till the fifties. But, due to the shaky position of the US dollar and other reasons such as speculation in gold, chaos in Euro-dollar market, etc., this system faced acute problems of international liquidity like balance of payments difficulties, inadequate growth of monetary reserves, and fragility of the gold exchange standard.

Economists have visualised three aspects–liquidity, adjustment, and confidence, as the problems of international liquidity. To solve these, a reform in the existing international monetary system was regarded inevitable. Many proposals and plans (as has been seen in the preceding section) had been suggested to evolve some alternative system to get rid of the difficulties faced by the existing system.

Under this scheme, the IMF is empowered to grant member governments special drawing rights (SDRs) on a specified basis, subject to ratification. SDRs are regarded as international reserve, allocated annually by the collective decision of participating members in the Fund. Possession of SDRs entitles a country to obtain a defined equivalent of currency from other participating countries and enable it to discharge certain obligations towards the General Account of the Fund. The creation of SDRs is, thus, intended to increase the resources available to IMF members to overcome their temporary foreign exchange difficulties without putting any additional strain on the IMF resources. SDRs are, thus, a method of supplementing the existing reserve assets in the international liquidity.

THE WORLD BANK

The International Bank for Reconstruction and Development (IBRD), better known as the World Bank, was established at the same time as the International Monetary Fund to tackle the problem of international investment. Since the IMF was designed to provide temporary assistance in correcting the balance of payments difficulties, an institution was also needed to assist long-term investment purposes. Thus, IBRD was established for promoting long-term investment loans on reasonable terms.

The World Bank (IBRD) is an inter-governmental institution, corporate in form, whose capital stock is entirely owned by its member governments. Initially, only nations that were members of the IMF could be members of the World Bank; this restriction on membership was subsequently relaxed.

Functions of IBRD

The principal functions of the IBRD are set forth in Article I of the agreement as follows:

1. To assist in the reconstruction and development of the territories of its members by facilitating the investment of capital for productive purposes.
2. To promote private foreign investment by means of guarantee of participation in loans and other investments made by private investors and when private capital is not available on reasonable terms, to make loans for productive purposes out of its own resources or from funds borrowed by it.
3. To promote the long-term balanced growth of international trade and the maintenance of equilibrium in balance of payments by encouraging international investment for the development of the productive resources of members.
4. To arrange loans made or guaranteed by it in relation to international loans through other channels so that more useful and urgent projects, large and small alike, will be dealt with first. It appears that the World Bank was created to promote and not to replace private foreign investment. The Bank considers its role to be a marginal one, to supplement and assist foreign investment in the member countries.

A little examination will show that the objectives of the IMF and IBRD are complementary. Both aim at increasing the level of national income and standard of living of the member nations. Both serve as lending institutions, the IMF for short-term and the IBRD for long-term capital. Both aim at promoting the balanced growth of international trade.

Organisation and Structure of IBRD

Like the Fund, the Bank's structure is organised on a three-tier basis; a Board of Governors, Executive Directors, and a President. The Board of Governors is the supreme governing authority. It consists of one governor (usually the Finance Minister) and one alternate governor (usually the governor of a central bank), appointed for five years by each member. The Board is required to meet once every year. It reserves to itself the power to decide important matters such as new admissions, changes in the bank's stock of capital, ways and means of distributing the net income, its ultimate liquidation, etc. For all technical purposes, however, the Board delegates its powers to the Executive Directors in the day-to-day administration.

At present, the Executive Directors are 19 in number, of which five are nominated by the five largest shareholders–the USA, the UK, Germany, France, and India. The rest are elected by the other members.

The Executive Directors elect the President who becomes their Ex-Officio Chairman holding office during their presence. He is the chief of the operating staff of the Bank and is subject to the direction of the Executive Directors on questions of policy and is responsible for the conduct of the ordinary business of the Bank and its organisation.

Lending Operations

Loans are granted to member countries only after the Bank is fully satisfied about the economic position of the borrowing country as well as the soundness of the specified projects for which assistance is sought. In granting loans, the Bank is prepared to take reasonable risks but insists that funds obtained from it should be used for purposes which are constructive and practical. The Bank has powers of supervision and control to ensure that funds are used for the purposes for which the loan is granted. Normally, the Bank makes medium or long-term loans, the term being related to the estimated useful life of the equipment or plant being financed.

The Bank makes or facilitates loans in any one or more out of its own following ways:

(a) by making or participating in direct loans out of its own funds; or

(b) out of the funds raised in the market of a member, or otherwise borrowed by the Bank; or

(c) by guaranteeing, in whole or in part, loans made by private investors through the investment channels.

In recent years, the Bank has made loans mainly for specific development projects in the field of agriculture, power, transport, and industry. Most of the loans have been made to the underdeveloped countries. India is the Bank's largest individual borrower.

Technical and Advisory Assistance

In addition to providing financial assistance to member countries, the Bank has been rendering significant service to its members by providing them suitable technical assistance to assess their total economic resources and to set up priorities to be followed in their development programmes. Technical assistance on a broader scale has also been provided, for instance, in development programming through Survey Missions, which make intensive studies of national resources and formulate recommendations to serve as the basis of long-term development programmes.

Criticism

The modus operandi of the Bank has been criticised on various counts from different quarters :

1. It is alleged that the Bank charges a very high rate of interest on loans. For example, some of the loans which India has received in recent years bear an interest of 53.4 per cent including the commission at 1 per cent which is credited to the Bank's special reserves.

2. The Bank's insistence, prior to the actual grant of loan, on the country having the capacity to transfer or repay, is open to criticism; The Bank should not apply orthodox standards to judge the transfer capacity of any borrowing country. Transfer capacity follows rather than precedes the loan.
3. The financial help given by the Bank does not amount to more than a drop in the big ocean of financial requirement so essential for various development projects.

Conclusion

World Bank has been instrumental to a very large extent in initiating and accelerating the work of economic reconstruction and development in different countries. No doubt, India has derived immense benefit from the World Bank. The Bank may have failed to finance most of the development projects, but it should be remembered that it has financed quite a large number of them which have proved a notable success. The Bank has also played a significant role outside financial matters by serving as a mediator between different countries on major economic and political issues. For instance, its help in the solution of the Indus Waters between India and Pakistan and the Suez Canal dispute between the UK and the UAR has been invaluable.

INTERNATIONAL DEVELOPMENT ASSOCIATION (IDA)

The International Development Association (IDA) was established in 1960, affiliated to the World Bank. It was started to provide finance to less developed member on a "soft" loan basis, that is, on terms imposing a lower servicing charge on loans than what the conventional bank charges.

Objectives of IDA

The following are the principal objectives of the IDA:

1. To provide development finance on easy terms to less developed member countries.
2. To promote economic development, increase productivity, and thus, raise the standards of living in the underdeveloped areas.

Working of IDA

Thus, IDA is looked upon as a means of furthering the development activities of the World Bank and as a supplementary to the Bank's activities. Under its charter, the IDA is to support projects which are calculated to contribute to the development of the country concerned, whether they are directly productive or not. The IDA credits would be called development credits to distinguish them from conventional loans, and these would be repayable mostly in the currency lent rather than in the currency of the borrower. Since IDA charges nominal rates of interest on its loans, it has also been nicknamed the "Soft-Loan Window."

IDA has granted a number of credits to India for her development schemes. The grant of credits for development projects given by IDA to India has been in the nature of a continuous flow. But for the funds that have been made available by IDA to India, our development pace would have been considerably slower.

In conclusion, it may be said that the IDA is expected to make a distinct contribution to the economic development of backward nations, furthering their development projects, and supplementing the activities of the World Bank. Moreover, unlike the World Bank loans which are meant to cover only the foreign exchange costs, the IDA loans can be utilised to finance both foreign exchange and local currency costs.

INTERNATIONAL FINANCE CORPORATION (IFC)

The International Finance Corporation was established in July 1956, with the specific subject of providing finance to the private sector. Though it is affiliated to the World Bank, it is a separate legal entity with separate fund and functions. Members of the World Bank are eligible for its membership.

Objectives of IFC

IFC's objective is to assist economic development by encouraging the growth of productive private enterprise in its member nations, particularly in the underdeveloped areas. *Thus, it laid down the following objectives:*

1. To invest in productive private enterprises, in association with private investors, and without government guarantee of repayment, in cases where sufficient private capital is not available on reasonable terms.
2. To serve as a clearing house to bring together investment opportunities, private capital (both foreign and domestic), and experienced management.
3. To help in stimulating the productive investment of private capital, both domestic and foreign.

THE WORLD TRADE ORGANISATION (WTO)

Introduction

The establishment of the World Trade Organisation (WTO) as the successor to the GATT on 1 January, 1995 under the Marrakesh Agreement places the global trading system on a firm constitutional footing with the evolution of international economic legislation resulted through the Uruguay Round of GATT negotiations.

A remarkable feature of the Uruguay Round was that it paved the way for further liberalisation of international trade with the fundamental shift from the negotiation approach to the institutional framework envisaged through transition from GATT to WTO Agreement.

The GATT 1947 and the WTO co-existed for the transitional period of one year in 1994. In January 1995, however, the WTO completely replaced the GATT. The membership of the WTO increased from 77 in 1995 to 127 by the end of 1996.

Features of the WTO

The distinctive features of the WTO are:

- Unlike the GATT, it is a legal entity.
- Unlike the international Monetary Fund (IMF) and the World Bank (WB), it is not an agent of the United Nations.

- Unlike the IMF and the World Bank, there is no weighted voting, but all the WTO members have equal rights.
- Unlike the GATT, the agreements under the WTO are permanent and binding to the member countries.
- Unlike the GATT, the WTO dispute settlement system is based not on dilatory but automatic mechanism. It is also quicker and binding on the members. As such, the WTO is a powerful body.
- Unlike the GATT, the WTO's approach is rule-based and time-bound.
- Unlike GATT, the WTO has a wider coverage. It covers trade in goods as well as services.
- Unlike the GATT, the WTO has a focus on trade-related aspects of intellectual property rights and several other issues of agreements.
- Above all, the WTO is a huge organisational body with a large secretariat.

Structure of the WTO

The Ministerial Conference (MC) is at the top of the structural organisation of the WTO. It is the supreme governing body which takes ultimate decisions on all matters. It is constituted by representatives of (usually, Ministers of Trade) all the member countries.

The General Council (GC) is composed of the representatives of all the members. It is the real engine of the WTO which acts on behalf of the MC. It also acts as the Dispute Settlement Body as well as the Trade Policy Review Body.

There are three councils, viz.: The Council for Trade in Goods , the Council for Trade in Services, and the Council for Trade-Related Aspects of Intellectual Property Rights (TRIPS) operating under the GC. These councils with their subsidiary bodies carry out their specific responsibilities.

Objectives of the WTO

The purposes and objectives of the WTO are spelled out in the preamble to the Marrakesh Agreement. In a nutshell, these are:

1. To ensure the reduction of tariffs and other barriers to trade.
2. To facilitate higher standards of living, full employment, a growing volume of real income and effective demand, and an increase in production and trade in goods and services of the member nations.
3. To eliminate discriminatory treatment in international trade relations.
4. To make positive effect, which ensures developing countries, especially the least developed, secure a level of share in the growth of international trade that reflects the needs of their economic development.
5. To facilitate the optimal use of the world's resources for sustainable development.
6. To promote an integrated, more viable, and durable trading system incorporating all the resolutions of the Uruguay Round's multilateral trade negotiations.
7. Above all, to ensure that linkages, trade policies, environmental policies with sustainable growth, and development are taken care of by the member countries in evolving a new economic order.

Functions of the WTO

The WTO consisting of a multifaceted normative framework, comprising institutional, substantive, and implementation aspects, undertakes the following functions:

1. To provide an integrated structure of the administration, thus, to facilitate the implementation, administration, and fulfilment of the objectives of the WTO Agreement and other Multilateral Trade Agreements.
2. To lay down a substantive code of conduct aiming at reducing trade barriers, including tariffs, and eliminating discrimination in international trade relations.
3. To provide the institutional framework for the administration of the substantive code which encompasses a spectrum of norms governing the conduct of member countries in the arena of global trade.
4. To ensure the implementation of the substantive code and to settle the trade-related disputes.
5. To act as a forum for the negotiation of further trade liberalisation.
6. To cooperate with the IMF and WB and its associates for establishing a coherence in trade policy-making.

The WTO Code/Agreements

The WTO through its code provides a framework for an integrated approach to tackle the trade-related economic issues which cannot be isolated from the world economic order.

The WTO code lies in the international instruments, such as, the GATT 1994, the Multilateral Trade Agreements (MTA), and the Preferential Trade Agreements (PTA). The clash/conflict between MTA and GATT 1994 is to be resolved by accepting the provisions of MTA.

In essence, the WTO Agreement is based on the results of the Uruguay Round of negotiations.

The WTO Agreement, thus, covers the following:

- Multilateral Agreements on Trade in goods
- General Agreement on Trade in services
- Agreement on TRIPs
- Rules and procedures regarding dispute settlement
- Preferential Trade Agreements (PTA)
- Trade Policy Review Mechanism (TPRM)

Among these, agreement on agriculture deserves attention of the developing agrarian nations. The Agreement seeks to deal with non-tariff measures affecting global competition. It specifically aims at reducing domestic and export subsidies on agricultural goods. It is laid down that the current total aggregate measurement of support–(in terms of non-product specific subsidies and product specific subsidies) should not exceed 10 per cent of the annual value of total agricultural product measured at international price.

Integration implies that trade in textile products and clothing will be governed by the General Rules of GATT as against the Multi-Fibre Agreement (MFA).

The WTO Agreement on anti-dumping sets out new and more detailed rules and the criteria, anti-dumping measures, and dispute settlement.

The WTO Agreement embraces all internationally traded services and aims at progressive liberalisation of the service sector.

The TRIPS Agreement pertains to the protection of following categories of intellectual property rights :

(i) copyright;
(ii) trademarks;
(iii) geographical indications;
(iv) industrial designs;
(v) patents;
(vi) integrated circuits; and
(vii) trade secrets.

Regarding copyrights, it is specified that the Berne Convention should be complied for the protection of literary and artistic works including computer programming.

The owner of the registered trade mark possess exclusive rights for its use.

The geographical indication relates to the identification of a product originating in the territory of the member state; and it should be legally protected.

Industrial designs are to be protected for at least 10 years and patents for 20 years.

Topography of integrated circuits are to be protected for 10 years. Trade secrets and know-how of commercial value are to be protected against breach of trust.

The member governments are required to enact suitable legislations in this regard. The Council for TRIPS is to monitor the members' compliance in this direction.

The Dispute Settlement Body is to be set up by the WTO to govern the dispute settlement system as per rules and procedures laid down.

Preferential Trade Agreements (PTA) consists of :

(i) Agreement on Trade in Civil Aircraft;
(ii) Agreement on Government Procurement;
(iii) International Bovine Meat Agreement, and
(iv) International Dairy Agreement.

TPRM is meant to review the trade policies and practices under MTA and PTA. The task is to be carried out by the Trade Policy Review Body.

The just approach of the DSB has, thus, strengthened the confidence of the developing countries in the WTO .

WTO and India

The Government of India has made the following major commitments to WTO:

Tariff Reduction : In a phased manner, customs duties are being reduced.

Removal of Quantitative Restrictions : The EXIM Policy of India announced removal of quantitative restrictions on 714 items in 2000 and further removal of 715 items were announced in 2001 .

TRIPS : The Government of India enacted the Patents (Amendment) Act, 1999 to provide for exclusive marketing rights. Patents (Amendment) Act 2005 was passed for product patents in drugs and farm products.

TRIMS : Notification was issued by the Government of India regarding local contents requirements in the production of certain pharmaceutical products and dividend balancing requirement for investments in 22 categories of consumer items.

Customs Valuation Rules : The Custom Valuation Rules, 1998 was amended to comply with the provisions of the WTO Agreement.

GATS : Under the General Agreement on Trade in Services (GATS), commitments were made relating to 33 activities and permitting the entry of foreign service providers.

Concluding Remarks

Most of the criticisms levelled against the GATT and Uruguay Round negotiations still hold true about the WTO. Economic implications of the WTO Agreement on various fields will be wide and varied. Though it may succeed in freeing trade and globalisation to an extent, it may fail to create a balanced growth of world economy.

It may also pave a greater way for the growth of economic imperialism of a few developed industrialised nations world over. A new economic order which may be envisaged through the operation of the WTO will certainly breed new problems and new issues with more complications and undesirable consequences in the new century to follow. A vicious circle of unending negotiations, disputes, and disagreements is not unlikely.

ASIAN DEVELOPMENT BANK

Some regional development banks have been established to assist the development of the developing countries of the respective regions-the African Development Bank, the Asian Development Bank, the Caribbean Development Bank, and the Inter-American Development Bank. The influence of the regional banks is growing as they are becoming more responsive to the special needs of their own constituencies.

The Asian Development Bank (ADB) was set up in December 1966 under the auspices of the United Nations Economic Commission for Asia and the Far East (ECAFE) to foster economic development of Asian countries, with its headquarters at Manila. It also has about two dozen other offices around the world. ADB is a multilateral development, finance institution dedicated to reducing poverty in Asia and the Pacific. In 2002, 61 nations, mostly from the region were members of ADB.

The funds of the ADB are contributed by developed countries such as Japan, USA, Canada, West Germany, Australia, etc.

Objectives of ADB

ADB's overarching goal is to reduce poverty in Asia and the Pacific. It helps improve the quality of people's lives by providing loans and technical assistance for a broad range of development activities. ADB is a non-profit, multilateral development finance institution that engages in mostly public sector lending for development purposes in its developing member countries.

The main objectives of the ADB are :

1. To promote investment in the ESCAP region of public and private capital for development.
2. To utilise the available resources for financing development, giving priority to those regional, sub-regional, as well as national projects and programmes which contribute more effectively to the harmonious economic growth of the region as a whole.

In the 23rd Annual Meeting of the Board of Governors of the ADB, the President has pointed out that the Bank's most appropriate response to Asian and Pacific development in future lies in following three broad directions:

1. Greater priority must be placed on alleviating poverty and protecting the environment.
2. The Bank must strengthen its assistance to the private sector to improve productivity and efficiency.
3. The Bank must work with its developing members to create a policy framework that makes the most efficient use of human and capital resources.

The adoption of poverty reduction as a strategy gave primacy to ADB's fight against poverty. ADB continues to carry out activities to promote economic growth, develop human resources, improve the status of women, and protect the environment, but these strategic development objectives now serve its poverty reduction agenda. Its other key development objectives, such as law and policy reform, regional cooperation, private-sector development, and social development, contribute significantly to this main goal.

Focus of ADB

ADB focusses on poverty reduction. In doing so, it emphasises on :

1. Promotion of the pro-poor, sustainable economic growth
2. Social development
3. Good governance

In support of the above, ADB concentrates on:

1. Protection of the environment
2. Promotion of gender and development
3. Private sector development
4. Regional cooperation

A major problem which the ADB is facing is shortage of funds. The Western donors now show a lot of interest in the development of the Eastern Europe.

UNCTAD

The widening trade gap between the developed and developing countries, the general dissatisfaction of the developing countries with the GATT, and the need for a new organisation for international economic cooperation in the field of trade and aid, designed to reduce the trade gap of developing countries, encouraged the establishment of the United Nations Conference on

Trade and Development (UNCTAD) in 1964 as a permanent organ of the UN General Assembly. The UNCTAD was designed to serve as a forum in which trade-related development issues could be discussed and analysed to lead to the negotiations of international understanding on issues that were in dispute.

Objectives of UNCTAD:

1. Aims at the development of friendly integration of developing countries into the world economy.
2. Aims to be the focal point within the United Nations for the integrated treatment of trade and development and the interrelated issues in the areas of finance, technology, investment, and sustainable development.
3. Act as a forum for intergovernmental discussions and deliberations, supported by discussions with experts and exchanges of experience, aimed at consensus-building. UNCTAD undertakes research, policy analysis, and data collection in order to provide substantive inputs for the discussions of experts and government representatives.
4. Co-operation with other organisations and donor countries, and provide technical assistance tailored to the needs of the developing countries, with special attention being paid to the needs of the least developed countries, and countries with economy in transition.

Functions of UNCTAD

The principal functions of UNCTAD are :

1. To promote international trade with a view to accelerating economic development.
2. To formulate principles of and policies on international trade and related problems of economic development.
3. To negotiate multinational trade agreements.
4. To make proposals for putting its principles and policies into effect.

The major activities of UNCTAD include research and support of negotiations for commodity agreements and technical elaboration of new trade activities designed to assist developing countries in the areas of trade and capital.

UNIDO

The United Nations Industrial Development Organisation (UNIDO), which was set up in January 1967, is an organ of the UN General Assembly. The primary function of UNIDO is to promote industrialisation in developing countries by encouraging the mobilisation of national and international resources. Particular attention is given to manufacturing industries. Unlike UNCTAD, UNIDO works directly with business firms, generally on an industry basis. The major activities of UNIDO fall into the following three categories:

Operational activities : These include direct, technical assistance to industries (at the request of the governments of the developing country) and in-plant limning programmes whereby groups of technicians and engineers from developing countries facing a common industrial problem arc brought together to consider, how industry in the more advanced countries avoids or solves similar problems

Research : In this area, UNIDO conducts feasibility studies on the requirements and potential industry in developing countries. Export-oriented industries are given special attention.

Coordination : The coordinating activities of UNIDO include mostly the organisation and sponsoring of inter-regional and international meetings, seminars, and symposia.

INTERNATIONAL TRADE CENTRE

The International Trade Centre (ITC) is the focal point in the United Nations System for technical cooperation with developing countries in trade promotion. ITC was created by the General Agreements on Tariffs and Trade (GATT) in 1964 and since 1968 has been operated jointly by GATT (now WTO) and the UN, the latter acting through the United Nations Conference on Trade and Development (UNCTAD). As an executing agency of the United Nations Development Programme (UNDP), ITC is directly responsible for implementing UNDP financed projects in developing countries related to trade promotion.

ITC can advise developing countries on their overall approach to marketing communications, as well as on individual information and publicity activities. This entails establishing a strategy with broad communication objectives that are in line with the firm's international marketing goals and defining specific actions to achieve those objectives. Trade fairs are one such specific activity. For instance, ITC can provide guidelines on choosing the most appropriate fairs for the firms and products concerned, preparing the exhibition budget, designing the stand, producing publicity material, briefing the participants, manning the stand, following up on business inquiries, and evaluating exhibition performance. Similar ITC services are available for planning and executing trade missions, solo exhibitions and store promotions, which all call for skills in conducting marketing research, electing participants and products, preparing promotional material, making detailed arrangements, and following through with business contacts.

For trade promotion publications, ITC can give advice on developing a publications plan and determining specific types of publications to be part of it, such as product and company brochures; export directories, and trade promotion bulletins, newsletters, and magazines. Suggestions on content. graphics, production, and distribution are part of this service. *Briefly, the ITC assists the developing countries by working with them in:*

1. Developing a national trade promotion strategy, including analysing export potential, choosing priority markets, and setting export targets.
2. Establishing appropriate government institutions and services, such as a central trade promotion organisation and services for exporters in trade information, export financing, export quality control, export costing and pricing, export packaging, trade fairs and commercial publicity, the legal aspects of foreign trade, international physical distribution

of goods, trade promotion services for small and medium-size enterprises, and commercial representation abroad.

3. Finding market opportunities for current export products, both non-traditional items and elected primary commodities, and using effective marketing techniques to promote them abroad; adapting other products to foreign market requirements and developing new items for export; and promoting exports of technical consulting services.

UN Reforms: A crying need and a trying deed

The clamour for reforms in the United Nations organisation is getting larger and louder every day. On the one hand there are those who want it to be disbanded; on the other there are those who seek to activate it to be a 'world governing body'. Agenda for reforms extends from democratising the Security Council to abolishing Trusteeship Council. The General Assembly is totally democratic with 'One country, one vote'; the Security Council is closed and confined to 'policing nations'. United States often bypasses the UN, but grumbles about its 22% share in funding. Russia, now much reduced from its post Soviet Union status is hardly the power it was. India, the second most populous country has neither a seat nor a say in the council on a basis of permanency. Anachronistic instruments of negation like 'vetoes' have hardly any place in today's world of openness, accountability and understanding. UN has to reinvent itself in a world that is now driven by technology and drawn by knowledge and developed by aspirations.

Economically the world is united as never before; it is time for the UN to take it forward. The various organs of that body need to be democratised to bring about transparency and accountability. New rules of engagement and enforcement are much needed. UN must expand its horizon to work for better handling of issues of poverty and hunger consistent with human dignity and human wants. UN which born to set the war torn world to order should reorient itself to put a world torn by inequalities to order.

INDIA and NSG..Milestones and Roadblocks

The Nuclear Supply Group (NSG), a consortium of 48 countries, controls the supply of materials needed for nuclear reactors. Entry into this group is by consensus and unanimity. India has been trying to get into this group for the sake of advancing its nuclear plans and programmes. However, its efforts have not been successful so far. China has been blocking India's entry on the grounds that India has not signed the NPT (Non Proliferation Treaty). India considers the NPT to be singularly discriminatory and arbitrary. It draws a line between those who are already nuclear and those not. In effect it bars other countries from becoming nuclear. It is not only China that is barring India's entry into NSG; other countries like New Zealand, South Africa, the Scandinavian countries, Poland, Egypt etc too have reservations.

The United States of America which had given India a special dispensation of civil-military facility is backing India, but given the intransigence and impediment from China, it is clearly helpless. Western countries and Russia see India as a huge prospect as also as a prosperous customer. France and Russia have entered into agreements with India for nuclear cooperation.

America, under Trump, has suggested that India take the other route of entry into other related groups like Australia Group, Wessener Group and the Missile Technology group first. India has recently joined the missile technology group.

International Relations

Model questions with answers

Q. Despite a strong political thrust on foreign policy in recent times, India's foreign policy architecture is still weak. Comment.

A. It is estimated that the present strength of the Indian Foreign Service (IFS) officers in India is 600, which is less than the number of diplomats Singapore has. With India's rising stature and global ambitions, the country is facing a woeful shortage of IFS personnel. The parliamentary standing committee on external affairs (2014-15) had mooted that experts in private industry and academicians should be made part of foreign policy team. They would be in touch with ground realities.

There is no inter-department postings so that Foreign Service officers learn about trade, say from the commerce department. Similarly, officers from commerce department are not sent for a stint in foreign affairs wings. In a world where diplomacy is now more concerned about trade, climate change, science and commerce, there is a need to change the traditional approach to foreign policy.

Q. Discuss the repercussions of the Doklam incident on India's foreign policy with China.

A. Unlike Bhutan, India does not have a claim on Doklam; however, India supports Bhutan's claim on the territory.

In June 2017, Doklam became the site of a stand-off between the armed forces of India and China following an attempt by China to extend a road from Yadong, further southward on the Doklam plateau. As the new move reached Bhutan army camp at Zornpelri and threatened India's highly strategic Siliguri corridor, it was a volatile situation. The 2007 friendship treaty of Bhutan and India allows our country's guidance in Bhutan's foreign policy.

On 18 June, Indian troops apparently crossed into the territory in dispute between China and Bhutan in an attempt to prevent the road construction. A truce was called between India and China, but it does not mean that China should not be watched closely. The reasons are:

- It is unclear whether China will patrol the region, which it claims to have been doing earlier.
- The Chinese media states that they may reconsider the decision of building road after taking into account 'different factors', which shows that it is again looking for an opportune moment to raise the issue again.

- China is playing for higher stakes in a globalised world. For instance, on the South China Sea, it has preferred confidence-building measures to deal with U.S. but is biding its time.
- China is currently seeking to reshape the regional and international order, and is keen to fine-tune its 'Great Power diplomacy'. It, hence, needs to be seen as preferring consensus over conflict.
- China's growth rate is declining, debt levels are dangerously high, and labour is getting more expensive. Embarking on military engagement could aggravate China's problems.

Q. It is said that "If executed properly, Aadhaar could become a central pillar of India's 'neighbourhood first" policy, culminating in the creation of a unique digital South Asian identity." Can Aadhaar be a foreign policy tool?

A. Aadhaar is a 12 digit unique-identity number issued to all Indian residents, based on biometric and demographic data. The data is collected by the Unique Identification Authority of India (UIDAI). Aadhaar is the world's largest biometric ID system, with over 1.154 billion enrolled members as of December 2017.

Aadhaar has received acclaim and approval from many parts of the world. The drive has been held to be a success by the international community. The technology developed by India can be utilised by exporting it to the neighbouring countries. Considering the stage of development of neighboiring countries of India, Aadhaar has great prospects in these countries.

- Aadhaar-like platforms catalyse innovation by managing and tailoring Big Data for governments and businesses alike. The political and economic leverage that will accrue to India will be huge and can be a foil to China.
- Once a critical mass of Aadhaar-enabled applications has been created; interoperability standards for the digital ecosystem will be determined by the Unique ID programme. Technological integrity would ensue as app developers, handheld manufacturers, and even Internet Service Providers will have to work around Aadhaar encryption standards and data protection guidelines.
- A digital identity-based scheme will not only authenticate the legitimate recipients of land, but also simplify future transactions for sale, leasing or commercial use. In Bangladesh, digital IDs could track loans made by multiple microfinance institutions to the same borrower and help check rural debt.

Countries in neighbourhood creating digital identification tools have got limited success. India has massively scaled up its bio-metric identification platform through Aadhaar successfully. Exchanging Aadhaar on the wheels of foreign policy can ensure profitable gains for our software companies too.

Q. Our focus on bilateralism is excessive and counterproductive and leading to India's isolation in our neighbourhood. Discuss.

A. India's 'neighbourhood first' policy was initiated because our greatest problems and biggest opportunities lie here. Making a unique effort to build ties with our big and small neighbours, India made a novel beginning. But, excessive focus on bilateralism, for example, with Pakistan and China has been not so fruitful

- Not much has been achieved in relations with neighbouring countries through a focus on bilateralism. Example, the Kashmir issue continues to fester; the Teesta Waters issue with Bangladesh is complicating matters. Unofficial blockade on Nepal over constitution issues took place
- Bilateral arrangements and treaties have not got off the ground

On other hand, multilateralism in neighbourhood can be of great use:

- Trade linkage, infrastructural developments and increased connectivity and people to people contacts can be initiated.
- Relations with our neighbours can improve by correlating with regional economies, especially those of countries like Bhutan, Nepal, Thailand, Myanmar via steps like Trilateral Highway, Bangladesh–China–India–Myanmar Forum for Regional Cooperation (**BCIM**, Kaladan Multi-modal project etc.
- A possible resolution to the Kashmir and the Northeast problems through economic interaction and connectivity
- Opportunity for India to lead the way by taking initiative to revamp multilateral projects like the BIMSTEC, SAARC etc; to further regional integration.

India should not be left out of profitable engagement with its neigbours through multilateral mechanisms. There are prospects in CPEC, OBOR for multilateral agreement and participation. India should build bridges with its immediate neighbours and also beyond.

Q. Write a critical note on One Belt and One Road Initiative of China and its possible repercussions on Pakistan.

A. Under the One Belt One Road (OBOR) scheme, Pakistan is hopeful that the China-Pakistan-Economic-Corridor (CPEC) flagship project will open up a corridor that will transform its economy. It is confident that infrastructure connectivity, huge foreign investment, creation of jobs would ensue. There will be a power boom in the energy deficient country and Chinese presence would aid Pakistan in putting pressure on Kashmir issue and also insurgents in Balochistan would be controlled.

But the flip side is that Pakistan's agricultural land will be leased out for China's demonstration projects in seeds and irrigation technology. Pakistan will also become a market for agricultural produce from western China, adversely impacting local producers.

A system of monitoring and surveillance will be built in cities from Peshawar to Karachi with 24-hour video recording starting on roads and busy marketplaces. A national fibre-optic backbone will be built for terrestrial distribution of broadcast TV, which will lead to "dissemination of Chinese culture".

China may offer concessional rates to Pakistan, but Islamabad could still find the final debt insurmountable. Recently, Sri Lanka has already reserved 29 exclusive economic zones situated in corridors for Chinese companies. Already, 10,000 Chinese work in Pakistan. The CPEC can be used for developing Milbus – the military business complex. The belt may result in loss of territorial sovereignty for Pakistan in the long run.

Q. What is the geostrategic significance of India's first bullet train project started with Japanese help?

A. India's first bullet train project – the Mumbai-Ahmedabad High Speed Rail (MAHSR) funded by the Japan International Cooperative Agency (JICA), will be the biggest project which Indian Railways has witnessed in post-Independence India. This technological transfer highlights the cordial relationship between the two countries.

Choosing Japan over cheaper Chinese technology shows geo strategic significance. It shows the independent stand taken by India.

This technology will reduce the dependence of India on Middle East countries for oil and other fuel products as there will be a shift to rail from road.

For Japan too, this deal has geostrategic meaning. Earlier Japan has lost to China in export of bullet trains in Thailand and Indonesia. This deal is a diplomatic win for Japan.

The low cost loan provided by Japan for this infrastructure project will save huge costs for Indian side. From a geostrategic point of view, both India and Japan have inked this pact by sidelining the mighty China giant and its assertive strategies.

Q. Discuss the potential of increasing with India's South Asian neighbours?

A. India's economy can improve and make rapids strides, if economic ties improve with South Asian countries. For example, Bhutan has huge potential for hydro power and India has already started some big projects. Transport of goods and passengers through Bangladesh would save time and labour. Myanmar's offshore and gas reserves make it the perfect investment destination. If Pakistan allows the Tapi pipeline, energy transmission costs would be greatly reduced. Fishing is important for our export basket. A number of fishermen from Tamil Nadu and Kerala are dependent on it. If the kidnapping of fishermen issue is settled with Sri Lanka, India would stand to gain. Maldives imports 12% items from India. Had India completed their airport project, it could have struck a deep friendship with the country. Mauritius has brought its first submarine from India.

Q. What are India's plans in Indian Ocean? Also specify the major challenges.

A. It is said, "One who controls the Indian Ocean will control entire Asia." For India, the strategic importance and regional significance of Indian Ocean makes it imperative for it to control the blue waters. The Indian Ocean carries two-thirds of world's oil shipments, one-third of bulk cargo and half of container shipments.

The Indian government has launched several initiatives to gain a strategic toehold in the Indian Ocean:

- It has launched Project Mausam to promote soft power to connect historical linkages
- It has started Sagar Mala which will give connectivity to economic and security domains
- Indian Ocean Rim Association has been formed to promote regional cooperation
- An Indian Ocean Naval Symposium would be held every two years where naval chiefs would hold discussions
- It has assured Sri Lanka that port of Trincomalee would be developed into a petroleum hub

But, there are challenges as well:

- India does not have forward posts and deep assets like China which has naval bases, growing cooperation with rim countries like Sri Lanka and heavy investment in Mynamar.
- India does not have civilian maritime infrastructure

India has to preserve interests in Indian Ocean, earmarking adequate funds in defence sector allocation. China is trying to change the name of 'Indian Ocean' by removing 'Indian.' Instead of too ambitious goals, India has to; nevertheless prepare moderate goals, which would ensure our significant presence over the blue waters.

Q. Mongolia can be a natural ally of India. Elucidate.

A. Mongolia and India have been friends for long, but there is a need to develop deeper relations. Being a landlocked country, Mongolia has been compelled to consider China and Russia as her two close neighbours. It now wants to make India, the third neighbour. India has to keep a strategic check over China's machinations and Mongolia can be cultivated by our country. China also has an eye on Mongolia's reserves of coal, uranium, copper, which has created Sino-phobia in mind of Mongolian people. By moving closer to Mongolia, India can assuage its fears. Buddhism came to Mongolia through India and hence there are civilisational links between the two countries.

To solve border problems, there should be dialogue and diplomacy, first. Roads and outposts must be improved to manage and supervise borders.

Q. What is meant by the term a 'de-hyphenated foreign policy"? Do you view it as aiding India's interests? Critically comment.

A. A 'de -hyphenated foreign policy' means a foreign policy with:

- More pragmatism and more need based approach than a policy based on traditional ethos.
- It also means not linking the particular relationship with any other country
- A rational public discourse on various foreign policy aspects.
- Active role of elected representatives in foreign policy.
- Use of economic strength to deal with the geo political goals
- Use of soft power in foreign policy strategies

Benefits

India has forged relationships with developing countries, especially South Africa, Brazil and Mexico. These countries often represent the interests of the developing countries through economic forums such as the G8+5, IBSA and WTO.

For example, it is very important to have a de-hyphenated approach while dealing with an assertive Chinese government. We should not let our relationship with China affect the cordial relationship with other neighbouring countries in the region.

Our economic compulsions to maintain de-hyphenated relationships with countries have increased to a large extent in recent times. The time has arrived to deal with geo political challenges with a combination of ideology and practical necessity.

Q. Discuss the steps taken by India to improve Indo-EU strategic relationship.

A. The resumption of EU-India summit, after a break of four years, was a massive strategic moment for India. Prime Minister Narendra Modi's visit to Brussels was another turning point. The attacks by suspected Islamic fundamentalists in France, Belgium and the menace of terrorism in India and EU closer. Marine Security can be another issue as there are islands like Reunion Island (France), Chagos archipelago (UK) and our own Indian Ocean issues. China is a common denominator to come together.

The Eurasian arc of instability, which stretches from Istanbul to Islamabad and from Moscow to Mauritius is of critical importance to Brussels and New Delhi's aim to stabilise their own regional peripheries. An EU-India-Afghanistan trilateral, with regular security consultations could be potential area for cooperation. Climate, trade and space can bring Delhi and Brussels close, too.

Q. In India's foreign approach, how is "Act East' policy different from "Look East" policy?

The Look East Policy was formulated in 1991, to open up to Southeast Asia and benefit from the South East Asian economies that were rapidly growing. Under this Look East Policy, India became a Sectoral Dialogue Partner with the ASEAN in 1992 and full Dialogue Partner in 1996. At the economic level India has signed the Free Trade Agreement with the 10 member ASEAN countries which will help increase trade between India and the ASEAN significantly. Thus, India's look east policy has been quite a success in its engagement with countries of the region.

The **ActEastPolicy** focusses on the Pacific countries in addition to the South East Asian countries. These include Fiji, Myanmar etc. The Act Easy Policy recognises the importance of the North East of India as the gateway to the East and thus the development of the North Eastern region is a priority in the policy. In this policy, apart from the ASEAN, India has also been actively engaged in regional fora such as Bay of Bengal Initiative for Multi-Sectoral Technical and Economic Cooperation (BIMSTEC), Asia Cooperation Dialogue (ACD), Mekong Ganga Cooperation (MGC) and Indian Ocean Rim Association (IORA).

Q. How is US President Donald Trump's new assertive policy in Afghanistan beneficial to India?

A. President Trump's policy is to enhance efforts to overcome the challenges facing Afghanistan and also confront safe havens. In his speech Trump had declared that the US can no longer be silent about Pakistan's safe havens for terrorist organisations, the Taliban and other groups that pose a threat to the region and beyond. He demanded that Pakistan's support to cross-border terror will have to change and change immediately. Restructuring Afghanistan is also India's policy. American efforts to remove the Pakistani base of terrorism that feeds the activity in Afghanistan may be beneficial to India.

Till now, Washington held that India's rivalry with Pakistan is part of the problem in Afghanistan. By invoking India's larger role in Afghanistan, Trump wants to pressurize Pakistan into toeing the American line.

President Trump has been strong and open, on Afghanistan issue, which is beneficial to India.

Q. What are the challenges faced by the Indian diaspora in West Asia, US,and UK?

A. The Indian Diaspora or people who migrated from territories in India, including their descendants ,is currently estimated to number over twenty million, which comprises "NRIs" and "PIOs" who have acquired the citizenship of some other country.

Challenges faced by Indian diaspora in West Asia-

- Due to low oil prices persisting for more than 4-5 years, economic slowdown in West Asian nations is affecting the Indian diaspora. Indians working there are facing difficulties in finding employment and are facing tough living conditions.
- West Asian nations have started preferring locals over South Asians.
- Further, tremendous competition from more skilled workers from countries such as the Philippines and cheaper labour from Nepal, is another problem.
- Also, the West Asian region is engulfed in terrorism and Shia-Sunni conflict. The Indian community is caught in the cross-fire.

Challenges faced by Indian diaspora in North America and UK

- Indians in these countries are facing racist and discriminatory treatment.
- With the election of Donald Trump as American President, employment opportunities may shrink for Indians as he is determined to make companies in America hire local talent.

Q. It is said that present terrorism problem has emanated from inefficiency of UN. Critically evaluate.

A. International terrorism endangers peace and security. The UN whose mandate is to ensure global security has failed miserably in this. In the 1960s, UN treated growing terrorism as a Palestinian issue and a local one. Even after a series of plane hijackings in September 1970 and murder of 11 athletes during 1972 Munich Olympics, UN Security Council refrained from passing a resolution to crack down on terrorist groups. Till 1990s, UN viewed terrorism as an Arab-Israel issue. After September 11 attacks, Resolution 13723 was passed, which was impressive as it outlawed terrorism and also terrorism financing. The lacuna was that it was not preventive. It could be invoked only when a terrorist act had occurred. It also failed to define terrorism, leaving each member state to rely on own interpretation and act accordingly. The UN has also failed to hold member states responsible for failing to pursue designated terrorist organizations. The groups like Islamic States, al-Qaeda, Taliban, Hamas, Lashkar no longer focus on local issues and have a worldwide reach.

Q. IMF could turn irrelevant unless it changes itself to keep up with rival global bodies. Critically evaluate.

A. The International Monetary Fund (IMF) an international organization of 189 countries works to foster global monetary cooperation, secure financial stability, facilitate international trade, promote high employment and sustainable economic growth, and reduce poverty around the world.

The economic architecture of IMF is skewed, as is evident from points below:

The clout of developing countries today vis-à-vis the developed ones is not commensurate with their quotas. Moreover the recent announcement of deferring the next round amendments in quota till 2019 could be hurtful.

The heads have historically been appointed from a coterie of developed nations leading to discrimination of developing countries

IMF's strong points are that

1. Given the successful experiences in dealing with BoP problems, it has tremendous relevance
2. A strong base of 150 members means a large Corpus and
3. Its recent decision to increase the quota share of developing countries signifies that it is open to change.

IMF facing strong competition from emerging institutions must be agile. It still remains relevant.

Practice Questions

1) Russia has shown a distinct inclination to move away from a very proactive stance of support to India lately. Do you agree?
2) Whatever be the political compulsions, it is the economics that matters. Can India take this view as paramount in its foreign policy?
3) United Nations Organisation is in urgent need for reforms. Give your arguments both for and against.
4) What are the outstanding issues between India and Myanmar? Elaborate.
5) A stable Afghanistan is in India's interests. Do you agree?
6) SAARC has outlived its purpose. It has now to further the road map for progress. Do you agree?
7) India needs to collaborate and not confront with China for its own interest. Do you agree?
8) India's look east policy is flawed. Comment.
9) Reforms in UN Security Council are nowhere in sight. What reforms are needed and what are the impediments?
10) The world cannot unite politically so long as economic barriers dominate. Do you agree?

Appendix-I

Scheme	Date of Launch	Provisions
Atal Pension Yojana	May 9, 2015	Social Sector Scheme pertaining to Pension Sector
Bachat Lamp scheme	2009	reduce the cost of compact fluorescent lamps
Central Government Health Scheme	1954	comprehensive medical care facilities to Central Government employees and their family members
Deendayal Disabled Rehabilitation Scheme	2003	Create an enabling environment to ensure equal opportunities, equity, social justice and empowerment of persons with disabilities.
Government Schemes	2015	List of all schemes launched by Central Government
Deen Dayal Upadhyaya Grameen Kaushalya Yojna	2015	It is a Goveronment of India Project to engage rural youth specially BPL and SC/ST segment of population, in gainful employment through skill training programmes.
Digital IndiaProgramme	July 1, 2015	Aims to ensure that government services are available to citizens electronically and people get benefited from the latest information and communication technology
Gramin Bhandaran Yojana	March 31, 2007	Creation of scientific storage capacity with allied facilities in rural areas to meet the requirements of farmers for storing farm produce, processed farm produce and agricultural inputs. Improve their marketability through promotion of grading, standardization and quality control of agricultural produce.
Pradhan Mantri Gramin Awaas Yojana	1985	Provides financial assistance to rural poor for constructing their houses themselves.[5]
The Indira Gandhi Matritva Sahyog Yojana	2010	A cash incentive of Rs. 4000 to women (19 years and above) for the first two live births.
Integrated Child Development Services	October 2, 1975	tackle malnutrition and health problems in children below 6 years of age and their mothers

Integrated Rural Development Program	1978	self-employment program to raise the income-generation capacity of target groups among the poor and The scheme has been merged with another scheme named Swarnajayanti Gram Swarozgar Yojana (SGSY) since 01.04 1999.
Janani Suraksha Yojana	2005	One-time cash incentive to pregnant women for institutional/home births through skilled assistance
Jawaharlal Nehru National Urban Renewal Mission (JnNURM)	December 3, 2005	a programme meant to improve the quality of life and infrastructure in the cities. To be replaced by Atal Mission for Rejuvenation and Urban Transformation.
Kasturba Gandhi Balika Vidyalaya	July 2004	Educational facilities (residential schools) for girls belonging to SC, ST, OBC, minority communities and families below the poverty line(BPL) in Educationally Backward Blocks
INSPIRE Programme		Scholarships for top Science students, Fellowships for pursuing PhD, Research Grants to researchers
Kishore Vaigyanik Protsahan Yojana	1999	Scholarship program to encourage students to take up research careers in the areas of basic sciences, engineering and medicine
Livestock Insurance Scheme		Insurance to cattle and attaining qualitative improvement in livestock and their products.
Mahatma Gandhi National Rural Employment Guarantee Act	February 6, 2006[8][9]	Legal guarantee for one hundred days of employment in every financial year to adult members of any rural household willing to do public work-related unskilled manual work at the statutory minimum wage of Rs. 120 per day in 2009 prices.

Members of Parliament Local Area Development Scheme	December 23, 1993	Each MP has the choice to suggest to the District Collector for, works to the tune of Rs.5 Crores per annum to be taken up in his/her constituency. The Rajya Sabha Member of Parliament can recommend works in one or more districts in the State from where he/she has been elected.
Midday Meal Scheme	August 15, 1995	Lunch (free of cost) to school-children on all working days
Namami Gange Programme	March 1995	Integrates the efforts to clean and protect the River Ganga in a comprehensive manner
National Literacy Mission Programme	May 5, 1988	Make 80 million adults in the age group of 15 – 35 literate
National Pension Scheme	January 1, 2004	Contribution based pension system
National Scheme on Welfare of Fishermen		Financial assistance to fishers for construction of house, community hall for recreation and common working place and installation of tube-wells for drinking water
National Service Scheme		Personality development through social (or community) service
National Social Assistance Scheme	August 15, 1995	Public assistance to its citizens in case of unemployment, old age, sickness and disablement and in other cases of undeserved want
Pooled Finance Development Fund Scheme		
Pradhan Mantri Adarsh Gram Yojana	July 23, 2010	Integrated development of Schedule Caste majority villages in four states
Pradhan Mantri Kaushal Vikas Yojna	April 2015[13]	To provide encouragement to youth for development of employable skills by providing monetary rewards by recognition of prior learning or by undergoing training at affiliated centres.
Pradhan Mantri Suraksha Bima Yojana [1]	May 9, 2015	Accidental Insurance with a premium of Rs. 12 per year.

Pradhan Mantri Jeevan Jyoti Bima Yojana	May 9, 2015	Life insurance of Rs. 2 lakh with a premium of Rs. 330 per year.
Pradhan Mantri Jan Dhan Yojana	August 28, 2014	National Mission for Financial Inclusion to ensure access to financial services, namely Banking Savings & Deposit Accounts, Remittance, Credit, Insurance, Pension in an affordable manner
Pradhan Mantri Gram Sadak Yojana	December 25, 2000	Good all-weather road connectivity to unconnected villages
Rajiv Awas Yojana	2013	It envisages a "Slum Free India" with inclusive and equitable cities in which every citizen has access to basic civic infrastructure and social amenities and decent shelter
Rajiv Gandhi Grameen Vidyutikaran Yojana	April 2005	Programme for creation of Rural Electricity Infrastructure & Household Electrification for providing access to electricity to rural households
Rashtriya Krishi Vikas Yojana	August 1, 2007	Achieve 4% annual growth in agriculture through development of Agriculture and its allied sectors during the XI Plan period
Rashtriya Swasthya Bima Yojana	April 1, 2008	Health insurance to poor (BPL), Domestic workers, MGNERGA workers, Rikshawpullers, Building and other construction workers, and many other categories as may be identified by the respective states
RNTCP	1997	Tuberculosis control initiative
Saksham or Rajiv Gandhi Scheme for Empowerment of Adolescent Boys	2014	Aims at all-round development of Adolescent Boys and make them self-reliant, gender-sensitive and aware citizens, when they grow up. It cover all adolescent boys (both school going and out of school) in the age-group of 11 to 18 years subdivided into two categories, viz. 11-14 & 14–18 years. In 2014–15, an allocation of Rs. 25 crore is made for the scheme.

Sabla or Rajiv Gandhi Scheme for Empowerment of Adolescent Girls	2011	Empowering adolescent girls (Age) of 11–18 years with focus on out-of-school girls by improvement in their nutritional and health status and upgrading various skills like home skills, life skills and vocational skills. Merged Nutrition Programme for Adolescent Girls (NPAG) and Kishori Shakti Yojana (KSY).
Sampoorna Grameen Rozgar Yojana	September 25, 2001	Providing additional wage employment and food security, alongside creation of durable community assets in rural areas.
Swabhiman	February 15, 2011	To make banking facility available to all citizens and to get 5 crore accounts opened by Mar 2012. Replaced by Pradhan Mantri Jan Dhan Yojana.
Swarnajayanti Gram Swarozgar Yojana	April 1, 1999	Bring the assisted poor families above the poverty line by organising them into Self Help Groups (SHGs) through the process of social mobilisation, their training and capacity building and provision of income generating assets through a mix of bank credit and government subsidy.
Swavalamban	September 26, 2010	pension scheme to the workers in unorganised sector. Any citizen who is not part of any statutory pension scheme of the Government and contributes between Rs. 1000 and Rs. 12000/- per annum, could join the scheme. The Central Government shall contribute Rs. 1000 per annum to such subscribers.
Udisha		Training Program for ICDS workers
Voluntary Disclosure of Income Scheme	June 18, 1997	Opportunity to the income tax/ wealth tax defaulters to disclose their undisclosed income at the prevailing tax rates.

National Rural Livelihood Mission(NRLM)	June 2011[16]	This scheme will organize rural poor into Self Help Group(SHG) groups and make them capable for self-employment. The idea is to develop better livelihood options for the poor.
National Urban Livelihood Mission(NULM)	24 Sep, 2013[18]	This scheme will reduce poverty of urban poor households specially street vendors who constitute an important segment of urban poor by enabling them to access gainful self-employment and skilled wage employment opportunities.
HRIDAY – Heritage City Development and Augmentation Yojana	Jan 2015[19]	The scheme seeks to preserve and rejuvenate the rich cultural heritage of the country.
Sukanya Samridhi Yojana (Girl Child Prosperity Scheme).	22 Jan 2015[16]	The scheme primarily ensures equitable share to a girl child in resources and savings of a family in which she is generally discriminated as against a male child.
Smart Cities Mission	June 25, 2015	To enable better living and drive economic growth stressing on the need for people centric urban planning and development.
AMRUT	June 25, 2015	To enable better living and drive economic growth stressing on the need for people centric urban planning and development.
Pradhan Mantri Awas Yojana(PMAY)	June 25, 2015	To enable better living and drive economic growth stressing on the need for people centric urban planning and development.
National Child Labour Projects(NCLP)	launched in 9 districts in 1987 and has been expanded in January 2005 to 250 districts in 21 different states of the country	The objective of this project is to eliminate child labour in hazardous industries by 2010.Under this scheme, the target group is all children below 14 years of age who are working in occupations and processes listed in the Schedule to the Child Labour (Prohibition & Regulation) Act, 1986 or occupations and processes that are harmful to the health of the child.

National Career Service (India)(NCS)	20 July 2015	The objective of this project is to help job-seekers land up at the job they deserve.Under this scheme, an online job-portal named as National Career Service portal has been launched which acts as a common platform for Job-seekers, employers, skill providers, govt. departments, placement organizations and counsellors. The portal possesses mre than 3.11 crore registered job-seekers and more than 9 lakh employers from across the country.
Antyodaya Anna Yojna	25 December 2000	Under the scheme 1 crore of the poorest among the (Below Poverty Line)BPL families covered under the targeted public distribution system are identified.Issue of Ration Cards Following the recognition of Antyodaya families, unique quota cards to be recognized an "Antyodaya Ration Card" must be given to the Antyodaya families by the chosen power. The scheme has been further expanded twice by additional 50 lakh BPL families each in June 2003 and in August 2004,thus covering 2 crore families under the AAY scheme
Pradhan Mantri Kaushal Vikas Yojana	July 15, 2015	Seeks to provide the institutional capacity to train a minimum 40 crore skilled people by 2022
National Food Security Mission	2007 for 5 years	It launched in 2007 for 5 years to increase production and productivity of wheat, rice and pulses on a sustainable basis so as to ensure food security of the country.The aim is to bridge the yield gap in respect of these crops through dissemination of improved technologies and farm management practices.

Pradhan Mantri Ujjwala Yojana	1 May 2016	Launched to provide free LPG connections to women from below poverty line families.
Pradhan Mantri Bhartiya Jan Aushadhi Kendra (PMBJK)	1 July 2015	[21] Pradhan Mantri Bhartiya Janaushadhi Pariyojana' is a campaign launched by the Department of Pharmaceuticals, Govt. Of India, to provide quality medicines at affordable prices to the masses through special kendra's known as Pradhan Mantri Bhartiya Jan Aushadhi Kendra. Pradhan Mantri Bhartiya Jan Aushadhi Kendra (PMBJK) have been set up to provide generic drugs, which are available at lesser prices but are equivalent in quality and efficacy as expensive branded drugs.
Standup India	April 5, 2016	The objective of the Stand-Up India scheme is to facilitate bank loans between INR 10 lakh (INR 1,00,000) and INR 1 Crore (INR 10,000,000) to at least one Scheduled Caste (SC) or Scheduled Tribe (ST) borrower and at least one woman borrower per bank branch for setting up a greenfield enterprise. This enterprise may be in manufacturing, services or the trading sector. In case of non-individual enterprises at least 51% of the shareholding and controlling stake should be held by either an SC/ST or Woman entrepreneur. Loans can be applied online through the Standup Mitra or Udyami Mitra portals.

Appendix-II

IMPORTANT JUDGEMENTS RELATED TO POLITY & CONSTITUTION

The judiciary has played an important and a pivotal role in ensuring that the fine balance between the various organs of the state is maintained and managed. It has also seen to it that citizens rights are held sacrosanct and are sustained. The very laudable work on environmental issues and public interest litigation too has earned it laurels. Besides, the Supreme Court has also stepped in to lay guidelines when it found the government lethargic or lagging; the guidelines in blood banks, sexual harassment of women at workplace and first aid for road accidents victims prove the point.

Listed below are some of the important judgements of the Supreme Court; more details can be collected rom other sources:

	SUBJECT MATTER	CASE REFERENCE
1.	Preamble	*Kesavananda Bharati vs State of Kerala* AIR SC 1973SC 1461
2.	Territory of India	*Amar Singh vs State of Rajasthan* AIR 1955 SC 504
3.	Citizenship	*State of Maharashtra vs Prabhakar* AIR 166 SC424
4.	Fundamanetal Rights (Basic Structure)	*Golaknath, Kesavananda Bharati (1973)* *Minerva Mills Ltd. Vs Union of India* AIR SC 1789
5.	Fundamental Rights (Personal Liberty)	*Maneka Gandhi vs Union of India* SC 597 AIR 1978
6.	Environment (Hazardous Chemicals)	*M C Mehta vs Union of India* 1987 SC 1086
7.	Preventive Detention	*ADM Jabalpur vs Shukla* AIR 1976 SC 1207
8.	Child Labour	*MC Mehta vs Union of India* AIR 1997 SC 699
9.	Public Interest Litigation Locus standi	*S P Gupta vs Union of India* AIR 1982 SC 149
10.	Directive Principles of State Policy	*State of Haryana vs Charanjeet Singh* AIR 2006 SC 16

11.	The Union (President) Art.72 with K S Puttaswamy	*Kehar Singh vs Union of India* 1989 SC 65
12.	Parliament (Office of Profit)	*Jaya Bachchan vs Union of India* AIR 2006 SC 2119
13.	Governor's powers to issue ordinances under Art 213	*D C Wadhwa vs State of Bihar* AIR 1987 SC 579
14.	Writs–Habeas Corpus	*Kishore Mohan vs State of WB* 1972 SC 1749
	– Mandamus	*Garg vs State of UP* 1991 SC 571
	– Certiorari	*Union of India vs Nambudiri* 1991 SC 203
	– Quo Warranto	*Mukhtiar vs State of Punjab* AIR 1991
15.	Right to Property A legal Right	*Bishamber vs State of UP* 1982 SC 34
16.	Article 356: Judicial Review	*S R Bommai vs Union of India* 1994 SC 215
17.	Powers, Privileges of Legislators	*ML George vs State of Kerala* 2010

PART VI

Previous Years' Solved Papers

Solved Paper 2013
General Studies
Paper II

*Each question carries **10 marks. Word limit** not more than **200.***

All questions are compulsory

Q1. The role of individual MPs (Members of Parliament) has diminished over the years and as a result healthy constructive debates on policy issues are not usually witnessed. How far can this be attributed to the anti-defection law which was legislated but with a different intention?

Ans. The 52nd amendment act of the Constitution, popularly known as the anti-defection law, while legislated with a good intention, tends to reduce the quality of debates in parliament. This legislation amended Articles 101,10 2, 190 and 191 of the Constitution regarding vacation of seats and disqualification from membership from parliament and State Legislatures. It also added in the 10th Schedule, which provides that a MP will lose his membership if he relinquishes his membership from the party on whose ticket he fought the election, or votes contrary to or abstains from voting despite the directive from his party. The Schedule also regulates splits in political parties and disallows independent members to join a party. Jurisdiction of courts is also excluded to decide questions of disqualification.

In a sense, the role of an MP is diminished to just a person who has to follow orders from the party bosses. Healthy, constructive debates in Parliament require that members are able to debate and vote on issues with an independent outlook, keeping in mind the interests of the people of their constituency. If debates become pre-decided by the leaders of the parties, those members who disagree with their party are also forced to vote with their party. For example, when the issue of FDI in retail was voted upon, all MPs voted on party lines. Maybe there were some in Congress who did not like FDI, maybe some in BSP wanted to vote and not abstain.

Knowing the situation, many members don't bother to raise independent issues. What is use of debates, if everything is known before?

Anti-defection law, which was legislated to prevent gross corruption, horse trading, splits and general instability in Parliament, particularly State Legislatures has come to restrain the essential facets of parliamentary democracy that is debates and discussions.

Q2. Discuss Section 66A of IT Act with reference to its alleged violation of Article 19 of the Constitution.

Ans. Article 19-1(a) of the Constitution provides the citizens of India with the freedom of speech and expression. Section 66A of the IT Act seeks to punish individuals with imprisonment for the following offences viz; sending any information which is grossly offensive or has a menacing character; sending information known to be false for causing annoyance, anger, inconvenience etc; persistently making use of a computer or a communication device to cause annoyance or inconvenience. Section 66A of the IT act seeks to prevent grossly offensive material from circulating freely on the internet.

However, its provisions are so vague and broad that they are liable to be misused as is clear from recent incidents. The potential impact was visible in the arrest of Shaheen Dhadha and Renu Srinivasan (Maharashtra), (who questioned the shutdown in the city after Shiv Sena supremo Bal Thackeray's death in Mumbai) Prof. Ambikesh Mahapatra (West Bengal) who was arrested for circulating cartoons of chief minister Mamta Banerjee, KV Rao and Mayank who were arrested for criticizing politicians through social media. Annoyance and anger are subjective questions which vary with individuals.

Clause 2 of Article 19 restricts freedom in the interest of sovereignty and integrity of India, security of the state, public sector, decency and morality and to prevent contempt of court. But Section 66A restricts the freedom of speech without clearly falling under any of the exceptions mentioned in Article 19. Though arrests are not to be made without the permission of an official below the rank of inspector general of police, individuals have been arrested for small offences. There is also a worry that such arrests might have been made to satisfy political leaders. The section goes a bit too far and curbs freedom; it should be made to conform to the Constitutional provisions.

Q3. Recent directives from Ministry of Petroleum and Natural Gas are perceived by the 'Nagas' as a threat to override the exceptional status enjoyed by the State. Discuss in light of Article 371A of the Indian Constitution.

Ans. The Nagaland state government regards oil exploration as parts of its land and resources, and regards itself competent to make laws on oil exploration. It is agitated over what it perceives as the Centre's "threat" to override the exceptional status enjoyed under Article 371A of the Constitution. The Article facilitated sovereignty of the Nagas on matters pertaining to their religious and social practices, customary laws and procedure, administration of civil and criminal justice, ownership and transfer of land and resources. The Naga Assembly can make any law of Parliament inapplicable by passing a resolution.

The Centre objected to the issuance of Nagaland Petroleum and Natural Gas Regulations saying that the state, under the Constitution could not regulate mining of natural wealth as it was a Central Subject. It argued that Article 371A only gives the state the right against implementing Central Acts in certain areas and not to make new law or regulations on these subjects. The Petroleum and Natural Gas Ministry terms as *ultra vires* of the Constitution the move by the Nagaland Government to invite expression of interest for exploration of 11 oil and gas blocks in the state. The state government on the other hand, regards it as its legal right under Article 371A of the Constitution. The move can be seen as challenging India's sovereignty and strengthening separatism. Instead of taking a confrontationist view, the whole issue needs sensitivity.

Q4. 'The Supreme Court of India keeps a check on arbitrary power of the Parliament in amending the Constitution.' Discuss critically.

Ans. There has been a conflict of interest between the Supreme Court and Parliament on the issue of amending the Constitution. Parliament wants to exercise discretionary use of power to amend the Constitution, while the Supreme Court wants to restrict that power. The Supreme Court through a judicial review and doctrine of basic features has evolved a system of keeping a check on what it feels are the arbitrary and undemocratic amendments of parliament.

Until the Supreme Court decision in the *Golaknath* case, there was no limitation on the power of parliament to amend any part of the Constitution. In that case however, the position was reversed and Fundamental Rights were held as transcendental and immutable. Parliament thus could not amend the Constitution even under Article 368 through the Constitution Amendment Act. In the *Kesavananda Bharati* case, the court said that parliament could amend any part of the Constitution as long as it did not alter the basic features of the Constitution. However, the definition of 'basic features' has not yet been given in any judgment.

The judges believe that if Parliament is allowed unlimited power to amend the Constitution, there is a danger that the democratic government could be converted into a dictatorship. But, if the Constitution makers wanted to limit the powers of Parliament to amend the Constitution, they would have done so in the Constitution itself.

The Supreme Court is not above the Constitution. It only has the power to interpret the Constitution and not to amend or add new features to it. Therefore the limitation on the power of the parliament to amend the Constitution does not seem right.

Q5. Many State Governments further bifurcate geographical administrative areas like Districts and Talukas for better governance. In light of the above, can it also be justified that more number of smaller States would bring in effective governance at State level? Discuss.

Ans. State Governments may bifurcate geographical administrative areas like Districts and Talukas for better governance, which is related to administrative convenience. But division of states is a different matter. Any state is badly governed until there is effective devolution of funds and powers to local authorities.

It takes about a decade for a new state and its government and administrative institutions to become stable. A small state faces natural (physical) and human resources limitations, lack of agro climatic diversity required for economic and developmental activities, and cannot raise resources internally. A new small state may find itself lacking in infrastructure (administrative and industrial), which requires time, money and effort to build. All these factors make it more dependent on the Centre for financial transfers and centrally-sponsored schemes.

But smaller administrative units bring the government closer to the people, have more uniformity and ensure that a specific and focused approach is taken up. Separation of poorer regions from the richer ones ensures that grants from the Centre will be spent on that particular region only. There is also evidence that smaller units have in general performed better on development as compared to their bigger counterparts.

But creation of new states increases administrative expenses since administrative infrastructure has to be repeated. There are also dangers that smaller states will create more intra-state conflicts particularly sharing of river waters, building of dams etc. Some people also fear threat to national unity and integrity. Therefore, a decision on creation of small states has to be taken carefully.

Q6. The Constitutional mechanisms to resolve the inter-state water disputes have failed to address and solve the problems. Is the failure due to structural or process inadequacy or both? Discuss.

Ans. Article 263 of the Constitution provides for the creation of interstate councils to inquire and advise upon the disputes, which have may arisen between states through a presidential order. Under Article 262, Parliament may by law also provide for the creation of tribunals to resolve interstate water disputes and exclude the jurisdiction of any court from such a dispute. Despite these provisions, many of these disputes have dragged on and haven't been resolved even after long years.

The Cauvery dispute tribunal was constituted in 1990 and the final award was given in 2007, after 17 years. The 2nd Krishna water dispute tribunal, constituted in 2004, gave its final award recently in December 2010. These long delays are partly due to elaborate judicial proceedings and deliberations. Two other disputes, namely the Mullaperiyar (between Kerala and Tamil Nadu) and the Bhabli (between Maharashtra and Andhra Pradesh) caused concerns about their potential impact over inter state relations in India.

In many cases, states have refused to comply with the award of the tribunal. In one particular case, the Supreme Court accepted a special leave petition under Article 136 of the Constitution despite the bar on jurisdiction provided under Article 262.

The disputes are not because of a structural or procedural problem. Water sharing is a very sensitive and political problem. Resolving water disputes thus requires a political solution. Both states should hold discussions and solve problems of inter-state rivers. The Centre must try to get a solution through discussion rather than directly opting for the judicial route. It must be remembered that frequent recurrence and long deliberations produce various kinds of insecurities and impact people's livelihoods.

Q7. Discuss the recommendations of the 13th Finance Commission which have been a departure from the previous commissions for strengthening the local government finances.

Ans. The recommendations of the 13th Finance Commission remap fiscal federalism in the country by conferring greater powers on the third tier of government, the local bodies, both urban and rural.

The commission for the first time recommended that local bodies be given a direct share in Union tax revenues bypassing the state governments. It provides for 2.5% share for local bodies from the divisible pool in the form of grants. This recommendation will unshackle the local bodies from state control and turn the grant into entitlements and thereby strengthening them.

It also proposed to increase the share of urban bodies vis-a-vis rural bodies in tune with the relative population. This would correct the earlier distortion which gave the rural bodies four times the resources irrespective of the fact that urban population has been increasing. To improve the performance of local bodies, only 1.5% of the 2.5% share would be constant while the rest should be based on performance.

The 13th Finance Commission holds local bodies as key to bringing about a developmental transformation. The State Governments fear that control over local bodies will pass from them to the party in power at the Centre. But the recommendations must be seen in totality. They seek to strengthen local bodies and many of them have also improved the position of state finances.

Q8. The product diversification of financial institutions and insurance companies, resulting in overlapping of products and services strengthens the case for the merger of the two regulatory agencies, namely SEBI and IRDA. Justify.

Ans. The recent dispute between SEBI and IRDA on the regulation of Unit Linked Insurance Plans (ULIPs) opened a Pandora's Box, which raised questions on the issue of regulation of the entire financial system. It was temporarily set right by putting ULIPs under the jurisdiction of IRDA.

The reality is that mutual funds are quite similar to ULIPs, but are placed under SEBI. Also, the regulations to be complied with under SEBI are much tougher as compared to IRDA. Hence, mis-selling by financial firms trying to come under a different regulator by making small changes in their products is a resultant problem.

There are eight regulators in the financial sector. While the stock market is regulated by SEBI, the commodities market is under the FMC (Forward Markets Commission) and pension under PFRDA. Products which exist or may come up in future may have features from some or all of these areas, thus, creating problems similar to the ULIP issue. Financial products and services are getting increasingly complicated and regulating them through multiple agencies will only lead to confusion and disputes.

The Financial Sector Legislative Reforms Commission suggested that financial sector regulators such as SEBI and IRDA should be merged into a Unified Financial Agency (UFA), which should aim to implement consumer protection provisions and micro-prudential provisions for the entire financial system which can bring clarity in the minds of the investors.

Consumers have received very little satisfaction in their grievance redressal from these regulators. A unified regulator would yield benefits in terms of economies of scope and scale in the financial system, reduce the identification of a regulatory agency with one sector and consistent approach towards consumer protection.

Q9. The concept of Mid Day Meal (MDM) scheme is almost a century old in India with early beginnings in Madras Presidency in pre-independent India. The scheme has again been given impetus in most states in the last two decades. Critically examine its twin objectives, latest mandates and success.

Ans. The Mid-Day Meal Scheme, introduced in government and government-assisted schools has two objectives, *one* to increase the nutritional content in children's daily food intake and *two,* to raise enrolment and attendance in schools. The aim is to provide hot cooked meals to children of primary and upper primary classes and encourage poor children to concentrate on classroom activities.

The scheme mandates to provide meals to ensure an energy content of 450 calories and 12 grams of proteins for children studying in primary classes and 700 calories of energy and 20 grams of proteins at the upper primary level.

According to recent studies, the scheme has achieved many successes and that too at a low cost. It has reduced protein deficiency of a primary school student by 10%, the calorie deficiency by 30% and the daily iron deficiency by nearly 10 %.

But the scheme also had several failures. The Ministry of Human Resource Development has confirmed that 95 per cent of meal samples prepared by NGOs in Delhi did not meet nutritional standards. Poor hygiene in the school kitchen and lack of food storage space are common. The monitoring committees at various levels are also not performing.

The government has taken steps to improve the scheme by raising the food norms to 'increase the quantity of pulses and vegetables, revising cooking costs upwards, increasing the honorariums of cooks and helpers and increasing funds to build kitchen sheds'.

Q10. Pressure group politics is sometimes seen as the informal face of politics. With regard to the above, assess the structure and functioning of pressure groups in India.

Ans. A pressure group's role is as vital as that of any political party existing in a country. Political scientist Samuel Finer has even said that a pressure group is an anonymous empire.

Pressure group is a living public behind the parties. It is an interest group working to secure certain interests by influencing the public policy. It is non-aligned with any political party and works as an indirect yet powerful group to influence decisions.

Pressure groups in India use several means to press for their demands; constitutional and unconstitutional; or legal and illegal. They may try to forge close relations with a political party to get their demands implemented. They may even fund the candidates of these political parties. They may also make resort to riots and demonstrations. For example, naxalites can be seen as a pressure group, which uses violence to get their demands accepted.

Pressure groups are distinct from political parties. They do not take part in the government, do not directly fight in elections, they espouse the interests of a narrow group of people and do not have any official recognition. Their functioning is however similar to the functioning of political parties.

Q11. The legitimacy and accountability of Self Help Groups (SHGs) and their patrons, the micro-finance outfits, need systematic assessment and scrutiny for the sustained success of the concept. Discuss.

Ans. A self-help group (SHG) is a village-based financial intermediary usually composed of local men or women. Members make small regular savings contributions over a few months until there is enough capital in the group to begin lending. Funds may then be lent back to the members or to others in the village for varied purposes. SHGs have reduced dependence on money lenders and also aided in women empowerment.

SHGs have emerged as an important part of the development strategy of the country with some significant successes to their name. But there are concerns about their patrons, the micro-finance institutions (MFIs).

MFIs are charging exorbitant interest rates which are directly affecting the poor. They also use coercive means in certain cases to get back their loans. Many self-help groups however are not able to link up with the formal banking system and have to rely on MFIs for finance.

Many loans were not given for income generating activities, which then led to members defaulting on payments. Lack of transparency in relation to interest rates and other charges, multiple lending, upfront collections of security deposits and over-borrowing are other problems.

The recommendations of the Malegam Committee on MFIs can be helpful. SHGs must be brought under the formal banking system instead of MFIs. Organisational and financial training of the SHG members must be set afoot. SHGs have so far been mainly functioning in south India and they have to be extended to the rest of the country so that maximum people avail of benefits.

Q12. The Central Government frequently complains on the poor performance of the State Governments in eradicating suffering of the vulnerable sections of the society. Restructuring of Centrally sponsored schemes across the sectors for ameliorating the cause of vulnerable sections of population aims at providing flexibility to the States in better implementation. Critically evaluate.

Ans. Centrally Sponsored Schemes (CSS) are schemes, which are designed by the Union Government but implemented by the States. Restructuring of these schemes is a key step which will help in improving the performance of State Governments in implementation. States were given very little flexibility in spending the money, for adjusting to local level variations. Less involvement by states followed as they did not take up ownership of these schemes.

Restructuring of CSS means states have been given many more powers. They can now spend 10% of the CSS funds on their own as long as the use remains within the broad guidelines of the scheme. Even regarding the remaining 90% of the funds, states will be involved in preparing the guidelines for the scheme. Also, funds will be provided through the Consolidated Fund of the state.

The implementation of the schemes will now improve. With reduction in schemes from 147 to 66, there would also be a focused approach. Resources will be spread evenly.

Q13. Electronic cash transfer system for the welfare schemes is an ambitious project to minimize corruption, eliminate wastage and facilitate reforms. Comment.

Ans. Electronic cash transfer system, mainly through Aadhaar can be a game changer, it is said. In this system, the money is directly transferred into the bank accounts of beneficiaries. LPG and kerosene subsidies, pension payments, scholarships, employment guarantee scheme payments and benefits under other government welfare programmes will be made directly to beneficiaries.

It can help the government reach out to identify beneficiaries and help plug leakages. Like in case of PDS scheme, some ration shop owners divert subsidised PDS grains or kerosene to open market and make a quick buck. Such leakages can be stopped by the implementation of the electronic cash transfer scheme.

Also by plugging leakages, the total burden of subsidies, which is Rs.3, 25,000 crores can be reduced in the long run. It will reduce the need for large administrative machinery and eliminate harassment of citizens. It will also solve the problem of targeting genuine and needy beneficiaries. Ghost and multiple beneficiaries will be eliminated and more funds can be made available for the eligible.

However, opening a bank account for every citizen of the country in a short time is a big task and identification of beneficiaries will remain a challenge. Corruption in the issuance of cards must be checked.

Q14. The basis of providing urban amenities in rural areas (PURA) is rooted in establishing connectivity. Comment.

Ans. Provision of Urban Amenities to Rural Areas (PURA) was launched to bridge the wide gap which exists in the provision of physical and social infrastructures between urban and rural areas. It is a strategy for rural development in India. This concept was given by former President Dr. A.P.J Abdul Kalam.

PURA proposes that urban infrastructure and services be provided in rural hubs to create economic opportunities outside of cities. Its aim is connecting rural hubs with urban areas. There are mainly three types of connectivity to be achieved, namely, physical connectivity by providing roads, electronic connectivity by providing communication network, and knowledge connectivity by establishing professional and technical institutions. PURA seeks to provide roads, communication networks and establishment of professional and technical institutions. All these connections are expected to lead to economic connectivity, thus creating economic growth and employment outside of the cities.

The scheme envisages the intertwining of rural infrastructure development with economic regeneration activities. It will now be implemented through the PPP mode so that private sector can be asked to manage assets and deliver services. The private partners would have to provide amenities like water supply and sewerage, roads, drainage, solid waste management, street lighting and power distribution and undertake some economic and skill development activities.

PURA thus seeks holistic development of rural areas around a potential growth centre.

Q15. Identify the Millennium Development Goals (MDGs) that are related to health. Discuss the success of the actions taken by the government for achieving the same.

Ans. Millennium Development Goals (MDGs) related to health are:

- To eradicate extreme poverty and hunger
- To reduce child mortality rates
- To improve maternal health
- To combat HIV/AIDS, malaria and other diseases
- To ensure environmental sustainability

Broadly, government is not likely to achieve the targets set by MDGs in reducing child mortality rates and maternal mortality rates. Poverty rates are reducing, though targets set by MDGs are hard to achieve. The maternal mortality rate (MMR) that highlights the number of mothers dying per 100,000 live births, may be on a decline, still about five women die every hour in India from complications developed during childbirth.

The recent World Bank data puts the MMR for India reported in 2015 at 174 per 100, 000 live births, which is a significant decline from the 215 figure that was reported in 2010.

In absolute numbers, nearly 45,000 mothers die due to causes related to childbirth every year that accounts for 17% of such deaths globally.

States do not present a uniform picture and many of them like Madhya Pradesh, Bihar and Orissa reveal a very depressing picture. Even in case of diseases such as TB, newer and more potent forms which are resistant to multiple drugs are seen.

India's record in combating HIV/AIDS is much better. HIV prevalence rates in India have almost halved in recent years. Cases of malaria have dropped significantly and incidence and mortality due to TB has also reduced. The success in combating these diseases can be attributed to the success of the third phase of the National AIDS Control Programme, the National Vector Borne Disease Control Programme and the Directly Observed Treatment Short Course.

Programmes for maternal and child health and nutrition and institutional deliveries are (i) Reproductive and Child Health Programme (i.e. immunisation, New Born Care Scheme etc), (ii) Janani Suraksha Yojana etc. However, a lot more needs to be done.

Q16. Though Citizen's Charters have been formulated by many public service delivery organizations, there is no corresponding improvement in the level of citizens' satisfaction and quality of services being provided. Analyse.

Ans. Citizen's Charters have failed to create an impact in India because they have several weaknesses. There is very little consultation with stakeholders in the design of the charters. They use jargonized language and are too brief or too large. Their aim is to be an extremely useful tool for improving the quality of service delivery and satisfaction of the people in dealings with the government. But many Charters don't have proper design. For example, a citizen's charter should provide the details of business transacted, clients served, services provided to each client group, grievance redressal mechanism and how to access it and the expectations of clients.

There is no mention of sharing of responsibility in such charters. There is very little consultation with stakeholders in the design of the charters. There is an absence of penal provisions in most charters.

Many times brochures, manuals and other publicity manuals of the organisation are taken as citizen's charter. Charters are not reviewed and updated periodically.

The Sevottam model presents an ideal model on which citizen's charters of the future have to be moulded.

Q17. 'A national Lokpal, however strong it may be, cannot resolve the problems of immorality in public affairs.' Discuss.

Ans. A National Lokpal is necessary for the fight against corruption, but however strong it may be, it will not be able to eliminate the problem of corruption in public affairs completely.

The exact judicial powers of Lokpal are rather unclear in comparison with its investigative powers. Without judicial review, Lokpal could potentially become an extra constitutional body with investigative and judicial powers whose decisions cannot be reviewed in regular courts.

It presumes that an act of corruption will be committed only by a government servant. This is evident from the partial inclusion of business entities and the total exclusion of NGOs, media and other similar categories of institutions from the Lokpal's ambit. The proposed Lokpal in India recommends a maximum punishment of life imprisonment for corrupt public servants, while the punishment for a Lokpal member found guilty of corruption is just "dismissal, removal or reduction or reduction in rank".

Legal factors of corruption arise due to the slow and expensive judicial process, protection offered to civil servants under Articles 311 and Section 197 of CrPC of the Constitution and lack of whistle-blower legislation. A National Lokpal only addresses the legal factors of corruption and that too on a small-scale.

Q18. The proposed withdrawal of International Security Assistance Force (ISAF) from Afghanistan in 2014 is fraught with major security implications for the countries of the region. Examine in light of the fact that India is faced with a plethora of challenges and needs to safeguard its own strategic interests.

Ans. The withdrawal of the ISAF from Afghanistan portends dangerous security implications for India and remains a big foreign policy challenge.

To safeguard India's own strategic interests:

- India does not want revival of extremist Taliban.
- India's energy interests in Iran, Turkmenistan can be protected with a stable and democratic Afghanistan.
- Friendly Afghanistan can also aid in containing Pakistan.

India seeks to expand its economic presence in Afghanistan by improving transport connectivity and economic collaboration with countries in Central and South Asia.

The Indian government is investing more than US$ 100 million in the expansion of the Chabahar port in south-eastern Iran, which will serve as a hub for transportation of transit goods.

The withdrawal of ISAF is taking place when Taliban has not been completely defeated. It implies that a final settlement will be done through negotiations, which would give Taliban a role in a future Afghan Government. The role of Pakistan in Afghanistan would also increase as ISI maintains close relations with Taliban. With war on the western front of Pakistan over, terrorists might increase their activities in Kashmir. Pakistan Army, released from the western front will start focusing on their eastern border. With Taliban in power in Afghanistan, Pakistan will try to use it to hurt Indian interests in Afghanistan. Regional terrorist activity in Xinxiang, Central Asia, may increase. India has over the past decade put substantial investments in Afghanistan. A lot of goodwill has been earned from the people there. All this hard work may be wiped out.

It is essential that the Afghan National Army is strengthened and world community commit itself towards Afghanistan's future. Regional powers and the UN need to be given a larger role in the final settlement. Pakistan, Saudi Arabia, Turkey, Qatar and the US must not be allowed to hog the entire space.

Q19. What do you understand by 'The String of Pearls'? How does it impact India? Briefly outline the steps taken by India to counter this.

Ans. The String of Pearls refers to the network of Chinese military and commercial facilities, and the relationships it builds along its sea lines of communication which extend from Chinese mainland to Port Sudan. Though China has not established any military facility in any of these countries, it has established commercial ports and other related projects in Bangladesh, Sri Lanka, Myanmar, Pakistan etc. Many of these will be owned and operated by Chinese companies. The threat is that some of them could be used in the future for military and espionage purposes.

As much as 90% of India's trade by volume and 77% by value are carried out through the sea. Many of India's industrial cities are located along the coast. India's oil and gas supplies are also mostly dependent on shipping and not so much on pipelines. This means that the String of Pearls can be potentially used to hurt India economically.

India has been conscious of the threat posed by this strategy and has taken steps to counter it. The *Malabar Exercise* is a multilateral naval exercise involving the United States, India, Japan, Australia, and Singapore. India's 'Look East' policy with the south-east Asian countries is also considered as a broad strategy to counter the String of Pearls. The newly evolving India-South Korea partnership is being seen as a vital component of India's game plan to counter China's increasing footprint in the Indian subcontinent. India is also developing our blue water navy so as to block Chinese naval movements along choke points such as the Strait of Malacca.

India has also forged relations with China's neighbours to cooperate with them since they share similar apprehensions. Frequent interactions with the Chinese are taking place to prevent a war like situation from coming up.

Q20. Economic ties between India and Japan while growing in the recent years are still far below their potential. Elucidate the policy constraints which are inhibiting this growth.

Ans. Japan is currently India's third largest source of foreign direct investment. Japan has assisted India in infrastructure development projects such as the Delhi Metro Rail Project. Both sides are discussing the Delhi-Mumbai Industrial Corridor (DMIC) Project and Dedicated Freight Corridor (DFC) Projects on the Mumbai-Delhi and the Delhi-Howrah routes. The Japanese government has also expressed interest to help establish a Chennai-Bengaluru Industrial Corridor and a Dedicated Freight Project in the south connecting the cities of Bengaluru and Chennai.

But the bilateral trade at $18 billion between the two countries is not very impressive, especially when the bilateral trade between India and China has crossed $70 billion. Japan's share in total FDI inflows into India has also been declining in recent years.

There are still some unresolved issues in India-Japan relations. One of the constraints is allowing the free movement of professionals between the two countries, which Japan is hesitant to provide. In the civil nuclear sphere, Japan has apprehensions regarding India's nuclear programme because of which it is reluctant to conclude a pact.

Another problem is the financial assistance under Japan's Official Development Assistance (ODA) requires the projects under DMIC and DFC to be given to Japanese companies. However, India is interested in competitive bidding between several contractors, including Indians. The CEPA (Comprehensive Economic Partnership Agreement) also needs to be renegotiated to bring more products and services under sphere. Japanese companies have been conservative while dealing with India.

The economies of India and Japan are complementary and show scope for cooperation. India provides a large market for Japanese products. India needs capital, technology and investment in infrastructure, which Japan can provide.

Q21. The protests in Shahbag Square in Dhaka in Bangladesh reveal a fundamental split in society between the nationalists and Islamic forces. What is its significance for India?

Ans. The 2013 Shahbag protests, associated with a central neighbourhood of Dhaka, spread to other parts of that country as people demanded capital punishment for Abdul Quader Mollah who had been sentenced to life imprisonment and for others convicted of war crimes by International Crimes Tribunal. On that day, the International Crimes Tribunal had sentenced Abdul Quader Mollah to life in prison after he was convicted on five of six counts of war crimes. Other demands included banning the Bangladesh Jamaat-e-Islami party from politics and a boycott of institutions supporting (or affiliated with) the party.

Finally, in September 2013, Bangladesh Supreme Court found Abdul Quader Mollah guilty of murders and other war crimes and ordered his execution, converting his life sentence to death sentence.

The protests in Shahbag Square reveal a tussle for a national identity between 'two groups' in Bangladesh. The youth who took part in protests showed that a large part of that country's population believe in a secular view. This is a positive and significant development from India's point of view. It will mean that Jihadi terrorism will get little support in that country. In the past, safe haven was given to terrorists, who were targeting India. Pakistan will also get less of a foothold in Bangladesh.

The protests also affirm the spirit of the Bangladeshi liberation war, in which India played a key role. It was a negation of the two-nation theory on which Pakistan is based. It also means that there will be little support in the future for politics based on anti-India propaganda.

Q22. Discuss the political developments in Maldives in the last two years. Should they be of any cause of concern to India?

Ans. The Maldives political crisis began as a series of peaceful protests that broke out in May 2011. A democratically elected President Mohamed Nasheed was ousted in an undemocratic fashion and close aide, Abdulla Yameen of the erstwhile authoritative ruler, Maumoon Abdul Gayoom, made a comeback into the government. The event raises a lot of issues of concern for India.

India lost a secular and pro-India leader in a neighbouring country. One of the first effects of the ouster was the cancellation of the contract of GMR group for airport development in Male. Maldives has also tried to forge closer ties with China and is close to offering several development projects to China. It may try to play China against India. Maldives might join the Chinese String of Pearls around India. Jihadi terrorists might get a safe haven in Maldives, who could target India through the coast. Many of the new people in power harbour anti-India feelings, rake up anti-India propaganda and are close to conservative Islamic forces.

India always maintained that it will not interfere in the internal affairs of another country. India wants democracy to be propagated among its neighbours and does not want the island nation to become a bastion of political Islam and religious extremism.

Q23. In respect of India-Sri Lanka relations, discuss how domestic factors influence foreign policy.

Ans. India-Sri Lanka relations in recent years have revealed how domestic politics can impact India's relations with foreign countries.

The issue of Sri Lankan Tamils played a role in Tamil politics as seen in the state elections. Tamil politicians consider the Centre's response to Sri Lanka's war crimes and human rights aberrations as inadequate and ineffective.

India supported a US-sponsored resolution against Sri Lanka in March 2013 in the UNHCR. It is true that there was pressure from state level political parties, but India's concerns regarding Sri Lanka's record are genuine.

None of our neighbours supported this resolution since they had no such pressure and were interested in safeguarding their bilateral relations with a neighbour. The other supporters of the resolution were countries from far away with much less at stake. It could be argued that in the absence of pressure from the state parties, India could have taken a different view on this matter.

Another area, which got impacted by state level politics, was that of defense exchanges between the two countries and the training of Sri Lankan armed forces personnel in India. The choice between saving the government, which relies on the support of a crucial ally and safeguarding India's long-term national interest came to the fore.

Significant lessons can be learnt. One, important issues of foreign relations should never be decided based on pressure from state level parties. Two, India should not be caught between taking decisions based on idealism and on practicality especially when it comes to relations with neighbours such as Sri Lanka. Third, India should take a stance on human rights issues in various international forums, while deciding its foreign policy.

Q24. What is meant by the Gujral doctrine? Does it have any relevance today? Discuss.

Ans. The Gujral doctrine was the foreign policy doctrine of former Prime Minister I K Gujral, which was first outlined by him, as External Affairs Minister. The doctrine enunciates a policy of non-reciprocal accommodation towards India's neighbours.

The Gujral Doctrine is a set of five principles to guide the conduct of foreign relations with India's immediate neighbours, notably Pakistan, as under:

1. With neighbours like Nepal, Bangladesh, Bhutan, Maldives and Sri Lanka, India does not ask for reciprocity but gives all that it can in good faith and trust.
2. No South Asian country will allow its territory to be used against the interest of another country of the region.
3. None will interfere in the internal affairs of another.
4. All South Asian countries must respect each other's territorial integrity and sovereignty.
5. They will settle all their disputes through peaceful bilateral' negotiations.

It is in pursuance of this policy that India concluded an agreement with Bangladesh in late 1996, on the sharing of Ganga waters. This pact enabled Bangladesh to draw slightly more water, in the lean season, than what the 1977 Agreement provided.

Another example could be the grant of MFN status to Pakistan without expecting much from that country.

The Gujral doctrine does retain relevance even today. India's neighbours are much smaller in size and many of our actions can raise apprehensions in their minds. As India is the dominant economy and bigger power, making unilateral concessions can create trust.

Q25. The World Bank and the IMF, collectively known as the Bretton Woods Institutions, are the two inter-governmental pillars supporting the structure of the world's economic and financial order. Superficially, the World Bank and the IMF exhibit many common characteristics, yet their role, functions and mandate are distinctly different. Elucidate.

Ans. The World Bank is an international financial institution that provides loans to developing countries for development programmes. Its official goal is reduction of poverty. It aims to promote foreign investment and international trade and the facilitation of capital investment. The IMF's goal is to assist in the reconstruction of the world's international payment system post World War II. The organization's stated objectives are to promote international economic co-operation, international trade, employment and exchange rate stability by making financial resources available to member countries to meet balance of payments needs among other measures.

Almost every country in the world is a member of both. However, the similarities between the two end there. The fundamental difference between the two institutions is that while the bank is primarily a development institution, the IMF is a cooperative institution that seeks to maintain an orderly system of payments and receipts between nations. The IMF and World Bank have a different purpose, a distinct structure; receive their funding from different sources and assist different categories of members. The IMF is a small organisation with no affiliates and subsidiaries while the World Bank is a big organisation itself composed of five institutions.

The World Bank is an investment bank, which borrows from one and lends to another. IMF is not a bank and does not intermediate between borrowers and lenders and receives its funds from the quota subscriptions of member nations. While the World Bank lends activities to poor and developing nations, the IMF can lend to any country depending on the foreign exchange position of the member. Despite differences, both these institutions complement each other's activities.

Solved Paper 2014

General Studies

Paper II

*Each question carries **10 marks. Word limit** not more than **200.***

All questions are compulsory

Q1. Starting from inventing the 'basic structure' doctrine, the judiciary has played a highly proactive role in ensuring that India develops into a thriving democracy. In light of the statement, evaluate the role played by judicial activism in achieving the ideals of democracy.

Ans. The basic structure doctrine came into practice after the landmark judgement in the *Kesavananda Bharati vs State of Kerala* case. With this judgement, Indian judiciary started a pro-active role in safeguarding the ideals of democracy such as equality, freedom, self-government, self-determination and, thus, the term judicial activism came into existence. Judicial activism is an innovative step of the Indian judiciary. It puts a brake on legislative adventurism and executive oppression by pointing to the Constitutional limits.

Judicial activism in India can be seen with reference to the review power of the Supreme Court and High Court under Articles 32 and 226 of the Constitution particularly in Public Interest Litigation (PIL) cases. Judicial activism has helped in issues from maintenance of public roads to environment pollution.

Judicial activism means that instead of judicial restraint, the Supreme Court and other lower courts become activists and compel the authority to act and sometimes also direct the government and government policies and also administration. It is a way through which justice is provided to the disadvantaged and aggrieved citizens. Failure on part of the legislative and executive wings of the Government to provide 'good governance' makes judicial activism an imperative. The violation of basic human rights has also led to judicial activism. Finally, due to the misuse and abuse of some of the provisions of the Constitution, judicial activism has gained significance. There are some very important cases where judicial activism plays an important role like Bhopal gas tragedy and the Jessica Lal murder case are among the top two. When our chosen representatives have failed to give us a welfare state, judiciary plays an active role.

Q2. Though the federal principal is dominant in our Constitution and that principle is one of its basic features, but it is equally true that federalism under the Indian Constitution leans in favour of a strong Centre, a feature that militates against the concept of strong federalism. Discuss.

Ans. India has the features of a federal government and also of a unitary government and is thus said to be a quasi-federal state. The Supreme Court also describes it as a federal structure with a strong bias towards the Centre.

Provisions such as two sets of government; one at the Centre and another at the state with division of powers (7th Schedule), a written Constitution, supremacy of the Constitution, supremacy of the judiciary, bicameral legislature (Lok Sabha and Rajya Sabha) are some of the main features of our federal system of government. To protect the diversity of our country and yet, maintain unity and integrity of our nation the Constitution makers rooted for a strong Centre.

Article 1 (1)of the constitution says India shall be union of states and its citizens shall have at least two tier governance. So the people of a UThave every right to opt for statehoodin India. However, the amended(in 1956) Article 3, allows the union government power with prior consent of the President (common head of states and union governments) to (a) form a new state/UT by separating a territory of any state, or by uniting two or more states/UTs or parts of states/UTs, or by uniting any territory to a part of any state/UT. (b) the power to establish new states/UT (which were not previously under India's territory) which were not in existence before.

In the case of a breakdown of constitutional machinery in a state, Article 356brings about state emergency which dissolves the state government and results in President's rule during which the Union Government can make laws for a state. There is no emergency at the centre which can dissolve the Union government unlike Government of India Act 1935.

Q3. The 'Powers, Privileges and Immunities of Parliament and its members' as envisaged in Article 105 of the Constitution leave room for a large number of un-enumerated privileges'. How can this problem be addressed?

Ans. Article 105 of the Constitution provides powers, privileges and immunities to Parliament and members. Freedom of speech is one such privilege. No member shall be liable to any proceedings in any court in respect of anything said or any vote given by him in parliament or any committee.

There is no legal codification of the parliamentary privileges as they are many and one of them is the nature of work that takes place in the parliament. By codifying the privileges, a limit on parliamentary freedom may be put which may not be helpful in its proceedings. Any violation of the limits imposed on parliament under Article 121 would still be a matter exclusively for parliament to deal with. Article 122 also puts a limitation on the courts from parliament. Parliament itself is the highest law making body which frames laws for the governance of the country.

The problem can be addressed by accepting the precedents of the parliamentary procedures as they incorporate the excellent practices of parliamentary procedure.

Q4. What do you understand by the concept "freedom of speech and expression"? Does it cover hate speech also? Why do the films in India stand on a slightly different plane from other forms of expression? Discuss.

Ans. Freedom of expression is interchangeably used for freedom of speech, but includes exchange of ideas or notions, no matter what medium is used. Freedom of speech is the right to express one's opinions and ideas.

But this freedom is not without any constraints and every government puts in curbs to some extent. This restriction is to curb the menace of hate speech, which attacks any person or a group on the basis of sex, cultural origin, faith, race, incapacity or sexual orientation and is thus, prohibited and outside the law.

As there is diversity in our country and political parties exploit this diversity in their favour by inciting communities against each other through hate speeches, freedom of speech must be restricted in some situations.

Films in India have a wide audience and are made in several regional languages. The Constitutional provision regarding films as a medium of speech and expression exists. But they are censored by a central authority and courts subject them to scrutiny, if the content is obscene or for maintenance of public order. Also, films have a much more emotional impact than other forms of media. A case in point is the recent controversy on the film *Padmavati* which created problems for the central and state governments as well as for the censor board. Finally, it was resolved with the title changed to *Padmavat*. This speaks volumes on the influence of films vis-à-vis other forms of media.

Q5. Instances of President's delay in commuting death sentences has come under public debate as denial of justice. Should there be a time limit specified for the President to accept/reject such petitions ? Analyse.

Ans. Article 72 of the Constitution gives power to the President to commute the death sentence of a convict with no time period within which to decide over the mercy petition.

But for petitioners, a delay over accepting and rejecting such mercy petitions adds to physical stress and trauma, which is harsh and also the question of human rights arises. It is said that justice delayed is justice denied. So, delay in death commutation is considered as denial of justice by many. Even in *Shatrughan Chauhan v. Union of India* case, the Supreme Court held that inordinate delay in deciding a petition of a convict sentenced to death by the president can be considered torture and inhuman punishment to the convict.

Such delays not only deprive a convict of his constitutional rights but also create adverse physical conditions and psychological stresses on him and his family.

The decision to accept/reject such mercy petitions is with the home ministry and is therefore an independent administrative procedure. This results in delay.

With regard to specifying a time limit for the President to accept/reject such mercy petitions, the apex court verdict in the Rajiv Gandhi assassination case (where it commuted the death sentence of convicts to life in view of the inordinate and unreasonable delay in considering their mercy petition), is very crucial. Hence, there should be a time limit for the President to accept or reject mercy petitions.

Q6. The size of the cabinet should be as big as governmental work justifies and as big as the Prime Minister can manage as a team. How far is the efficacy of a government then inversely related to the size of the cabinet? Discuss.

Ans. In India, the size of Council of Ministers is fixed at 15 % of the size of the Lok Sabha, which takes the collective decisions of the government. But this 15 % also becomes too big a size. Sometimes, this cabinet size becomes too large due to coalition partners in government, which turns counter-productive.

The Cabinet which is the supreme decision making body of the government has membership of important ministries such as home, finance, defense, external affairs and is led by the Prime Minister who ultimately decides on the decisions. It has to meet every day and take decisions of day-to-day work and also meet from time to time to take important decisions.

The cabinet's purpose is to reach unanimous agreements outlining government's policy and thus, a large size puts impediments in reaching a consensus due to differing opinions of the members and leads to paralysis. If the size of the cabinet is small, decisions can be made quickly. In case of coalition governments, the government has to accommodate the interests of the coalition partners and this results in increase in size of the cabinet. A bigger cabinet may become unwieldy and crucial decisions may be delayed.

Q7. Though 100 percent FDI is already allowed in non-news media like a trade publication and general entertainment channel, the Government is mulling over the proposal for increased FDI in news channel for quite some time. What difference would an increase in FDI make? Critically evaluate the pros and cons.

Ans. The government is considering a proposal to increase foreign direct investment (FDI) limit in print media sector to 49 per cent from 26 per cent at present.

Currently, the FDI policy permits 26 per cent foreign direct investment in the publishing of newspapers and periodicals dealing with news and current affairs through government approval route.

The cap of 26% in news media has led to stunted growth of the sector. FDI in news media is need of the hour. Indian media is yet to produce its BBC or Al-Jazeera news channel. We should bring more Foreign Direct Investment or FDI in news. The 100% FDI in sectors like retail, pharmaceuticals, manufacturing and telecom has benefitted them immensely. FDI means advanced technology, processes and training, more jobs and smart returns. It boosts the economy, gives increased employment and income levels as increased competition starts. FDI in news media should be allowed with proper checks and balances to keep out the riff-raff and anti-national elements from participating. This sector is very sensitive as it reaches millions of people in our country and FDI, if not regulated would pose a threat to country. FDI must take in views of all the stakeholders involved viz, citizens, media, industry etc.

Q8. The setting up of a Rail Tariff Authority to regulate fares will subject the cash strapped Indian Railways to demand subsidy for obligation to operate nonprofitable routes and services. Taking into account the experience in the power sector, discuss if the proposed reform is expected to benefit the consumers, the Indian Railways or the private container operators.

Ans. The Rail Tariff Authority (RTA) has been given green signal to act as an advisory body with a Chairperson and four other members. It would advise the government on prices for both passenger trains and goods trains depending on input cost and volatile market conditions. The body is armed with powers to develop an integrated, transparent and dynamic pricing mechanism for the freight segment of the Indian Railway's business. Indian railway is a commercial entity earning revenue, but also meets social obligation through suburban passenger services, concessionary travel to certain section of travelers and concessional freight movement of certain commodities, particularly to remote and inaccessible areas which are always running below cost.

The power sector which was given a social obligation, offered subsidy to the agricultural sectors, but this resulted in huge losses, inefficiency and poor performance.

From the consumer view point, setting up of RTA would increase fare prices as it would try to rectify the problem of cross subsidization wherein to keep the fare of passenger trains low, freight prices are kept higher. But if this cross subsidization is taken care of, it would bring relief to industrial sector and boost economy. This would also bring succour to private container operators as due to high freight prices, these operators were facing stiff competition from road transportation, which generally run along the railways tracks.

Q9. National Human Rights Commission (NHRC) in India can be most effective when its tasks are adequately supported by other mechanisms that ensure the accountability of a government. In the light of the above observation, assess the role of NHRC as an effective complement to the judiciary and other institutions in promoting and protecting human rights standards.

Ans. The National Human Rights Commission is an independent body, which safeguards rights relating to life, liberty, equality and self-respect of the individual and which hold pride of place in the Constitution as Fundamental Rights, or are enumerated in international agreements.

To cite some NHRC functions :

(a) examining human right violations or disregard on part of public servants in preventing such violations, (b) visiting jail or other such institutions where persons are detained, (c) undertaking and promoting research in the field of human rights, (d) look into cases of human rights violations involving NGOs and encouraging their participation in protection of human rights.

(e) providing advice and assistance to governments, creating awareness, promoting interaction, exchange, and better coordination among other national human rights institutions in the region and worldwide, promoting interaction and exchange with non-governmental organisations, and publishing annual reports.

All these involve large number of public and private institutions. It becomes necessary that NHRC is supported by these institutions to be really effective in preventing human rights violations. In India, NHRC has gone beyond its jurisdiction of civil rights to social and economic rights.

Q10. The penetration of self-help groups (SHGs) in rural areas in promoting participation in development programmes is facing sociocultural hurdles. Examine.

Ans. In India, Self Help Groups (SHGs) are basically rural based and aim at imparting entrepreneurship skills among the members, so that additional livelihood avenues among the village folks become a reality.

As these SHGs are women centric, the parochial mind-set, still active, poses difficulties. In male dominated rural society, women don't generally have property rights, which they can show as collateral to obtain funds from banks. Illiteracy among women in rural areas means they are not aware of many business opportunities. Also, many rural women feel insecure and are not aware of their own abilities as potential entrepreneurs.

Finance is also a problem and finance in rural economies is still controlled by the menfolk leaving the women dependent on the whims and fancies of men.

The socio-economic structure in tribal communities is markedly different from that of the non-tribal or advanced groups of people. This also places SHGs in a spot.

Custom made policies, keeping in mind diversity of race, religion, languages and other socio-cultural practices among different states, must be started. Decentralization with involvement of all people must be attempted for SHGs to make a mark.

Q11. Do government's schemes for uplifting vulnerable and backward communities by protecting required social resources for them, lead to their exclusion in establishing businesses in urban economies?

Ans. Government schemes for vulnerable and backward communities, which seek to uplift the masses from social and economic backwardness, provide social resources such as roads, hospitals, schools, financial services, food and housing facilities among others.

These schemes are aimed at assisting the underprivileged and backward communities in their endeavors, and not give them freebies that discourage them from taking up initiatives of their own. The schemes target to provide them with certain social resources because they have been excluded from mainstream society for decades, and are still reeling under the consequences of the same. The focus on the disadvantaged communities will help put them on an equal footing and integrate them with the rest of society.

But, such schemes disincentivize the rural folk from migrating to urban centres, because of the availability of facilities and infrastructure in nearby vicinity as they can start business activities in their surroundings. They don't need to move out. Why will they then migrate to set up business in urban areas?

Admittedly, the schemes do create opportunities for them near their vicinity which is very beneficial. But the country needs contribution from every nook and corner and hence, if these masses keep away from towns, it would hurt the economy.

Q12. An athete participates in Olympics for personal triumph and nation's glory; victors are showered with cash incentives by various agencies, on their return. Discuss the merit of state sponsored talent hunt and its cultivation as against the rationale of a reward mechanism as encouragement.

Ans. State sponsored talent hunt is a holistic approach towards creating a sporting culture in the country. It is a superior approach as it searches hidden talent.

The policy of Indian sport authorities to reward the successful players with large amount of cash and other incentives is not as productive as the policy of state-sponsored talent hunt. China, Russia, US and other top sporting nations have all followed a holistic and long-term approach to creating a sporting culture. In such a system the primary focus is to search for talent in sports and then provide them the required sports infrastructure. *It has the following merits*

(1) It enables sport agencies to find suitable talents and nurture them into world class players.

(2) Talented players who are financially weak also get the opportunity to motivate their talents and become successful.

(3) There is transparency and an environment of equal opportunities in the system.

(4) Future uncertainties do not derail the confidence of talented sportsperson.

Felicitating with rewards recognises and honours the achievement of victors. It does motivate them to perform better and also acts as an incentive for others, leading to a culture of competitiveness. But state sponsored talent hunt gives economic and continuous security to individuals, who want to dedicate their life for sports. India lags behind in sports arena as sportspersons are not given financial security and stability.

Q13. Should the premier institutes like IITs/ IIMs be allowed to retain premier status, allowed more academic independence in designing course and also decide mode/ criteria of selection of students. Discuss in light of the growing challenges.

Ans. Premier institutes like IITs and IIMs which are the backbone of India's research and development are far behind international institutes. The reason is too much centralisation and a pathetic lack of autonomy.

Various reports like the Radhakrishnan Commission (1948-49), the Kothari Commission (W64-66), NPE-1968, the NPE-1986 and Review of NPE by Acharya Ramamurthy Commission (1992) have strongly advocated autonomous character for our universities.

Indian higher education is significantly over regulated, stifling private effort; which is not conducive to innovation or creativity. Inappropriate resources, mismanaged regulatory mechanism and political interference are causing qualitative problems.

There is demand for knowledge economy in present scenario which makes it all the more important for such premier institutes to be updated in their curriculum. Regarding the question of selection of students, it should always be done on merit.

In fact, less than 9% (of eligible population in India) as compared to 40-80 % in developed countries has access to higher education. The IITs and IIMs should ponder on this.

Q14. Has the cadre based Civil Services organization been the cause of slow change in India? Critically examine.

Ans. Cadre based Civil Services Organisation means that members are allotted each state based on merit and choice of preference. Once a cadre is allotted to a civil servant, he/she have to spend a major part of his/her service period in the allocated cadre.

This permanency of cadre of civil servant results in inefficiency and ineffectiveness which is exactly opposite of purpose for which cadre based civil services was designated. The career prospects of civil servants are in the hands of the state government.

The system of a cadre based civil services organization has limited recruitment of persons to important positions in the government to those within a particular cadre. This has made lateral entries nearly impossible, thus reducing chances for recruitment of talent suitable to the position. This issue was raised and analysed in the 2nd Administrative Reforms Commission's Report. Specialized knowledge of the sector concerned is an important asset that could help in performance of the task at hand. Such expertise could help in dealing with the various complexities that the task presents. Rapid and fundamental changes are taking place in the country as fast economic growth, urbanisation, environmental degradation, technological change and increased local awareness and identity are seen. The response time to adapt to these changes is much shorter than it used to be and as instrument of public service, civil servants have to be ready to manage such changes keeping aside all individual goals.

Q15. Two parallel run schemes of the Government, viz the Aadhar Card and NPR, one as voluntary and the other as compulsory, have led to debates at national levels and also litigations. On merits, discuss whether or not both schemes need run concurrently. Analyse the potential of the schemes to achieve developmental benefits and equitable growth.

Ans. Aadhaar card is a 12- digit number that is provided against a person's biometric data after the same has been reduplicated. National Population Register (NPR), is a comprehensive identity database of Indian nationals. The aim of Aadhar is to eliminate duplicate and fake identities whereas that of NPR is to help in better utilisation and implementation of benefits and services under government schemes.

Both the schemes are of similar nature, creating a database of Indian nationals and thus, need not run concurrently. Instead of rolling out different schemes for same purpose, only one scheme can be implemented.

Both the schemes can serve as the access mechanism to a unified payment infrastructure that could centralise all financial transactions, including wages, salaries and subsidies under a single number to an Aadhaar enabled bank account of the recipient.

With a database of Indian nationals, under NPR, it becomes very easy to identify beneficiaries for various government schemes. Since, the Aadhaar scheme provides a unique identity to all the citizens it eliminates fraud and bogus activity. The deprived and needy can access services like banking facilities and other government services in the form of food subsidies, thus, preventing leakages. This would definitely help in reducing unnecessary expenditure and using the money on developmental activities.

The need of the hour is systems which run easily, efficiently, effectively and economically.

Q16. With respect to the South China sea, maritime territorial disputes and rising tensions, affirm the need for safeguarding maritime security to ensure freedom of navigation and over flight throughout the region. In this context, discuss the bilateral issues between India and China.

Ans. Territorial disputes in the South China Sea involve many countries within the region, which are in direct confrontation with China. India, being in near vicinity of China should develop friendly ties with countries like Sri Lanka, Nepal, Maldives and others whom China is actively wooing.

South China Sea is also important strategically and economically due to its important shipping lanes and proven offshore reserves of crude oil and natural gas. China enjoys indisputable sovereignty over the South China Sea and thus even a small presence of India is not acceptable to China. India, on other hand, supports freedom of navigation in international waters, including South China Sea and the right of passage in accordance with accepted principles of international law.

A stable Asia depends highly on cordial relations between India and China.

Another Indo-China conflict in land or sea can greatly affect the peace and stability of the entire region.

Hence, the bilateral relations become all the more important and are closely monitored by the international community.

India and China are not only immediate neighbours, but they also share a strong geographical bond. Hence, maritime relations between China and India are crucial for stability in Asia.

Q17. The aim of Information Technology Agreements (ITAs) is to cut all taxes and tariffs on information technology products by signatories to zero. What impact would such agreements have on India's interests?

Ans. Information Technology Agreements (ITAs) provide for participants to completely eliminate duties on IT products covered by the agreement. The ITAs represent about 97% of world trade in information technology products.

India had joined ITA-1, but it had a shocking impact on domestic electronics hardware sector. There is hence a reluctance to join ITA-2 which is expected to be worth \$ 1 trillion and add about 200 products to the list.

India's reasons for hesitation are that such agreements benefit only those countries whose domestic manufacturing is robust and also signing the agreement would go against the recent slogan of 'Make in India' push, as it would make importing goods cheaper than manufacturing in the country. India, of course, stands to gain as all IT exports will enjoy zero tariffs. However, the immediate impact will be negligible as India hardly exports any IT hardware and all member countries have to slash import duties on their products to zero.

These pacts would help India only if we have a large manufacturing base along with an increase in exports and in the longer run would give our local firms access to big markets.

Q18. Some of the international funding agencies have special terms for economic participation stipulating a substantial component of the aid to be used for sourcing equipment from the leading countries. Discuss the merits of such terms and if there exists a strong case not to accept such conditions in the Indian context.

Ans. The IMF and World Bank exert enormous leverage over the economies of more than 60 countries. Having a global membership, their role is crucial. Nowadays, international funding agencies like the World Bank, IMF, Ford Foundation and Rockefeller Foundation among others are increasingly tightening their grip over developing countries and dictating terms to them to be eligible for funding.

These international institutions decide how much a debtor must spend on education, healthcare and environmental protection, and force structural adjustment policies so that countries have to cut spending on education and health, make exports cheaper and privatise national assets. These are not conducive for developing countries.

Also, these funding agencies prop up interests of wealthy countries by making debtor countries prioritise exports over the development of diversified domestic production. Multinational corporations of affluent countries are given precedence to undertake developmental projects, and forcibly labour costs are cut so that small businesses and farmers can't compete.

India which often faces resource crunch needs funding of these agencies to undertake developmental projects and cannot ignore such funds. But a lot of precaution needs to be taken while accepting such funding. National interest must be kept in mind. Policies must be framed, in the backdrop of globalization and the world becoming integrated economically.

Q19. India has recently signed to become founding member of New Development Bank (NDB) and also the Asian Infrastructure Bank (AIIB). How will the role of the two Banks be different? Discuss the strategic significance of these two Banks for India.

Ans. Asian Infrastructure Investment Bank (AIIB) is a multilateral development bank which exclusively lends money to Asia for infrastructural projects. New Development Bank (NDB) is also a multilateral bank operated by BRICS (Brazil, Russia, India, China and South Africa) as an alternative to Bretton Woods's institutions viz, World Bank (WB), IMF and WTO.

NDB is formed to help defend BRICS countries from volatility in dollar exchange, help finance high tech projects, infrastructure and sustainable development in member nations, and also to escape from the dictates of World Bank and IMF.

With the coming of these two institutions, India stands to gain immensely as it would have an equal say in governance of these institutions unlike the WB and IMF. With soft loans coming from these new institutions without any terms, we would be able to cater to development needs of our economy.

These institutions have the potential to give tough competition to Bretton Wood institutions, thus making loans further cheaper and on the terms and conditions of the debtor, which can greatly help in developmental activities of a country like India.

BRICS nations have become a collective superpower with one-fifth of world GDP and two-fifths of world population.

Q20. WTO is an important international institution where decisions taken affect countries in a profound manner. What is the mandate of WTO and how binding are their decisions? Critically analyse India's stand on the latest round of talks on food security.

Ans. The World Trade Organisation (WTO) is a multilateral organisation that works for the harmonisation and unification of international trade and to reduce barriers to world trade. Outdated laws unsuited to commercial practices in this globalised world are modified, domestic laws of countries are altered to enhance predictability in cross border commercial transactions, and common legal standards governing particular aspects of international business transactions are embraced.

The decisions of WTO are legally binding on the member countries. Flouting of rules and regulations of WTO can be resolved by making an official complaint to the dispute settlement body of the WTO, where parties go for mutual consultation and if that fails, formal adjudication by an expert panel ensues.

India with its huge population, without adequate food availability had a tiff with WTO over its food security programme. In July 2016, India had refused to ratify the Trade Facilitation Agreement(TFA) which is meant to ease custom norms and is being pushed by developed countries like USA among others, to boost their economies through unhindered international trade. For developing countries like India, public stockholding for food security is a paramount issue and with TFA in place under WTO rules, it threatens our food security programme. As of now the impasse has been resolved as developing countries like India can continue procurement and stocking of food grains without attracting any kind of action from WTO, even if it crosses the 10% cap.

Solved Paper 2015
General Studies
Paper II

Each question is of ***12.5 marks and maximum word limit is 200.***

All questions are compulsory

Q1. Discuss the possible factors that inhibit India from enacting for its citizens a uniform civil code as provided for in the Directive Principles of State Policy (DPSP).

Ans. Article 44 of the Indian Constitution that aims to secure a uniform civil code for all the citizens has been a controversial issue right from independence. No consensus could be reached due to a variety of factors.

Firstly, India is a land of diversity as far as population composition is concerned. People come from different religious and ethnic groups that make it difficult to agree on a uniform civil code.

Secondly, there are ideological differences among various sections of the population. While one section readily welcomes uniform code, others driven by orthodoxy want existing laws to continue.

Thirdly, it is said that uniform civil code if enacted, would be in conflict with the existing religious laws and as such it is not acceptable to various religious groups.

Fourthly, civil laws pertain to social change. It cannot be forced from above without taking citizens into confidence.

Also, a lack of political will can also be partly blamed for non-enactment of a uniform civil code. Finally, the very nature of DPSP that makes its implementation non-binding on government is also a bottleneck in its quick implementation.

Goa is only state in India that has an active and enforced uniform civil code for all citizens. The way forward is an evolutionary process that aspires for a consensus based solution rather than legislative measure.

Q2. The concept of cooperative federalism has been increasingly emphasized in recent years. Highlight the drawbacks in the existing structure and the extent to which cooperative federalism would answer the shortcomings.

Ans. Granville Austin called Indian federalism as a, Cooperative Federalism'. In recent years, the concept of cooperative federalism has been increasingly emphasized.

The existing structure of federalism has given more focus on 'top-to-bottom' approach, under which Centre proposed laws, policies, programmes and schemes which all states irrespective of ground realities and requirements have to implement. This 'one size fits all' approach, leads to poor implementation and wastage of resources.

In recent times, the Government is however emphasising more on competitive, cooperative federalism in which states not only help each other (e.g. resource mobilisation to less developed states) but also compete with each other for investment, trade, and other growth and development parameters. For example, Andhra Pradesh Government is providing various incentives (e.g. land, water etc) for attracting foreign companies and foreign investment and is in a healthy competition with Telangana.

The scrapping of the erstwhile Planning Commission and creation of NITI Aayog in its place has also reduced the Centre's role and empowers states to make their plan according to their requirement. The 14th Finance Commission has also provided provision for greater transfer of funds (42%) to the state.

All these provisions made in recent times for cooperative federalism not only promote growth and development of states but also will help India to emerge as a global super power.

Q3. In the absence of a well-educated and organised local level government system, 'panchayats' and 'samitis' have remained mainly political institutions and not effective instruments of governance. Critically discuss.

Ans. The development and evolution of local self-government institutions takes the reins of democracy in India to the common people at the grass root level. Post-independence, the Balwant Rai Mehta Committee, Ashok Mehta Committee, the 73rd & 74th Constitutional Amendment Acts set the stage for the development of Panchayati Raj system. After the 14th Finance Commission recommendation and governments' greater focus on decentralised development, greater funds are being provided to PRIs. Earlier, the lack of funds, functions and functionaries hampered the functioning of these institutions and made them a mere political tool. Now with greater funds allocation and functions under their command, the need is educated, skilled and trained functionaries. Acting through the Block Development Officer (BDO) who functions as CEO, the Panchayat Samiti is entrusted with such functions which not only require some degree of expertise and financial resources, but also involves the employment of a host of government employees, thereby introducing the element of interface between the people's representatives and the government functionaries in a structured and intimate manner.

Panchayat Samitis also plan and execute most of the developmental activities for the betterment of rural life. So a well-educated person can ensure the soul of the Panchayati Raj system is intact, otherwise it becomes a bone of contention between government and citizens.

Q4. Khap Panchayats have been in the news for functioning as extra constitutional authorities, often delivering pronouncements amounting to human rights violations. Discuss critically the actions taken by the legislative, executive and the judiciary to set the things right in this regard.

Ans. *Legislative actions taken:*

(i) Many states tried to bring legislation to ban khap panchayats, but due to lack of consensus it has not been passed successfully.

(ii) Law Commission had drafted a Bill , The Prohibition of Unlawful Assembly (Interference with the Freedom of Matrimonial Alliances) Bill' 2011. It tried to address the issue of khap panchayats.

Executive actions taken:

(i) District administration has taken many steps to tackle the menace of khap panchayats in the affected districts. It has declared such assembly to be illegal, subject to severe punishments.

(ii) Political executives have taken steps to reform these khap panchayats, as their view is that social change cannot happen immediately.

Judicial actions taken:

(i) Supreme Court has declared the khap panchayats unconstitutional and illegal and they must be "ruthlessly stamped out".

(ii) Condemning honour killings and khap panchayats, the Bench directed the administrative and police officials to take strong measures to prevent such atrocious acts.

These steps have been effective, but more of the following steps need to be taken.

(i) Lok Adalats: These institutions need to be strengthened at the grassroots level. It will help in eliminating the unconstitutional khap panchayats as well as in delivering justice.

(ii) Legislation: Effective legislation needs to be enacted in the States to ban khap panchayats.

(iii) Executive action: They need to be proactive in implementing the law and in taking action against khap panchayats.

(iv) Attitude change: Elders of the village needs to be persuaded for attitude change in order to bring social change.

Q5. Resorting to ordinance has always raised concern on violation of the spirit of separation of powers doctrine. While noting the rationale justifying the power to promulgate ordinances, analyse whether the decisions of the Supreme Court on the issue have further facilitated resorting to this power. Should the power to promulgate ordinances be replaced?

Ans. The Constitution provides for Ordinance making power to the President under Article 123 and to the Governor under Article 213.

In *RC Cooper vs. Union of India (1970)* the Supreme Court held that the President's decision could be challenged on the grounds that 'immediate action' was not required; and the ordinance had been passed primarily to by-pass debate and discussion in the legislature. It was argued in *DC Wadhwa vs. State of Bihar (1987)* the legislative power of the executive to promulgate ordinances is to be used in exceptional circumstances and not as a substitute for the law making power of the legislature. The Supreme Court argued that if ordinance making was made a usual practice and creating an 'ordinance raj', the courts could strike down repromulgated ordinances.

However, the general rule in the Wadhwa verdict came with an exception. It was stated that the government may, occasionally be unable "to introduce and push through" a Bill to convert an ordinance either because "the Legislature [has] too much legislative business" or the time at its disposal is short. In such a case, the verdict stated, the President may "legitimately find that it is necessary to repromulgate the ordinance". And such "repromulgation of the ordinance", the Court said, "may not be open to attack".

So, this exception in the Wadhwa judgment has enabled the government to resort to re-promulgation of ordinances, though they need to show that the situation is extraordinary. No, the power to promulgate ordinances should not be repealed. It is a method of last resort for the executive when there is immediate need and legislature is not in session. So, it is not the use of ordinances, but its misuse which is a cause of concern and must be checked.

Q6. What are the major changes brought in the Arbitration and Conciliation Act, 1996 through the recent ordinance promulgated by the President? How far will it improve India's dispute resolution mechanism? Discuss.

Ans. The President promulgated the Arbitration and Conciliation (Amendment) Ordinance, 2015 which amends the Arbitration and Conciliation Act, 1996. ***The important changes brought in are the following:***

(i) *Relevant court for domestic and international arbitration matters:* The Ordinance states that in the case of international arbitration, the relevant court would only be the high court having original ordinary jurisdiction.

(ii) *Powers of court to refer a party to arbitration if agreement exists:* The ordinance states that the power of referral is to be exercised by a court even if there is a previous court judgment to the contrary.

(iii) *Interim order by a court:* The ordinance amends the provision to specify that if the court passes an interim order before the commencement of arbitral proceedings, the proceedings must commence within 90 days from the making of the order, or within a time specified by the court.

(iv) *Appointment of arbitrators:* The 1996 Act permits parties to appoint arbitrators. If they are unable to appoint arbitrators within 30 days, the matter is referred to the court to make such appointments. The ordinance states that, at this stage, the court must confine itself to the examination of the existence of a valid arbitration agreement.

(v) *Time period for arbitral awards:* The ordinance introduces a provision that requires an arbitral tribunal to make its award within 12 months. This may be extended by a six month period.

(vi) *Time period for disposal of cases by a court:* The ordinance states that any challenge to an arbitral award that is made before a court must be disposed of within a period of one year.

(vii) *Fast track procedure for arbitration:* The ordinance permits parties to choose to conduct arbitration proceedings in a fast track manner. The award would be granted within six months.

Q7. Does the right to clean environment entail legal regulations on burning crackers during Diwali? Discuss in the light of Article 21 of the Indian Constitution and Judgement(s) of the Apex Court in this regard.

Ans. The Supreme Court in a landmark judgement has pronounced right to clean environment as a fundamental right enshrined under right to life and personal liberty under Article 21 of the Constitution. Though no law has been enacted on regulating the burning of crackers, but the apex court has issued guidelines in this regard. So it entails legal regulation on burning fire crackers on account of these guidelines. In the landmark case of 2005; "*Prevention of Environment & Sound Pollution v. Union of India*", the apex court laid down a few essential guidelines relating to firecrackers and addressing other problems of sound pollution. *The key highlights being:*

(a) The Department of Explosives may divide the firecrackers into two categories (i) Sound emitting firecrackers, and (ii) Colour/light emitting firecrackers.

(b) There shall be a complete ban on bursting sound emitting firecrackers between 10 p.m. and 6 a.m. It is not necessary to impose restrictions as to time on bursting of colour/light emitting firecrackers.

(c) Every manufacturer shall on the box of each firecracker mention details of its chemical contents and that it satisfies the requirement as laid down by Department of Explosives.

Bursting crackers has been a custom in our society which is now proving to be lethal for the coming generations. Article 21-Right to Life, is a basic human right and subsequently a Fundamental Right for Indian citizens, and to breathe clean air constitutes the same. Hence, it is necessary to exercise certain prudence and caution in this situation and one must give precedence to various rights in terms of their necessity.

Q8. Examine critically the recent changes in the rules governing foreign funding of NGOs under the Foreign Contribution (Regulation) Act (FCRA), 1976.

Ans. The government has drawn up new guidelines which stipulate that NGOs must not use foreign funds for activities "detrimental to national interest, likely to affect public interest, or likely to prejudicially affect the security, scientific, strategic or economic interest of the state." The draft Foreign Contribution (Regulation) Amendment Rules, 2015, also require any NGO receiving foreign funds to register themselves and to report the receipt of such funds on its website or a government prescribed website within 7 days. The rule replaces the older rule under which only foreign donations in excess of Rs. 1 crore were to be notified at the end of the year. Another rule requires banks to disclose information regarding the entry of foreign funds for NGOs in India within 48 hours. Earlier, banks were only mandated to disclose details of contributions in excess of Rs. 1 crore, within 30 days. The rules also provide for new forms for registration, renewal of registration and disclosure of receipt of foreign funds, which need to filled and uploaded on government portals. The new rules have not only increased the frequency with which NGOs are required to file information with the government, they also have provisions that require the disclosure of additional information. NGOs will now have to reveal the details of their social media accounts, and disclose whether their office bearers are part of other NGOs, to help in profiling them.The present crackdown on foreign-funded NGOs in India began after the Intelligence Bureau submitted a report on NGOs last year that said that some NGOs are deliberately trying to restrict India's developmental projects. So these new guidelines will help in better regulation of NGOs and their funding.

Q9. The Self-Help Group (SHG) Bank Linkage Programme (SBLP), which is India's own innovation, has proved to be one of the most effective poverty alleviation and women empowerment programmes. Elucidate.

Ans. Self Help Groups (SHGs) are informal associations of people who choose to come together to find ways to improve their living conditions. They help to build social capital among the poor especially women. Consequently, SHGs have emerged as the most effective mechanism for delivery of micro-finance services to the poor.

Self Help Groups, today, play today a major role in poverty alleviation in rural India. Growing number of poor people (mostly women) in various parts in India are members of SHGs and actively engage in saving and credit, as well as in other activities of income generation, natural resources management, literacy, child care and nutrition. There is ample evidence that the SHG approach is a very effective, efficient and relevant tool for organising and empowering the poor.

The SHG bank Linkage Programme helps these SHGs to get easy access to loans at low interest rate. The loans can be returned in number of installments. There is also no requirement of collaterals. After repayment, they can avail much larger amount.

There are several agencies that regulate the finances to the SHG. Other bodies like Small Industries Development Bank of India (SIDBI), Rashtriya Mahila Kosh (RMK), SEWA in Ahmedabad, MYRADA in Karnataka, Nav Bharat Jagriti Kendra and Ramakrishna Mission in Jharkhand and ADITHI in Bihar are some of the names which took the lead in promoting SHGs mostly of women.

Q10. How can the role of NGOs be strengthened in India for development works relating to protection of the environment? Discuss throwing light on the major constraints.

Ans. NGOs have played important role towards protection and conservation of environment and imparting environmental education in India. There is need to empower NGOs for development works.

NGOs need to move beyond their traditional role of passive participants in developmental work to become active participants in environmental protection. Public Private Partnership (PPP) on lines of infrastructure development projects need to be taken in environmental field.

In discharging their functions, NGOs face a number of constraints; lack of financial resources is one of them. Recently, many NGOs have come under scrutiny for financial irregularities. It is alleged that foreign funding has been provided by Western countries to stall developmental projects. The protest against Kudankulam nuclear power plant was seen in this context.

While Foreign Contribution Regulation Rules (FCRR) was amended recently to bring in transparency, it should not be utilised to deprive NGOs of necessary foreign funding.

Providing NGOs with necessary expertise to deal with environmental issues will go a long way in dealing with environmental concern. For this, a few NGOs like Centre for Science and Environment (CSE) could be identified and appropriately equipped with necessary expertise.

Evolution of a legal framework to simplify the procedures and bring in transparency would be steps in right direction to strengthen NGOs.

Among other constraints are lack of coordination between voluntary agencies and state agencies. Groups like *Narmada Bachao Aandolan* (NBA) often come in conflict with government. This mutual distrust has done more harm than good for protection of environment. Government could work constructively by looking into genuine grievances of NGOs and arrives at consensus.

Q11. The quality of higher education in India requires major improvements to make it internationally competitive. Do you think that the entry of foreign educational institutions would help improve the quality of higher and technical education in the country? Discuss.

Ans. The higher educational scenario in India lacks the edge to match up to the global competitiveness. When we compare global rankings, Indian universities fare rather poorly. Out of the top 500, it has just 1 in the Academic Ranking of World Universities, 6 in QS World Universities Rankings.

The greatest challenge that higher education in India faces is chronic shortage of faculty. According to reports, around 30-40% of faculty positions are lying vacant.

Other issues that compound the problems include

- Outdated rigid curricula and absence of employer engagement in course content and skills development.
- Pedagogies and assessment are focused on input and rote learning.
- High student: teacher ratio, due to lack of teaching staff.

Now government is looking towards foreign educational institutions to address the issues of quality in education. Their entry has many advantages. The mere presence of foreign institutions will increase competition among Indian institutions to improve quality. It will also bring the culture of rigor and excellence in research and academic standards.

Foreign educational institutions will help supplement India in content-rich curricula with activity based learning and bridge the gap between academics and industry. This will also help in filling the 'skill gap' that hurt the current technology boom.

However, there is also a need of caution. The danger of leading foreign institutions garnering our best faculty can be debilitating for existing institutions. Global experiences shows that majority of institutions entering foreign market are not prestigious universities, but rather low-end institutions seeking market access and income opportunities. To address these concerns, a revised foreign Universities Education Bill subjected to intensive consultation with all stakeholders is the need of the hour.

Q12. Public health system has limitations in providing universal health coverage. Do you think that the private sector could help in bringing the gap? What other viable alternatives would you suggest?

Ans. *The public health system in India faces many difficulties in providing universal health coverage (UHC).*

- Availability of healthcare services is quantitatively inadequate due to massive shortage of healthcare professionals.
- India's public spending on health (1.2% of GDP) is among the lowest in the world.
- Insufficient funding of public facilities, combined with faculty planning and inefficient management over the years, has resulted in a dysfunctional health system that has been yielding poor health outcomes.

It is believed by many policy makers that "private healthcare, properly subsidized, or private health insurance, subsidised by the state, can meet the challenge. In most of the countries, a mix of private and public services is a reality.

Private sector could definitely come in to supplement the efforts of public sector to deliver UHC.

In addition to partnering with private sector, other-viable alternatives should also be considered. India could possibly learn from international best practices. In countries like Canada and Australia, where UHC is already operational, universal public insurance programme is publicly financed through tax revenue. In Germany, statutory health insurance is funded by 'sickness funds'.

It is now widely accepted that, though private sector could help in realisation of goals of UHC, there is no alternative to a progressive strengthening of the public facilities. Beginning could be made by increasing public expenditure on health from current level of 1.2% to atleast 2.5% of the GDP by the end of 12th Five Year Plan. A national health package should be developed that offers essential health services at different levels of the healthcare delivery system.

Q13. Though there have been several different estimates of poverty in India, all indicate reduction in poverty levels over time. Do you agree? Critically examine with reference to urban and rural poverty indicators.

Ans. The extent of poverty in India is depicted by the following measures such as Head Count Ratio or Poverty Ratio, Poverty Gap Index, Sen Index of Poverty, Multi-Dimensional Poverty Index, Human Poverty Index (HPI) Fisher Price Index (FPI) and Conditional Cash Transfers (CCTs).

Several different expert groups have been estimated poverty in India.

The Suresh Tendulkar Committee in its finding has moved away from just calorie-criterion definition to a broader definition of poverty that also includes expenditure on health, education and clothing in addition to food. As per Tendulkar Committee Report, poverty has declined on an average by 1.5 percentage points per year between 2004-05 and 2009-10.

Uniform Recall Period (URP) and Mixed Recall Period (MRP) is another estimate of poverty in India.

Dr NC Saxena Committee reviewed the methodology for conducting BPL census in rural areas. The committee has recommended automatic exclusion of some privileged sections and automatic inclusion of certain deprived and vulnerable sections of society and a survey for the remaining population to rank them on a scale of 10. Based on the above methodology, the committee estimated the population below the poverty line at 50% of the total population.

SR Hashim Committee determined the methodology and identification of BPL families in the urban areas. Hashim suggested methodology for identifying urban poor households having three or four items like refrigerators, motorised two wheelers; landline telephone or washing machines should not be treated as poor. The expert group recommended that the urban poverty has declined.

C Rangarajan, former Governor of RBI submitted his report on the state of poverty in India. According to Rangarajan estimate, the poverty ratio has come down from 38.2% in the 10th Plan to 29.5% in the 12th Plan. The rural poverty has declined from 39.6% to 30.9% and urban poverty from 35.1% to 26.4%.

Thus, we can say that the different findings regarding the poverty declining in India is true, which can be seen both in villages and towns.

Q14. In the light of the Satyam Scandal (2009), discuss the changes brought in corporate governance to ensure transparency, accountability.

Ans. The Satyam scam brought about many corporate governance, disclosure and audit reforms to plug the loopholes in the existing system.

Immediately after the scandal the Confederation of Indian Industries (CII) set-up a task force to suggest reforms and the National Association of Software and Services Companies (NASSCOM) established a corporate governance and ethics committee.

The report of this committee addressed reforms relating to audit committees, shareholder's rights and whistleblower policy. Subsequently, the Ministry of Corporate Affairs released a set of voluntary guidelines for corporate governance, dealing with independence of directors, roles and responsibilities of audit committees and other provisions relating to directors.

The newly introduced Companies Act 2013 clearly establishes responsibility and accountability of independent directors and auditors. It provides for compulsory rotation of auditors and audit firms.

An auditor cannot perform non-audit services for a company. Auditors are required to report fraudulent acts noticed during performance of their duties.

Further, the act mandates that at least one third of the board of a company has to consist of independent directors. Independent directors have been prohibited from receiving stock options or remuneration.

To ensure greater transparency, additional disclosure norms such as formal evaluation of performance of the board of directors, filing returns with the registrar of companies with respect to any change in share holding positions of the promoters has been made mandatory.

Adoption of new accounting system IND-AS may also help to check any fraud in accounting.

Also, statutory status for Serious Fraud Investigation Office (SFIO) has been proposed. Investigation report of SFIO filed with court for framing charges shall be treated as report filed by police officer.

With these steps in place, transparency, accountability of corporate governance in India stand at better position than before the Satyam scandal.

Q15. "If amendment bill to the Whistleblowers Act, 2011 tabled in the Parliament is passed, there may be no one left to protect." Critically evaluate.

Ans. The amendment bill to the Whistleblowers Protection Act, 2011 contains a long list of restrictions that is likely to dissuade anyone from whistle blowing the cases of corruption in the government or bureaucracy.

The bill primarily seeks to amend the act in order to incorporate necessary provisions to strengthen safeguards against disclosures which may prejudicially affect the integrity and sovereignty of the country and security of the States among other things.

To begin with, whistleblowers will not be allowed to reveal any documents classified under the Official Secrets Act, 1923, even if the purpose is to disclose acts of corruption, misuse of power or criminal activities. Further, the proposed amendments allow whistleblowers to disclose some kinds of information, only if it has been obtained under the Right to Information Act. This includes intellectual property, trade secrets and even information that can be considered "unwanted invasion of privacy" of an individual.

Critics point out that the 'excuse' of national security could be used by a public authority to scuttle any investigation into a whistleblower complaint. No public servant will come forward to blow the whistle on corruption in government for fear of inviting prosecution under the Official Secrets Act.

Under the amendment, whistleblowers would be entitled to official protection only if all the conditions stipulated in the bill are met and could face action if they are not. Also as Central and State Governments would be the final authority with the power to judge each case, protection of whistleblowers might become a process of victimisation.

Providing whistleblower with safe alternative to silence is the foundational principle of every whistleblower protection law. Indian law should also conform to this principle by making suitable changes in the bill.

Q16. "For achieving the desired objectives, it is necessary to ensure that the regulatory institutions remain independent and autonomous". Discuss in the light of experience in the recent past.

Ans. The desired objective of India is to ensure national unity, integrity, sovereignty, democracy, minorities' rights and parliamentary form of government. To become an economic power is also a desired objective. The Constitution and many laws made by Parliament mention about some regulatory bodies.

These regulatory bodies regulate the financial malpractices as well as political crisis. The Reserve Bank of India (RBI) is a regulatory institution which control and supervise the financial activities like inflation and deflation. Further, the National Human Rights Commission (NHRC), CVC, CBI, the Central Information Commission (CIC), Lokpal and Lokayukta are some political regulatory institutions.

However, these regulatory bodies are autonomous in nature but their appointment, functions and termination are governed by legislative and political parties. This causes these institutions to become inefficient and subordinate to politicians, which dismantle the soul of these regulatory bodies.

The Supreme Court dubbed the country's premier investigating agency as a 'caged parrot' and expressing anguish over the CBI's lack of autonomy, gave the agency an opportunity to push for reforms.

The Supreme Court ordered the CBI to initiate probe against coal scam, Augusta Westland corruption case where former Air Chief SP Tyagi was named as one of the accused. The financial powers of the CBI chief have got a boost. The Supreme Court pointed to conspiracy among politicians, public officials and private companies in Nira Radia Case. Hence it is in national interest that the regulatory institutions must be free and depoliticised.

Q17. Increasing interest of India in Africa has its pros and cons. Critically examine.

Ans. India shares cordial relations with Africa since the era of decolonisation. These engagements have been taken to a higher level with recognition of potential of the 'dark continent'.

India and Africa find themselves on the same page on various issues of global importance. India shares similar thought with Africa on the question of global institutional governance reform and climate change negotiations. Most African countries also support India's candidature in an expanded UN Security Council.

Africa is important for ensuring energy security of India in long-run. Crude oil and mineral resource are present in South Africa, Morocco, Egypt, Sudan, Nigeria and Angola. Uranium is found in Namibia.

Greater engagement with Africa will also help India in fighting maritime piracy in Indian Ocean, off the east African coast. India could coordinate its strategy with Africa's integrated maritime strategy.

On the other hand, there are certain areas where India needs to be cautious.

Africa has remained a conflict ridden region with civil war like conditions. Terrorist organisations like Al-Qaeda in Somalia and Boko Haram have potential to harm India's interest and developmental initiatives. China has already enhanced its engagement with Africa, especially in maritime infrastructure development and naval presence. China's presence might create conflict like situation as observed in Vietnam.

However, unlike China, India's soft power stand and policies would give more space to India in building a long-term relationship.

Beginning has already been made with India sponsored Pan-African e-Network that links 53 African countries through tele-medicine, tele-education and tele-governance and plays a crucial role in fostering skill and human resources that are critical for Africa to develop in sustainable way.

Q18. Discuss the impediments India is facing in its pursuit of a permanent seat in UN Security Council.

Ans. India has been actively pursuing its quest for permanent membership of UNSC. While its economic stature, large population, democratic credentials and contribution towards peacekeeping operations supports its candidature, there are many impediments also in the realisation of this goal.

Permanent members like France and Britain are in favour of India's inclusion, others like USA and China are opposed to any sudden expansion of UN Security Council. Now that the reform requires an affirmative vote from all permanent members, any immediate expansion seems a distant possibility.

The text-based negotiation introduced by India has already been rejected by permanent members like China and Russia. Uniting for Consensus (UFC) countries like Pakistan, Italy, Mexico and Egypt also sees text-based negotiation as a breach of their strategy of open ended discussions.

Another impediment in India's claim comes from other strong contenders for the permanent seat. While G-4 countries (India, Germany, Brazil, and Japan) support each other's candidature, others like Italy, Mexico, Argentina and Pakistan has also led claims. Also, that no country from either Africa or Latin America is presently among the permanent members with Asia already having one, India's chances are further weakened in the context of any expansion. India's refusal to sign Nuclear Non-Proliferation Treaty (NPT) and long pending border disputes with Pakistan and China are also seen as hurdles in India's claim.

Among other impediments are allegations of human rights violation in Kashmir and North-Eastern India and issues associated with Armed Forces Special Power Act (AFSPA). Also that India is still struggling with issues like poverty and unemployment and perform poorly on various socio-economic indicators also reflects negatively on India's prospects.

Q19. Project 'Mausam' is considered as a unique foreign policy initiative of the Indian government to improve relationship with its neighbours. Does the project has a strategic dimension? Discuss.

Ans. Project *Mausam* is a ministry of culture project that aims to understand how the knowledge and manipulations of monsoon wind has shaped interactions across the Indian Ocean and led to the spread of shared knowledge systems, traditions, technologies and ideas along the maritime route.

Its objectives are firstly, to re-connect and re-establish communication between countries of Indian Ocean world, leading to enhanced understanding of cultural values and concerns and secondly, concentrate on understanding national cultures in their regional maritime milieu.

There is talk that *Project Mausam* is a strategy to counter China's Maritime Silk Route (MSR) initiative. It can be said that the project is essentially a cultural project that spotlights on India culture, more than economic and trade activities.

Admittedly, the project has some strategic components. One of the sub-themes of "mausam' is sharing of knowledge systems and ideas between coastal centres and maritime routes connecting India with its maritime neighbours. This signifies a desire for greater influence in Indian Ocean region over the years. China's plan for maritime infrastructure creation in the Indian Ocean region is well-known. India would also make keen efforts to have a strategic hold in these areas through such projects.

Q20. Terrorist activities and mutual distrust have clouded India-Pakistan relations. To what extent the use of soft power like sports and cultural exchanges could help to generate goodwill between the two countries? Discuss with suitable examples.

Ans. India and Pakistan have a long and complicated history with each other. There have been numerous attempts to improve the relationship notably, the Shimla Summit, the Agra Summit and Lahore Summit.

Since the early 1980s, relations between the two nations soured particularly after the Siachen conflict, the intensification of Kashmir insurgency in 1989, Indian and Pakistani nuclear tests in 1998 and the 1999 Kargil War.

The peace efforts have been impeded by periodic terrorist attacks. The 2001 Indian Parliament attack almost brought the two nations to the brink of a nuclear war. 2007 Samjhauta Express bombings, which killed 68 Pakistani civilians was also a chapter in deteriorating India-Pakistan relations. Additionally, the 2008 Mumbai attacks carried out by Pakistani militants resulted in a severe blow to the ongoing India-Pakistan peace talks. However, both the countries have started many confidence building measures like-economic ties, MFN status, trade infrastructure, business exchanges and other economic initiatives. Delhi-Lahore bus services was started in 1999, but was discontinued in light of the Kargil conflict. Passenger and freight rail services between Attari and Lahore and air linkages between the two countries were resumed in 2004.

The first bus service between Srinagar and Muzaffarabad was started in 2005. The first overland truck route between the two countries was opened at the Wagah border. Humanitarian aid in terms of food, medicine and the like was extended by India and accepted by Pakistan in the aftermath of the earthquake in Pakistan in 2005. Some right wing nationalists in India also oppose the efforts of normalisation. In present day, these nationalists opposed the concert of Ghulam Ali and cricket matches between the two countries.

However, humanitarian and cultural exchanges and cricket diplomacy can accelerate the good relations between the two countries.

Solved Paper 2016
General Studies
Paper II

Each question carries ***12.5 marks*** *and* ***maximum word limit is 200.***

All questions are compulsory

Q1. Discuss the essentials of the 69th Constitutional Amendment Act and anomalies, if any, that have led to recent reported conflicts between the elected representatives and the institution of the Lieutenant Governor in the administration of Delhi. Do you think that this will give rise to a new trend in the functioning of the Indian federal politics?

Ans. The 69th Constitutional Amendment designated Delhi as National Capital territory and provided a legislative assembly. However, it was not conferred with full statehood and is administered by Union government through the Lieutenant Governor.

Anomalies of the 69th amendment

- Delhi is more than a Union Territory but less than a full State. As per Article 239AA, public order, police and land are under the Central government.
- The article is vague. It reads identical to Article 163(1) that pertains to state and means that Delhi's power and jurisdiction is analogous to state government.
- LG has full powers to appoint bureaucrats

The crux is that Delhi does not enjoy full powers like a regular state. The law passed by Delhi Assembly regarding local bodies has to be sent to Urban Development Ministry for approval. The ongoing tussle between Delhi government and the Centre reflects strained federal relations, portending an ominous trend affecting the administration.

Q2. To what extent is Article 370 of the Indian Constitution, bearing marginal note "temporary provision with respect to the State of Jammu and Kashmir", temporary? Discuss the future prospects of this provision in the context of Indian polity.

Ans. Article 370 of Constitution is a temporary provision which grants autonomous status to Jammu and Kashmir. Except defence, foreign affairs finance and communication, Parliament needs state concurrence for applying other laws. The marginal note 'temporary provision' means it is not a permanent clause. There is a demand to repeal 'temporary' and replace it with 'special.' But Article 370 can be amended only if J & K Assembly approves. There are two views on the subject. Some constitutional experts hold that Article 370 can be amended, only if the Constituent Assembly passes a resolution. But that is hardly possible. The second view is that of the Supreme Court, which in 2013 held that Parliament, in view of Article 368 can take a call on scrapping Article 370. Also in ***Kesavananda Bharati***case (1973), Parliament was given power to amend any part of Constitution. Article 370 can be hence abolished or abrogated, subject to judicial review.

The future prospects are that rest of states may also demand a status, similar to J & K, like the north-eastern states are already demanding. Unity and integrity of country may be threatened in the face of such demands.

Q3. "The Indian party system is passing through a phase of transition which looks to be full of contradictions and paradoxes." Discuss.

Ans. There is lack of unity and maturity in ideological terms among political parties in India now.

Hundreds of parties have been recognised by the Election Commission which has led to a proliferation of parties. There is no common ideological strand uniting the various parties. On religious, social and economic issues, parties have different views making consensus building a difficult task. This has resulted in hurdles in implementation. India's multi-party systems make look attractive to the outside world, but internally it has stymied development and progress.

Regionalism has also resulted in parties toeing a narrow regionalistic stance on issues that has affected national unity.

Ideologies are shed and principles compromised for the sake of power. Parties with opposing views are forming coalitions.

Although defections have reduced after the Tenth Schedule, the whip controls everybody.

On views like donations, criminalisation of parties and electoral reforms, parties are as silent as before.

Q4. Exercise of CAG's powers in relation to the accounts of the Union and the States is derived from Article 149 of the Indian Constitution. Discuss whether audit of the Government's policy implementation could amount to overstepping its own (CAG) jurisdiction.

Ans. According to Article 149, CAG has powers to audit the accounts of the Union and the States. But as CAG had started auditing policy implementation aspects like questioning the method of auction in 2G spectrum and coal mine allocations, checking beneficiaries of farm loan waiver schemes, his jurisdiction has been questioned. He has started looking into "wisdom, faithfulness and economy" of government measures, which is being questioned.

The benefits of CAG auditing government accounts are that it would lead to performance budgeting. Ideal practices like e-auction started only after CAG reported scams.

In the Coalgate scam case, the Supreme Court had said CAG is not merely an accountant. The office of CAG had also said it has the mandate to examine and scrutinize public policies.

But critics feel as CAG is responsible to PAC (Public Accounts Committee), his actions come within the role of CAG and Parliamentary committees. Hence CAG should understand the limits of his office.

The way forward is the CAG should do constructive audit rather than fault finding alone.

Q5. Discuss each adjective attached to the word 'Republic' in the 'Preamble'. Are they defendable in the present circumstances?

Ans. The Preamble provides that India is a sovereign, socialist, secular, democratic Republic.

Sovereign: It means independence and autonomy in deciding internal and external policies. But issues like intellectual property rights and environment have led to pacts with other countries.

Yet, India has major say in all policies. For example, India did not allow US participation in naval exercise in South China Sea.

Socialist: Under 'democratic socialism,' government allows private sector to flourish. But government is now withdrawing, allowing privatization. However, corporate social responsibility has come in to fill the void of welfare socialism.

Secular: India treats all religions equally. However, communal violence and bigotry threaten our secular credentials. Yet, India remains one, despite divisive tendencies.

Democratic Republic: Representative democracy exists in India, as Parliament and state legislatures function. But corruption, criminalization, frequent disruptions to Parliament and State legislatures are blots on democracy. Yet, the 73rd and 74th constitutional amendments have ensured participatory democracy.

We can say adjectives attached to Republic are very much defendable, despite the increasing attacks on them.

Q6. What was held in the Coelho case? In this context, can you say that judicial review is of key importance amongst the basic features of the Constitution?

Ans. In the *I.R.Coelho v State of Tamil Nadu case* (AIR 2007SC 861), the Supreme Court held that the Ninth Schedule of the Constitution is not immune from judicial review if it violates the fundamental rights of the citizens. It also reaffirmed the concept of basic structure. The idiom"basic structure" itself cannot be found in the Constitution of India. The Supreme Court recognised this concept for the first time in the historic *Kesavananda Bharati case* in 1973. Since then the Supreme Court has been the interpreter of the Constitution and the arbiter of all amendments made by Parliament.

Judicial review is important as:

- it is a basic tool which *suo moto* protects other elements of the basic structure
- it ensures checks and balances, protecting citizens from the executive and legislature
- discretionary powers of various functionaries are kept in check
- If executive is delaying or failing in its duties, judicial review comes to aid as in Singur land acquisition act, harassment of women in workplace etc.

Q7. Did the Government of India Act 1935 lay down a federal constitution? Discuss.

Ans. The **Government of India Act 1935**was the last constitution of British Indiawhich split Burma from it. It lasted until 1947, when British territory was split into Pakistan and India. Provision was made for the establishment of an All India Federation at the center, consisting of Provinces of British India and the Princely states.

The Government of India Act 1935 is called the 'mini constitution,' because it laid down several features, one such being federalism.

The federal features were:

- an all-India federation of British Indian provinces and princely states was envisaged
- division of subjects between central and federal provinces
- a council of states and federal assembly were enumerated, suggesting bicameral legislature
- federal court to adjudicate inter-state disputes

However, a complete federal system was not announced as:

- residuary powers were retained by British officers like Governor General
- major powers like financial were retained by the Centre
- emergency powers were retained which meant provincial governments could be dismissed at will

It was a quasi-federal constitution.

Q8. What is a quasi-judicial body? Explain with the help of concrete examples.

Ans. A quasi-judicial body is an entity like arbitrator or tribunal board, generally of a public administrative agency. Powers resemble those of court of law or judge, which is obliged to objectively determine facts and draw conclusions. Powers are related to specific areas of excellence like financial markets, employment, immigration etc;

Important quasi-judicial bodies

Constitutional bodies

- Central Administrative Tribunal (under Article 323A) and other tribunals (under Article 323B) are quasi-judicial bodies as their decisions are like laws, but they are not bound by laws of evidence like the judiciary. Administrative officials can also head them and give rulings different from earlier decisions
- The National Commission for Scheduled Castes and National Commission for Schedules Tribes. These can summon witnesses and ask for production of documents.

Statutory bodies

- Central Vigilance Commission, SEBI, National Human Rights Commission .These are established by an act of Parliament. But like civil courts, they can enforce punishment.

Q9. Professor Amartya Sen has advocated important reforms in the realms of primary education and primary healthcare. What are your suggestions to improve their status and performance?

Ans. Professor Amartya Sen has pointed out that high out- of- pocket- expenditure (70%) and low quality are present in education and health sectors. Government spending on health is akin to that of Haiti and Sierra Leone.

Suggestions to improve education and primary healthcare involve:

- Three A's viz, Availability, Affordability and Assurance are must for improving status and performance on the health front
- Spending on health and education is 1%, compared to 4% in other countries
- Teacher- pupil ratio, child friendly pedagogy and outcome based education are in need of urgent reforms
- public and private sector must cooperate. For example, if public facilities are insufficient, private hospitals must step in to the extent possible

- Use of digital tools like Aadhar, online payments, etc can be utilised to improve the standards of education and healthcare.

Q10. "In the Indian governance system, the role of non-state actors has been only marginal." Critically examine this statement.

Ans. Non- state actors mean NGOs, community based organizations, women's groups , human rights associations etc. They have played a role by promoting child rights (*Bachpan Bachao Andolan* of Kailash Satyarthi), environmental protection (Survival International worked in Niamgiri area to stop bauxite mining by Vedanta), as watchdog against violation of human rights (Amnesty International) , promoting quality education (like Pratham) and electoral reforms (NOTA, submission of criminal cases against candidates), holding flagship conferences (Observer Research Foundation) and promoting business (FICCI).

But their role in actual governance is limited because there is not significant collaboration with the governments. Governments also view activities of these organisations with some suspicion. On various important occasions eg; budget formulation activity etc, the role of the non-state actor is not as high as in other developed democratic countries. Their activities invite allegations of non-transparency putting their credibility at stake.

Q11. "Effectiveness of the government system at various levels and people's participation in the governance system are inter-dependent." Discuss their relationship in the context of India.

Ans. Governance means providing an enabling environment along with basic public utilities efficiently and equitably, thereby allowing citizens to develop their full potential. Peoples' participation enhances the quality of governance as suggestions are given, public functionaries are made accountable, and implementation of infrastructure projects is given priority. For example, during plans made for construction of dams, it would be ideal to know how many people would be displaced and then efforts can be made to rehabilitate them. The concept of panchayat raj is also derived from people's participation. Panchayats play a crucial role in ensuring development at the grassroot level. Only the Panchayats can ensure that funds are utilised to reach the deserving beneficiaries. Decentralisation is the key to development of rural and backward areas. The use of digital technology at the panchayat level for digitization of records etc can also help in quickening the pace of development. Corruption at grassroots level can be eradicated if people involve themselves in governance.

The colonial *mai-baap* system has been altered completely. The government and governed have come closer due to citizen charters, use of information technology, grievance redressal systems. Hence both citizens and government must play a complementary role in governance and development.

Q12. In the integrity index of Transparency International, India stands very low. Discuss briefly the legal, political, social and cultural factors that have caused the decline of public morality in India.

Ans. Transparency International which released integrity index for 180 countries has placed India on 76th position. The current ranking is definitely consider as an improvement over previous years but in reality , while we aiming for corruption free India and implementing many measures for eradication of black money from system the ranking seems to be quite low. Where the small landlocked country like Bhutan performing much better than India , rank 27, its time to take a deep insights on factors which are causing decline in public morality .

The reasons for decline in public morality in India are:

- ***Legal factors***

  Multiplicity of laws and complexity are responsible for corruption. There are nearly100 laws relating to labour. Many interpretations arise due to varied laws.

- ***Role of judicial delays***

  There are over 30 million cases pending in courts. This may force people to resort to corrupt methods to influence, delay and change judgements. The complexity of economic laws, taxation laws etc also lead to varied interpretation and loopholes resulting in endless litigation and evasion of tax. For example, double tax avoidance agreement has been misused for round tripping.

- ***Political factors***

  Political parties are outside RTI ambit. This shows the apathy towards tracking corruption. Misuse of power through political patronage also leads to lack of morality.

Q13. Has the Indian governmental system responded adequately to the demands of Liberalization, Privatization and Globalization started in 1991? What can the government do to be responsive to this important change?

Ans. The general philosophy of governments after the 1991 liberalisation is "government has no business, to be in business.' The economic reforms of 1991, known as LPG (Liberalization, Privatization and Globalization), have been a great turning point for the Indian economy. Under liberalisation, the license/quota raj has been dismantled. Deregulation, delicensing and disinvestment is the new mantra. The policy has done away with trying to revive various sick PSUs. Miniratna, Maharatna and Navratna tags gave operational and financial autonomy to the public sector industries. Under privatization, the airline industry took off in a big way with private players like Indigo, SpiceJet, etc taking a huge share of the market. The government must continue this process of moving from businesses which are not its core competence. The proper functions of a government are providing law and order, ensuring transparency and uniformity in laws and focusing on improving infrastructure like roads, railways, ports etc. It can also ensure that the legislature, executive and judiciary work in tandem to ensure there is no overlapping and interference in each other's domain. Important economic legislations must be pushed through and efforts made to bring the States to agree on reforms. For example, liberal trade reforms through FDI have limited government interference in various sectors. Doing away with many export/import duties has increased free flow of trade. Jan Dhan-Aadhar-Mobile (JAM) has been introduced to rationalize social sector reforms. Insolvency and Bankruptcy Code, Public Asset Rehabilitation Agency are some legislative reforms to tackle economic challenges. New IPR policy is in line with global standards.

Q14. "Traditional bureaucratic structure and culture have hampered the process of socio-economic development in India."

Ans. The bureaucratic structure is a colonial relic. British laws still prevail. For example, Indian Police Act, 1861 is in operation. Hampering of socio-economic development has taken place, due to following factors:

- Red tapism

  India's rank was 130 out of 189 countries in World Bank's Ease of Doing Business report. Complex laws cause confusion and lead to overall increase costs.
- Centralised decision making

  The delegation of powers to states is important for speedy economic development. Traditionally, because of the colonial influence, governance has been a Delhi-centric one. It is only in recent times that delegation of powers to the states is the focus of governance.
- Political interference

  Traditionally, politicians and bureaucrats consider the public as beneficiaries of their policies and not as equals. The citizens, politicians and bureaucrats have to be seen as equal partners.
- Lack of effective decentralization

  A top heavy bureaucracy has been the bane of Indian polity. It has resulted in delayed decision making and implementation. The need is for effective decentralization through institutions like the Panchayati raj. Also, in this digital age, it is necessary that we use technology to penetrate deep into the rural heartland. Human interference must be reduced to a minimum and the common man must be empowered to take decisions on his own.

Q15. Examine the main provisions of the National Child Policy and throw light on the status of its implementation.

Ans. The National Policy for Children, 2013 aims to protect and encourage the rights of the children to survival, health, nutrition, education, development, protection and participation. It has incorporated major inputs of various organizations regarding the needs of children with disabilities.

The salient features of the children's policy include the following:

- It is the first policy document in India that specifically highlights "disability" as a ground for discrimination that must be countered.
- It focuses on the prevention of disabilities. Since it has been estimated that a large percentage of disabilities in India are preventable, so it is expected that with early interventions, further disabilities could be treated and managed, after which rehabilitation and social support measures need to be provided.
- It highlights the need for schools to be inclusive and for the availability of trained teachers and special educators, appropriate pedagogy and education material, barrier-free access for mobility, functional toilets and co-curricular activities towards the development of a child's fullest potential and autonomy. It specifically states that the views of children with disabilities must be promoted and strengthened.
- India New Born Action Plan, National Deworming Mission and Indradhanush are some notable plans.

  Various initiatives like Right to Education Act, *Pade Bharat, Badhe Bharat* and *Beti Bachao, Beti Padhao* have been started.

As a step in right direction,the Draft National Action Policy for Children, 2016 provides a roadmap for linking objectives and goals.

Q16. "Demographic Dividend in India will remain only theoretical unless our manpower becomes more educated, aware, skilled and creative." What measures have been taken by the government to enhance the capacity of our population to be more productive and employable?

Ans. Demographic dividend means economic growth potential that can result from shift on population age structure mainly when age of working populace is from 15-64 and higher than non-working age group. To reap this demographic dividend, government has taken several steps like:

- National Skill Development Mission aims at a well-trained skilled workforce
- Relaxed education policy means more women can join work force. *Nai Roshni* improves leadership qualities of women.
- Vocational training is provided under *Pradhan Mantri Kaushal Vikas Yojana, Paryatak Mitra* (for tourism), National Policy for Skill Development, Atal Innovation Mission fosters innovation,
- *Deen Dayal Upadhyay Grameen Kaushalya Yojana* is a special placement linked scheme for poor rural youth
- *Hunar Haat* for handicrafts and artisans
- *Stand Up India* is aimed at creating the spirit of entrepreneurship among people

The National Skills Development Corporation (NSDC), which has made significant progress at a pan-India level by promoting, sponsoring and financing skill development programme implementation agencies, and facilitating the creation of nearly 30 industry-led Sector Skills Councils (SSCs) that are laying down sector-specific national occupational standards. The NSDC provides a robust framework for states to take the work forward. Private entities need to be encouraged to take up vocational training and skilling activities. The incentives for such partners have to be carefully structured and should be linked to assessment and employment outcomes with sound monitoring and evaluation mechanisms.]

Q17. "The broader aims and objectives of WTO are to manage and promote international trade in the era of globalization. But the Doha round of negotiations seem doomed due to differences between the developed and the developing countries." Discuss in the Indian perspective.

Ans. The Doha Round of WTO commenced in November 2011. Their aims were to lower trade barriers across the world and facilitate increase in global trade. The main point of contention was that developed countries were ignoring the developmental challenges of the developing and least developing countries.

India's perspective

- Agriculture and subsidy issues

  India felt generous effort is needed for reducing trade distortions in domestic agriculture. Subsidies have to be provided for farmers because of food security, marginal land holdings, and rural distress due to drought
- Patent and Medicine issues

  India argued for balance of interests between pharma companies in developed countries that hold patents and health needs in developing countries. Trade related aspects of

TRIPS were another issue. An agreement was reached allowing member countries to export pharmaceutical products made under compulsory license to least developed and certain other members.

- Traditional knowledge, yoga and digital library are benefits which Indian can derive from WTO talks
- Because of poverty and inequality, Brazil and India should not be treated at par with developed countries

Members agreed that developing and under-developed countries would continue to get favourable treatment, when special and differential treatment were discussed.

Q18. Evaluate the economic and strategic dimensions of India's *Look East Policy* in the context of the post Cold War international scenario.

Ans. India's *Look East Policy* aims at cultivating extensive economic and strategic relations with Southeast Asian countries. The policy was developed in the 1990s after the end of the Cold War. The objective is to carve a legitimate place for India in the larger Asia-Pacific region.

Economic dimensions

Commerce with Southeast Asian countries accounts for 45% of India's trade. With a total population of 1.8 billion and a combined GDP of $3.8 trillion, both form an important economic space in the world. A host of bilateral agreements have been signed with Singapore, South Korea, Thailand, Sri Lanka, Malaysia and Japan. In fact, Japan has also signed a civil nuclear pact. South Korea's huge corporations have made rapid strides in Indian markets. Myanmar, Vietnam and Malaysia can contribute to energy security. Regional Comprehensive Economic Partnership (RCEP) pacts will boost trade and investment in the region.

Strategic Dimensions

As India's trade traverses the Straits of Malacca, the Indian Navy is patrolling the site. India is conducting military and naval exercise with Japan, Malaysia, Thailand and Indonesia. Ties with Japan, Vietnam, Korea and Thailand have been upgraded to 'strategic partnership' status.

Q19. "Increasing cross-border terrorist attacks in India and growing interference in the internal affairs of member-states by Pakistan are not conducive for the future of SAARC (South Asian Association for Regional Cooperation)." Explain with suitable examples.

Ans. India was not willing to attend the 19th SAARC summit along with Bhutan, Afghanistan and Bangladesh, which has brought a question mark on the geopolitical union called SAARC. India was reluctant because of cross border terrorism and interference in member countries affairs by Pakistan. Bhutan was willing to join others on issue of deterioration of regional peace and security dues to terrorism. Bangladesh cited lack of congenial atmosphere in region.

As regards India, the Mumbai attack, Uri encounter and Pathankot assault are examples of Pakistan-sponsored terrorist attack. The reaction by Pakistan, after execution of criminals in Bangladesh, shows interference in another sovereign country's affairs. Afghanistan has been vocal against Pak-sponsored terrorism in its areas.

Pakistan, through China, is also increasing interference in domestic matters of regional nations. Thus, Pakistan is isolated in the region because of its terrorism policies and interference in other countries' affairs.

Q20. What are the aims and objectives of the McBride Commission of the UNESCO? What is India's position on these?

Ans. ***Many Voices One World***, also known as the **MacBride report**, was a 1981 UNESCO publication written by the **International Commission for the Study of Communication Problems**, chaired by Irish Nobel laureate Seán MacBride. Its aim was to analyze communication problems in modern societies, particularly relating to mass media and news, consider the emergence of new technologies, and to suggest a kind of communication order (New World Information and Communication Order) to diminish these problems to further peace and human development.

Among the problems the report identified were concentration of the media, commercialization of the media, and unequal access to information and communication. The commission called for democratization of communication and strengthening of national media to avoid dependence on external sources, among others.

Problems identified in report:

- Concentration of media
- Commercialization of media
- Unequal access to information and communication
- Democratization of communication and strengthening of national media to avoid dependence on external sources was mooted.

India's position on Mac Bride report:

- It is of extreme importance to give weight age to facts and policies
- Social media's binary stand sometimes is of concern.

  Example: Nationalist v Anti-national debate
- There is growing demand to revive AIR, Prasar Bharti etc; so that national media is available f or accessible and transparent communication.

Solved Paper 2017

General Studies

Paper II

There are twenty questions. All Questions are Compulsory.
*Questions **1-10** are 10 marks each and **150 words.***
*Questions **11-20** are 15 marks each and **250 words.***

Q1. "The local self government system in India has not proved to be effective instrument of governance". Critically examine the statement and give your views to improve the situation.

Ans. Though there is Panchayat Raj in over half a million villages and 3 million elected representatives, local self-government has not made a mark. The reasons are:

- State government retains core functions, like water supply, sanitation, roads
- Punjab, Haryana and Rajasthan have abolished local taxes, starving panchayats of funds
- Zero investment in technology

Steps to Improve Panchayats

- Elections should be held every five years
- Timely release of funds is a must
- Local expenditure as percentage of GDP should be increased from 2% to at least 7%, as in Brazil

There has been some success in schemes like MNREGA and women empowerment, which means panchayat raj is not a total failure.

Q2. Critically examine the Supreme Court's judgment on 'National Judicial Appointments Commission Act, 2014' with reference to appointment of judges of higher judiciary in India.

Ans. The National Judicial Appointment Commission (NJAC) was created to select, appoint and transfer judges of high courts and Supreme Court. It consisted of six persons, namely the Chief Justice of India, two other senior judges of Supreme Court, Union Law Minister and two eminent jurists/persons, who would be nominated by a committee consisting CJI, PM and opposition leader.

NJAC was declared unconstitutional by Supreme Court, enunciating that it violates independence of Supreme Court, provided under Article 50 and Article 124 to 128. Also, the balance of power shifts in favour of the executive. Therefore, the, Supreme Court quashed the NJAC.

However, the present collegium system suffers from nepotism, favouritism and corruption. Therefore, Supreme Court should have recommended changes like

1. Removing Law minister
2. Mention qualification of eminent persons
3. Stipulate NJAC composition in Constitution, by amending Art. 125 and not the law itself.

Q3. 'Simultaneous election to the Lok Sabha and the State Assemblies will limit the amount of time and money spent in electioneering but it will reduce the government's accountability to the people' Discuss.

Ans. Post- coalition era since 1977 and especially after 1996, there has been abnormal increase in number of elections due to hung Parliament (Lok Sabha) or Assemblies or mismatch between completion of terms of Lok Sabha or Assemblies. Therefore, there is increasing demand for simultaneous elections.

Advantages

- More stability in governments
- Reduced policy paralysis due to reduction in imposition of Model Code of Conduct .
- Logistically it would be a cost-effective step.
- Helps in taking long term policy decisions7

Disadvantages

- Logistically, it can be a challenge for the Election Commission
- Anti-federal in nature
- Voter may get confused, mixing up regional and local issues with national issues
- Simultaneous electioneering not possible, if a state gets hung assembly or state had to dissolve its assembly in between.

Yet, simultaneous elections can be given a chance. At experimental level, half of the states' elections can be conducted in midterm and another half of the states during Lok Sabha elections.

Q4. How do pressure groups influence Indian political process? Do you agree with this view that informal pressure groups have emerged more powerful than formal pressure groups in recent years?

Ans. When a group of people unite having a common objective to get their demands accepted or implemented by political parties or authorities, pressure groups are formed. They use tactics, mass media campaign, vote bank politics and directly or indirectly political funding too, to influence decision making and policy making.

Informal Pressure Groups

Caste Panchayats, Khap Panchayats, cults etc ; which are not registered under the Society registration Act or a Trust are examples of informal pressure groups.

Formal Pressure groups

These pressure groups are organised and registered under the Societies Registration Act or Trust. Examples: FICCI, ASSOCHAM

Formal Groups have become powerful to get concessions such as tax break , changes in land acquisition act 2013, PPP projects etc; But, vote bank politics has given ample scope for informal pressure groups to put pressure and get concessions.

Therefore, informal pressure groups are stronger and dominant and an informal group can becomes formal in the long run like the Aam Aaadmi Party.

Q5. Discuss the role of Public Accounts Committee in establishing accountability of the government to the people. (150 words)

Ans. Public Accounts Committee (PAC) examines the CAG reports, tables them in Parliament and provides its interpretation in layman's language so that everyone understands the financial conduct of Executive and ensures the financial accountability of the Executive towards Parliament.

A minister cannot be a member of PAC. From 1967, its chairman is conventionally from the Opposition party.

Functions of PAC

1. To examine appropriation accounts and finance accounts of Union Government
2. To scrutinise audit reports of CAG
3. To examine accounts of State corporations, PSUs and audit reports of CAG on PSUs
4. To examine accounts of autonomous and semi-autonomous bodies
5. To examine accounts of stores and stocks

Limitations of PAC

1. Only recommendatory in nature, therefore no legal effectiveness
2. It has power to summon but not of questioning if no answers are received (It was seen in 2G scam case where the Prime Minister refused to answer the questions)
3. Cannot investigate financial reports

Q6. 'To ensure effective implementation of policies addressing water, sanitation and hygiene needs, the identification of beneficiary segments is to be synchronized with the anticipated outcomes' Examine the statement in the context of the WASH scheme.

Ans. WASH is UNICEF's scheme, which is spelt out as 'water sanitation and hygiene'. According to UNICEF, there are 2.4 million people without access to sanitation and 663 million people without improved water sources. India too suffers from the lack of adequate water, sanitation and hygiene facilities for its urban and rural population.

India has launched *Swachh Bharat Abhiyan* and WASH at different geographical and social levels. For example, WASH has been started, as under:

1. Plain vs hilly areas
2. Urban vs rural area
3. Slum versus organised settlement
4. Individual and community resources

Significant success (open defecation reduced by 30% in rural areas and 45% in urban areas) has been achieved.. But, targeting of beneficiaries and their segmentation is missing. The one-size-fits-all approach is not working.

The human life-cycle approach can be adopted, for WASH, under which, segments like below can be selected:

School going (Young children and Adolescent)

Adults (male and female)

Old age

Q7. Does the Rights of Persons with Disabilities Act, 2016 ensure effective mechanism for empowerment and inclusion of the intended beneficiaries in the society? Discuss

Ans. According to 2011 Census around 2.2% of the population are disabled in India, including blind people. The new act, Rights of Persons with Disabilities Act, 2016 replaces the 1995 act and confers more rights. It has expanded the list of disabilities from 7 to 21 (including mental health, sickle cell disease and anaemia etc) . It outlines that transport, and information and communication should be 50% disabled- friendly by 2022.

Improvements

It confers 4% reservation in education and employment (in public sector) and preference in government schemes.

Two types of Guardianship provided by the District Court for mentally ill persons.

National and state Commission would identify laws, policies inconsistent with act and enquire into safeguards. Central and state advisory board would undertake periodic review and make policies.

Limitations

No clear cut sustainable financial mechanism

Policy mainly caters to urban areas in transport, public bodies and education.

40% cut off in declaring disabled is high and open to subjectivity.

Q8. Hunger and Poverty are the biggest challenges for good governance in India still today. Evaluate how far successive governments have progressed in dealing with these humongous problems. Suggest measures for improvement.

Ans. Hunger and poverty are interlinked and create a vicious cycle of burden.

Strategies by successive governments

Five Year Plans, Nationalisation of banks, 20- point programme, MGNREGA, Atal Pension Yojana, Rashtriya Swasthya Bima Yojana, Pradhan Mantri Fasal Bima Yojana etc;

The previous decades, steps and impact

Years: 60s - 70s

Steps: Trickle-down approach, food for work, Jawahwar Rojgar Yojana

Impact – Poverty remained, 45% of population below BPL level

Years: 80s -90s

Steps: Welfare scheme

Impact: Poverty reduced to 35-40% of population under BPL.

Years: Late 90s and till mid-2000s

Steps: PM Gram Sadak Yojana, Infrastructure, LPG reforms

Impact: Hunger remained, Relative Poverty decreased to 30% (approx.) of population,

Years: Post 2005-2013

Steps: MGNREGA, RTE, Food Security Act, NRLM, NRUM,

Impact: Strategy for food

Years: Post 2013

Steps: Address hidden hunger and malnourishment

Impact: Poverty reduced to 22-23% of population,

Measures for Improvement:

i. Food fortification and bio-fortification to attack hidden hunger.
ii. WASH (Water, Samitation and Hygiene) scheme
iii. Reforming PDS [Direct Benefit Transfer (DBT) and biometrically authenticated physical uptake (BAPU) to be adopted]

Q9. 'China is using its economic relations and positive trade surplus as tools to develop potential military power status in Asia', In the light of this statement, discuss its impact on India as her neighbour.

Ans. China is using its trade surplus to reinvest along all the South Asian neighbours of India.

China's moves

- String of pearls: Ports in Myanmar, Hambantota (Sri Lanka,) Gwadar, Maldives etc to encircle India .
- Land based blocking or five fingers (Ladakh, Nepal, Bhutan, Sikkim, and Arunachal Pradesh) and Palm (Tibet) theory of Mao
- Nepal's strategic location is being used to make inroads into Indian border.
- Nuclear powered submarine docked at Colombo
- Oil and gas pipeline via Yemen to Bay of Bengal through Myanmar.

Thus, the pattern of encirclement of India is such that all neighbours facing huge trade deficit would allocate strategic and commercial ports and infrastructure projects to China, which can be used to check India on land via sea.

In spite of huge trade between Britain and Germany, World War II broke out. So, China's trade moves with India's neighbours has strategic and security implications for India. Conversely, a strategic open alliance of like-minded nations can check a belligerent China such as India-USA-Japan or India-USA-Japan-Australia.

Q10. What are the main functions of the United Nations Economic and Social Council (ECOSOC)? Explain different functional commissions attached to it.

Ans. ECOSOC is one of the six principal organs of the UN responsible for economic, social and related work of 15 UN specialised agencies, their functional commissions and five regional commissions

It serves as the international forum for discussing the main socio-economic issues and comes up with policy recommendations to states and UN. To boost quality of decision and making it more inclusive, NGOs are also given observer status.

Its functional commissions

1. Commission for social development Matter related with poverty, education, employment, inequality.
2. Commission on human rights Matter related with human rights and coordinating the activity country wise. (Recently involved- Rohingya crisis).
3. Commission on narcotic drugs Mainly focus on drug trafficking and watchdog over Golden Triangle to Golden Crescent.
5. Commission on science and tech Exploring, promoting innovations and research in S&T for socio-economic development.
6. Commission on sustainable development Stick to Sustainable Development Goals SDG (2030 Agenda) and coordinate accordingly.
7. Commission on women development Recently incorporated, to focus on half of population of world.
8. Commission on crime prevention and criminal justice Human trafficking, trade malpractices, terrorism.

In 2015, UN-ECOSOC was mandated to review the (Intended Nationally Determined Contribution) INDC targets to be fulfilled by various countries by 2020 and create a report. This Foundation has been added to fulfill some Sustainable Development Goals targets.

Q11. Explain the salient features of the Constitution (One Hundred and First Amendment) Act, 2016. Do you think it is efficacious enough 'to remove cascading effect of taxes and provide for common national market for goods and services'?

Ans. GST, the mother of all tax reforms was introduced by the Constitution's 101st Amendment Act. It inserts article 246 A to subsume all indirect taxes levied by Centre (excise, service tax, central sales tax, additional custom duty etc.) and States (entertainment tax, VAT, entry tax).

The salient features of GST are

1. GST Council will consist of Union finance minister (chairman), Union Minister of state revenue/finance, member- minister in charge (Finance) of each state. Quorum is 50% and decision is by 75% weighted votes. Central government has one third vote, therefore, effectively having veto power.
2. States will be compensated for 5 years in case of any loss.
3. Centre has already devolved 42% of tax collected to the states.

How GST creates common market

GST has led to "one nation, one tax" situation. As there is one tax, there is one market too, from manufacturer to consumer. It removes all barriers of States' borders. By doing away with myriad taxes imposed by various states, it leads to a unified market. It promotes free flow of goods in every part of the country, envisaging a common market. GST removes economic distortions. It promotes exports across the country.

How GST removes cascading tax effect

GST avoids "tax upon tax "situation. Previously, a consumer used to be taxed at various points. He even suffered double taxation. But GST has removed the cascading effect of taxes, by bringing one tax (although there are various slabs now). The input tax credit system makes doubly sure that a person is not harassed by tax after tax.

Q12. Examine the scope of Fundamental Rights in the light of the latest judgement of the Supreme Court on Right to Privacy.

Ans. "Human beings deserves privacy space for so-called "self-regarding actions"- John Stuart Mill

Right to privacy has been declared as part of Article 21 and 19 of the Constitution by 9-0 bench of Supreme Court. Justice Chandrachud gave its definition as

- Spatial control: private space and bodily integrity.
- Decisional autonomy: protects the intimate personal choices.
- Informational privacy: control over personal information.

Therefore, right to privacy will enable a person to control what information about him/her should be known to others.

Effect of judgement on fundamental rights

- It will expand the ambit of Article 21 under which innate dignity, autonomy of man, and choices will also come. Hence a woman can terminate pregnancy without losing privacy or getting permission.
- It will expand and also put reasonable restrictions under Article 19. Corporate houses will have right to privacy over their data, content but can't violate the right to privacy of individuals. Therefore data theft, collection, sale or use of private data, e-commerce will be hit.
- Under Article 19, freedom to choose profession (butchering of bovine etc or selling of alcohol) or freedom to choose any food (consuming beef) will have constitutional protection
- Data protection (Aadhaar issue):

New man is techno- social, for which right to privacy is required.

What you earn, sell or where you live and privacy of choice should not suffer erosion due to Aadhaar Data Collection. Data (biometrics) collection in the name of welfare should protect private data.

Q13. The Indian Constitution has provisions for holding joint session of the two houses of the Parliament. Enumerate the occasions when this would normally happen and also the occasions when it cannot, with reasons thereof.

Ans. The joint session of Parliament's two houses can take place, under some circumstances, under the constitution:

Joint session (Article 108)

i. Ordinary bills

ii. Finance bills involving imposition, abolition, alteration, regulation of tax, license

iii. Finance bills which have been introduced only with prior consent of President

When joint session of both cannot take place:

i. Money bill

ii. Constitutional Amendment Bill

Reasons why joint session should not happen in the above cases

i. Money bill

- House of People (Lok Sabha) should have control over the purse and no other house.
- There are the bills which are introduced only in Lok Sabha and the Upper House can only suggest amendments but cannot vote on grants. Therefore, joint sitting doesn't make sense for money bills.
- As per Article 110, Money bill deals with expenditure incurred from the Consolidated Fund of India that is money of tax payer of India and the Lok Sabha alone represents the people of India, not the Rajya Sabha.

ii. Constitutional amendment

- Due to the gravity of the matter and constitutional principle of parliamentary democracy, joint sitting for constitutional amendment is not allowed.
- Constitution require equal importance of Union and States while amending the constitution. The lower house with its majority will overshadow the upper house in the case of joint amendment session.
- Numerical majority cannot decide constitutional amendments
- Bill will pass through ordinary majority, not special majority, which is absolutely essential for such grave matters.
- Elaborate discussion is not going to happen in joint session. For constitutional amendment, detailed analytical discussions are a must.

Q14. To enhance the quality of democracy in India the Election Commission of India has proposed electoral reforms in 2016. What are the suggested reforms and how far are they significant to make democracy successful?

Ans. The Election Commission of India (ECI) has proposed the following reforms to enhance quality of democracy:

i. Systemic and legal reforms.

a. Making a Model Code of Conduct part of Representation of Peoples Act, 1951.(RPA).

b. Curb paid news

c. Lifetime ban on convicts from election.

d. Power to deregister a party

f. To make all following offences cognizable such as:

- Undue influence and bribery
- Publishing false statement

g. Inclusion of caste and religious appeal to voters as a corrupt practice.

ii. Procedural changes

a. Introduction of VVPAT (Voter Verifiable Paper Audit Trail).

b. Compulsory voting

c. Right to reject (on experimental level) and right to recall (on experimental level)

d. Changing 'first past the post' system based on deliberation via Parliament.

iii. Financial changes

a. The expenditure of ECI needs to be charged on the consolidated fund of India

b. Curb black money in election and anonymous funding.

c. Reducing cash donation to political parties.

d. Introduction of State funding (partial) and electoral bonds.

e. Compulsory maintenance of accounts by political parties.

iv. Other reforms demanded by ECI

a. A ban on exit polls and opinion polls totally.

b. Ban on Government sponsored ads before election.

e. Form 26 should be amended to include a column for declaring sources of income

According to the Association for Democratic Reforms (ADR), 35% of our MPs and MLAs have criminal background or are facing convictions in various courts. In order to remove role of money and muscle power, and make the election process transparent, these reforms are very useful.

Q15. Is the National Commission for Women able to strategize and tackle the problems that women face at both public and private spheres? Give reasons in support of your answer.

Ans. The National Commission of Women reviews constitutional and legal safeguards, recommends remedial legislative measures apart from facilitating grievance redressal and giving advice to the government on all policy matters affecting women.

We can categorise two places, home and away and can list the issues involved in each.

i. Domestic violence (private)

Issues involved.

a. Non legislation of marital rape.

b. Multiple personal laws.

c. Patriarchal families.

ii. Violence outside home (public)

Issues involved.

a. Patriarchal society, state and institutions

b. Less number of women in the State, Police and administration.

c. Ineffective gender budgeting.

d. Sexual harassment at workplace

e. Only 53% of companies have set up ICC (internal complaint committee)

Other problems faced by NCW.

a. It's powers are limited. It does not have investigation powers and is only a recommendatory body.

b. Only has power to recommend compensation which Centre or State have to pay and NCW is effective in ensuring compliance on such cases.

c. Appointment of members and Chairperson lack transparency and affected by nepotism and favouritism.

d. Dilution of Section 498 of IPC and making it gender neutral goes against the theory of women as a weaker section.

e. State police agencies treat their orders as a burden.

f. NCW affected by political pressure, as in case of Mangalore pub attack controversy in 2009.

Following steps should be taken to empower NCW :

a. Make it constitutional body and empower it on the lines of NHRC.

b. Giving suo-moto powers of investigation.

c. Providing adequate and autonomous funding

Q16. 'The emergence of Self Help Groups(SHGs) in contemporary times points to the slow but steady withdrawal of the state from developmental activities'. Examine the role of the SHGs in developmental activities and the measures taken by the Government of India to promote the SHGs.

Ans. SHGs are informal and formal grouping of 10 to 20 people (generally women), who build an activity cluster based on resources and occupational skills and availability of market.

Role of SHGs

a. They help in financial inclusion.

b. Generate social capital.

c. Help in capability enhancement

d. Improvement in gender relations.

e. Help in Poverty alleviation.

f. Provide community platform to the vulnerable.

Post LPG reforms and the rolling back of the State, SHGs are becoming drivers of development based on bottom-up approach.

There are 7.4 million SHGs and 6.2 of them are exclusively by women. The total participation in these SHGs exceeds 97 million.

SHGs Problems

SHGs are not able to scale up and are restricted to rural or semi urban areas. There is the problem of adequate and timely credit. The poorest are still left out.

Government measures to promote SHGs

a. MUDRA (Micro Units Development and Refinance Agency) scheme to refinance micro lending. The corpus of the scheme currently stands at 36000 crores.

b. Funding by NABARD to provide 100% refinance to the banks, lending to SHGs.
c. Priority sector lending by banks and especially for micro finance institutions (MFI) linked bank institutions
d. Finance to new banks, especially small finance banks
e. Integrating NRLM with SHGs and MFI credit linked subsidy schemes.
f. Startup India – Standup India to support SHGs.

For women, there are special schemes:

- Sewa Shakti Kendra
- Swayamsiddha Scheme
- Swawalamban Scheme

SHG is a holistic microenterprise, covering all aspects of self-employment. Successful uses of the SHGs can be seen in projects like Lijjat Papad, SEWA (Self Employed Women's Association) etc

Q17. 'Poverty Alleviation Programmes in India remain mere show pieces until and unless they are backed by political will'. Discuss with reference to the performance of the major poverty alleviation programmes in India.

Ans. *The major government measures for poverty alleviation, over the years can be sketched as under:*

1. Five year plans, land reforms, Green Revolution and Operation Flood.

Political will: Strong from 1950 till 1980.

Performance: Partial success, it brought down poverty from 65% inR1950 to 35% in 1980.

2. Twenty point programme

Political will: Strong initially, due to emergency, but later fizzled out. Funds crunch made it a burden by late 1980s.

Performance: Inefficient, i.e. more spending and little result.

3. Comprehensive plan of latter 1980s, embracing education, health and technology.

Political will: Strong initially during Rajiv Gandhi era but due to growing Balance of Payment (BoP) crisis lost steam.

Performance: Partial success. Real increase in wages was low.

3. LPG (Liberalisation, Privatisation and Globalisation) reforms

Political will: Strong

Performance: Government boost to income and demand in market economy but reduced welfare programs and social protection.

Infrastructure Projects: *Pradhan Mantri Gram Sadak Yojana*, Bharat Nirman etc.

Political will: Moderately strong

Performance: inequality reduced.

6. MGNREGA (Mahatma Gandhi National Rural Employment Guarantee Act)

Political will: Strong

Performance: Economy and rural income improved which reduced poverty by 10%.

6. Food Security Act, 2013.

Political will: Initially strong but by 2016, more focus of government on reducing subsidies.

Performance: Foodgrain production already a success but hidden hunger (micronutrient shortage) remains.

Therefore, none of the policies such as Land Reforms, Green Revolution, LPG reforms, MGNREGA etc would have been possible without a strong political resolve. Without strong political will, poverty alleviation can remain only a dream, on a piece of paper.

Q18. Initially the Civil Services in India were designed to achieve the goals of neutrality and effectiveness, which seems to be lacking in the present context. Do you agree with the view that drastic reforms are required in the Civil Services. Comment

Ans. The Indian Civil Services is based on the principle of Weberian (Max Weber) Bureaucracy, where neutrality and effectiveness should be prime characteristics.

But due to archaic IPC and CRPC and status-quo orientation, red-tapism has crept in. The concept of 'Committed Bureaucracy' has done harm. Continuous political interference in postings, transfers has made civil servants subservient to the whims and fancies of political masters. Motivation to take decisions and work pro-actively is missing.

Reforms needed:

1. Neutrality

a. A Civil Services Board needed for transfer and postings of higher officers based on merit

b. A Service Selection Board essential for promotion and grievance redressal

c. Early implementation of *TSR Subramanian Vs Union of India* judgement and *Prakash Singh Vs Union of India case* guidelines of Supreme Court in order to protect civil services neutrality.

2. Effectiveness

a. Civil Services Exam should be more holistic to test candidate's merit and aptitude

b. New training (value based, ethics, conduct)

3. Reforms during service

a. Mid-term career review.

b. Amending article 310 and 311, which provide protection to civil servants would increase performance

c. Lateral entry to the civil services for ensuring quality

d. Mid-term career training.

4. Exit Reforms

a. Protection of honest officers after retirement by amending section 13 (1)(a) of prevention of corruption act, POCA.

5. **Other Reforms**

a. Collusion and bribery should be made offence under POCA

b. Tenure assurance for officials, above the rank of joint secretary, for minimum 2 years.

c. Section 7 of POCA must be amended to break nexus of politician- bureaucracy- businessman.

d. Article 309 should shield civil servants against arbitrariness

Therefore, civil services reforms are the need of day but they should not be drastic. They should be incremental.

Q19. The question of India's energy security constitutes the most important part of India's economic progress. Analyse India's energy policy cooperation with West Asian countries. (250 words)

Ans. India imports 80% of its oil (70% from West Asia) and 60% of gas. This shows our dependence on West Asia for our energy security. *India's energy policy cooperation is as under:*

1. UAE

- Comprehensive Strategic Partnership with UAE to develop and provide oil for India's strategic reserves at Mangalore and two other locations. It will help India set up 36.87 billion barrels of crude oil in underground storage.
- UAE will channelise its strategic and sovereign wealth fund for energy (oil and gas) exploration in India, investing in renewable energy

2. Iran

- India will source Iranian oil after embargo has been lifted, thereby diversifying need and imports.

3. Saudi Arabia.

- India imports large chunk of oil from Saudi Arabia and India is pushing for lower rates after Russia's Essar deal.

4. Qatar and Bahrain.

- India aims for gas based economy, therefore, it is concentrating on deal with Qatar to provide for LNG under long- term contracts and terminals and an under-sea pipeline.

5. Iraq.

- India bought oil fields during Saddam era, from which it wants to produce oil

6. Oman.

- India signed long- term oil purchasing contracts and is considering 1,100 km long underwater natural gas pipeline from Oman, called South Asian Gas Enterprise, SAGE, an alternative to IPI (Iran-Pakistan-India) pipeline.

India is shifting its energy needs to renewables and is focusing on developing infrastructure for electric mobility and vehicles and aims to produce 35% of its energy from renewable energy by 2030. Thus, our present relations are crucial in transitioning our economy from fossil fuels to clean energy.

Q20. Indian Diaspora has an important role to play in South-East Asian countries' economy and society. Appraise the role of Indian Diaspora in South- East Asia in this context.

Ans. The Indian diaspora in Southeast Asia has been present since ancient times, with migrants contributing to literature, religion, philosophy, art and architecture of the region. Examples are Angkor Vat and other Hindu temples in Cambodia, Indonesia, Java and Bali, Thailand and Myanmar.

A lot of emigration took place during the colonial period. Punjabis from Gujranwala migrated to Thailand. The *baniyas* of UP, *marwaris* from Rajputana, *chettiyars* from Madras, Gujaratis and Maharashtrians migrated to South East Asia, who later became middle class and upper class elites.

The Indian National Army (INA) in Malaysia got support from Indian Independence League, which was supported by Indian diaspora in the South East Asia.

In post-independence period, foreign trade saw 20-fold increase. Tourism witnessed 10-fold increase since 1950; cultural exchanges-in shape of *Aashiyaan-India* took place. Professional exchanges were seen especially in Singapore.

All the above successes have been due to collaborated efforts of the diaspora and the Indian government, which have also led to:

i. Grant of dual citizenship in India.

ii. Voting rights in India.

iii. Introduction of direct Air India flights.

iv. Free trade and collaboration in the field of science and technology.

v. Increased tourism, trade, connectivity (Trilateral Highway).

vi. Increased people to people ties.

The diaspora is into politics and administration of their respective nations. India should leverage this to complete its 'Look and Act East policy'.

Solved Paper 2018
General Studies
Paper II

There are twenty questions. All Questions are Compulsory.

*Questions **1-10** are 10 marks each and **150 words.***

*Questions **11-20** are 15 marks each and **250 words.***

Q1. In the light of recent controversy regarding the use of Electronic Voting Machines (EVM), what are the challenges before the Election Commission of India to ensure the trustworthiness of elections in India? (150 words)

Ans. Electronic Voting Machines (EVMs) ensure speed and ease in conducting elections. However, in the light of certain controversies regarding EVMs, the Election Commission has a task cut out, i.e to bring back confidence in the EVMs. The challenges are many: some owing to perception, some due to technological glitches, and others owing to the need to involve all stakeholders.

As for perception, the Commission has to bring in more transparency and openness, by ample demonstration, before political parties. As for integrity of the technology and process, paper trail (VVPAT) is a way forward, but there are financial and practical constraints. As far as stakeholders are concerned, the Commission may organize demonstration before representatives of political parties and use such machines only. It can also actually carry out live sample voting before the actual voting. In short, the Commission should see the whole issue objectively and analytically. Years back, there was afurore about 'vanishing ink,' but the Election Commission handled the issue with care, concern and caution.

Q2. Whether National Commission for Scheduled Castes (NCSC) can enforce the implementation of constitutional reservation for the Scheduled Castes in the religious minority institutions? Examine.

Ans. The provisions of constitution under Article 15(5) are pointed, specific and relevant. This section was inserted by the 93rd Amendment, 2008.

'Nothing in this article or in sub-clause (g) of clause (1) of Article 19 shall prevent the state from making any special provisions, by law, for the advancement of any socially and educationally backward classes of citizens or for the scheduled castes or the scheduled tribes in so far as special provisions relate to their admission to educational institutions include private educational institutions , whether aided by the state, other than the minority educational institutions referred to in clause (1) of Article 30.'

Article 30 provides for 'Right of minorities to establish and administer educational institutions' and this is a fundamental right.

Scheduled Castes are part of Hindu religion and therefore, cannot have a right to reservation in religious minority institutions. The controversy emanated from Aligarh Muslim University, whose 'minority status' is itself sub-judice in the Supreme Court.

Q3. Under what circumstances can the Financial Emergency be proclaimed by the President of India? What consequences follow when such a declaration remains in force?

Ans. A financial emergency is declared under Article 360, if the President is satisfied that a situation has arisen whereby the financial stability or the creditworthiness of India or of any part of the territory thereof isthreatened.

Effects of Financial Emergency

The executive authority of the Union extends to the giving of directions to any State to observe such canons of financial propriety as may be specified, and to the giving of such other directions as the President may deem necessary and adequate for the purpose.

Directions given by or powers assumed by Union or President are as follows:

- Reduction of salaries and allowances of all or any class of persons serving in connection with the affairs of a State is allowed.
- All Money Bills or other Bills to which the provisions of article 207 apply are to be reserved for the consideration of President after being passed by State Legislature.
- Salaries and allowances of Judges of Supreme Court and High Courts can be reduced.

Q4. Why do you think the committees are considered to be useful for parliamentary work? Discuss, in this context, the role of the Estimates Committee.

Ans. Committees are an integral and inevitable part of parliamentary democracy.

In parliamentary work, committees are governed by conventions and precedents, both of which lay foundation for smooth functioning. As committees have a fair and adequate representation of all parties, they effectively become mini parliaments. Committees also provide ample space and opportunity for give and take, as also dissent. At times, committees act as 'safety valves' to absorb shocks emanating from contentious issues.

Estimates committee comprising of elected members on the principle of proportional representation through single transferable vote exclusively from Lok Sabha is an important committee. It does not have any ministers and is headed by representative of ruling party, nominated by Speaker.

The committee scrutinizes the estimates and as both ruling and opposition parties are there, the survey is intense and serious. It functions round the year. As its members are all elected, it represents the people.

Q5. "The Comptroller and Auditor General (CAG) has a very vital role to play." Explain how this is reflected in the method and terms of his appointment as well as the range of powers he can exercise.

Ans. The Comptroller and Auditor General (CAG), is a constitutional entity under Article 148 and is appointed by the President of India by warrant under his hand and seal. The CAG makes and subscribes an oath of affirmation, before appointment. Like a judge of the Supreme Court, the CAG can be removed only by the President.

Terms of appointment incorporate adequate safeguards. Salary of CAG is charged to the Consolidated Fund of India. His salary is decided only by the Parliament of India [Article 148(3)]. .

The CAG's powers (Article 149) state that he performs such duties and exercises such powers in relation to accounts of Union and States, and of any other authority or body as may be prescribed by or under any law made by Parliament.

The CAG submits an annual report to President who causes it to be laid before each House of Parliament. Similarly, report to Governor is sent, regarding states. The CAG, thus, is independent and acts as a watchdog over the entire accounts of the Union and States.

Q6. "Policy contradictions among various competing sectors and stakeholders have resulted in inadequate 'protection and prevention of degradation to environment." Comment with relevant illustrations.

Ans. Resources are scarce, demands on them are aplenty. There is always a crisis with conflicting demands and competing desires.

Industrial sector is in conflict with agriculture, while agriculture is in conflict with forestry and there is a conflict between forestry and environment and so on. It is, to an extent, inevitable but not irreversible.

The obvious way forward is integrated mechanism for decision making where all concerns and considerations are given due evaluation. Cabinet committee on clearance of projects is one such example. The mandatory Environmental Impact Asssessment (EIA) frames guidelines for evaluation of projects is another example.

The Sardar Sarovar dam on the Narmada is a case in point of conflict between development and environment, where ultimately Supreme Court had to step in. Conflict in demand over land for agriculture and industry in West Bengal is another example. Environmental damage due to mining for meeting demands of industry in Goa is one more example.

Q7. Appropriate local community level healthcare intervention is a prerequisite to achieve 'Health for All' in India. Explain.

Ans. China stunned the world with its 'barefoot doctor' scheme which entailed that trained people would attend people in rural areas. In India, the emphasis is on 'health for all' with a different approach but covering traditional and modern systems.

The government, from the Ninth Plan onwards, has been seriously expanding infrastructural facilities, particularly in the remote areas. Given the feel and faith in alternate therapies like ayurveda, homoeopathy, naturopathy etc, the Department of Ayush has been created to advance these systems, with encouraging results.

A new National Health Policy has been has been unfolded in 2017, with focus on inclusiveness and upgradation of features and facilities, particularly child and maternal care. Rural Health Mission, being well organized has a good launch pad.

To ensure treatment for poor and place affordability, the Ayushman Bharat scheme, with a noble objective seeks to cover treatment upto Rs 5 lac through medicare in this year's budget. A very imaginative and bold step, this will make 'Health for All' a reality.

Q8. E-governance is not only about utilization of the power of new technology, but also much about critical importance of the 'use value' of information. Explain.

Ans. E-governance is all about feasibility and utility. In feasibility, E-governance brings to fore the power of technology to access information in an open, transparent and speedy manner. In utility, E-governance accords the possibility of using it to focus on utility through 'use value.'

E-governance makes it feasible to access a whole range of data but it is the 'use value' that matters. Organizations collect lot of data, but in the end hardly find 'use value' for the same. Some keep reviewing their data but never reach a point where they can find 'use value.' Often static information is not very relevant. Yet organisations keep insisting in reviewing static information. This defeats the purpose of E-governance.

Much also depends on how designing is done for collection of data. In the ultimate analysis, it is how the data is used or interpreted or analysed that matters. 'Use value,' when given attention, breaks barrier between user and recipient.

Q9. "India's relations with Israel have, of late, acquired a depth and diversity, which cannot be rolled back." Discuss.

Ans. Israel is India's leading trade partner, though actual trading started in 2002. With Jordan and Egypt extending recognition and friendship to Israel, India, no longer anticipating adverse reaction from the Arab world, began to cautiously develop trade relations.

Israel is now a leading supplier of military hardware to India, alongside helping in indigenous production. The mobility and fire power of Israel is India's need.

India can offer help in information technology and bio-technology. India is seeking Israel's assistance in development of horticulture and desalination of sea water. With a vast coastline and chronic shortage of potable water, India is looking towards Israel.

A glitch is that India has not shown much interest in 'Free Trade Agreement,' owing to reservations from domestic industry. Israel is under pressure from US not to sell some items of military hardware like missiles (stinger missiles).

The trade between India and Israel has, however, entered a stage from where it can only move 'North.'

Q10. A number of outside powers have entrenched themselves in Central Asia, which is a zone of interest to India. Discuss the implications, in this context, of India's joining the Ashgabat Agreement, 2018.

Ans. With the collapse of the erstwhile Soviet Union and emergence of the independent Central Asian Republics, it was to be expected that these would be open to influence and interference. Russia may wield influence, given past association. Iran wants to connect as these republics have sizeable Shia Muslims. Meanwhile, China is extending its footprints all over Asia. Pakistan feels it can also have a share of the influence, because of its strategic location.

It's all happening because these republics are rich in natural gas and endowed with minerals. These countries are also strategically located between Asia and Europe which is another factor for its growing influence and relevance. India, with centuries of ties with the republics feels there's potential for trade, ties and travel. However there are two critical factors that may limit India's efforts.

(a) Remoteness and terrain

(b) India would need the support of Iran and Afghanistan to reach out to these countries. In this context, the Chabahar port in Iran has paramount importance.

In the light of the above factors, the Ashgabat treaty (2018) on 'International transport and trade,' linking Oman, Iran, Turkmenistan, Uzbekistan, Afghanistan and Kazakhstan is highly important to India for reaching out to these republics. India has therefore has a lot at stake in the success of this treaty.

Q11. Whether the Supreme Court Judgement (July 2018) can settle the political tussle between the Lt. Governor and elected government of Delhi? Examine.

Ans. The Supreme Court of India in its judgement of July 2018, took a balanced view of the ongoing tussle between the Lieutenant Governor and the elected government of Delhi by declaring that the Lt. Governor ought to respect the will of the elected government. Most certainly, the role of Governor is pivotal and he must honour constitutional niceties. Even so, the outstanding issues plentiful as they are, do not get resolved by this.

Both the Lt. Governor and elected government of Delhi have constitutional status and footing; the former has some defined subjects, wherein the elected government has no role. Similarly, the latter has assigned subjects where it has responsibility but needs approval of Lt. Governor. It is here that Supreme Court has shown ire that Lt. Governor must respect the constitutional authority and validity of the decisions of the elected government of Delhi.

Notwithstanding the ruling by the apex court, there are many issues remaining, which have the potential to sour matters. The constitution has special provisions for Delhi under Article 239AA and the elected government must conform and confine itself to these articles. But, the elected government is, forever, looking at powers, functions and responsibilities of full-fledged states and is seeking parity. It is wistfully looking at subjects that are in the domain of Lt. Governor, who would have no interference in that.

The role of central government is vital in this matter and it needs to balance caution and optimism so that both Lt. Governor and elected government of Delhi operate within the limits of constitutional space with mutual understanding and respect.

Q.12. How far do you agree with the view that tribunals curtail the jurisdiction of ordinary courts? In view of the above, discuss the constitutional validity and competency of the tribunals in India.

Ans. Ordinary courts in the country are overburdened with litigation and even higher courts are saddled with cases dating back to years. Tribunals have been created to handle cases which have substantive administrative and judicial (legal) content. These cases need a certain level of experience and expertise in handling which ordinary courts may not have. Even so, under the existing set-up, the litigants always have the right to appeal in high courts and ultimately the Supreme Court. Should they feel aggrieved with denial of justice; citizens can always approach courts of law in case of infringement of fundamental rights. Tribunals do not curtail the jurisdiction of ordinary courts; rather they complement it.

Tribunals are of two types, the Administrative Tribunal and the Departmental. They have quasi-judicial functions. To this extent they are bound to follow the law of the land; based on principles of natural justice and as guaranteed by the Constitution. Assistance of legal aides can also be taken in these tribunals. Further, the chairman of the Administrative Tribunal is always handpicked from the judiciary with sufficient seniority and exposure.

Creation of tribunals is provided under Article 323-A for Administrative Tribunals and Article 323-B for Departmental Tribunals. This gives validity and sanctity.

Regarding competence, there is some room for concern. Cases are finding their way into High Courts and Supreme Court. Reasons are many, but not all can be traced back to lack of competence. Litigants too seem to clutch at the last straw; it's their legal right or even a fundamental right.

Q13. India and USA are two large democracies. Examine the basic tenets on which the two political systems are based.

Ans. India and the USA are both thriving and pulsating democracies. Their functioning is based on some basic tenets and principles which ensure freedom and equality. Both countries have 'liberty' at the very root in their constitutions. A necessary concomitant of liberty is 'freedom' which both countries value high; with USA placing in its preamble and India in its fundamental rights.

Both India and USA recognize that for democracy to thrive, a spirit of cooperation and respect is a must. This is found in their constitutions, both of which are federal in nature. Both have states that are federated and have reasonable degree of freedom within the framework of the constitution. The essence of democracy is rooted in the tenets of 'power and accountability' or 'authority and responsibility'. Both India and USA have ensured this by having systems that are vested with powers yet accountable. In case of India, it's Parliament and in case of USA it's Senate and House of Representatives. People's mandate is at the heart of system in both the countries.

India and USA have recognized the importance of tenets of justice and created independent mechanisms of judiciary. In India, there is Supreme Court, while in the USA it is the US Supreme Court. It must be said that America's Supreme Court is more powerful and pervasive.

Equality is another important right, which both countries have recognized with India placing it in Fundamental Rights making it justifiable and justiciable and USA in its very preamble. 'All men are created equal.'

In short, 'liberty, equality and fraternity' are the very foundation of the constitutions of both India and the USA.

Q.14. How is the Finance Commission of India constituted? What do you know about the terms of reference of the recently constituted Finance Commission? Discuss.

Ans. The Finance Commission is constituted under Article 280 by the order of President of India. It is appointed once every five years, with a chairman and four members, all appointed by the President.

At present, the 15th Finance Commission headed by Shri N K Singh has terms of reference as follows:

(a) Review the current status of finance, deficit, debt levels, cash balances, fiscal discipline efforts of Union and States

(b) Recommend fiscal consolidation roadmap for sound financial management

(c) Take into account the responsibility of central government and state governments to adhere to appropriate levels in general and consolidated debt and deficit levels

(d) Foster higher inclusive growth guided by principles of equity, efficiency and transparency

(e) Examine whether revenue deficit grants be provided at all

(f) Review present arrangements on financing disaster managementinitiatives

Other key issues for consideration are:

1. Impact on union government's fiscal situation following substantial tax devolution to states following 14th Finance Commission recommendations. Also the impact of various national development programmes including New India 2022.
2. GST impact and efforts made by states in expanding and deepening GST tax net and progress in moving towards replacement rate of population growth.

Criticism of 15th Finance Commission:

1. Terms of reference have gone beyond those outlined under Article 280
2. It uses data of 2011 census while 14th Finance Commission used 1971 census. This will hurt southern states which have shown good progress in control of growth of population.

Q15. Assess the importance of the Panchayat system in India as a part of local government. Apart from government grants, what sources the Panchayats can look out for financing developmental projects?

Ans. Panchayats are at the grassroots of our democracy and their optimal functioning is of essence to the success of our democratic system of participatory and inclusive arrangement. With the 73rd amendment (1992) to the constitution, 'Panchayat Raj' was heralded in the country. The administrative set up being in place, the need was to evolve a financial system of sustenance and self-sufficiency. However, the devolution envisaged did not go very much in the manner desired. Panchayats are the first visible face of governance to the citizens and their progress is vital to the democratic functioning in the country. Local government is by far the best face of any governance, especially if it built on participatory and inclusive model.

As for finances, the constitution under Article 280 (3)(ba) of the same has tasked the State Finance Commissions to augment the resources of the panchayats (through 73rd amendment).

The way forward to supplement income by Panchayats is through organisation of cooperatives, use of NGOs, opening of health centres, engagement of women in small scale industries, opening of cooperative banks, innovative use of garbage in generation of energy, entertainment shows etc;

The 14th Finance Commission increased the states' share from 32 percent to 42 per cent of central collection proceeds. There was a good opportunity to increase the funding of Panchayats. It was missed by most states.

Individually, panchayats may not either be viable or fully equipped to raise funds for development projects. Need of the hour is to combine panchayats to harness resources, particularly, those that are unique to the areas. Voluntary and philanthropic organizations should also be tapped.

Q16. Multiplicity of various commissions for the vulnerable sections of the society leads to problems of overlapping jurisdiction and duplication of functions. Is it better to merge all commissions into an umbrella Human Rights Commission? Argue your case.

Ans. India is a union of states with federal spirit and richness in diversity. In the first instance, it means both the Union and states have powers to constitute commissions. This ensured multiplicity of commissions.

Commissions for the vulnerable, like the ones for women, children, scheduled caste, scheduled tribes, backward castes are all statutory, just as is the commission for human rights. In a pluralistic, diverse, fragmented and hierarchy-ridden society, they all serve a purpose– a purpose of social standing and exclusiveness, a purpose of considered attention and a purpose of identity.

These commissions meet a social need just as much as a political necessity. There would be cases of duplication of functions and overlapping jurisdiction, but it is understandable.

Two issues become important and these justify the need to have commissions as they exist now.

(a) Commissions for the vulnerable can only investigate but have no compelling powers to prosecute or even insist on attendance.

(b) Functional commissions give confidence and consideration to the vulnerable but bringing these under one composite commission will be counterproductive. For instance, if national commission for women is brought under the umbrella 'National commission for human rights', the affected women may not feel ease or freedom.

What is needed today is constitution of fast track courts to prosecute cases and change in penal systems and codes to align with current needs.

Q17. How far do you agree with the view that the focus on lack of availability of food as the main cause of hunger takes the attention away from ineffective human development policies in India?

Ans. "An army can't march on an empty stomach; a nation cannot sleep on empty stomachs." There is a lot of truth in both these statements. Hunger is so primary that it takes away focus from all other issues.

The example of India fully illustrates the point that spotlight on lack of availability of food takes attention away from many issues. After independence, the country faced an acute crisis of food shortage. The entire focus of the five-year plans was on augmenting food supplies; we even had to accept humiliating terms of PL480 from USA for food imports. The Third Plan fell away dues to crisis of 1962, 1965 wars and the annual plans (1966 to 1969) saw the first seeds of Green Revolution sown.

As the country slowly but surely moved toward food sufficiency, the attention now shifted to human development policies. From the Fifth Plan onwards, we saw development of human policies. The emergence of service sector and development of right skills ensured it progressed further. Simultaneously, there was a focus on policies that led to a growth in the manufacturing sector.

The 1991 economic reforms were mainly on manufacturing and service sector, while agriculture and food issues hardly figured in liberalization, privatization and globalization reforms. Unshackling of private sector gave an impetus to human development policies. Indian entry at WTO (1995) was easy due to strong agriculture and self-sufficiency. Further development of human skills became possible due to WTO entry.

The spectre of famine and hunger is no longer looming in the horizon now. Now is the time to devote our attention to the problems of human development and social justice.

Q18. The Citizen's Charter is an ideal instrument of organisational transparency and accountability, but it has its own limitations. Identify the limitations and suggest measures for greater effectiveness of the Citizen's Charters.

Ans. The Citizen's charter, as the name suggests, is a document that showcases the expectations of citizens. These may relate to quality, cost, delivery, value, service and goodwill. No doubt, the concept is laudable and it is expected to keep the organizations focused. Yet there are limitations; these often defeat the very purpose of the charter.

To list a few limitations :

(a) Quite often the charter remains a mere declaration on paper; management has no commitment to it. It is neither followed nor enforced

(b) The charters promise much but perform little. The gap between promise and performance makes the charter a non-starter

(c) Frequent changes in management are often the cause of charters being forgotten. Sometimes, charters are put in place only to please the superiors, not actually follow

(d) Resources of organisations are too inadequate to meet the charters

(e) Many organisations hide behind the cloak of 'confidentiality' and 'secrecy' to make charters redundant

(f) Not following up issues from charter or resorting to legalities are also problems

(g) Layers of bureaucratic hierarchy can finish off expectations.

Notwithstanding all these limitations, improvements are feasible. Many organizations are showing excellent results.

To list a few suggestions:

(i) The charter should be time-bound, with clear indications as to time limits for the expectations to be fulfilled

(ii) If no response or failure occurs, provision for appeal to higher- ups must exist, with time-bound limits

(iii) Periodic meetings must be organized with all stakeholders to pre-empt problems

(iv) Incentives should be given to those who work extra hard to meet expectations of charters

Q19. What are the key areas of reform if the WTO has to survive in the present context of 'Trade War', especially keeping in mind the interest of India? (15)

Ans. The World Trade Organisation (WTO) is built around the principles of 'positive outreach' of consensus, most favoured nation concept , tariff reduction, pluralisation of bilateral, regional and multilateral treaties, and dispute redressal mechanism, as also the significant 'Intellectual Property Rights.'

In 23 years, WTO has seen enormous growth in trade and services but fissures are developing and disputes and dissensions are out in the open.

Key reasons of concern are:

(a) Tariff related issues, including 'dumping'

(b) Lack of faith in Dispute Redressal Mechanism

(c) Role, scope and functions of WTO in specific issues like agriculture, environment and human resources etc;

(d) Treaties outside WTO; bilateral agreements, regional and multilateral

These are the areas where reform is needed, if WTO is to survive. Championing for new changes is USA under its President Donald Trump. Ever since WTO was established (1995), world trade has increased but share of USA has not, in terms of percentage. The US, under President Trump is highly critical of tariffs, raised notably by China and India. It is also raising its voice against the mechanism of arbitration and dispute redressal, even though it is winning a number of cases (notably solar battery case against India). The US also has serious issues with India's stand on agriculture and subsidies. It also feels many bilateral, regional and multilateral treaties, are to its disadvantage. Treaties with Mexico, Canada etc and those under NAFTA, treaties with EU etc, are all under the scanner. In this context, Trump has even gone to the extent of calling India a 'tariff king.'

According to Trump, China, which has worked to build treaties on its own, against the rules of the WTO regime is classified as a 'developing country' that behaves likes a 'developed one.'

Q.20. In what ways would the ongoing US-Iran Nuclear Pact controversy affect the national interest of India? How should India respond to its situation? (15)

Ans. The US-Iran pact on nuclear issues signed by the Obama administration has been put on reversal by the Trump administration. It has brought back the issue of sanctions against Iran to the forefront. These sanctions affect India, as Iran is a significant partner in trade. Even during the Obama regime, Hillary Clinton as Secretary of State, put across strong sentiment against oil imports from Iran by India, and insisted on cuts.

India has no involvement in the issue of US stand against Iran. However, it is the trade embargo on Iran that hurts India. As a developing country, India has a huge need for energy and its own resources, particularly in oil, are very limited. Iran, therefore, becomes important as other sources like Venezuela and Central Asian republics are either far or inaccessible.

Iran is the third largest supplier of oil to India after Saudi Arabia and Iraq, and has agreement to trade in rupees. India has, therefore to negotiate larger supplies from Saudi Arabia and Iraq or work to get a waiver from USA. What is worrisome is that an embargo on Iran could lead to escalation in world oil prices, something India would be hard-pressed to adjust given the fiscal pressure the country is facing.

Chabahar port is another issue that India will find a tight rope walk. Would Iran enter into agreements like SCO? It remains to be seen. In the long run, India has to focus on solar energy and in the short run, on increased coal production. Nuclear energy is an option but has its own hassles.

Solved Paper 2019

General Studies

Paper II

- *Total Marks: 250 marks, Time duration: 3 hours.*
- *There are 20 questions printed both in ENGLISH and HINDI.*
- *All questions are compulsory.*
- *The number of marks carried by a question/part is printed against it.*
- *Answers must be written in the medium authorized in the admission certificate which must be stated clearly on the cover of this question-cum-answer (QCA) booklet in the space provided.*
- *No marks will be given for answers written in the medium other than authorized one.*
- *Answers to questions no. 1 to 10 should be in 150 words, whereas answers to questions no. 11 to 20 should be in 250 words.*
- *Keep the word limit indicated in the questions in mind.*
- *Any page or portion of the page left blank, must be struck off clearly.*

1. Do you think that Constitution of India does not accept principle of strict separation of powers rather it is based on the principle of 'checks and balance'? Explain. (10 Marks)

Ans. Articles 73 and 74 for the Union, and Articles 163 and 164 for the states, outline the structure of Parliamentary form of democracy. Executive is responsible to the Parliament and the government can be removed by Parliament. Even so, the executive too has a sizeable role in evolving rules through subordinate legislation that is framed by Parliament.

Legislature controls finance that is the lifeline of the executive and keeps check on the executive through CAG and other parliamentary committees. Excesses by the executive in defiance of the legislature can also be investigated by the legislature. Even contempt issues are known of being investigated.

Judiciary keeps check on both the legislature as well as the executive. Cases of *Golaknath* and *Kesavananda Bharati* concerned the judicial 'outreach' in the former case, and 'over each' in the latter. Overall, it is a system not of dependence, nor independence but interdependence that is understood, understandable and understanding. **(153 words)**

2. The Central Administrative Tribunal which was established for redressal of grievances and complaints by or against central government employees nowadays is exercising its powers as an independent judicial authority." Explain. (10 Marks)

Ans. Over the period from 1985 when the Tribunal came into existence, the number of cases has steadily been on the rise; chiefly due to increasing levels of awareness among employees and also due to rising tendency among government departments to push cases to the Tribunal. These factors are responsible for the Tribunals to act as an independent judicial authority, for one.

Secondly, government departments are showing increasing signs of ignorance of law causing the Tribunal to wield the stick and thereby putting matters in the right perspective.

Thirdly, cases relating to infringement of fundamental rights of employees are now being heard by the Tribunal. This follows the decision in the *L. Chandra Kumar v. Union of India,* the landmark case which decided on the constitutionality of Articles 32A and 323B as they dealt with the exclusion of jurisdiction of High Court in service matters This has brought added pressure to the Tribunals to act as independent judicial authority.

(158 words)

3. What are the methods used by the farmers' organisations to influence the policymakers in India and how effective are these methods? (10 Marks)

Ans. Farmers' organisations have both a case and a cause to agitate for; on the one hand, they are actively pursuing a course of debate and discussion to highlight their issues. On the other hand, the farmers' organisations are on the warpath, out on the streets in marches, road blockades and meetings.

Farmers' organisations are demonstrating by throwing away excess produce as a mark of protest against low prices; these are often lesser than investment or sunk costs. Spilling milk is another method of recording protest. A rather unusual way of protest at Jantar Mantar Delhi by farmers from Tamil Nadu was seen when they came with human skulls.

Long marches, as seen in Maharashtra, to cities like Mumbai are another way of recording angst. Television debates too are being used to propagate burning issues of remuneration suggested by Swaminathan Commission.

Some of these agitations are partially successful as some state governments have given concessions and the Centre has raised the MSP (Minimum Support Price) for crops.

(166 words)

4. From the resolution of contentious issues regarding distribution of legislative powers by the courts, 'Principle of Federal Supremacy' and 'Harmonious Construction' have emerged. Explain. (10 Marks)

Ans. 'Principle of Federal Supremacy' has emerged from the evolution of constitutional development in the United States. It means that in the event of contention or conflict, the federal laws would prevail and not the state laws. 'Harmonious Construction' is the tenet that matters should be seen in a certain context and not in isolation.

Courts in India have, over the years, supported these constructions to bring a 'chain of thought' that irons out all conflicts of opinion. The road map is clear; the 'federal interests' prevail and 'whole' has predominance over the 'parts'.

Article 246(3) of the constitution expressly lays down the principle of federal supremacy, noting that 'Parliament has exclusive power to make laws with respect to any of the matters enumerated in List I in the Seventh Schedule'.

The constitution does not expressly mention about 'harmonious construction', rather it has evolved through the interpretation by Supreme Court which held that if 'part' cannot be reconciled with the 'whole', the 'whole' must prevail. **(160 words)**

5. What can France learn from the Indian Constitution's approach to secularism? (10 Marks)

Ans. France is a catholic country that is now in the throes of an adjustment crisis in matters of ethnic, cultural and religious assimilation and integration. The issues are manifesting themselves in the matter of dress too, as seen in the recent controversy about instructions to girls of Muslim faith to remove headscarves. The clear division of society and the state on religious matters too is also a hindrance.

India presents a different picture with the state being positively neutral and seen to be so. The constitution guarantees equality to all as a matter of fundamental right and special protection to minorities in the matter of practicising their faith and preservation of their institutions. These rights, are not only justifiable but also justiciable.

France can see and sense how positivity in secularism is not only an imperative article of faith but also an ingrained arrangement of fidelity. France was the pioneer in 'Liberty, Equality and Fraternity,' Secularism is the keystone of Fraternity. **(162 words)**

6. Despite consistent experience of high growth, India still goes with the lowest indicators of human development. Examine the issues that make balanced and inclusive development elusive. (10 Marks)

Ans. Growth and Distribution are two different matters; former may result from capital, innovation and involvement; latter is served well with imagination, consideration and application.

India has done well to register steady growth but these indices do not mean much to the people at large. The rise of private sector and relegation of the public sector have meant that while the fruits of growth are being enjoyed by the former, the latter is getting confined to "facilitating". Growth of population has outstripped distribution schemes for human development. Health, education, housing are woefully inadequate for the masses. The fact that a vast majority of population that is working is in the informal sector is no help either. This sector is hopelessly inadequately covered by social welfare schemes.

Low levels of literacy and equally low levels of awareness too are responsible for human development indices to be low. Gender issues affecting women are a lot more pernicious than we imagine.

(156 words)

7. There is a growing divergence in the relationship between poverty and hunger in India. The shrinking of social expenditure by the government is forcing the poor to spend more on non-food essential items squeezing their food-budget. Elucidate. (10 Marks)

Ans. Poverty and hunger are inter-related with hunger being a consequence of poverty. Poverty is multi-dimensional and in the case of absolute poverty, hunger assumes a manifestly significant role. In the multi-dimensional matrix of poverty, parameters like health, education, unemployment, lack of housing, absence of clean drinking water, lack of sanitation too occupy high positions.

In today's situation, hunger is not the only index of poverty. Dignity of life may take precedence over hunger.

The government is constrained by force of circumstance to cut on social expenditure forcing people to divert their income to meet these needs. It could be a case of finding proper education for children in private schools or medical treatment through private healthcare.

The informal and unorganised sector is growing rapidly and forms the backbone of our economy. Those employed therein have no social sector benefits or coverage. They have to fall back on services offered by the private dispensation. **(151 words)**

8. **Implementation of Information and Communication Technology (ICT) based Projects/Programmes usually suffers in terms of certain vital factors. Identify these factors and suggest measures for their effective implementation. (10 Marks)**

Ans. Despite the benefits, there are inherent problems in ICT too if we considered the overall perspective. These problems are part human, part technological, part managerial and part social.

(i) **Human Factors:** No effect is made to make the population equipped to adapt to the technology and its usage thereby affecting assimilation.

(ii) **Technological Factors:** Obsolete technology or inappropriate technology causes problems. Frequent up-gradation or changes also cause concern.

(iii) **Managerial Factors:** At times there is acute shortage of skilled personnel who can understand and adapt the system to the technology.

(iv) **Social Factors:** One must always be alert about negative campaigns. Even a good project/programme can be run down on purpose through social media by detractors.

Issues like digital illiteracy, non-familiarity with English, lack of broadband connectivity, lack of continuous electric supply, non availability of mobile coverage etc can hamper the spread of technology.

Often, ICT based projects / programmes are launched without any 'preparatory work' and proper awareness campaign. **(159 words)**

9. **'The time has come for India and Japan to build a strong contemporary relationship, one involving global and strategic partnership that will have a great significance for Asia and the world as a whole.' Comment. (10 Marks)**

Ans. India and Japan have commonality of interests and mutuality of concerns. Japan is technologically rich, but resource wise poor; India needs technology, but is resource wise blessed.

(a) Japan has signed civil nuclear agreement that signified mutual faith and trust in strategic terms.

(b) Japan alongside United States is partnering India in Malabar naval exercises which has a clear strategic intent and thrust.

(c) Japan is investing in development of Andaman and Nicobar Islands as also in the development of North-Eastern states in India, like Meghalaya which is a strategic push against future eventualities.

In the sphere of global matters, both India and Japan are apprehensive and anxious about the increasing role being played by China. The United States too is also viewing the developments with caution, if not concern.

(a) The marked thrust by China in Africa is sought to be countered by Japan and India with suitable investments there.

(b) Japan, India, Australia and the United States are conjoined into an informal thinking group to counter China.

(c) The rapid advancement of China in its economic corridor network is bringing India and Japan together to explore alternatives. (159 words)

10. 'Too little cash, too much politics, leaves UNESCO fighting for life.' Discuss the statement in the light of US' withdrawal and its accusation of the cultural body as being 'anti-Israel bias.' (10 Marks)

Ans. UNESCO being a frontline body of the United Nations Organisation, so much was expected of it. The truth is that it does not count for much today. The reasons are not far to seek. Firstly, today, UNESCO has got associated solely with branding of 'world heritage sites' as countries only want branding to the exclusion of conservation. Secondly, UNESCO has faced hostile attitude from USA. The US pulled out in 1984 only to rejoin in 2003. The UNESCO sponsored MacBride commission report on Media and its domain took many western countries to crying 'foul' as their interests were called to question.

Further, the recognition by the UNESCO of Palestinians rights to sites around and in Jerusalem where Israel was carrying out archaeological work incensed the US. This led to the US to call it 'bias'. The US is again leaving the world body. UNESCO is grappling with political matters, not so much the matters it is mandated to handle. (159 words)

11. On what grounds a people's representative can be disqualified under the Representation of Peoples Act, 1951? Also mention the remedies available to such person against his disqualification. (15 Marks)

Ans. Article 84 of the Indian Constitution lays down the conditions that a candidate must fulfil to be a member of the Parliament. If these conditions are not met, the elected representative stands disqualified.

Representation of Peoples Act 1951, lays down the grounds under which an elected representative can be disqualified.

(i) A member must not have been found guilty of corrupt practices or certain electoral offences in the elections.

(ii) He must not be imprisoned for more than two years for any offence.

(iii) Must not have been punished for committing social offences like practising untouchability.

(iv) Must not be having any interest in government works, contracts and services.

(v) Must not have been convicted for offences for promoting enmity among different sections.

(vi) Must not have failed to submit expenses account on election.

(vii) Must not have been dismissed from a government service on grounds of corruption or disloyalty.

The President of India takes the decision on disqualification in consultation with Election Commission which is final.

The disqualification period is for six years from the date of conviction. It is also relevant to note that conviction for an offence under certain acts of Indian Penal Code, Protection of Civil Rights Act, 1955, Unlawful Activities (Prevention) Act, 1967, Prevention of Corruption Act, 1988, Prevention of Terrorism Act, 2002 etc the convicted person is sentenced to:

(a) only fine, disqualification for six years from the date of such conviction.

(b) Imprisonment, from the date of such conviction and shall continue for a further period of six years since release.

The normal remedy of filing a case in the High Court and appeal in the Supreme Court is available. (277 words)

12. "Parliament's power to amend the Constitution is a limited power and it cannot be enlarged into absolute power." In the light of this statement explain whether Parliament under Article 368 of the Constitution can destroy the Basic Structure of the Constitution by expanding its amending power? (15 Marks)

Ans. The two landmark cases, namely *Golaknath and others vs. State of Punjab (1967) and Kesavanada Bharti and others vs. State of Kerala (1973)* were both decided by the Supreme Court of India. In the Golaknath case it was held that article 368 merely dealt with the procedure to amend the constitution and not the inherent power. The view, prevailed through a 6:5 judgement, simply held that, 'Parliament's power to amend the constitution is a limited power and it cannot be enlarged into absolute power'. It set the stage for a confrontation, with the parliament reinforcing that it was supreme.

In the Kesavananda Bharti judgement (1973) Supreme Court reconsidered its rigidity and held that the Parliament indeed could amend the constitution but subject to the limitation that it could not amend the basic structure of the constitution. Interestingly, the Supreme Court

(a) did not define or distinctly state what that basic structure would be

(b) the Supreme Court held to itself the power as to what the final interpretation of basic structure would be. Issues like sovereignty, rule of law, independence of judiciary fundamental rights, secularism, federal structure, republican and democratic form of government etc. were seen to be constituting the basic structure.

In the *Minerva Mills (1980)* case the Supreme Court provided key clarifications on the interpretation of the basic structure doctrine. The court unanimously ruled that the power of the parliament to amend the constitution is limited by the constitution.

In a way, it was the reaffirmation of the older view that held 'constitution is not a plaything of the parliament'.

(262 words)

13. "The reservation of seats for women in the institutions of local self-government has had a limited impact on the patriarchal character of the Indian political process." Comment. (15 Marks)

Ans. The 73rd and 74th amendments to the constitution paved the way for local self government bodies, both in rural as well as urban areas. It was also ensured that $33\frac{1}{3}$ percent of seats would be for women. A commendable initiative, no doubt, but some whispers were heard that no proper or adequate preparatory work had been done.

Historically, Indian society has been dominated by men, made more so with the institution of joint family and the preeminent position of its head, the Karta. In the event, two points remained paramount.

(a) The political process of electioneering and campaigning has been with the men folk.

(b) Even with elected women taking charge, the men in the family call the shots. Women are guided in making decisions by men.

It is also important to note that even today many women are dependent on men for money and security. Add to this, social norms don't permit the women to defy or deny the men folk in public.

In the context, a few more issues are also pertinent. One, the winning possibility remains a prime concern and this leads to women of merit being denied opportunity to contest. Passive and ignorant women make no difference. Two, the system of joint family ensures that interests of it are not harmed at all. This reduces the degree of freedom of elected women folk of the family; the patriarchal character gets reinforced, even revitalised. India has a long way to traverse but at least the voice of women is being heard; this itself is a gain.

(256 words)

14. "The Attorney-General is the chief legal adviser and lawyer of the Government of India." Discuss. (15 Marks)

Ans. The Attorney General of India holds a constitutional position by virtue of the provisions of the constitution as per Article 76(1). He is appointed by the President of India based on the advice of the Union Cabinet.

Attorney General who is appointed should be qualified to be appointed a judge of the Supreme Court, meaning thereby that he should be a judge of some high court for five years or an advocate of some high court for ten years.

As the chief legal advisor, he gives advice to the President upon such legal matters which are referred or assigned to him by the President.

The Attorney General appears on behalf of the Government of India in all the cases in the Supreme Court in which the government is concerned. He appears on behalf of the government in any reference made under Article 143 of the constitution by the President. He also appears in the High Court when the government so desires.

The Attorney General has a right of audience in all courts within the country. He can take part in proceedings of both houses of parliament, including joint sitting but without the right to vote. He enjoys all the privileges and immunities available to members of parliament; he can be a member of committee of the parliament without the right to vote.

Attorney General should not advise or hold a brief against the government. He should not defend in criminal cases the accused persons without the permission of Government of India. **(250 words)**

15. Individual Parliamentarian's role as the national law maker is on a decline, which in turn, has adversely impacted the quality of debates and their outcome. Discuss. (15 Marks)

Ans. There are many reasons for the decline of individual parliamentarian as a law maker; chiefly, due to the nature of our parliamentary democracy and also due to changing nature of our polity. The parliamentarian today is bound by his party diktats and discipline and not by his convictions and conscience. Besides, our electoral system of universal adult franchise and non-insistence on qualifications of candidates throws up candidates who are not equipped to deal or debate, let alone add quality to discussions.

Also, 52nd constitutional amendment, 1985 which inserted the Tenth Schedule banning defections was another reason. Dissent has been banned. Parliamentarians now have to vote as per party diktat, not as per conscience.

In the event of a party getting a brute majority or commanding position, the chances of individual parliamentarians recede further to contribute by debate or discussion. As the outcome is known, individual members resign themselves to the fact of it all.

The rapid polarisation among parties is further reducing the scope for quality debates as members go by political considerations, not the core of the issue. The lack of education and proliferation of criminals among elected members is a sure matter to reduce debates to a farce.

The only little scope parliamentarians find to vent their feelings is during the question, answer time. One vividly remembers the helplessness of a nominated member of parliament, himself a 'Bharat Ratna', when he was not allowed to speak due to ruckus on an issue of importance when he had the core competence to do so. **(252 words)**

16. 'In the context of neo-liberal paradigm of development planning, multi-level planning is expected to make operations cost-effective and remove many implementation blockages.' – Discuss. (15 Marks)

Ans. Planning in the country, after independence was 'top down' and singularly linear; the government ruled the roost too. Post-1991, the scenario changed with the rise of private sector in the relaxed scenario of liberalisation and globalisation. The approach became 'bottom up'. In the event, development planning became broad based and multi-layered. Planning became consensus based to an extent, stakeholders multiplied and soon planning moved closer to reality too. 'One size fits all' approach gave way to 'differences respected, always expected'. The onset of local government model at rural and urban levels through the constitutional 73rd and 74th amendments in 1992 marked the beginning.

Multi-level planning empowers the number of layers thereby reducing the extra functionaries which also means cost reduction. Unlike in the past, all decisions, even for lower level planning need not go to the top. In effect it means 'democratisation of government' as opposed to 'bureaucratisation of government'. Multilevel planning significantly brings lot of advantages, some of which are in the direction of removal of blockages and some towards cost reduction. Planning done at the lower level means removal of blockages as decisions can be taken on the spot. This also means cost effectiveness as time is saved.

Wastages and pilferages too get eliminated through multilevel planning as closer accountability is ensured. India has seen the benefits of multilevel planning with huge reduction in poverty levels. Schemes like MGNREGA have been successfully implemented. Multilevel planning has also shown how country progressed in making national highways, in implementation of Swachh Bharat drive, in literacy programmes, in rural electrification etc.

(259 words)

17. The need for cooperation among various service sectors has been an inherent component of development discourse. Partnership bridges the gap among the sectors. It also sets in motion a culture of 'collaboration' and 'team spirit'. In the light of statements above examine India's development process. **(15 Marks)**

Ans. Development process, by its very nature, presupposes an element of interdependence among the various sectors. Cooperation is the life blood of development narrative among sectors. Besides, development process is forever evolving, being dynamic and diverse, it needs the spirit of collaboration and team work.

Indian constitution recognised this essence and inserted article 280 that deals with Finance Commission which seeks to work for collaboration and team spirit.

Right from 1950 to 1991, the development discourse was led by a strong centre aided by a highly centralised planning commission. Collaboration was enforced and team spirit extracted. The model of development was 'top down'. The enveloping crisis of balance of payment led to the 1991 reforms of liberalisation, privatisation and globalisation. Reforms unshackled the private sector which made rapid strides, notably in the service sector. The collaboration now centred round 'Public Private Partnership' discourse. This was further reinforced with the coming of WTO (World Trade Organisation) regime. The centre now moved to its new role of being a 'facilitator' and its focus shifted to furthering social welfare. Collaboration now assumed a new role and meaning, centre looked hard at distribution of wealth.

Development discourse took a new turn from 2014 with focus on 'cooperative federalism', justly emphasising on collaboration and team spirit. Initiative for rolling Goods and Service Tax (GST) came from this endeavour. Centre and the states are now conjoined in the urgent state of progress.

NITI Aayog has now moved to the centre stage to lead the discourse, more a 'think tank' than a planner, with the task of implementation assumed. The focus now is on collaboration in putting heads together.

(270 words)

18. Performance of welfare schemes that are implemented for vulnerable sections is not so effective due to absence of their awareness and active involvement at all stages of policy process. – Discuss.
(15 Marks)

Ans. For a variety of reasons, performance of welfare schemes is not so effective in so far as the intended beneficiaries namely the vulnerable sections of the society are concerned. The design and the devolution of the schemes are crucial factors, while the implementation and the initiative are the other factors. Those charged with the implementation, for a good part, are either not initiated or motivated or have the resources or the reason to make awareness an imperative principle of action. Creating awareness involves breaking barriers, showing empathy, demonstrating bond, apply it on self and standing by it. Awareness cannot be spread if there's a gap in communication; either oral or technological. 'Pulse Polio' programme has been a success because awareness was created door to door, dawn to dusk. The Swachch Bharat campaign is another example where all forms of communication was utilised to connect to the masses and drive home the message.

Involvement at all stages of policy process is a desirable target or an end all planners seek, but the ground situation is dismally different. There are of course two ways of looking at this issue. One, if the vulnerable sections have been involved in samples at the various stages of the design process of policy; two, while implementing the policy, if the vulnerable sections have been involved at all stages. In either event, voluntary involvement levels always go up when peer pressure builds up; women to women, aged to aged etc.

(246 words)

19. 'The long-sustained image of India as a leader of the oppressed and marginalised nations has disappeared on account of its new found role in the emerging global order.' Elaborate. (15 Marks)

Ans. After the Second World War, India took the lead to carve a niche for itself as a non-aligned nation which would maintain itself distance from both the capitalist and communist blocs. This role found favour with many nations, notably Egypt, Yugoslavia and Indonesia.

At the United Nations and other World Organisations, India crafted its role and carried a voice that resonated well with the oppressed, marginalised nations.

All that changed in 1990s with the rapid and real collapse of Soviet Union, leaving United States dominant in a decisive manner.

Economically, the world moved over to the new world order in 1995 with the World Trade Organisation becoming a reality. Bilateral trade of tariffs and quotas gave way to open, expanding order of trust, transparency and rights; trade included services too; a fact that helped India immensely. Two events redefined the political landscape; one, China emerged as a power of consequence; two, the 9/11 attacks on United States woke that country to harsh realities of new order. India's position in the new global order too was conditioned by the need to succeed, not merely survive. Its advancement on many parameters made it a developing country with the mindset of a developed country.

The coming together of China and Pakistan forced India to redefine her relationship with the United States. Along with shared values and vision of freedom and democracy, India and the United States have the common, considered enemy in terrorism.. Naturally, in these set of circumstances, India has ceased to be seen as a leader of downtrodden nations. Colonialism and imperialism are now past narratives. **(264 words)**

20. 'What introduces friction into the ties between India and the United States is that Washington is still unable to find for India a position in its global strategy, which would satisfy India's national self-esteem and ambitions.' Explain with suitable examples. (15 Marks)

Ans. In the global strategy of the United States, the position of India is piquant. India, as a developing country and with regional concerns and global outreach, cannot find itself suitably accommodated by the United States.

India's self-esteem does not allow it to play the role of a subservient country that perhaps would send troops to Afghanistan, much as the United States would want it to do. In the same vein, India finds it incredibly appalling that it would be dictated by the United States as to how it should shape its relations with Iran in so far as oil transactions are concerned.

The United States has issues with India in matters of trade and tariffs, intellectual property rights, immigration, issuance of visas, military hardware etc. India has a surplus trade equation with the United States and it is an irritant with the US; uncertainties over visas are also a sore point with India.

India's arms deals with Russia are also an issue with the United States over the years. However, today the main issues are China and Pakistan. The US is engaged in a battle of sorts with China over tariffs. In this, India does not fit in a major way for the US. Pakistan presents a different picture; India sees it as the epicentre of global terrorism and the root cause of disruption in Afghanistan and disturbance in Kashmir; United States is more concerned of Pakistan's nexus with China. In the event, United States does not feel India has any role to its liking. **(255 words)**

Solved Paper 2020
General Studies
Paper II

There are twenty questions. All Questions are Compulsory.
*Questions **1-10** are 10 marks each and **150 words.***
*Questions **11-20** are 15 marks each and **250 words.***

1. "There is a need for simplification of procedure for disqualification of persons found guilty of corrupt practices under the Representation of Peoples Act". Comment. ***(Answer in 150 words)***

Ans: There is an urgent and pressing need for simplification of procedure for disqualification of persons found guilty of corrupt practices under the Representation of People's Act 1951. While on the one hand there's marked increase in number of cases, on the other hand there's the delay in prosecution that brings gloom and lack of faith all round.

Section 123 of RP Act, outlines all such activities that constitute corrupt practices towards disqualification.

Section 8A of RP Act relates to disqualification on grounds of corrupt practices.

Section 9 of the RP Act covers disqualification on grounds of corruption and disloyalty. While the provisions exist for combating cases of corruption and malpractices, the ground situation is indeed tricky.

Courts have held that while the election process is on, they cannot intervene. Similarly, the cases in the courts are huge and till disposal and appeals no one can be held guilty. The obvious way forward is to put in place special courts and speed up disposal of cases. Many new and ingenious ways of corruption are seen these days. 'Paid News' is one such practice and it needs to be curbed. (188 words)

2. "Recent amendments to the Right to Information Act will have profound impact on the autonomy and independence of the Information Commission". Discuss. ***(Answer in 150 words)***

Ans: The Right to Information Act is a transformational Act whose acceptance, application and advancement depend on independence and involvement of public authorities. Autonomy and Independence of the Information Commission is essential. Accountability of public service authorities is the key issue.

The recent amendments to the Right to Information Act are aimed at checking the independence and autonomy of the Commission. The term of the office of the Chief Information Commissioner of the Central Information Commission and State Information

Commissioners will be prescribed by the Central Government. Secondly, the salaries allowances and other terms of service shall be prescribed by the Central Government. These two amendments take away the autonomy of the commissioners who are expected to pursue the objectives of the Right to Information Act.

The original tenure of 5 years is now at the pleasure of the government at the centre as also the salaries and perks. The previous status of CICs and state information commissioners stands lowered. This affects the functioning of the setup and with central government making inroads the image of the information commission and the functioning will take a hit. **(185 words)**

3. How far do you think cooperation, competition and confrontation have shaped the nature of federation in India? Cite some recent examples to validate your answer. (Answer in 150 words)

Ans: The Constitution of India vide Article 246 has spelt out in Schedule 7 the division of powers between the Union, State and concurrent items being common. The basic objective is to foster cooperation, promote competition and avoid confrontation. Although the division is not watertight, yet very substantially the division is understood and appreciated. There's competition between centre and the states in social sector areas.

As for cooperation, the roll out of GST (Goods and Service Tax) so seamlessly and systematically is a shining example of the same. Another worthwhile instance is the setting up of NIA (National Investigative Agency) which combats terror. Rural employment under MGNREGA too is an instance of cooperation.

As for confrontation, the position of Governor has come into sharp contention. Art 356 dealing with imposition of 'President's Rule' has always been the subject matter of discussion; many commissions have looked into it. Recent farm laws by the centre are at the centre stage with dissent, doubt and distrust. Another area of confrontation is the imposition of AFSPA Act in some states, notably in the north-east. **(168 words)**

4. The judicial system in India and UK seem to be converging as well as diverging in recent times. Highlight the key points of convergence and divergence between the two nations in terms of their judicial practices. *(Answer in 150 words)*

Ans: The judicial practices in the UK and India have evolved differently over the years. Both follow rule of law and rule as prescribed by law. UK's Constitutional Reform Act, 2005 in October 2009 abolished the appellate jurisdiction of the House of Lords and transferred it to a new body, the Supreme Court of the United Kingdom. In India, the Supreme Court of India already has an independent status under the constitution.

Both countries have integrated hierarchy of courts with provisions of judgments and appeals.

There are many points of divergence too. In the United Kingdom, Parliament is supreme whereas in India, the Constitution is supreme. Public Interest Litigation (PIL) has a commanding position in the judicial setup in India whereas in the United Kingdom no such practice exists.

In sedition matters Indian judiciary is quite elaborately engaged with it whereas UK judiciary's concerns are mild and muted. In the matter of selection of judges the UK there's a selection commission whose recommendations are sent to the Queen. In India there are constitutional provisions prescribing establishment of a 'collegium'. **(178 words)**

5. 'Once a Speaker, Always a speaker'! Do you think this practice should be adopted to impart objectivity to the office of the Speaker of Lok Sabha? What could be its implication for the robust functioning of parliamentary business in India? ***(Answer in 150 words)***

Ans: 'Once a Speaker, always a Speaker' is a tradition embedded in the British Constitution exemplifying the concept of neutrality of the office of the Speaker. He is to be not merely neutral but seen to be so. In our parliamentary democracy also the Speaker of Lok Sabha is seen as someone who is neutral and non-partisan.

The practice of 'once a Speaker, always a Speaker,' can be applied to Lok Sabha more vigorously. The Speaker plays a prominent role in the matter of settling the issue of defections. Given the parameters set by the 52nd Amendment (1985), the Speaker comes under strain to pursue his party's interests. The Supreme Court has recently suggested creation of a tribunal to decide on fate of defectors by amending the constitution (10th schedule) since speaker cannot be neutral given his party loyalties.

Another point of contention is the power given to the speaker of Lok Sabha to decide whether a Bill is a money bill or not; the debate is on and opinions are divided. The onus lies on the speaker to be seen as non-partisan by being objective. **(185 words)**

6. In order to enhance the prospects of social development, sound and adequate healthcare policies are needed in the fields of geriatric and maternal health care. Discuss ***(Answer in 150 words)***

Ans: Geriatric (old age related) and maternal health care issues need care, concern and consideration as these are rooted among the weaker sections of the society. The state has a definite duty to attend to the old and infirm as also the expectant mothers who must be given nutritional support and sustenance.

Healthcare policies for the old must be evolved in a manner that the aged population is not put to any financial burden. Old age pension is one such outcome, free healthcare being another. Geriatric care also extends to emotional support and a life with dignity and honour. The state has a bounden duty to put in place adequate and affordable health care polices.

Maternal health care is equally important; pre-natal and post-natal care matter too. A healthy child is an asset for the society.

Many old age homes for the senior citizens now exist, mostly from the initiatives of social welfare organisations. Maternal healthcare is well supported by very liberal assistance from the government, including maternity leave, paternity leave etc. **(171 words)**

7. "Institutional quality is a crucial driver of economic performance". In this context, suggest reforms in Civil Service for Strengthening Democracy. ***(Answer in 150 words)***

Ans: Reforms in Civil Service for strengthening democracy with quality of institutions as the mode centres around two aspects; one, to improve the infrastructure; two, to bring out responsiveness, transparency and accountability. The prime need is to ensure that the Civil Services deliver quality service on time with ease and transparency.

The role of technology is the key; Civil Services must adopt and adapt technology as the prime driver. It would bring in responsiveness and transparency in the services. Accountability too would follow.

Use of technology would also facilitate innovation and speed, both being the keystones in furthering reforms in Civil Services. Services should be available 'online' thereby eliminating corruption.

Democracy is best served and strengthened by reaching out to the last man in the queue. Robust and requisite grievance redressal machinery is the need of the hour. Measures like strengthening Right to Information, service availability at 'doorstep', reaching out to the less privileged and following of rule of law are of the essence. **(163 words)**

8. "The emergence of Fourth Industrial Revolution (Digital Revolution) has initiated e-Governance as an integral part of the government". Discuss. ***(Answer in 150 words)***

Ans: The Fourth Industrial Revolution has initiated e-governance bringing forth lot of advantages. Foremost, e-Governance has ready, relevant and reliable solutions to all the problems that Governance today is facing. Secondly, e-Governance only can take governance to the doorstep of the citizens. Thirdly, e-Governance only can handle the sheer volumes of work that modern Governance is up against. Fourthly, the complexities of modern day Governance are daunting and can only be handled by e-Governance. Fifthly, Governance today is required to be open and transparent; e-Governance only can be the option to provide this.

Essentially, e-Governance offers speed, accuracy and accessibility. These are at the base of Governance today. Speed is of great significance as delays or dithering can put Governance in a tight spot. Accuracy and accessibility is central to Governance that is required to deliver. Another big advantage that e-Governance provides is the 'faceless contact'; this is so essential for Governance to be free of bias. e-Governance is can operate 24/7, 365 days and be available seamlessly. **(167 words)**

9. Critically examine the role of WHO in providing global health security during the COVID-19 Pandemic ***(Answer in 150 words)***

Ans: The World Health Organisation (WHO) is mandated with advocating for universal healthcare, monitoring public health risks, coordinating responses to health emergencies and promoting human health and well being. Covid-19 certainly was an emergency and its manifestation in China was surely a case and a cause for alarm. WHO sounded its highest alarm on 30th January, 2020, a good 20 days after first cases surfaced in Wuhan, China; it was called by WHO a 'public health emergency.' It was signaling that a pandemic might be imminent. Many felt the WHO should have declared a week earlier. The bigger failure however was that many countries ignored the call.

The situation changed by March, 2020 when the virus spread and China declared it to be 'out of control' and WHO called it a 'pandemic'. Countries started listening to WHO only after the word 'pandemic', gained currency. The main flaw in WHO's working seems to be linked to the process of declaring a situation to be 'pandemic' and this needs looking at.

A significant point however is that WHO didn't see the dangers emanating from travel and trade, including with China. **(187 words)**

10. "Indian Diaspora has a decisive role to play in the politics and economy of America and European countries". Comment with examples. ***(Answer in 150 words)***

Ans: The Indian diaspora plays a very significant and substantial role in the political and economic sectors of America and Europe. The diaspora is well backed by experience, expertise and excellence. It has a good standing and acceptability.

Politically, the diaspora shares the values and ethos of the host country with remarkable ease. The integration is complete and law abiding people from the diaspora are an asset. They infuse new ideas and push the frontiers for greater development and productivity. Political parties, both in America and Europe, acknowledge this. Many from the diaspora have reached high in professions and their endorsements are valued high.

Economically, the contribution has been immense too. With high levels of productivity and willingness to work with lower wages, Indian diaspora has been much in demand. The Indian diaspora has a significant presence in IT, hotel, transport, education, space, medicine and a whole host of other sectors in America and Europe. Their contribution to the economies of these continents is far above their population size. **(168 words)**

11. Indian Constitution exhibits centralising tendencies to maintain unity and integrity of the nation. Elucidate in the perspective of the Epidemic Diseases Act, 1897; The Disaster Management Act, 2005 and recently passed Farm Acts. ***(Answer in 250 words)***

Ans: The Indian constitution has a clear tilt towards the Union over the states in both legislative as well as administrative relations. It means that the Union, which is charged with maintaining unity and integrity of the country, has been empowered and armed to act.

Article 249 outlines that Parliament can legislate with respect to a matter in the state list in the national interest.

Article 257(1), covering administrative relations between the Union and the states stipulates, 'The executive power of every state shall be so exercised as not to impede or prejudice the exercise of the executive power of the Union and the executive power of the Union shall extend to giving of such directions to a state as may appear to the Government of India to be necessary for that purpose.'

It is clear between the two articles that while the Parliament in a set of given circumstances can make legislation from the state list in the national interest, provisions exist for the administrative relations between the Union and the States to be so regulated that the Government of India's orders are given the predominance.

In the event, Union makes legislation through Parliament which must be enforced throughout the country just as the Government of India issues executive orders that take prominence over the orders of the state.

The Epidemic Diseases Act, 1897, a legacy from the colonial era and the other two acts, namely Disaster Management Act and the Farm Acts passed recently are all the result of Union's initiatives to enact legislation for the states. NIA Act, 2008 is another ready example.

(265 words)

12. Judicial legislation is antithetical to the doctrine of separation of powers as envisaged in the Indian Constitution. In this context justify the filing of large number of public interest petitions praying for issuing guidelines to executive authorities. ***(Answer in 250 words)***

Ans: In the matter of separation of powers, India stands on a different footing with lot of flexibility and accommodation. In the United Kingdom, Parliament is Supreme; in the United States, the separation of powers between Legislature, Judiciary and the Executive is water tight.

India's judiciary has a role that involves watch over the Parliament and the Executive to course correct to curb over enthusiasm.

The Constitution has allowed the judicial remedy or recourse through the instrument of writs. These writs concern fundamental rights for their violation or neglect. Public authorities can be proceeded against through writs (Article 32) by citizens in the Supreme Court. High Courts too, under Article 226, are empowered by the constitution to handle writs. Although the mechanism of writs gives that opportunity, yet the prohibitive costs and nuances of litigation and ground realities of hassles make approaching courts very difficult. The obvious solution was use of PIL (Public Interest Litigation) through which any matter of Public Interest could be agitated.

Public Interest Litigation petitions are on the rise given the apathy of public authorities and the disinterestedness of the Legislature to move forward with the political compulsions. PILs are for seeing that course-corrections are made where needed and for making the rules/laws when necessary. In the Vishaka case (1978) of sexual harassment, the Supreme Court was compelled to issue guidelines considering the intransigence by the government.

Article 32(2) states that, 'The Supreme Court shall have power to issue directions or order or writs, including writs in the nature of habeas corpus, mandamus, prohibition, quo warranto and certiorari whichever may be appropriate, for the enforcement of any of the rights conferred.' It clearly shows that judicial legislation is not antithetical to the doctrine of separation of powers as the constitution inherently allows for judiciary to issue orders in writ applications. PIL petitions seek enforcement of rights through writs. **(268 words)**

13. The strength and sustenance of local institutions in India has shifted from their formative phase of 'functions, functionaries and funds' to the contemporary stage of' functionality'. Highlight the critical challenges faced by local institutions in terms of their functionality in recent times. ***(Answer in 250 words)***

Ans: Ever since local institutions got a constitutional status through 73rd/74th amendments in 1992, their progress has been steady. With the initial skepticism and scoffing being over, the institutions came to be accepted increasingly. Political parties too began to see the visible and viable platform it offered in settling local issues.

With the Finance Commission stepping in to lay the roadmap for flow of funds to local institutions, political parties started taking huge interest in reaching out to the public and there was a need to operate with responsiveness and transparency. The focus gradually shifted.

The focus now began to be on 'functionality', meaning operating with freedom, franchise, function, farsightedness and flavour. On the one hand, the urgent need was to push for reservation of one third seats for women to give them the freedom they deserved being one half of the humanity, on the other hand, the need was to work for 'capacity building' using all resources even with franchise for the NGOs, Self Help Groups etc.

Functions of local self government too increased with greater need for accessing people. e-applications found increased acceptance; digital illiteracy and non-availability of computers posed problems. This meant that functions of local government had to digitised; it brought transparency and visibility.

In the political paradigm, local government has found a new meaning. It is seen as crucial and critical to political survival. Being the most visible face of governance with relatively less strain, local government is the obvious bet to gain people's confidence. **(250 words)**

14. Rajyasabha has been transformed from a 'useless Stepney tire' to the most useful supportive organ in past few decades. Highlight the factors as well as areas in which this transformation could be visible. (Answer in 250 words)

Ans: Rajya Sabha or 'the House of the Elders' has a prominent and pivotal place in our parliamentary democracy. Its permanency as a body with the Vice President as its Chairman gives it the vitality that commands respect. The wisdom and the erudition of its members who examine issues objectively and dispassionately go a long way in stabilizing our democracy. The in-built mechanism of one third of the members of Rajya Sabha retiring after every two years provides for induction of fresh members.

With the advent of coalition politics and emergence of smaller parties, Rajya Sabha has witnessed transformational changes. The notable change is that opinions and views have become broad based. Secondly, political parties are now fielding erudite and highly qualified candidates who cannot handle the rough and tumble of electoral politics. The contribution of such members in the Rajya Sabha is at once visible.

Far from being a 'useless stepney tire', Rajyasabha has brought both balance and buoyancy to our parliamentary democracy putting a brake on legislative adventurism. It has stepped in to calm, calibrate and construct in a way that the proposed legislation is enriched.

The upper house has facilitated socio-economic transformation in the country. It has shown great maturity in being in tune with the realities of the times by lending support to long overdue legislations such as Right to Information Act, Environmental Legislation, Right to Education etc. One must also note that Rajyasabha has avoided all confrontation with the other house, unlike in the past. **(250 words)**

15. Which steps are required for constitutionalisation of a commission? Do you think imparting constitutionality to the national commission for woman would ensure greater gender justice and empowerment in India? Give reasons. ***(Answer in 250 words)***

Ans: A Commission is constitutionalised by moving constitutional amendment in the Parliament. For example, National Commission for Backward Classes became a constitutional body through 123rd constitutional amendment bill 2017 and 102nd amendment 2018 in constitution. National Commission for Women was setup as a 'Statutory Body' in January 1992 under the National Commission for Women Act, 1990. The Commission has worked for the upliftment of women and safeguards their rights and interests.

Imparting constitutionality to the commission for women would bring about change that is both desirable as well as discernible. A constitutional body is endowed with more powers and is enabled to function with more freedom.

Women in India suffer from many infirmities, indignities and injustices. Whether it is social disabilities or economic deprivation or gender discrimination, women are put to severe challenges. Some of the issues are rooted in tradition, some in history and some in obnoxious taboos or practices. Safety is a prevalent challenge that transcends barriers of age and status. Worse is the discrimination at work place or in terms of wages for similar work as done by men.

Giving the commission for women the constitutional status will ensure that annual reports on status are placed before the President who in turn will send them to the Parliament. Moreover, as a constitutional body, the commission can summon the concerned persons. This will bring about sea change in the outlook of the society and the commission too would be seen as an organ that matters and that means.

It is also a fact that being a constitutional body means that the commission would have lesser dependence on the government. The salaries of those working in the commission would be drawn from the consolidated fund (voted by the Parliament). **(289 words)**

16. "Incidence and intensity of poverty are most important in determining poverty based on income alone". In this context analyze the latest United Nations Multi Poverty Index report.

(Answer in 250 words)

Ans: In determining poverty based on income alone, economists and planners looked initially at calorie intake, firm in the belief that lower calorie intake was due to lower income. The idea could not be faulted, malnutrition being surely linked to compulsive deficient calories. The Tendulkar committee came up with linkages between calorie intake and income; the results were to shock some, sadden some and surprise many. The reason was that a very low threshold was prescribed to be under poverty line. The Rangarajan committee came forth to do some urgent revisions.

The debate was raging, 'can poverty be measured by calorie intake alone?' What about dignity of life, what of education, what of housing, decent cloths, comfort etc.?

Multidimensional Poverty Indices use a range of indicators to calculate a summary poverty figure for a given population, in which a larger figure indicates a higher level of poverty. Global Multidimensional Poverty Index (MPI) was developed in 2010 by Oxford Poverty and Human Development Initiative and United Nations Development Programme and it uses health, education and standard of living indicators to determine the incidence and intensity of poverty. Multidimensional poverty indices use a household as their unit and a household is deprived for a given indicator if it fails to meet a given 'cutoff'. Each dimension is given equal weightage and each indicator within the dimension is also weighted equally.

The Heath dimension has child mortality and nutrition as indicators; Education has school attendance; standard of living has cooking fuel, sanitation, drinking water, electricity, housing and assets.

The method is markedly better since it helps in identifying the most vulnerable and the poorest. The findings are useful in allocation of resources to target the greater intensity of poverty. **(285 words)**

17. "Microfinance as an anti-poverty vaccine is aimed at asset creation and income security of the rural poor in India". Evaluate the role of Self Help Groups in achieving twin objectives along with empowering women in rural India. ***(Answer in 250 words)***

Ans: Self Help Groups (SHGs) are created to harness skills that are available to be productively used with the aid and assistance of microfinance. Finance is made available without hassles of collaterals or conditions. In simple terms, SHGs are the medium to convert raw materials available locally by labour available locally and marketed on sustained basis to generate profits that create sufficient incentive to go on and on.

The success story of `Lijjat Papad' is a fascinating example of enterprise and engagement. 'Rural Telephony' in Bangladesh was another instance of ingenuity and inclusion.

Self Help Groups (SHGs) make their impact felt in more ways than one; two points are paramount. One, the success of SHGs leads to lesser dependence on moneylenders and middlemen, a remarkable point of note that is borne out by statistics. Two, the SHGs contribute eventually to the economic development of the country. A notable feature of SHGs is that hidden unemployment is taken care of with productive usage.

Women Self Help Groups are of particular significance in many ways. They look at making women economically self-reliant and empowered. It helps in saving for the future, better care of the children and creation of assets that provide insurance for the family.

In a country like India with its historic and holistic boundaries and barriers of social limitations, emancipation of women with self-reliance adds a new dimension in dignity.

Government too must come forward with initiatives and incentives to help SHGs run by women. Organising them into cooperatives and availability of soft loans could be a fair deal. Certainly, extending marketing facilities is a much needed help. Good practices of SHGs and success stories must be showcased to encourage women seeking help to break forth. **(286 words)**

18. National Education Policy 2020 is in conformity with the Sustainable Development Goals-4 (2030). It intended to restructure and re-orient the education system in India. Critically examine the statement. ***(Answer in 250 words)***

Ans: The 42nd amendment to the constitution shifted 'Education' from the state list to the concurrent list with a view to improving the quality of education. Prior to this, the central government unfolded its policy on education in 1968; later in 1986 and subsequently in 1992, the policy was revisited to attune it to the needs of changing times.

Two issues have remained with us; one, it takes a long while to bring about desired changes given the intransigence of states and flip flops by the centre. Two, emphasis on quantity has led to decline in quality.

Now another dimension has also added to the criticality; technological advancement in education. As the country is progressing, the need for technology is increasing too. The SDF-4 (2030) agenda of 'plan of action for people, planet and prosperity' is looking at the aim to ensure inclusive and equitable quality education and promote lifelong learning opportunities for all. It has a total of ten targets with five other SDGs with direct reference to education.

The New Education Policy, 2020 is attuned to the objectives of SDG-4 keeping in view the ground realities and compulsions of constitutional arrangements.

Emphasis is on use of technology in education, planning, teaching and learning assessment. Plans are mooted to remodel higher education and establish reputed universities. The idea is to make education quality based and competitive.

The thrust is to create knowledge economy which would make available critical inputs for all round growth.

Vocational education in schools is part of the action plan. More importantly, digital learning in eight regional languages is a big step forward.

Overall, NEP, 2020 is a positive step in a planned way for purposeful growth. **(280 words)**

19. Quadrilateral Security Dialogue is transforming itself into a trade block from the military alliance, in present times. Discuss *(Answer in 250 words)*

Ans: Quad or Quadrilateral Security dialogue is an initiative of maritime democracies with India, United States, Australia and Japan. What began primarily as military exercises together with respective Navies of the countries, it soon expanded to cover trade related matters.

It all began in 2007 with India and the United States joint naval exercises at Malabar in Western India. Quad or Quadrilateral Security is a strategic thrust that seeks to bring about stability in the region.

The prime aim of Quad is to secure and stabilise sea-routes and lines. Alongside this, the effort is to bring about military cooperation and preparedness. Modern day situation in warfare demands strategic connect and availability of open sea-lines. China has been ensuring this with steady expansion in the world; aggressive patrolling and fortification of islands in South China seas is a visible example of it.

Over the years, it has transpired that Quadrilateral Security dialogue has moved steadily towards trade becoming trading blocs. The reasons for this are part due to compulsions and part due to considerations. Compulsions are rooted in the fact that all the four countries that is United States, India, Australia and Japan are thriving economies which have much to gain by cooperation. Moreover, these countries are compelled to protect their sea trade routes. Another compulsion is that communication lines have to be maintained as trade and commerce are dependent on communication.

The overriding considerations for promotion of cooperation are that all these four countries have democracies in place; it makes easy to come together. Ideologically there is seamless bonding. Another important consideration is that military cooperation is strengthened by steady supplies which can be ensured by facilitated trade. Trade bloccs promote ease of business which in turn ensures ready positioning of all materials so essential for defense.

(296 words)

20. What is the significance of Indo-US deals over Indo-Russian defense deals? Discuss with reference to stability in the Indo-Pacific region ***(Answer in 250 words)***

Ans: Indo-US relations over Indo-Russian relations in defense sector are significant in many ways, notably concerning reliability in supplies. Known as NATO arms and ammunition, US supplies have widespread acceptance the world over while Russian supplies are limited in spread. Moreover, Russian defense supplies are fraught with many uncertainties after the overthrow of communist regime due to closure of Defense sector industries. With growing demand for consumer goods in Russia, the priorities are changing fast; many defense sector units in Russia have been converted to meet the surge in demand for consumer goods. A case in point is the severe crisis being faced by India's crying need for spares for Battle Tanks made under Russian defense deals. India had to fall back on Russia, then under Soviet Union dispensation, for want of choice as USA and NATO countries were manifestly disinclined to oblige.

After the twin tower terror attack in US in 2001, Indo-US relations have undergone sea change. India's growing economic clout has given it the leeway and leverage to seek US arms. With the emergence of Israel as a robust and reliable supplier of defense items, US has been ever so keen to be game too. US supplies, even if costlier, are served well by good backup service and spares. Rate of obsolescence too is low compared to Russian arms and ammunition.

In the Indo-Pacific region, US has a huge advantage over Russian supplies with logistics. The supply lines are well protected. All weather connectivity is a clinching advantage too. Even fuelling facilities would be a critical consideration. Indo-US Defense deals present the decided and determinable advantage in as much as they are stable and settled compared to uncertainties and unevenness of Russian deals. **(285 words)**